iLife '05

THE MISSING MANUAL

*The book that
should have been
in the box*

iLife '05

THE MISSING MANUAL

David Pogue

POGUE PRESS™

O'REILLY®

Beijing • Cambridge • Farnham • Köln • Paris • Sebastopol • Taipei • Tokyo

iLife '05: The Missing Manual
by David Pogue

Published by O'Reilly Media, Inc., 1005 Gravenstein Highway North, Sebastopol, CA 95472.

O'Reilly Media books may be purchased for educational, business, or sales promotional use. Online editions are also available for most titles: *safari.oreilly. com*. For more information, contract our corporate/institutional sales department: (800) 998-9938 or *corporate@oreilly.com*.

August 2005:   First Printing

RepKover™ This book uses RepKover™, a durable and flexible lay-flat binding.

ISBN: 0-596-10036-1

Table of Contents

Part Three: iMovie

The Missing Credits

About the Authors

David Pogue is the weekly computer columnist for the *New York Times,* an Emmy-winning correspondent for *CBS News Sunday Morning,* and the creator of the Missing Manual series. He's the author or co-author of 37 books, including 16 in this series and six in the "For Dummies" line (including *Macs, Magic, Opera,* and *Classical Music*). In his other life, David is a former Broadway show conductor, a magician, and a pianist. News and photos await at *www.davidpogue.com.*

He welcomes feedback about his books by email at *david@pogueman.com.*

J. D. Biersdorfer (iTunes chapters) writes the weekly computer Q & A column for the Circuits section of *The New York Times.* She also writes an occasional Circuits feature story and has penned articles for *The New York Times Book Review,* the *AIGIA Journal of Graphic Design,* and *Rolling Stone.* After living all over the country as a former Air Force brat and theater technician, she planted herself in New York City in 1989. In her limited spare time, she plays the banjo and watches far too much CNN Headline News. Email: *jdbiersdorfer@mac.com.*

Erica Sadun (iDVD chapters) holds a Ph.D. in Computer Science from the Georgia Institute of Technology. She has written, co-written and contributed to almost two dozen books about technology, particularly in the areas of programming, digital video, and digital photography. An unrepentant geek, Erica has never met a gadget she didn't need. Her checkered past includes run-ins with NeXT, Newton, and a vast array of both successful and unsuccessful technologies. When not writing, she and her geek husband parent three adorable geeks-in-training, who regard their parents with unrestrained bemusement. Email: *erica@mindspring.com.*

Derrick Story (contributor to the iPhoto chapters) is the managing editor of O'Reilly Network (*www.oreillynet.com*) and Mac DevCenter (*www.macdevcenter.com*), which he created in December, 2000 for O'Reilly Media. His other books include *Digital Photography Pocket Guide, 2nd Edition; Digital Video Pocket Guide;* and *Digital Photography Hacks.* Derrick continues to hone his shooting skills through his photo business, Story Photography (*www.storyphoto.com*), which specializes in digital imaging and special events. His photographs are featured in this book.

About the Creative Team

This book is the sum of its parts—the individual Missing Manuals about iTunes, iMovie and iDVD, iPhoto, and GarageBand. Those books, in turn, were made possible by the talent and cheerful attitudes of the following team:

Copy editors: Nan Barber, Teresa Noelle Roberts

Technical editors: Dennis Cohen, Karl Petersen, Gary Drenan

Production and graphics editor: Lesa Snider

Proofreaders: John Cacciatore, Stephanie English, Danny Marcus, Sada Preisch, Sohaila Abdulali, Kate Chase, Linley Dolby, Dawn Mann

Cover illustration: Rose Cassano

Book design and layout: Phil Simpson

Indexer: David Pogue

Contributors: Joseph Schorr (iPhoto), Tim Franklin (QuickTime Web pages), Steve Alper (musical typesetting)

Acknowledgments

The Missing Manual series is a joint venture between Pogue Press (the dream team introduced on these pages) and O'Reilly Media (a dream publishing partner).

From Apple, I had insanely valuable assistance from Fred Johnson, Paul Towner, Xander Soren, Greg Scanlon, and Gary Drenan. Thanks, too, to Adam Goldstein, Boy Genius, for production assistance; Glenn Reid for tech-editing two iMovie editions; and to David Rogelberg. Lesa Snider and Jackie Samwick, for assisting immensely with this book's massive index.

Finally, thanks to Kelly, Tia, and Jeffrey, my favorite iMovie stars, and my wife, Jennifer, who made this book—and everything else—possible.

The Missing Manual Series

Missing Manuals are witty, superbly written guides to computer products that don't come with printed manuals (which is just about all of them). Each book features a handcrafted index; cross-references to specific page numbers (not just "see Chapter 14"); and RepKover, a detached-spine binding that lets the book lie perfectly flat without the assistance of weights or cinder blocks.

Recent and upcoming titles include:

- *Mac OS X: The Missing Manual,* Tiger Edition by David Pogue
- *GarageBand 2: The Missing Manual* by David Pogue et al.
- *iPhoto 5: The Missing Manual* by David Pogue and Derrick Story
- *iMovie HD & iDVD 5: The Missing Manual* by David Pogue

- *iPod & iTunes: The Missing Manual,* Third Edition by J.D. Biersdorfer
- *AppleScript: The Missing Manual* by Adam Goldstein
- *iWork: The Missing Manual* by Jim Elferdink
- *Office 2004 for Macintosh: The Missing Manual* by Mark H. Walker, Franklin Tessler, and Paul Berkowitz
- *FileMaker Pro 7: The Missing Manual* by Geoff Coffey
- *Switching to the Mac: The Missing Manual,* Tiger Edition by David Pogue and Adam Goldstein
- *Photoshop Elements 3: The Missing Manual* by Barbara Brundage
- *Google: The Missing Manual* by Sarah Milstein and Rael Dornfest
- *Dreamweaver MX 2004: The Missing Manual* by David Sawyer McFarland
- *AppleWorks 6: The Missing Manual* by Jim Elferdink and David Reynolds
- *Windows XP Home Edition: The Missing Manual,* 2nd Edition by David Pogue
- *Windows XP Pro: The Missing Manual,* 2nd Edition by David Pogue, Craig Zacker, and Linda Zacker

THE MISSING CREDITS

Introduction

At its best, Apple has always focused on one particular mission: identifying powerful but complex technologies and distilling them into far simpler packages. You shouldn't have to be a professional working for a media conglomerate, says Apple, to harness cutting-edge technology for your own creative expression and entertainment.

That's the philosophy behind the iLife software suite. Each of the five programs in this $80 package is a streamlined, attractive, easy-to-use version of software that was once hopelessly complex (or hopelessly expensive).

Each of the five programs is designed to serve as the digital hub for a different kind of artistic expression:

- **iTunes 4,** for managing, playing, buying, and sharing digital music.

- **iPhoto 5,** for downloading photos from your digital camera, and organizing, sharing, and printing them.

- **iMovie HD,** for editing footage from a digital camcorder, adding effects, sound, and credits, and then presenting the result.

- **GarageBand 2,** for composing and recording terrific-sounding songs of your own.

- **iDVD 5,** for burning DVDs containing the movies, music, and photos from iTunes, iPhoto, iMovie, and GarageBand. Professional DVDs in every way—except you get to make them yourself!

Technically speaking, you can perform all of the same tasks using other software brands and other kinds of computers. But not as easily, not as consistently, not as pleasurably, and certainly not for a grand total of $80 (or free with a new Mac).

iLife Integration

Leaning the five programs of iLife isn't really as difficult as learning, say, five Windows programs, because Apple has designed these programs to work alike—and to work together.

Now, as Figure I-1 illustrates, the integration of the five iLife programs isn't quite as fluid as popular mythology would have it. You can't move information from any program into any other; you can move it only in directions that make sense.

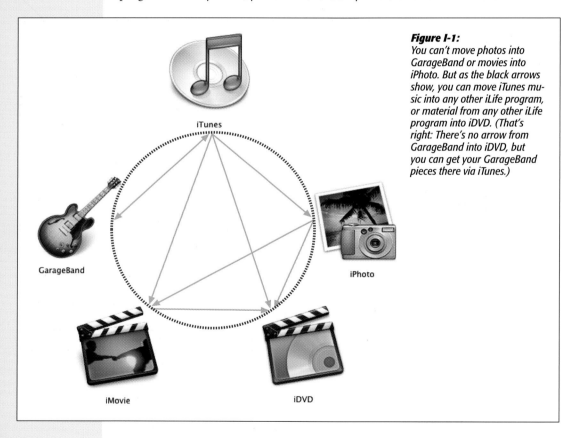

Figure I-1:
You can't move photos into GarageBand or movies into iPhoto. But as the black arrows show, you can move iTunes music into any other iLife program, or material from any other iLife program into iDVD. (That's right: There's no arrow from GarageBand into iDVD, but you can get your GarageBand pieces there via iTunes.)

The real payoff of adopting Apple's version of all five programs is that you save so much time learning them. Over and over again, Apple reuses the same elements: a color picker, a spell-checker, and so on. Learn once, use often.

Here are some of the most important iLife software conventions. You'll see these controls and windows in many different circumstances, no matter which program you're using at the time.

The iTunes Selection Panel

Three of the iLife programs—iMovie, iDVD, and iPhoto—come with a window into your iTunes music collection. (To see it in iMovie, click the Audio button. In iPhoto, click the Slideshow button. In iDVD, open the Customize panel, click the Media button, and choose iTunes from the pop-up menu.) Having direct access to your music files saves you a lot of hunting around on your hard drive when you want to use this or that song as the background music for a DVD, movie, or slideshow.

You can see the basic mini-iTunes window in Figure I-2.

Figure I-2:
In general, the mini-iTunes window found in iMovie, iPhoto, and iDVD works a lot like the list of songs in the real iTunes. For example, you can double-click a song to listen to it (or click once and then click the triangular Play button). Click the same button–now shaped like a square Stop button–when you've heard enough.

Note that above the list, the pop-up menu lists all of your iTunes playlists (subsets of songs), for your browsing convenience. And below the list is a search box that lets you pluck one song out of the haystack just by typing a few letters of its name, album, or performer.

Other tips:

- Rather than scroll through a huge list, you can locate the tracks you want by using the capsule-shaped Search box near the bottom of the window. Click in the Search field, and then type a word (or part of a word) to filter your list. iPhoto searches the Artist, Song, and Album fields of the iTunes Library and displays only the matching entries. To clear the search and view your whole list again, click the X in the Search field.

- Click one of the three headers—Artist, Song, or Time—to sort the iTunes music list alphabetically by that criterion.

- You can also change the arrangement of the three columns by grabbing the headers and dragging them into a different order.

- Better yet, if you place your cursor carefully on the vertical dividing line between the column headings, you'll find that you can drag it sideways to change the relative sizes of the columns. That's especially handy when all you can see of the Electric Light Orchestra's name is, for example, Elect...estra.

Check Your Spelling

You can use Mac OS X's built-in spelling checker to proofread your prose in all kinds of useful places. You can check iPhoto's text boxes (for the coffee-table books that you order), iMovie's titles and credits, and iDVD's onscreen text boxes.

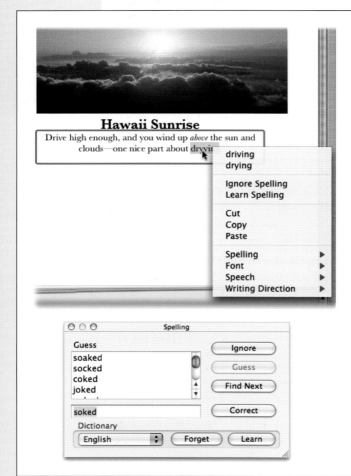

Figure I-3:
Top: Control-click any word that's underlined with a red, dashed line. If the resulting shortcut menu contains the correct spelling, choose it. Otherwise, choose Ignore or Add (to teach Mac OS X that word for future spell checks).

Bottom: If you prefer a more word processor–like spelling check, you can summon this box.

The first "misspelled" word already appears. If the correct version appears in the list, double-click it (or single-click it and then click Correct). If not, type the correct word into the box below the list and then click Correct.

On the other hand, if the word in your text box is fine as it is, click either Ignore ("I want this word spelled this way; stop underlining it and move on") or Add ("Not only is this name or word spelled correctly, but I may use it again. Add it to your dictionary so you'll never flag it again").

As in a word processor, you can ask the Mac to check your spelling several ways:

- **Check a single word or selection.** Highlight a word, or several, and then choose Edit→Spelling→Check Spelling (⌘-semicolon). If the word is misspelled in iPhoto's opinion, a red, dashed line appears under the word. Proceed as shown in Figure I-3.

- **Check a whole text block.** Click inside a title or comment box and then choose Edit→Spelling→Spelling (⌘-colon). The standard Mac OS X Spelling dialog box appears, also shown and described in Figure I-3.

- **Check as you type.** The trouble with the spelling commands described here is that they operate on only a single, tiny text block at a time. To check your entire photo book, you must click inside each title or caption and invoke the spelling command again. There's no way to have iPhoto sweep through your entire book at once.

  Your eyes might widen in excitement, therefore, when you spot the Edit→Spelling→Check Spelling As You Type command. You'd expect it to make the Mac flag words it doesn't recognize *as you type them*. Sure enough, when this option is turned on, whenever you type a word not in the Mac's dictionary, a colorful dashed underline appears. To correct a misspelling, Control-click it. A shortcut menu appears. Proceed as shown in Figure I-3.

  But don't get too excited: This option turns itself *off* every time you click into a new text box. Using the mouse (there's no keyboard shortcut), you have to turn it on again for every title and caption. The regular Check Spelling command looks positively effortless by comparison.

The Color Picker

Here and there—in iMovie's Title generator and iPhoto's Web-page design dialog box, for example—Mac OS X offers you the opportunity to choose a *color* for the text, background, and so on.

The dialog box that appears (Figure I-4) offers a miniature color lab that lets you dial in any color in the Mac's rainbow. There are actually several color labs, arrayed across the top, each designed to make color-choosing easier in certain circumstances:

- **Color Wheel.** Drag the scroll bar vertically to adjust the brightness, and then drag your cursor around the ball to pick the shade (Figure I-4, left).

- **Color Sliders.** From the pop-up menu, choose the color-mixing method you prefer. *CMYK* stands for cyan, magenta, yellow, and black. People in the printing industry will feel immediately at home, because these four colors are the component inks for color printing. (These people may also be able to explain why *K* stands for *black*.)

- **RGB** is how a TV or computer monitor thinks of colors: as proportions of red, green, and blue. And *HSB* stands for Hue, Saturation, and Brightness—a favorite color-specifying scheme in scientific circles.

In each case, just drag the sliders to mix up the color you want, or type in the percentages of each component.

- **Color Palettes** presents canned sets of color swatches. They're primarily for programmers who want quick access to the standard colors in Mac OS X. (The Web Safe Colors list is useful for Web designers, so they can tell whether a color will display properly on other computers.)

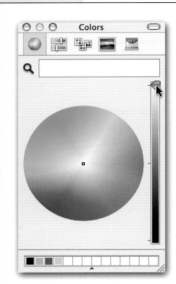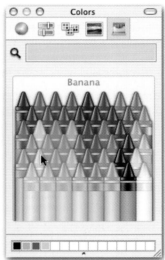

Figure I-4:
The buttons along the top offer different ways to specify a color; two examples are shown here.

You can store frequently used (or frequently admired) colors in the mini-palette squares at the bottom of the Colors box. To do that, drag the big rectangular color swatch (next to the magnifying glass) directly down into one of the little squares, where it will stay fresh for weeks.

If you don't have space for all the colors you want, drag down the small circular dot at the bottom of the window to make room for more.

- **Image Palettes** offers the visible rainbow arrayed yet another way: in cloudy, color-arranged streaks. (Cool tip: If you drag a graphics file directly into the dialog box, it will appear in the spectrum's place. That's a handy trick if you're trying to identify the color of a certain spot of an image, for example. And don't miss the pop-up button at the bottom of the dialog box, which offers a few other stunts).

- **Crayons.** Now *this* is a good user interface (Figure I-4, right). You can click each crayon to see its color name: "Mocha," "Fern," "Cayenne," and so on. (Some interior decorator in Cupertino had a field day naming these crayons.)

In any of these color pickers, you can also "sample" a color that's outside the dialog box—a color you found on a Web page, for example. Just click the magnifying-glass icon and then move your cursor around the screen. You'll see the sliders and numbers change inside the dialog box automatically when you click.

Preferences

Just about every Mac program has a Preferences command tucked into its application menu (the menu named after the program, like iPhoto or iMovie). What's nice about the iLife suite, though, is that its keystroke is the same in every program: ⌘-comma.

It's also nice that the resulting dialog box is a separate window that you can leave open as you work (you don't have to close it after making a selection). When you're finally finished with the Preferences dialog box, just click its upper-left, red Close button (or press ⌘-W).

About This Book

The iLife programs may be simple, but they're not simplistic. They offer a wide range of powerful, flexible features that let you create music, movies, pictures, and DVDs worthy of professional work. Unfortunately, many of the best techniques aren't covered in the only "manual" you get with iLife—its sparse electronic help screens.

This book is designed to serve as the iLife manual, as the book that should have been in the box. It explores each program in depth, offers shortcuts and workarounds, and unearths features that the online help doesn't even mention.

About the Outline

iLife '05: The Missing Manual is divided into six parts. The first five correspond to the iLife programs: iTunes, iPhoto, iMovie, iDVD, and GarageBand. At the end of the book, you'll find troubleshooting chapters that correspond to those programs.

FREQUENTLY ASKED QUESTION

The Sum of All Books?

I see that you've also written individual Missing Manual books on iTunes, iMovie & iDVD, GarageBand, and iPhoto. If I have this book, do I need those too?

Probably not.

iLife '05: The Missing Manual is adapted from those four other books, but it's not exactly the same. It's been slimmed down somewhat from the component source book. Otherwise, it would be over 1,400 pages long, which would put it over that 20-pound weight limit that bookstores are so picky about.

So what do you get in the individual books that's missing from this one? Here are some examples: *iMovie HD & iDVD 5: The Missing Manual* includes three chapters about good camcorder and film technique. *iPhoto 5: The Missing Manual* has several chapters about how to use your

digital camera for best results. *GarageBand 2: The Missing Manual* offers a crash course in music, plus coverage of shareware plug-ins and add-ons for GarageBand. And *iPod & iTunes: The Missing Manual* includes lots more detail on the iPod, including a good deal of information for Windows PC owners.

If you find yourself spending most of your time in one particular program, it may be worth checking the relevant book out of the library to soak in the extra detail that's not in this all-in-one book.

Otherwise, though, everything you need is right here: The tips, the tricks, the shortcuts, the behind-the-scenes details on how iLife programs store your projects on the hard drive, and 500 illustrations. This book offers such complete coverage of the i-programs, in fact, it could have been called *iBook*—but that one was taken.

About→These→Arrows

Throughout this book, and throughout the Missing Manual series, you'll find sentences like this one: "Open your Home→Library→Preferences folder." That's shorthand for a much longer instruction that directs you to open three nested folders in sequence, like this: "In the Finder, choose Go→Home. In your Home folder, you'll find a folder called Library. Open that. Inside the Library window is a folder called Preferences. Double-click to open it, too."

Similarly, this kind of arrow shorthand helps to simplify the business of choosing commands in menus, as shown in Figure I-5.

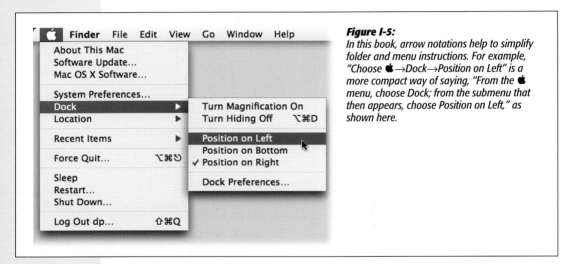

Figure I-5:
In this book, arrow notations help to simplify folder and menu instructions. For example, "Choose ⌘→Dock→Position on Left" is a more compact way of saying, "From the ⌘ menu, choose Dock; from the submenu that then appears, choose Position on Left," as shown here.

About MissingManuals.com

At *www.missingmanuals.com*, you'll find news, articles, and updates to the books in this series.

But if you click the name of this book and then the Errata link, you'll find a unique resource: a list of corrections and updates that have been made in successive printings of this book. You can mark important corrections right into your own copy of the book, if you like.

In fact, the same page offers an invitation for you to submit such corrections and updates yourself. In an effort to keep the book as up-to-date and accurate as possible, each time we print more copies of this book, we'll make any confirmed corrections you've suggested. Thanks in advance for reporting any glitches you find!

In the meantime, we'd love to hear your suggestions for new books in the Missing Manual line. There's a place for that on the Web site, too, as well as a place to sign up for free email notification of new titles in the series.

The Very Basics

You'll find very little jargon or nerd terminology in this book. You will, however, encounter a few terms and concepts that you'll see frequently in your Macintosh life. They include:

- **Clicking.** This book offers three kinds of instructions that require you to use the mouse or trackpad attached to your Mac. To *click* means to point the arrow cursor at something onscreen and then—without moving the cursor at all—press and release the clicker button on the mouse (or laptop trackpad). To *double-click*, of course, means to click twice in rapid succession, again without moving the cursor at all. And to *drag* means to move the cursor while keeping the button pressed.

  When you're told to ⌘-*click* something, you click while pressing the ⌘ key (next to the Space bar). Such related procedures as *Shift-clicking, Option-clicking,* and *Control-clicking* work the same way—just click while pressing the corresponding key on the bottom row of your keyboard. (The Option key is called the Alt key on some non-U.S. keyboards, by the way.)

- **Menus.** The *menus* are the words in the lightly striped bar at the top of your screen. You can either click one of these words to open a pull-down menu of commands (and then click again on a command), or click and *hold* the button as you drag down the menu to the desired command (and release the button to activate the command). Either method works fine.

UP TO SPEED

The Requirements

Officially, Apple lists the requirements to run the iLife programs like this. First, you need a Mac with a G3, G4, or G5 processor inside. It should have at least 256 megabytes of memory and 4.3 gigabytes of free hard-drive space (if you plan to install all five programs). And it has to be running Mac OS X version 10.3.4 or later. (You also need QuickTime 6.5.2 or later, but it comes with iLife.)

You also need a monitor that can display at least 1024 by 768 pixels. And you can't easily install iLife unless your Mac has a DVD-playing drive.

Some of the programs, however, are more demanding. You can't use GarageBand's built-in instrument sounds, for example, unless your Mac has a G4 or G5 processor. iDVD won't even run unless you have a 733-megahertz G4 chip or something faster, and iMovie requires a 1-gigahertz chip

if you want to edit high-definition video.

In the real world, however, savvy Mac fans consider some of those requirements the Computer Jokes of the Day. Thes Apple specs aren't just the minimums—they're the bare, desperate, stranded-on-a-desert-island minimums.

For example, 256 megabytes isn't nearly enough to get any meaningful work done with GarageBand or iDVD. And running iPhoto on a G3 Mac might be theoretically possible, but it's crushingly slow.

Bottom line: A much more practical minimum for running the iLife programs is a Mac with 512 megabytes of memory (or more—much more), with at least a G4 processor, running Mac OS X 10.3 and QuickTime 6.5.1 or later.

After that, the only requirement is a creative gene in your body.

Note: Apple has officially changed what it calls the little menu that pops up when you Control-click something on the screen. It's still a contextual menu, in that the menu choices depend on the context of what you click—but it's now called a *shortcut menu*. That term not only matches what it's called in Windows, but it's slightly more descriptive about its function. Shortcut menu is the term you'll find in this book.

- **Keyboard shortcuts.** Every time you take your hand off the keyboard to move the mouse, you lose time and potentially disrupt your creative flow. That's why many experienced Mac fans use keystroke combinations instead of menu commands wherever possible. ⌘-P opens the Print dialog box, for example, and ⌘-M minimizes the current window to the Dock.

  When you see a shortcut like ⌘-Q (which closes the current program), it's telling you to hold down the ⌘ key, and, while it's down, type the letter Q, and then release both keys.

If you've mastered this much information, you have all the technical background you need to enjoy *iLife '05: The Missing Manual.*

Part One: iTunes

1

Getting Music Into iTunes

As the MP3 music craze of the late 1990s swept across the globe, software programs for playing the new music files on the computer began to pop up around the Internet. If you're old enough, you may even remember using Mac programs like SoundApp, SoundJam MP, and MacAmp.

When iTunes debuted in January 2001, Apple reported that 275,000 people downloaded it in the first week. The iTunes software proved to be a versatile, robust all-around music management program made exclusively for Macintosh. And it was *free*.

Even in that first version of iTunes, you could import songs from a CD and convert them into MP3 files; play MP3s, audio CDs, and streaming Internet radio; create custom playlists; burn audio CDs without having to spring for extra CD burning software; zone out to groovy animated laser-light displays in the iTunes window while songs played; and transfer music to a few pre-iPod, Mac-friendly portable MP3 players.

Today, iTunes is much more. In fact, it's the hub of the digital hub; it's the only iLife program that communicates directly with all four of the *other* iLife programs. Among many other feats, it lets you download perfectly legal music files from well-known artists using the Music Store feature and zip them over to your iPod in no time, all from within iTunes and without buying a single CD.

The version that came with your copy of iLife '05 is probably outdated at this point; Apple releases another version of iTunes every few months. But unlike the other iLife programs, iTunes is free. Each time Apple unleashes a new version, you'll be notified by Mac OS X's Software Update feature, which pops up on the screen and offers to update your copy via the Internet. Accept its invitation without fail.

A Quick Tour

This chapter is all about *filling* your copy of iTunes with music. Chapter 2 is all about *playing* that music (but here's the gist of it: Double-click a song to hear it).

Before you go about stocking up on tunes, though, it's worth taking a moment to get your bearings. The round-ended display at the center top of the iTunes window—the status area—tells you what song is playing, who's playing it, which album it came from, and how much playing time remains. To the left are volume and song naviga-tion controls; to the right is a search box for hunting down or looking up specific singers or songs. Figure 1-1 presents a guided tour of the controls and functions on the iTunes screen.

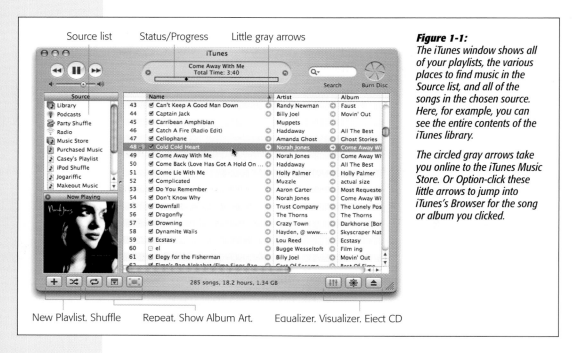

Source list   Status/Progress   Little gray arrows

New Playlist. Shuffle   Repeat. Show Album Art.   Equalizer. Visualizer. Eject CD

Figure 1-1:
The iTunes window shows all of your playlists, the various places to find music in the Source list, and all of the songs in the chosen source. Here, for example, you can see the entire contents of the iTunes library.

The circled gray arrows take you online to the iTunes Music Store. Or Option-click these little arrows to jump into iTunes's Browser for the song or album you clicked.

The Source panel at the left of the iTunes window displays all of the audio sources you can tap into at the moment. If you have a CD in the computer's drive, for example, it shows up in the Source list, as does your iPod when it's connected.

Clicking a name in the Source column makes the main song-list area change accord-ingly, like this:

- Click the icon of a CD you've inserted; the disc's track list appears.

- Click a playlist (page 53); the contents of that music mix appear in the window.

- Click the Radio icon for a list of Internet radio stations, or the Party Shuffle icon to—well, see page 36.

- Click the Podcasts icon to see the list of those home-brewed and professional programs you can download and listen to within iTunes or on your iPod.

Tip: You can show or hide the Radio and Party Shuffle icons in the Source list by visiting the General pane of iTunes's Preferences dialog box. If you find those little gray arrows all over your nice song titles in the iTunes window deeply annoying, you can turn them off in the iTunes Preferencs box as well.

- Click the Music Store icon; you jump to Apple's online music emporium where you can browse, preview, and buy songs (Chapter 4).

As shown in Figure 1-1, the iTunes window is brimming with tools for managing your music, all of which are described in detail in the following chapters. But first you'll need some music to work with. The next section explores one of the most popular uses for iTunes—ripping digital audio files from compact discs.

Window Fun

Don't be misled by the brushed-aluminum look of the iTunes window. In fact, you can push and pull the various parts of the window like taffy.

- You can resize the panes within the iTunes window. Look for a shallow dot between panes; it denotes strips that you can drag to resize adjacent panes.

- The main song list is separated into columns, which you can sort and rearrange. Click a column title (like Artist or Album) to sort the list alphabetically by that criterion. Click the black triangle next to the column title to reverse the sorting.

UP TO SPEED

Box Full of Buttons

The round button up in the top-right corner of iTunes changes depending on what you're doing. Here's what each one means and when you see it.

 The Import button indicates you've inserted a CD into your computer and are ready to rip some songs into your iTunes library.

 The Browse button appears when you click the Library icon to look through your collection or shop in the iTunes Music Store.

 When the iTunes Visualizations are turned on, clicking the Options button lets you adjust the frame rate and other visual settings.

 This version of the Burn CD button shows up when a playlist is selected in the Sources area or you have a separate playlist window open onscreen.

 To check for new radio stations and other new content available in the iTunes Radio or Podcasts areas , click the Refresh/Update button.

 If you have taken iTunes up on its offer to burn a CD by clicking on the previous button, this icon appears as the disc-burning process begins.

- Change the order of the columns by dragging them. For example, if you want to have Album right next to the Song Name, drag the word Album horizontally until it's next to Song Name.

- To adjust the width of a column, drag the vertical divider line on its right side.

- To resize all the columns so that they precisely fit the information in them, Control-click any column title and choose, from the contextual menu, Auto Size All Columns. Double-clicking on the vertical column lines automatically resizes them to fit the text as well.

- To add more columns (or less), Control-click any column title. From the pop-up list of column categories (Bit Rate, Date Added, and so on), choose the name of the column you want to add or remove. Column names with checkmarks are the ones that are currently visible.

Tip: Want to track your own listening habits? Turn on the Play Count in iTunes Options. Now you can see just how many times you have played "I Want You Back" by the Jackson 5 since you ripped that CD of old Motown gems to your hard drive. Checking out the Top 25 Most Played playlist in the Source window can also let you know where your ears have been lately.

If you intend to make a *lot* of adjustments to your list of columns, though, it's much faster to make the changes all at once. Choose Edit→View Options to produce the dialog box shown in Figure 1-2, where you can turn columns on and off en masse.

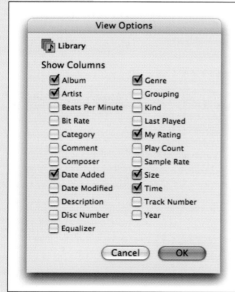

Figure 1-2:
The View Options box from the iTunes Edit menu lets you see as many—or as few—categories for sorting your music as you can stand.

Even in this tiny, unassuming dialog box, a trick or two awaits. If you Option-click any checkbox that's turned on, you turn all of them off. And vice versa.

If you want to turn all of them off except Album and Artist, for example, you'll save time by Option-clicking a turned-on box to turn them all off—and then turning the two you want back on.

Minimizing the window

Lovely as the iTunes window may be, it can take up a heck of a lot of screen real estate. When you're just playing music while you work on other things, you can shrink iTunes down to a svelte display panel that takes up a fraction of the size of the full window.

In fact, iTunes can run in three size modes: small, medium, or large (Figure 1-3). Here's how you pull this off:

Figure 1-3:
And what size music would you like today? You can choose large, medium, or small. Only the large version has the space to serve as command central for MP3s, Internet radio, visual effects, and the kitchen sink.

Arbitrary Groupings

Speaking of the iTunes information columns: The column called Grouping lets you override the usual sorting criteria and keep together a bunch of songs of your own choosing. (If you don't see the Grouping column, Control-click *any* column heading and choose Grouping, so that a checkmark appears next to its name.)

Many classical albums, for example, contain different symphonies, concertos, and other musical forms, all on one disc. How can you make sure that all of Mozart's *Concerto for Piano No. 5 in D Major (K 175)* stays together, and doesn't get mixed in with concertos 6 and 8 from the same CD?

Easy. Select all the "songs" that belong together (by ⌘-clicking them). Then choose File→Get Info. iTunes asks if you're sure you want to edit the file information for all of the selected pieces at once; yes, you do.

In the Get Info box, type *Piano Concerto 5* (or whatever group name you want). Now, when you click OK, you return to the main iTunes list.

To sort your list by grouping name, so that grouped pieces appear consecutively in the list, just click the word Grouping at the top of the column.

- **Large.** This is what you get the first time you open iTunes.

- **Medium.** You can switch between large and medium by clicking the green zoom button at the top- or middle-left corner (or choosing Window→Zoom).

- **Small.** If your desktop isn't big enough for even the small iTunes window in Figure 1-3 at lower left, try taking it down a notch. To create the mini bar shown at lower right in Figure 1-3, start with the medium-size window. Then drag the resize handle (the diagonal lines in the lower-right corner) leftward. To expand it, just reverse the process.

Music from CDs

Ripping a CD means "converting its recordings into digital files on the computer." (Too bad recording industry executives didn't know that when they accused Apple's "Rip, Mix, Burn" ad campaign of promoting piracy. They evidently—and incorrectly—thought that "rip" meant "rip off.")

With the proper iTunes settings, ripping a CD track and preparing it for use with the iPod is fantastically easy. Here's how to go about it.

Phase 1: Choose an Audio File Format

Before you get rolling with ripping, decide which format you want to use for your music files: MP3, AAC, AIFF, WAV, or Apple Lossless (Figure 1-4). This may be more choice than you really wanted, but learning the pros and cons of each format is worth

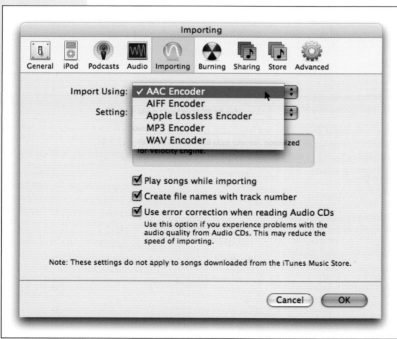

Figure 1-4:
To choose the CD-ripping and file-converting format you prefer, choose iTunes→Preferences, click the Importing tab, and choose the format you want.

"Create files names with track number" arranges the songs you import in the same order in iTunes as they were on the CD—even if you don't choose to rip every song on the album.

The Apple Lossless option works only on dock-connecting 2003 iPods and later, including the iPod Mini. Owners of the pre-dock iPods that came out in 2001 and 2002 are out of luck.

the effort, especially if you're about to commit a huge stack of CDs to digital format. You don't want to have to convert them all a second time.

MP3

Suppose you copy a song from a Sheryl Crow CD directly onto your computer, where it takes up 47.3 MB of hard disk space. Sure, you could now play that song without the CD in your CD drive, but you'd also be out 47.3 megs of precious hard drive real estate.

Now say you put that Sheryl Crow CD in your computer and use your favorite encoding program to convert that song to an MP3 file. The resulting MP3 file still sounds really good, but only takes up about 4.8 MB of space on your hard drive—about 10 percent of the original. Better yet, you can burn a lot of MP3 files onto a blank CD of your own—up to 11 hours of music on one disc, which is enough to get you from Philadelphia to Columbus on Interstate 70 with tunes to spare.

MP3 files are so small because the compression algorithms use *perceptual noise shaping,* a method that mimics the ability of the human ear to hear certain sounds. Just as people can't hear dog whistles, most recorded music contains frequencies that are too high for humans to hear; MP3 compression discards these sounds. Sounds that are blotted out by louder sounds are also cast aside. All of this space-saving by the compression format helps to make a smaller file without overly diminishing the overall sound quality of the music.

New portable MP3 player models come out all the time, but many people consider the iPod's arrival in 2001 to be a defining moment in the history of MP3 hardware.

Tip: MP3 is short for MPEG Audio, Layer 3. And MPEG stands for Moving Pictures Experts Group, the association of engineers that also defined the specifications for the DVD video format, among others.

AAC

The Advanced Audio Coding format may be relatively new (it became official in 1997), but it has a fine pedigree. Scientists at Dolby, Sony, Nokia, AT&T, and those busy folks at Fraunhofer collaborated to come up with a method of squeezing multimedia files of the highest possible quality into the smallest possible space—at least small enough to fit through a modem line. During listening tests, many people couldn't distinguish between a compressed high-quality AAC file and an original recording.

What's so great about AAC on the iPod? For starters, the format can do the Big Sound/Small File Size trick even better than MP3. Because of its tighter compression technique, a song encoded in the AAC format sounds better (to most ears, anyway) and takes up less space on the computer than if it were encoded with the same quality settings as an MP3 file. Encoding your files in the AAC format is how Apple says you can stuff 15,000 songs onto a 60 GB iPod.

The AAC format can also be copy-protected (unlike MP3), which is why Apple uses it on the iTunes Music Store. (The record companies would never have permitted Apple to distribute their property without copy protection.)

> *Note:* You can think of AAC as the Apple equivalent of WMA, the copy-protected Microsoft format used by all online music stores except Apple's. For better or worse, the iPod doesn't recognize copy-protected WMA files; it can download $1-a-song music only from Apple's iTunes Music Store.

Since the iPod can play several different audio formats, you can have a mix of MP3 and AAC files on the device if you want to encode your future CD purchases with the newer format. If you want to read more technical specifications on AAC before deciding, Apple has a page on the format at *www.apple.com/mpeg4/aac.*

> *Note:* AAC is the audio component of MPEG-4, a video format that's designed to get high-quality video compressed enough to travel over computer networks (even pokey old modem lines) and still look good onscreen.

WAV

The iPod was designed to handle AAC and MP3 formats the most efficiently, but it's not limited to them.

WAV, for example, is a standard Windows sound format, going all the way back to Windows 95. (Macs can play WAV files, too.) Windows fans download WAV recordings for everything from TV-show snippets to start-up sounds. A WAV song usually sounds better than the same song in MP3—but takes up more room.

AIFF

The AIFF standard (Audio Interchange File Format) can create sound files that sound spectacular—in fact, these are the audio files on commercial music CDs—but they hog hard drive space. For example, if you stick Prince's Purple Rain CD into your computer, double-click the disc icon, and drag the song file for "Let's Go Crazy" onto your desktop, you'll soon have a 46.9 MB AIFF file on your hard drive. Although the sound fidelity is tops, the files are usually ten times bigger in size than MP3s.

Apple originally developed the AIFF standard, but AIFF files play on other operating systems, too.

> *Note:* If you insist on putting gargantuan files like AIFFs on your iPod, you'll have to worry about running out of battery power as well as disk space.

A modern iPod comes with a 32 MB memory chip. Yes, it serves as skip protection, because it stores 25 minutes' worth of MP3 or AAC music. But it also serves as a battery-life enhancer, because the hard drive stops spinning whenever the music plays from the memory buffer.

If you have big song files on the iPod, the memory buffer holds less music. When it runs out of music data, the iPod has no choice but to read from the hard drive, which runs your battery down much faster.

Audible

You can listen to more than just music on your iPod; you can also listen to the spoken word. Not books on tape, exactly, but more like books on MP3—courtesy of *www.audible.com.*

There, you can find over 25,000 spoken recordings to download. These are downloadable versions of the same professionally produced audio books you see in stores: the latest bestsellers in popular genres, children's books, and even old science fiction faves like Neal Stephenson's *Snow Crash*. Details on page 74.

Apple Lossless Encoder

As you probably know, a program like iTunes creates MP3 and AAC files by throwing away some of the audio data (mostly stuff you can't hear). Geeks call these *lossy* formats. But for true audiophiles with impeccable taste and bionic ears, lossy formats make music sound thin, tinny and screeching.

Of course, WAV and AIFF are *lossless*—no audio data is lost—but these files take up a huge amount of hard-drive space, to the tune of 40 to 50 MB per pop song.

In iTunes 4.5 and later, you can use the Apple Lossless Encoder instead. It offers great-sounding files that take up about half the space of an uncompressed CD track. (It requires not only iTunes 4.5 or later, but also QuickTime 6.5.1. and iPod Update 2004-04-28 or later.)

Tip: Before you stack up the CDs next to the computer for an afternoon of ripping, you may want to test your format preferences by ripping test songs in various formats. Let your ears tell you which format and bit rate sounds best to you.

Phase 2: Choose a Bit Rate

That's a lot of sound-file formats to choose from, so here's some simple advice: most people use either the familiar old MP3 format or the spunky new AAC option. AIFF and WAV formats may offer better sound quality than MP3 and AAC, but result in larger file sizes, which takes up more space on your hard drive and your iPod, if you have one. AAC usually creates files sound significantly better than an MP3 recorded at the same *bit rate*, given you high audio quality in a small file size.

Now, bit rate may sound like one of those unbelievably geeky computer terms (which it is), but it plays a big role in how your music sounds when you snag a song from a CD and convert it to MP3 or AAC format. When it comes to sound quality, all digital audio files are not created equal.

The bit rate has to do with the number of *bits* (binary dig*its*—tiny bits of computer data) used by one second of audio. The higher the number of bits listed, the greater the amount of data contained in the file, and the better the sound quality.

Tip: Eight bits make a byte. So why are audio files measured in kilobits (thousands of bits), and not the more familiar kilobytes?

Force of habit. Geeks measure size and storage capacity in bytes, but network speeds and data-transfer speeds have always been measured in bits. When you encode an MP3 file, the transfer and compression of the audio data into the new format is measured in kilobits.

Files encoded with lower bit rate settings—like 64 kilobits per second—don't include as much audio information from the original sound file. They sound thin and tinny compared to a file encoded at, say, 160 kbps.

Just as you can't compare megahertz ratings across different chip families (like Pentium III vs. Pentium 4), you can't compare bit rates between AAC and MP3 files. A 128 kbps AAC file generally sounds much better than a 128 kbps MP3 file. In fact, tests by the group that developed the AAC standard found that a 96 kbps AAC file generally sounds better than a 128 kbps MP3 file. (Your ears may differ.) As a bonus, the AAC version takes up much less space on your hard disk and iPod. You probably don't want to encode AAC files lower than 128 kbps, though, as the sound quality will begin to suffer noticeably.

For both formats, the higher the bit rate, the larger the file size. For example, an MP3 file encoded at 160 kbps sounds a heck of a lot better than one recorded at 96—but takes up over twice as much disk space (1.5 MB vs. 700 KB).

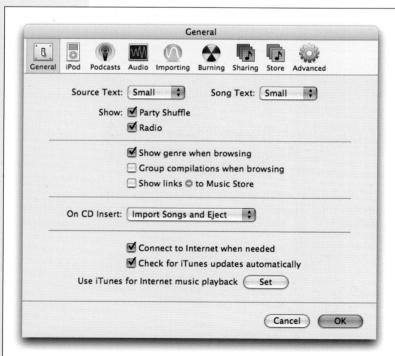

Figure 1-5:
The iTunes Preferences dialog box is where you give iTunes permission to go to the Internet to bring back CD information. You can also set the size of the program's display font for the Source and Song lists to either "Small" or "Large," and opt to show the Genre column in your iTunes browser window.

Got a lot of CDs to rip but no time to burn? From the "On CD Insert" pop-up menu, choose "Import Songs and Eject" to make iTunes automatically snag the track names, rip the tunes, and hand the CD back to you.

For MP3s, most people find that 128 kbps is a good compromise of file size and sound quality. At that rate, MP3 files take up roughly one megabyte of space per minute of music. The 128 kbps rate is considered high quality for the AAC format—which is why iTunes comes factory set to 128 kbps. (Songs for sale in the iTunes music store are 128 kbps AAC files, too.)

You're not stuck with the 128 kbps rate for your own home-ripped tracks. If you're a classical music fan and want to hear every nuance of a symphony, go for 160 or even 192 kbps. On the other hand, if you're listening to garage rock while strolling city streets, 96 kbps may sound fine, while giving you plenty of room on your iPod.

To make this kind of change, choose iTunes→Preferences and click the Importing icon (Figure 1-5).

Note: The iPod can also play files encoded in the MP3 VBR format, in which sophisticated software has adjusted the song's bit rate continuously along its length. (VBR stands for Variable Bit Rate.) The song winds up using more data during sonically complex parts of a song (higher bit rates) and lower settings during simpler parts. By constantly adjusting the bit rate, a MP3 VBR file conserves space more efficiently than a song encoded at a high bit rate all the way through.

To set up iTunes for MP3 VBR, go to Preferences, select Importing→MP3 Encoder. From the Setting pop-up menu, choose Custom to find the option for VBR encoding.

Phase 3: Download Song Names and Track Information

When you first insert a music CD, you may be disappointed to discover that to the computer, the album is named "Audio CD," and the songs on it are called "Track 1," "Track 2," and so on. It turns out that most audio CDs don't include any digital information about themselves. So if you don't do anything to solve the problem, after you've ripped, say, seven CDs into iTunes, you'll find that you have seven songs called Track 1, seven songs called Track 2, and so on—not the easiest way to organize your music.

There are two ways to remedy the problem: You can type the information in manually, or let iTunes go on the Internet to find out for itself.

The manual method

After you load up a CD, you can type in all of the song information for each track. To do so, click the track's name once to highlight its row, and then a second time to open up the renaming box. Edit away.

Tip: You can edit the information in the Artist, Album, or Genre columns the same way.

You should consider this purely theoretical information, however; you'd be nuts to go about naming your CDs and tracks this way. Read on.

The online way

If you have an Internet connection, choose iTunes→Preferences (or press ⌘-comma). The Preferences dialog box opens. Make sure that the settings in the bottom half of the dialog box match Figure 1-5. This setup allows the computer to zip out to the Internet to get the specific song information for the CD you've just inserted.

Behind the scenes, it's consulting a massive, comprehensive CD Database (CDDB), maintained by a company called Gracenote (*www.gracenote.com*). After iTunes sends information from the disc to the Gracenote CDDB servers, the database identifies the album and sends back the song titles and other data for iTunes to display.

(Firewall software may interfere with downloading CD track information. If you suspect that problem, ask your administrator to confirm that your computer's Internet settings are correct.)

If you don't have a high-speed connection, you may not want the computer dialing up every time you insert a CD. In that case, turn off "Connect to the Internet when needed." Instead, you may prefer to ask for the CD information when you're already connected to the Internet. Just choose Advanced→Get CD Track Names.

Phase 4: Convert the Song to a Digital Audio File

Once the songs on the CD have been identified, the song and artist names, time, and other information pops up in the main part of the window, as shown in Figure 1-6. Each song has a checkmark next to its name, indicating that iTunes will convert and copy it onto the computer when you click the Import button.

If you don't want the entire album—who wants anything from Don McLean's *American Pie* album besides the title track?—you can turn off the songs you *don't* want. Once you've picked your songs, click Import in the upper-right corner of the screen.

Tip: You can ⌘-click any box to deselect all checkboxes at once. To do the reverse, ⌘-click a box next to a list of unchecked songs to turn them all on again. This is a great technique when you want only one or two songs in the list; turn *all* checkboxes off, then turn those *two* back on again.

Another way to select a single song is to click it in the iTunes window and then choose Advanced→Convert Selection to MP3 (or whatever format you have chosen for importing). You can also use this menu item to convert songs that are *already* in your library to different audio formats.

As the import process starts, iTunes moves down the list of checked songs (Figure 1-6), ripping each one to a file in your Home→Music→iTunes→iTunes Music folder. Feel free to switch into other programs, answer email, surf the Web, and do other work while the ripping is under way.

Once the importing is finished, each imported song bears a green checkmark, and iTunes signals its success with a little melodious flourish. And now you have some brand new files in your iTunes music library.

Phase 4: Add Cover Artwork

Songs you download from the iTunes Music Store (Chapter 4) often include artwork, usually a picture of the album cover. iTunes displays the pictures in the lower-left corner of its main window.

But you shouldn't have to be a slave to the artistic tastes of some faceless, monolithic record company; you can install any art you like for any song. If Pachelbel's *Canon in D* makes you think of puppies, you can have baby dachshund photos appear in the iTunes window every time you play that song.

The only stipulation is that the graphic you choose must be in a format that QuickTime can understand: JPEG format, GIF, PNG, TIFF, or Photoshop, for example. Just keep in mind that the bigger the image size, the bigger the overall file size of the audio file and the more hard drive space you fill up.

Figure 1-6:
When you click Import, iTunes converts the selected songs from the CD to MP3, AAC, AIFF, Apple Lossless, or WAV files on your hard drive (depending on what you've selected in Preferences). The status bar at top shows the song being imported, the amount of time left, and the speed of the conversion. Songs in progress sport a wavy line in an orange circle.

Adding an image to an individual song: drag-and-drop method

To add an image file to a song you're listening to in iTunes, click the Show/Hide Song artwork button at the bottom of the iTunes window. The artwork pane appears. As shown in Figure 1-7, faint gray words appear in the pane, telling you exactly where to drag the image file. Just drag any graphics file right off of the desktop (or any other Finder folder) and into this space to install it there.

Tip: If you find an image on the Web that you love, right-click (or Control-click) it and choose Download Image to Disk to save it to your hard drive (the wording depends on your browser). Most browsers nowadays let you drag images off the Web page onto your desktop, too. Either way, you can drag the resulting graphic into the iTunes artwork pane.

Figure 1-7:
To copy a picture into the iTunes artwork pane, just drag it into the designated spot in the corner of the window (after you've selected the song you want to illustrate), as shown here before and after. You can also double-click any image that appears in this panel to view it in a separate window.

And speaking of CD cover art: Right there in iTunes, you can print out a perfectly sized CD jewel-case insert, complete with song list, by choosing File→Print, selecting a format, and clicking the Print button.

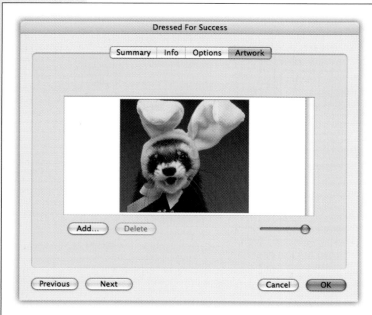

Figure 1-8:
Click a song and press ⌘-I, or choose File→Get Info, and click the Artwork tab. Click the Add button to select a digital photo from your hard drive. You can use almost any kind of photo or image file with your music. If you like the result, click OK.

Adding an image to an individual song: dialog box method

Instead of dragging a graphic off your desktop, you may prefer to use the Get Info dialog box, where at least you can inspect the image before accepting it. Figure 1-8 shows the way.

Tip: You can even install *multiple* graphics for an individual song. Just drag multiple images into the artwork pane; thereafter, you can click through them with the arrows at the top of the Selected Song bar. If you use the Get Info dialog box shown in Figure 1-8, you can click Add, and then ⌘-click the multiple graphics files to achieve the same result.

If you decide you want to get rid of any artwork or change what's attached to your songs, click the track and press ⌘-I. Click the Artwork tab, then click the art in the window. Click the Delete button to remove the image.

Artwork Made Easy

If you have a scanner, the original CD, and a large amount of free time, you can scan in album cover artwork yourself.

Alas, life is too short already. If that scenario doesn't appeal to you, there are plenty of places around the Web to download pictures of album covers that have been previously scanned and are just hanging out for you to copy.

Amazon.com and AllMusic.com have comprehensive selections, as do most sites that sell CDs. That's still a lot of manual effort, though: looking up an album, Control-clicking or right-clicking its artwork, choosing Copy from the contextual menu, and finally pasting into iTunes.

Fortunately, a great little free Mac OS X program called Clutter can spare you even that effort. (You can download it from *http://sprote.com/clutter.*) After you launch Clutter while playing a song in iTunes, it recognizes the song and automatically downloads an image of the album cover from Amazon.com.

The program has a pretty good track record, so to speak, for finding pop and rock album covers, but more esoteric fare may come up blank.

The album cover art appears both in Clutter's Now Playing window and the Dock. You can also drag the image onto your desktop to create a sea of tiny, floating album-cover windows, as shown here. When you click a cover, iTunes jumps to that album and starts playing it.

If you want to add your Clutter covers to your iTunes tracks. Choose File→Copy Cover to iTunes to quickly attach a copy of the artwork to your selected iTunes track.

Adding art to your tracks has another benefit besides making your iTunes window look pretty: if you ever decide to burn a playlist to an audio CD to give to someone, iTunes gives you the option to print out a jewel-case cover decorated with a mosiac made from the all artwork attached to all tracks on the playlist.

Adding an image to an entire album

To select the same art for *all* the songs on an album (or by the same artist), saving yourself a little time, open the iTunes browser by clicking the eyeball icon at the top right of the screen. Click the name of an artist or album in the browser, and then press ⌘-I to open the Multiple Song Information box. (You'll see a worrisome alert box from iTunes, asking if you're sure about editing multiple items. Click Yes.)

In the Multiple Song Information dialog box (Figure 1-9), turn on the Artwork checkbox, and then double-click in the white area. In the window that opens, navigate to and select the image file you want to use for all the songs on the album, and then click OK. (Of course, you can also drag a graphic into this white box, right off your desktop.) You'll see a progress bar as iTunes applies the artwork and any other group settings you've chosen for the files.

Click OK, confirm your decision one last time, and then enjoy the new album art.

Tip: You can apply the same image over and over again into all the songs in the same *playlist*. Visit *http:// malcolmadams.com/itunes* and download a copy of the "Selected Artwork to All in Playlist" AppleScript. The next time you have an image that you want to associate with all the songs on a particular playlist, just fire up that script.

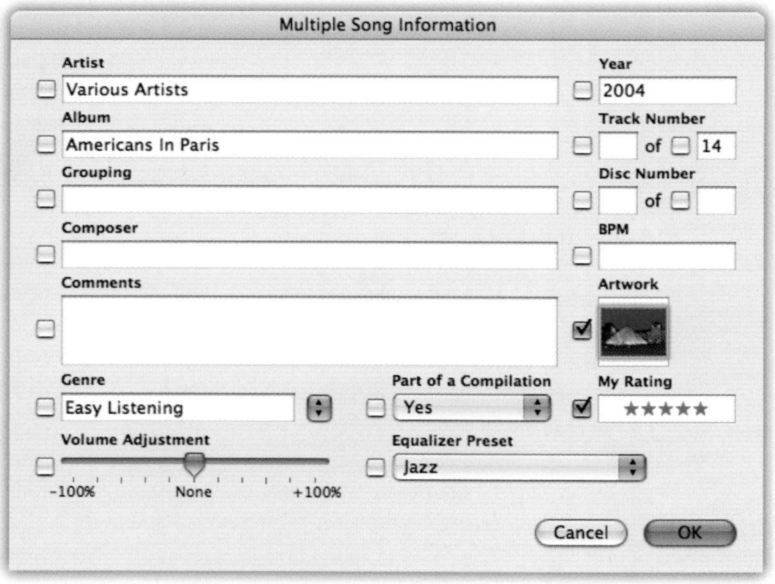

Figure 1-9:
The Multiple Song Information box can save a lot of time because it allows you to change information all at once for all the songs listed in the Artist, Album, or Genre categories. For example, you can assign the Equalizer's "Classical" preset to all your files in the Classical genre, add a picture of a yellow submarine to all of your Beatles tracks, or adjust the title of all the songs at once on a mislabeled album.

Importing Other Music Files into iTunes

Not all sound files come directly from the compact discs in your personal collection. As long as a file is in a format that iTunes can comprehend (MP3, AAC, AIFF, WAV, Apple Lossless, or Audible), you can add it to the iTunes music library by any of several methods.

Figure 1-10:
Select the file you'd like to add to your expanding iTunes library with the File→Add File to Library command. In iTunes 4.8 and later, you can even import video files in the .mov or .mp4 formats and watch them right within your album artwork window. If you find the Fig Newton-sized screen too small, you can also watch videos in a separate window or in glorious full-screen view by clicking the full-screen icon at the bottom of the iTunes window (page 76).

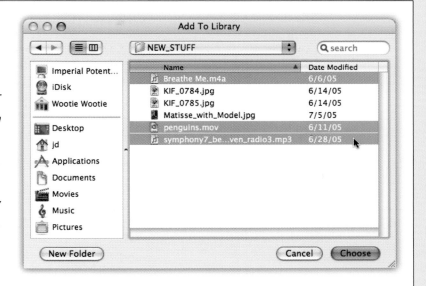

FREQUENTLY ASKED QUESTION

A Trip to the Library

Where exactly does iTunes store its music library on my computer's hard drive? Can I move the music library if my hard drive starts to get full?

The music library is the program's personal database. It stores all of the songs you've imported into the program, as well as all of the playlists you created from those songs. This database file sits in your Home→Music→iTunes Music folder.

If you rudely drag the iTunes Music folder to a different place without telling iTunes, it will think the songs are gone. The next time you start the program, you'll find it empty. (While iTunes remains empty but calm, *you* may have heart palpitations as you picture your music collection vanishing in a puff of bytes.)

To move the iTunes Music folder to a new drive, just let the program know where you're putting it. Move the folder to the desired location, then choose iTunes→Preferences and click the Advanced icon or tab. In the area labeled iTunes Music Folder Location, click the Change button, and navigate to the place where you moved the iTunes Music folder. Finally, click OK.

Exhale.

Note: The AAC format includes a copy-protection feature that MP3 doesn't have. Songs you buy from the iTunes Music Store and music encoded from your own CDs with iTunes work, but you may have trouble playing or moving other copy-protected AAC files (like those bought from, for example, LiquidAudio.com).

- If menus are your thing, choose File→Add File to Library. In the resulting dialog box (Figure 1-10), locate and click the file you wish to add, or ⌘-click several files to highlight them all at once. Click Choose to bring it, or them, into iTunes.

- You can drag a file or folder full of sound files onto the iTunes icon on the Dock to add the music to the library.

- You can also drag the files or folders straight into the iTunes window.

Now, when you read about iPhoto later in this book, you'll discover that dragging graphics into the iPhoto window from your hard drive creates a copy of them, which iPhoto stashes safely into its own private collection, deep within your Home folder.

Ordinarily, iTunes does the same with music files: When you drag one into its window, the program duplicates it, placing the copy into its own iTunes Music folder. That way, if you wind up moving or discarding the original during a frenzied cleanup binge, you won't return to iTunes to discover the song missing.

The copying business does, however, use up your hard-disk space faster, since every music file is getting doubled. Fortunately, you can override this behavior. Just choose iTunes→Preferences, click the Advanced tab, and turn off "Copy files to iTunes Music folder when adding to library."

From now on, iTunes will merely note the original locations of any music files you introduce, rather than making copies. If you move or delete those files, iTunes will no longer be able to track or play them.

Note: Don't have an iPod but still find yourself craving your iTunes tracks when you have to drag yourself away from the Mac? Thanks to a tidy deal between Apple and Motorola, you'll soon be able to download iTunes songs (including tracks you've purchased from the Music Store) to certain Motorola wireless phones by way of a Bluetooth or USB connection. The mobile-phone version of iTunes won't be available until the second half of 2005, but keep it in mind when you need to pick out that new cellphone.

Getting Music Out of iTunes

The first chapter of this section is all about getting music into iTunes, whether from a CD or by dragging audio files onto your hard drive. Now comes the payoff: the chance to hear and even see your songs playing, to burn them onto a CD, or to share them with friends and family over a network.

Playing Music

To turn your computer into a jukebox, click the triangular Play button in the upper-left corner of the iTunes window, or press the Space bar. The computer immediately begins to play the songs whose names have checkmarks in the main list. (You can also double-click a song's name to make it start playing.)

The central display at the top of the window shows not only the name of the song and album, but also where you are in the song, as represented by the diamond in the horizontal strip. Drag this diamond, or click elsewhere in the strip, to jump around in the song.

Or just click the tiny triangle at the left side of this display to see a pulsing VU meter, indicating the current music's sound levels at various frequencies.

Tip: You can also control CD playback from the Mac's Dock. Just Control-click or right-click the iTunes icon (or click and hold on it) to produce a pop-up menu offering playback commands like Pause, Next Song, and Previous Song, along with a display that identifies the song currently being played.

As music plays, you can control and manipulate the music and the visuals of your Mac in all kinds of interesting ways. As a result, some people don't move from their machines for months at a time.

Visuals

Visuals is the iTunes term for an onscreen laser-light show that pulses and dances in perfect sync to the music you're listening to. The effect is hypnotic and wild. (For real party fun, invite some people who grew up in the 1960s to your house to watch.)

To summon this psychedelic display, click the flower-power icon in the lower-right corner of the window (see Figure 2-1). The show begins immediately—although it's much more fun if you choose Visualizer→Full Screen so that the movie takes over your whole monitor. True, you won't get a lot of work done, but when it comes to stress relief, visuals are a lot cheaper than a hot tub.

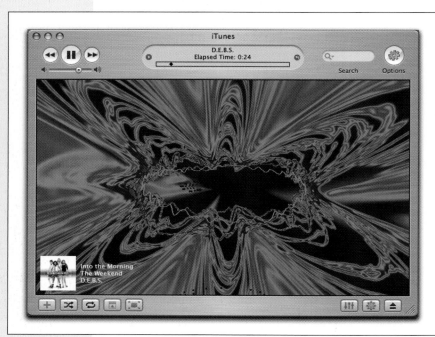

Figure 2-1:
No matter what you're listening to, the animated full-color patterns produced by the iTunes Visualizations feature can make it a more interesting experience. (This feature works really well with the original cast album from "Hair" or anything by Jimi Hendrix.)

Once the screen is alive with visuals, you can turn it into your personal biofeedback screen by experimenting with these keys:

Key	Function
?	Displays a cheat sheet of secret keystrokes. (Press it repeatedly to see the other shortcut keys.)
F	Displays, in the upper-left corner of your screen, how many frames per second iTunes' animation is managing—a quick, easy way to test the power of your graphics circuitry.

T	Turns *frame rate capping* on or off—a feature that limits the frame rate to 30 frames per second, to avoid sapping your Mac's horsepower when you're working in other programs (not really much of an issue in Mac OS X, of course).
I	Shows/hides information about the current song.
C	Shows/hides the current Visuals configuration (the name of the current waveform, style, and color scheme) in the upper-right corner of the screen.
M	Turns slide show mode on or off. In slide show mode, the visuals keep changing color and waveform as they play. (Otherwise, the visuals stick with one style and color.)
B	Turns on an Apple logo in the center of the Visuals screen.
R	Chooses a new waveform/style/color at random.
Q or W	Cycles through the various waveform styles stored in iTunes.
A or S	Cycles though *variations* on the currently selected waveform.
Z or X	Cycles through color schemes.
Number keys	Cycles through the ten different preset, preprogrammed waveform/color/style configurations.
D	Restores the default waveform settings.

Tip: These are the secret keystrokes for the *built-in* visuals. The Web is crawling with add-on modules that have secret keystrokes of their own.

Keyboard Control

You can control iTunes' music playback using its menus, of course, but the keyboard can be far more efficient. Here are a few of the control keystrokes worth noting:

Function	Keystroke
Play, Pause	Space bar
Next song/previous song	Right arrow, left arrow
Next source/previous source	Down arrow, up arrow
Louder	⌘-up arrow
Quieter	⌘-down arrow
Mute	⌘-M
Fast-forward, rewind	Option-⌘-right arrow, -left arrow
Eject	⌘-E
Turn Visuals on	⌘-T
Turn Visuals off	⌘-T or mouse click
Full-screen visuals	⌘-F
Exit full-screen visuals	⌘-T, ⌘-F, or mouse click

Shuffle, Repeat

iTunes has all the shiny controls you'd expect to find on a decent CD player, and more. In the Controls menu, for example, you'll find playback controls like these:

- The **Shuffle** command tells iTunes to get randomly funky with the order of the songs currently listed in your iTunes window at the time—an album listing, a single playlist, or all the songs in the library. A checkmark next to the Shuffle command means that the setting is already turned on; select Shuffle again to toggle it off. *Shortcut:* Click the Shuffle button, second from left at the bottom of the iTunes window.

- The **Repeat Off, All,** and **One** choices on the Controls menu make iTunes automatically play current playlists or albums over and over (Repeat All) or just once (Repeat One). **Repeat Off** disables the repeat function altogether. (You can choose only choose one of these commands at a time, and the checkmark shows you which setting is active.)

The Graphic Equalizer

If you click the Graphic Equalizer button (third from bottom right in Figure 2-1), you get a handsome floating control console that lets you adjust the strength of each musical frequency independently (Figure 2-2). (Or just press ⌘-2 to get the console onscreen.)

Tip: You can also make an Equalizer pop-up tab appear as one of the iTunes columns. Choose Edit→View Options and turn on the Equalizer checkbox.

To apply Equalizer settings to a specific selected song, press ⌘-I or choose File→Get Info, and click the Options tab, shown at bottom in Figure 2-2.

You can drag the Preamp slider (at the left side of the Equalizer) up or down to help compensate for songs that sound too loud or soft. To design your own custom preset pattern with the Preamp and the other ten sliders, click the pop-up tab at the top of the Equalizer and select Make Preset.

FREQUENTLY ASKED QUESTION

Auto-Playing Music CDs

In Mac OS 9, you could set the QuickTime Settings control panel to play music CDs automatically when they're inserted into the Mac. Can Mac OS X do that?

Sure!

First, make sure that iTunes is slated to open automatically when you insert a music CD. You do that on the CDs & DVDs panel of System Preferences (use the "When you insert a music CD" pop-up menu).

Then all you have to do is make sure iTunes knows to begin playing automatically once it launches. Choose iTunes→Preferences, click the General icon, and from the On CD Insert pop-up menu, choose Begin Playing, and click OK.

Preventing Ear-Blast Syndrome

No longer must you strain to hear delicate Chopin piano compositions on one track, only to suffer from melted eardrums when the hyperkinetic Rachmaninoff cut kicks in right after it. The Sound Check feature attempts to bring the disparate volumes onto line, making the softer songs louder and gently lowering the level of the more bombastic numbers in the iTunes library. Audiophiles may nitpick about the Sound Check function, but it can be quite useful, especially for times, like bicycling uphill, when constantly grabbing at the iPod's volume controls on the remote or scroll wheel are inconvenient.

The first step using Sound Check is to turn it on. In iTunes, open the Preferences box (⌘-comma). Click the Audio icon or tab and turn on the box for Sound Check.

If you have an iPod, also connect your iPod and select it from the iTunes Source list when it pops up. Then click the iPod Preferences button at the lower right side of the iTunes window.

Figure 2-2:
Top: Drag the sliders (bass on the left, treble on the right) to accommodate the strengths and weaknesses of your speakers or headphones (and listening tastes). Or save yourself the trouble by using the pop-up menu above the sliders to choose a canned set of slider positions for Classical, Dance, Jazz, Latin, and so on. These settings even transfer to the iPod.

Bottom: You can also apply preset or customized equalizer settings to individual songs under the Options tab in the song's Get Info box. If you have a live track with a lot of noodling or goofing around at the beginning or end of the song, you can use the Start and Stop Time controls in the Options area to edit out the borning parts.

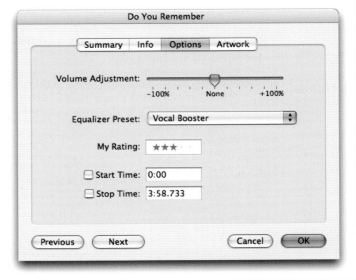

In the resulting dialog box, click the Effects icon and turn on the Sound Check dialog box. You also need to turn on Sound Check on the iPod itself: From the iPod's main screen, choose Settings→Sound Check and click the Select button.

Internet Radio

Not satisfied with being a mere virtual jukebox, iTunes also serves as an international, multicultural radio without the shortwave static. You can find everything from mystical Celtic melodies to American pop to programming from Japan, Italy, Germany, and other spots around the globe.

Computers with high-speed Internet connections have a smoother streaming experience, but the vast and eclectic mix of musical offerings is well worth checking out even if you have a dial-up modem. Just click the Radio icon in the Source list to see a list of stations, as shown in Figure 2-3.

Party Shuffle On, Dude

The standard iTunes Shuffle feature can be inspiring or embarrassing, depending on which songs the program happens to play. Especially when your guests discover the Milli Vanilli tracks buried in the depths of your collection.

Party Shuffle lets you control which songs iTunes selects when it's shuffling at your next wing-ding. It also shows you what's already been played and what's coming up in the mix, so you'll know what to expect.

To use it, click the Party Shuffle icon on the iTunes Source list. (If you don't see it, visit the Preferences dialog box, click General, and turn on Party Shuffle.) Until you turn it off, iTunes will display a message each time that describes what Party Shuffle does.

Now you see an extra panel at the bottom of the iTunes window, as shown here. Using the pop-up menu, select a music source for the mix—either an existing playlist or your whole Library. If you don't like the song list that iTunes proposes, click the Refresh button at the top of the iTunes window to generate a new list of songs from the same source.

Next, use the pop-up menus in the Display area to specify how many songs you want to see coming up in the mix, and how many recently played ones you want to see. iTunes can show you anywhere from 0 to 100 songs, either coming or going, and it can play tracks more often according to their play counts and ratings.

As in any iTunes playlist, you can manually add songs, delete them from the playlist, or rearrange the playing order. Party Shuffle may grab the same track multiple times, especially if you turn on "Play higher ranked songs more often," so watch for unwanted dupes.

(The shortcut menu that appears when you Control-click a song lets you add it again into the Party Shuffle mix—or, if you're seized with a sudden inspiration for your mix, designate it to play next.)

Once you're satisfied, click the Play button and let the music play on. With plenty of upcoming tracks displayed, you can feel free to mingle with guests without having to worry about your less-favorite songs crashing the party mix out of the blue.

If you find your radio streams are constantly stuttering and stopping, try this: Choose iTunes→Preferences. In the Preferences dialog box, click the Advanced icon or tab. From the Streaming Buffer Size pop-up menu, choose Large. Click OK.

Having the buffer set to Large may increase the waiting time before the music starts flowing through your computer from the Internet, but it allows iTunes to hoard more music at once to help make up for interruptions caused by network traffic.

Tip: It's possible to save music streams to your computer's hard drive, although the practice dances dangerously close to copyright infringement. Programs like Streamripper X (from *http://streamripperx.sourceforge. net*) let you save radio streams as MP3 files.

Figure 2-3:
The Radio list displays the categories and subcategories that can take you around the world in 80 stations with iTunes. Click the Refresh button to update the station list.

There are even more streaming radio stations around the Web at sites like www.live365.com and www. shoutcast.com. If you find a stream you like, click its link the link to listen and play the station through iTunes.

Podcasts

In addition to bringing an eclectic selection of Internet radio streams to your computer's speakers, iTunes 4.9 and later can round up, play, and organize *podcasts* for you as well. The podcast name itself is a tad misleading—you don't need an *iPod* to play them and they aren't broad*cast* over the airwaves.

Podcasts are just radio-like shows, recorded as an audio file and posted online. Just about anybody with a computer, a microphone, and something to say can whip up and post a podcast on the Internet for everyone else to download and play. And because the podcasts are just regular audio files, you can play them anytime you want to hear them. You can even play them on your iPod.

Podcasts can be about anything, from a weekly show about Scottish music to a daily rant about politics. Professional organizations like National Public Radio and the British Broadcasting Corporation even post some of their regular shows as podcast downloads. (In fact, some of the grass-roots amateur podcasters are mightily annoyed that podcasting has been "discovered" by the big faceless corporate entities.)

Before Apple included podcast support in iTunes, people had to hunt around the Web for the shows at sites like *www.podcastalley.com* and *www.podcast.net*, but iTunes 4.9 changed all that.

To get started casting around for podcasts from the comfort of your on iTunes window, click the purple Podcasts icon in the Source list. As show in Figure 2-4, any podcasts you've signed up for will appear in the list. Since you haven't signed up for any shows, click the Podcasts Directory button down at the bottom of the window to get a quick trip into the podcasts area of the iTunes Music Store.

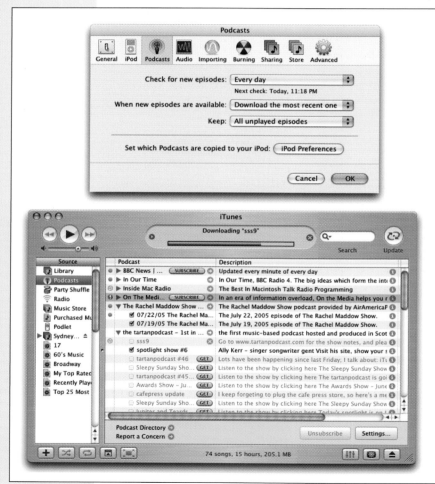

Figure 2-4
The iTunes Podcast feature lets you search for and subscribe to any of the hone-brewed radio shows available for free in the iTunes Music Store. In the Settings box (top), you can choose how often you'd like iTunes to check for new episodes of a particular show for you, and you also tell the progarm how many installments you'd like to keep on your hard drive.

With the Podcasts icon selected in the Source list (bottom), you can see just what you're subscribed to and how many episodes you have around. To find out more about a particular podcast, click the ❶ icon ext to its name. An exclama-tion point means you haven't paid attention to that podcast in awhile.

Unlike the iTunes Store music tracks that you pay for, most podcasts are free. To catch a 'cast, just click the Subscribe button to download it to your Mac. When you subscribe to a podcast, iTunes saves you the hassle of going back to the Store for updated episodes ; it automatically downloads your chosen podcasts right to your Podcasts playlist when new installments are available.

Note: An exclamation mark next to the name of a show in your Podcasts playlists means that you haven't updated the show in a while. iTunes is wondering if you till want to stay subscribed to it.

If you want to adjust your podcast settings, like how often you want iTunes to check for new episodes and how many old shows it should keep around at any given time, click the Settings button at the bottom of the window. If you want to update your podcast shows manually, turn off the automatic updating feature and click the Update button in the iTunes window to fetch fresh shows.

If you decide that a certain podcast is not for you, click the title in your Podcasts playlist and then click Unsubscribe at the bottom of the window. The show will stay in your list with a forlorn Subscribe button next to its title in case you ever want to you back to it. If you don't, select the name and hit the Delete key.

Tip: Love a podcast and want to know more about where it came from? Click the ❶ icon in your podcast playlist. A window pops up, listing the show's homepage and other pertinent information.

Burning a CD or DVD

If want to record a certain playlist on a CD for posterity—or for the Mr. Shower CD player in the bathroom—iTunes gives you the power to burn. In fact, it can burn any of three kinds of discs:

- **Standard audio CDs.** This is the best part. If your computer has a CD burner, it can serve as your own private record label. (Apple has a list of external CD recorders that work with iTunes at *www.apple.com/support/itunes.*) iTunes can record selected sets of songs, no matter what the original sources, onto a blank CD. When it's all over, you can play the burned CD on any standard CD player, just like the ones from Tower Records—but this time, you hear only the songs you like, in the order you like, with all of the annoying ones eliminated.

Tip: Use CD-R discs. CD-RW discs are not only more expensive, but may not work in standard CD players. (Not all players recognize CD-R discs either, but the odds are better.)

- **MP3 CDs.** A standard audio compact disc contains high-quality, enormous song files in the AIFF format. An *MP3* compact disc, however, is a data CD that contains music files in the MP3 format.

  Because MP3 songs are much smaller than the AIFF files, many more of them fit in the standard 650 or 700 MB of space on a recordable CD. Instead of 74 or 80 minutes of music, a CD-R full of MP3 files can store *10 to 12 hours* of tunes.

Just about any computer can play an MP3 CD. But if you want to take the disc on the road or even out to the living room, you'll need a CD player designed to read both standard CDs and discs containing MP3 files. Many modern players can play both CDs and MP3 CDs, and the prices are not much higher than that of a standard CD player. Some DVD players and home-audio sound systems can also play MP3 CDs.

Note: You can't easily convert copy-protected AAC files into MP3 files, so you can't burn an MP3 CD from a playlist that contains purchased music. If you're determined to do that, certain workarounds are available. You could use certain frowned-upon utility programs from the Web. Or you could burn the AAC files onto a CD and then rip *that* into iTunes, exactly as described earlier in this chapter. At that point, the songs are MP3 files.

- **Backup DVDs.** If your Mac has an Apple SuperDrive that can play and record both CDs and DVDs, you have another option. iTunes can also back up 4.7 gigabytes of your music collection at a time by copying it to a blank DVD. (The disc won't play in any kind of player, of course; it's just a glorified backup disk for restoration when something goes wrong with your hard drive.)

You pick the type of disc you want to make in the Preferences dialog box (Figure 2-5). Then proceed as follows:

1. **Select the playlist you want to burn. Check to make sure you have all the songs you can fit, in the order you want them in.**

   Consult the readout at the bottom of the window, which lets you know how much playing time is represented by the songs in the playlist.

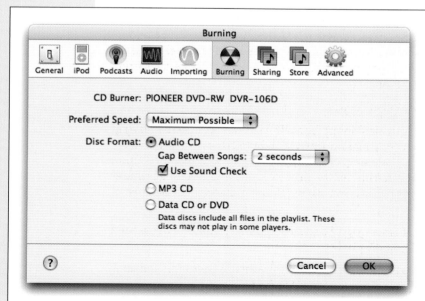

Figure 2-5:
Choose iTunes→Preferences, and then click Burning. Here, you select the recorder you wish to use, as well as what kind of CD to make: a standard disc that will play in just about any CD player, an MP3 CD that will play in the computer's CD drive (and some newer home decks), or a backup just for safekeeping.

Note: Although earlier versions of iTunes would stop burning a long playlist once it got to the last full song it could fit on a disc, your version is smart enough to ask you to insert another disc if it runs out of room on the first one—and then it picks up where it left off.

2. **When you're ready to roll, click the Burn Disc button at the top-right corner of the iTunes window.**

   The icon changes into a yellow-and-black graphic that resembles the symbol used for fallout shelters in the 1950s.

3. **Insert a blank CD into your computer's drive when prompted. Click the Burn Disc button again after the program acknowledges the disc.**

   iTunes prepares to record the CD, which may take a few minutes. In addition to prepping the disc for recording, iTunes has to convert the music files to the standard format used by audio CDs.

   Once iTunes has taken care of business, it lets you know that it's now burning the CD. Again, depending on the speed of your computer and CD burner, as well as the size of your playlist, the recording process could take several minutes.

   When the disc is done, iTunes pipes up with a musical flourish. Eject the CD (by pressing the Eject key at the upper right of your keyboard, for example) and label the top of the newly minted music storehouse with a magic marker (or your favorite method).

CD Covers and Printed Playlists

In versions of iTunes before 4.5, you had to do a lot of gymnastics just to make a nice-looking song list to tuck into the CD jewel case of a freshly burned disc. Not to make you relive any bad memories, or anything, but you had to export the playlist as a text file, import it into a word-processing program, format the type, and then, six hours later....*Print.* Nowadays, you just choose File→Print, select a formatting option, and click the Print button.

The iTunes Print box is now full of choices:

- You can print out a perfectly sized insert for a CD jewel case, complete with song list on one side and a miniature mosaic of all your album artwork on the other, as you can see in Figure 2-6. For a simpler CD insert, there's also a text-only option on a plain background. (If you opt for the CD jewel case, your resulting printout even comes with handy crop marks you can use to guide your X-Acto blade when trimming it down to size.)

- If you want something simpler, select Song Listing from the pop-up menu for a plain vanilla list of tracks on the playlist.

- The Album Listing option prints out a comprehensive list of all the original albums that you used when cherry-picking the songs for the playlist.

The Theme menu in the Print dialog box offers even more formatting fun, like adding User Ratings to a Song Listing sheet.

Tip: Want to use one of your own personal photos for the cover of your CD case? Just add artwork to a track (described on page 26) and then choose Edit→Print→Theme: Single Cover to place your own picture on the front.

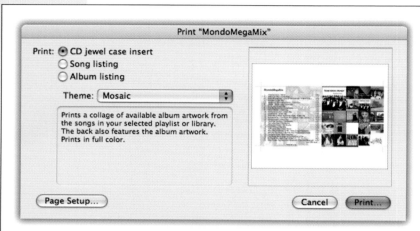

Figure 2-6:
With a playlist selected, go to File→Print to call up the iTunes print box. Pick and click the Print format you desire, select a theme (single picture or a mosaic, plain old text, etc.), and click the Print button for hard-copy proof of your CD-mixing prowess.

Playing Songs Across a Network

If you've taken the trouble to set up a home network so your family can share a printer, an Internet connection, and so on, more treats await. With iTunes 4, you share songs and playlists with up to five networked computers—Macs, PCs, or a mix of both. You could, for example, tap into your roommate's jazz collection without getting up from your desk, and she can sample the zydeco and tejano tunes from your World Beat playlists. The music you decide to share is streamed over the network to the other computer.

Note: In iTunes 4.0, you could even listen to music on Macs *elsewhere on the Internet,* as long as you knew their IP addresses (network addresses). It didn't take long for people to figure out how to exploit this feature and share music all over the Internet in sneaky ways that Apple had never intended.

In response to hysterical phone calls from the record companies, Apple removed this feature (and the Advanced→Connect to Shared Music command) in version 4.0.1 ad beyond. Now you can connect only to other machines on your own office network.

Machines involved in sharing music must meet a few requirements:

• All the computers involved in the sharing—both Macs and Windows boxes—need to be using at least iTunes 4.5.

- The computers must be on the same *subnet* of the network. (If you don't know what that means, read on.)

- The Sharing preferences for each computer involved must be set up properly.

Preparing to Share

The *Subnet Mask* (that is, the chunk of the network you're on) is identified by four numbers separated by periods, like this: 255.255.255.0. (Nobody ever said networking was user-friendly.)

Figure 2-7:
Top: The Sharing Preferences box lets you share as much of your music collection as you would like with other people on the same network. It also allows you to seek out music on other connected computers yourself. To share your music, you must first turn on the sharing feature and indicate what you want to put out there for others to sample.

Bottom: Once you've decided to share, your subnet pals can sample your collection right from their iTunes Source lists.

To check your Mac's subnet number, open System Preferences and click the Network icon. In Mac OS X 10.3 and later, double-click Built-In Ethernet, AirPort, or whatever line appears at the top of the summary list. You'll see your network info displayed, including the subnet mask.

Sharing Your Own Music

To "publish" your tunes to the network, choose iTunes→Preferences and click the Sharing icon. Turn on "Share my music" (see Figure 2-7 at top). You can choose to share your entire collection, or just selected playlists.

Tip: You can even share your tunes with another account holder who's logged into the *same* Mac simultaneously, using Mac OS X's *fast user switching* feature. You just have to make sure iTunes is open in both accounts.

Sharing music can get a little wacky if the first account is already playing a song when you start playing a second one; you get both songs playing at once, with no way to turn off the first person's music from the second person's account. It's one way to get Elvis to duet with Usher, but probably not the most listenable.

Whatever you type in the Shared Name box in the Sharing preferences will show up in your friend's iTunes Source list. You can also require a password as a key to your own music library—a handy feature if you feel that your colleagues mooch off you quite enough in other areas of life.

You can share AAC, MP3, AIFF, WAV, Apple Lossless files, and radio station links with your network buddies, but not Audible or QuickTime files. And sharing means "streaming" here. You can listen to shared music, but you can't burn someone else's music files to a CD, copy them to an iPod, or add them to your own library.

Finally, remember that songs bought from the iTunes Music Store can play on a maximum of five machines. If you want to listen to such a song across the network, one that hasn't been authorized on your computer, you must first enter the Apple account name and user password that was used to purchase the song.

Listening to Someone Else's Tunes

Once they've been shared, other people's iTunes libraries generally appear right in your Source list, labeled with whatever name your benevolent buddies have chosen for the shared collection. (See Figure 2-6, bottom.)

Double-click the desired song to fire it up and play through your computer's speakers. (Type the password first, if your pal has set one up.)

Tip: Want to know if a certain song is shared? Select the title and press ⌘-I, or choose File→Get Info. If the word "Remote" appears next to Kind in the Summary area, you're looking at a shared file.

If the other person's tunes aren't showing up, choose iTunes→Preferences and click the Sharing icon. In the preferences box (Figure 2-6), turn on "Look for shared music."

Turning Off Music Sharing

If you want a little privacy for your music collection, go back to the iTunes Preferences box (Figure 2-6) and click the Sharing icon. Turn off "Share my music" and click OK to disable the feature until the next time you're feeling generous. Your playlists are no longer visible to other people on the network.

AirPort Express and AirTunes

The AirPort Express, which resembles a PowerBook AC adapter after a few months of gym workouts, is a handy-dandy 802.11g Wi-Fi base station for a wireless network, just like its big brother, the AirPort Extreme.

"So," you say, "Why do I care about wireless networking in a book about my iLife '05 programs? I just want to learn how to use iTunes."

This is why: AirPort Express was made with iTunes in mind. Thanks to a built-in feature called AirTunes, you can wirelessly stream your iTunes music from your Mac, through the air, and out from your home stereo speakers (which are plugged into the AirPort Express)—all without tripping over a long and pesky cable connecting your Mac upstairs to your home audio system downstairs. All you need are these:

Figure 2-8:
Use the pop-up menu in the lower corner of the iTunes window (top) to choose where you want your music to be heard. If you have more than one AirPort Express base station (bottom)—in Apple's dreams!—then you can use this pop-up menu to specify which stereo you want to pump out the music.

When your remote speakers are turned off, by the way, don't forget to choose Computer from this pop-up menu. Otherwise, you'll hear nothing at all from iTunes.

- An AirPort Express mobile base station, which Apple will gladly sell you for $130 at *www.apple.com/airportexpress*. It includes the AirTunes software.

- A Mac with an AirPort card and Mac OS X 10.3 or later. (If you have a wireless network in place, you already have one of these. By the way, both Macs and PCs can pump music out to an AirPort Express.)

- Version 4.6 or later of iTunes.

- A cable that connects your home sound system (or powered speakers) to the Line Out port on the bottom of the AirPort Express. It can be either a digital fiber-optic cable or analog Y-shaped cable (that is, the stereo miniplug-to-dual-RCA connectors common on audio equipment).

Once you buy the pocket base station, some set-up software gently guides you through the chores like naming the base station and getting iTunes ready for its broadcast debut. Make sure to plug the AirPort Express into an electrical outlet close to your stereo system and use the proper cable to connect the two.

After the setup process is finished, a new little pop-up menu appears at the bottom of your iTunes window (Figure 2-8), displaying the name you just bequeathed to AirPort Express. Choose that and then click the iTunes Play to start broadcasting.

Tip: The AirPort Express also has a port to connect a USB-enabled printer, which lets all of the computers on your wireless network share the same printer.

Managing Your Music

A t its heart, iTunes is nothing more than a glorified database. Its job is to search, sort, and display information, quickly and efficiently. Here, for example, are some powerful managerial tasks it stands ready to handle.

Deleting Songs

If you want to delete a song or songs—like when you outgrow your Britney Spears phase and want to reclaim some hard drive space by dumping those tracks from the *Oops…I Did It Again* album—click the title in the Albums pane, select the songs you want to delete from the song list, and press Delete.

Tip: Selecting songs works just like selecting files in the Finder. For example, you can select a consecutive batch by clicking the first song's name, then Shift-clicking the last. Or you can add individual songs to the selection (or remove them from the selection) by ⌘-clicking their names.

When iTunes asks if you're sure you want to delete the music, click Yes. You'll usually be asked twice about deleting a song, the first time for deleting it from a list, the second time about deleting the music file from your iTunes music library altogether. If you want your hard drive space back, click Yes to both.

Searching for Songs

You can call up a list of all the songs that have a specific word in their title, album name, or artist attribution, just by typing a few letters into the Search box at the top of the window. With each letter you type, iTunes shortens the list of songs that are visible, confining it to tracks that match what you've typed.

For example, in Figure 3-1, typing *train* brings up a list of songs by different performers that all have the word "train" somewhere in the song's information—maybe the title of the song, maybe the band name. This sort of thing could be useful for creating themed playlists, like a mix for a Memorial Day barbecue made from songs that all have the word "sun" or "summer" in the title.

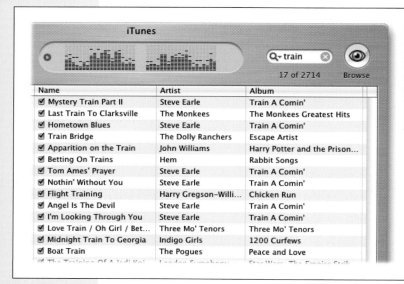

Figure 3-1:
The Search box in the iTunes window can quickly find all the songs in the library that match the keyword you enter. To erase the Search box so that you see all of your songs again, click the little circled X button at the right side of the box.

Figure 3-2:
When you click an Artist name in the left column, you get a list of all attributed albums on the right side. To see the songs you've imported from each listed album, click the album name. The songs on it appear in the main list area of the iTunes window, beneath the Browser panes.

If you see duplicate songs and suspect there might be more lurking around your iTunes library, choose Edit→Show Duplicate Songs to round up the doubles and clear up some hard drive space.

The Browser

The Browse button is the eyeball in the upper-right corner of the window. (It appears only when the Library icon is selected in the source list at the left side of the screen.) It produces a handy, supplementary view of your music database, this time organized like a Finder column view (shown in Figure 3-2).

Tip: Can't get back that full list of albums on the right Album pane after you've clicked on a name in the Artist list in the left pane? Go to the top of the Artist list and click All. The complete album list reappears.

It's worth noting, by the way, that this two-panel Browser can become a *three*-panel browser, much to the delight of people who enjoy the phrase "drill down." Figure 3-3 has details.

Figure 3-3:
The Genre pane in iTunes preferences can add another whole layer of categorizing for your music collection. If you don't see the Genre pane when you start iTunes for the first time, you need to turn it on in Preferences. Press ⌘-comma, or choose iTunes →Preferences→General, and then turn on "Show genre when browsing."

Ratings

Although there's no way to give a song two thumbs up within iTunes, you can label each song in your collection with a star rating (one to five). Not only can you, too, now feel like a *Rolling Stone* record critic, but you can also use your personal rating system to spontaneously produce playlists of the hits, nothing but the hits.

To add a rating to a song in the Song list window, first make sure the My Rating field is turned on in the iTunes Options box (⌘-J). Then proceed as shown in Figure 3-4.

Once you've assigned ratings, you can sort your list by star rating (click the My Rating column title), create playlists of only your personal favorites, and so on.

Tip: One the newer iPods, you can even rate songs on the go; your ratings will transfer back to iTunes. To rate a song on the iPod, start playing it and tap the Select button twice from the Now Playing screen. Use the scroll wheel to spin across the ghostly gray dots onscreen and transform them into the number of stars you feel the song deserves.

Figure 3-4:
Click inside the My Rating column. The position of your click determines how many stars you're giving. You can also add a rating by selecting a song, pressing ⌘-I to open its Get Info box, and then clicking the Options tab.

Ratings are helpful for snagging the best songs in your collection if you're making a Smart Playlist or using Party Shuffle.

Song Information

You have a couple different ways to change song titles in iTunes—to fix a typo or other incorrect information, for example.

In the song list, click the text you want to change, wait a moment, then click again to make the renaming rectangle appear. Type to edit the text, exactly as when you change a file name on the desktop.

Another way to change the song's title, artist name, or other information is to click the song in the iTunes window and press ⌘-I to bring up the Get Info box. (Choose File→Get Info if you forget the keyboard shortcut.) Click the Info tab (Figure 3-5) and type in the new track information. This is the way to go if you have several pieces of information to change.

Remember, too, that you can change the information for a whole batch of selected songs at once. See page 28 for details on the Multiple Song Info dialog box.

Tip: Once you've got a song's Get Info box up on the screen, you can use the Previous and Next buttons to navigate to the other tracks grouped with it in the iTunes song list window. This way, if you want to rapidly edit all the track information on the same playlist, on the same album, in the same genre, or by the same artist, you don't have to keep closing and opening each song's Get Info box.

Converting Between File Formats

iTunes isn't just a cupboard for music; it's also a food processor. You can convert any song or sound file into almost any other format: MP3 to AIFF, AAC to WAV, MP3 to AAC, and so on.

Tip: If you're going from a compressed format like MP3 to a full-bodied, uncompressed format like AIFF, you shouldn't hear much difference in the resulting file. Quality could take a hit, however, if you convert a file from one compressed format to another, like MP3 to AAC. If you're a stickler for sound but still want the space-saving benefit of the AAC format, it's best just to set the iTunes preferences to encode in AAC format and re-rip the song from the original CD.

To get the conversion underway, choose iTunes→Preferences and click the Importing button. From the Import Using pop-up menu, pick the format you want to convert to, then click OK.

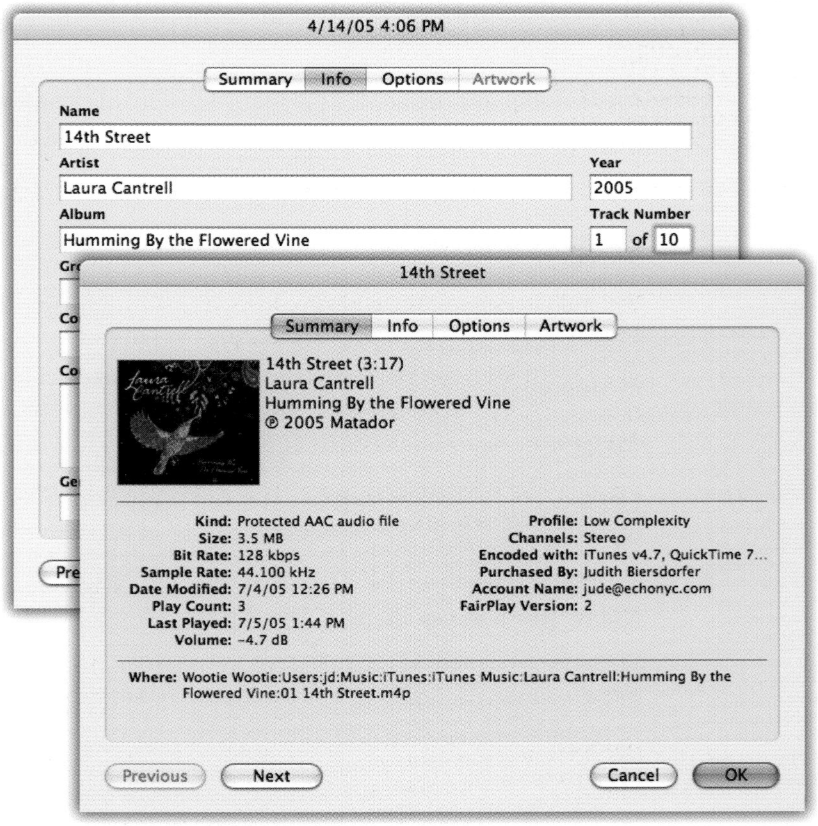

Figure 3-5:
Lower right: The Get Info box for each is where you can add, correct, and customize information for each song.

Upper left: Click the Summary tab for the lowdown on the song's bit rate, file format, and other fascinating technical details.

Now, in your iTunes library, select the song file you want to convert, and then choose Advanced→Convert Selection to AAC (or MP3 or AIFF or whatever you just picked as your import preference).

If you have a whole folder or disk full of potential converts, hold down the Option key as you choose Advanced→Convert to AAC (or your chosen encoding format). A window pops up, which you can use to navigate to the folder or disk holding the files you want to convert. The only files that don't get converted are protected ones: Audible.com tracks and AAC songs purchased from the iTunes Music Store.

The song or songs in the original format, as well as the freshly converted tracks are now in your library.

Joining Tracks

If you want a seamless chunk of music without the typical two-second gap of silence between CD tracks, you can use the Join Tracks feature to stitch together a sonic sampler in one big file. This feature is great for live albums or other CDs that run one song into the next.

To rip multiple songs as one track, pop in the CD you want to use, download the song information, make sure the list is sorted by track number, and then Shift-click to select the tracks you want to join during the ripping process. You can only join tracks that are in sequential order on the CD.

Once you've got the tracks selected, go to Advanced→Join CD Tracks. iTunes displays a bracket around the selected tracks, and indents the names of the tacked-on ones. If you change your mind and want to separate one of the tracks from the group, select it and go to Advanced→Unjoin CD Tracks. (You can Shift-click to peel off multiple tracks from the group, too.)

Click the Import button to rip the selected songs to one big track.

Tip: Suppose you're trying to join up some tracks, but iTunes is having none of it—it's dimming the Join Tracks command in the menu. The solution: Make sure that the tracks on the CD are sorted according to ascending Track Number. (If not, click the top of the very first column on the left of the iTunes window. The top of the column should be colored blue and the triangle pointing upward.) Then try Join Tracks again.

Start and Stop Times for Songs

Most of the time, there's musical interest in every juicy moment of the songs that you download, buy, or rip from CDs. Every now and then, though, some self-indulgent musician releases a song with a bunch of onstage chitchat before the music starts. Or maybe you've got a live album with endless jamming at the end, as a song plays out.

Fortunately, you don't have to sit there and listen to the filler each time you play the file. You can adjust the start and stop times of a song, so that you'll hear only the juicy middle part.

As you play the song you want to adjust, observe the iTunes status display window; watch for the point in the timeline where you get bored (Figure 3-6, top). Say, for example, that the last two minutes of that live concert jam is just the musicians riffing around and goofing off. Note where *you* want the song to end.

Then select the track you want to adjust. Choose File→Get Info to call up the information box for the song, and proceed as shown in Figure 3-6 at bottom.

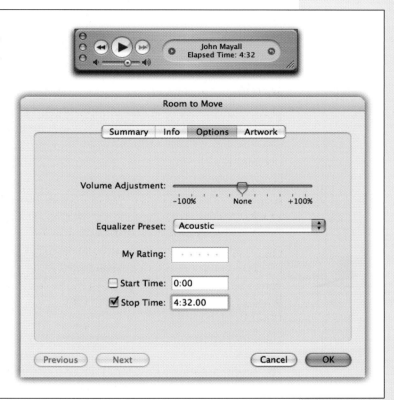

Figure 3-6:
Top: Song too long for your taste?

Bottom: Click the Options tab and take a look at the Stop Time box, which shows the full duration of the song. Change the number to the length of time you want the song to run, as you noted earlier. iTunes automatically turns on the Stop Time box. Click OK to lop off those last boring minute of the song. (You can do the exact same trick at the beginning of a song by adjusting the time value in the Start Time box.)

The shortened version plays in iTunes and on the iPod, but the additional recorded material isn't really lost. If you ever change your mind, you can go back to the song's Options box, turn off the Stop Time box, and return the song to its full length.

Playlists

A *playlist* is a list of songs that you've decided should go together. It can be made up of pretty much any group of songs arranged in any order. For example, if you're having a party, you can make a playlist from the current Top 40 and dance music in your music library. If you're in a 1960s Brit Girl Pop mood, you can make a playlist that alternates the hits of Dusty Springfield, Lulu, and Petula Clark. Some people may question your taste if you, say, alternate tracks from *La Bohème* with Queen's *A Night at the Opera*, but hey—it's *your* playlist.

Making a New Playlist

To create a playlist, press ⌘-N, or, if you're being paid by the hour, choose File→New Playlist or click the + button below the Source area of the iTunes window.

All freshly minted playlists start out with the impersonal name Untitled Playlist. Fortunately, its renaming rectangle is open and highlighted; just type a better name. As you add them, your playlists alphabetize themselves in the Source window.

Once you've created and named this spanking new playlist, you're ready to add your songs. You can do this in two different ways.

If this is your first playlist, opening the playlist into its own window might make it easier for you to see what's going on. To do so, double-click the new playlist's icon in the Source list, which opens a window next to your main iTunes window. From here, drag the song titles you want over to the new playlist window. Figure 3-7 demonstrates the process. (You can also open the iTunes Music Store into its own window with the double-click trick.)

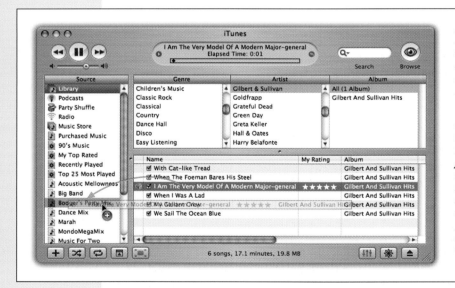

Figure 3-7:
Making a playlist is as easy as dragging song titles from your library window to your new playlist window. The other way to add songs to a playlist is to drag them over from the Songs window and just drop them on the new playlist's icon in the Source list. (If you have a lot of playlists, though, you risk accidentally dropping songs on the wrong icon.)

Don't worry about clogging up your hard drive. When you drag a song title onto a playlist, you don't *copy* the song; you're just giving iTunes instructions about where to find the files. In essence, you're creating an *alias* or *shortcut* of the original. You can have the same song on several different playlists.

Note: Anytime you see an exclamation mark next to a title in the iTunes song list, iTunes is alerting you that it can no longer find that song in its library. The song may have been moved or deleted by accident.

If you think you know where you moved it, double-click the song title and navigate to where you think the song is living. Once you find it, select the song file and click Choose.

Modifying a Playlist

If you change your mind about the order of the tunes you've selected for a playlist, just drag the song titles up or down within the playlist window to reorder them.

You can also drag more songs into a playlist, or delete the titles from the list if you find your playlist needs pruning. (Click the song in the playlist window and hit Delete or Backspace to get rid of it. When iTunes asks you to confirm your decision, click Yes.) Remember, deleting a song from a playlist doesn't delete it from your music library—it just removes the title from your *playlist.* (Only pressing Delete when the *Library* icon is selected gets rid of the song for good.)

Tip: If you want to mix up the songs on a playlist but don't feel like thinking about it, iTunes can do it for you. Click the Shuffle button at the bottom of the iTunes window. You'll hear your playlist songs in a random order.

Deleting a Playlist

The party's over and you want to delete that playlist to make room for a playlist for next week's bash. To delete a playlist, click it in the Source list and press Delete. (Again, this just zaps the playlist itself, not all the stored songs you had in it. Those are still in your iTunes Music folder.)

Tip: Want to change the name of your iPod? Once you've connected the iPod to the computer, click the iPod's name to select it and then click again to highlight the text. Type whatever name you'd like to call your iPod, and then click somewhere else. If you're using your iPod as a FireWire disk, you can also click it on the desktop and type a new name for it, just as you can with any file or folder.

Smart Playlists

Just as you can have iTunes vary your song order for you, you can also have the program compose playlists all by itself. Once you give it some guidelines, a *Smart Playlist* can go shopping through your music library and come up with its own mix for you. The Smart Playlist even keeps tabs on the music that comes and goes from your library and adjusts itself on the fly.

You might tell one Smart Playlist to assemble 45 minutes' worth of songs that you've rated higher than four stars but rarely listen to, and another to play your most-often-played songs from the Eighties. Later, you can listen to these playlists with a turn of the iPod's control dial, uninterrupted and commercial-free.

To start a Smart Playlist in iTunes, press Option-⌘-N or choose File→New Smart Playlist. A Smart Playlist box opens: It has a purple gear-shaped icon next to the name in the Source list, while a regular playlist has a blue icon with a music note icon in it.

Tip: When you press Option, the + button for Add New Playlist at the bottom of the iTunes window turns into a gear icon. Click the gear button to get a new Smart Playlist to appear in the Source list, all ready for you to set up.

Now you can give the program detailed instructions about what you want to hear. You can select the artists you want to hear and have iTunes leave off the ones you're not in the mood for, pluck songs that only fall within a certain genre or year, and so on. You can make a Smart Playlist using information from any field in the song's tag, like a collection of every tune in your library that's track 17 on an album.

Click the little + sign at the end of each line to keep adding criteria, or click the – sign to remove one. See Figure 3-8 for an example.

Then, provided the "Live updating" checkbox is turned on, iTunes will always keep this playlist updated as your collection changes, as you change your ratings, as your Play Count changes, and so on.

A Smart Playlist is a dialogue between you and iTunes: You tell it what you want in as much detail as you want, and the program responds back with what it thinks you want to hear. Once you lay out the boundaries, iTunes pores through the current contents of your music library and generates the playlist.

Tip: If you find Smart Playlists are becoming an obsession, take a browser ride over to *www.smartplaylists. com*. There, you will find many like-minded individuals exchanging tips, tricks, and tales about Smart Playlists, iTunes, and what they'd like Apple to add to the *next* version of the program.

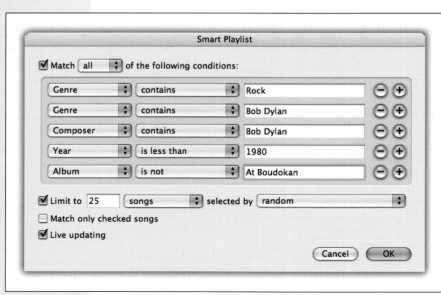

Figure 3-8:
This Smart Playlist seeks out all Bob Dylan songs in your collection, either written or performed by Bob, on albums released before 1980, but not including any songs from the Dylan At Budokan *album. This playlist would even include versions of his songs performed with other musicians, too.*

The iTunes Music Store

T he recent explosion in Internet song swapping presented the recording industry with a paradoxical challenge: to stop music lovers from freely trading
files over the Internet, while trying to make money themselves by selling copy-
protected music online. The early attempts, backed by the major record companies,
featured a monthly fee, a puny song catalog, and no ability to burn the bought music
to CDs or save it onto music players. What a deal!

Needless to say, people stayed away in droves. The free (and free-form) world of KaZaA,
LimeWire, and similar file-trading services were much more attractive.

Then Apple took a whack at it. In April 2003, the iTunes Music Store debuted, an
online component of iTunes that scored the hat trick that other companies had yet to
achieve: digital audio downloads that were easy, cheap, and—drum roll, please—legal.
Here's a look inside the store, and how to shop it.

Welcome to the Music Store

The iTunes Music Store has the backing (and the song catalogs) of five big music
companies, plus an increasing number of independent ones. Its inventory contains
more than 1.5 million songs from major-label artists like Bob Dylan, U2, Missy El-
liott, Jewel, Sting, and hundreds of other musicians in a range of popular styles like
Rock, Pop, R & B, Jazz, Folk, Rap, Latin, Classical, and more—and the collection grows
by thousands of songs a week. You can also browse, sample, or buy any of 11,000
audiobooks from Audible.com.

You can also find thousands of podcasts (page 37) free of charge in the Store, as well
as music videos and digital booklets of liner notes that come with some albums.

Tip: To see what songs have been added recently, click the Just Added link at the left side of the main Music Store page.

Farther down the page, you can also see and hear what famous people are listening to in the store's Celebrity Playlist section. It never hurts to know what Wynton Marsalis and Kevin Bacon are listening to these days.

You can browse the virtual CD racks from the comfort of your own computer, listen to a sample 30 seconds free from any track in the store, and download desired songs for 99 cents each with a click of the mouse. There are no monthly fees. And your digitally protected downloads don't go *poof!* into the ether if you decide to cancel your subscription, as they do with certain rival services. All your downloaded songs go right into iTunes, where they are just a sync away from your iPod's traveling music collection.

You can play the downloaded songs on up to five different iTunes 4–equipped Macs or PCs (in any combination), burn them onto an unlimited number of CDs, and download them to as many iPods as you like. Thousands of people use the Music Store every day, in fact, without even realizing that the songs are copy protected.

Apple's success with the iTunes Music Store—over 500 million downloads by mid-2005—caught its rivals' attention. These days, Apple's imitators in the dollar-a-song biz include Napster 2.0, Yahoo, Microsoft, Sony, and even Wal-Mart. (Remember, though, that music from these services come in Microsoft's Windows Media Audio format, which won't work on the iPod. Except Sony's music service, which uses its own proprietary file format—but that doesn't play on the iPod, either.)

Figure 4-1:
The Browse button and Search box in the iTunes window perform their song-locating duties on the Store's inventory. Each listing in the Choose Genre pop-up menu has its own set of pages.

Below it, you can see a lot of the latest Music Store bells and whistles: movie trailers, radio charts, etc. The Store itself is now available in more than 15 countries, including Canada and members of the European Union.

In the summer of 2004, Real Networks announced that the songs on its own Rhapsody music-download service were now iPod-playable, meaning that the company somehow reverse-engineered Apple's song file format. Apple wasted no time in announcing that (a) it was furious, and (b) it would simply change the iPod's software so that songs from non-Apple music stores would once again stop working.

A Store Tour

With iTunes running, click the Music Store icon in the iTunes Source list on the left pane of the program's window (Figure 4-1). If you use a dial-up modem, fire it up as you would to check email or surf the Web. If you have a cable modem or DSL, a message about connecting to the store appears in the status display at the top of the iTunes window.

Note: As you can imagine, the whole Music Store business (like just about everything else on the online these days), works *much* better over high-speed Internet connections.

Setting Up an Account

After you click the Music Store icon in the iTunes Source list and connect to the store, you land on the home page, which works like a Web page.

If you're in the mood to buy, you might as well take care of setting up your Apple Account now. To do so, click the Account: Sign In button on the right side of the iTunes window. A Sign In box appears.

If you've ever bought or registered a product on Apple's Web site, signed up for the AppleCare tech-support plan, have a .Mac membership, ordered an iPhoto photo book, or used another Apple service, you probably have an Apple ID already. All you have to do is remember your user name (usually your email address) and password.

FREQUENTLY ASKED QUESTION

Changing the Information in Your Apple Account

I moved and need to change my billing address for the iTunes Music Store. How do I do that?

You can change your billing address, switch the credit card you have on file for your music purchases, or edit other information in your Apple Account without calling Apple. Just start up iTunes, click the Music Store icon on the Source list, and sign in to your account by clicking the Sign In button.

Once you've signed in, you'll see your account name (email address) next to the Account button. Click it. In the box that pops up, type in your password again and click View Account, then click the Edit Credit Card button. You're ready

to change your billing address or credit-card information. In the main account area, you can also set up an allowance or buy iTunes Music Store gift certificates.

If you want to change your user name, password, or secret identity-proving question, click the Edit Account Info button. (Click Done when you're done.)

Note, by the way, that any changes you make to your Apple Account through iTunes affect other programs or services you might also use with your account, like ordering picture prints with iPhoto.

If you've never had an Apple ID, click Create Account. The iTunes Music Store Welcome screen lists the three steps you need to follow to set up your Apple account:

1. **Agree to the terms for using the store and buying music.**

2. **Create an Apple Account.**

3. **Supply a credit card number and billing address.**

As your first step to creating an Apple Account, you must agree to the long scrolling legal agreement on the first screen. The 23-part statement informs you of your rights and responsibilities as an iTunes Music Store customer. (It boils down to this: *Thou shalt not download an album, burn it to CD, and then sell bootleg copies of it down at your local convenience store.*)

Click the Agree button to move on to Step 2. On the next screen, you're asked to create a user name, password, and secret question and answer. If you later have to email Apple because you've forgotten your password—hey, it could happen—this is the question you'll have to answer to prove that you're you. Apple also requests that you type in your birthday to help verify your identity.

On the third and final screen, provide a valid credit card number with a billing address. After you click Done, a screen congratulates you on your account-setup prowess.

Click Done. From now on, you can log into the Music Store by clicking the Account Sign In button in the upper-right corner of the iTunes window.

Figure 4-2:
If you connect with a dial-up modem, you may want to turn on "Buy using a Shopping Cart," so that you won't have to wait for each song to download before proceeding with your next purchase. You might want to turn on "Load complete preview before playing," which prevents gaps and stops in listening to the sound clips because of slow connection speeds or network traffic. Click OK when you're done.

The Shopping Cart

Thanks to Apple's 1-Click option, iTunes can instantly download a selected track as soon as you click the Buy Song button. That's a quick and painless experience for people with high-speed Internet connections.

If you have a dial-up modem, though, you may not want to sit there and wait for each song to download. Each song may take several minutes, which can severely impede your shopping rhythm.

To solve this problem, iTunes offers a Shopping Cart option. When you use it, all the songs you buy pile up until the end of the session; then iTunes downloads them all at once when you click the Shopping Cart icon in your iTunes Source list (and then click Buy Now). This way, you can go off and do something productive (or unproductive) while the stack of tracks takes its time squeezing through the dial-up connection.

If this idea appeals to you, choose iTunes→Preferences. In the Preferences dialog box, click the Store icon, and proceed as shown in Figure 4-2.

Searching and Shopping

You don't have to log in to browse the store—only when you want to buy music or audiobooks. And music is everywhere you turn in the iTunes Music Store. Click any album cover or text link to zoom right to it. The upper left corner area of the Music Store home page offers a pop-up menu to jump straight to the Genres you want.

You can also use the Power Search tool, shown at top in Figure 4-3, to zero in on a specific song, artist, album, genre, or composer—or just peruse the text-based lists, as shown in Figure 4-3 at bottom.

When you find a performer you're interested in, click the name to see a list of songs or albums on hand for purchase. If you click an album name, all of the songs available from it appear below in the Details window. Double-click a track to hear a 30-second snippet of it to see how it suits you, or to make sure that's really the song you were thinking of, before buying it.

You navigate the iTunes Music Store aisles just like a Web browser. Most song and artist names are hyperlinked—that is, you can click their names, or album cover images, to see what tracks are included.

Click the Back button in the Store window to go back to the page you were just on, or click the button with the small house on it to return to the Music Store home page.

Tip: When browsing the store, you may see a small, gray, circular icon bearing a white arrow in some columns of the Details window. That's the "More Info this way!" button. Click it to jump to a page bearing details about the subject, like a discography page next to a singer's name in the Artist column, or to the main page of artists for the genre listed.

The main iTunes Music Store page also displays links to new releases, exclusive songs that can be purchased only from the Music Store, Apple staff favorites, songs scheduled to become available in the near future, sneak peeks at unreleased tunes, and the Billboard Top 100 charts going back to 1946.

Figure 4-3:
Top: Click the Power Search link on the Music Store's home page to do some serious sleuthing .

Bottom: Click Browse, then pick a Genre, a Subgenre (if there is one), and then click an Artist on the next list to see the albums available by that musician or group. Once you have settled on a Subgenre, the store unfurls a list of all the artists in that category.

Adjusting the Columns

Just as you can modify the look and information displayed for your own music library in iTunes, you can customize your columns in the iTunes Music Store. See Figure 4-4 for an example of how to modify which columns of detail information to display.

Figure 4-4:
Left: When the Browser is open, choose Edit→View Options to specify which columns of information appear.

Right: Or just right-click (Control-click) any column heading to produce this secret pop-up menu of available columns.

Remember, too, that you can drag column headings (like Time, Artist, or Price) horizontally to rearrange them, or drag the divider lines between them to adjust the column widths.

Buying a Song or Album

Making a purchase is as easy as clicking the Buy Song button next to a song (Figure 4-5).

Figure 4-5:
When you download an album, or even just one song from an album, you get music files in the AAC format. A color picture of the album cover is attached to the song file, which you can display in the artwork pane of the iTunes program window when you're playing that song.

The songs for sale in the iTunes Music Store cost 99 cents each. Most albums cost $10 to $14, which is quite a bit cheaper than the $17 or so you'd pay to buy the same album on CD. Plus, you don't have to worry about finding a parking space at the mall.

Tip: Many musicians in the Featured Artists area also have a free video that you can watch right in iTunes. Depending on your connection speed, it may take a few minutes for the video to download. Unfortunately, iTunes stops playing other songs, so that it can concentrate on snagging the clip. You're forced to download in silence.

The solution: Double-click it in the Source list to open it in a separate window. Now the iTunes tunes can keep spinning away in the background, giving you something to listen to as the video download proceeds.

Once you click that Buy Song button, the iTunes Music Store comes to your service. Now you see an "Are you sure?" alert box. Click the glowing Buy button to confirm your purchase decision, or Cancel if you suddenly remember that your credit card is a bit close to the edge this month. (You can also turn on "Don't warn me about buying songs" if you feel that there's quite enough nagging in your life already.)

Tip: Don't see a song or album in the iTunes Music Store that you really want to buy? Click the Requests & Feedback link on the Music Store's home page and send your plea to Apple. There's no guarantee they'll add it, but it can't hurt to make your wishes known.

Publishing Your Own Playlists (iMixes)

An *iMix* is a playlist that you publish on the Music Store, so everyone on earth can see your masterwork. You can name it, write your own liner notes explaining your mixing inspiration, and put it out there for everyone to see (Figure 4-6).

Figure 4-6:
Here's a typical iMix in the iTunes Music Store, posted by someone who listens to the same songs over and over again. If you like someone's mixing skills, you can give the collection a 5-star rating, tell your friends about it, or even buy all the songs on the list.

Start by signing into your Music Store account. Then, in the iTunes Source list, select the playlist you want to publish. (If it contains any songs that Apple doesn't sell, they'll get knocked off the list—which may ruin your carefully constructed mix.)

When you click the playlist, a gray arrow appears next to its title. Click the arrow to begin the publishing process (or choose File→Publish Playlist to Music Store). In the warning box, click Publish (and turn on "Do not show this message again" if you're sick of naggy little alerts in your face).

On the next screen, name your iMix and add your thoughts on making it.

Finally, in the iMix window, click Publish. Now other people can see your playlist, rate it, be inspired by it, or—and let's face it, here's the main thing—buy the songs for themselves.

To tell all your pals about your brand new iMix, click the Tell a Friend button on your new iMix page. iTunes sends a virtual birth announcement by email, complete with album-cover art.

GEM IN THE ROUGH

Charting History

Quick! What was the Number One song during your senior year in high school? What tunes were topping the music charts during your college years? If you've ever paid attention to any sort of a Top Ten list, odds are you were looking at a Billboard chart.

Billboard, something of an industry bible among music professionals, is a weekly magazine that's been tabulating and reporting lists of the popular songs and albums for over 50 years. These days, the company now uses high-tech methods to chart the hits in several music categories. SoundScan, for example, is a computerized system that tracks retail music sales. The tabulators also keep a close ear on what songs are spilling out of radio stations around the country. All these numbers get crunched together into a formula that's part of the Billboard chart recipe.

In addition to all the other ways to find and buy your favorite

songs, the iTunes Music Store lets you riffle through the Billboard top 100 charts going all the way back to 1946. (Missing entries in the song list—like the top three songs for 1968—reflect songs that iTunes doesn't have for sale, usually because the record companies or the bands haven't given permission for online sale yet.)

To see the charts, click the Charts link at the left side of the main page. Glancing at an old Billboard chart can serve as a sonic snapshot of a particular musical era: You see the songs listed, and you're instantly transformed back to the time when you heard them first (if, that is, you were even *alive* then).

Check out charts from the early Sixties, and you learn just how hip the girl-group sound was. Go back a few years further, and you discover the hip-shaking Reign of Elvis. Jump forward several decades, and you see hip hop transforming the cultural airwaves.

Tip: Want to e-mail a friend a direct link to your brand new iMix, or anybody else's? Control-click the playlist's icon on the iMix page and, from the shortcut menu, choose "Copy iTunes Music Store URL." Next, create a new message in your e-mail program and paste in the link you just copied.

Apple will send you an e-mail message congratulating you on your successful iMixing along with a link for your iMix. The Store keeps iMixes on its site for a year.

Gift Certificates

Gift certificates make perfect presents for People Who Have Everything, especially when purchased by People Who Are Lousy Shoppers. These redeemable email coupons are also an excellent way to save face in potentially unpleasant situations (*"Honey, you may think I forgot our anniversary again, but…check your email!"*).

With iTunes Music Store gift certificates, available both from the iTunes store or from Apple's Web site, you can send your friends and family $10 to $200 worth of credit to go hog-wild in Apple's music emporium.

To buy one, click Gift Certificates on the main page of the iTunes Music Store. After you choose delivery by either email or U.S. Mail, the process is like buying anything on the Web: You fill in your address, gift amount, personalized message, and so on.

If you already have an Apple ID, you can log in and request to have your credit card billed; if not, sign up for one. Once you complete all the pixel paperwork, your gift certificate will be on its way.

Tip: Before sending off a gift certificate, discreetly check whether your recipient's computer meets the iTunes 4 requirements. People on Windows 98, Windows Me, and older operating systems may be in for an even bigger pang of disappointment than if you gave them a box of cheap tube socks.

Figure 4-7:
Receiving and redeeming an iTunes Music Store gift certificate is as easy as opening your email and clicking Redeem Now to add the gift credits to your account. You can also send paper gift certificates through the U.S. mail.

Spending

Whether they come in the mailbox by the front door or the one on the computer, iTunes Music Store gift certificates are meant to be spent. Here's how they work:

- If you're lucky enough to be the recipient of an iTunes email gift certificate (Figure 4-7), redemption is just a click away. The Redeem Now button at the bottom of the message takes you straight to the Music Store, where the certificate's confirmation number pops up automatically. Click Redeem in the Music Store window to credit your account and start shopping.

- If the gift arrived by postal mail, start up iTunes and click Music Store in the Source list. On the main Music Store page, click the link for Gift Certificates. On the next screen, click Redeem Now. Type in the confirmation number printed on the lower edge of the gift certificate and click Redeem.

If you already have an iTunes Music Store account, log in and start shopping. If you've never set your mouse pointer inside the store before, you'll need to create an Apple Account. You have to provide your name and address, but you don't have to surrender a credit card number. If you choose None, you can use your gift certificate as the sole payment method—and end your shopping experience once you've burned through it.

iTunes Allowance Accounts

Allowance accounts are a lot like iTunes store gift certificates. You, the parent (or other financial authority), decide how many dollars' worth of music or audiobooks you want to give to a family member or friend (from $10 to $200, in increments of $10). Unlike gift certificates, however, allowance accounts automatically replenish themselves on the first day of each month—an excellent way to keep your music-loving kids out of your wallet while teaching the little nippers how to budget their money throughout the month.

Both you and the recipient need to have Apple IDs. To set up a monthly allowance, click the Allowance link on the main page of the iTunes Music Store and fill out the form on the next screen. After you select the amount of credit you want to deposit each month, fill in your recipient's Apple ID and password. (There's also an option to create a new account for the monthly allowance.)

Once the giftee logs into the designated Apple Account, the spending can begin—no credit card required. Once the allowance amount has been spent, that's it for music until the following month. (Of course, if the recipient *does* have a credit card on file, he can always put the difference on the card.) If you need to cancel an allowance account, go to your Account Info page (page 73) to take care of the matter.

Tip: Can't remember how much money you have left on your gift certificate or in your allowance account? Look at your iTunes window the next time you're logged into the store. Your balance appears right next to your account name.

The Interrupted Download

If your computer crashes or you get knocked offline while you're downloading your song purchases, iTunes is designed to pick up where it left off after you restart the program and reconnect to the Internet. If for some reason it doesn't go back to downloading, choose Advanced→Check for Purchased Music to log back into the Music Store to resume your downloading business.

Signing Out

If other people have access to your computer when you're not around, consider wrapping up your shopping session by clicking your name (next to the Account button on the Music Store window) and then Sign Out. Unless you're one of those exceedingly benevolent types, you probably don't want anyone else to come along and charge up your credit card with a music-buying marathon.

Locating Your New Tracks

You can find your new tracks by clicking Purchased Music in the iTunes Source list (Figure 4-8). As the dialog box says, you can work with the Purchased Music playlist as though it were any other playlist. That is, even if you delete a track from it, the song itself still remains in the iTunes music library. And behind the scenes, the corresponding music file stays in your Home→Music→iTunes→iTunes Music folder.

Figure 4-8:
When you click the Purchased Music playlist after buying music, iTunes offers an explanation of how the playlist works (top) and fills out your list with the newly bought songs (bottom). From here, you can play the songs, drag them into other playlists, transfer them to your iPod, or burn them to a CD to play on the stereo.

What to Do with Music You've Bought

As you know, the iTunes Music store gives you a lot more freedom to use your downloaded songs than other music services. There are a *few* restrictions, though.

Play It on Five Computers

You can play Music Store–bought songs only on an *authorized* computer. Authorization is Apple's copy protection scheme.

Between work, home, and the family network, not everyone spends time on just one computer these days. So Apple lets you play your Music Store songs on up to five computers at once: Macs, PCs, or any combination. You just need to type in your Apple user name and password on each computer. Each must make an Internet connection to relay the information back to Music Store headquarters.

Authorizing Computers

You authorized your first machine when you signed up for an Apple Account for the iTunes store.

To authorize a song to play on another computer, follow these steps:

1. **Find the song you want to transfer.**

   This step, of course, involves *finding* the song on your hard drive.

   Method 1: Open your Home→Music→iTunes→iTunes Music folder. Music Store files are easily recognizable by their .m4p file name extensions.

   Method 2: Just drag the song you want out of the iTunes window and onto your desktop.

2. **Copy the song to the second computer.**

   Copy the song file onto a CD or USB flash drive; email it to yourself; transfer it across the network; or whatever method you prefer for schlepping files from machine to machine.

   Deposit the songs in the Home→Music→iTunes→iTunes Music folder on the Computer #2.

3. **Bring the copied song into iTunes on the second computer.**

   To do that, you can either choose File→Add to Library (and then select and open them), or just drag their icons right into the iTunes window.

4. **In your iTunes list, select a transferred song and click the Play button.**

   iTunes asks for your Apple Account user name and password.

5. **Type your Apple ID and password, and click OK.**

This second computer is now authorized to play that song—and any other songs you bought using the same Apple Account.

Note: Although you may feel like AAC stands for Always Authorizing Computers, remember that this whole authorizing business is necessary only to play songs you've *bought.* To play songs you've ripped into AAC format from CDs, for example, or to play everyday MP3 files, you don't have to authorize anything.

Deauthorizing Computers

You won't be able to play the purchased music on a sixth computer if you try to authorize it. When you connect to the authorization system over the Internet, it will see five other computers already on its list, and deny your request.

That's a drag, but copy protection is copy protection—and it's much better than rival music services, which permit you to play downloaded music only on *three* machines (just like iTunes did before 2004).

In any case, you have to deauthorize one of the other computers if you want to play the music on Number 6. To deauthorize a computer, choose Advance→Deauthorize Computer, and then type in your Apple Account user name and password. The updated information zips back to Apple over the Internet.

Tip: Thinking of putting that older computer up for sale? Before you wipe the drive clean and send it on its way, be sure to deauthorize it, so your new machine will be able to play your songs from the iTunes Music Store. Erasing a hard drive, by itself, does not deauthorize a computer.

And what if it's too late? What if you've already sold the old Mac without remembering to deauthorize it first? Or what if you're slamming into the five-machine limit, and you *can't remember* which five you've authorized? You're in luck. Click the Sign In button the next time you're in the Music Store, and then click the View Account button after you type in your Store name and password. On the main account page, click the Deauthorize All button. Then log out and go re-authorize the machines you still own.

Copy It to Your iPod

Not only can you download your purchased songs to your iPod, but you can download it to *unlimited numbers* of iPods. Apple placed no copy restrictions on iPod joy.

Tip: If your iPod is a pre-2003 model, you must first update its software to version 1.3 or later. Otherwise, the iPod won't recognize files in the AAC format.

When you buy a song, it lands in the iTunes playlist called Purchased Music. But you can easily drag it into other playlists you've concocted within iTunes. The songs, artists, and albums appear just like any other tracks in iTunes.

Burn It to a CD

You can also burn purchased tracks to blank CDs, so you can listen to them in the car or on the big component rack in the living room. Here, Apple has put in only one tiny, almost irrelevant form of copy protection: If you've made store-bought songs part of a certain playlist, you can't burn more than seven CD copies of it in a row without making at least one change to the song list.

And if you find *that* limitation restrictive, you must be so dedicated a music pirate that you wear an eye patch and a parrot on your shoulder.

Share it Across the Network

You can also share purchased music tracks with other people on your same office network—by playing them live, not by copying the actual files. Details on page 40.

Back It Up

If your hard drive croaks and takes your entire music library with it, you have two alternatives. (a) Buy all of your Music Store songs all over again. (b) Calmly reach for the backup CD or DVD you had the foresight to make before disaster struck.

Backing up your music library

To back up your entire music collection, you want to copy the *iTunes* folder in your Home→Music folder.

Backing up this folder, huge though it may be, backs up not just your songs, but all the other work you've done in iTunes (creating and naming your playlists, organizing your columns, and so on).

You can use any standard backup method for this:

- Copy the folder to another computer via network cable.

- Burn it onto a blank CD (if the folder fits) or a DVD (if you have a DVD-burning computer).

- Use a program like Dantz Retrospect to back it up onto Zip disks, multiple CDs, or whatever you've got.

Figure 4-9:
Choose iTunes→ Preferences, click Burning, and click the button for data CD or DVD. Selecting the Data format for your disc will copy your files in their original MP3, AAC, or Audible formats without converting them to standard audio CD files, which would happen if you created an audio CD.

When your hard drive croaks, restore your backed-up iTunes folder by dragging it back into your Music folder. You're saved.

Backing up playlists

iTunes also has a built-in backup feature. Note, however, that it can back up only one playlist at a time.

This backup procedure isn't the same thing as burning an *audio* CD. Here, you're burning a *data* disc. That's important if you want to preserve the original file formats in your iTunes music library and avoid turning your high-quality AIFF files, for example, into squished-down MP3 files. To make this important change to your Burning desires, see Figure 4-9.

After you've chosen the Data format for your backup disc, make a playlist that includes all the files you want to copy to the CD or DVD. Keep an eye on the total size at the bottom of the window to be sure it will fit on one disc: about 650 megabytes for a CD, 4.7 gigabytes for a DVD. (If not, you'll have to file your songs away into multiple playlists—one per backup disc—to spread out your collection over multiple discs.)

Burn it to disc by clicking the Burn Disc button on the iTunes window. Insert a blank disc when the Mac asks, and then click the Burn Disc button again to start copying.

If your hard drive ever dies, copy this data disc's files back onto the computer and re-import them into iTunes to rebuild your library from the backup disc.

GEM IN THE ROUGH

Back Up Only What Needs Backing Up

They say that backing up is hard to do—but mainly, it's hard to remember what you've already backed up and what still needs attention.

Here, however, is a sneaky trick that makes iTunes help you make backups of all the songs you've bought or ripped since the last time you backed up your iTunes Music folder. This means you won't have to burn the whole darn library to a stack of CDs or DVDs each time, and can just fill a disc with the new stuff you've added.

After you've backed up your files to disc for the first or latest time, open iTunes and choose File→New Smart Playlist.

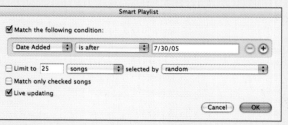

In the Smart Playlist set-up box, change the pop-up menus to say *Date Added—is after—[today's date]*. Make sure Live Updating is turned on, and that there's no limit set for the amount of songs on the playlist. When you click OK, give your new playlist a name, like Smart Backup.

The next time you're ready to burn a data backup disc, back up only your Smart Backup playlist to get the only latest library additions.

Then, once you've burned it to CD, choose File→Edit Smart Playlist change the Date Added to today's date, so that iTunes starts keeping track of the new stuff for your next backup.

Backing up non-music data

If you've got a .Mac account (Apple's $100-a-year suite of online services), you can use the handy Backup program to save copies of your personal files to a remote Web site, recordable disc, or external hard drive—including your list of iTunes playlists.

Music Store Billing

The iTunes Music store keeps track of what you buy and when you buy it. If you think your credit card was wrongly charged for something, or if you suspect that one of the kids knows your password and is sneaking in some forbidden downloads before you get home from work, you can contact the store or check your account's purchase history page to see what's been downloaded in your name.

The Customer Service Page

If you have general questions about using the iTunes Music Store, have a problem with your bill, or want to submit a specific query or comment, the online Customer Service center awaits. To get there, connect to the Internet and then choose Help→—Music Store Customer Service.

Click the link that best describes what you want to learn or complain about. For billing or credit-card issues, click Purchase Information.

Note: The iTunes Music Store sends out invoices by email, but they don't come right after you buy a song. You usually get an invoice that groups together all the songs you purchased within a 12-hour period, or every $20 worth of tunes that you buy.

UP TO SPEED

AAC, Copy Protection, and You

Apple's AAC files are copy-protected, but not all AAC files are. Some, which you may have collected from other Web sites, are freely copyable.

How can you tell the difference?

In iTunes, click the questionable track in the music library and then press ⌘-I. The Summary tab of the song shows the album cover, technical information about its encoding, who bought it, and where it lives on the computer. If the Kind says "Protected AAC audio file," well, you've got your answer.

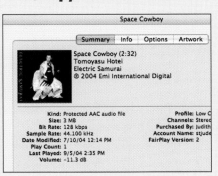

(In this picture, the phrase [remote] means that you're checking out a song that's on another computer on the network.)

Incidentally, the suffix on a protected AAC file (as viewed on your desktop, for example) is .m4p. iTunes 4 can play AAC files that were ripped in iTunes, and it can play protected AAC files downloaded from the iTunes Music Store.

But beware: you may have problems playing non-iTunes AAC tracks from another online music service or Web site.

Your Purchase History

To have a look at just how addicted you've grown to buying songs, open iTunes, click the Music Store icon in the Source List, and sign into the store. When you see your user name appear next to the Account button in the iTunes Music Store window, click it. In the box that pops up, click the View Account button.

When you get to the Account Information screen, click Purchase History. In the list that comes up, you see all of the songs you've bought (Figure 4-10).

Tip: Every wonder how something would play in Peoria? Now you can see for yourself *what's* playing in Peoria, thanks to the Radio Charts feature of the iTunes Music Store. Just click the Radio Charts link on the Store's main page to see what's at the top of the pops on 1,000 stations around the country.

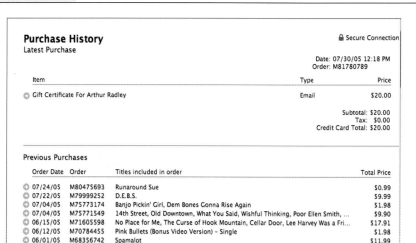

Figure 4-10:
The Purchase History area records all of the songs and albums downloaded and charged to an Apple Account, which can be useful for bracing yourself for the coming credit card bill. The list starts with the most recent ones.

Purchase History
Latest Purchase

🔒 Secure Connection

Date: 07/30/05 12:18 PM
Order: M81780789

Item	Type	Price
Gift Certificate For Arthur Radley	Email	$20.00

Subtotal: $20.00
Tax: $0.00
Credit Card Total: $20.00

Previous Purchases

Order Date	Order	Titles included in order	Total Price
07/24/05	M80475693	Runaround Sue	$0.99
07/22/05	M79999252	D.E.B.S.	$9.99
07/04/05	M75773174	Banjo Pickin' Girl, Dem Bones Gonna Rise Again	$1.98
07/04/05	M75771549	14th Street, Old Downtown, What You Said, Wishful Thinking, Poor Ellen Smith, ...	$9.90
06/15/05	M71605598	No Place for Me, The Curse of Hook Mountain, Cellar Door, Lee Harvey Was a Fri...	$17.91
06/12/05	M70784455	Pink Bullets (Bonus Video Version) - Single	$1.98
06/01/05	M68356742	Spamalot	$11.99

"Books on Tape" from Audible

Audible.com, which you can shop right from within the iTunes Music Store, is a virtual store filled with digital "books on tape"—not just books, but also everything from vocalized versions of the New York Times to programs like National Public Radio's All Things Considered. There are more than 25,000 spoken-word recordings on the site and you can hear free samples of most files for sale before you buy.

If you choose to subscribe, $15 a month gets you one recorded book a month, plus a daily, weekly, or monthly magazine or radio show. You can also skip the subscription business and just buy the books you want for a flat fee. Prices vary, but the audio file usually costs less than the hard copy and fits in your pocket better. "The Da Vinci Code," a popular mystery novel selling for $25 in book stores, was $20 on Audible. com when the book first appeared.

Formats within formats

Audible.com files that come from its Web site (and not from the iTunes Music Store) use the .aa file name extension. You can't convert .aa files to MP3, but you can burn them to an audio CD to play on the stereo, and you can copy them to your iPod.

Most recordings from Audible.com come in a variety of sound resolutions, from low-fi, AM radio–like sound to a really good MP3 quality. The Audible resolutions that work on the iPod are called Formats 2, 3, and 4 (from worst to best quality). Better audio quality, of course, means a bigger file to download.

For example, the 18-hour audio book for Snow Crash is split into two files. The first half is a 34 MB download in Format 2, a 63 MB download in Format 3, or a 127 MB download in Format 4. The various formats cost the same, but unless you have a broadband connection, you'll probably want to stick with the smaller file size.

Tip: If you decide you don't like the way a format sounds, you can download your selection again in a different format by logging back into your account on the Audible.com page—a benefit you don't get at the iTunes Music Store.

To make sure that iTunes is set to handle Audible files, choose iTunes→Preferences, click the General icon, and next to "Use iTunes for Internet Music Playback," click the Set button. When you download a book file from Audible.com, it shows up right in iTunes.

Before you listen to it, iTunes asks you to type in the name and password you set up for your listener account with the Audible.com site. After you type the Aubible pass-

Figure 4-11:
Whether you get it from Audible.com's Web site or you buy it right within the Music Store, iTunes plays your audio book just like any other track in your library. Longer books are split into multiple parts for easier downloading from the Audible.com site.

word the first time, you can listen to your book or show at your desk (Figure 4-11) or transfer it to your iPod like any other track.

You play them just like regular audio files; the iPod even remembers where in the audio book you stopped listening, so you can pick up where you left off the next time. Better yet, these little electronic bookmarks are synchronized between iTunes and the iPod; if you're listening to a certain chapter on your iPod while walking home from work, you can continue listening at your desk later, in iTunes, without missing a sentence.

Tip: It's fun to wander around in the iTunes Music Store as your own music plays, but it's extremely easy to drift away from your playlist-in-progress. If you want to go directly back to the song that's currently playing, just click the curled arrow on the right side of the oval iTunes display window.

This handy icon is called the Snapback arrow, and it serves as a one-click shortcut to the File→Show Current Song menu dance (or the keyboard shortcut ⌘-L). It only works when there's a song actually playing, but you can use it in your own collection or when while traipsing around song previews in the Music Store.

GEM IN THE ROUGH

iTunes Video on the Big, Medium, or Small Screen

When iTunes 4.8 hit the ground in the spring of 2005, geeks and bloggers quickly got very excited about an underpublicized feature of the new edition: iTunes could now download and play video clips right in its own Artwork window—or even over the Mac's entire screen—wth the click of a button.

To check it out, first make sure that iTunes is set for video fun: Choose iTunes→Preferences→Advanced, turn on Play Videos, and then choose what window type you'd like to view them in: the Artwork pane of the main iTunes window, in a separate floating medium-sized window, or at the full-screen size. (You can also summon the full-screen view at any time by clicking the full-screen button under the Source list.)

You can add video clips to your iTunes library just like you add songs, by dragging them into the window or by using the File→Add to Library command. Make sure the clips are in the .mov or the .mp4 formats before you import them,

though, or iTunes won't know what to do with them.

And you're not just limited to your own clips, either. In the summer of 2005, the iTunes Music Store began selling "bonus" video clips along with certain albums, including works by the Shins, Coldplay, and the Dave Matthews Band. You'll know when a video is available, thanks to the little gray video camera icon next to the song's name. (Videos are usually included with album-only purchases. Some albums include a PDF file of the liner notes as well as the video, which means you're getting everything the CD buyer gets except for a breakable plastic jewel box.)

Sure, your album download times are a little longer because you're pulling down a big 50- or 60-megabyte video file, but when you get it to your Mac, you have a cool extra feature alongside your new album's tracks—and, one day soon, maybe even on the screen of your iPod.

The iPod Connection

i Tunes is a lot of things to a lot of people. But for millions of people, iTunes is primarily the loading dock for an iPod. Once connected to the Mac, the iPod is ready to accept whatever you want to give it.

This chapter is dedicated to that concept of iPod as Satellite to Your Computer. All you need is the FireWire or USB 2.0 cable for the connection that gets songs and files off the mother ship and onto the ultraportable, ready-to-go iPod. And if you have an iPod Shuffle model, you don't even need the cable; the player itself plugs right into the USB port.

Your Very First Sync

Connecting an iPod or iPod Mini is simple: Just plug its FireWire cable (or its dock) to the FireWire jack on your Mac. iTunes opens automatically and begins copying your entire music library to the player (see Figure 5-1). If you have Mac OS X 10.3.4 or later and a recent iPod model (or iPod Mini), you can use a USB 2.0 cable instead.

If you have a light 'n' sporty iPod Shuffle, on the other hand, odds are you can't fit your entire iTunes library onto the smaller player, which comes in much smaller capacities than the bigger iPods. If you don't want to manually add the music yourself, you can click the handy Autofill button that appears at the bottom of the iTunes window when your Shuffle is plugged in, as shown in Figure 5-2. Autofill does what it says, and randomly fills up your Shuffle with songs.

Tip: If you *don't* want iTunes to appear automatically every time the iPod is connected, you can turn off this option in the iPod Preferences dialog box (Figure 5-3).

Variations on the Auto-Transfer Theme

The beauty of the iTunes/iPod system is that whatever music you add to your Mac gets added to the iPod automatically, effortlessly. You've always got your entire music collection with you. Just plugging in the iPod inspires iTunes to open up and sync.

It's conceivable, however, that you won't always want complete and automatic syncing to take place whenever you connect the 'Pod. Maybe you use the iPod primarily as an external hard drive, so you don't especially care to have iTunes jumping up like a West

Figure 5-1:
The Source list (left side) displays an icon for the iPod when it's connected, as well as your music library, list of playlists, songs from the iTunes Music Store, podcasts, and Internet radio stations. The bottom of the window shows the amount of space left on the iPod, the number of songs, and consecutive days the iPod can play music without repeating songs.

Figure 5-2:
With the Autofill function, you can have iTunes automatically fill your iPod Shuffle to the brim with tracks from your music library. In the Autofill panel at the bottom of the window, you can tell iTunes where to look for songs to snag, whether or not you want higher-rated tracks, or if you want it all to be a random adventure.

Highland terrier every time you plug in the iPod. Maybe you want to synchronize only *some* of your music, not all of it. Or maybe you have an iPod Shuffle.

Fortunately, you're in complete control of the situation.

Stop Auto-Opening iTunes

If you like, you can command your jukebox software to open only when *you* want it to, rather than every time the iPod is plugged in.

When the iPod plugged in, click its icon in the Source list. Then click the iPod-shaped icon in the bottom right part of the iTunes window (identified in Figure 5-3). The

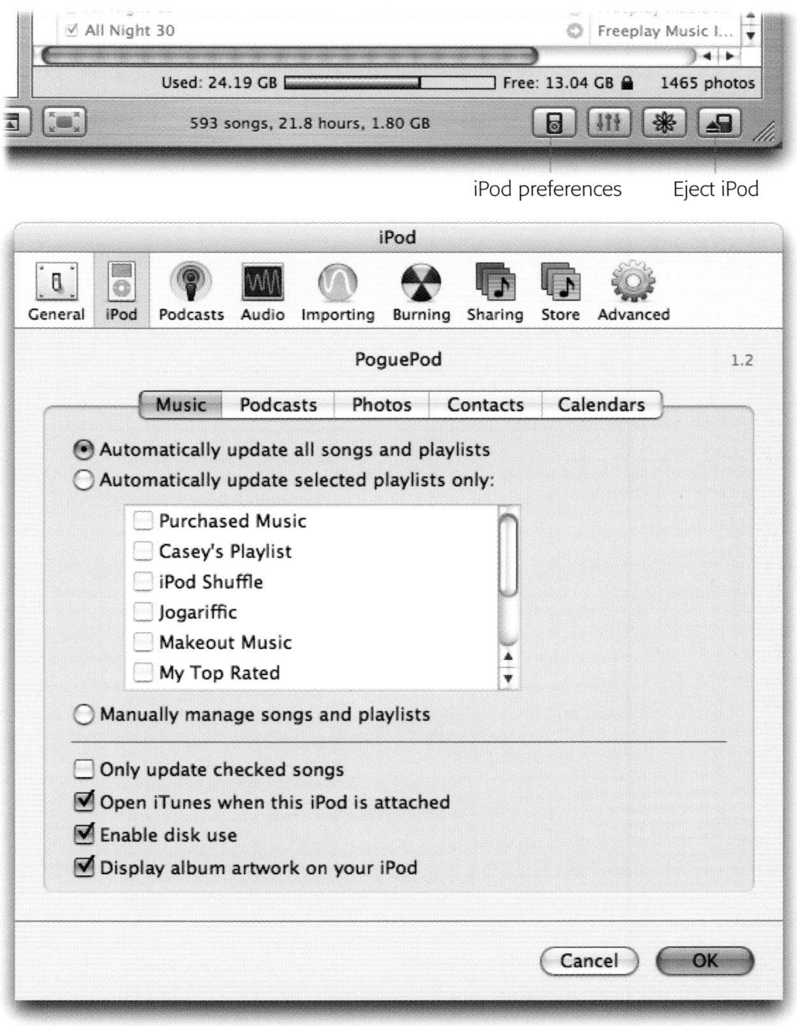

Figure 5-3:
Top: Click the identified button to call up the iPod Preferences dialog box. (The second button provides access to equalizer settings; the third controls screen displays. The Eject iPod button dismounts the iPod from the computer.)

Bottom: In the iPod Preferences box, you can choose to have the iPod update everything automatically or just certain playlists. "Manually manage songs and playlists" lets you move just the songs you want to the iPod.

The "Display album artwork on your iPod" option appears only if your iPod has a color screen.

iPod preferences   Eject iPod

iPod's Preferences box appears, where you can turn off the "Open iTunes when attached" checkbox.

Transfer Only Some Songs

The auto-sync option for iPod and iPod Minis pretty much removes any thought process required to move music to the iPod. But if you'd rather take control of the process, or you just want to transfer *some* songs or playlists, you can change the synchronization settings.

With the main iTunes window open, click the name of your iPod in the Source list on the left side of the window. Look at the bottom of the iPod window for the four small buttons along the right side (Figure 5-3). Click the first button, which has a small graphic of an iPod on it, to open the iPod Preferences dialog box.

Once the Options dialog box is open, click the third tab, labeled Synchronization.

The dialog box before you lets you control how the syncing of your library goes:

Complete automatic synchronization

"Automatically update all songs and playlists" means that your computer's music collection and your iPod's will be kept identical, no matter what songs you add or remove from the computer.

Figure 5-4:
You can add songs to the iPod playlists by dragging them out of your main Library list, delete them by clicking their names and then pressing the Delete key, drag playlists onto playlists to merge them, and so on.

Manually adding songs and playlists to the iPod Shuffle works the same way: You see what you want to add and drag it over to the iPod icon.

If you have a PalmPilot or PocketPC, you may be thinking to yourself: "*Ah, sweet synchronization! I won't have to worry about losing any data, because everything is updated all the time no matter where I input them!*"

There is a difference, however: Unlike a palmtop, the iPod's synchronization with the computer is a one-way street. If a song isn't in iTunes, it won't be on your iPod. Delete a song from iTunes, and it disappears from the iPod the next time you sync up.

This, of course, is the iPod's system for preventing piracy. If song copying were a two-way street, people could wander around with their iPods, collecting songs from any computers they encountered, and then copy it all to their home computers.

On the bright side, the autosync system means that you never worry about which songs are where. With the autosync option, what is in the computer's music library is on the iPod, and that's that.

Sync up selected playlists only

Choosing to only sync up only certain playlists can save you some time, because you avoid copying the entire music library each time. This tactic is helpful when, say, you have a workout playlist that you fuss with and freshen up each week. You can choose to update only that playlist instead of waiting around for the whole iPod to sync. (This feature is also handy if you're a multi-iPod household. Each iPodder can maintain a separate playlist.)

Once you turn on "Automatically update selected playlists only," you're shown a list of the playlists you've created. Turn on the ones you want synced.

Manually manage songs and playlists

There may be times when you don't want any automatic synchronization at all. Maybe, for example, you've deleted some audio files from your hard drive that you still want to keep on your iPod. If you leave automatic syncing turned on, iTunes will erase any songs from the iPod that it doesn't have itself.

Turning on "Manually manage songs and playlists" means that no music will be auto-copied to the iPod. You'll have to do all the copying yourself.

TROUBLESHOOTING MOMENT

"Do Not Disconnect"

The universal symbol for NO!, pictured as a circle with a slash through it ($\varnothing$), is a common sight when the iPod is connected to the Macintosh. It appears whenever the two drives are busy exchanging music and data (and probably a little hard-disk humor on the side). If you're using the iPod as an external hard disk, or you've turned off the iPod's automatic synchronization feature, you'll see a lot of this Dr. $\varnothing$.

Breaking the connection while all this is going on can result in lost files and possibly a scrambled song. So if you need to unplug the iPod and get going for work, be sure to *unmount*

it properly (remove its icon from the screen) first.

To do that, click the ⏏ button in the iTunes window; by dragging the desktop icon of the iPod into the Mac's Trash; or by Control-clicking (or right-clicking) the iPod icon on your screen and choosing Eject from the shortcut menu.

When you've ejected the iPod correctly, its screen flashes a large happy check mark (older iPods) or pulls up the standard main menu, ready for action (2003 and later models).

Note: When you turn on this option, iTunes says, "Disabling automatic update requires manually unmounting the iPod before each disconnect." It's saying that from now on, when you're finished with the iPod, you'll have to click the ⏏ button in the lower-right corner of the iTunes window. This action safely releases the iPod from the computer connection.

From now on, you'll have to drag songs onto the iPod manually (Figure 5-4). After you close the iPod Preferences box, click the small triangle next to your iPod in the Source list. It reveals all the songs and playlists on the iPod, which work just like any other iTunes playlists.

If you have an iPod Shuffle and you opt *not* to use the Autofill button, you can manually add music without having to fiddle with any iPod preferences box. Just drag tracks or playlists and drop them on the Shuffle's icon in the iTunes Source list.

To delete songs off the iPod or Shuffle , click its icon in your iTunes Source list. Then, in the main song-list window, click the songs you don't want anymore, and press Delete. The songs vanish, both from the iPod's list in iTunes and from the iPod itself.

Tip: The Only Update Checked Songs option in the iPod Preferences box (Figure 5-3) can be useful in this situation. It ensures that iTunes will update the iPod only with songs whose title checkmarks you've turned on. If you have songs that aren't part of your iTunes music library, make sure they're unchecked—and therefore unerased—during an automatic synchronization.

The Unspeakable Act: iPod to Mac Copying

The iPod was designed to be the destination of a one-way trip for your tunes: music slides down the cable *to* the iPod, but songs on the player never make the trip back to the Mac.

This design was perfectly intentional on the part of its creators. As noted earlier, Apple's position appears on a sticker on every iPod: "Don't steal music." If the iPod let you copy music both ways, people might be tempted to turn the device into a pocket music-sharing service, capable of copying free copyrighted songs from computer to computer.

The truth is, though, that not everyone who wants to upload songs from the iPod to a computer is stealing music. You may have perfectly legitimate reasons for wanting to be able to do so.

For example, say your computer's hard drive self-destructs, vaporizing the 945 MP3 files that you've made from your paid-for CD collection. You legally own those copies. Shouldn't you have the right to retrieve them from your own iPod?

Most people would answer "yes." Some might even thump their fists on the table for emphasis.

And then they would clear their throats and ask, "Well, how can I do it, should I ever need to copy files off my iPod?"

Note: Once again, the following methods are printed here not to encourage you to steal music, but instead to help you back up and manage the songs that you already own.

The Hidden World of the iPod

Turning the iPod into a FireWire hard drive lets you copy everyday computer files back and forth from your Mac. But when it comes to your *music* files, you won't even be able to *find* them. The iPod and its music management programs use a special database for storing and organizing the music files—and it's invisible.

The name of the super-secret invisible iPod music folder is called iPod_Control, and there are software utilities that can make it visible. (You can download them from the "Missing CD" page of *www.missingmanuals.com.*) For example:

iPod Viewer

For beginners, the nicely designed iPod Viewer program (Figure 5-5) makes the whole copying-to-the-Mac procedure very simple.

Once you install iPod Viewer, open the program with your iPod attached to the Mac; click your Poddy little pal in the list. The program's preferences let you arrange your songs in the order you want. Then, when you click the Import From iPod button at the top of the iPod Viewer window (Figure 5-5), the program pulls in the list of everything on the iPod.

Figure 5-5:
The free iPod Viewer program lets you select all or just some of the songs you want to copy over to the Mac. The program also gives you the option of deciding what folder to put the imported songs into. Just click the Transfer Songs button at the top of the window to start copying. You can also transfer entire playlists, or make a CD of the imported files by clicking the Burn Data CD button.

OmniWeb

Yes, OmniWeb is a Web browser. But in addition to surfing the Net with it, you can also surf the hidden contents of your iPod and copy songs back to your computer. The OmniWeb browser sells for $30, but you can download a trial copy from the "Missing CD" page at *www.missingmanuals.com*. (Although paying for a Web browser may seem like a bizarre idea, OmniWeb has some wonderful features like saved browsing sessions, ad-blocking, and automatic bookmark-updating.)

To use OmniWeb to browse the iPod, drag the iPod icon off your desktop and into the browser window.

A list of all the files on the iPod appears, including the elusive iPod_Control folder. Double-click iPod_Control, and then the folder within it titled Music. You see a list of folders, all starting with F. Within these folders lie your songs. Double-click the songs you want to copy to the Mac; OmniWeb does the rest.

iPod.iTunes

Built for speed, iPod.iTunes keeps the Mac and iPod constantly in sync with each other, and only copies songs *not* found in the iTunes library. In case of a disastrous hard Mac drive crash, iPod.iTunes can fully restore music files and playlists in the iPod, and can even fix those accidents where you mistakenly delete music from iTunes.

The program also makes it possible to *clone* an iPod, making an exact duplicate of its contents, and can synchronize music and playlists together or separately. Once installed, iPod.iTunes walks you through its synchronization procedure in great detail.

Senuti

No, it's not the Latin verb meaning "to rock out." The name Senuti doesn't look like much until you read it backwards, and then the name of this clever little free program becomes all too clear, especially when you consider its tag line: *Everything in reverse.*

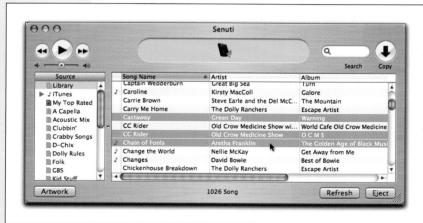

Figure 5-6:
Senuti's window looks just like the iTunes main window, except for the Copy button at the top. To use the program, just connect your iPod and start Senuti so it can display the contents of your player. Once you find the tracks you're looking for, click to select them and then tap the Copy button to send them to the Mac's hard drive.

Senuti, as shown in Figure 5-6, sports a decidedly familiar iTunesey look, with one big exception—a big ol' Copy button in the top right corner. Once you get your iPod connected to the Mac and start up Senuti, the program displays all the music tracks and playlists nestled inside your Pod friend.

As with iTunes, you can click the top of a column in the Senuti window to sort the list by artist, album, or song name for easy picking, depending on what you need to collect from the iPod's drive. Click a playlist's icon on the left side of the window or click to select the tracks you want to grab from the iPod's library, and then click the Copy button to bring the selected music home to your Mac's hard drive.

TinkerTool

You know how in those Invisible Man movies, people could only see him if he had a hat or a coat or a mask on, or spilled something on his invisible self? It was all about revealing the hidden aspects.

You can do the same thing with your invisible iPod files with the aid of some helpful freeware by way of Germany. TinkerTool, available on the "Missing CD" page at *www.missingmanuals.com,* is a system utility for Mac OS X that can make hidden files visible.

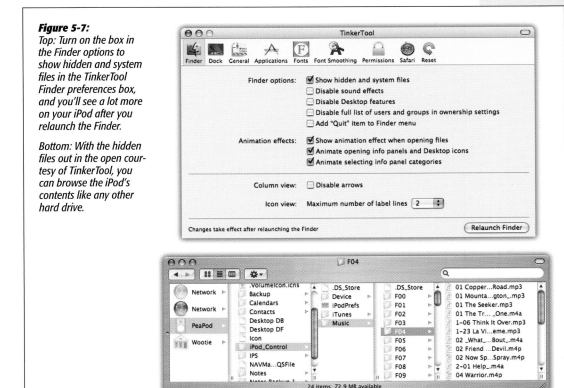

Figure 5-7:
Top: Turn on the box in the Finder options to show hidden and system files in the TinkerTool Finder preferences box, and you'll see a lot more on your iPod after you relaunch the Finder.

Bottom: With the hidden files out in the open courtesy of TinkerTool, you can browse the iPod's contents like any other hard drive.

Once you have installed TinkerTool on your Mac, you'll see an icon for it in System Preferences. Click TinkerTool; in the box that pops up, turn on "Show hidden and system files," and then click the Relaunch Finder button. Figure 5-7 shows the way.

When the Finder restarts, you see all the formerly secret invisible system files right there on your screen, as though someone had spilled paint on the Invisible Man. You see a lot of .DS_Stores all over the place, but step over them and connect your iPod to the Mac.

Double-click the iPod's icon to see all the files that live on it, including the iPod_Control folder that holds all of your music files (Figure 5-7, bottom). You can click through the folders from iPod_Control→Music→F00 (all the iPod's music folders are named F-something) and drag the files you wish to copy to your Mac's own hard drive.

Part Two: iPhoto

2

Camera Meets Mac

In case you haven't heard, the digital camera market is exploding. In 2004, digital cameras—close to *53 million* of them—outsold traditional film cameras for the first time. It's taken a few decades; the underlying technology used in most digital cameras was invented in 1969. But film is finally on the decline.

And why not? The appeal of digital photography is huge. When you shoot digitally, you never have to pay a cent for film or photo processing. You get instant results, viewing your photos just moments after shooting them, making even Polaroids seem painfully slow by comparison. As a digital photographer, you can even be your own darkroom technician—without the darkroom. You can retouch and enhance photos, make enlargements, and print out greeting cards using your home computer. Sharing your pictures with others is far easier, too, since you can burn them to CD, email them to friends, or post them on the Web. As one fan puts it: "There are no 'negatives' in digital photography."

On the other hand, while digital photography is full of promise, it's also been full of headaches. During the early years of digital cameras, just making the camera-to-computer connection was a nightmare. You had to mess with serial or USB cables; install device drivers; and use proprietary software to transfer, open, and convert camera images into a standard file format. If you handled all these tasks perfectly—and sacrificed a young male goat during the spring equinox—you ended up with good digital pictures.

iPhoto Arrives

Apple's answer to all these problems is iPhoto, a simple and uncluttered program designed to organize, edit, and distribute digital photos without the nightmarish hassles. Like Apple's other iPrograms (iMovie, iTunes, iDVD, and so on), its design subscribes to its own little 80/20 rule: 80 percent of us really don't need more than about 20 percent of the features you'd find in a full-blown, $650 digital-asset management program.

iPhoto approaches digital photo management as a four-step process:

- **Import.** Working with iPhoto begins with feeding your digital pictures into the program. During the import process, iPhoto duplicates your pictures and stores them in its Photo Library folder on the Mac's hard drive.

  In general, importing is literally a one-click process. This is the part of iPhoto covered in this chapter.

- **Organize.** This step is about sorting and categorizing your chaotic jumble of pictures so you can easily find them and arrange them into logical groups. You can add searchable keywords like Vacation or Kids to make pictures easier to find. You

Figure 6-1:
Top: This message appears to get you all excited about your voyage into the not-so-unknown. It acknowledges that you're about to use iPhoto for the first time, and is therefore a clue that you'll probably arrive at an empty iPhoto library window (Figure 6-2).

Bottom: If you're upgrading from an earlier version of iPhoto, this warning is the first thing you see when you launch iPhoto. Once you click the Upgrade button, there's no going back—your photo library will no longer be readable with iPhoto 1, 2, or 4.

Welcome to iPhoto!
iPhoto is your best choice for importing, organizing, and sharing your digital photos. Best of all, it's already right here on your Mac. There's no other software needed.

Optimized for Mac OS X.
iPhoto is engineered to take advantage of the speed and power of Mac OS X, so you can do more with your photos, faster.

No Drivers Necessary.
iPhoto does not require any additional drivers or software, so you can begin enjoying your digital photos the second you plug in your camera.

So Many Ways to Share
Send photos via email, print them on your home printer, or create your own customized photo books to share with friends and family. iPhoto lets you do more with your favorite shots.

OK

The Photo Library needs to be upgraded to work with this version of iPhoto.
Your Photo Library will not be readable by previous versions of iPhoto after the upgrade. The upgrade process may take several minutes depending on the number of photos in the library.

Quit   Upgrade

can change the order of images, and group them into "folders" called albums. As a result, instead of having 4,300 randomly named digital photos scattered about on your three hard drives, you end up with a set of neatly categorized and immediately accessible photo collections. Chapter 7 thoroughly covers all of iPhoto's organization tools.

- **Edit.** This is where you fine-tune your photos to make them look as good as possible. iPhoto provides everything you need for rotating, retouching, resizing, cropping, color-balancing, straightening, and brightening your pictures. More significant image adjustments—like editing out an ex-spouse—require another image-editing program. Editing your photos is the focus of Chapter 8.

- **Share.** iPhoto's best features have to do with sharing your photos, either onscreen or on paper. In fact, iPhoto offers nine different ways of publishing your pictures. In addition to printing pictures on your own printer (in a variety of interesting layouts and book styles), you can display images as an onscreen slideshow, turn the slideshow into a QuickTime movie, order professional quality prints or a professionally bound book, email them, apply one to your desktop as a desktop backdrop, select a batch to become your Mac OS X screen saver, or post them online as a Web page.

Chapters 9 through 11 explain how to undertake these self-publishing tasks.

Note: Although much of this portion of the book is focused on using digital cameras, remember this: You don't have to shoot digital photos to use iPhoto. You can just as easily use it to organize and publish pictures you've shot with a traditional film camera and then digitized using a scanner (or had Kodak convert them to a Photo CD). Importing scanned photos is covered later in this chapter on page 97.

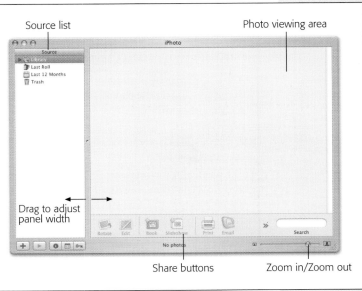

Figure 6-2:
Here's what iPhoto looks like when you first open it. The large photo-viewing area is where thumbnails of your imported photos will appear. The icons at the bottom of the window represent all the stuff you can do with your photos.

Source list

Photo viewing area

Drag to adjust panel width

Share buttons

Zoom in/Zoom out

Getting Your Pictures into iPhoto

With iPhoto installed and ready to run, it's time for you to import your own pictures into the program—a process that's remarkably easy, especially if your photos are going directly from your camera into iPhoto.

Of course, if you've been taking digital photos for some time, you probably have a lot of photo files already crammed into folders on your hard drive or on Zip disks or CDs. If you shoot pictures with a traditional film camera and use a scanner to digitize them, you've probably got piles of JPEG or TIFF images stashed away on disk already, waiting to be cataloged using iPhoto.

This section explains how to transfer files into iPhoto from each of these sources.

Connecting with a USB Camera

Every modern digital camera can connect to a Mac using the USB port. If your Mac has more than one USB jack, any of them will do.

Plugging a USB-compatible camera into your Mac is the easiest way to transfer pictures from your camera into iPhoto. In fact, the whole process practically happens by itself:

1. **Connect the camera to one of your Mac's USB jacks.**

   To make this camera-to-Mac USB connection, you need what is usually called an *A-to-B* USB cable; your camera probably came with one. The "A" end—the part you plug into your camera—has a small, flat-bottomed plug whose shape varies by manufacturer. The Mac end of the cable has a larger, flatter, rectangular, standard USB plug. Make sure both ends of the cable are plugged in firmly.

   If iPhoto isn't already running when you make this connection, the program opens and springs into action as soon as you switch on the camera (that is, unless you've changed the factory settings in Image Capture, a little program that sits in your Applications folder).

   A few cameras require a step that would be numbered 1.5 right about here: turning the Mode dial on the top to whatever tiny symbol means "computer connection." If yours does, do that.

Note: If this is the first time you've ever run iPhoto, it asks if you always want it to run when you plug in the camera. If you value your time, say yes.

   In iPhoto 5, there's no wondering whether iPhoto is ready to do its job; the entire screen changes to show you the "ready" message shown in Figure 6-3.

Tip: If, for some reason, iPhoto doesn't "see" your camera after you connect it, try turning the camera off, then on again.

In addition, your camera's icon appears in the Source list. That's handy, because it means that you can switch back and forth between the importing mode (click the camera's icon) and the regular working-in-iPhoto mode (click any other icon in the Source list), even while the time-consuming importing is under way.

(Incidentally, as long as the camera's appearing in the Source list—wouldn't it be cool if you could drag photos *onto* the camera too? Maybe next year.)

2. **If you like, type in a *roll name* and description for the pictures you're about to import.**

Each time you import a new set of photos into iPhoto—whether from your hard drive, a camera, or a memory card—that batch of imported photos is called a *film roll*.

Of course, there's no real film in digital photography, and your pictures aren't on a "roll" of anything. But if you think about it, the metaphor makes sense. Just as in traditional photography, where each batch of photos you shoot is captured on a separate roll of film, each separate batch of photos you download into iPhoto gets classified as its own film roll.

You'll learn much more about film rolls in Chapter 7. For the moment, typing in a name for each new batch—*Disney, First Weekend* or *Baby Meets Lasagna,* for example—will help you organize and find your pictures later. (Use the Description box for more elaborate textual blurbs, if you like. You could specify the date, who was on the trip, the circumstances of the shoot, and so on.)

3. **Turn on the "Delete items from camera after importing" checkbox, if you like.**

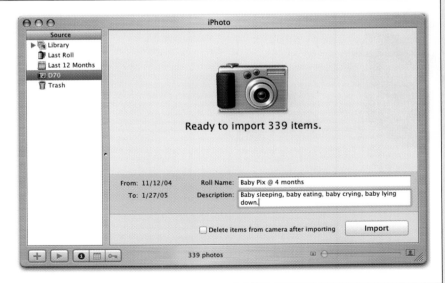

Figure 6-3:
iPhoto is ready to import, captain! If you have to wait a long time for this screen to appear, it's because you've got a lot of pictures on your camera, and it takes iPhoto a while to count them up and prepare for the task at hand. (The number may be somewhat larger than you expect if you forgot to erase your last batch of photos.)

If you turn on this box, iPhoto will automatically delete all photos from your camera's memory card once they're safely on the Mac. Your camera's memory card will be all ready for you to fill with more pictures.

Now, iPhoto won't delete your pictures until *after* it has successfully copied them all to the Photo Library. However, it's not beyond the realm of possibility that a hard disk could fail during an iPhoto import, or that a file could get corrupted when copied, thereby becoming unopenable. If you want to play it safe, leave the "Delete items from camera after importing" option turned off.

Then, after you've confirmed that all of your photos have been copied safely, you can use the camera's own menus to erase its memory card.

4. **Click the Import button.**

If you chose the auto-erase feature, you'll see a final "Confirm Move" dialog box, affording you one last chance to back out of that decision. Click Delete Originals

Figure 6-4:
Top: If you're not in the habit of using the "Delete items from camera after importing" option, you may occasionally see the "Import duplicates?" message. iPhoto notices the arrival of duplicates and offers you the option of downloading them again, resulting in duplicates on your Mac, or ignoring them and importing only the new photos from your camera. The latter option can save you a lot of time.

Bottom: A nice new feature in iPhoto 5: As the pictures get slurped into your Mac, iPhoto shows them to you, nice and big, as a sort of slideshow. You can see right away which ones were your hits, which were the misses, and which you'll want to delete the instant the importing process is complete.

if you're sure you want the camera erased after the transfer, or Keep Originals if you want iPhoto to import *copies* of them, leaving the originals on the camera.

A different message appears if you're about to import photos you've *already* imported (see Figure 6-4, top).

In any case, iPhoto swings into action, copying each photo from your camera to your hard drive. You get to see them as they parade by (Figure 6-4, bottom).

When the process is over, your freshly imported photos appear in the main iPhoto window, awaiting your organizational talents.

Tip: If you receive any kind of error message, you might have an older camera that requires "unmounting" from the screen before disconnecting. To do this, Control-click the camera's icon and choose Unmount. Even if the camera's still attached to your Mac, its icon disappears from the Source list.

GEM IN THE ROUGH

The Memory Card's Back Door

When you connect an older digital camera to the Mac, its memory card shows up as a disk icon at the upper-right corner of your desktop, as shown here.

The icons of newer cameras don't show up this way—but you can get the same effect by inserting your memory card into a card reader attached to your Mac.

Inside the disk window, you'll generally find several folders, each cryptically named by the camera's software. One of them contains your photos; another may contain movies.

Opening this "disk" icon is one way to *selectively* delete or copy photos from the card. (If you do that, though, make sure you eject and reconnect the camera before importing into iPhoto, to avoid thoroughly confusing the software.)

Finding the folder that contains the memory card's photos also offers you the chance to copy photos *from* your hard

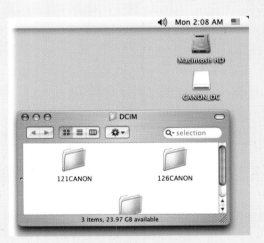

drive *to* your camera—just drag them to the "disk" icon in the Finder.

The downside of having your card icon show up is that you must eject it manually after importing your photos into iPhoto. You can drag it to the Trash, Control-click it and choose Eject, click its ⏏ button in the Sidebar (Mac OS X 10.3 or later), or use any other disk-ejecting tactic you want. You can also use the Unmount command within iPhoto, as described in the Tip on the next page.

If your camera *doesn't* show up as an icon, you can always open the Image Capture program in your Applications folder. It's capable of selectively deleting or importing photos and can also import your digital movies.

Then, after you've confirmed that all of your photos have been copied into the iPhoto Library folder, you can use the camera's own command to erase its memory card.

---

6. **Turn off the camera, and then unplug it from the USB cable.**

You're ready to start having fun with your new pictures.

USB Card Readers

A USB *memory card reader* offers another convenient way to transfer photos into iPhoto. Most of these card readers, which look like tiny disk drives, are under $20, and some can even read more than one kind of memory card.

If you have a reader, then instead of connecting the camera to the Mac, simply remove the camera's memory card and insert it into the reader (which you can leave permanently connected to the Mac). iPhoto recognizes the reader as though it's a camera and offers to import (and erase) the photos, just as described on the previous pages.

This method offers several advantages over the camera-connection method. First, it eliminates the considerable battery drain involved in pumping the photos straight off the camera. Second, it's less hassle to pull a memory card out of your camera and slip it into your card reader (which is always plugged in) than it is to constantly plug and unplug camera cables. Finally, this method lets you use almost *any* digital camera with iPhoto, even those too old to include a USB cable connector.

Tip: iPhoto doesn't recognize most camcorders, even though most models can take still pictures. Many camcorders store their stills on a memory card just as digital cameras do, so a memory card reader is exactly what you need to get those pictures into iPhoto.

Connecting with a USB-compatible memory card reader is almost identical to connecting a camera. Here's how:

1. **Pop a memory card out of your camera and insert it into the reader.**

Of course, the card reader should already be plugged into the Mac's USB jack.

As when you connect a camera, iPhoto acknowledges the presence of the memory card reader. A huge camera icon appears in the main window, you see the number of images on the card, and you're offered a chance to type in a roll name and description. As described on page 93, you can also turn on the "Delete items from camera after importing" checkbox if you want iPhoto to automatically clear the memory card after copying the files to your Mac.

2. **Click Import.**

iPhoto swings into action, copying the photos off the card.

3. **Click the tiny Eject button (⏏) next to the card's name in the Source list, and then remove the card from the reader.**

Put the card back into the camera, so it's ready for more action.

Importing Photos from Non-USB Cameras

If your camera doesn't have a USB connection *and* you don't have a memory card reader, you're still not out of luck.

First, copy the photos from your camera/memory card onto your hard drive (or other disk) using whatever software or hardware came with your camera. Then bring them into iPhoto as you would any other graphics files.

Tip: *If your camera or memory card appears on the Mac desktop like any other removable disk, you can also drag its photo icons, folder icons, or even the "disk" icon itself directly into iPhoto.*

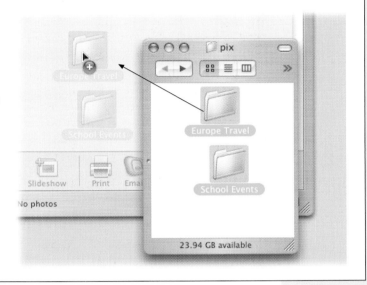

Figure 6-5:
When you drop a folder into iPhoto, the program automatically scans all the folders inside it, looking for pictures to catalog. It creates a new film roll (page 109) for each folder it finds. iPhoto ignores irrelevant files and stores only the pictures that are in a format it can read.

Importing Existing Graphics Files

If you've already got digital photos—or any other kinds of graphics files—stored somewhere on your computer, the easiest way to import them into iPhoto is simply to drag their icons into the main iPhoto window, using one of these two methods:

- Drag the files directly into the main iPhoto window, which automatically starts the import process. You can also drop an entire *folder* of images into iPhoto to import the contents of the whole folder, as shown in Figure 6-5.

  What's especially nice in iPhoto 5 is that you can drag a *bunch* of folders at once.

Tip: *Take the time to name your folders intelligently before dragging them into iPhoto, because the program retains their names. If you drag a folder directly into the main photo area, you get a new film roll named for the folder (page 109); if you drag the folder into the Source list at the left side of the screen, you get a new album named for the folder. And if there are folders inside folders, they, too, become new film rolls and albums. Details on all this reside in Chapter 7.*

- Choose File→Add to Library (or press ⌘-O) in iPhoto and select a file or folder in the Open dialog box, shown in Figure 6-6.

Note: Apple changes both the wording and the keystroke for this command, which, before iPhoto 5, was called Import. The change is logical enough, as it usefully suggests what's really going to happen. (You're about to create a duplicate of whatever you import, adding a copy of the original to iPhoto's own internal library folder.) However, it may come as a bewildering surprise to iPhoto veterans.

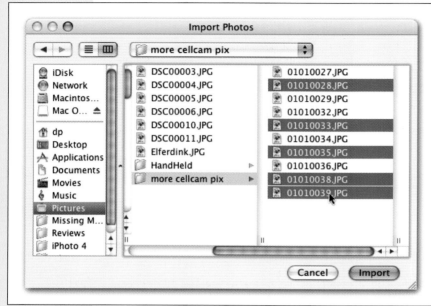

Figure 6-6:
When the Import Photos dialog box appears, navigate to and select any graphics files you want to bring into iPhoto. You can ⌘-click individual graphics to select more than one simultaneously, as shown here. You can also click one, then Shift-click another one, to highlight both files and everything in the list in between.

These techniques also let you select and import files from other hard drives, flash drives, 4CDs, DVDs, Jaz or Zip disks, or other disks on the network.

If your photos are on a Kodak Photo CD, you can insert the CD (with iPhoto already running), and then click the Import button on the Import pane, just as if you were importing photos from a connected camera. As always, iPhoto makes fresh copies of the files you import, storing them in one centralized photo repository (the iPhoto Library folder) on your hard drive. The program also creates thumbnail versions of each image for display in the main iPhoto window.

Through this process and all other importing processes, remember this: iPhoto *never moves* a file, whether from a memory card or disk; it only copies it.

The File Format Factor

iPhoto can't import digital pictures unless it understands their file format, but that rarely poses a problem. Just about every digital camera on earth saves photos as JPEG files—and iPhoto handles this format beautifully. (JPEG is the world's most popular file format for photos, because even though it's compressed to occupy a lot less disk space, the visual quality is still very high.)

Note: While most digital photos you work with are probably JPEG files, they're not always called JPEG files. You may also see JPEG referred to as JFIF (JPEG File Interchange Format). Bottom line: The terms JPEG, JFIF, JPEG JFIF, and JPEG 2000 all mean the same thing.

But there's more to this story—in iPhoto 5, much more. The program now imports and recognizes some very useful additional formats.

RAW format

Most digital cameras work like this: When you squeeze the shutter button, the camera studies the data picked up by its sensors. The circuitry then makes decisions pertaining to sharpening level, contrast and saturation settings, color "temperature," white balance, and so on—and then saves the resulting processed image as a compressed JPEG file on your memory card.

For millions of people, the resulting picture quality is just fine, even terrific. But all that in-camera processing drives professional shutterbugs nuts. They'd much rather preserve *every last iota* of original picture information, no matter how huge the resulting file on the memory card—and then process the file *by hand* once it's been safely transferred to the Mac, using a program like Photoshop.

That's the idea behind the RAW file format, which is an option in many pricier digital cameras. (RAW stands for nothing in particular, and it's usually written in all capital letters like that just to denote how imposing and important serious photographers think it is.)

A RAW image isn't processed at all; it's a complete record of all the data passed along by the camera's sensors. As a result, each RAW photo takes up much more space on your memory card. For example, on a 6-megapixel camera, a JPEG photo is around 2 MB, but over 8 MB when saved as a RAW file. Most cameras take longer to store RAW photos on the card, too.

But for image-manipulation nerds, the beauty of RAW files is that once you open them up on the Mac, you can perform astounding acts of editing on them. You can actually change the lighting of the scene—retroactively! And you don't lose a single speck of image quality along the way.

Until recently, most people used a program like Photoshop or Photoshop Elements to do this kind of editing. But amazingly enough, humble, cheap little iPhoto 5 can now edit them, too. For details on editing RAW images, see Chapter 8.

Note: Not every camera offers an option to save your files in RAW format—and among those that do, not all are iPhoto compatible. Apple maintains a partial list of compatible cameras at *www.apple.com/ilife/iphoto/import.html*.

Movies

With iPhoto 5, Apple has brought the software one delicate step into the 21st century. In addition to still photos, most consumer digital cameras these days can also capture cute little digital movies. Some are jittery, silent affairs the size of a Wheat Thin; others are full-blown, 30-frames-per-second, fill-your-screen movies (that eat up a memory card plenty fast). Either way, iPhoto can now import and organize them. (The program recognizes .mov files, .avi files, and many other movie formats.

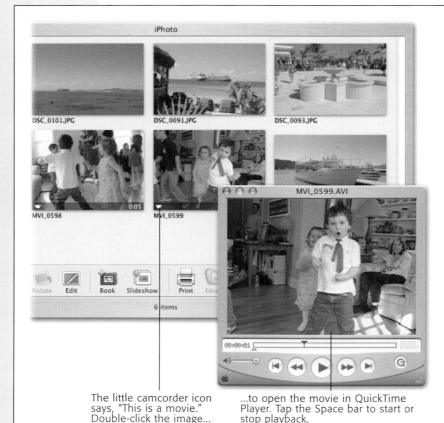

Figure 6-7:
The first frame of each video clip shows up as though it's a photo in your library; only a little camera icon and the total running time let you know that it's a movie and not a photo. iPhoto is no iMovie, though; it can't even play these video clips. If you double-click one, it actually opens up in QuickTime Player, a different program on your Mac that's dedicated to playing digital movies.

The little camcorder icon says, "This is a movie." Double-click the image...

...to open the movie in QuickTime Player. Tap the Space bar to start or stop playback.

In fact, it can import any format that QuickTime itself recognizes, which is a very long list indeed.)

You don't have to do anything special to import movies, since they get slurped in automatically. To play one of these movies once they're in iPhoto, see Figure 6-7.

Other graphics formats

Of course, iPhoto also lets you load pictures that have been saved in a number of other file formats, too—including a few unusual ones. They include:

• **TIFF.** Most digital cameras capture photos in a graphics-file format called JPEG. Some cameras, though, offer you the chance to leave your photos *uncompressed* on the camera, in what's called TIFF format. These files are huge—in fact, you'll be lucky if you can fit one TIFF file on the memory card that came with the camera. Fortunately, they retain 100 percent of the picture's original quality.

Note, however, that the instant you *edit* a TIFF-format photo (Chapter 8), iPhoto converts it into JPEG. That's fine if you plan to order prints or a photo book (Chapter 10) from iPhoto, since JPEG files are required for those purposes. But if you took that once-in-a-lifetime, priceless shot as a TIFF file, don't do any editing in iPhoto—don't even rotate it—if you hope to maintain its perfect, pristine quality.

- **GIF** is the most common format used for non-photographic images on Web pages. The borders, backgrounds, and logos you typically encounter on Web sites are usually GIF files—as well as 98 percent of those blinking, flashing banner ads that drive you insane.

- **PNG** and **FlashPix** are also used in Web design, though not nearly as often as JPEG and GIF. They often display more complex graphic elements.

- **BMP** is a popular graphics file format in Windows.

- **PICT** was the original graphics file format of the Macintosh prior to Mac OS X. When you take a screenshot in Mac OS 9, paste a picture from the Clipboard, or copy an image from the Scrapbook, you're using a PICT file.

- **Photoshop** refers to Adobe Photoshop, the world's most popular image-editing and photo-retouching program. iPhoto can even recognize and import *layered* Photoshop files—those in which different image adjustments or graphic elements are stored in sandwiched-together layers.

- **MacPaint** is the ancient file format of Apple's very first graphics program from the mid-1980s. No, you probably won't be working with any MacPaint files in iPhoto, but isn't it nice to know that if one of these old, black-and-white, 8 x 10 pictures, generated on a vintage Mac SE, happens to slip through a wormhole in the fabric of time and land on your desk, you'll be ready?

- **SGI** and **Targa** are specialized graphics formats used on high-end Silicon Graphics workstations and Truevision video-editing systems.

- **PDF** files are Portable Document Format files that open up in Preview or Acrobat Reader. They can be user manuals, brochures, or Read Me files that you downloaded or received on a CD. Apple doesn't publicize the fact that iPhoto can import PDF files, maybe because iPhoto displays only the first page of multipage documents. (Most of the PDFs you come across probably aren't photos; they're usually multipage documents filled with both text and graphics.)

If you try to import a file that iPhoto doesn't understand, you see the message shown in Figure 6-8.

The Post-Dump Slideshow

Once you've imported a batch of pictures into iPhoto, what's the first thing you want to do? If you're like most people, this is the first opportunity you have to see, at full-screen size, the masterpieces you and your camera created. That's the beauty of iPhoto's slideshow feature, which comes complete with the tools you need to perform an initial screen of the new pictures—like deleting the baddies, rotating the sideways ones, and identifying the best ones with star ratings.

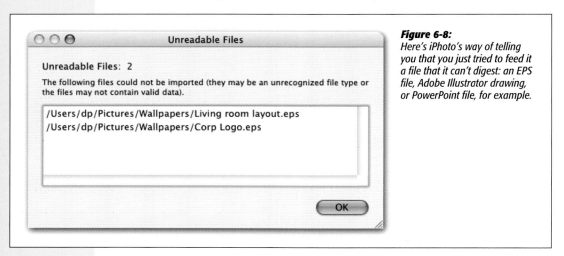

Figure 6-8:
Here's iPhoto's way of telling you that you just tried to feed it a file that it can't digest: an EPS file, Adobe Illustrator drawing, or PowerPoint file, for example.

To begin the slideshow, click the Last Roll icon in the Source list at the left side of the screen to identify which pictures you want to review.

Note: On a freshly installed copy of iPhoto, this icon is labeled Last Roll. If you've fiddled with the iPhoto preference settings, it may say, for example, "Last 2 Rolls" or "Last 3 Rolls," and your slideshow will include more than the most recent batch of photos. If that's not what you want to see, just click the actual photo that you want to begin the slideshow (in the main viewing area).

Now *Option-click* the Play triangle underneath the Source list. iPhoto fades out of view, and a big, full-screen slideshow of the new photos begins, accompanied by music.

Tip: If you just click the Play triangle (instead of adding the Option key), you summon the Slideshow dialog box instead of starting the show. This dialog box has lots of useful options; for instance, you can choose the music for your slideshow, for example. If you merely want a quick look at your new pix, however, Option-clicking is the way to bypass it.

You can read more about slideshows in general in Chapter 9. What's useful here, though, is the slideshow control bar shown in Figure 6-9. You make it appear by wiggling your mouse as the show begins.

As Figure 6-9 points out, this is the perfect opportunity to throw away lousy shots, fix the rotation, and linger on certain photos for more study—all without interrupting the slideshow. You can even apply a rating by clicking the appropriate star in the band of five; later, you can use these ratings to sort your pictures or create *smart albums*. See Chapter 7 for full detail on rating stars and smart albums.

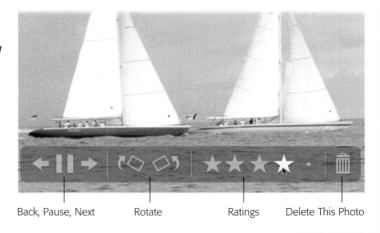

Figure 6-9:
As the slideshow progresses, you can pause the show, go backward, rotate a photo, delete a bad shot, or apply your star rating to a picture, all courtesy of this new control bar.

Back, Pause, Next   Rotate   Ratings   Delete This Photo

Here's the full list of things you can do when the onscreen control bar is visible:

- Click the Play/Pause button to start and halt the slideshow. The space bar toggles these controls—and the control bar doesn't have to be visible when you press it.

- Click the left and right arrows to browse back and forth through your photos. The left and right arrow keys on your keyboard do the same thing.

- Press the up or down arrow keys on your keyboard to make the slides appear faster or slower.

- Click the rotation icons to flip photos clockwise or counterclockwise, 90 degrees at a time.

- Click one of the five dots to apply a rating in stars, from one at the left to five all the way at the right. Or use the number keys at the top of the keyboard or on the numeric keypad; press 3 to give a picture three stars, for example.

- Click the Trash can icon to delete a photo from the album you're viewing (but not from the Photo Library). Or simply hit Delete (or Del) on your keyboard.

Tip: There are keyboard shortcuts for all of these functions, too, that don't even require the control bar to be on the screen (page 193).

Click the mouse somewhere else on the screen to end the slideshow.

Where iPhoto Keeps Your Files

Having entrusted your vast collection of digital photos to iPhoto, you may find yourself wondering, "Where's iPhoto putting all those files, anyway?"

Most people slog through life, eyes to the road, without ever knowing the answer. After all, you can preview, open, edit, rotate, copy, export, and print all your photos right in iPhoto, without actually opening a folder or double-clicking a single JPEG file.

Even so, it's worthwhile to know where iPhoto keeps your pictures on the hard drive. Armed with this information, you can keep those valuable files backed up and avoid the chance of accidentally throwing them away six months from now when you're cleaning up your hard drive.

A Trip to the Library

Whenever you import pictures into iPhoto, the program makes *copies* of your photos, always leaving your original files untouched.

- When you import from a camera, iPhoto leaves the photos right where they are on its memory card (unless you use the "Erase" option).

- When you import from the hard drive, iPhoto leaves the originals in whichever folders they're in. As a result, transferring photos from your hard drive into iPhoto *more than doubles* the amount of disk space they take up. In other words, importing 1 GB of photos requires an additional 1 GB of disk space, because you'll end up with two copies of each file: the original, and iPhoto's copy of the photo. In addition, iPhoto creates a separate thumbnail version of each picture, consuming about another 10 K to 20 K per photo.

iPhoto stores its copies of your pictures in a special folder called iPhoto Library, which you can find in your Home→Pictures folder. (To find your Home folder, begin in the Finder and choose Go→Home.) If the short name you use to log into Mac OS X is *mozart,* the full path to your iPhoto Library folder from the main hard drive window would be Macintosh HD→Users→mozart→Pictures→iPhoto Library.

FREQUENTLY ASKED QUESTION

Moving the iPhoto Library

Do I have to keep my photos in the iPhoto Library folder? What if I want them stored somewhere else?

No problemo! iPhoto has come a long way since the days when it could keep track of photos only if they were in its own folder structure within the iPhoto Library folder.

Just quit iPhoto. Then move the *whole* iPhoto Library folder (currently in your Home→Pictures folder) to another location—even onto another hard drive.

Then open iPhoto again. It will proclaim that it can't find your iPhoto Library folder. Now click the Find Library button to show the program where you put the folder. Done deal!

Tip: You should back up this iPhoto Library folder regularly—using the Burn command to save it onto a CD or DVD, for example. After all, it contains all the photos you import into iPhoto, which, essentially, is your entire photography collection. Chapter 12 offers much more on this file management topic.

What all those numbers mean

Within the iPhoto Library folder, you'll find a set of mysteriously numbered files and folders. At first glance, this setup may look bizarre, but there's a method to iPhoto's madness. It turns out that iPhoto meticulously arranges your photos within these numbered folders according to the *creation dates* of the originals, as explained in Figure 6-10.

Folders inside the year/month/date folders

A few mysterious icons appear inside each year/month/date photo folder, too, right alongside your JPEG photo files. They include:

Figure 6-10:
Behold the mysteries of the iPhoto Library. Once you know the secret, this seemingly cryptic folder structure actually makes sense, with all the photos in the library organized by their creation dates.

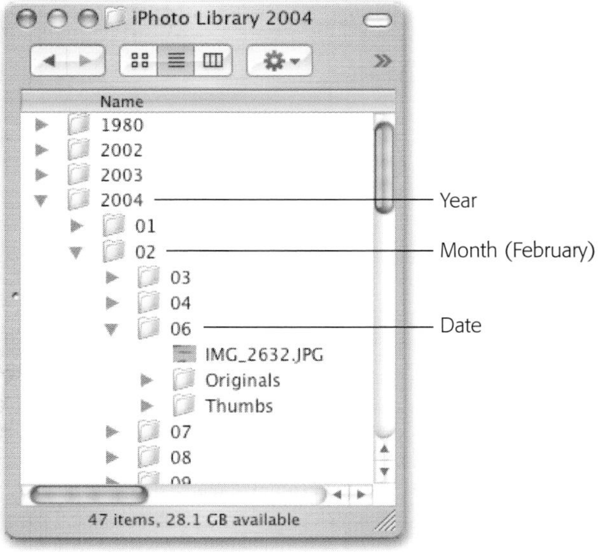

- **Thumbs folder.** Here, iPhoto stores the small thumbnail versions of the pictures in your Photo Library—the "slides" that actually appear in the iPhoto window.

  These images are numbered in the order in which they were imported.

- **Originals folder.** Some photo folders may contain an Originals folder. It doesn't appear until you use one of iPhoto's editing tools (Chapter 8) to touch up a photo. The Originals folder is the key to one of iPhoto's most remarkable features: the Revert to Original command.

Before it applies any potentially destructive operations to your photos—like cropping, red-eye removal, brightening, black-and-white conversion—iPhoto *duplicates* the files and stuffs pristine, unedited copies of them in the Originals folder. If you later decide to scrap your changes to a photo using the Revert to Original command—even months or years later—iPhoto moves the unedited file back into its original location, returning your photo to its originally imported state.

Note: Don't confuse the files in the Originals folders with your true originals: the files on your hard drive, camera, or memory card that you first imported into iPhoto. As mentioned earlier, iPhoto never touches those originals; they stay exactly where they were when you imported them.

Look, don't touch

While it's enlightening to wander through the iPhoto Library folder to see how iPhoto keeps itself organized, don't rename or move any of the folders or files in it. Making such changes will confuse iPhoto to the point where it will either be unable to display some of your photos or it'll just crash.

The Digital Shoebox

I f you've imported your photos into iPhoto using any of the methods described in the previous chapter, you should now see a neatly arranged grid of thumbnails in iPhoto's main photo-viewing area. You're looking at what iPhoto refers to as your *Photo Library*—your entire photo collection, including every last picture you've ever imported. This is the digital equivalent of that old shoebox you've had stuffed in the closet for the last 10 years, brimming with snapshots waiting to be sorted and sifted, often never to be seen again.

You're not really organized yet, but at least all your photos are in one place. Your journey out of chaos has begun. From here, you can sort your photos, give them titles, group them into smaller sub-collections (called *albums*), and tag them with keywords so you can find them quickly. This chapter helps you tackle each of those organizing tasks as painlessly as possible.

The Source List

Even before you start naming your photos, assigning them keywords, or organizing them into albums, iPhoto imposes an order of its own on your digital shoebox.

The key to understanding it is the *Source list* at the left side of the iPhoto window. This list will grow as you import more pictures and organize them—but right off the bat, you'll find icons like Library, Last 12 Months, and Last Roll.

Library

The first icon in the Source list is called Photo Library. This is a very reassuring little icon, because no matter how confused you may get in working with subsets of photos later in your iPhoto life, clicking Photo Library returns you to your entire picture collection. It makes *all* of your photos appear in the viewing area.

Library by Year

In early versions of iPhoto, the Library got a bit unwieldy if you had 2,000 pictures in it. But now that iPhoto can easily handle 25,000 photos, Apple realized that people needed a way to break down this tidal wave of pixels.

Enter the year icons, shown at top in Figure 7-1. When you click the Photo Library flippy triangle, iPhoto's Source list now shows small yellow calendar icons, one for each year going back to 2001 (and a catch-all for earlier images).

When you import your entire digital photo collection (or upgrade from an earlier version of iPhoto), the program files each photo by the date you took it. You can click Library to see all your photos amassed in one window, or click, say, the 2004 icon to see just the ones you took during that year.

The year icons are also very helpful when you're creating an iPhoto slideshow or trying to pinpoint one certain photo. After all, you usually can remember what year you took a vacation or when someone's birthday was. The year icons help you narrow down your search without requiring that you scroll through your entire Library.

Figure 7-1:
Top: You can specify how far back the "Last ___ Months" album goes and how many downloads the "Last ___ Rolls" album includes on the General panel of iPhoto Preferences (bottom).

Don't forget, by the way, that iPhoto 5 isn't limited to grouping your pictures by year. It can also show you the photos that you took on a certain day, in a certain week, or during a certain month. See page 132 for details.

Bottom: While you're in Preferences, don't miss the "Show photo count for albums" option. It places a number in parentheses after each album name in the Source panel, representing how many pictures are inside.

Photo Library by Month

The Last 12 Months icon is the same idea as the calendar-year icons, except that it puts the most recent photos at your fingertips. The idea, of course, is that most of the time, the freshest photos are the most interesting to you.

Actually, it doesn't even have to say "Last 12 Months." You can specify how many months' worth of photos appear in this heap—anywhere from one month to a year and a half—by choosing iPhoto→Preferences and going to the General panel (see Figure 7-1). Like the new iPhoto 5 calendar, this feature is very useful when you want to find the pictures from this past Christmas, photos from your kid's most recent birthday, or wedding pictures from your most recent marriage.

Last Roll

Each batch of imported photos is called one *film roll*.

Most of the time, you'll probably work with the photos that you just downloaded from your camera. Conveniently, iPhoto always keeps track of your most recently added film roll, so you can view its contents without much scrolling.

That's the purpose of the roll-of-film icon called Last Roll in the Source list. With one click, iPhoto displays only your most recent photos, hiding all the others. This feature can save you a lot of time, especially as your Photo Library grows.

In fact, iPhoto lets you specify how *many* film rolls you want listed here; choose iPhoto→Preferences and click the General icon (again, see Figure 7-1). Simply change the number where it says "Show last __ rolls album." (In the unlikely event that you don't find this icon useful, you can also hide it entirely by turning off the corresponding checkbox.)

For example, if you've just returned from a three-day Disney World trip, you probably want to see your last *three* imports all at once. In that case, you'd change the last rolls setting to *3*.

Tip: If you delete everything from the Last Roll category, iPhoto promptly displays the previous roll's contents—whatever was the Last Roll before this latest one. It's a handy way to rewind into the past, even if it was many weeks or months ago, in your quest for a lost picture.

Other Icons in the Source List

Library, year icons, and Last Roll icons aren't the only items you'll find in the Source list. Later in this chapter, you'll find out how to create your own arbitrary subsets of pictures called albums, and—thanks to a new feature in iPhoto 5—even how to stick a bunch of related albums into an enclosing entity called a *folder*.

Later in this book, you'll find out how to swipe photos from other people's collections via iPhoto sharing. And later in life, you may discover the geeky joy of dumping photos onto CDs or DVDs—and then loading them back into iPhoto whenever you darned well feel like it.

Shared photo collections, CD icons, and DVD icons can all show up in the Source list, too.

iPhoto 5 even introduces the notion of saved slide shows and book layouts. These, too, get their own icons in the Source list (and can be filed, alongside albums, in folders).

As you go, though, remember this key point: Photos in your Library, Last Roll, and Last Months icons are the *real* photos. Delete a picture from one of these three collections, and it's gone forever. (That's *not* true of albums, which store only aliases—phantom duplicates—of the real photos.)

More on Film Rolls

iPhoto starts out sorting your Library by film roll, meaning that the most recently imported batch of photos appears at the bottom of the window. Your main iPhoto window may look like a broad, featureless expanse of pictures, but they're actually in a logical order.

Tip: If you'd prefer that the most recent items appear at the top of the iPhoto window instead of at the bottom, choose iPhoto→Preferences, click Appearance, turn on "Place most recent photos at the top," and close the Preferences window. This option also affects the Sort Photos→by Date option described below.

Using the View→Sort Photos submenu, you can make iPhoto sort all the thumbnails in the main window in a number of useful ways:

- **by Date.** This sort order reflects the *creation* date of the photos (rather than the date they were imported).

- **by Title.** This arrangement is alphabetical by the photos' *names*. (To name your photos, see page 129.)

- **by Rating.** If you'd like your masterpieces at the top of the window, with the losers way down below, choose this option. (To rate your photos, see page 142.)

- **Manually.** If you choose this option, you can drag the thumbnails around freely within the window, placing them in any order that suits your fancy. To conserve your Advil supply, however, make no attempt to choose this item when you're viewing one of the *film rolls*' contents—do so only in an *album*. See the box on the facing page for details.

FREQUENTLY ASKED QUESTION

Your Own Personal Sorting Order

I want to put my photos in my own order. I tried using View→Sort Photos→Manually, but the command is dimmed out! Did Apple accidentally forget to turn this on?

No, the command works—but only in an album, not in the main Photo Library. If you create a new photo album (as explained later in this chapter) and fill it with photos, you can then drag them into any order you want.

Displaying film rolls

If you choose View→Sort Photos→by Film Roll, iPhoto returns to sorting your photos by film roll, even if you had previously chosen to sort the photos by rating, title, or date. (This option is available in the menu only when you've clicked Library or one of the "__Rolls" icons in the Source list.)

Tip: To hide or show the film roll dividers, just choose View→Film Rolls. Better yet, use the keyboard shortcut Shift-⌘-F. (The presence or absence of the dividers doesn't affect the sorting order.) You can see these film-roll dividers in Figure 7-2.

Figure 7-2:
This tidy arrangement is the fastest way to use iPhoto. Display the photos grouped by film roll, and then hide the photo batches you're not working with. Click the triangle beside each header to expand or collapse the film roll, just like a folder in the Finder's list view.

Note that the header for each roll lists the date that you imported this batch. If you dragged a folder of files into iPhoto—or if you named the roll as the pictures were imported—the film-roll header also lists the name of the enclosing folder.

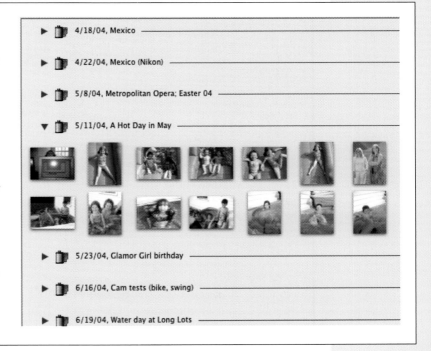

You'll probably find this arrangement so convenient that you'll leave it on permanently. As your Photo Library grows, these groupings become excellent visual and mnemonic aids to help you locate a certain photo—sometimes even months or years after the fact.

Furthermore, as your Photo Library becomes increasingly massive, you may need to rely on these film-roll groupings just for your sanity. By collapsing the flippy triangles next to the groups you're *not* looking at right now (Figure 7-2), you speed up iPhoto considerably. Otherwise, iPhoto may grind almost to a halt as it tries to scroll through ever more photos. (About 25,000 pictures is its realistic limit for a single library on everyday Macs. Of course, you can always start new libraries, as described in Chapter 12.)

Collapsing film rolls en masse

On a related note, here's one of the best tips in this entire chapter: *Option-click* a film roll's flippy triangle to hide or show all of the film rolls' contents. When all your photos are visible, scrolling is slowish, but at least you can see everything. By contrast, when all your film rolls are collapsed, you see nothing but their names, and scrolling is almost instantaneous.

Tip: Click anywhere on the film-roll divider line—on the film roll's name, for example—to simultaneously select all the photos in that roll.

By the way, even if you opt not to display the film-roll divider lines in the photo-viewing area, you can still *sort* the pictures in your Library by film roll. Just choose View→Sort Photos→by Film Roll. You won't be able to see where one film roll ends and the next begins, but the photos will be in the right order.

Creating film rolls manually

Film rolls are such a convenient way of organizing your pictures that Apple even lets you create film rolls manually, out of any pictures you choose.

This feature violates the sanctity of the original film-roll concept: that each importing batch is one film roll, and that *albums* are what you use for arbitrary groupings. Still, in this case, usefulness trumps concept—and that's a good thing.

You just select any bunch of pictures in your Photo Library (using any of the techniques described on page 115), then choose File→Create Film Roll. iPhoto creates and highlights the new roll, like any normal film roll. It then gives the newborn roll a generic name like "Roll 54" or whatever number it's up to, but you can always rename it, as described on the facing page.

Merging film rolls

You can *merge* film rolls using this technique, too. Just select photos in two or more existing film rolls, and then choose File→Create Film Roll. iPhoto responds by removing the pictures from their existing film rolls, and then placing them into a new, unified one. (If you selected all the photos in a couple of film rolls, the original film rolls disappear entirely.) The power and utility of this tactic will become more attractive the more you work with big photo collections.

Tip: Speaking of cool film-roll tips: You can move any photo (or group of selected photos) into another film roll just by dragging it onto the film roll's row heading!

Renaming and dating film rolls

As you know from Chapter 6, iPhoto gives you the opportunity to name each film roll as it's created—that is, at the joyous moment when a new set of photos becomes one with your iPhoto library.

If you don't type anything into the Roll Name box that appears at that time, though, iPhoto just labels each film roll with a roll number. In any case, you can easily change any film roll's name at any time.

To edit the name of a roll, see Figure 7-3.

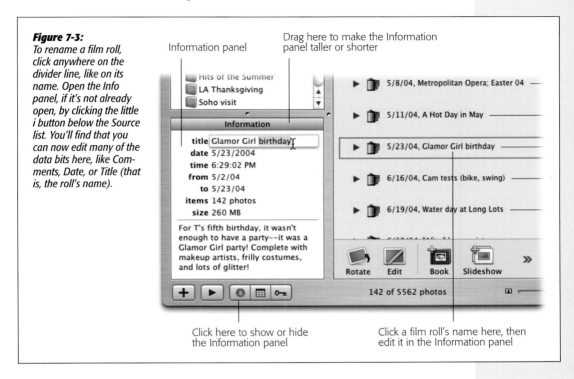

Figure 7-3:
To rename a film roll, click anywhere on the divider line, like on its name. Open the Info panel, if it's not already open, by clicking the little i button below the Source list. You'll find that you can now edit many of the data bits here, like Comments, Date, or Title (that is, the roll's name).

Information panel

Drag here to make the Information panel taller or shorter

Click here to show or hide the Information panel

Click a film roll's name here, then edit it in the Information panel

Using the same technique, you can also change the *date* that appears in the film-roll header. This date usually identifies when you imported the photos, but for most purposes, that date is relatively unimportant. What you probably care more about is the day or month that the photos were actually *taken*.

Once again, start by clicking the roll-of-film icon in the film-roll divider. This time, type a new date in the Information pane's Date text box. You can type the date in a variety of formats—*4 September 2005, September 4, 2005,* and *4/9/05* all work—but you must use a complete date, including day, month, and year. If you don't, iPhoto will take a guess, filling in the missing information for you—and sometimes getting it wrong.

Tip: Another effective way to redate a bunch of pictures at once is to use iPhoto's batch-processing feature, described on page 129.

Working with Your Photos

All right: You've gotten the hang of the Source list, the Library, and film rolls. Enough learning about iPhoto already…now it's time to start *using* it.

Scrolling Through Your Photos

Browsing, selecting, and opening photos is straightforward. Here's everything you need to know:

- Use the vertical scroll bar to navigate through your thumbnails. (Pressing your Page Up and Page Down keys work, too. They scroll one screenful at a time.)

Tip: If your photos scroll by too fast for you to find the ones you want, try using iPhoto's Slow Scroll mode. Hold down the Option key while dragging the scroll box in the scroll bar. You get a much slower, smoother scroll, making it easier to navigate to a specific row of thumbnails.

- Scrolling can take awhile if you have a full library, especially if you haven't collapsed the film rolls you're not using. But you can use this standard Mac OS X trick for faster navigation: Instead of dragging the scroll box or clicking the scroll bar arrows, *Option-click* the spot on the scroll bar that corresponds to the location you want in your Library. If you want to jump to the bottom of the Library, Option-click near the bottom of the scroll bar. To find photos in the middle of your collection, Option-click the middle portion of the scroll bar, and so on.

Note: By turning on "Scroll to here" in the General panel of your System Preferences, you can make this the standard behavior for all Mac OS X scroll bars—that is, you won't need the Option key.

- Press Home to jump to the very top of the photo collection, or End to leap to the bottom.

- To create the most expansive photo-viewing area possible, you can temporarily hide the Source list at the left side of the window. To do so, drag the divider bar (between the Source list and the main photo-viewing area) all the way to the left edge of the window. You've just hidden the Source list.

  To reveal that panel again, grab the left edge of the iPhoto window and drag it to the right.

Tip: You can speed up iPhoto's scrolling by turning off the Drop Shadow option in the Appearance section of iPhoto's Preferences window.

Size Control

You can make the thumbnails in iPhoto grow or shrink using the Size Control slider (on the right side of the iPhoto window, just under the photo-viewing area). Drag the slider all the way to the left, and you get micro-thumbnails so small that you can fit 200 or more of them in the iPhoto window. If you drag it all the way to the right, you end up with such large thumbnails that you can see only one picture at a time.

Tip: You don't have to drag the Size Control slider; just click anywhere along the controller bar to make the slider jump to a new setting. Using this technique, you can instantly change the size of thumbnails from large to small, for example, by clicking once at the left end of the controller.

By the way, you might notice that this Size Control slider performs different functions, depending on which mode iPhoto is in. When you're editing a photo, it zooms in and out of an individual image; when you're designing a photo-book layout (Chapter 10), it magnifies or shrinks a single page.

Tip: You may want to adopt a conservative dragging approach when using the Size Control slider, since iPhoto may respond slowly in enlarging or shrinking the photos. Just drag in small movements so the program can keep pace with you.

Selecting Photos

To highlight a single picture in preparation for printing, opening, duplicating, or deleting, click the icon once with the mouse.

That much may seem obvious. But many first-time Mac users have no idea how to manipulate *more* than one icon at a time—an essential survival skill.

To highlight multiple photos in preparation for deleting, moving, duplicating, printing, and so on, use one of these techniques:

- **To select all photos.** Select all the pictures in the set you're viewing by pressing ⌘-A (the equivalent of the Edit→Select All command).

- **To select several photos by dragging.** You can drag diagonally to highlight a group of nearby photos, as shown in Figure 7-4. You don't even have to enclose the thumbnails completely; your cursor can touch any part of any icon to highlight it. In fact, if you keep dragging past the edge of the window, iPhoto scrolls the window automatically.

Figure 7-4:
You can highlight several photos simultaneously by dragging a box around them. To do so, start from somewhere outside of the target photos and drag diagonally across them, creating a whitish enclosure rectangle as you go. Any photos touched by this rectangle are selected when you release the mouse.

- **To select consecutive photos.** Click the first thumbnail you want to highlight, and
  then Shift-click the last one. All the files in between are automatically selected,
  along with the two photos you clicked (Figure 7-5, top). This trick mirrors the
  way Shift-clicking works in a word processor, the Finder, and many other kinds
  of programs.

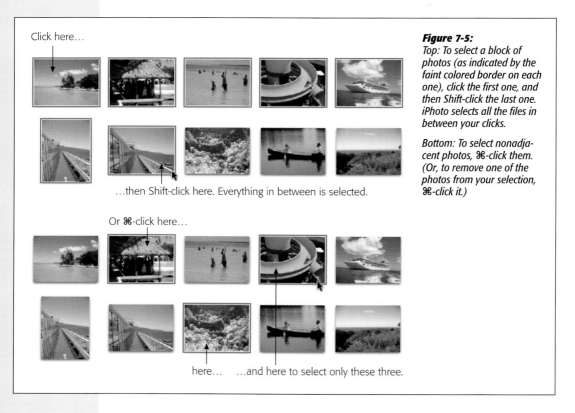

Click here...

...then Shift-click here. Everything in between is selected.

Or ⌘-click here...

here...   ...and here to select only these three.

Figure 7-5:
*Top: To select a block of
photos (as indicated by the
faint colored border on each
one), click the first one, and
then Shift-click the last one.
iPhoto selects all the files in
between your clicks.*

*Bottom: To select nonadja-
cent photos, ⌘-click them.
(Or, to remove one of the
photos from your selection,
⌘-click it.)*

- **To select random photos.** If you only want to highlight, for example, the first,
  third, and seventh photos in a window, start by clicking photo icon No. 1. Then
  ⌘-click each of the others. Each thumbnail sprouts a colored border to indicate
  that you've selected it (Figure 7-5, bottom).

If you're highlighting a long string of photos and then click one by mistake, you
don't have to start over. Instead, just ⌘-click it again, and the dark highlighting
disappears. (If you do want to start over from the beginning, however, just deselect
all selected photos by clicking any empty part of the window.)

The ⌘ key trick is especially handy if you want to select *almost* all the photos in a window. Press ⌘-A to select everything in the folder, then ⌘-click any unwanted photos to deselect them. You'll save a lot of time and clicking.

Tip: You can also combine the ⌘-clicking business with the Shift-clicking trick. For instance, you could click the first photo, then Shift-click the tenth, to highlight the first ten. Next, you could ⌘-click photos 2, 5, and 9 to remove them from the selection.

Once you've highlighted multiple photos, you can manipulate them all at once. For example, you can drag them en masse out of the window and onto your desktop—a quick way to export them. (Actually, you may want to drag them onto a *folder* in the Finder to avoid spraying their icons all over your desktop.) Or you can drag them into an album at the left side of the iPhoto window. Just drag any *one* of the highlighted photos; all other highlighted thumbnails go along for the ride.

In addition, when multiple photos are selected, the commands in the File, Edit, Photos, and Share menus—including Duplicate, Print, Revert To Original, and Email—apply to all of them simultaneously.

Opening Photos

iPhoto wouldn't be a terribly useful program if it let you view only postage stamp versions of your photos (unless, of course, you like to take pictures *of* postage stamps). Fortunately, iPhoto lets you open photos at full size, zoom in on details, and even edit them to enhance their appearance. (Editing photos is covered blow-by-blow in the next chapter.)

The easiest way to open a photo is simply to double-click a thumbnail. Unless you've changed iPhoto's settings, the photo opens in the main iPhoto window, scaled to fit into the viewing area.

This is the way most people start out opening pictures using iPhoto, and there's nothing technically wrong with this method. Nevertheless, it does have several drawbacks:

- You can have only one picture open at a time.

- Pictures opened by double-clicking are always scaled to fit within the iPhoto window, even if that means scaling them *upward,* over 100 percent of their actual size. As a result, smaller pictures wind up pixellated and distorted as they're stretched to fill the whole window.

  Worse yet, at this point, there's no way to zoom *out.* You can zoom in further, but you can't reduce the magnification.

- Double-clicking a thumbnail catapults you directly into iPhoto's *Edit mode*, hiding all your other thumbnails and transforming the lower panel in the iPhoto window into the Edit pane, with its various cropping, red-eye removal, and color-changing tools. That's great if you're ready to start editing photos. But if you opened the picture simply because you wanted to see it at full size, you now have to click the

Done button (at the bottom-right corner of the screen) to return to viewing and sorting your photo collection.

Tip: Here's a really cool shortcut for exiting Edit mode and returning to your full photo collection: *Double-click* the photo you're editing.

The better way to open photos

You can avoid all of these problems by using iPhoto's much smarter, but less obvious, method of opening photos: Open each picture *in its own window*.

There are two ways to do this:

- Go to iPhoto→Preferences and change the photo-opening setting. On the General panel, select the "Opens in edit window" button. Then close the window.

Tip: Pressing Option reverses whichever choice you make here. That is, if you've chosen "Changes to edit view" in the Preferences window, then Option-double-clicking a thumbnail opens the photo into a separate window instead. Conversely, if you've chosen "Opens in edit window," Option-double-clicking a thumbnail overrides your choice and opens it into the main iPhoto viewing area.

(Option-double-clicking has no effect if you've selected the third Preferences option, "Opens in other," which is described in Chapter 8.)

- Control-click the photo. Choose "Open in separate window" from the shortcut menu.

When a photo opens in its own window, all kinds of control and flexibility await you. First, you can scale it up *or* down simply by making the window larger or smaller (by dragging its lower-right corner). You can close an open photo from the keyboard by pressing ⌘-W. And best of all, you can open multiple pictures and look at them side by side, as shown in Figure 7-6.

Albums

No matter how nicely you title, sort, and arrange photos in your digital shoebox, it's still a *shoebox* at this point, with all your photos piled together in one vast collection. To really become organized and present your photos to others, you need to arrange your photos into *albums*.

In iPhoto terminology, an album is a subset of pictures from your Library. It's a collection of photos that you group for easy access and viewing. Represented by a little album-book icon in the Source list at the left side of the screen, an album can consist of any photos that you select, or it can be a *smart album* that iPhoto assembles by matching certain criteria that you set up—all pictures that you took in 2004, for example, or all photos that you've rated four stars or higher.

While your Photo Library as a whole might contain thousands of photos from a hodgepodge of unrelated family events, trips, and time periods, a photo album has a focus: Steve & Sarah's Wedding, Herb's Knee Surgery, and so on.

Figure 7-6:
When you open photos in their own windows, you can look at several at the same time—a critical feature when comparing similar shots. Plus, you can keep your other thumbnails in view, allowing you to easily open additional photos without closing the open ones. Note that the title bar no longer tells you which magnification level iPhoto's using to display each photo, as it did in iPhoto 4.

As you probably know, mounting snapshots in a *real* photo album is a pain—that's why so many of us still have stacks of Kodak prints stuffed in envelopes and shoeboxes. But with iPhoto, you don't need mounting corners, double-sided tape, or scissors to create an album. In the digital world, there's no excuse for leaving your photos in hopeless disarray.

Of course, you're not required to group your digital photos in albums with iPhoto, but consider the following advantages of doing so:

- You can find specific photos much faster. By opening only the relevant album, you can avoid scrolling through thousands of thumbnails in the Photo Library to find a picture you want—a factor that takes on added importance as your collection expands.

- Only in a photo album can you drag your photos into a different order. To change the order of photos displayed in a slideshow or iPhoto hardbound book, for example, you need to start with a photo album (see Chapters 9 and 10).

Creating an Album by Clicking

Here are a few ways to create a new, empty photo album:

- Choose File→New Album.

- Press ⌘-N.

- Control-click in a blank area of the Source list and choose New Album from the shortcut menu.

- Click the + button in the iPhoto window, below the Source list.

In each case, a dialog box appears, prompting you to name the new album. Type in a descriptive name (*Summer in Aruba, Yellowstone 2005, Edna in Paris,* or whatever), click OK, and watch as a new photo album icon appears in the Source list (several are on display in Figure 7-7).

Now you can add photos to your newly spawned album by dragging in thumbnails from your Library, also as shown in Figure 7-7. There's no limit to the number of albums you can add, so make as many as you need to satisfactorily organize all the photos in your Library.

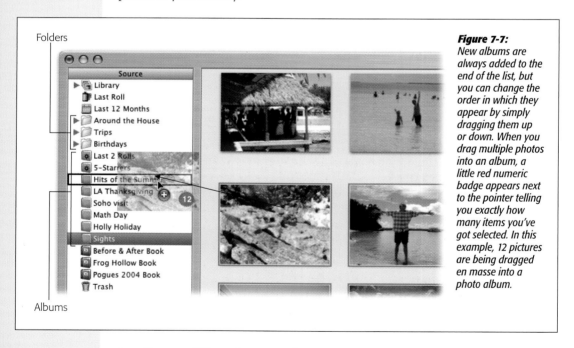

Folders

Albums

Figure 7-7:
New albums are always added to the end of the list, but you can change the order in which they appear by simply dragging them up or down. When you drag multiple photos into an album, a little red numeric badge appears next to the pointer telling you exactly how many items you've got selected. In this example, 12 pictures are being dragged en masse into a photo album.

Creating an Album by Dragging

Creating a new, empty album, however, isn't always the best way to start. It's often easier to create an album and fill it with pictures all in one fell swoop.

For example, you can drag a thumbnail (or a batch of them) from the photo-viewing area directly into an empty portion of the Source list. In a flash—well, in about three seconds—iPhoto creates a new album for you, named Album-1 (or whatever number it's up to). The photos you dragged are automatically dumped inside.

Similarly, you can drag a bunch of graphics files from the *Finder* (the desktop behind iPhoto) directly into the Source list. In one step, iPhoto imports the photos, creates a new photo album, names it after the folder you dragged in, and puts the newly imported photos into that album.

Tip: Remember that you can drag photos directly from the Finder onto a photo album icon in the Source list, forcing iPhoto to file them there in the process of importing.

Creating an Album by Selecting

Here's a handy, quick, album-creation command: File→New Album From Selection. Scroll through your Library and select any pictures you like using the methods described on page 115. (They don't have to be from the same film roll, or even the same year.) When you're done, choose New Album From Selection, type a name for the new album, and click OK.

Tip: To rename an existing photo album, double-click its name or icon in the Source list. A renaming rectangle appears around the album's name, with text highlighted and ready to be edited.

Adding More Photos

To add photos to an existing album, just drag them onto its icon. Figure 7-7 illustrates how you can select multiple photos and drop them into an album in one batch.

The single most important point about adding photos to an album is this: Putting photos in an album doesn't really *move* or *copy* them. It makes no difference where the thumbnails start out—whether it's the Photo Library or another album. You're just creating *references*, or pointers, back to the photos in your master Photo Library. This feature works a lot like Macintosh aliases; in fact, behind the scenes, iPhoto actually does create aliases of the photos you're dragging. (It stashes them in the appropriate album folders within the iPhoto Library folder.)

What this means is that you don't have to commit a picture to just one album when organizing. One photo can appear in as many different albums as you want. So, if you've got a killer shot of Grandma surfing in Hawaii and you can't decide whether to drop the photo into the Hawaiian Vacation album or the Grandma & Grandpa album, the answer is easy: Put it in both. iPhoto just creates two references to the same original photo in your Photo Library.

Viewing an Album

To view the contents of an album, click its name or icon in the Source list. All the photos included in the selected album appear in the photo-viewing area, while the ones in your Photo Library are hidden.

You can even browse more than one album at a time by highlighting their icons simultaneously:

- To view the contents of several adjacent albums in the list, click the first one, then Shift-click the last.

- To view the contents of albums that aren't consecutive in the list, ⌘-click them.

Tip: Viewing multiple albums at once can be extremely useful when it's time to share your photos. For example, you can make prints or burn an iPhoto CD archive (as explained in Chapters 10 and 12) containing the contents of multiple albums at the same time.

Remember, adding photos to albums doesn't remove them from the Library itself, your master collection. So if you lose track of which album contains a particular photo, just click the Library icon at the top of the Source list to return to the overview of your *entire* photo collection.

Tip: You can put your albums in any order. Just drag them up or down in the Source list.

Moving Photos Between Albums

There are two ways to transfer photos from one photo album to another:

- To *move* a photo between albums, select it and then choose Edit→Cut (or press ⌘-X), removing the photo from the album. Click the destination photo album's name or icon, and then choose Edit→Paste (or press ⌘-V). The photo is now a part of the second album.

- To *copy* a photo into another album, drag it onto the icon of the destination album in the Source list. That photo is now a part of both albums.

Removing Photos from an Album

If you change your mind about the way you've organized your photos and want to remove a photo from an album, open the album and select the photo. (Caution: Be sure that you're viewing the contents of a blue photo *album* in the photo-viewing area and not the main Photo Library, the Last 12 Months collection, or the Last Roll collection. Deleting a photo from those sources really does delete it for good.)

Then do one of the following:

- Choose Edit→Cut (or press ⌘-X) or Edit→Clear.

- Drag the photo's thumbnail onto the little Trash icon.

- Press the Delete key.

- Press the Del (forward delete) key.

- Control-click the photo, and then, from the shortcut menu, choose Remove from Album.

The thumbnail disappears from the album, but of course it's not really gone from iPhoto. Remember, it's still in your Photo Library.

Duplicating a Photo

You can't drag the same photo into an album twice. When you try, the thumbnail simply leaps stubbornly back into its original location, as though to say, "Nyah, nyah, you can't drag the same photo into an album twice."

It's often useful to have two copies of a picture, though. As you'll discover in Chapters 9 and 10, a photo whose dimensions are appropriate for a slideshow or photo book (that is, a 4:3 proportion) are inappropriate for ordering prints (4 x 6, 8 x 10, or whatever). To use the same photo for both purposes, you really need to crop them independently.

In this case, the old adding-to-album trick isn't going to help you. This time, you truly must duplicate the file, consuming more hard drive space behind the scenes. To do this, highlight the photo and choose Photos→Duplicate (⌘-D). iPhoto switches briefly into Import mode, copies the file, and then returns to your previous mode. The copy appears next to the original, bearing the same name plus the word "copy."

Note: If you duplicate a photo in an album, you'll see the duplicate both there and in the Library, but not in any other albums. If you duplicate it only in the Library, that's the only place you'll see the duplicate.

Putting Photos in Order

If you plan to turn your photo album into an onscreen slideshow, a series of Web pages, or a printed book, you'll have to tinker with the order of the pictures, arranging them in the most logical and compelling sequence. Sure, photos in the main Library or in a smart album (page 126) are locked into a strict sort order—either by creation date, rating, or film roll—but once they're dragged into a photo album, you can shuffle them manually into a new sequence.

To custom-sort photos in an album, just drag and drop, as shown in Figure 7-8.

Figure 7-8:
Arrange photos any way you like by dragging them to a new location within a photo album. In this example, two selected photos from the top-left corner are being dragged to a new location in the next row. The 2 indicates the number of photos being moved; the black vertical bar indicates where iPhoto will insert them when you release the mouse.

Duplicating an Album

It stands to reason that if you have several favorite photos, you might want to use them in more than one iPhoto presentation (in a slideshow and a book, for example). That's why it's often convenient to *duplicate* an album: so that you can create two different sequences for the photos inside.

Just highlight an album and then choose Photos→Duplicate. iPhoto does the duplicating in a flash—after all, it's just duplicating a bunch of tiny aliases. Now you're free to rearrange the order of the photos inside, to add or delete photos, and so on, completely independently of the original album.

Tip: For quick duplicating, you can also Control-click an album in the list and choose Duplicate from the shortcut menu. Duplicating an album creates an identical album, which you can then edit as described on the preceding pages.

Merging Albums

Suppose you have three photo albums that contain photos from different trips to the beach, called Spring Break at Beach, Summer Beach Party, and October Coast Trip. You'd like to merge them into a single album called Beach Trips 2004. No problem.

Select all three albums in the Source list (⌘-click each, for example); the photos from each now appear in the photo-viewing area. Now create a new, fourth album, using any of the usual methods. Finally, select all of the visible thumbnails and drag them into the new album.

You now have one big album containing the photos from all three of the original albums. You can delete the three source albums, if you like, or keep all four around. Remember, albums contain only references to your photos—not the photos themselves—so you're not wasting space by keeping the extra albums around. The only penalty you pay is that you have a longer list of albums to scroll through.

Deleting an Album

To delete an album, select its icon in the Source list, and then choose Edit→Clear or press the Delete (or Del) key. You can also Control-click an album and choose Delete Album from the shortcut menu. iPhoto asks you to confirm your intention.

Deleting an album doesn't delete any photos—just the references to those photos. Again, even if you delete *all* your photo albums, your Library remains intact.

Tip: If you're a person of steely nerve and unshakable confidence, there is a way to make iPhoto delete an album forever—including all the photos inside it. All you need is the Delete Album and Contents script that's part of the free AppleScripts for iPhoto collection. You can find this collection on this book's "Missing CD" at *www.missingmanuals.com.*

Folders

Obviously, Apple hit a home run when it invented the album concept. Let's face it: If there were a Billboard Top Software-Features Hits chart, the iPhoto albums feature would have been number one for months on end.

Albums may have become *too* popular, however. It wasn't long before iPhoto fans discovered that their long list of albums had outgrown the height of the Source list. As a result, people grew desperate for some way to organize albums *within* albums, to create subfolders somehow.

Apple's response in iPhoto 5 consisted of one word: "folders."

If you choose File→New Folder, iPhoto promptly creates a new, folder-shaped icon in the Source list called "untitled folder." (Type a name for it and then press Return or Enter.) Its sole purpose in life is to contain *other* Source-list icons—albums, smart albums, saved slideshow icons, book layouts, and so on. Figure 7-9 shows the details.

What's really nice about folders is that they can also contain *other* folders. That is, iPhoto is capable of more than a two-level hierarchy; you can actually create folders within folders within folders within folders, also as shown in Figure 7-9.

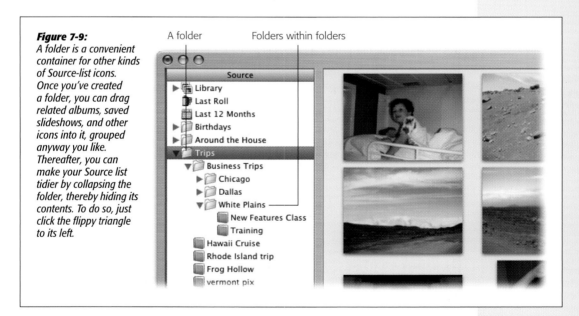

Figure 7-9:
A folder is a convenient container for other kinds of Source-list icons. Once you've created a folder, you can drag related albums, saved slideshows, and other icons into it, grouped anyway you like. Thereafter, you can make your Source list tidier by collapsing the folder, thereby hiding its contents. To do so, just click the flippy triangle to its left.

A folder   Folders within folders

Otherwise, folders work exactly like albums. You rename them the same way, drag them up and down the Source list the same way, delete them the same way, and duplicate them the same way.

Clearly, the people have spoken.

Smart Albums

Albums, as you now know, are the primary organizational tool in iPhoto. Since the dawn of iPhoto, you've had to create them yourself, one at a time—by clicking the + button beneath the Source list, for example, and then filling up the album by dragging photo thumbnails.

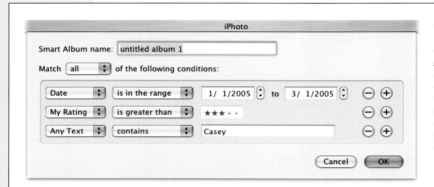

Figure 7-10:
The Smart Album dialog box is really just a powerful search command, because iPhoto is really just a powerful database. You can set up certain criteria, like this hunt for photos taken during a certain time period.

iPhoto, though, can fill up albums *for* you, thanks to *smart albums.* These are self-updating folders that always display pictures according to certain criteria that you set up—all pictures with "Aunt Edna" in the comments, for example, or all photos that you've rated four stars or higher. (If you've ever used smart playlists in iTunes, you'll recognize the idea immediately.)

To create a smart album, choose File→New Smart Album (Option-⌘-N), or Option-click the + button below the Source list. Either way, the Smart Album sheet slides down from the top of the window (Figure 7-10).

The controls here are designed to set up a search of your Photo Library. Figure 7-10 illustrates how to find pictures that you took in the first two months of 2005—but only those that have four- or five-star ratings and mention your friend Casey in the title or comments.

Click the + button to add a new criterion row to be even more specific about which photos you want iPhoto to include in the smart album. Use the first pop-up menu to choose a type of photo feature (keyword or date, for example) and the second pop-up menu to tell iPhoto whether you want to match it ("is"), eliminate it ("is not"), and so on. The third part of the criterion row is another pop-up menu or a search field where you finally tell iPhoto what to look for.

- You can limit the smart album's reach by limiting it to a certain **Album**. Or, by choosing "is not" from the second pop-up menu, you can *eliminate* an album from consideration. All your albums are listed in the third pop-up menu.

- **Any Text** searches your Library for words or letters that appear in the title, comments, or keywords that you've assigned to your photos.

Tip: If you can't remember how you spelled a word or whether you put it in the Comments or Title field, choose "Any Text," choose "contains" from the second pop-up menu, and in the search field type just the first few letters of the word ("am" for Amsterdam, for example). You're bound to find some windmills now!

- **Comments, Filename, Keyword, and Title** work the same way, except they search *only* that part of the photo's information. Search for "Keyword" "is" "Family" (choose "Family" from the third pop-up menu) to find only those pictures that you specifically assigned the keyword "Family," for example, and not just any old photos where you've typed the word "family" somewhere in the comments.

- **Date** was once one of iPhoto's most powerful search criteria. By choosing "is in the range" from the second pop-up menu, you can use it to create an album containing, for example, only the pictures you took on December 24 and 25 of last year, or for that five-day stretch two summers ago when your best friends were in town. In iPhoto 5, the new calendar serves this function much more conveniently.

- The **My Rating** option on the first pop-up menu really puts the fun into smart albums. Let's suppose you've been dutifully giving your pictures star ratings from 1 to 5, as described on page 142.

   Here's the payoff: You can use this smart album feature to collect, say, only those with five stars to create a quick slideshow of just the highlights. Another option is to choose "is greater than" two stars for a more inclusive slideshow that leaves out only the real duds.

- **Roll** lets you make iPhoto look only in, for example, the last five film rolls that you took (choose "is in the last" from the second pop-up menu and type 5 in the box). Or, if you're creating an album of old shots, you can eliminate the last few rolls from consideration by choosing "is not in the last."

- Click the – button next to a criterion to take it out of the running. For example, if you decide that date shouldn't be a factor, delete any criterion row that tells iPhoto to look for certain dates.

When you click OK, your smart album is ready to show off. When you click its name in the Source list (it has a little gear icon), the main window displays the thumbnails of the photos that match your criteria. The best part is that iPhoto will keep this album updated whenever your collection changes—as you change your ratings, as you take new photos, and so on.

Tip: To change or review the parameters for a smart album, click its icon in the list and then choose Photos→Get Info (⌘-I). The Smart Album sheet reappears.

Three Useful Panels

Just below the Source list, iPhoto can display any of three useful panels:

- **Information.** On this panel, you can view and edit general data about a photo, album, roll, or whatever else you've selected.

- **Calendar.** This feature, new in iPhoto 5, is fantastically useful. It helps you pluck a photo out of your thousands according to the timeline of your life.

- **Keywords.** This option was in previous versions of iPhoto, but its location is new. As before, the idea is that you can use this list of keywords for tagging your pictures with text labels, from "Robin" to "sunny day" to "prize winner."

To open one of these panels, click the corresponding button beneath the Source list: the blue circled i for the Information panel, the tiny grid for the Calendar panel, and the little key for the Keywords panel. (You close the panel by clicking the same button again.) Note, too, that you can adjust the relative height of the panel by dragging the gray divider bar just above it, as illustrated in Figure 7-11.

This chapter covers all three displays, beginning with the information panel.

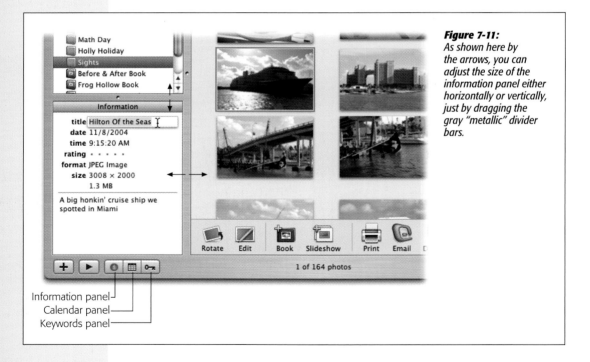

Figure 7-11:
As shown here by the arrows, you can adjust the size of the information panel either horizontally or vertically, just by dragging the gray "metallic" divider bars.

Information Panel: Titles, Dates, and Comments

When the Information panel is visible, as described in the previous section, you may see any number of different displays (Figure 7-11):

- When a single photo is selected, iPhoto displays that picture's name, rating, creation time and date, dimensions (in pixels), file size, and any comments you've typed.

- When multiple photos are selected, you see the *range* of their creation dates, plus how many photos are selected, and how much disk space they occupy.

- When no photos are selected, the Info area displays information about whatever container is selected in the Source list—the current album or film roll, for example. You get to see the name of the container, the range of dates of its photos, the number of photos, and their total file size on the hard drive.

- When a photo-book icon is selected (Chapter 10), you get to see its name, theme, dimensions, number of photos, and number of pages, plus any comments you added.

Titles (Renaming Photos)

Just about everything in iPhoto has its own title: every photo, album, folder, film roll, photo book, slideshow, and so on. You can rename them easily enough: Just edit the "title" box in the Information panel, as shown in Figure 7-11.

Most people find this feature especially valuable when it comes to individual photographs. When you import them from your digital camera, the pictures bear useless gibberish names like CRS000321.JPG, CRS000322.JPG, and so on. To change a photo's name to something more meaningful, just select its thumbnail, click once in the Title field, and type in a new title.

While you can make a photo's title as long as you want, it's smart to keep it short (about 10 characters or so). This way, you can see all or most of the title in the Title field (or under the thumbnails).

Tip: A new keystroke in iPhoto 5 makes life a lot easier when naming a whole bunch of photos in a row (like a batch you've just imported). Edit the title box for the first photo, and then press ⌘-] (right bracket) to select the next one. Each time you press ⌘-], iPhoto not only highlights the next picture, but also pre-highlights all of the text in its "title" box so you don't need to click anything before typing a new name for it. (Pressing ⌘-[takes you back one photo, of course.)

This simple keystroke is your ticket to quickly naming a multitude of unique photos, without ever taking your hands off the keyboard.

Changing titles, dates, or comments en masse

The trouble with naming your photos is that hardly anybody takes the time. Yes, the keystroke described in the Tip above certainly makes it easier to assign every photo its own name with reasonable speed—but are you really going to sit there and make up individual names for 25,000 photos?

Mercifully, iPhoto lets you change the names of your photos all at once, thanks to a new "batch processing" command. No, each photo won't have a unique, descriptive name, but at least they can have titles like *Spring Vacation 2* and *Spring Vacation 3* instead of *IMG_1345* and *IMG_1346*.

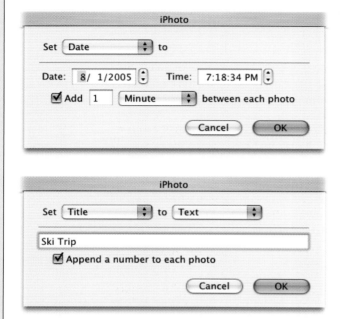

Figure 7-12:
iPhoto's batch-processing feature lets you specify Titles, Dates, and Comments for any number of photos you select.

Top: When you assign a date and time to a batch of pictures, turn on "Add ___ minute between each photo" to give each a unique time stamp, which could come in handy later when you're sorting them. Besides, you didn't take them all at the exact same moment, did you?

Bottom: When you title a batch of pictures, turn on "Append a number to each photo" to number them in sequence as well.

To use it, choose Photos→Batch Change, or press Shift-⌘-B, or Control-click some selected photos and choose Batch Change from the shortcut menu. The Batch Change sheet drops down from the top of the window (see Figure 7-12). Make sure that the first pop-up menu says Title.

Tip: Don't be fooled by the command name Batch Change. iPhoto still can't edit a batch of photos. You can't, for example, scale them all down to 640 x 480 pixels, or apply the Enhance filter to all of them at once.

Your options, in the second Batch Change pop-up menu, are as follows:

- **Empty.** Set the titles to "empty" if you want to un-name the selected photos, so they're all blank. You might appreciate this option when, for example, you're working on a photo book (Chapter 10) and you've opted for titles to appear with each photo, but you really want only a few pictures to appear with names under them.

- **Text.** This option produces an empty text box into which you can type, for example, *Ski Trip*. When you click OK, iPhoto names all of the selected pictures to match.

If you turn on "Append a number to each photo," iPhoto adds digits after whatever base name you choose—for example, *Ski Trip 1, Ski Trip 2,* and so on.

- **Roll Info.** Choose this command to name all the selected photos after the roll's name—"Grand Canyon 2005," for example. iPhoto automatically adds the photo number after this base name.

- **Filename.** If you've been fooling around with naming your photos, and now decide that you want their original, camera-blessed file names to return (IMG_1345 and so on), use this command.

- **Date/Time.** Here's another approach: Name each photo for the exact time it was taken. The dialog box gives you a wide variety of formatting options: long date, short date, time of day, and so on.

Tip: Once you've gone to the trouble of naming your photos, remember that you can make these names appear right beneath the thumbnails for convenient reference. Choose View→Titles to make it so.

Photo Dates

When you select a single photo, you can actually *change* its creation date by editing the Info pane's Date field. For example, you can switch the date from the day the digital file was created to the day the photo was actually taken.

In fact, you can also use the Batch Change command to rewrite history, resetting the dates of a group of photos all at once, as shown in Figure 7-11.

(We trust you won't use this feature for nefarious ends, such as "proving" to the jury that you were actually in Disney World on the day of the office robbery.)

Comments

Sometimes you need more than a one- or two-word title to describe the contents of a photo, album, folder, book, slideshow, or film roll. If you want to add a lengthier description, you can type it in the Comments field in the Photo Info pane.

Even if you don't write full-blown captions for your pictures, you can use the Comments field to store little details such as the names, places, dates, and events associated with your photos.

The best thing about adding comments is that they're searchable. After you've entered all this free-form data, you can use it to quickly locate a photo using iPhoto's search command.

Tip: If you speak a non-English language, iPhoto makes your life easier. As you're typing comments, you can choose Edit→Special Characters. Mac OS X's Character Palette opens, where you can add international letters like É, ø, and ß. Of course, it's also ideal for classic phrases like "I ♥ my cat."

Keep the following in mind as you squirrel away all those bits and scraps of photo information:

- You don't have to manually *type* to enter data into the Comments field. You can paste information in using the standard Paste command, or even drag selected text from another program (like Microsoft Word) right into the Comments box.

- If you feel the need to be verbose, go for it; the Comments box holds thousands of words. Careful, though: The field has no scroll bars, so there's a limit as to how much of what you paste or type will actually be visible. (You can, however, scroll the text by pressing the Page Up and Page Down keys, or by pressing the up or down arrow keys, or by dragging the cursor until the insertion point bumps the top or bottom edge of the box. If you've got a lot to say, your best bet is to make the box taller and the Source list wider.)

- If no photos, or several photos, are selected, the notes you type into the Comments box get attached to the current *album*, rather than to the pictures.

- You can add the same comment to a group of photos using iPhoto's Batch Change command. For example, ⌘-click all the pictures of your soccer team, choose Photos→Batch Change, choose Comments from the first pop-up menu, and type a list of your teammates' names in the Comments field. Years later, you'll have a quick reminder of everyone's name.

You can just as easily add comments for an album, folder, slideshow icon, book, or film roll whose name you've highlighted.

Comments as captions

While the Comments field is useful for storing little scraps of background information about your photos, you can also use it to store the *captions* that you want to appear with your photos. In fact, some of the book layouts included with iPhoto's book-creation tools (Chapter 10) automatically use the text in the Comments field to generate a caption for each photo.

(On the other hand, you don't *have* to use the Comments box text as your captions. You can always add different captions when you're editing the book.)

The Calendar

iPhoto has always offered a long list of ways to find certain photos: visually, by film roll, by album, by searching for text in their names or comments, and so on. But as the years went by, rival programs like Photoshop Album added what, in retrospect, seemed like an obvious and very natural method of finding specific pictures: by consulting a calendar.

After all, you might not know the file names of the pictures you took during your August 2003 trip to Canada. You might not have filed them away into an album. But one thing's for sure: You know you took that trip in August of 2003, and the new iPhoto calendar will help you find those pictures fast.

To use the calendar, start by indicating what container you want the calendar to search: an album or folder, for example, or one of the Library or Last __ Roll icons.

Now make the calendar appear by clicking the tiny blue calendar-grid button at the bottom of the Source list (see Figure 7-13).

At first, you get a year-at-a-glance view. This display may look clear and crisp and simple, but it contains a lot of power—and, if you look closely, a lot of different places to click the mouse. Here's how you can use the calendar to pinpoint photos taken in a certain time period.

- **Photos in a certain month.** See the names of the months in the year view? The names in **bold type** are the months where you took some photos. Click the name of a boldfaced month to see, the thumbnails of those photos; they'll appear in the main viewing area. (To scroll to a different year, click the tiny up and down triangle buttons on either side of the word Calendar at the top of the display, as shown in Figure 7-13.)

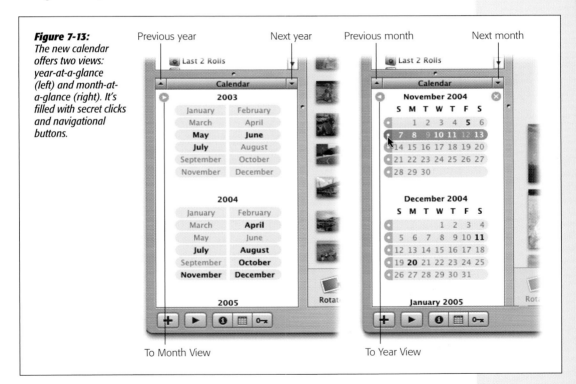

Figure 7-13:
The new calendar offers two views: year-at-a-glance (left) and month-at-a-glance (right). It's filled with secret clicks and navigational buttons.

Previous year   Next year   Previous month   Next month

To Month View   To Year View

- **Photos on a certain date.** In Year view, start by double-clicking the appropriate month name. The calendar now changes to show you the individual dates within that month, shown in Figure 7-13 at right. Once again, bold type lets you know that photos are awaiting. Click a date square to see the photos you took that day. (Here again, the up and down triangle arrows above the calendar let you scroll to different months. You can return to the year view by clicking the left-pointing arrow next to the uppermost month's name.)

- **Photos in a certain week.** Once you've drilled down into the Month view, as described above, you can also round up the photos taken during an entire week: Just click the little dot to the left of the week in question. (It's indicated by the cursor in Figure 7-13.) The horizontal week bar of the calendar is now highlighted in color, and the photos taken during any of those seven days appear in the main viewing area.

It's possible to develop some fancy footwork when you work with this calendar, since, as it turns out, you can select more than one week, month, or day at a time. In fact, you do that using exactly the same keyboard shortcuts that you would use to select individual photo thumbnails. For example:

- You can select multiple adjacent time units by clicking the first and then shift-clicking the last. For example, in Year view, you can select all the photos from June through August by first clicking June, and then Shift-clicking August. (You can use the same trick to select a series of days or weeks in the month view.)

Tip: Alternatively, you can just drag the mouse across the dates on the Month view, the days of the week, or the months on the Year view to select consecutive time periods.

- You can select multiple time units that *aren't* adjacent by ⌘-clicking them. For example, in Month view, you can select November 1, 5, 12, 20, and 30 by ⌘-clicking those days. In the photo-viewing area, you'll see all the photos taken on all of those days combined.

- Here's an offbeat shortcut that might actually be useful someday: You can round up all the photos taken during a specific month, week, or day *from every year in your collection* by holding down the Option key as you select.

  For example, you can round up six years' worth of Christmas shots by Option-clicking the December button in the Year view. Or you can find the pictures taken every year on your birthday (from all years combined) by Option-clicking that date in the month view.

Apple really went the extra mile on behalf of shortcut freaks when it designed the calendar. Here are a few more techniques that you probably wouldn't stumble upon by accident:

- In Year view, select all the days in a month by double-clicking the month's name. In Month view, you can do the same by triple-clicking any date number.

- Return to Year view by quadruple-clicking any date, or by clicking the month's name.

- Skip ahead to the next month or year (or the previous month or year) by turning the scroll wheel on your mouse, if you have one.

- Deselect anything that's selected in the calendar by clicking the small gray circular X button at the top-right corner of the calendar.

Keywords

Keywords are descriptive words—like *family*, *vacation*, or *kids*—that you can use to label and categorize your photos, regardless of which album they're in.

The beauty of keywords in iPhoto is that they're searchable. Want to comb through all the photos in your library to find every closeup taken of your children during summer vacation? Instead of browsing through multiple photo albums, just perform an iPhoto search for photos containing the keywords *kids, vacation, close-up,* and *summer*. You'll have the results in seconds.

Keywords are also an integral part of iPhoto's smart albums feature, as described on the previous pages.

Editing Keywords

Apple offers you a few sample entries in the Keywords list to get you rolling: Favorite, Family, Vacation, Kids, and Birthday. But these are intended only as a starting point. You can add as many new keywords as you want—or delete any of Apple's—to create a meaningful, customized list:

- To add, delete, or rename keywords, choose iPhoto→Preferences. Click the Keywords button to reveal the panel shown in Figure 7-14. Now click Add to produce a new entry called "untitled" in the Keywords list, ready to be edited. Finally, just type in your new keyword name and then press Return or Enter.

Figure 7-14:
Apple completely rejiggered the whole Keyword process in iPhoto 5 so that it's a lot easier to figure out—unless, of course you're used to the old way. Now, you create and destroy keywords in iPhoto's Preferences dialog box.

- To delete a keyword, select it in the list and then click Remove. As usual in iPhoto, you can select multiple keywords for deletion by Shift-clicking or (for noncontiguous selections) ⌘-clicking them in the list before clicking Remove. (When you remove a keyword from the list, iPhoto also removes that keyword from any pictures to which it had been applied.)

- To rename a keyword, select it in the list, click the Rename button below the list, and then edit the name.

Note: Be careful about renaming keywords after you've started using them; the results can be messy. If you've already applied the keyword Fishing to a batch of photos, but later decide to replace it with Romantic in your keyword list, all the Fishing photos automatically inherit the keyword Romantic. Depending on you and your interests, this may not be what you intended.

It may take some time to develop a really good master set of keywords. The idea is to assign labels that are general enough to apply across your entire photo collection, but specific enough to be meaningful when conducting searches.

Here's a general rule of thumb: Use *albums* to group pictures of specific events—a wedding, family vacation, or beach party, for example. (You can use *film rolls* for the same purpose, if you prefer.) Use *keywords* to focus on general characteristics that are likely to appear through your entire photo collection—words like Mom, Dad, Casey, Robin, Family, Friends, Travel, and Vacation.

Suppose your photo collection includes a bunch of photos that you shot during a once-in-a-lifetime trip to Rome last summer. You might be tempted to assign *Rome* as a keyword. Don't…because you probably won't use *Rome* on anything other than that one set of photos. It would be smarter to create a photo album or film roll called *Trip to Rome* to hold all those Rome pictures. Use your keywords to tag the same pictures with descriptors like Travel or Family. It also might be useful to apply keywords that describe attributes of the photos themselves, such as Closeup, Landscape, Portrait, and Scenic—or even the names of the people *in* the photos, like Harold, Chris, and Uncle Bert.

Assigning and Unassigning Keywords

iPhoto 5 offers two different methods of applying keywords to your pictures. No matter which method you prefer, keep one fortunate fact in mind: You can apply as many keywords to an individual photo as you like. A picture of your cousin Rachel at a hot dog eating contest in London might bear all these keywords: Relatives, Travel, Food, Humor, and Medical Crises. Later, you'll be able to find that photo no matter which of these categories you're hunting for.

Method 1: Drag the picture

One way to apply keywords to photos is, well, to apply the *photos* to the *keywords*.

If it's not already visible, expose the Keywords panel by clicking the little key button below the Source list (Figure 7-15).

Once your keyword buttons are visible, you can drag relevant photos directly onto them, as shown in Figure 7-15. You can drag them one at a time, or you can select the whole batch first, using any of the selection techniques described on page 115.

This method is best when you want to apply a whole bunch of pictures to one or two keywords. It's pretty tedious, however, when you want to apply a lot of different keywords to a single photo. That's why Apple has given you a second method, described next.

Note: If you press the Option key as you drag a thumbnail onto a keyword button, you *remove* that keyword assignment from the picture.

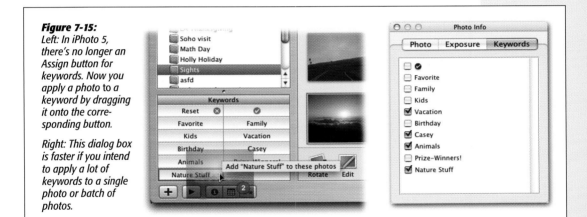

Figure 7-15:
Left: In iPhoto 5, there's no longer an Assign button for keywords. Now you apply a photo to a keyword by dragging it onto the corresponding button.

Right: This dialog box is faster if you intend to apply a lot of keywords to a single photo or batch of photos.

Method 2: Get Info

Highlight a pictures thumbnail and then choose Photos→Get Info. The Photo Info dialog box appears (Figure 7-15, right).

Now click the Keywords tab. Here, you find a simple checklist of all your keywords. Turn on all the checkboxes that correspond to the currently selected photo.

The beauty of this system is that you can keep the little Keywords window open on the screen as you move through your photo collection. Each time you click a photo—or, in fact, select a group of them—the checkboxes update themselves to reflect the keywords of whatever is now selected. Select some pictures, turn on Travel, select some others, turn on Family, and so on, without ever having to close the palette.

(It should be pretty obvious how you can use this method to *remove* keyword assignments from a certain picture or group of pictures, too—just turn off the checkboxes.)

Viewing Keyword Assignments

Once you've tagged a few pictures with keywords, you can see those keywords in either of two ways:

- Look at the Keywords window described above. When you select a photo, its assigned keyword checkboxes light up in the Keywords list.

- Set up iPhoto to show the actual text of the keywords right in the main photo-viewing area. To do this, choose View→Keywords, or press Shift-⌘-K. Figure 7-16 shows the resulting effect.

The Checkmark "Keyword"

You may have noticed that one entry in the keyword panel is not a word, but a symbol—a small checkmark. You can't edit this particular entry; it's always just a checkmark.

The checkmark works just like the other keyword entries, with one exception. Instead of assigning a particular keyword to photos, it flags them with a small checkmark symbol, as shown in Figure 7-17.

So what does the checkmark mean? Anything you want it to mean; it's open to a multitude of personal interpretations. The bottom line, though, is that you'll find this marker extremely useful for temporary organizational tasks.

For example, you might want to cull only the most appropriate images from a photo album for use in a printed book or slideshow. As you browse through the images, use the checkmark button to flag each shot you want. Later, you can use the Search function (described next) to round up all of the images you checkmarked, so that you can drag them all into a new album en masse.

You remove checkmarks from photos just as you remove any other keywords, as described in the previous sections.

Tip: Just after moving your checkmarked photos to an album, remember to remove the checkmark from all of them while they're still selected. This way, you won't get confused the next time you want to use the checkmark button for flagging a batch of photos.

Using Keywords

Whether you tag photos with the checkmark symbol or a series of keywords, the big payoff for your diligence arrives when you need to get your hands on a specific set of photos, because iPhoto lets you *isolate* them with one quick click.

Start by opening the Keywords panel below the Source list. (Click an album, folder, or roll in the Source list at this point, if you like, to confine your search.)

Here's where the fun begins: When you click one of the keyword buttons, iPhoto immediately rounds up all photos labeled with that keyword, displays them in the photo-viewing area, and hides all others.

Here are the important points to remember when using iPhoto's keyword searches:

- To find photos that match multiple keywords, click additional keyword buttons. For example, if you click Travel and then click Holidays, a photo reveals all the pictures that have *either* of those keywords. (There's no way to perform an "and" keyword roundup—that is, to find only pictures that have *both* Travel and Holidays keywords.)

Every button stays "clicked" until you click it a second time; you can see several of the keyword buttons "lit up" in Figure 7-16.

Figure 7-16:
You might find it easier to keep track of which keywords you've assigned by displaying them right in the photo-viewing area. Choose View→Keywords, or press Shift-⌘-K, to make them appear.

Figure 7-17:
The idea behind the checkmark button is to provide an easy, uncomplicated way of earmarking a series of photos while sifting through your collection.

- Suppose you've rounded up all your family pictures by clicking the Family keyword. The trouble is, your ex-spouse is in half of them, and you'd really rather keep your collection pure.

  No problem: *Option*-click the Ex-Spouse keyword button. iPhoto obliges by removing all photos with that keyword from whatever is currently displayed. In other words, Option-clicking a keyword button means, "find photos that don't contain this keyword."

- You can confine your search to a single album by selecting it before searching. Similarly, clicking the Library (or Last Roll, or Last 12 Months) in the list before searching means that you want to search that photo collection. You can even select multiple albums and search only in those—a first in this version of the software.

- Click Reset to restore the view to the whole album or whole Photo Library you had visible before you performed the search.

Searching for Photos by Text

The keyword mechanism described above is an adequate way to tag photos with textual descriptions. But as you know by now, there are other ways. The name you give a picture might be significant; its original file name on the hard drive might be important; and maybe you've typed some important clues into its Comments box or given its film roll an important name.

Anyhow, that's the purpose of the Search box in the lower-right corner of the iPhoto window.

The Photo Info Window

The small Information pane below the Source list displays only the most basic information about your photos: title, date, and size. For more detailed information, you need the Get Info command. It opens the Photo Info window, where iPhoto displays a surprisingly broad dossier of details about your photo: the make and model of the digital camera used to take it, for example, and even exposure details like the f-stop, shutter speed, and flash settings.

To open the Photo Info window (Figure 7-18), select a thumbnail and then choose Photos→Get Info (or press ⌘-I). (If more than one photo is selected, you'll get only a bunch of dashes in the info window.)

In addition to the Keywords tab described above, the Photo Info window contains Photo and Exposure tabs. The Photo panel contains information about the image file itself—when it was originally created, when it was first imported, and when it was last modified. If the image was shot with a digital camera (as opposed to being scanned or imported from disk), the make and model of the camera appear at the bottom of the window (see Figure 7-18).

Tip: Reading the details on the Exposure panel can be eye-opening. For example, if you put your camera into its automatic mode and snap a few pictures, you can find out—and learn from—the shutter and lighting settings the camera used.

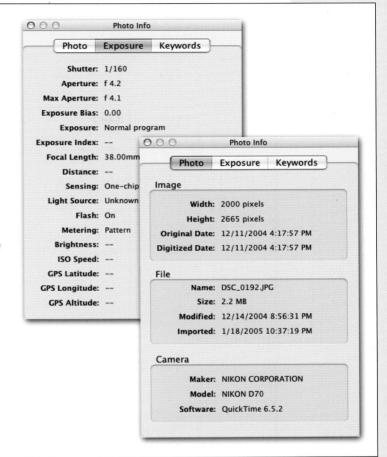

Figure 7-18:
The Photo Info window reports details about your photos by reading the EXIF tags that your camera secretly embeds in your files.

Left: On the Exposure panel, you can tell at a glance that this photo was shot with a flash, at a shutter speed of 1/160, and with an f-stop setting of 4.2. Tracking this information can be useful in determining which settings on your camera produce the best-quality digital photos in a certain set of conditions.

Right: iPhoto uses the Original Date (or lacking that, Modified date) information to sort your photos in the Photo Library and place them in their respective year albums.

How on earth does iPhoto know so much about how your photos were taken? Most digital cameras embed a wealth of image, camera, lens, and exposure information in the photo files they create, using a standard data format called *EXIF* (Exchangeable Image Format). With that in mind, iPhoto automatically scans photos for EXIF data as it imports them.

Note: Some cameras do a better job than others at embedding EXIF data in photo files. iPhoto can extract this information only if it's been properly stored by the camera when the digital photo is created. Of course, most (if not all) of this information is missing altogether if your photos didn't come from a digital camera (if they were scanned in, for example).

Rate Your Photos

iPhoto offers a great way to categorize your pictures: by how great they are! You can assign each picture a rating of 1 to 5 stars, then use the ratings to sort your Photo Library, or gather only the cream of the crop into a slideshow, smart album, or photo book.

Here are the ways you can rate your digital masterpieces:

- Select a photo (or several) and choose Photos→My Rating; from the submenu, choose from 1 through 5 stars. You can even do this while you're editing a single photo.

Tip: If the top of the screen is just too far away, you can also Control-click any one of the selected thumbnails (or, in Edit mode, anywhere on the photo) and choose the My Rating command from the shortcut menu. Its submenu is exactly the same as what you'd find in the Photos→My Rating command.

- If you're not a mousy sort of person, you can perform the same stunt entirely from the keyboard. Press ⌘-1 for one star, ⌘-2 for two stars, and so on. Press ⌘-0 to strip away any existing ratings.

- During a slideshow, twitch the mouse to bring up the onscreen control bar. In the bar, click the row of dots to turn them into rating stars (click the third dot to give the current photo 3 stars, for example). Or just press the number keys on the keyboard to bestow that number of stars as the slides go by.

- To remove a rating, select the photo and choose Photos→My Ratings→None. You're saying, in effect, "This photo has not yet been rated." Keyboard shortcut: ⌘-0.

Tip: Once you've applied your star ratings, you can view the actual little stars right under the corresponding thumbnails by choosing View→My Ratings (or pressing Shift-⌘-R).

FREQUENTLY ASKED QUESTION

Undeletable Photos?

iPhoto won't delete photos of my sister. I thought I got rid of a bunch of unflattering pictures of her the other day, and then I found them again when browsing through my Library. Why aren't they staying deleted?

Possibility 1: You deleted the pictures from an album instead of the Library itself (the first icon in the list). When you remove a photo from an album, it removes only a reference to that picture from the album, leaving the photo itself untouched in the Library.

If the pictures of your sister are really horrendous, click the Library icon in the Source list, move the offending photos to the Trash, and then empty the Trash. That'll get rid of them once and for all.

Possibility 2: You're trying to delete the photo from inside a smart album (page 126). Remember, you have to delete such photos from the Library itself, or from the Last __ Months or Last __ Rolls collections.

Deleting Photos

As every photographer knows—make that every *good* photographer—not every photo is a keeper. So at some point, you'll probably want to delete some of your photos.

The iPhoto Trash

iPhoto has a private Trash can that works just like the Finder's Trash. It's sitting there at the bottom of the Source list. When you want to purge a photo from your Library, simply drag it to the Trash. Instead of deleting the photo immediately, iPhoto lets it sit there in the Trash "album," awaiting permanent disposal via the Empty Trash command. This feature gives you one more layer of protection against accidentally deleting a precious picture.

In the main thumbnails view, you can relegate items to the Trash by selecting one or more thumbnails in the Library (not in an album) and then performing one of the following:

Figure 7-19:
When you dump a photo into iPhoto's Trash, it's not really gone—it's just relocated to the Trash folder. Clicking the Trash icon in the Source list displays all the photos in the Trash and makes the Info panel show the total number of trashed photos, their date range, and their sizes.

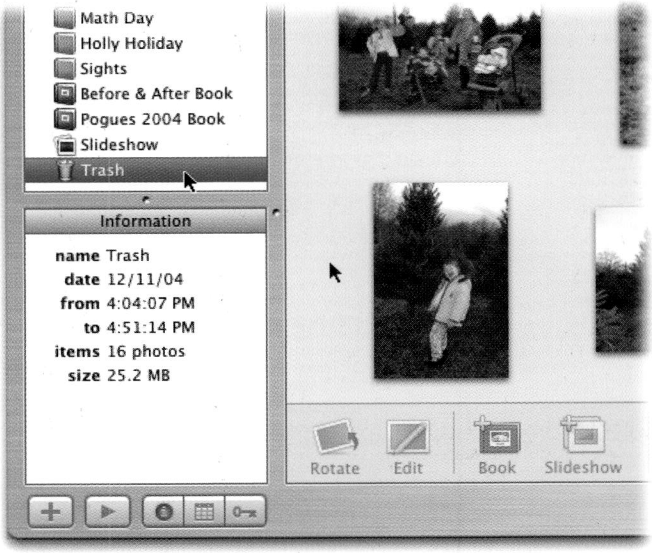

- Drag the thumbnails into the Trash.

- Control-click a photo and choose Move to Trash from the shortcut menu.

- Press ⌘-Delete or choose Photos→Move to Trash.

Tip: To delete a photo from a smart album or from Edit mode, press Option-⌘-Delete.

To view the photos that you have sentenced to the great shredder in the sky, click the Trash icon, as shown in Figure 7-19. However, if you suddenly decide you don't really want to get rid of any of these trashed photos, it's easy to resurrect them: Just drag the thumbnails out of the Trash and onto the Library icon in the Source list. (Alternatively, you can Control-click the photo or photos and, from the shortcut menu, choose Restore to Photo Library.)

You've just rescued them from photo-reject limbo and put them back into your main photo collection.

Tip: You can also move photos from the Trash back into your Library by selecting them—yes, in the Trash "album"—and then pressing ⌘-Delete. Think of it as the un-Trash command.)

To *permanently* delete the photos in the Trash, choose iPhoto→Empty Trash, or Control-click the Trash icon to access the Empty Trash command via a shortcut menu. iPhoto then displays an alert message, warning you that emptying the Trash removes these photos permanently and irreversibly.

(Of course, if you imported the photos from files on disk or haven't deleted them from your camera, you can still recover the original files and reimport them.)

Note: As you might expect, dragging photos into the Trash doesn't reduce the total size of your iPhoto Library by a single byte, because iPhoto is still storing a copy of each photo in its Trash folder. Only when you empty the Trash does the iPhoto Library folder actually shrink in size.

Whatever pictures you throw out by emptying the Trash also disappear from any albums you've created. (Deleting a photo from an *album* is different.)

Customizing the Shoebox

iPhoto starts out looking just the way you probably see it now, with each picture displayed as a small thumbnail against a plain white background. This view makes it easy to browse through photos and work with iPhoto's various tools.

But hey, this is *your* digital shoebox. With a little tweaking and fine-tuning, you can completely customize the way iPhoto displays your photos.

Start with a visit to iPhoto→Preferences and click the Appearance button.

Tip: You can open the iPhoto Preferences window at any time by pressing ⌘-, (comma). This keystroke is blissfully consistent across all the iLife programs.

Changing the View

The controls in the Appearance panel of the Preferences window let you make some pretty significant changes to the overall look of your Photo Library. See Figure 7-20 for an example.

Here are your options:

- **Add or remove a border or shadow.** The factory setting, Drop Shadow, puts a soft black shadow behind each thumbnail in the photo-viewing pane, a subtle touch that gives your Photo Library an elegant 3-D look.

As pretty as this effect is, however, there's also a decent reason to turn it *off*: It slows iPhoto down slightly, as the program has to continually redraw or resize those fancy shadows behind each thumbnail whenever you scroll or zoom. Switch to either the Border or No Border setting and you'll be rewarded with faster scrolling and smoother zooming whenever you change the size of thumbnails (as described in

Figure 7-20:
Here's a typical Library with a very different look. Instead of the usual white background with drop-shadowed thumbnails, this view presents large thumbnails, with borders, against a dark gray background. The Source list is hidden, but the titles for each photo are displayed.

Figure 7-21:
The "Align to grid" option does nothing if all photos have the same orientation. But with mixed horizontal and vertical images, photos stay in strict rows and columns (right) despite their shape differences. At left:- an "unaligned" version of the same thumbnails.

the next section). The Border setting puts a thin white frame around each picture. You won't see this border unless you change the background color, as explained in the next paragraph.

- **Change the background color.** Right under the No Border radio button, a slider lets you adjust the background color of the photo-viewing pane. Actually, the term "color" is a bit of an overstatement, since your choices only include white, black, or any shade of gray in between. Not exactly a rainbow of colors.

- **Adjust the Alignment.** Turn on the "Align photos to grid" checkbox if you want the thumbnails in your Photo Library to snap into evenly spaced rows and columns, even if your collection includes thumbnails of varying sizes and orientations, as shown in Figure 7-21.

- **Change the date order.** Turning on "Place most recent photos at the top" puts them at the top of the main iPhoto window. It's sort of like seeing your most recent email messages at the top of your inbox. If you turn this checkbox off, you'll have to scroll all the way down to see your most recent pictures.

- **Choose text size.** The pop-up menu at the bottom of the Appearance panel lets you choose Small or Large for the album names in the Source list, depending on your eyesight. As for keywords and the other text in the iPhoto window, you're stuck with one size—tiny.

Showing/Hiding Keywords, Titles, and Film Roll Info

If you want to display thumbnails along with the titles and keywords you assign your pictures using iPhoto, you can switch these view options on or off by choosing View→Titles (Shift-⌘-T) and View→Keywords (Shift-⌘-K). Titles and keywords appear under each thumbnail.

As with most of iPhoto, your formatting options are limited. You can't control the font, style, color, or size of this text. Your only choice is to either display the title and keywords or to keep them hidden.

Editing Your Shots

Y ou can't paint in additional elements, mask out unwanted backgrounds, or
apply 50 different special effects filters in iPhoto, as you can with editing programs like Photoshop and GraphicConverter. Nonetheless, iPhoto is designed
to handle basic photo fix-up tasks in two categories: one-click fixes and advanced
fine-tuning.

One-Click Fixes

These are the original iPhoto editing tools, the ones that were present in the previous
version and are nearly idiot-proof:

- **Enhance.** With one click, this tool endeavors to make photos look more vibrant
  by tweaking the brightness and contrast settings and adjusting the saturation to
  compensate for washed-out or oversaturated colors.

- **Cropping.** The cropping tool lets you cut away the outer portions of a photo to
  improve its composition or to make it the right size for a printout or Web page.

- **Retouch.** This little brush lets you paint out minor imperfections like blemishes,
  freckles, and scratches.

- **Red-Eye.** This little filter gets rid of a very common photo glitch—those shining
  red dots that sometimes appear in a person's eyes as the result of flash photography.
  Who wants to look like a werewolf if it's not necessary?

- **Black & White.** Turns your color photos into moody black-and-white art shots.

- **Sepia.** Makes new photos look faded and brownish, for that old-time daguerreotype
  look.

Advanced Fine-Tuning

iPhoto 5 introduces a new floating panel for power users who used to go galloping off to Photoshop every time they needed greater control over photo editing. It includes sliders for these parameters:

- **Brightness/Contrast.** These sliders can tone down bright, overexposed images or lighten up those that look too dark and shadowy. While the Enhance button takes an all-or-nothing approach to fixing a photo, the Brightness and Contrast controls let you make tiny adjustments to the settings.

- **Saturation, Temperature, Tint.** These sliders affect the overall color of a picture: its vividness, warmth, and color cast.

- **Sharpness.** There's no rescuing a completely out-of-focus shot. But this slider can take a photo a few percentage points closer to sharp, or—in situations where a traditional photographer might smear a little Vaseline on the lens—blur the picture softly to hide your subject's wrinkles and flaws.

- **Straighten.** Here's a really fun new control. In one quick twitch of the mouse, you can rotate a crooked shot slightly so that it appears square with the horizon.

- **Exposure.** Like magic, this slider lets you fix most over- and underexposed shots, allowing you to crank up the flash or bring details out of shadow.

- **Levels.** Using these sophisticated controls, you can compress or expand the lights and darks across a photo's spectrum—a function that will make a lot more sense when you try it.

For anything beyond these touch-up tasks, you need to manipulate your photos in a more powerful editing program—which you can easily do within iPhoto, as explained later in this chapter.

Using the Editing Tools

All iPhoto editing is performed in a special editing mode, in which the photo appears at nearly full-screen size, and tool icons appear along the bottom (Figure 8-1). You enter Edit mode either by double-clicking a photo's thumbnail (the quick way) or by highlighting the thumbnail and then clicking the Edit icon at the bottom of the screen (the long way).

As you may recall, however, iPhoto can take you to either of two alternate Edit worlds. First, there's the one where the photo appears right in the iPhoto window. Second, there's the one where the photo opens up in a separate window of its own.

A reminder: You specify which arrangement you prefer in the iPhoto→Preferences dialog box. Then again, you can decide on an individual basis, too. To do so, Control-click a thumbnail or a photo in its own window, then from the shortcut menu, choose "Edit" or "Edit in separate window," depending on your preference. (If you've bought a two-button mouse for your Mac, just right-click instead.)

If you've opted to open the photo within iPhoto's window, by the way, you'll see a parade of other photo thumbnails at the top of the window. Feel free to edit any other photo by clicking its little postage-stamp icon up there (or by clicking the big Previous/Next arrows at the bottom of the window).

Or, if you'd rather hide the thumbnail browser to reclaim the space it's using, choose View→Thumbnails (Option-⌘-T) so that the checkmark disappears.

Note: If you're used to the way previous versions of iPhoto handled photo editing, here are three important differences. First, the editing tools always appear in the same place (the bottom of the window), regardless of whether you're editing a picture right in the iPhoto or in its own separate window. Second, you can no longer edit the toolbar; the same set of tools always appears in the same order.

Finally, Apple eliminated the mode buttons in iPhoto 5 (Organize, Share, Edit, and so on). As a result, when you're finished editing a photo, either click the Done button (or close the window, if you're editing in a separate window) to return to the normal thumbnails view, or switch to another photo using the arrow buttons or the thumbnail browser at top.

Figure 8-1:
iPhoto's editing tools appear in the toolbar when you open a photo for editing. A >> symbol at the right end of the toolbar (as shown here) means that the window is too narrow to display all the tools. Just drag the window wider to show all tools, or click the double-arrow to access the tools via a pop-up menu.

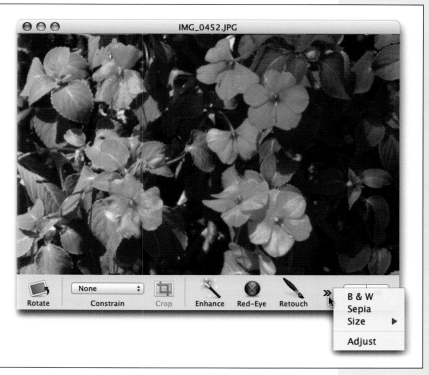

One-Click Fixups: The Enhance Button

The Enhance button provides a simple way to improve the appearance of less-than-perfect digital photos. You click one button to make colors brighter, skin tones warmer, and details sharper. (If you've used Photoshop, the Enhance button is a lot like the Auto Levels command.)

But if you want to know *exactly* what the Enhance button does, well, good luck. Apple guards that information as though it's a top-secret meatloaf recipe. iPhoto's online help makes only a nebulous statement about it "improving colors," but provides no explanation as to *how* they're improved.

What's clear is that the Enhance button analyzes the relative brightness of all the pixels in your photo and attempts to "balance" the image by dialing the brightness or contrast up or down and intensifying dull or grayish-looking color. In addition to this overall adjustment of brightness, contrast, and color, the program makes a particular effort to identify and bring out the subject of the photo. Usually, this approach at least makes pictures look somewhat richer and more vivid, as shown in Figure 8-2.

Figure 8-2:
The Enhance command works particularly well on photos that are slightly dark and that lack good contrast, like the original photo on the left. Using iPhoto's Brightness and Contrast sliders alone might have helped a little, but the Enhance button produces a faster and overall better result, as shown at right.

Using the Enhance Button

If you're editing a photo in iPhoto's main window, you'll find the Enhance button on the lower pane of the window, along with iPhoto's other editing tools. To enhance a photo, just click the Enhance button. That's it...there's nothing to select first, and no controls to adjust.

Tip: You can also Control-click a photo to choose Enhance from the shortcut menu.

As you use the Enhance button, remember that iPhoto's image-correcting algorithms are simply best guesses at what your photo is supposed to look like. It has no way of knowing whether you've shot an overexposed, washed-out picture of a vividly colored sailboat, or a perfectly exposed picture of a pale-colored sailboat on an overcast day.

Consequently, you may find that Enhance has no real effect on some photos, and only minimally improves others. Remember, too, that you can't enhance just one part of a photo. When you click the Enhance button, iPhoto runs its enhancement routine on the entire picture. If you want to selectively adjust specific portions of a picture, you need a true photo-editing program like GraphicConverter or Photoshop Elements.

Tip: If using the Enhance command does improve your photo, but just not enough, you can click it repeatedly to amplify its effect—as many times as you want, really. It's just that applying Enhance more than three times or so risks turning your photo into digital mush.

If you go too far, remember that you can press ⌘-Z (or choose Edit→Undo) to backtrack. In fact, you can take back as many steps as you like, all the way back to the original photo.

In some cases, you'll need to do more than just click the Enhance button to coax the best possible results from your digital photos. You may have to tweak away with the Brightness and Contrast sliders, as explained later in this chapter.

Cropping

Think of iPhoto's cropping tool as a digital paper cutter. It neatly shaves off unnecessary portions of a photo, leaving behind only the part of the picture you really want.

You'd be surprised at how many photographs can benefit from selective cropping. For example:

- **Eliminate parts of a photo you just don't want.** This is a great way to chop your brother's ex-girlfriend out of an otherwise perfect family portrait, for example (provided she was standing at the end of the lineup).

- **Improve a photo's composition.** Trimming a photo allows you to adjust where your subject matter appears within the frame of the picture. If you inspect the professionally shot photos in magazines or books, for example, you'll discover that many pros get more impact from a picture by cropping tightly around the subject, especially in portraits.

- **Get rid of wasted space.** Huge expanses of background sky that add nothing to a photo can be eliminated, keeping the focus on your subject.

- **Fit a photo to specific proportions.** If you're going to place your photos in a book layout or turn them into standard size prints (Chapter 10), you may need to adjust their proportions. That's because there's a substantial discrepancy between the *aspect ratio* (length-to-width proportions) of your digital camera's photos and those of film cameras—a difference that will come back to haunt you if you order prints. The following discussion covers all the details.

How to Crop a Photo

Here are the steps for cropping a photo:

1. **Open the photo for editing.**

   You can use any of the methods mentioned earlier in this chapter.

2. **Make a selection from the Constrain pop-up menu, if you like (Figure 8-3).**

Figure 8-3:
When you crop a picture, you drag out (draw) a rectangle in any direction using the crosshair pointer to define the part of the photo you want to keep. (To deselect this area—when you want to start over, for example—click anywhere in the foggy area.)

Top: The three different cursor shapes you may see, depending on where you move the pointer: the + crosshair for the initial drag, the black double arrow when you're near a boundary (for reshaping), or the pointing-hand for sliding the entire rectangle around the photo.

Bottom: Once you've drawn the rectangle and clicked Crop, the excess margin falls to the digital cutting room floor, thus enlarging your subject.

The Constrain pop-up menu controls the behavior of the cropping tool. When the menu is set to None, you can draw a cropping rectangle of any size and proportions, in essence going freehand.

When you choose one of the other options in the pop-up menu, however, iPhoto constrains the rectangle you draw to preset proportions. It prevents you from coloring outside the lines, so to speak.

The Constrain feature is especially important if you plan to order prints of your photos (Chapter 10). When doing so, you'll notice that you can order prints only in standard photo sizes: 4 x 6, 5 x 7, 8 x 10, and so on. You may recall, however, that most digital cameras produce photos whose proportions are 4 to 3 (width to height). This size is ideal for DVDs and iPhoto books (Chapter 10), because your television and iPhoto book layouts use 4 to 3 dimensions, too—but it doesn't divide evenly into standard print photograph sizes.

That's why the Constrain pop-up menu offers you canned choices like 4 x 6, 5 x 7, and so on. Limiting your cropping to one of these preset sizes guarantees that your cropped photos will fit perfectly into Kodak prints. (If you don't constrain your cropping this way, Kodak—not you—will decide how to crop them to fit.)

Note: Even though the Constrain menu ensures the right proportions, it doesn't in any way guarantee that the total size of the final photos is adequate. See the box "When Cropping Problems Crop Up" on page 155 for more about properly sizing your photos.

Other crop-to-fit options in the Constrain menu let you crop photos for use as a desktop picture ("1024 x 768 [Display]," or whatever your actual monitor's dimensions are), as a 4 x 6-inch print, to fit into one of the Book layouts available in iPhoto's Book mode, and so on.

Tip: Here's a bonus feature: the item in the Constrain pop-up menu called Custom. Inside the two text boxes that appear, you can type any proportions you want: 4 x 7, 15 x 32, or whatever your eccentric design needs call for.

As soon as you make a selection from this pop-up menu, iPhoto draws a preliminary cropping rectangle—of the proper dimensions—on the screen, turning everything outside it dim and foggy.

In general, this rectangle always appears in either landscape (horizontal) or portrait (vertical) orientation, according to the shape of the photo itself. If you've selected "4 x 3" (Book), you can reverse the orientation of the starter rectangle by opening the pop-up menu a second time and choosing Constrain as Portrait (or Constrain as Landscape).

Tip: Actually, there's a quicker way to rotate the selection from horizontal to vertical (or vice versa): Option-drag across the photo to draw a new selection rectangle, as described in the next step. The selection rectangle crisply turns 90 degrees.

Now, the cropping area that iPhoto suggests with its foggy-margin rectangle may, as far as you're concerned, be just right. In that case, skip to step 5.

More often, though, you'll probably want to give the cropping job the benefit of your years of training and artistic sensibility by *redrawing* the cropping area. Here's how:

3. **Click anywhere in the foggy area to get rid of the rectangle. Then position the mouse pointer (which appears as a crosshair) at one corner of your photo. Drag diagonally across the portion of the picture that you want to *keep*.**

    As you drag a rectangle across your photo, the portions *outside* of the selection—the part of the photo that iPhoto will eventually trim away—are dimmed out once again (Figure 8-3).

Tip: Even if you've turned on one of the Constrain options in step 2, you can override the constraining by pressing ⌘ after you begin dragging.

Don't worry about getting your selection perfect, since iPhoto doesn't actually trim the photo until you click the Crop button.

4. **Adjust the cropping, if necessary.**

    If the shape and size of your selection area are OK, but you want to adjust which part of the image is selected, you can move the selection area without redrawing it. Position your mouse over the selection so that the pointer turns into a hand icon. Then drag the existing rectangle where you want it.

    You can even change the *shape* of the selection rectangle after you've released the mouse button, thanks to an invisible quarter-inch "handle" that surrounds the cropping area. Move your cursor close to any edge or corner so that it changes to a + shape (near the corner) or a double-headed arrow (near the edge). Now you can drag the edge or corner to reshape the rectangle (see Figure 8-3).

    If you get cold feet, you can cancel the operation by clicking once anywhere outside the cropping rectangle (to remain in Edit mode), or by double-clicking anywhere on the photo (to return to thumbnails mode). Or, if the photo is open in its own window, just close the window.

Note: Despite its elaborate control over the relative dimensions of your cropping rectangle, iPhoto won't tell you its actual size, in pixels. Therefore, if you want to crop a photo to precise pixel dimensions, you must do the job in another program, like GraphicConverter or Photoshop Elements. (See page 172 for instructions on flipping into a different editing program.)

---

5. **When the cropping rectangle is just the way you want, click the Crop button.**

    Alternatively, Control-click the photo and choose Crop from the shortcut menu.

    If throwing away all those cropped-out pixels makes you nervous, relax. When you click Crop, iPhoto, behind the scenes, makes a duplicate of the original photo before doing the deed—a handy safety net for the day you decide to revert back to the uncropped version, months or years later.

If you realize immediately that you've made a cropping mistake, you can choose Edit→Undo Crop Photo to restore your original.

If you have regrets *weeks* later, on the other hand, you can always select the photo and choose Photos→Revert to Original. After asking if you're sure, iPhoto promptly reinstates the original photo from its backup, discarding every change you've ever made.

Note: When you crop a photo, you're changing it in all albums in which it appears. If you want a photo to appear cropped in one album but not in another, you must first duplicate it (highlight it and then choose Photos→Duplicate), then edit each version separately.

Painting Over Freckles, Scratches, and Hairs

Sometimes an otherwise perfect portrait is spoiled by the tiniest of imperfections—a stray hair or an unsightly blemish, for example. Professional photographers, whether working digitally or in a traditional darkroom, routinely remove such minor imperfections from their final prints—a process known as *retouching*, for clients known as *self-conscious*.

iPhoto's Retouch brush lets you do the same thing with your own digital photos. You can paint away scratches, spots, hairs, or any other small flaws in your photos with a few quick strokes.

UP TO SPEED

When Cropping Problems Crop Up

Remember that cropping always shrinks your photos. Remove too many pixels, and your photo may end up too small (that is, with a resolution too low to print or display properly).

Here's an example: You start with a 1600 x 1200 pixel photo. Ordinarily, that's large enough to be printed as a high-quality, standard 8 x 10 portrait.

Then you go in and crop the shot. Now the composition is perfect, but your photo measures only 800 x 640 pixels. You've tossed out nearly a million and a half pixels.

The photo no longer has a resolution (pixels per inch) high enough to produce a top-quality 8 x 10. The printer is forced

to blow up the photo to fill the specified paper size, producing visible, jaggy-edged pixels in the printout. The 800 x 640 pixel version of your photo would make a great 4 x 5 print (if that were even a standard size print), but pushing the print's size up further noticeably degrades the quality.

Therein lies a significant advantage of using a high-resolution digital camera (5 or 6 megapixels, for example). Because each shot starts out with such a high resolution, you can afford to shave away a few hundred thousand pixels and still have enough left over for good-sized, high-resolution prints.

Moral of the story: Know your photo's size and intended use—and don't crop out more photo than you can spare.

The operative word here is *small*. The Retouch brush can't wipe out a big blob of spaghetti sauce on your son's white shirt or completely erase somebody's mustache. It's intended for tiny fixups that don't involve repainting whole sections of a photo. (For that kind of photo overhaul, you need a dedicated photo-editing program.)

The Retouch brush works its magic by blending together the colors in the tiny area that you're fixing. It doesn't cover the imperfections you're trying to remove, but *blurs* them out by softly blending them into a small radius of surrounding pixels. You can see the effect in Figure 8-4.

Tip: The Retouch brush is particularly useful if your photo library contains traditional photographs that you've scanned in. You can use it to wipe away the dust specks and scratches that often appear on film negatives and prints, or those that are introduced when you scan the photos.

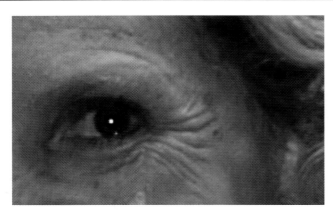
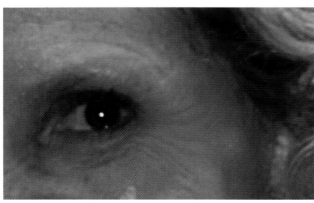

Figure 8-4:
The key to using the Retouch brush is to target small areas and use restraint so that you don't overblur the area you're working on. Notice how the Retouch brush was used on the original photo (top) to soften wrinkles around the eye and remove imperfections in the upper-left corner (bottom), like an application of digital Botox.

Using the Retouch Brush

The Retouch brush appears at the bottom of the window as soon as you open a photo for editing. You can also switch to it whenever you're in Editing mode, by Control-clicking a photo and choosing Retouch from the shortcut menu.

Once you've selected the Retouch brush, your pointer turns into a small crosshair with a hole in the middle. Using the center of the crosshair, target the imperfection and "paint" over it, using a series of short strokes to blend it with the surrounding portion of the picture. Don't overdo it: If you apply too much retouching, the area you're working on starts to look noticeably blurry and unnatural, as if someone smeared Vaseline on it.

Fortunately, you can use the Edit→Undo command (⌘-Z) to take back as many of your brush strokes as necessary.

Note: On high-resolution photos, it can take a moment or two for iPhoto to process each individual stroke of the Retouch brush. If you don't see any results, wait a second for iPhoto to catch up with you.

Red-Eye

Red-eye is actually light reflected back from your subject's eyes. The bright light of your camera's flash passes through the pupil of each eye, illuminating the blood-red retinal tissue at the back of the eye. This illuminated tissue, in turn, is reflected back into the camera lens. Red-eye problems worsen when you shoot pictures in a dim room, because your subject's pupils are dilated wider, allowing even more light from the flash to illuminate the retina.

If it's too late to avoid red-eye to begin with (by using an external flash, for example), and people's eyes are already glowing demonically, there's always iPhoto's Red-Eye tool. It lets you alleviate red-eye problems by digitally removing the offending red pixels. Here's how:

1. **Open your photo for editing.**

   Change the zoom setting, if necessary, so that you have a close-up view of the eye with the red-eye problem.

2. **Click the Red-Eye button.**

   If you're editing in a separate window, as shown in Figure 8-5, you may have to use the >> menu at the right end of the toolbar to find the Red-Eye command.

3. **Use the crosshair pointer to click inside each red-tinted eye.**

   With each click, iPhoto neutralizes the red pixels, painting the pupils solid black.

   Of course, this means that everybody winds up looking like they have *black* eyes instead of red ones—but at least they look a little less like the walking undead.

B & W, Sepia

The B & W (Black and White) and Sepia tools, meanwhile, don't correct anything. They simply drain the color from your photos. B & W converts them into moody grayscale images (a great technique if you're going for that Ansel Adams look); Sepia repaints them entirely in shades of antique brown (as though they were 1865 daguerreotypes).

Open a photo in Edit mode, and then click the Black & White or Sepia buttons. That's all there is to it. If you change your mind, you can use Edit→Undo Convert to B&W to restore the color immediately, or choose Photos→Revert to Original at any point to return to your original file.

Tip: If you don't see the B & W or Sepia buttons, you can always Control-click the photo and choose the corresponding command from the shortcut menu.

Figure 8-5:
Top: When you click the Red-Eye tool, a pop-up message informs you of the next step: Click carefully inside each affected eye.

Bottom: Truth be told, the Red-Eye tool doesn't know an eyeball from a pinkie toe. It just turns any red pixels black, regardless of what body part they're associated with. Friends and family members look more attractive—and less like Star Trek characters—after you touch up their phosphorescent red eyes with iPhoto.

Rotate

Unless your digital camera has a built-in orientation sensor, iPhoto imports all photos in landscape orientation (wider than they are tall). The program has no way of knowing if you turned the camera 90 degrees when you took your pictures. Once you've imported the photos, just select the sideways ones and rotate them into position (if you didn't do so during your first slideshow, as described in Chapter 7).

Remember, you don't have to be in Edit mode to rotate photos. You can select thumbnail images when you're in Organize mode and then use one of the following methods to turn them right-side up:

- Choose Photos→Rotate→Counter Clockwise (or Clockwise).

- Click the Rotate button at the bottom of the main iPhoto window. (Option-click this button to reverse the direction of the rotation.)

- Press ⌘-R to rotate selected photos counter-clockwise, or Option-⌘-R to rotate them clockwise.

- Control-click a photo and choose Rotate→Clockwise (or Counter Clockwise) from the shortcut menu.

Tip: After importing a batch of photos, you can save a lot of time and mousing if you select all the thumbnails that need rotating first (by ⌘-clicking each, for example). Then use one of the rotation commands above to fix all the selected photos in one fell swoop.

Incidentally, clicking Rotate (or pressing ⌘-R) generally rotates photos counter-clockwise, while Option-clicking that button (Option-⌘-R) generally rotates them clockwise. If you want, you can swap these directions by choosing iPhoto→Preferences and changing the Rotate setting on the General tab of the dialog box.

Note: When you rotate an image saved in GIF format in iPhoto, the resulting rotated picture is saved as a JPEG file. The original GIF is stored unchanged in an Originals folder in the iPhoto Library folder.

The Adjust Panel

For thousands of people, the handful of basic image-fixer tools described on the previous pages offered plenty of power. But many others wound up disappointed with previous iPhoto versions.

Power users were irked at having to trot off to some other program like Photoshop to make more advanced changes to their pictures, like fiddling with the saturation (the intensity of colors) or the sharpness of the image. Meanwhile, Apple clearly detected that the landscape of inexpensive photo editors was changing; even the most basic free digital shoebox program for Windows offered full-blown image controls.

All of which sets the stage for one of iPhoto 5's most important new features: the Adjust panel (Figure 8-6). It appears whenever you click the Adjust button in editing mode.

Note: Except for the Brightness and Contrast controls, the Adjust palette doesn't work unless your Mac has at least a G4 processor. And if you want to apply these effects to photos in the RAW format, you'll need Mac OS X 10.3.6 or later.

Now, before you launch yourself into the following pages and turn yourself into a tweak geek, here are some preliminary words of advice concerning the Adjust panel:

- **When to use it.** Plenty of photos need no help at all. They look fantastic right out of the camera. And plenty of others are ready for prime time after only a single click on the Enhance button, as described earlier.

  The beauty of the Adjust panel, though, is that it permits infinite *gradations* of the changes that the Enhance button makes. For example, if a photo looks too dark and murky, you can bring details out of the shadows without blowing out the highlights. If the snow in a skiing shot looks too bluish, you can de-blue it. If the colors don't pop quite enough in the prize-winning soccer goal shot, you can boost their saturation levels.

  In short, there are fixes the Adjust panel can make that no one-click magic button can touch.

- **How to play.** You can fiddle with an Adjust panel slider in any of three ways, as illustrated in Figure 8-6.

- **Backing out.** You can always apply the Undo and Revert to Original commands to work you perform with the Adjust panel. But the panel also has its own Reset Sliders button, which essentially means, "undo all the Adjust-panel changes I've made during this session."

Tip: The Reset Sliders button is also useful when you just want to play around with an image. You can make some adjustments, see how they look, then hit Reset Sliders before closing the window or clicking the Done button. In this case, iPhoto leaves the photo just as it was.

- **Moving on.** The Adjust panel is a see-through, floating entity that lives in a plane of its own. You can drag it anywhere on the screen, and—here's the part that might not occur to you—you can move on to a different photo without having to close the panel first. (Click another photo among the thumbnails at the top of the screen, for example, or click the big Previous and Next arrows at the bottom.)

Introduction to the Histogram

Learning to use the Adjust panel effectively involves learning about its *histogram,* the colorful little graph at the bottom of the panel.

The histogram is the heart of the Adjust palette. It's a self-updating visual representation of the dark and light tones that make up your photograph. If you've never encountered a histogram before, this all may sound a little complicated. But the Adjust palette's histogram is a terrific tool, and it'll make more sense the more you work with it.

Within each of the superimposed graphs (red, blue, green), the scheme is the same: The amount of the photo's darker shades appears toward the left side of the graph; the lighter tones are graphed on the right side.

Therefore, in a very dark photograph—a coal mine at midnight, say—you'll see big mountain peaks at the left side of the graph, trailing off to nothing toward the right. A shot of a brilliantly sunny snowscape, on the other hand, will show lots of information on the right, and probably very little on the left.

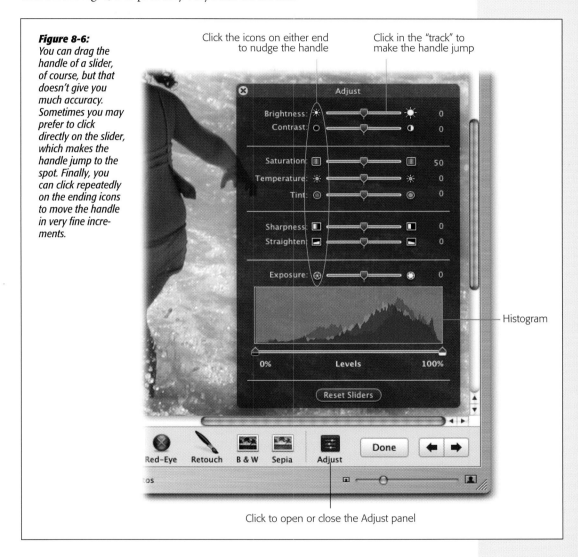

Figure 8-6:
You can drag the handle of a slider, of course, but that doesn't give you much accuracy. Sometimes you may prefer to click directly on the slider, which makes the handle jump to the spot. Finally, you can click repeatedly on the ending icons to move the handle in very fine increments.

Click the icons on either end to nudge the handle

Click in the "track" to make the handle jump

Histogram

Click to open or close the Adjust panel

The best-balanced pictures have some data spread across the entire histogram, with a few mountain-shaped peaks here and there. Those peaks and valleys represent the really dark spots (like the background of a flash photo) and bright spots (a closeup face in that flash picture). Those mountains are fine, as long as you have some visual information in other parts of the histogram, too.

The histogram for a *bad* photo, on the other hand—a severely under- or overexposed one—has mountains all bunched at one end or the other. Rescuing those pictures involves spreading the mountains across the entire spectrum, which is what the Adjust palette is all about.

Three Channels

As noted on the previous page, the histogram actually displays three superimposed graphs at once. These layers—red, green, and blue—represent the three "channels" of a color photo.

When you make adjustments to a photo's brightness values—for example, when you drag the Exposure slider just above the histogram—you'll see the graphs in all three channels move in unison. Despite changing shape, they essentially stick together. Later, when you make color adjustments using, say, the Temperature slider, you'll see those individual channels move in different directions.

Exposure

Most of the sliders in the Adjust palette affect the histogram in some way. But where do you begin?

Here's a general suggestion: Make exposure adjustments first. In the simplest terms, the Exposure slider makes your picture lighter when you move it to the right and darker when you move it to the left.

Its effects differ slightly depending on which file format a photo has:

- When you're editing **JPEG** graphics (that is, most photos from most cameras), the Exposure slider primarily affects the middle tones of a photo (as opposed to the brightest highlights and darkest shadows). If you're used to advanced programs like Photoshop, you may recognize this effect as a relative of Photoshop's gamma controls. (Gamma refers to the middle tones in a picture.)

- When you're working with **RAW** files, however (page 98), Exposure is even more interesting. It actually changes the way iPhoto interprets the dark and light information that your camera recorded when it took the picture. A photographer might say that it's like changing the ISO setting before snapping the picture—except that now you can make this kind of change long *after* you snapped the shutter.

  The Exposure slider demonstrates one of the advantages of the RAW format. In a RAW file, iPhoto has a lot more image information to work with than in a JPEG file. As a result, you can make exposure adjustments without sacrificing the overall quality of the photograph.

Watch the data on the histogram as you move the Exposure slider. Make sure you don't wind up shoving any of the "mountain peaks" beyond the edges of the Histogram box. If that happens, you're discarding precious image data; when you print, you'll see a loss of detail in the darks and lights.

The first step in fine-tuning a photo, then, is to drag the Exposure slider until the middle tones of the picture look acceptable to you (Figure 8-7).

Figure 8-7:
Top: Here's a promising landscape shot that will serve as the basis for all the Adjust-panel manipulations described in this chapter. The camera was in Program mode, with Auto White Balance turned on. Unfortunately, you can see by looking at the histogram that much of the tonal information is bunched in the middle of the graph. As a result, the photo looks a little "flat," without much contrast.

Bottom: Step one in the repair job, then, is to move the Exposure slider a little to the right to improve the midtones. Because the graph in the histogram is elongated as a result, you've also improved the contrast.

You can't add details that simply aren't there, but brightening a dark shadowy image, or deepening the contrast on a washed-out image, can coax out elements that were barely visible in the original photo.

If the dark and light areas aren't yet perfect, don't worry; you'll improve those areas next with the Levels control.

Adjusting the Levels

After you've spent some time working with the middle tones of your picture, you can turn your attention to the endpoints on the histogram, which represent the darkest and lightest areas of the photo.

If the mountains of your graph seem to cover all the territory from left to right, you already have a roughly even distribution of dark and light tones in your picture...so you're probably in good shape. But if the graph comes up short on either the left (darks) or the right (lights) side of the histogram, you might want to make an adjustment.

To do so, drag the right or left pointer on the Levels slider *inward,* toward the "base" of the "mountain" (Figure 8-8). If you're moving the *right* indicator inward, for example, you'll notice that the whites become brighter, but the dark areas stay pretty much the same; if you drag the *left* indicator inward, the dark tones change, but the highlights remain steady.

Figure 8-8:
Here's that same photo, now showing the results of the second Adjust-panel tweak: You've moved the endpoints of the Levels slider inward, boosting the shadow and highlight tones. In this case, moving them all the way to the point where they're touching the sides of the "mountains" would overdo it, creating too much contrast for this particular image. The base of the mountains is usually your target, but the visual results should always be your primary guide. Besides, you can always perform additional tweaks using the Brightness and Contrast sliders.

Tip: Instead of dragging these handles inward, you may prefer to simply click the slider track itself at the outer base of the mountain. That's faster and gives you better control of the handle's landing point.

In general, you should avoid moving these endpoint handles inward *beyond* the outer edges of the mountains. Doing so adds contrast, but also throws away whatever data is outside the handles, which generally makes for a lower quality printout.

Brightness and Contrast Sliders

Once you've massaged the Exposure and Levels controls, the overall exposure for a picture usually looks pretty good. In effect, you've managed to create a full range of tones from dark to light.

So why, then, does Apple include Brightness and Contrast sliders, which govern similar aspects of your photo's appearance?

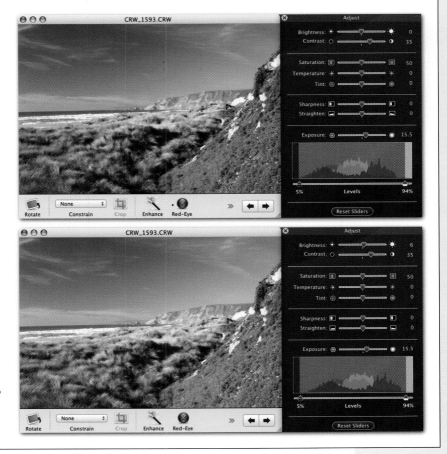

Figure 8-9:
Top: Moving the Contrast slider to the right added more punch. Instead of moving the Levels endpoints inward, the mountains moved outward toward the endpoints. Remember, the farther outward you stretch the graph, the more difference you create between the darkest and lightest tones.

Bottom: Once the contrast looks right, you can use the Brightness slider. This control moves the entire graph to the left or right of the histogram. Here, moving it a little to the right brightened the image—a good preparation for the color corrections that will follow in the next steps, because they usually darken the picture slightly.

Reason #1: They've always been part of iPhoto, and millions of people are used to them.

Reason #2: They're not quite the same as Exposure and Levels.

Brightness

When you move the Brightness slider, you're making the *entire* image lighter or darker. You're literally sliding the entire histogram to the left or right without changing its shape (Figure 8-9). (Remember that the Exposure and Levels controls affect the midtones, highlights, and shadows independently.)

In other words, if the picture's contrast is already exactly as you want it, but the whole picture could use darkening or lightening, Brightness should be your tool of choice.

Contrast

The Contrast slider, on the other hand, does change the shape of the histogram. Contrast is the difference between the darkest and lightest tones in your picture. If you increase the contrast, you "stretch out" the shape of the histogram, creating darker blacks and brighter whites. When you decrease the contrast, you're scrunching the shape of the histogram inward, shortening the distance between the dark and light endpoints. Since the image data now resides in the middle area of the graph, the overall tones in the picture are duller. Photographers might call this look "flat" or "muddy."

Color Balance

If all you ever shoot is black-and-white photos, then Exposure/Levels or Brightness/Contrast may be all you ever need. If you're like most people, though, you're also concerned about a little thing called color.

One of the most common failings of digital cameras (and scanners, too) is that they don't capture color very accurately. Digital photos sometimes have a slightly bluish or greenish tinge, producing dull colors, lower contrast, and sickly looking skin tones.

FREQUENTLY ASKED QUESTION

Battle of the Sliders

All right, first you said that I can create a well-balanced histogram with the Exposure and Levels sliders. Then you said that the Brightness and Contrast sliders do pretty much the same thing. So which should I use?

Photography forums everywhere are overflowing with passionate comments advocating one approach over the other.

The bottom line is, for most normal JPEG photos, you can use whichever you prefer, as long as you wind up creating a histogram whose peaks generally span the entire graph.

If you have no preference, you may as well get into the habit of using the Exposure and Levels sliders. One day, when you begin editing super-high-quality RAW files (page 98), you'll appreciate the clever way these controls interpret the data from the camera's sensors with virtually no loss of quality.

In fact, the whole thing might have a faint green or magenta cast. Or maybe you just want to take color adjustment into your own hands, not only to get the colors right, but to also create a specific mood for an image. Maybe you want a snowy landscape to look icy blue so friends back home realize just how darned cold it was!

The Adjust panel offers three sliders that wield power over this sort of thing: Tint, Temperature, and Saturation. And it offers two ways to apply such changes: the manual way and the automatic way.

Manual Color Adjustment

These three sliders in the middle of the Adjust Palette provide you with plenty of color adjustment power. In particular, the Tint and Temperature sliders govern the *white balance* of your photo. (Different kinds of light—fluorescent lighting, overcast skies, and so on—lend different color casts to photographs. White balance is a setting that eliminates or adjusts the color cast according to the lighting.)

For best results, start at the bottom slider and work your way upward.

- **Tint.** If you've ever fiddled with the tint control on a color TV, you already have a decent idea how this slider works. It adjusts the photo's overall tint along the red-green spectrum. Nudge the slider to the right to add a greenish tint, left to add red. As you go, watch the histogram to see how iPhoto is applying the color.

  Adjusting this slider is particularly helpful for correcting skin tones and compensating for difficult lighting situations, like pictures you took under fluorescent lighting. (See Figure 8-10.)

Figure 8-10:
Moving the Tint slider just a little to the right removed a little red. Nudging the Temperature slider to the right warmed up the colors, making the grass more appealing. To make the colors more vibrant, move the Saturation slider to the right—not too far, unless you're after a Mars-like, otherworldly effect.

- **Temperature.** This slider, on the other hand, adjusts the photo along the blue-orange spectrum. Move the slider to the left to make the image "cooler," or slightly bluish. Move the slider to the right to warm up the tones, making them more orangish—a particular handy technique for breathing life back into subjects that have been bleached white with a flash. A few notches to the right on the Temperature slider, and their skin tones look healthy once again!

Professional photographers *love* having color-temperature control; in fact, many photographers could handle the bulk of their image correction with nothing but the Exposure and Temperature controls.

• **Saturation.** Once you're happy with the color tones, you can increase or decrease their intensity with the Saturation slider. Move it to the right to increase the intensity and to the left for less saturation.

When you increase the saturation of a photo's colors, you make them more vivid; essentially, you make them "pop" more. You can also improve photos that have harsh, garish colors by dialing *down* the saturation, so that the colors end up looking a little less intense than they appeared in the original snapshot. That's a useful trick in photos whose *composition* is so strong that the colors are almost distracting.

(iPhoto's Enhance button automatically adjusts saturation when "enhancing" your photos, but provides no way to control the *degree* of its adjustment.)

Automatic Color Correction

Dragging the Tint, Temperature, and Saturation sliders by hand is one way to address color imbalances in a picture. But there's an easier way: iPhoto also contains a fairly secret feature that adjusts all three sliders *automatically.*

Technically, this tool is a *gray balance* adjuster. It relies on your ability to find, somewhere in your photo, an area of what *should* appear as medium gray. If you can adjust the color balance so that this spot does in fact appear the correct shade of gray, iPhoto can take it from there—it can adjust all of the other colors in the photo accordingly, shifting color temperature, tint, and saturation, all with a single click. This trick works amazingly well on some photos.

Before you use this feature, though, make sure you've already adjusted the overall *exposure* of the photo, using the steps described on the previous pages.

Next, scan your photo for an area that should appear as a neutral gray. Slightly dark grays are better for this purpose than bright, overexposed grays. (See Figure 8-11.)

Once you've found such a spot, ⌘-click it.

Instantly, iPhoto automatically adjusts the color-balance sliders to balance the overall color of the photo. If you don't like iPhoto's correction, choose Edit→Undo and try again on a different gray area.

Thankfully, there's a good way to check how well iPhoto corrected the image. Find a spot in the picture that should be plain white. If it's clean (no green or magenta tint), you're probably in good shape; if not, undo the gray balance adjustment and try again on another area of gray.

Tip: If you're a portrait photographer, you can use the gray-balance control to correct skin tones with almost magical efficiency. The trick is to plan ahead by stashing a photographer's gray card somewhere in the composition (somewhere that can be cropped out of the final print). Make sure the gray card receives about the same amount of lighting as the subject.

Later, when you're adjusting the image in iPhoto, you can ⌘-click the gray card in the composition, and presto: perfect skin tones. Now crop out the gray card and make your print, grateful for the time you've just saved.

Figure 8-11:
Indoor settings often present tricky lighting situations. Here, this existing light shot has a greenish cast to it.

Bottom: By ⌘-clicking a gray midtone spot—in this case, the case of the inkjet printer on the desk (see the cursor?), you tell iPhoto, "This is supposed to be gray. Use this information to correct all the other colors appropriately."

If you don't like iPhoto's correction, choose Edit→Undo and try again on a different gray area.

Straightening

Many a photographer has remarked that it's harder to keep the horizon straight when composing images on a digital camera's LCD screen than when looking through an optical (eyepiece) viewfinder. Whether that's true or not, off-axis, tilted photos are a fact of photography, and especially of scanning—and a new iPhoto 5 feature makes fixing them incredibly easy. Figure 8-12 shows the secrets of the Straighten slider.

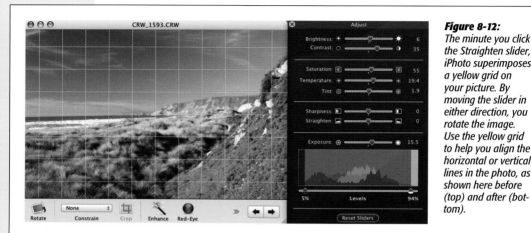

Figure 8-12:
The minute you click the Straighten slider, iPhoto superimposes a yellow grid on your picture. By moving the slider in either direction, you rotate the image. Use the yellow grid to help you align the horizontal or vertical lines in the photo, as shown here before (top) and after (bottom).

Now, if you think about it, you can't rotate a rectangular photo without introducing skinny empty triangles at the corners of its "frame." Fortunately, iPhoto sneakily eliminates that problem by very slightly magnifying the photo as you straighten it. Now you're *losing* skinny triangles at the corners, but at least you don't see empty triangular gaps when the straightening is over.

In other words, the straightening tool isn't a free lunch. Straightening an image decreases the picture quality slightly (by blowing up the picture, thus lowering the resolution) and clips off tiny scraps at the corners. You have to view the before and after pictures side by side at high magnification to see the difference, but it's there.

So as cool as the Straighten slider is, it's not a substitution for careful composition with your camera. However, it can help you salvage an otherwise wonderful image that's skewed. (And besides—if you lose a tiny bit of clarity in the straightening process, you can always apply a little sharpening afterward. Read on.)

Sharpening

The Sharpen command (see Figure 8-13) seems awfully tempting. Could technology really solve the problem of blurry, out-of-focus photos?

Um, no.

Instead, the Sharpen tool that now appears in iPhoto works by subtly increasing the contrast among pixels in your photo, which seems to enhance the crispness of the image. In pro circles, applying a soupçon of sharpening to a photo is a regular part of the routine.

In iPhoto, move the Sharpen slider to the right to increase the sharpness, or to the left to soften the look.

Figure 8-13:
Top: As a final stop in the Adjust panel, visit the Sharpen slider. By nudging it to the right, you make the photo a tad crisper (or "crispier," as Kellogg's would say). In this example, the slider's been moved a bit farther than was strictly necessary, just to make the effect more visible. The 30.0 mark would ordinarily do nicely.

Bottom: To see just how far you've come, hold down the Control key to see the photo as it originally looked, before you started fiddling with the Adjust panel. Amazing how much better this picture looks after adjusting; when you first looked at it, the picture might not have struck you as an especially dull, ineffective shot.

Now, lest you think otherwise, too much sharpening can also ruin a photo, since, eventually, the pixels become grainy and weird-looking. Fortunately, Apple has mostly protected you from this sort of disaster by keeping both the effects and the side effects of the Sharpen control to a minimum. You can help matters by moving the slider in small increments.

Generally speaking, sharpening should be the last Adjust-panel adjustment you make to the picture. If you apply other corrections after sharpening, you may discover that you have to return and sharpen again.

Also, keep in mind that *softening* (or unsharpening) can be effective for portraits that are "too sharp," or for landscapes where you want to create a more dreamy effect. Sometimes applying just a little softening will smooth out skin tones and take the edge off the overall appearance of the portrait.

Beyond iPhoto

Thanks to the Adjust panel, iPhoto's editing tools have come a long, long way. There's a lot less reason now to invest in a dedicated editing program like Photoshop.

But that doesn't mean that there are *no* reasons left. The Auto Levels command (in Photoshop and Photoshop Elements) is still a better overall color-fixer than iPhoto's Enhance button. Photoshop-type programs are also necessary if you want to scale a photo up or down to specific pixel dimensions, superimpose text on a photo, combine several photos into one (a collage or montage), apply special-effect filters like Stained Glass or Watercolor, or adjust the colors in just a *portion* of the photo.

In all of these situations and more, you still have to spring for a more full-featured image-editing program.

Photoshop is by far the most popular tool for the job, but at about $600, it's also one of the most expensive. Fortunately, you can save yourself some money by buying Photoshop Elements instead. It's a trimmed-down version of Photoshop with all the basic image-editing stuff and just enough of the high-end features. It costs less than $100, and a free trial version is available online. (Your digital camera may even have come with Photoshop Elements right in the box.)

Before you go software shopping, though, check out your own hard drive. If you bought your Mac recently, you may already have the image-editing software you need. Apple includes GraphicConverter—a simple but powerful editing program with Photoshop-like tools—on some Mac models.

Opening Photos in Other Programs

To open a photo in a "real" editing program, first install that program's icon on your Dock. (For example, drag the Photoshop icon onto the Dock from your Applications folder.)

Then, any time you want to edit a photo in iPhoto, drag its thumbnail image directly onto the program's Dock icon. (Of course, you can also drag a picture from iPhoto's window onto the application's *desktop* icon, or an alias of it.) In fact, you can even drag several thumbnails at once to open all of them simultaneously.

If you've already been working in, say, Photoshop, you might be tempted to use its File→Open command to open an iPhoto photo directly. But, alas, the drag-and-drop method is far more efficient. If you use File→Open, you'll have to navigate through the oddly numbered folders of the labyrinthine iPhoto Library folder just to locate the picture you want.

Tip: When you edit a photo in another program, you're essentially going behind iPhoto's back; the program doesn't have a chance to make a safety copy of the original. Therefore, you're sacrificing your ability to use the Revert to Original command to restore your photo to its original state in case of disaster (page 175).

The sneaky workaround: Just make one tiny change to the photo *in iPhoto* before you drag its thumbnail onto another program's icon. Any small change, even rotating it all the way around, forces iPhoto to create a backup. Thereafter—whether you edit the photo in another program or not—you can restore the photo to its original condition at any time.

In iPhoto, Less Is More

I just finished editing a batch of photos, cropping each picture to a much smaller size. But now my iPhoto Library folder is taking up more space on my hard drive! How can making the photos **smaller** *increase the size of my photo collection? Shouldn't throwing away all those pixels have the opposite effect—shrinking things down?*

Your cropped photos do, in fact, take up much less space than they previously did. Remember, though, that iPhoto doesn't let you monkey with your photos without first stashing away a copy of each original photo, in case you ever want to use the Revert to Original command to restore a photo to its original condition.

So each time you crop a picture (or do any other editing) for the first time, you're actually creating a new, full-size file on your hard drive, as iPhoto stores both the original and the edited versions of the photo. Therefore, the more photos you edit in iPhoto, the more hard drive space your photo collection will occupy.

Incidentally, it's worth noting that iPhoto may be a bit over-zealous when it comes to making backups of your originals. The simple act of rotating a photo, for example, creates a backup (which, considering how easy it is to re-rotate it, you might not consider strictly necessary). If you've set up iPhoto to open a double-clicked photo in another program like Photoshop, iPhoto creates a backup copy even if you don't end up changing it in that external program.

If this library-that-ate-Cleveland effect bothers you, you might investigate the free program iPhoto Diet (available from the "Missing CD" page of *www.missingmanuals.com,* for example). One of its options offers to delete the backups of photos that have simply been rotated. Another option deletes perfect duplicates that iPhoto created when you opened those photos in another program without editing them.

There's even an option to delete *all* backups—a drastic measure for people who believe that their photos will never be better than they are right now.

Setting up a default editing program

The drag-and-drop approach is fine if you *occasionally* want to open a photo in another program. But if you find yourself routinely editing your photos in another program, there's a much easier method: Just set up iPhoto to open your photos in that program automatically when you double-click. You set up this arrangement as follows:

1. **Choose iPhoto→Preferences.**

   The Preferences window opens.

2. **Click the General button, if necessary. For the "Double-click photo" preference settings, select the "Opens photo in" radio button, then click Select Application.**

   A standard Open dialog box appears so you can navigate to your favorite photo-editing program.

3. **Choose the program you want to use for editing, then click Open.**

   When you're done, close the Preferences window.

Now, whenever you double-click a thumbnail, iPhoto launches the designated editing program and uses it to open your photo.

One big advantage of this method is that it lets iPhoto track your editing activity—yes, even in other programs. iPhoto can subsequently update its thumbnail versions of your photos to reflect the changes. It can also preserve the original version of the photos you edit externally, so that you can later use the Revert to Original command if disaster should ever strike, as explained later in this chapter.

Freedom of choice

Sure, it's nice to be able to edit photos in external programs, but it's a lot of trouble to switch that feature on and off, since a trip to iPhoto→Preferences is involved every time. If you're like many photo fans, what you want is to use iPhoto's convenient editing features *most* of the time, ducking out to other programs only when you need more industrial-strength features.

Fortunately, iPhoto offers a couple of tricks that let you switch to an external editor only on demand:

- Clicking the Edit button below the photo-viewing area *always* opens a selected photo for editing right in iPhoto, regardless of your Preferences setting.

- If you Control-click a thumbnail, the shortcut menu offers you three choices: "Edit" (in the main iPhoto window), "Edit in separate window," or "Edit in external editor." (The last option is available only if you've selected an editing program as described above.) No matter what your settings in Preferences may be, this route always gives you the choice of all three editing modes.

Reverting to the Original

iPhoto includes built-in protection against overzealous editing—a feature that can save you much grief. If you end up cropping a photo too much, cranking up the brightness of a picture until it seems washed out, or accidentally turning someone's lips black with the Red-Eye tool, you can undo all your edits at once with the Revert to Original command. Revert to Original strips away *every change you've ever made* since the picture arrived from the camera. It leaves you with your original, unedited photo.

The secret of the Revert to Original command: Whenever you use any editing tools, iPhoto—without prompting and without informing you—instantly makes a duplicate of your original file. With an original version safely tucked away, iPhoto lets you go wild on the copy. Consequently, you can remain secure in the knowledge that in a pinch, iPhoto can always restore an image to the state it was in when you first imported it.

Note: The unedited originals are stored in an Originals folder inside each date-labeled photo folder, deep in your Home→Pictures→iPhoto Library folder. (The Originals folder doesn't exist until you edit at least one photo.)

To restore an original photo, undoing all cropping, rotation, brightness adjustments, and so on, select a thumbnail of an edited photo or open the photo in Edit mode. Then choose Photos→Revert to Original, or Control-click a photo and choose the command from the shortcut menu. Now iPhoto swaps in the original version of the photo—and you're back where you started.

As noted earlier, iPhoto does its automatic backup trick whenever you edit your pictures (a) within iPhoto or (b) using a program that you've set up to open when you double-click a picture. It does *not* make a backup when you drag a thumbnail onto the icon of another program. In that event, the Revert to Original command will be dimmed when you select the edited photo.

Bottom line: If you want the warmth and security of Revert to Original at your disposal, don't edit your pictures behind iPhoto's back. Follow the guidelines in the previous two paragraphs so that iPhoto is always aware of when and how you're editing your pictures.

Editing RAW Files

As noted in Chapter 7, iPhoto can now handle the advanced photographic file format called RAW—a special, unprocessed file format that takes up a lot of space on your memory card but offers astonishing amounts of control when editing later on the Mac. (Also as noted in Chapter 7, the RAW format is available only on certain high-end cameras.)

Actually, iPhoto can do more than handle RAW files. It can even edit them...sort of.

iPhoto is, at its heart, a program designed to work with JPEG files. Therefore, when it grabs a RAW file from your camera, it instantly creates a JPEG version of it, which is what you actually see onscreen. The RAW file is there on your hard drive (deep within the labyrinth known as the iPhoto Library folder). But what you see onscreen is a JPEG interpretation of that RAW file. (This conversion to JPEG is one reason iPhoto takes longer to import RAW files from a camera than other kinds of files.)

This trick of using JPEG lookalikes as stand-ins for your actual RAW files has two important benefits. First, it lets you work with your photos at normal iPhoto speed, without the lumbering minutes of calculations you'd endure if you were working with the original RAW files. Second, remember that your iPhoto photos are also accessible from within iDVD, iMovie, Pages, and so on—and these programs don't recognize RAW files.

So the question naturally comes up: What happens if you try to edit one of these RAW-file stunt doubles?

No problem. iPhoto accepts any changes you make to the JPEG version of the photo, applies them behind the scenes to the original RAW file, and then generates a new JPEG for you to view.

The iPhoto Slideshow

i Photo's slideshow feature offers one of the world's best ways to show off your digital photos. Slideshows are easy to set up, they're free, and they make your photos look fantastic—and in iPhoto 5, the whole slideshow mechanism has been gutted and renovated. This chapter details not only how to put together an iPhoto slideshow, but how to give presentations that make you and your photos look their absolute best.

About Slideshows

When you run an iPhoto slideshow, your Mac presents the pictures in full-screen mode—no windows, no menus, no borders—with your images filling every inch of the monitor. Professional transitions take you from one picture to the next, producing a smooth, cinematic effect. If you want, you can even add a musical soundtrack to accompany the presentation. The total effect is incredibly polished, yet creating a slideshow requires very little setup.

You always begin by selecting the pictures you want—by clicking an album or a Library icon, for example. At this point, you can kick off a slideshow in three different ways, each one offering a different degree of instant gratification and flexibility:

- **Option-click.** Option-click the triangular Play button under the Info pane (see Figure 9-1). A moment later, your Mac's screen fades to black, and then the show begins. Each photo is displayed full screen for two seconds, and then softly fades out as the next one dissolves into view. The default musical soundtrack—J. S. Bach's Minuet in G—plays in the background.

  As noted in Chapter 6, this is a terrific feature for reviewing photos you've just dumped into the Mac from the camera. In fact, that delicious moment when you first see the pictures at full-screen size—after having viewed them only on the camera's two-inch screen—is just what Apple's engineers had in mind when they designed the Play button.

Remember to wiggle your mouse during the slideshow when you want to summon iPhoto's onscreen control bar (page 103).

When you've had enough, click the mouse or press almost any key to end the show and return to the iPhoto window. (Otherwise, iPhoto will run the show in a continuous loop forever.)

Figure 9-1:
The quickest way to kick off a slideshow in iPhoto is to Option-click the Play button in the main iPhoto window, shown here by the cursor (and the helpful tooltip label). While there's no keyboard shortcut, you can hit any key except the arrow keys and the Space bar to stop a show once it's running.

- **Instant.** If you click the triangular Play button without the Option key, you get the Slideshow dialog box shown in Figure 9-2. It lets you choose the music for the slideshow, adjust its speed, and make other settings. Only when you dismiss the dialog box by clicking the Play button does the show begin.

Tip: Once you've made changes in this dialog box, iPhoto applies them to the currently selected album or folder and memorizes them—even if you don't click the Save Settings button. Thereafter, you can Option-click the Play button to start the show without interruption by the dialog box; iPhoto will recreate the show just the way you had it last.

- **Saved.** In the days before iPhoto 5, each album had its own associated slideshow settings. The album was, in essence, the container for the slideshow.

  In iPhoto 5, Apple has introduced *saved* slideshow, a new kind of icon that can appear in the Source list and be saved forever, independent of any album. It works a lot like an album in many ways. For example, the photos inside are only "pointers" to the real photos in the Library, and you can drag them into any order you like. On the other hand, unlike an album, a saved slideshow contains special advanced controls for building a really sophisticated slideshow.

This chapter covers each of these three slideshow techniques in order.

Option-Click Slideshows

There's mercifully little to learn about instantaneous slideshows—the ones that begin when you Option-click the Play button beneath the Source list. The slideshow begins automatically and instantaneously, leaving nothing for you to do but sit back and enjoy the show. (All right, truth be told, you can have *some* involvement, as described later in this chapter.) Finish the show by clicking the mouse.

Which Photos

Among the virtues of this slideshow type is the freedom you have to choose which pictures you want to see. For example:

- If no photos are selected, iPhoto exhibits all the pictures currently in the photo-viewing area, starting with the first photo in the album, book, or Photo Library.

  Most people, most of the time, want to turn one *album* into a slideshow. That's easy: Just click the album before starting the slideshow. It can be any album you've created, a smart album, the Last Roll album, or one of iPhoto's built-in monthly yearly albums. As long as no individual pictures are selected, iPhoto will reveal all the pictures in the album currently open.

Tip: For the first time, iPhoto 5 lets you create an Option-click or instant slideshow from multiple albums. That is, you can select more than one album simultaneously (by ⌘-clicking them); then, when you click Play, iPhoto creates a slideshow from all of their merged contents, in order.

- If one photo is *selected*, iPhoto uses that picture as its starting point for the show, ignoring any that come before it. Of course, if you've got the slideshow set to loop continuously, iPhoto will eventually circle back to display the first photo in the window.

- If you've selected more than one picture, iPhoto includes *only* those pictures.

Tip: If a slideshow icon (described momentarily) is highlighted in the Source list, you don't need the Option key to begin a slideshow immediately. Use the Option key only if an album or a batch of photos are selected.

Photo Order

iPhoto displays your pictures in the same order you see them in the photo-viewing area. In other words, to rearrange your slides, drag the thumbnails around within their album. Just remember that you can't drag pictures around in the Photo Library, a smart album, the Last 12 Months collection, or the Last Roll folder—only within a photo album.

Note: If iPhoto appears to be shamelessly disregarding the order of your photos when running a slideshow, it's probably because you've got the "Present slides in random order" option turned on in the Slideshow dialog box, as described in the following section.

Instant Slideshows

An *instant* slideshow, for the purposes of this book, is one that you begin by clicking the triangular Play button beneath the Source list *without* the Option key. It makes the Slideshow dialog box appear, so that you can make a few quick changes to the slideshow settings. (Slide selection and slide sequence, as described in the previous paragraphs, work the same way.)

The Slideshow dialog box has two panels—Settings and Music—as shown in Figure 9-2. In iPhoto 5, you have more ways than ever to customize your slideshow:

Transitions

In iPhoto 4, you were offered a mere four types of transition effects between slides—for example, the crossfade or *dissolve,* in which one slide gradually fades away as the next "fades in" to take its place. These days, you have a choice of 13 transition effects:

- **None.** An abrupt switch, or simple cut, to the following image.

- **Cube.** Imagine that your photos are pasted to the sides of a box that rotates to reveal the next one. If you've ever used the Fast User Switching feature introduced in Mac OS 10.3, you've got the idea.

- **Dissolve.** This classic crossfade should be familiar to users of previous versions of iPhoto or the screen saver feature in Mac OS X.

- **Droplet.** New in iPhoto 5, this wild effect resembles animated, concentric ripples expanding from the center of a pond—except that a new image forms as the ripples spread.

- **Fade Through Black.** Here's another new one…and an incredibly useful one to boot. After each slide has strutted and fretted its time upon the stage, the screen fades momentarily to black before the next one fades into view. The effect is simple and clean, like an old-fashioned living-room slideshow. Along with Dissolve, you should consider this effect one of the most natural and least distracting choices.

- **Flip.** The first photo seems to flip around, revealing the second photo pasted onto its back.

- **Mosaic Flip Large, Mosaic Flip Small.** The screen is divided into several squares, each of which rotates in turn to reveal part of the new image, like puzzle pieces turning over. (The two options refer to two sizes of the puzzle pieces.)

- **Page Flip.** Apple's just showing off here. The first photo's lower-right corner actually peels up like a sheet of paper, revealing the next photo "page" beneath it.

- **Push, Reveal, Wipe.** Three variations of "new image sweeping onto the screen." In Push, Photo A gets shoved off the other side of the screen as Photo B slides on. In Reveal, Photo A slides off, revealing a stationary Photo B. And in Wipe, Photo A gets covered up as Photo B slides on.

- **Twirl.** Photo A literally spins, furiously, shrinking to a tiny dot in the middle of the screen—and then Photo B spins onscreen from that spot. The whole thing feels a little like the spinning-newspaper effect used to signify breaking news in old black-and-white movies.

In most cases, choosing a transition effect makes two additional controls "light up" just below the pop-up menu:

- **Direction.** Determines the direction the new image enters from. Choose Right to Left, Top to Bottom, or vice versa in both cases. (Most people find left to right the most comfortable way to experience a transition, but a slow top-to-bottom wipe is pleasant, too.)

- **Speed.** Move the slider to the right for a speedy transition, or to the left for a leisurely one. Take into account your Timing setting, described below. The less time your photo is onscreen, the better off you are with a fast transition, so that your audience has time to see the picture before the next transition starts. However, moving the Speed slider *all* the way to the right produces a joltingly fast change.

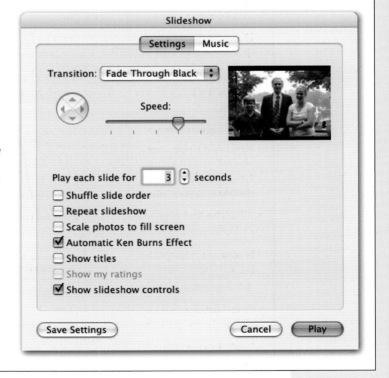

Figure 9-2:
The Slideshow dialog box is where you set slideshow timing for each show. You can set it to go as fast as 1 second per slide, or bump the number up to 60 seconds each for a very leisurely presentation. (You can type a number larger than 60 in the "Play each slide for..." field, but iPhoto will ignore you. It refuses to spend any more than one minute on each shot, no matter how good a photographer you are.)

Using the pop-up menus and Speed slider at the top of this dialog box, you can choose from five transition effects and decide how quickly you want them to go by.

Slide Timing

If left to its own devices, iPhoto advances through your pictures at the rate of one photo every two seconds. If that seems too brisk or too slow, you can simply change the rate. In the Slideshow dialog box, use the "Play each slide for __ seconds" controls to specify a different interval, as shown in Figure 9-2.

Tip: You can also adjust the speed *during* the slideshow, just by pressing the up or down arrow keys. Behind the scenes, iPhoto adjusts the number of seconds in the Slideshow dialog box accordingly.

Shuffle Slide Order

An iPhoto slideshow normally displays your pictures in the order they appear in the photo-viewing area. But if you'd like to add a dash of surprise and spontaneity to the proceedings, turn on the "Shuffle slide order" checkbox. iPhoto will then shuffle the pictures into whatever order it pleases.

Repeat Slideshow

When iPhoto is done running through all your photos in a slideshow, it ordinarily starts playing the whole sequence from the beginning again. If you want your photos to play just once through, turn off the "Repeat slideshow" checkbox.

Scale Photos to Fill Screen

If any photos in your slideshow don't match your screen's proportions, you may want to turn on "Scale photos to fill screen." For example, if your slideshow contains photos in portrait orientation—that is, pictures taken with the camera rotated—iPhoto fills up the unused screen space on each side with vertical black bars.

Turning on "Scale photos" makes iPhoto enlarge the picture so much that it completely fills the screen. This solution, however, comes at a cost: Now the top and bottom of the picture are lost beyond the edges of the monitor.

When the middle of the picture is the most important part, this option works fine. If the black bars bother you, the only other alternative is to crop the odd-sized pictures in the slideshow album so that they match your monitor's shape. (See "Cropping" on page 151.)

UP TO SPEED

How Big Is My Monitor?

To know if your photos are large enough to be displayed distortion-free on your monitor, you first must know how many pixels it takes to fill your screen.

And to know that, you need to know your screen's resolution. Choose →System Preferences, and open the Displays panel. In the Resolutions list, you'll find all the resolutions that your monitor can handle, with the current resolution highlighted. If the selection says, for example, 1024 x 768, you know that photos must be at least 1024 pixels by 768 pixels to fill your screen without iPhoto having to stretch them to fit.

Note: This option doesn't mean "Enlarge smaller photos to fill the screen"; iPhoto always does that. This option affects only photos whose *proportions* don't match the screen.

Automatic Ken Burns Effect

Apple first introduced what it calls the "Ken Burns effect" in iMovie, not iPhoto. It's a special effect designed to address the core problem associated with using still photos in a movie: namely, that they're *still!* They just sit there without motion or sound, wasting much of the dynamic potential of video.

And now your own humble slideshows can have that graceful, animated, fluid Ken Burns touch. No photo ever just sits there motionless on the screen. Instead, each one flies gracefully inward or outward, sliding and zooming.

Show Titles

Every photo in your collection can have a name—a title, in other words. If you turn on this option, iPhoto superimposes each photo's title during the slideshow in a small white-on-black box in the upper-left corner of the screen.

Needless to say, the cryptic file names created by your digital camera (IMG00034. JPG) usually don't add much to your slideshow. But if you've taken the time to give your photos helpful, explanatory names ("My dog age 3 mos"), then by all means turn on the "Show titles" checkbox.

WORKAROUND WORKSHOP

Small Photos, Big Show

You can't control the size of your pictures as they appear during a slideshow, as they always fill the screen. To ensure that the results look professional, you must make sure all your photos are sized to fill the screen properly, as mentioned earlier in this chapter.

But what if you're stuck with photos that simply aren't big enough? Suppose you're charged with putting together a slideshow for the family reunion, and the only pictures you have of Uncle Rodney happen to be scanned photos that are only 640 x 480 pixels?

You can't cut Rodney out of the slideshow, but at the same time, you know Aunt Lois won't take kindly to having her husband appear onscreen hideously distorted. ("Why does Rod look so jagged?" you can imagine her saying. "What did you do to him?") Here's one simple way to display smaller photos in a slideshow and keep everyone happy:

Using a program like GraphicConverter or Photoshop Elements, create a new document that's exactly the right size for your screen. If your monitor's set to 1024 x 768 pixels, create a document that's 1024 x 768 pixels. Fill the background of the blank document so that it's black, to match the black between slides. (Actually, you can use whatever background you like.)

Now open the small photo that you want to include in your slideshow. Paste a copy of it into the center of your blank document. Save the results and then import the image file into iPhoto.

You now have a new picture, perfectly sized for your slideshow. Your small photo will appear onscreen at the proper size, with a black border around it. No, the photo won't fill the screen, but at least it will appear just as clear and distortion-free as the larger photos.

Show My Ratings

As described on page 142, you can differentiate your stunning award-winners from the photographic dogs by adding ratings to each, on a one-to-five-star scale. If you turn on this option, iPhoto superimposes a small ratings bar on the bottom of each slideshow picture. (Unfortunately, you can't change the rating using this mini-bar, since it's for display purposes only. Of course, a quick mouse wiggle summons the full-blown control bar, complete with its own star-rating panel that you *can* change.)

Note: The control bar and the star-rating panel occupy the same space near the bottom of the slideshow "canvas," so they can't both be onscreen at the same time. That's why the "Show my ratings" checkbox is grayed out whenever "Show slideshow controls" is turned on.

Show Slideshow Controls

You can always summon iPhoto's new onscreen control bar by twitching the mouse during a slideshow; then, if a few seconds go by without any mouse activity, the bar politely fades away again.

If you turn on "Display slideshow controls," however, then the control bar appears automatically every time this slideshow begins—no mouse wiggling required—and remains onscreen all the time.

iTunes: The Soundtrack Store

Perhaps more than any other single element, *music* transforms a slideshow, turning your ordinary photos into a cinematic event. When you pair the right music with the right pictures, you do more than just show off your photos; you create a mood that can stir the emotions of your entire audience. So if you really want your friends and family to be transfixed by your photos, add a soundtrack.

That's especially easy if, like many Mac OS X fans, you've assembled a collection of your favorite music in iTunes. For the background music of an iPhoto slideshow, you have the choice of an individual song from your iTunes Library or an entire *playlist*. Gone are the days of listening to the same tune repeating over and over again during a lengthy slideshow—a sure way to go quietly insane (unless, of course, you *really* like that song).

The possibilities of this new feature are endless, especially combined with iPhoto's smart albums feature. You can create a smart album that contains, say, only photos of your kids taken in December, and give it a soundtrack composed of holiday tunes, created effortlessly using a smart playlist in iTunes. Instant holiday slideshow!

Your first iPhoto slideshow is born with a ready-to-use soundtrack—J. S. Bach's Minuet in G. In fact, Apple sends iPhoto to you equipped with *two* Bach classics—the Minuet in G and *Jesu, Joy of Man's Desiring*. They're listed in the Sample Music category.

Not to knock Bach, but it's fortunate that you're not limited to two of his greatest hits. To switch to a soundtrack of your own choosing, click the Music button at the top of the Slideshow dialog box (Figure 9-3). If you use iTunes, every track in your iTunes

Library automatically appears here. You can search and sort through your songs and playlists, just as though you were in iTunes itself.

To get started, click the Music button near the top of the Slideshow dialog box. As shown in Figure 9-3, a folder called Sample Music appears at the top, containing the two Bach pieces mentioned above. If you have songs of your own in iTunes, click the Library icon to access them (this option is grayed out if you don't have any music files in iTunes).

Figure 9-3:
The Music tab of the Slideshow dialog box lets you choose a playlist (or your entire iTunes Library). By clicking the column headings, you can sort the list by Song, Artist, or Time. You can also use the Search box, as shown here, to pinpoint an individual song.

If you have a long slideshow, use the list to choose an iTunes playlist rather than an individual song. iTunes will repeat the song (or playlist) for as long as your slideshow lasts.

Your iTunes playlists appear on this menu, too. (For iTunes songs, a playlist represents what an album is in iPhoto: a hand-picked subset of the larger collection.) In other words, you can use this list either to select an entire playlist to use as your soundtrack, or to call up a playlist for the purpose of listing the individual songs in it, thereby narrowing your search for the one song you seek.

- To listen to a song before committing to it as a soundtrack, click its name in the list and then click the triangular Play button. (Click the same button, darkened during playback, when you've heard enough.)

- To use an entire playlist as a soundtrack for your slideshow, select it from the list. At slideshow time, iPhoto will begin the slideshow with the first tune in the playlist and continue through all the songs in the list before starting over.

- To use an individual song as a soundtrack, click its name in the list. That song will now loop continuously for the duration of the slideshow.

- Rather than scroll through a huge list, you can locate the tracks you want by using the capsule-shaped Search field below the song list. Click in the Search field, and then type a word (or part of a word) to filter your list. iPhoto searches the Artist, Song, and Album fields of the iTunes Library and displays only the matching entries. To clear the search and view your whole list again, click the X in the search field.

- Click one of the three headers—Artist, Song, or Time—to sort the iTunes music list alphabetically by that header.

- You can also change the arrangement of the three columns by grabbing the headers and dragging them into a different order.

Once you've settled on (and clicked) an appropriate musical soundtrack for the currently selected album, click Save Settings (to memorize that choice without starting the slideshow) or Play (to begin the slideshow right now). From now on, that song or playlist will play whenever you run a slideshow from that album. (It also becomes the *proposed* soundtrack for any new slideshows you create.)

Alternatively, if you decide you don't want any music to play, turn off the "Play music during slideshow" checkbox above the list.

Note: You can select multiple songs from the song list in the Slideshow dialog box, using the Shift-click and ⌘-click keystrokes that work in so many Mac dialog boxes. Keep in mind, though, that iPhoto will play back only the last one you click. If you have in mind a group of several songs that would make a perfect backdrop for your slideshow, the solution is to create a new playlist in iTunes, taking care to drag into it the desired songs from your Music Library, in the order that you want them to play. Switch back to iPhoto, and choose that playlist from the pop-up menu in the Slideshow dialog box (see Figure 9-3).

Different Shows, Different Albums

You can save different slideshow settings for each icon in your Source list.

To save settings for a specific photo album, for example, first choose the album from the Source list, then click the Slideshow icon in the lower pane of the iPhoto window to open the Slideshow dialog box. Pick the speed, order, repeat, and music settings you want, then click Save Settings. The settings you saved will automatically kick in each time you launch a slideshow from that album.

Saved Slideshows

iPhoto 5 introduces the notion of *saved* slideshows, each of which appears as an icon in your Source list. As noted earlier, the beauty of this system is that you can tweak a slideshow to death—you can even set up different transition and speed settings for *each individual slide*—and then save all your work as an independent clickable icon, ready for playback whenever you've got company.

The key to all of this is the Slideshow icon at the bottom of the iPhoto window (Figure 9-4). It tosses you into the new Slideshow editing mode, which has some features of Edit mode and some features of regular old thumbnail-organizing mode.

Figure 9-4:
In the new slide-show editor, the window shape is designed to mimic your Mac's monitor shape (or whatever screen proportions you've specified in the Settings box); that's why gray bars may appear. Some of the settings affect the entire slideshow, and some affect only the currently displayed photo, as identified here.

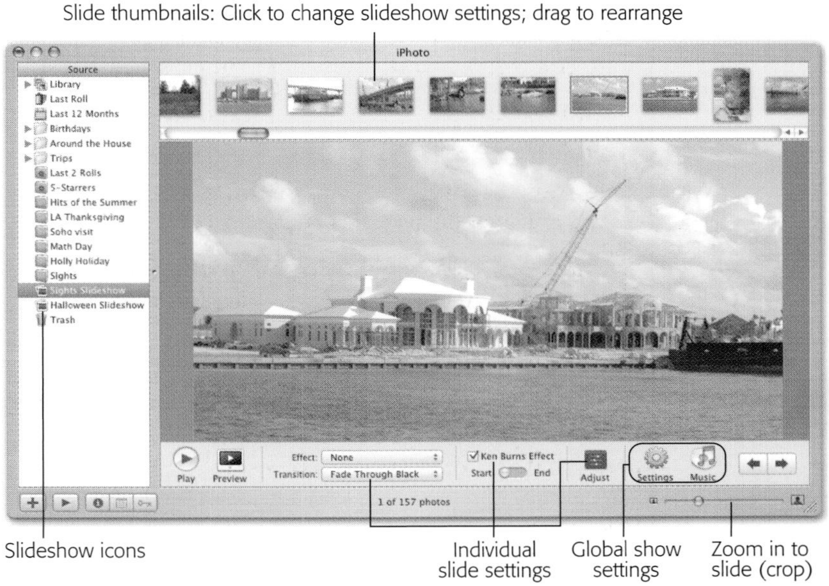

Slide thumbnails: Click to change slideshow settings; drag to rearrange

Slideshow icons

Individual slide settings

Global show settings

Zoom in to slide (crop)

To create a saved slideshow, select the photos you want to include (or the album), and then click the Slideshow button beneath the photo-viewing editor. You wind up in the slideshow editing mode shown in Figure 9-4. At the same time, a new icon appears in the Source list, with the word "Slideshow" tacked onto the name. (The icon looks like a little pile of actual slides.)

Choose a playback order for your pictures by dragging thumbnails horizontally at the top of the window.

Next, by clicking the Settings and Music buttons, set up the preferences that will affect all slides in the show (like timings and transitions), using the controls at the bottom of the window. You can read about what these controls do in the next section.

If you like, walk through the slides one at a time, taking the opportunity to set up their individual characteristics.

For example, you can choose one slide to linger longer on the screen, another to dissolve (rather than wipe) into the next picture, and so on. These options, too, are described below.

At this point, if you click the Preview button, iPhoto plays a quick, miniature, abbreviated slideshow. It's only two slides long, featuring the currently selected slide (in the thumbnails up top) and whatever follows it. The idea is that you can judge the timing of the currently selected slide, as well as its transition into the next one. (There's no music, and the entire thing plays right in the editing window instead of filling your screen.)

When everything looks ready, click the Play button (the big one, next to Preview) to play the actual slideshow.

When it's over, you can do three things with the slideshow icon that now resides in your Source list:

- **Delete it.** Drag it onto the iPhoto Trash icon, as you would an album. When you're asked if you're sure, click Delete or press the Return key.

- **File it away.** Drag it into an iPhoto folder (page 125) to keep it organized with the related albums and books.

- **Edit it.** Click its icon and then change the bottom-of-screen controls.

Global Settings

As indicated by the preceding steps, you can make two kinds of changes to a saved slideshow: global ones (which affect all slides) and individual ones.

Most of the global options are hiding behind the Settings and Music buttons, which summon the two dialog boxes shown in Figure 9-5.

The Music dialog box

The Music dialog box should look familiar; it's identical to the dialog box shown in Figure 9-3. Here's where you choose the music that will accompany your slideshow, using the techniques described on page 185.

The Settings dialog box

The Settings button, however, brings up a dialog box that only *seems* familiar (Figure 9-5, top right). It contains many of the same options described on pages 182 through 188 (transition style, slide duration, Ken Burns effect, choice of music track or playlist, options to show your photos' titles and ratings, and so on).

In this incarnation, though, you get a few new options. First, iPhoto wants to know how it should handle slideshows that aren't exactly the same length as the music you've selected for their soundtracks. Your options are "Repeat music during slideshow" (loops the music as necessary to fit the slides) or "Fit slideshow to music" (plays the music only once, but squeezes or stretches the slides' time on the screen to fit the music).

Second, you get a Slideshow Format pop-up menu. Here, you can tell iPhoto what *shape* the screen will be.

Now, that may strike you at first as a singularly stupid statement; after all, doesn't the Mac know what shape its own screen is? But there's more to this story: In iPhoto 5 more than ever, you can build slideshows that aren't intended to be played on your screen. You might want to export a slideshow to play on other people's screens, or even on their TV sets by burning the slideshow to a DVD. That's why this pop-up menu offers three choices: Current Display, 4:3 iDVD, TV (that is, a standard squarish TV set), and 16:9 Widescreen (for high-definition TV sets and other rectangular ones).

In any case, the changes you make here affect *all* photos in the slideshow. Click OK when you're done, confident in the knowledge that you can always override these settings for individual slides.

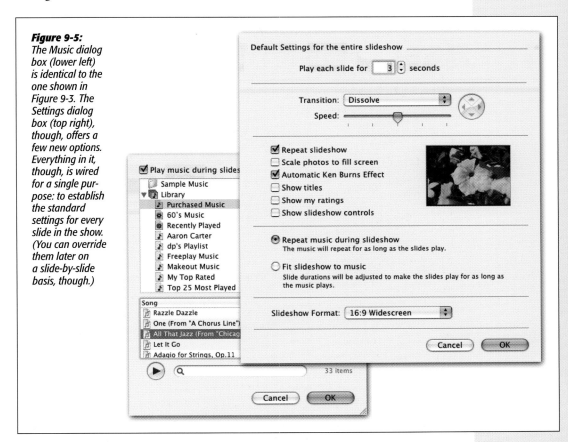

Figure 9-5:
The Music dialog box (lower left) is identical to the one shown in Figure 9-3. The Settings dialog box (top right), though, offers a few new options. Everything in it, though, is wired for a single purpose: to establish the standard settings for every slide in the show. (You can override them later on a slide-by-slide basis, though.)

The Effect pop-up menu

This pop-up menu lists three choices: None, Black and White, and Sepia (that is, brownish, old-fashioned monochrome). You could argue that Black and White makes a slideshow look artsier and more Ansel Adamsish, and that Sepia makes the pictures look more nostalgic and old-fashioned.

You could also argue that both of these options are pretty gimmicky and should be used only as a last resort.

Individual-Slide Options

The Settings and Music dialog boxes offer plenty of control, but the changes you make there affect *all* slides in the show. For the first time, though, iPhoto 5 also offers control over *individual* slides. For example:

Transition

The options in this pop-up menu are the different crossfade effects (Cube, Dissolve, and so on) that you can specify for the transition from one slide to another. (Whatever you choose here governs the transition *out* of the currently selected slide; every slideshow *begins* with a fade in from black.)

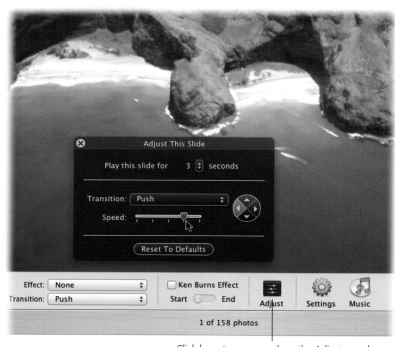

Figure 9-6:
The Adjust panel offers some less frequently used individual-slide settings. For example, it lets you change the speed of a transition effect and the amount of time an individual slide remains onscreen. (The Transition pop-up menu here is identical to the one at the bottom of the iPhoto window.)

Click here to open or close the Adjust panel

Transition speed and direction

You can also control the speed of the transitions on a slide-by-slide basis, and even which direction the transition effect proceeds across the screen (for transition styles that offer a choice). Because Apple figures this isn't the sort of control most people need every day, it hid these controls away.

To see them, click the black Adjust button shown in Figure 9-6. Dragging the Speed slider left or right gets through the transition slower or faster.

Tip: The idea behind the design of the strangely see-through Adjust panel is that you can leave it open. You can park it anywhere onscreen as you work through the slides in your show. Simply put, as you click a new slide, the Adjust panel changes to reflect whatever settings are in place for that photo. In other words, don't waste your time closing and reopening it.

Slide timing

As you know, the Settings dialog box (Figure 9-5) is where you specify how long you want each slide to remain onscreen—in general. But if you want to override that setting for a few particularly noteworthy shots, the Adjust panel (Figure 9-6) is once again the solution.

With the specially blessed photo on the screen before you, summon the Adjust panel (click the Adjust button, if the panel isn't already open). Use the "Play this slide for __ seconds" control to specify this slide's few seconds of fame.

Tip: If you click the Reset to Defaults button in the Adjust panel, iPhoto wipes out any individual-slide customizations. It then reapplies your global transition and slide-timing settings to the selected photo.

Cropping and zooming

Here's another brand new (and totally undocumented) feature in iPhoto 5: You can choose to present only *part* of a photo in a slideshow, in effect cropping out portions of it, without actually touching the original.

To enlarge the photo (thus cropping out its outer margins), just drag the Size slider at the lower-right corner of the iPhoto window. Whatever photo size you create here is how it will appear during the slideshow.

What you may not realize, though, is that you can also drag *inside* the picture itself to shift the photo's position onscreen. Between these two techniques—sizing and sliding—you can set up a very specific portion of the photo. (Heck, you could even present the photo *twice* in the same slideshow, revealing half of it the first time, half of it the next.)

The Ken Burns Effect checkbox

If you flip back a few pages, you'll be reminded that the Ken Burns effect is a graceful, panning, zooming effect that brings animation to the photos of your slideshow, so that they float and move instead of just lying there.

You'll also be reminded that when you apply the effect to an entire slideshow, you have no control over the pans and zooms. iPhoto might begin or end the pan too soon, so that the primary subject gets chopped off. Or maybe it zooms too fast, so that your viewers never get the chance to soak in the scene—or maybe it pans or zooms in the *wrong direction* for your creative intentions.

Fortunately, the Ken Burns Effect controls located here let you control every aspect of the panning and zooming for one photo at a time. (Note: The settings you're about to make *override* whatever global Ken Burns setting you've made.) As you can see in Figure 9-7, it works like this:

1. **Select the photo. Turn on the Ken Burns Effect checkbox (bottom of window).**

If more than one is selected, iPhoto will apply the effect only to the first one.

Figure 9-7:
The idea behind the Ken Burns effect is that you set up the start and end points for the gradual zooming/panning effect. iPhoto, meanwhile, will automatically supply the in-between frames, producing a gradual shift from the first position to the second. In this case, the Ken Burns effect lets you save the "punch line" of this story-telling photo for the end of its time onscreen.

Top: Click Start. Use the Size slider (lower right) to magnify the photo, if you like. Once you've magnified it, you can drag inside the photo to reposition it inside the "frame" of your screen.

Bottom: Click End. Once again, use the Size slider and then drag inside the photo, if you like, to specify the final degree of zoom and movement. In this shot, you can see the tiny "grabbing hand" cursor that appears whenever your mouse wanders into the magnified-photo area.

2. **Click Start. Drag the Size slider (at the lower-right corner of the iPhoto window) until the photo is as big as you want it at the *beginning* of its time onscreen. Drag inside the picture itself to adjust the photo's initial position.**

In other words, you're setting up the photo the way it appears at the beginning of its time onscreen. If you hope to create a zooming *out* effect, you'd begin here by dragging the Size slider to the right, thus magnifying the photo, and then dragging the picture itself to center it properly.

3. **Click End. Use the Size slider to set up the picture's final degree of magnification. Drag inside the photo to specify the photo's final position.**

You've set up the starting and ending conditions for the photo.

Take a moment now to click the Preview button. The animated photo goes through its scheduled motion inside the window, letting you check the overall effect. Repeat steps 2 and 3 as necessary.

Now that you've specified the beginning and ending positions of the photo, iPhoto will interpolate, calculating each intermediate frame between the starting and ending points you've specified. Click the Preview button to see the fully animated results of your programming.

Control Over the Show

All types of iPhoto slideshows run themselves, advancing from photo to photo according to the timings you've specified. However, you can still control a slideshow after it starts running in a number of ways. Although some of these functions are represented by icons on the control bar (see page 103), it's nice to know that you can also trigger them from the keyboard, with or without the control bar. Your options:

- **Pause it.** Press the Space bar at any point to pause a slideshow. The music keeps playing, but the photos stop advancing. If the control bar isn't onscreen, a glowing Pause indicator briefly appears in the lower portion of the picture. When you're ready to move to the next slide and resume the auto-advancing of pictures, press Space again. A small Play indicator appears onscreen momentarily to confirm that iPhoto understands your command.

- **Manual advance.** Press the right or left arrow keys to advance to the next or previous photo, overriding the preset timing. In fact, once you hit either arrow key, the slideshow shifts into manual mode and stops advancing the photos altogether. A small translucent bar with arrows and a Play button appears onscreen to indicate that iPhoto is listening to your key presses.

At this point, you can continue to use the arrow keys to move through all the photos—or stay on one photo for the rest of your life, for all iPhoto cares. As with the pause command, the music track keeps on playing. (To stop the music, you must end the slideshow.)

In short, this is a terrific setup for a slideshow that you're narrating in person.

- **Back to auto-advance.** To return a slideshow to autoplay mode after you've used one of the arrow keys, press the Space bar. The photos advance automatically once again. Another option is to just wait a moment. As the onscreen arrows or control bar fade away, auto-advancing will resume.

- **Speed it up or slow it down.** Press the up or down arrow keys to speed up or slow down the slideshow on the fly. You'll discover that iPhoto can't create a stroboscopic, three-frames-per-second effect; one picture per second is about its maximum speed. (Give the poor thing a break—it's got a *lot* of data to scoop off the hard drive and throw onto your screen.)

Note: The changes you make manually are temporary. The next time you run a slideshow, you'll start again with the timing set in the Slideshow dialog box.

- **Rate the photos.** Even if you haven't summoned the control bar, you can rate photos as they flash by just by tapping the corresponding number keys on your keyboard: 1, 2, 3, 4, or 5 for the corresponding number of stars, or 0 to remove the rating altogether.

- **Rotate the photos.** If a photo appears sideways, press ⌘-R to rotate it counter-clockwise, or Option-⌘-R to rotate it clockwise. (Or vice versa, if you've fooled around with iPhoto's Preferences dialog box.)

- **Delete the duds.** When a forgettable photo appears, press the Delete or Del key on your keyboard to move it to the iPhoto Trash, without even interrupting the show. (Unless you have very understanding family and friends, you may want to do this *before* you show the pictures to others for the first time.)

Slideshows and iDVD

If you have a Mac equipped with a DVD-burning SuperDrive, you have yet another slideshow option: Instead of running a presentation directly from iPhoto, you can send your slideshow—music and all—from iPhoto to iDVD, Apple's simple DVD-authoring software. Using iDVD, you can transform the pictures from your album into an interactive slideshow that can be presented using any DVD player. (Just picture the family clicking through your photos on the big-screen TV in the den!)

Learn how to perform the iPhoto-to-iDVD conversion in Chapter 21.

Prints and Books

There's a lot to love about digital photos that remain digital. You can store hundreds of them on a single CD; you can send them anywhere on earth by email; and they won't wrinkle, curl, or yellow until your monitor does.

Sooner or later, though, most people want to get at least some of their photos on paper. You may want printouts to paste into your existing scrapbooks, to put in picture frames on the mantle, to use on homemade greeting cards, or to share with your Luddite friends who don't have computers.

Using iPhoto, you can create such prints using your own printer. Or, for prints that look, feel, and smell like the kind you get from a photo finishing store, you can transmit your digital files to Kodak Print Services, an online photo processing service. In return, you receive an envelope of professionally printed photos on Kodak paper that are indistinguishable from their traditional counterparts.

This chapter explains how to use each of iPhoto's printing options, including the features that let you print greeting cards, contact sheets, and other special items from your digital photo collection.

Making Great Prints

Using iPhoto to print your pictures is pretty easy. But making *great* prints—the kind that rival traditional film-based photos in their color and image quality—involves more than simply hitting the Print command.

One key factor, of course, is the printer itself. You need a good printer that can produce photo-quality color printouts. Fortunately, getting such a printer these days is pretty easy and inexpensive. Even some of the cheapo inkjet printers from Epson, HP, and

Canon can produce amazingly good color images—and they cost less than $100. (Of course, you make it up to the printer company on the back end when you buy more ink cartridges. Depending on how many prints you make, what you spend on these expensive cartridges can easily double or triple the cost of the printer in a year.)

Tip: If you're really serious about producing photographically realistic printouts, consider buying a model that's specifically designed for photo printing, such as one of the printers in the Epson Stylus Photo series or the slightly more expensive Canon printers. What you're looking for is a printer that uses *six* or even *seven* different colors of ink instead of the usual "inkjet four." The extra colors do wonders for the printer's ability to reproduce a wide range of colors on paper.

Even with the best printer, however, you can end up with disappointing results if you fail to consider at least three other important factors when trying to coax the best possible printouts from your digital photos. These factors include the resolution of your images, the settings on your printer, and your choice of paper.

Resolution and Shape

Resolution is the number of individual pixels squeezed into each inch of your digital photo. The basic rule is simple: The higher your photo's resolution, or *dpi* (dots per inch), the sharper, clearer, and more detailed the printout will be. If the resolution is too low, you end up with a printout that looks blurry or speckled.

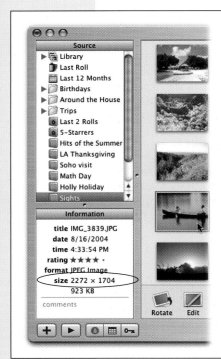
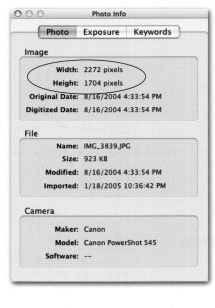

Figure 10-1:
To select the best size for a printout, you must know a photo's size in pixels. iPhoto reveals this information in two convenient places. First, when a photo is selected, its dimensions appear in the Info panel in the main window (left). Second, you can choose Photos→Show Info to see the same information in the Photo Info window (right).

Low-resolution photos are responsible for more wasted printer ink and crumpled photo paper than any other printing snafu, so it pays to understand how to calculate a photo's dpi when you want to print it.

Calculating resolution

To calculate a photo's resolution, divide the horizontal or vertical size of the photo (measured in pixels) by the horizontal or vertical size of the print you want to make (usually measured in inches).

Suppose a photo measures 1524 x 1016 pixels. (How do you know? See Figure 10-1.) If you want a 4 x 6 print, you'll be printing at a resolution of 254 dpi (1524 pixels divided by 6 inches = 254 dpi), which will look fantastic on paper. Photos printed on an inkjet printer look their best when printed at a resolution of 220 dpi or higher.

But if you try to print that same photo at 8 x 10, you'll get into trouble. By stretching those pixels across a larger print area, you're now printing at just 152 dpi—and you'll see a noticeable drop in image quality.

While it's important to print photos at a resolution of 250 to 300 dpi on an inkjet printer, there's really no benefit to printing at higher resolutions—600 dpi, 800 dpi, or more. It doesn't hurt anything to print at a higher resolution, but you probably won't notice any difference in the final printed photos, at least not on inkjet printers. Some inkjets can spray ink at finer resolutions—720 dpi, 1440 dpi, and so on—and using these highest settings produces very smooth, very fine printouts. But bumping the resolution of your *photos* higher than 300 dpi doesn't have any perceptible effect on their quality.

Aspect ratio

You also have to think about your pictures' *aspect ratio*—their proportions. Most digital cameras produce photos with 4-to-3 proportions, which don't fit neatly onto standard print paper (4 x 6 and so on). You can read more about this problem on page 151. (Just to make sure you're completely confused, some sizes of photo paper are measured *height by width*, whereas digital photos are measured *width by height*.)

If you're printing photos on letter-size paper, the printed images won't have standard Kodak dimensions. (They'll be, for example, 4 x 5.3.) You may not particularly care. But if you're printing onto, say, precut 4 x 6 photo paper (which you choose in the File→Page Setup dialog box), you can avoid ugly white bands at the sides by first cropping your photos to standard print sizes.

Tweaking the Printer Settings

Just about every inkjet printer on earth comes with software that adjusts various print quality settings. Usually, you can find the controls for these settings right in the Print dialog box that appears when you choose File→Print. To reveal these printer-specific controls in iPhoto, click the Advanced Options button in the Print dialog box, and then choose an additional command from the pop-up menu (Figure 10-2).

Before you print, verify that you've got these settings right. On most printers, for example, you can choose from several different quality levels when printing, like Draft, Normal, Best, or Photo. There might also be a menu that lets you select the kind of paper you're going to use—plain paper, inkjet paper, glossy photo paper, and so on.

Choose the wrong settings, and you'll be wasting a lot of paper. Even a top-of-the-line Epson photo printer churns out awful photo prints if you feed it plain paper when it's expecting high-quality glossy stock. You'll end up with a smudgy, soggy mess. So each time you print, make sure your printer is configured for the quality, resolution, and paper settings that you intend.

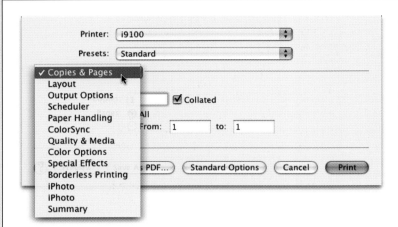

Figure 10-2:
Click Advanced Options in the standard iPhoto Print dialog box to open this important box. Here, choose Print Settings, Quality & Media, or a similar command from the pop-up menu (depending on your printer type) to see the controls for paper type, print quality, and so on.

Paper Matters

When it comes to inkjet printing, paper is critical. Regular typing paper—the stuff you'd feed through a laser printer or copier—may be cheap, but it's too thin and absorbent to handle the amount of ink that gets sprayed on when you print a full-color digital photo. If you try to print large photos on plain paper, you'll end up with flat colors, slightly fuzzy images, and paper that's rippled and buckling from all the ink. For really good prints, you need paper designed expressly for inkjets.

Most printers accommodate at least five different grades of paper. Among them:

- Plain paper (the kind used in most photocopiers)

- High Resolution paper (a slightly heavier inkjet paper—not glossy, but with a silky-smooth white finish on one side)

- Glossy Photo paper (a stiff, glossy paper resembling the paper that developed photos are printed on)

- Photo Matte paper (a stiff, non-glossy stock)

- Most companies also offer an even more expensive glossy *film*, made of polyethylene rather than paper (which feels even more like traditional photographic paper)

These better photo papers cost much more than plain paper, of course. Glossy photo paper, for example, might run $25 for a box of 50 sheets, which means you'll be spending about 50 cents per 8 x 10 print—not including ink.

Still, by using good photo paper, you'll get much sharper printouts, more vivid colors, and results that look and feel like actual photographic prints. Besides, at sizes over 4 x 6 or so, making your own printouts is still less expensive than getting prints from the drugstore, even when you factor in printer cartridges and photo paper.

Tip: To save money and avoid wasting your high-quality photo paper, use plain inkjet paper for test prints. When you're sure you've got the composition, color balance, and resolution of your photo just right, load up your expensive glossy photo paper for the final printouts.

Printing from iPhoto

When you choose File→Print (⌘-P) in iPhoto, you don't see the standard Mac OS X Print dialog box—the one that asks you how many copies you want to print, which pages you want included, and so on. (As shown in Figure 10-2, you must click Advanced Options to see these controls.)

Instead, you're presented with iPhoto's own private version of the Print command, with six photo-specific printing options at your disposal: Standard Prints, Full Page, Greeting Cards, Contact Sheet, N-Up, and Sampler.

Each of these six printing styles is discussed in detail below.

Standard-Sized Prints

Use this method to print out photos that conform to standard photo sizes, like 5 x 7 or 8 x 10. This is especially useful if you intend to mount your printed photos in store-bought picture frames, which are designed to handle photos in these standard dimensions.

1. **Select the thumbnail(s) of the photo(s) you want to print.**

   Alternatively, you can open the photo in Edit mode before you print it; the Print command is accessible in all of iPhoto's modes. You can also select more than one photo—a good idea if you want to get the most out of your expensive inkjet paper (see step 5). Just highlight the ones you want, using the using clicking, Shift-clicking, and ⌘-clicking techniques.

2. **Choose File→Print, or press ⌘-P.**

   The iPhoto Print dialog box appears.

3. **From the Style pop-up menu, choose Standard Prints.**

   This is the factory setting, but if you've been printing other formats, you may have to switch it back.

4. **Using the Size pop-up menu, choose the print size you want.**

   You have several standard photo sizes to choose from—4 x 6, 5 x 7, and so on. Remember, though, that choosing a larger size stretches the pixels of your photo across a larger area, reducing the photo's resolution and potentially degrading its print quality. For best results, don't choose 8 x 10 unless the picture you're print-ing is at least 1200 x 1800 pixels. (A yellow triangle warns you if the resolution is too low; see Figure 10-3.)

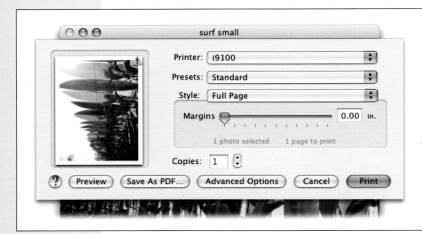

Figure 10-3:
See that warning icon on the top right corner of the preview? That's iPhoto's warning that the selected print size is too large, given the resolution of your photo. If you ignore the warning, your printout will likely have jagged edges or fuzzy detail.

   The Preview panel displays how your photo will be positioned on the paper, as shown in Figure 10-3.

5. **Select the number of photos you want printed on each page.**

   When the "One photo per page" checkbox is turned off, iPhoto fits as many photos as it can on each page, based on the paper size (which you select using the File→Page Setup command) and the photo size that you've chosen. Conversely, when the checkbox is turned on, you get one photo at the center of each page.

   On letter-size paper, iPhoto can fit nine 2 x 3, four 3 x 5, two 4 x 6, or two 5 x 7 pictures on each page. (If you're printing one photo per sheet—on 4 x 6 paper, for example—use the Full Page option described below, not "One photo per page.")

6. **Choose the number of copies you want to make.**

   You can either type the number into the Copies field or click the arrows to increase or decrease the number.

7. **Click the Print button (or press Enter).**

Your printer scurries into action, printing your photos as you've requested.

Tip: Printing photos using these standard sizes works best if your digital photos are trimmed so that they fit perfectly into one of the three preset dimensions—4 x 6, 5 x 7, or 8 x 10. Use iPhoto's Constrained Cropping tool, explained on page 152, to trim your photos to precisely these sizes.

Greeting Cards

When you choose Greeting Card from the Style pop-up menu of the Print dialog box, iPhoto automatically rotates and positions your photo (Figure 10-4). You could conceivably print out cards on standard letter-size paper and then fold it into halves or quarters, but this option is actually designed for printing on special blank inkjet greeting cards. This kind of glossy or matte paper stock, made by Epson and others, comes prescored and perforated for tidy edge-to-edge printing and crisp folding.

Figure 10-4:
iPhoto's Greeting Card printing doesn't create any actual greeting card content—no titles, holiday-themed icons, fancy borders, or pithy verses here. All you get is a printout of your photo on an otherwise blank sheet of paper, ready for you to fold over like a greeting card.

Here's how you print out a greeting card:

1. **Select or open the photo(s) you want to print.**

   Only one photo goes on each card. If you've selected more than one picture, you'll see only the first one illustrated in the preview.

2. **Choose File→Print, press ⌘-P, or click the Print button at the bottom of the iPhoto window.**

   The Print dialog box appears.

3. **From the Style menu, choose Greeting Card. Pick a greeting card style using the radio buttons.**

   You have two choices: Single-fold, which prints your photo onto a half sheet of paper; or Double-fold, which fits your photo into a quarter-page printing area.

The Preview panel on the left side of the Print dialog box illustrates how each of these options will appear in the final printout.

4. **In the Copies field, enter the number of copies you want to make.**

If you selected multiple photos in Step 1, iPhoto will print multiple greeting cards, one per photo. The number you enter here is different, in that it tells iPhoto how many *duplicates* of each one to print.

5. **Click the Print button (or press Enter).**

Your cards emerge from your printer, ready to fold, sign, and mail.

Printing Full Page Photos

iPhoto's Full Page printing option reduces or enlarges each photo so that it completely fills a single page.

With Full Page printing, it takes ten pages to print ten photos, of course. But when you make Standard, N-Up, Sampler, or Contact Sheet prints, iPhoto can fit more than one photo on each page.

Tip: iPhoto's print dialog box tells you how many photos you've selected and how many pages it will take to print them all. However, this information is easy to miss because it appears in dim, grayed-out text near the center of the dialog box, under the Margins slider.

Contact Sheets

The Contact Sheet option prints out a *grid* of photos, tiling as many as 120 pictures onto a single letter-size page (eight columns of fourteen rows, for example).

Photographers use contact sheets as a quick reference tool when organizing photos—a poor man's iPhoto, if you think about it. But this printing option is also handy in some other practical ways:

• By printing several pictures side by side on the same page, you can easily make quality comparisons among them without using two sheets of paper.

FREQUENTLY ASKED QUESTION

Changing Page Sizes

iPhoto's Print command lets me choose the size of the photos I want to print, but not the size of the paper *I'm printing them on. Can't I pick a different paper size?*

Yes, but remember that you change this kind of setting in the Page Setup dialog box, not the Print dialog box. Choose File→Page Setup, and then select the paper size you want using the Paper Size pop-up menu.

- Use contact sheet printing to make test prints, saving ink and paper. Sometimes a 2 x 3 print is all you need to determine if a picture is too dark or if its colors are wildly off when rendered by an inkjet printer. Don't make expensive full-page prints until you're sure you've adjusted your photo so that it will print out correctly.

- You can easily print multiple copies of a *single* picture if you want to produce lots of wallet-sized (or smaller) copies. (You can also make wallet sizes using the N-Up option.)

Contact Sheet printing options

To make Contact Sheet prints, choose Contact Sheet from the Style pop-up menu in the Print dialog box. Your printing options vary:

- If you've selected no specific photos, the Contact Sheet option prints *all* the photos in the Photo Library (or the current album, if you've selected one). Use the Across slider (Figure 10-5) to change the size of the grid and, therefore, the number of photos that appear on each printed page. iPhoto will print as many pages as needed to include all the photos in your current view.

- If you select several photos, iPhoto prints a contact sheet containing only those.

Figure 10-5:
To fit even more pictures on a contact sheet, turn on the Save Paper checkbox, which appears only when you're printing more than one photo. It not only squishes the pictures closer together on the page, but also automatically rotates vertical photos so that they fit into an evenly spaced grid, again reducing white space. With more photos squeezed onto each page (bottom), you end up using less paper than you would otherwise (top).

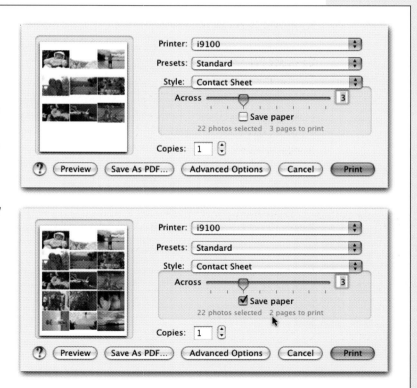

• When you select only *one* photo, iPhoto clones that one photo across the whole grid, printing one sheet of duplicate images at whatever size you specify using the slider control.

N-Up

With the N-Up option, you can tell iPhoto exactly how many photos you want printed on each page. The five preset grid configurations let you tile 2, 4, 6, 9, or 16 pictures on each sheet of paper. iPhoto automatically rotates photos as needed to make them fit perfectly into the grid size you choose.

N-Up printing may sound an awful lot like the Contact Sheet option just described, but it's slightly different. When printing Contact Sheets, you specify how many *columns* you want in your photo grid and, based on your choice, iPhoto crams as many photos on the page as it can—even if they end up the size of postage stamps. With N-Up Printing, you control the total number of pictures printed on each page, with a maximum of 16 photos in a 4 x 4 grid.

Tip: If you need your photos to be printed at a specific size—to fit in a 5 x 7 picture frame, for example—use the Standard Prints option instead of N-Up. With Standard Prints, you can specify the exact *size* of the photos; with N-Up, you can't.

N-Up printing options

As with printing contact sheets, your N-Up printing options depend on what you've got selected in the iPhoto window when you choose the Print command and choose N-Up from the Style menu.

• If you've selected no specific photos, the Contact Sheet option prints *all* the photos in the Photo Library (or the current album, if you've selected one). Use the "Photos per page" pop-up menu (Figure 10-6) to change the size of the grid and, therefore, the number of photos that appear on each printed page. iPhoto will print as many pages as needed to include all the photos in your current view.

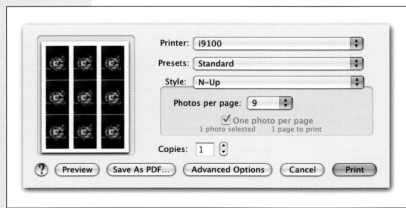

Figure 10-6:
Need a sheet of wallet-sized photos to send to relatives? One way to make them is via the N-Up printing option. Just turn on the "One photo per page" checkbox so that you have two, three, or four rows of duplicate pictures. You can print up to sixteen copies of a photo on each sheet.

- If you select several photos, iPhoto prints a grid containing only those.

- When you select only *one* photo, iPhoto prints one sheet of duplicate images at whatever grid size you specify.

Sampler Pages

While the Contact Sheet and N-Up options produce a straight grid of evenly-sized photos on each printed page, the Sampler option lets you print a grouping of photos at *different sizes* on a single page—just like the portrait galleries you might get from a professional photographer. For example, you can print a sheet that contains a combination of one large photo and five smaller photos, as shown in Figure 10-7.

Once you choose Sampler from the Style menu in the Print dialog box, you can choose from two different Sampler templates from the Template pop-up menu. Sampler 1 puts three pictures on each page—one large photo on the top, with two smaller ones beneath it. Sampler 2 produces the six-photo layout shown in Figure 10-7.

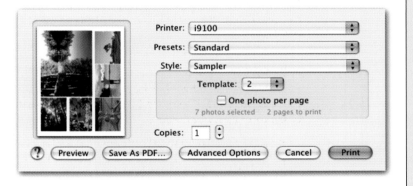

Figure 10-7:
You can print a neatly arranged combination of large and small photos on each page using one of the Sampler templates.

The Sampler option offers the same "One photo per page" checkbox available with N-Up printing (explained in Figure 10-6). Turn it on to fill each page with multiple copies of a single photo, just like the school photos brought home by fourth-graders worldwide each year.

Positioning photos in Sampler templates

You can pick exactly which of the photos from your collection are included in Sampler printouts by selecting them in the iPhoto window *before* choosing the Print command. If you have no photos selected, iPhoto will build Sampler pages using *all* the photos currently visible in the iPhoto window. If you have just one photo selected, iPhoto will fill the Sampler page with duplicates of the single photo. The order of the photos in your Photo Library determines how they're positioned in the printout, as explained in Figure 10-8.

The Preview Button

A mini-preview of your printout-to-be is always visible on the left side of the Print dialog box. But this postage stamp preview is far too small to show much detail. Worse, it shows you only the *first page* of a multipage job.

For a better preview, click Preview. iPhoto processes the print job, just as if you had hit Print—a "Print" progress bar appears at this point, indicating that the job is "on its way" to the printer. Instead of transmitting the job to your printer hardware, however, iPhoto creates a temporary PDF (Acrobat) file. It opens in Preview, the free graphics-viewing program that comes with Mac OS X.

Tip: Depending on the size of your print job, building a preview can take awhile. iPhoto must process all the image data involved, just as if it were really printing.

Figure 10-8:
The thing to keep in mind when setting up Sampler pages is that the first photo in your current selection is always the one that iPhoto picks as the "large" photo in the layout. If you want a specific photo to end up in the jumbo photo slot, make sure it's either the first one in the album or first among those you select. If you decide to rearrange the photos on the soon-to-be-printed page, close the Print dialog box, drag the thumbnails into a different order in the main iPhoto window, and then choose Print again.

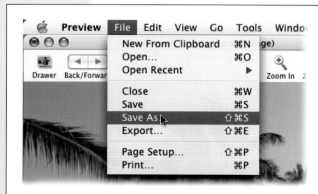

Figure 10-9:
The documents generated by the Preview command are temporary. If you close one, it disappears without even asking if you want to save it.

To save a preview document permanently, choose File→Save As or File→Export. The difference between the two commands: Save As lets you save only as a PDF document; Export lets you choose other formats, like JPEG or TIFF. Save As can create a multipage PDF from a bunch of selected pictures; Export saves only the first page in a selection.

You end up with a full-size, full-resolution electronic version of your printout. Using the commands in Preview's Display menu, you can zoom in or out to view details, scroll across pages, and move from page to page (to preview every page of a contact sheet, for example). You're seeing exactly how iPhoto is going to render your printout when it actually hits the printer, using the print options you selected.

If you like what you see in the PDF preview, you have the following two choices:

- Close the Preview window, return to iPhoto, and choose File→Print again (the Print dialog box will have closed itself automatically). Now, confident that you're going to get the results you expect, click the Print button and send the printout to your printer.

- If you want to *keep* the preview—in order to distribute an electronic version of a contact sheet, for example—you can save it, using one of the options shown in Figure 10-9. You can save it, for example, as a PDF file, which anyone with a Mac, Windows PC, or Unix machine can open using the free Acrobat Reader program that comes on every computer.

Save As PDF

The Save As PDF button, a standard part of all Mac OS X Print dialog boxes, lets you save a printout-in-waiting as a PDF file instead of printing it on paper. A click on this button lets you convert any type of iPhoto printout—greeting card, contact sheet, sampler, and so on—to PDF. After opening the Print dialog box, set up your print options the way you want, click the Save As PDF button, name the PDF in the Save to File dialog box, and click Save. (Saving the file can take awhile if you're converting several pages of photos into the PDF.)

Tip: You can also save a print job as a PDF file *after* you've previewed the results. See Figure 10-9 for details.

Ordering Prints Online

Even if you don't have a high-quality color printer, traditional prints of your digital photos are only a few clicks away—if you have an Internet connection and you're willing to spend a little money, that is.

Thanks to a deal between Apple and Kodak, you can order prints directly from within iPhoto. After you select the size and quantity of the pictures you want printed, one click is all it takes to have iPhoto transmit your photos to Kodak Print Services and bill your credit card for the order. The rates—some of which are much lower than they were in iPhoto 4—range from 19 cents for a single 4 x 6 print to about $23 for a jumbo 20 x 30 poster. Within a couple of days, Kodak sends you finished photos printed on high-quality glossy photographic paper.

Tip: If you plan to order prints, first crop your photos to the proper proportions (4 x 6, for example), using the Crop tool as described in Chapter 8. Most digital cameras produce photos whose shape doesn't quite match standard photo-paper dimensions. If you send photos to Kodak uncropped, you're leaving it up to Kodak to decide which parts of your pictures to lop off to make them fit. (More than one Mac fan has opened the envelope to find loved ones missing the tops of their skulls.)

By cropping the pictures to photo-paper shape before you place the order, *you* decide which parts get eliminated. (You can always restore the photos to their original uncropped versions using iPhoto's Revert to Original command.)

Click an album in the album list to order prints of everything in it, or select only the specific photos you want. Only the photos you select will appear in the Order Prints window.

Next, below the main iPhoto window, click the Order Prints icon. Now the Mac must go online to check in with the Kodak processing center. (If you've never before ordered an iPhoto book or iPhoto prints, click Set Up Account to surrender your identity and credit card info.)

Figure 10-10:
The Order Prints window lets you order six different types of prints from your photos—from a set of four wallet-sized prints to mammoth 20" x 30" posters. Use the scroll bar on the right to scroll through all the photos you've selected to specify how many copies of each photo you want to order. If you need to change your shipping, contact, or credit card information, click the Account Info button to modify your Apple ID profile.

If you want 4 x 6 or 5 x 7 prints of every photo you've selected, use the Quick Order pop-up menu at the top of the dialog box; otherwise, fill in the quantities individually for each photo, scrolling down through the dialog box as necessary.

As you order, pay heed to the alert icons (little yellow triangles) that may appear on certain lines of the order form (visible in Figure 10-10). These are iPhoto's standard warning symbols, declaring that certain photos don't have a high enough resolution to be printed at the specified sizes.

Click the Buy Now button to order the prints. Your photos are transferred, your credit card is billed, and you go sit by the mailbox. A batch of 24 standard 4 x 6 snapshots costs about $5, plus shipping, which is about what you'd pay for processing a roll of film at the local drugstore.

Better yet, you get to print only the prints that you actually want, rather than developing a roll of 36 prints only to find that only two of them are any good. It's far more convenient than the drugstore method, and it's a handy way to send top-notch photo prints directly to friends and relatives who don't have computers. Furthermore, it's ideal for creating high-quality enlargements that would be impossible to print on the typical inkjet printer.

Publishing a Photo Book

The program's Book feature lets you design and order (via the Internet) a gorgeous, professionally bound photo book, printed at a real bindery and shipped to the recipient in a slipcover. Your photos are printed on glossy, acid-free, single-sided pages, complete with captions, if you like.

A 20-page book costs $10 to $30, depending on the page size and whether you choose soft cover or hardback. When you think about it, that's about the least you could hope to pay for a handsome, emotionally powerful gift *guaranteed* never to wind up in an attic, at a garage sale, or on eBay. In short, it's a home-run gift every time.

In iPhoto 5, Apple's engineers gave the photo-book feature a massive overhaul. They did more than update this feature; they gutted it and rebuilt it from scratch.

Phase 1: Pick the Pix

The hardest part of the whole book-creation process is winnowing down your photos to the ones you want to include. Many a shutterbug sits down to create his very first published photo book—and winds up with one that's 99 pages long (that is, $109).

In general, each page of your photo book can hold a maximum of six or seven pictures. (iPhoto also offers canned book designs called Catalog and Yearbook, which hold up to 32 tiny pictures per page in a grid. At this size, however, your pictures don't exactly sing. Instead, the whole thing more closely resembles, well, a catalog or yearbook.)

Even the six-per-page limit doesn't necessarily mean you'll get 120 photos into a 20-page book, however. The more pictures you add to a page, the smaller they have to be, and therefore the less impact they have. The best-looking books generally have varying numbers of pictures per page—one, four, three, two, whatever. In general, the number of pictures you'll fit in a 20-page book may be much lower—50, for example.

You can choose the photos for inclusion in the book using any selection method you like. You can select a random batch of them (page 115), or you can file them into an album as a starting point. You can even select a group of albums that you want included, all together, in one book.

If you opt to start from an album, take this opportunity to set up a preliminary photo *sequence*. Drag them around in the album to determine a rough order. You'll have plenty of opportunity to rearrange the pictures on each page later in the process, but the big slide-viewer-like screen of an album makes the process easier. Take special care to place the two most sensational or important photos first and last (for the cover and the last page of the book).

Phase 2: Publishing Options

Once you've selected an album or a batch of photos, click the Book button below the main picture area (Figure 10-11), or choose File→New Book.

Now you see something like Figure 10-11: a dialog box in which you can specify what you want your book to look like. The dialog box looks pretty simple, but it's crawling with important design options, many of which are offered in iPhoto 5 for the first time.

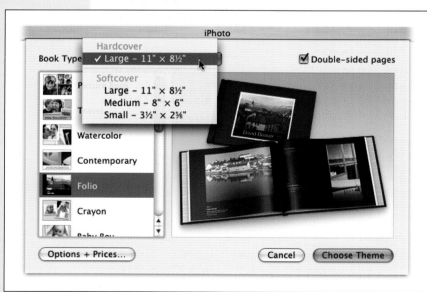

Figure 10-11:
You can change these settings later, even after you've started laying out your book pages. But if you have the confidence to make these decisions now, you'll save time, effort, and (if you want captions for your photos) possibly a lot of typing.

Book Type

This pop-up menu, shown open in Figure 10-11, lets you specify whether you want to publish your book as a hardbound volume (classier and more durable, but more expensive) or as a paperback. If you choose the softcover option, you can also choose one of three book sizes. The options are 11 x 8½ inches, which feels the slickest and most formal; 8 x 6, which is more portable; and 3½ x 2⅝.

This last option gives you a tiny, wallet-size flip book, with one photo filling each page, edge to edge. You must order these in sets of three (for $12), which suggests that Apple imagines them to serve as simultaneous giveaways to relatives, wedding guests, business clients and so on. In any case, they're absolutely adorable (the booklets, not the business clients).

Double-Sided Pages
The pages of *all* softcover book styles are printed with photos on both sides.

If you choose a hardback book, though, you can choose either double-sided printing or single-sided, meaning that each left-hand page is blank. The single-sided printing style tends to give each photo page more weight and drama because it's isolated, but of course your book winds up costing more because it's longer.

Theme Choices
And now, the main event: choosing a *theme*—a canned design, typography, and color scheme—for the cover and pages of your book. The scrolling list of named icons at the left side of the dialog box contains 15 professionally designed page templates, each dedicated to presenting your photos in a unique way.

The first eight of them are new in iPhoto 5. Some are designed to cover even the background of the page with textures, shadows, passport stamps, ripped-out clippings, and other photorealistic simulations.

If you scroll down far enough into the list of design templates, you'll find a second set of them called Old Themes. These were the design choices in iPhoto 4. True, they may be old in computer time (2004—ooh! Ancient!), but they're still perfectly usable (at least for hardback books; they're not available in softcover). In fact, because iPhoto 5 offers double-sided printing for the first time, these older designs have been given new life.

Once you've settled on a design theme for your book, your initial spate of decision-making is mercifully complete. Click Choose Theme.

"Drag photos from the top of the iPhotow indow onto your book pages, or click the Autoflow button to lay out your book automatically," says a message.

Phase 3: Design the Pages
When you click OK, two things happen. First, a new icon appears in your Source list, representing the book layout you're about to create. You can work with it as you would other kinds of Source-list icons. For example, you can delete it by dragging it to the iPhoto Trash, rename it by double-clicking, file it in a folder by dragging it there, and so on.

Note: If you're used to previous iPhoto versions, this is a happy bit of news. It means that a book is no longer tied to an album. Therefore, rearranging or reassigning photos to the original album no longer wreaks havoc with the book design that's associated with it.

Second, you now see something like Figure 10-12. The page you're working on always appears at nearly full size in the main part of the window. Up above, you see a set of thumbnails, either of your photos or of your book pages (more on this in a moment); that's the *photo browser*. iPhoto has just turned into a page-layout program.

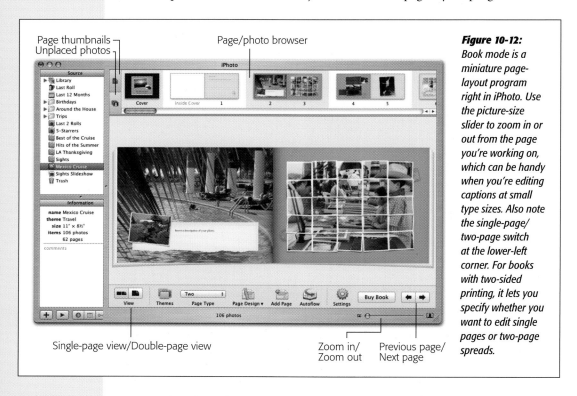

Page thumbnails
Unplaced photos

Page/photo browser

Figure 10-12:
Book mode is a miniature page-layout program right in iPhoto. Use the picture-size slider to zoom in or out from the page you're working on, which can be handy when you're editing captions at small type sizes. Also note the single-page/two-page switch at the lower-left corner. For books with two-sided printing, it lets you specify whether you want to edit single pages or two-page spreads.

Single-page view/Double-page view

Zoom in/ Zoom out

Previous page/ Next page

Once you've selected an album and a theme, the most time-consuming phase begins: designing the individual pages.

The initial pour

If you're in a hurry or you're not especially confident in your own design skills, click the AutoFlow button at the bottom of the window. iPhoto springs into action, arranging photos, in the sequence you've specified, on successive pages of the book.

Of course, you may not agree with iPhoto's choices. It may clump that prizewinning shot of the dog nosing the basketball through the hoop on the same page as three less impressive pictures. But it's a start; you can always override the initial layout as described on the following pages.

Open a page

That photo browser at the top of the window has two functions, as represented by
the two tiny icons at its left edge.

When you click the top one (the blue page button), you see miniatures of the pages
in your book. This is your navigation tool, your master scroll bar. When you click one
of the page thumbnails, the full-sized (well, fuller-sized) image of that page appears
in the main editing area.

The lower icon presents a desktop, a pasteboard, a temporary scrapbook, for *unplaced
photos*—pictures that you've said you want in your book, but haven't yet inserted.
(You can see this view of the photo browser in Figure 10-12.) The unplaced-photos
area is also convenient for dragging the photos into a satisfying sequence before you
transfer them onto the book's pages.

In any case, the first step in building your book is to click a page to work on. Most
people start with the Cover page—the first thumbnail in the row. When it's selected,
the cover photo appears in the main picture area. This is the picture that will appear,
centered, on the linen or glossy cover of the actual book. You can't do much with the
cover except to change the title or subtitle; see "Edit the Titles and Captions" on page
220. You'll choose the cover color in a later step.

Tip: The picture you see here is the first picture in the album or selected group. If it's not the photo you want
on the cover, you can drag a different photo into its place, as described in the following pages.

Choose a page type

After you're finished working with the cover, open the next page you want to work
on. If you did some preliminary photo-arranging work (in an album, for example),
your photos should already be in roughly the right *order* for the book pages—but not
necessarily the right *groupings*.

Whether you opted to have your photos placed into the book manually or automatically, you can see that iPhoto cheerfully suggests varying the number of photos per
page. Two-per-page on the first page, a big bold one on the next, a set of four on the
next, and so on. (In the case of a manual layout, these placements are represented on
the screen by empty gray rectangles.)

If you approve of the photos-per-page proposal, great. You can go to work choosing
which photos to put on each page, as described in the following pages.

Sooner or later, though, there will come a time when you want three related photos
to appear on a page that currently holds only two. That's the purpose of the Page
Type pop-up menu shown in Figure 10-13. It's a list of the different page designs that
Apple has drawn up to fit the overall design theme you've selected.

You control how many pictures appear on a page by choosing from the Page Type
pop-up menu. Your choices include Cover, Introduction (a big blank text box),
One/Two/Three (indicating how many photos will appear on the selected page), or
Blank. Some themes, especially the Folio theme, offer their own private page designs

(with names like One with Text, Title Page, Text Page, About Page, and Contact Page). In general, they're designed to hold specialized blobs of text that are unique to that book design.

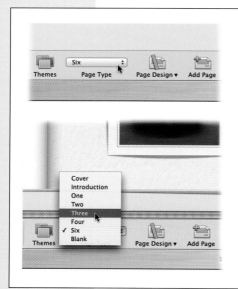 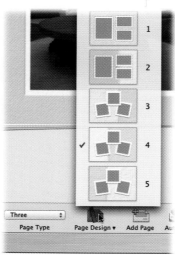

Figure 10-13:
The Page Type pop-up menu (top left, lower left) lets you specify how many photos you want on this page, and lists bonus page types like Cover and Introduction.

Right: Once you've chosen a Page Type, you can use the Page Design pop-up menu. It shows tiny previews of the different layouts available for the Page Type you've selected.

Pick a layout variation

Once you've chosen how *many* photos you want on a page, the Page Design pop-up menu becomes available to you. As shown in Figure 10-13, it contains tiny thumbnail representations of the various photo layouts available. If you chose Three as the number of photos, for example, the Page Design pop-up menu may offer you a choice of page background (for a three-photo layout) or a couple of different arrangements of those three photos—big one on top, two down the side, or whatever.

In some themes, especially the older ones, you're not offered any choices at all. There's only one arrangement for a two-photo layout, one for a three-photo layout, and so on. In some of the new iPhoto 5 themes, a page type may offer over a dozen variations. Try before you buy.

FREQUENTLY ASKED QUESTION

Doubling the Cover Photo

I want to use my cover photo as one of the pages in the book, just like they do in real coffee-table photo books. How do I do it?

Find the photo in its album, or in your Library; click the photo and then choose Photos→Duplicate (⌘-D).

Now you have two copies of the photo. Use one as the cover, and then drag the other onto the desired interior page layout.

Lay out the book

The key to understanding iPhoto 5's book-layout mode is realizing that all photos are *draggable*. Dragging is the key to all kinds of book-design issues (see Figure 10-14).

In fact, between dragging photos and using a handful of menu commands, you can perform every conceivable kind of photo- and page-manipulation trick there is.

Figure 10-14:
iPhoto's book-layout mode is absolutely crawling with tricks that let you move photos around, add them to pages, remove them, and so on. The fun begins when you finally understand the difference between the page browser (top) and the unplaced-photo browser (bottom).

For example, you can add new photos to your book only via the unplaced-photo browser. Use the page browser more as a navigational tool.

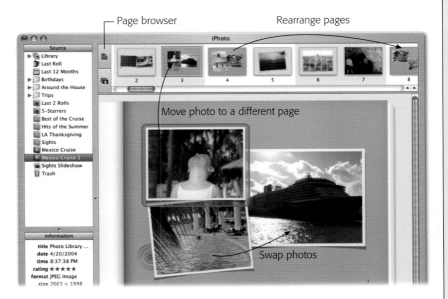

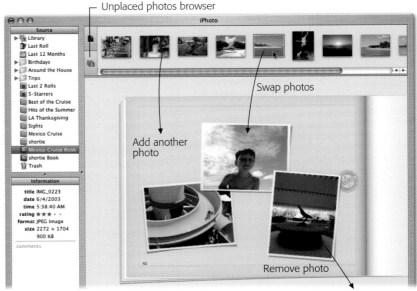

Here are all the different ways to move photos around in your book (see Figure 10-14 for a summary):

- **Swap two photos on the same page (or two-page spread)** by dragging one directly on top of the other. When the existing picture sprouts a colored border, let go of the mouse button; the two pictures swap places.

- **Move a photo to a different page of the book** by dragging it onto a different page in the photo browser.

- **Remove a photo from a page** by clicking its icon and then pressing your Delete key. Its icon moves up into the unplaced-photos area (Figure 10-14). (You can also drag the photo directly into the unplaced-photo browser, if it's visible.) There it will remain until you move it back onto a book page or delete it.

- **Remove a photo from the book altogether** by (a) moving it to the unplaced-photo area as described above (or just dragging it off the page), then (b) clicking it *again* (in its current photo-browser location) and, finally, (c) pressing Delete *again*.

  Note that removing a photo also changes the resulting page type from a four-photo page layout (for example) to a three-page layout. In other words, the three remaining pictures snap into a different arrangement to fill up the new space. (And if you delete the last photo on a page, you wind up with a big gray placeholder.)

- **Shove one overlapping photo "under" another** by Control-clicking it and, from the shortcut menu, choosing Send to Back.

- **Add an unplaced photo to a page** by dragging it out of the unplaced-photos browser (Figure 10-12) onto a *blank* spot of the page. iPhoto automatically increases the number of photos on that page, even changing the Page Type pop-up menu to match.

Note: This won't work if the page already has the maximum number of photos on it, according to the theme you've chosen. For example, the Folio theme permits a maximum of two pictures per page.

- **Swap in an unplaced photo** by dragging it out of the unplaced-photos browser *onto* a photo that's already on a page of your book. iPhoto swaps the two, putting the outgoing photo back into the unplaced-photo browser.

- **Add new photos to the unplaced-photo area** by dragging them onto the book's Source-list icon. For example, you can click any album, smart album, slideshow, or Library icon to see what photos are inside—and then drag the good ones onto your book icon.

  Once these photos have arrived in the unplaced-photo area, you can drag them onto individual pages as described above.

- **Fill in an empty gray placeholder frame** by dragging a photo onto it from the unplaced-photos area.

- **Fill in *all* the gray placeholders with photos** by clicking the Autoflow button at the bottom of the window. (Those gray placeholders appear when you first create the book and haven't yet clicked the Autoflow button, or whenever your book has more pages than photos you've put on them.)

Either way, clicking Autoflow "pours" all of the unplaced photos into the gray placeholders of your book, front to back. When they arrive, they'll be in the same order as they appeared in the thumbnails browser.

If the results aren't quite what you expected, you can always use the Edit→Undo command to backtrack.

- **Enlarge or crop a picture,** right there on the page, by double-clicking it. A tiny zoom slider appears above the photo, which you can use to magnify the picture or shift it inside its boundary "frame" (see Figure 10-15). For now, it's worth remembering that this trick is helpful when you want to call attention to one part of the photo, or to "crop" a photo for book-layout purposes without actually editing the original.

Figure 10-15:
At this point, you can drag inside the photo to adjust its position within its "frame."

None of this affects the actual photo (as using the iPhoto cropping tool would). You're basically just changing the relationship between the photo and its boundary rectangle on the page template. Of course, you'll have to be careful not to enlarge the photo so much that it triggers the dreaded yellow-triangle low-resolution warning.

They don't call her Flipper for nothing!

- **Edit a photo** by Control-clicking it and, from the shortcut menu, choosing Edit Photo. In a flash, book-layout mode disappears, and you find yourself in the editing mode described in Chapter 8. (Either the picture appears in its own window, or the Edit tools fill the bottom toolbar, depending on your iPhoto preference settings.)

When you're finished editing, click the Done button (or, if you're editing in a separate window, close it). You return to the layout mode, with the changes intact.

Photos aren't the only ones having all the fun. You can drag and manipulate the pages themselves, too:

- **Move pages around within the book** by dragging their thumbnails horizontally in the photo browser.

- **Remove a page from the book** by clicking its photo-browser icon and then either pressing Delete or choosing Edit→Remove Page. (If you use the Delete-key method, iPhoto asks if you're sure you know what you're doing.)

  Note that removing a page never removes any *pictures* from the book. They just fall into the unplaced-photos area, ready to use later if you like. But removing a page *does* vaporize any captions you've carefully typed in.

- **Insert a new page into the book** by clicking the Add Page button at the bottom of the window, or by choosing Edit→Add Page.

  Before you go nuts with it, though, note that iPhoto inserts the new page *after* the page you're currently viewing. It's helpful, therefore, to begin by first clicking the desired page thumbnail (in the page browser at the top of the window).

  If you have some leftover pictures in the unplaced photos area, iPhoto uses them to fill the new page; if not, you just get empty gray placeholders. (iPhoto takes it upon itself to decide how many photos appear on the new page.) In any case, now you know how to change the number of photos on that page, or at least how to replace the pictures that iPhoto put there.

Tip: As a shortcut, you can also Control-click a blank spot on any page and, from the shortcut menu, choose Add Page or Remove Page.

Making your photos shape up

iPhoto's design templates operate on the simple premise that all of your photos have a 4:3 aspect ratio. That is, the long and short sides of the photo are in four-to-three proportion- (four inches to three inches, for example).

In most cases, that's what you already have, since those are the standard proportions of standard digital photos. If all your pictures are in 4:3 (or 3:4) proportion, they'll fit neatly and beautifully into the page-layout slots iPhoto provides for them.

But not all photos have a 4:3 ratio. You may have cropped a photo into some other shape. Or you may have a camera that can take pictures in the more traditional 3:2 film dimension (1800 x 1200 pixels, for example), which work better as 4 x 6 prints.

When these photos land in one of iPhoto's page designs, the program tries to save you the humiliation of misaligned photos, which was a chronic problem in iPhoto 4. Rather than leave unsightly strips of white along certain edges (therefore producing photos that aren't aligned with each other), iPhoto 5 automatically blows up a mis-cropped photo so that it perfectly fills the 4:3 space allotted to it. Figure 10-16 shows the effect.

Unfortunately, this solution isn't always ideal. Sometimes, in the process of enlarging a nonstandard photo to fill its 4:3 space, iPhoto winds up lopping off an important part of the picture—somebody's forehead, say.

Here, you have two alternatives. First, you can use the Fit Photo to Frame Size command described in Figure 10-16.

Figure 10-16:
Top: When you first start working on a book, the photos all look nice together. They nestle nicely side by side. Every now and then, however, you may be disheartened to find that iPhoto is lopping off a dear one's head.

Bottom: If you Control-click a photo and choose Fit Photo to Frame, you'll discover that the problem is a photo that doesn't have 4:3 proportions (on this page, that's three of them). iPhoto thought it was doing you a favor by blowing it up enough to fill the 4:3 box. Now you get ugly white gaps, but, hey, at least you're seeing the entire photo.

Second, you can crop your non-4:3 photos using the Constrain pop-up menu (page 152) set to "4 x 3 (Book)." This way, *you* get to decide which parts of the photo get lopped off. (Or just use the adjustment technique shown in Figure 10-15.)

Page Limits

The book can have anywhere from 10 to 100 pages (or 20 to 100 for double-sided pages). If you try to create more than that, iPhoto scolds you and dumps the excess photos onto your unplaced-photo shelf.

Of course, if you really have more than 100 pages' worth of pictures, there's nothing to stop you from creating multiple books. ("Our Trip to New Jersey, Vol. XI," anyone?)

Hiding Page Numbers

Don't be alarmed if iPhoto puts page numbers on the corners of your book pages— that's strictly a function of the theme you've chosen (some have numbering, some don't). In any case, you never have to worry about a page number winding up superimposed on one of your pictures. A picture *always* takes priority, covering up the page number.

Even so, if it turns out that your theme *does* put numbers on your pages, and you feel that they're intruding on the mood your book creates, you can eliminate them. Click the Settings button at the bottom of the window. In the resulting dialog box, you'll see a "Show page numbers" checkbox that you can turn off.

Tip: As a shortcut, you can also Control-click a blank spot on any page and, from the shortcut menu, choose Show Page Numbers to turn it on or off.

Phase 5: Edit the Titles and Captions

Depending on the theme you're using, iPhoto may offer you any of several kinds of text boxes that you can fill with titles, explanations, and captions:

- **The book title.** This box appears on the book's cover and, if you've added one, Introduction page. When you first create a book, iPhoto proposes the *album's* name as the book name, but you're welcome to change it.

  A second text box, all set with slightly smaller-type formatting, appears below the title. Use it for a subtitle: the date, "A Trip Down Memory Lane," "Happy Birthday Aunt Enid," "A Little Something for the Insurance Company," or whatever.

- **The introduction.** Applying the Introduction-page design to a page produces a huge text block that you can fill with any introductory text you think the book needs.

- **Photo titles.** In some layouts—primarily the old, iPhoto 4 ones—iPhoto can display the name of each photo. (Of the new designs, only the Folio template offers such an option.) When you first create the layout, the program labels each photo with whatever its title is.

If you haven't already named each picture, you'll get only the internal iPhoto name of each one—"IMG_0030.JPG," for example. Once the book layout has been created, though, you can edit the name only in one place: directly on the book page. See Figure 10-17 for details.

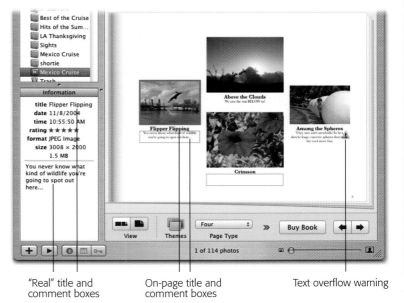

Figure 10-17:
When you first create the book layout, iPhoto inherits its initial photo name and caption text from the existing photo titles and Comments-box information. Unlike previous versions, however, iPhoto 5 doesn't link these two sources; if you change the photo's name in the Info panel, it doesn't change on the page layout. At right: A yellow, nonprinting warning sign appears if the text box is too small to display all of the comment text (or the full photo name).

"Real" title and   On-page title and   Text overflow warning
comment boxes   comment boxes

- **Comments.** The larger text box that appears for each photo (in some layouts) is for a caption. At the moment of the book's creation, iPhoto automatically fills in this box with any comments you've typed into the picture's Comments box at the left side of the iPhoto screen (see page 129).

Or, to be precise, it displays the first *chunk* of that text. Most layouts don't show nearly as much text as the "real" Title or Comments box does. In these cases, iPhoto has no choice but to chop off the excess, showing only the first sentence or two. A yellow, triangular exclamation point appears next to any text box with overflow of this kind—your cue to edit down the text to fit the text box on the layout (see Figure 10-17).

Tip: If iPhoto copies the photo names and comments onto the book pages and you don't want it to, click the Settings button below the book layout. Turn off "Automatically enter photo information." This option is also available in the shortcut menu that appears whenever you Control-click a blank spot on any page.

Editing Text

In general, editing text on the photo page is straightforward: Click inside a text box to activate the insertion-point cursor, so you can begin typing. Zoom in on the page (using the size slider at lower-right) and scroll it, if necessary, so that the type is large enough to see and edit. Click outside a text box—on another part of the page, for example—to finish the editing.

Tip: To make typographically proper quotation marks (curly like "this" instead of like "this"), press Option-[and Shift-Option-[, respectively. And to make a true long dash—like this, instead of two hyphens—press Shift-Option-hyphen.

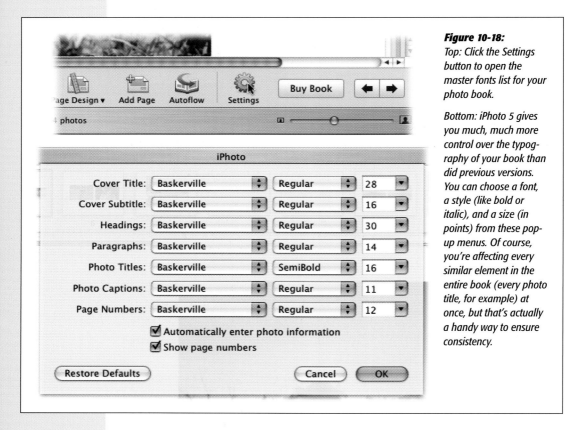

Figure 10-18:
Top: Click the Settings button to open the master fonts list for your photo book.

Bottom: iPhoto 5 gives you much, much more control over the typography of your book than did previous versions. You can choose a font, a style (like bold or italic), and a size (in points) from these pop-up menus. Of course, you're affecting every similar element in the entire book (every photo title, for example) at once, but that's actually a handy way to ensure consistency.

Formatting Text

iPhoto 5 offers infinitely more control over the fonts, sizes, colors, and styles of the text in your book than previous versions did. Here's a summary of your newfound typographical freedom:

- **Standard typefaces.** To choose the basic font for each *category* of text box—book title, photo name, caption, or whatever—throughout the entire book, click the Settings button at the bottom of the window. (If the iPhoto window is very narrow, the Settings command may be hiding in the >> menu at the lower-right corner of the window.)

You get the dialog box shown in Figure 10-18, where you can make your selections.

- **Font exceptions, text colors.** If you want to override the standard typeface for a certain text box, you can. Choose Edit→Fonts→Show Fonts (⌘-T); the standard Mac OS X Fonts panel appears. Here, you have complete access to all of your Mac's fonts. You can choose special text effects, shadowing, and even colors for individual text selections. Yes, the bright, multicolored result might look a little bit like it was designed by Barney the Dinosaur, but the Color option is worth keeping in mind when you're preparing books describing, say, someone's fourth birthday party.

- **Character formatting.** If you select some words and then Control-click them, a shortcut menu appears. It offers Bold, Italic, and Underline choices, which iPhoto will apply to the highlighted text. (The Edit→Fonts menu also works, but it offers only Bold and Italic.)

Phase 6: Preview the Masterpiece

Ordering a professionally bound book is, needless to say, quite a commitment. Before blowing a bunch of money on a one-shot deal, you'd be wise to proofread and inspect it from every possible angle.

Print It

As any proofreader can tell you, looking over a book on paper is a sure way to discover errors that somehow elude detection onscreen. That's why it's a smart idea to print out your own, low-tech edition of your book at home before beaming it away to Apple's bindery.

While you're in Book mode, choose File→Print. After the standard Mac OS X Print dialog box appears, fire up your printer and click Print when ready. The result may not be linen-bound and printed on acid-free paper, but it's a tantalizing preview of the real thing—and a convenient way to give the book one final look.

Turn It into a PDF File

Sooner or later, almost everyone with a personal computer encounters PDF (Portable Document Format) files. Many a software manual, Read Me file, and downloadable "white paper" come in this format. When you create a PDF document of your own, and then send it off electronically to a friend, it appears to the recipient *exactly* as it did on your screen, complete with the same fonts, colors, page design, and other elements. They get to see all of this even if they don't *have* the fonts or the software you used to create the document. PDF files open on Mac, Windows, and even Linux machines—and you can even search the text inside it.

If you suspect other people might want to have a look at your photo book before it goes to be printed—or if they'd just like to have a copy of their own—a PDF file makes a convenient package.

Here's how to create a PDF file:

1. **With your book design on the screen in front of you, choose File→Print.**

   The print dialog box appears.

2. **Click the Save as PDF button, if you have one, or choose "Save PDF" from the PDF pop-up button.**

   The Save sheet appears.

3. **Type a name for the file, choose a folder location for it, and click Save.**

   Your PDF file is ready to distribute. (Fortunately, the recipients will be able to correct the rotation within Adobe Acrobat using its View→Rotate Counterclockwise command.)

Phase 7: Send the Book to the Bindery

When you think your book is ready for birth, click Buy Book.

After several minutes of converting your screen design into an Internet-transmittable file, iPhoto offers you a screen like the one shown in Figure 10-19.

That is, assuming you don't get any of iPhoto's pre-publication warnings first, namely, that you haven't filled in all the default text boxes, like the title and subtitle; that some of your text boxes or photos bear the yellow-triangle low-resolution warning (see the

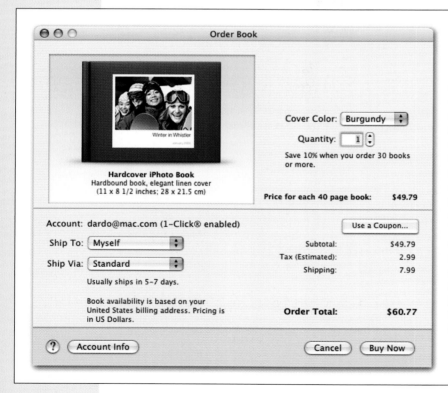

Figure 10-19:
Choose a color, a quantity, and a recipient. You won't be allowed to choose a quantity or recipient, though, until you've first signed up for an Apple account, which you'll enjoy using over and over again to order books and stuff from the Apple online stores. To sign up for an account, click the Set Up Account button (not shown here, but it would appear in place of Buy Now if this were your first time).

box below); that your book is "incomplete" (you didn't fill in all the gray placeholder rectangles with pictures); and so on.

At this stage, your tasks are largely administrative. Chooes a cover color (hardback books only), inspect the charges, and indicate the quantity.

Your Apple ID and One-Click Ordering
You can't actually order a book until you've signed up for an Apple account and turned on "1-Click Ordering."

The Heartbreak of the Yellow Exclamation Point

As you work on your book design, you may encounter the dreaded yellow-triangle-exclamation-point like the one shown here. It appears everywhere you want to be: on the corresponding page thumbnail, on the page display, on the page preview (which appears when you click Preview), and so on.

If you actually try to order the book without first eliminating the yellow triangles, you even get a warning in the form of a dialog box.

Sometimes the problem is that you've tried to put too much text into a text box. So no big deal, just edit it down.

But if the triangle appears on a photo, you have a more worrisome problem: At least one of your photos doesn't have enough resolution (enough pixels) to reproduce well in the finished book. If you ignore the warning and continue with the ordering process, you're likely to be disappointed by the blotchy, grainy result in the finished book.

As you may already know, the resolution of your digital camera is relatively irrelevant if you'll only be showing your pictures onscreen. It's when you try to print them that you need all the megapixels you can get—like *now*.

The easiest solution is to shrink the photo on its page. And the easiest way to do that is to increase the number of pictures on that page. Or, if your page design has places that hold both large and small photos, you can drag the problem photo onto one of the smaller photos, swapping the large and small positions.

Decreasing a picture's size squeezes its pixels closer together, improving the dots-per-inch shortage that iPhoto is so boldly warning you about.

If even those dramatic steps don't eliminate the yellow warning emblems, try to remember if you ever cropped the photo in question. If so, your last chance is to use the Photos→Revert To Original command (page 175). Doing so will undo any cropping you did to the photo, which may have jettisoned a lot of pixels that you now need. (If Revert To Original is dimmed, then you never performed any cropping, and this last resort is worthless.)

Finally, if nothing has worked so far, your only options are to eliminate the photo from your book, or to order the book anyway.

However, you may well already have an Apple account if, say, you've ever bought something from an online Apple store or the iTunes Music Store. Whether you have or not, ordering your first iPhoto book requires completing some electronic paperwork.

In the Order Book dialog box (Figure 10-19), click Set Up Account. (This button appears only if you've never ordered an iPhoto book before.) In any case, an Apple Account Sign-In screen appears. If you already have an Apple account, type in your Apple ID and account password here by all means. (An Apple ID is your email address; it's your .Mac address, if you have that.)

And if you've never established an Apple account before, click Create Account and fill in the blanks.

When your account info is taken care of, open the Ship To pop-up menu. Choose the lucky recipient of your book. If it's you, choose Myself. If not, you can choose Add New Address from this pop-up menu.

Note: You can order books if you live in Europe, Japan, or North America, but Apple offers shipping only to people in your own region.

From the Ship Via pop-up menu, indicate how you want the finished book shipped. For U.S. orders, "Standard" shipping takes about four days and costs $8. "Express" means overnight or second-day shipping (depending on when you place the order) and costs $15. An additional book sent to the same address costs another $1 for Standard shipping, or $2 for Express.

Indicate how many copies of the book you want, using the Quantity control. Click Buy Now. Go about your life for a few days, holding your breath until the book arrives.

And when it does, you'll certainly be impressed. The photos are printed on Indigo digital presses (fancy, digital, four-color offset machines). They're not what you'd call Kodak quality—or even photo-inkjet-on-glossy-paper quality. But the book itself is classy, it's handsome…and it smells good!

Photos Online—
and on Your Network

Holding a beautifully rendered glossy color print created from your own digital image is a glorious feeling. But unless you have an uncle in the inkjet cartridge business, you could go broke printing your own photos. Ordering high-quality prints with iPhoto is terrific fun, too, but it's slow and expensive. For the discerning digital photographer who craves both instant gratification and economy, the solution is to put your photos *online*—either by emailing them to others or posting them on the Web.

Emailing Photos

The most important thing to know about emailing photos is this: *full-size photos are usually too big to email.*

Suppose, for example, that you want to send three photos along to some friends— terrific shots you captured with your 5-megapixel camera. First, a little math: A typical 5-megapixel shot might consume two or three megabytes of disk space. So sending along just three shots would make at least a 6-megabyte package.

Why is that bad? Let us count the ways:

- It will take you 24 minutes to send (using a dial-up modem).

- It will take your recipients 24 minutes to download. During that time, the recipients must sit there, not even knowing what they're downloading. And when you're done hogging their time and account fees, they might not consider what you sent worth the wait.

• Even if they do open the pictures you sent, the average high-resolution shot is much too big for the screen. It does you no good to email somebody a 5-megapixel photo (3008 x 2000 pixels) when his monitor's maximum resolution is only 1024 x 768. If you're lucky, his graphics software will intelligently shrink the image to fit his screen; otherwise, he'll see only a gigantic nose filling his screen. But you'll still have to contend with his irritation at having waited 24 minutes for so much superfluous resolution.

• The typical Internet account has a limited mailbox size. If the mail collection exceeds 5 MB or so, that mailbox is automatically shut down until it's emptied. Your massive 6-megabyte photo package will push your hapless recipient's mailbox over its limit. She'll miss out on important messages that get bounced as a result.

For years, this business of emailing photos has baffled beginners and enraged experts—and for many people who haven't yet discovered iPhoto, the confusion continues.

It's all different when you use iPhoto. Instead of unquestioningly attaching a multi-megabyte graphic to an email message and sending the whole bloated thing off, its first instinct is to offer you the opportunity to send a scaled-down, reasonably sized version of your photo instead (see Figure 11-1). If you take advantage of this feature,

Figure 11-1:
The Mail Photo dialog box not only lets you choose the size of photo attachments, it also keeps track of how many photos you've selected and estimates how large your attachments are going to be, based on your selection.

FREQUENTLY ASKED QUESTION

Using iPhoto with PowerMail, QuickMail Pro, MailSmith…

Hey, I don't use Entourage, Eudora, AOL, or Apple Mail! How can I get iPhoto to send my photos via QuickMail? It's not listed as an option in the iPhoto's Mail Preferences.

You're right. Even if you have a different email program selected in the Internet panel of System Preferences, iPhoto won't fire up anything but Entourage, Eudora, or Mail when you click the Compose button.

There's a great workaround, though, thanks to the programming efforts of Simon Jacquier. Using his free utility, iPhoto Mailer Patcher, you can make iPhoto work obediently with MailSmith, PowerMail, QuickMail Pro, or even the aging Claris Emailer. It replaces the Mail button on iPhoto's bottom-edge panel with the icon of your preferred email program. You can download iPhoto Mailer Patcher from *http://homepage.mac.com/jacksim/software.*

your modem-using friends will savor the thrill of seeing your digital shots without enduring the agony of a half-hour email download.

The Mail Photo Command

iPhoto doesn't have any emailing features of its own. All it can do is get your pictures ready and hand them off to your existing email program. iPhoto's Mail Photo command works with four of the most popular Mac email programs—Microsoft Entourage, America Online, Qualcomm's Eudora, and Apple's own Mail (the free email program that came with your copy of Mac OS X).

If you currently use Apple's Mail program to handle your email, you're ready to start mailing your photos immediately. But if you want iPhoto to hand off to AOL, Entourage, or Eudora, you have to tell it so. Choose iPhoto→Preferences (or press ⌘-comma), click General, and then choose the email program you want from the Mail pop-up menu.

Once iPhoto knows which program you want to use, here's how the process works:

1. **Select the thumbnails of the photo(s) you want to email. Click the Email icon at the bottom of the iPhoto window.**

   The dialog box shown in Figure 9-1 appears.

2. **Choose a size for your photo(s).**

   This is the critical moment. As noted above, iPhoto offers to send a scaled-down version of the photo. The Size pop-up menu in the Mail Photo dialog box, shown in Figure 9-1, offers four choices.

   Choose **Small (240x320)** to keep your email attachments super small—and if you don't expect the recipient of your email to print the photo. (A photo this size can't produce a quality print any larger than a postage stamp.) On the other hand, your photos will consume less than 100 K apiece, making downloads quick and easy for those with dial-up connections.

Note: Don't be weirded out by the fact that iPhoto, for the first and only time, displays these dimensions backwards (height x width). What it should say, of course, is "Small (320x240)."

Choosing **Medium (640x480)** yields a file that will fill a nice chunk of your recipient's screen, with plenty of detail. This setting can trim a 2 MB, 4-megapixel image down to an attachment of less than 150 K.

The **Large (1280x960)** setting downsizes even your large photos to about 450 K, preserving enough pixels to make good 4 x 6 prints and completely fill the typical recipient's screen. In general, send these sparingly. Even if your recipients have a cable modem or DSL, these big files may still overflow their email boxes.

Despite all the cautions above, there may be times when a photo is worth sending at **Full Size (full quality)**, like when you're submitting a photo for printing or

---

publication. This works best when both you and the recipient have high-speed Internet connections and unlimited-capacity mail systems.

In any case, this option attaches a copy of your original photo at its original dimensions.

3. Include Titles and Comments, if desired.

Turn on these checkboxes if you want iPhoto to copy the title of the photo and any text stored in the Comments field into the body of the email. When Titles is turned on, iPhoto also inserts the photo's title into the Subject line of the email message.

Note: If multiple photos are selected when you generate an email message, the Titles option produces a generic subject line: "5 great iPhotos" (or whatever the number is). You can edit this proposed text, of course, before sending your email.

---

4. Click Compose.

At this point, iPhoto processes your photos—converting them to JPEG format and, if you requested it, resizing them. It then launches your email program, creates a new message, and attaches your photos to it. (Behind the scenes, iPhoto uses AppleScript to accomplish these tasks.) Type your recipient's email address into the "To:" box, and then click Send.

Your photos are on their merry way.

Tip: iPhoto always converts photos into JPEG format when emailing them. If you to want preserve the files' original format when emailing Photoshop files or PDFs, *don't* use the Mail Photo feature. Instead, create a new email message manually, and then drag the thumbnails from iPhoto directly into the message window to attach them. (If you want to resize the photos, export them first using the Share→Export command, which offers you a choice of scaling options.)

Publishing Photos on the Web

Putting your photos on the Web is the ultimate way to share them with the world. If the idea of enabling the vast throngs of the Internet-using public to browse, view, download, save, and print *your* photos sounds appealing, read on. It's amazingly easy to get your photos from iPhoto to the Internet.

Before you can post your photos online—and on your network using iPhoto's built-in Web tools—you need a *.Mac* account. That's Apple's suite of Internet services: email accounts, secure file-backup, Web-site hosting, and a few other extras. If you don't already have a .Mac account, see the "Getting a .Mac Account" box on the next page. Follow the directions, and you'll have one in less than five minutes. (A .Mac membership costs $100 per year; a two-month trial account is free.)

Three Roads to Webdom

iPhoto actually provides three different Web-publishing routes (two of which require a .Mac account), offering varying degrees of sophistication and complexity.

- **The easiest, most hands-off approach:** Use the HomePage feature within iPhoto. With only a couple of mouse clicks, this feature lets you construct Web pages, transfer them to the Internet, and make them available to the public. (A .Mac account is required.)

What's especially nice about the resulting Web page is that it presents a tidy collection of thumbnail images—a gallery that downloads relatively quickly into your audience's browsers. Then, when visitors click one of the thumbnails, a new window opens up to display the picture at full size (see Figure 11-2).

Figure 11-2:
You'd be nuts to stuff your full-size pictures onto the Web. The 70 percent of the population that uses dial-up modems would come after you with a lynch mob.

Fortunately, iPhoto adopts a respectful approach: It uploads only a gallery of smallish thumbnails (top). When visitors click one of them, a larger version of it opens (bottom right). This way, they wait only for the pictures they really want to see at full size. At this point, the left and right arrow buttons conduct a tour of the larger photos.

- **More effort, more design and layout options:** Copy photos from iPhoto to the Pictures folder of your iDisk (a 125 MB Internet-based "virtual hard drive" that comes with a .Mac account). Then use the HomePage features at Apple's Web site (instead of the layout tools in iPhoto) to set up your pages.

- **For the experienced Web page designer:** If you already have a Web site, you can use iPhoto's Export command to generate Web pages (HTML documents) that already contain your photos. You can upload these files, with the accompanying graphics, to your Web site, whether that's a .Mac account or any other Web-hosting service. (Most Internet accounts, including those provided by America Online, Earthlink, and other service providers, come with free space for Web pages uploaded in this way.)

  This is the most labor-intensive route, but it offers much more flexibility if you know how to work with HTML to create more sophisticated pages. It's also the route you should take if you hope to incorporate the resulting photo gallery into an existing Web site (that is, one in which the photos aren't the only attraction).

All three of these methods are detailed in the following pages.

Method 1: Use HomePage in iPhoto

Web publishing doesn't get any easier than it is with iPhoto's built-in HomePage feature. Your photos end up on a handsome-looking Web page in just a few quick steps—and you don't have to know the first thing about HTML.

1. **In iPhoto, select the photos you want to put on the Web, or click the album that contains them.**

   The selection can be one you've dragged pictures into, a smart album, the Last Roll(s) album, a year album, and so on. Or use the selection techniques described on page 115 to isolate a bunch of photos within an album.

Note: The HomePage feature in iPhoto can't handle more than 48 photos per Web page. If you want to "publish" more than that, you'll have to create a series of separate pages.

---

2. **Click the HomePage button.**

   After it connects to the Internet, iPhoto opens its Publish HomePage window, which offers a visual menu of predesigned frame styles for your photos (see Figure 11-3).

3. **Click a frame style.**

   The Publish HomePage window immediately displays a mock-up of how your finished Web page is going to look (Figure 11-3), displaying the thumbnails in whatever order they appear in iPhoto. You can choose from 23 different frame and text styles by clicking the photo thumbnails in the drawer alongside the window.

4. **Edit the page title, subtitle, and individual photo titles.**

   Just click inside a text block to edit it. You can use iPhoto's spelling checker, if you need the help (page 4). If you don't bother changing the photo names, iPhoto will simply use whatever titles the photos have in the program itself. (On the other hand, be careful: Any changes you make to the photo titles here are reflected in iPhoto.)

5. Select the layout options you want.

Use the Layout radio button in the lower-left corner of the window to switch between a two-column or three-column layout.

Figure 11-3:
Before you even open a Web browser, iPhoto shows you what your yet-to-be-created Web page is going to look like in the Publish HomePage window. In iPhoto 5, you can choose from among 14 canned Web designs, complete with frame styles, background colors, font schemes, and so on. Better yet, you're not looking at a page of HTML code.

The "Send Me a Message" option lets you include a link on your Web pages that lets your fans send their gushing admiration via email to your .Mac address. Turning on the Counter option adds an odometer-style counter to your page, so you can marvel (or despair) at the number of visitors who hit your pages once you publish them.

6. Click Publish.

This is the big moment: iPhoto connects to the .Mac Web site, scales down your photos to a reasonable size, and then transfers them to the server (Figure 11-4, top). When the process is complete, as indicated by the alert dialog box (Figure 11-4, bottom), you can go to the page and see your results.

Note: If you include larger photos in your Web page, iPhoto automatically scales them down to 800 x 600 pixel JPEG files, so that they can be more easily loaded and displayed in a Web browser. If you want your Web pages to include *exact* copies of your original photos—regardless of size or file format—you must copy them to your iDisk yourself and then use the online HomePage tools to create your Web pages, as described later in this chapter. Or use the "Export Web Pages" option described on page 237.

In any case, beware: Your iDisk holds only 125 MB of data—a limit that's easy to hit once you're addicted to self-publishing. (If you're *really* addicted, Apple is happy to raise the ceiling to 200 MB or even a gigabyte—for an additional annual fee.)

Figure 11-4:
Top: Click Publish to upload the photos to your .Mac account. Depending on the size and number of photos, this can take some time.

Bottom: Your new Web page has been born. You can see your finished page on the Web by click-ing Visit Page Now, but pay heed to the URL listed above the buttons; that's the Web address you need to give out if you want others to visit the page. (You can either click this address to visit the page, or drag across it to copy it.)

What you get when you're done

When you see what you've created with iPhoto, you'll be impressed: It's a professional-looking, stylishly titled Web page with thumbnails neatly arranged in a two- or three-column grid. Clicking a thumbnail opens an enlarged version of the picture, complete with Previous and Next buttons (Figure 11-2). You can return to your main index page at any time, or use the buttons in the slideshow window to navigate through the larger versions of your pictures.

Tip: In the URLs for your .Mac-hosted Web sites (such as *http://hompage.mac.com/yackell/PhotoAlbum2 .html*), capitalization counts—a point not to be forgotten when you share the site's address with friends. If you type one of these addresses into a Web browser with incorrect capitalization, you'll get only a "missing page" message.

Then again, maybe it's better to send your friends a much shorter, easier to remember address. You can convert long URLs into shorter ones using a free URL redirection service. At *http://www.here.is*, for example, you can sign up to turn *http://hompage.mac.com/gladys/PhotoAlbum22.html* into *www.here.is/gladys*. (And if the *here.is* service isn't working as you read this, do your own shopping for free redirection services by searching Google for "free URL redirection.")

Editing or deleting the Web page

The easiest way to edit your Web page is just to republish it from within iPhoto.

That is, make your changes (add or delete photos, rearrange them, rename them, and so on) and then click the HomePage button again at the bottom of the iPhoto screen. You'll be offered the chance to replace the existing gallery pages.

Deleting a Web page is easy once you've signed onto the .Mac HomePage Web site. Click the name of the page you want to delete, and then click the Delete button. When asked, "Are you sure?" click Yes.

Method 2: Use .Mac

Although using iPhoto's HomePage feature is incredibly simple, there's another way to go about creating, editing, and managing your photo galleries online: visit your .Mac Web site. The advantage here is that you can make changes to your photo gallery even when you're far from home, using any Web-connected computer. As a bonus, Apple offers templates that lets you use your photos in Web pages that aren't photo-gallery designs—there's a nice baby announcement page, for example.

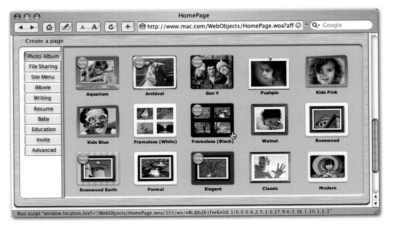

Figure 11-5:
Your Web-publishing options multiply considerably once you hit HomePage. In addition to the photo album themes shown here, you can also create resumés, personal newsletters, baby announcements, and party invitations. You can find these other options by clicking the "Create a page" tabs along the left side of the screen in the main HomePage screen.

To get started with HomePage, you first must copy the photos you want to publish from iPhoto to the Pictures folder of your iDisk—in fact, into a *new folder* in the Pictures folder, one folder per Web page. (If your iDisk isn't already onscreen, just choose Go→iDisk→My iDisk in the Finder, so that its icon appears on your desktop.) You can drag thumbnails directly out of iPhoto and into the Pictures folder on the iDisk.

Once your photos are in the iDisk's Pictures folder, you're ready to create your Web pages. Go to *www.mac.com*, sign in, click the HomePage icon, then click one of the "Create a page" tabs on the HomePage screen to view the styles of pages you can create. Some of the formatting options available are shown in Figure 11-5.

The first tab, Photo Album, offers much the same photo-gallery layouts that you find in iPhoto itself. But you're free to use your photos in the other Web page designs here, too, like the baby announcements, writing samples, invitations, and so on.

If you choose Photo Album, click the miniature image of the design you want. HomePage next asks which photos folder in your Pictures folder you want to place on your new Web page, as shown in Figure 11-6. Select a folder of pictures, and then click Choose. After a few moments, your new photo album page appears with photos already inserted in the appropriate spots.

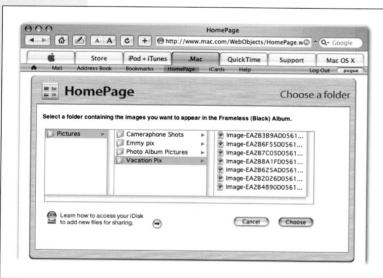

Figure 11-6:
Tell HomePage which photos to use. Two things to remember here: First, the pictures you choose must be in the Pictures folder of your iDisk, or HomePage won't see them; second, you can only choose a folder, not individual files. To include specific photos on a page, put them into a folder of their own in your Pictures folder before you start building the page.

(If you choose any other Web page design, like Baby, the routine is pretty much the same, except that you have to click Edit at the top of the page in order to choose the photos you want.)

To finish the project, click Edit at the top of the page to change the chunks of dummy text on the page. (Make an effort to avoid misspellings and typos, unless you want an audience of 400 million to think you slept through fourth-grade English.)

Finally, click Preview to see how the Web page will look. When everything is just the way you want it, click Publish. The page goes live, as indicated by the confirmation dialog box shown at the bottom of Figure 11-4.

Tip: You can create as many Web pages as your iDisk will hold, by the way. When you return to the main HomePage screen, a list of your existing Web pages appears, complete with New Page, Edit Page, and Delete Page buttons.

Corporations and professional Web designers may sniff at the simplicity of the result, but it takes *them* a lot longer than two minutes to do their thing.

Method 3: Export Web Pages

If you already have your own Web site, you don't need .Mac or HomePage to create an online photo album. Instead, you can use iPhoto's Export command to generate HTML pages that you can upload to any Web server. You're still saving a lot of time and effort—and you still get a handy, thumbnail gallery page like that shown back in Figure 11-2.

The Web pages you export directly from iPhoto don't include any fancy designs or themed graphics. In fact, they're kind of stark; just take a look at Figure 11-10.

But they offer more flexibility than the pages made with HomePage. For example, you can select the background color (or image) that appears on each page, specify the dimensions of thumbnails and images, and choose exactly how many thumbnails you want included on each page.

This is the best method if you plan to post the pages you create to a Web site of your own—especially if you plan on tinkering with the resulting HTML pages yourself.

Preparing the export

Here are the basic Web exporting steps:

1. **In iPhoto, select the photos you want to include on the Web pages.**

   Unlike the HomePage feature, the Export command puts no limit on the number of photos you can export to Web pages in one burst. Select as many photos as you want; iPhoto will generate as many pages as needed to accommodate all the pictures into your specified grid.

Tip: If you don't select any photos, iPhoto assumes you want to export all the photos in the current album, including the Photo Library or Last Roll(s) album.

---

2. **Choose Share→Export, or press Shift-⌘-E.**

   The Export Photos dialog box now appears.

3. **Click the Web Page tab.**

   You see the dialog box shown in Figure 11-7.

---

4. Set the Page attributes, including the title, grid size, and background.

The title you set here will appear in the title bar of each exported Web page, and as a header in the page itself.

Tip: For maximum compatibility with the world's computers and operating systems, use all lowercase letters and no spaces.

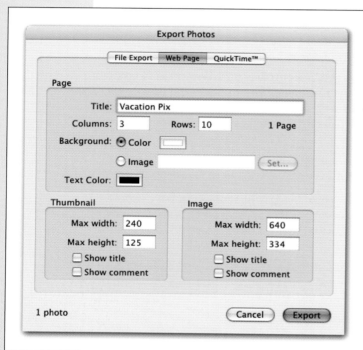

Figure 11-7:
As you change the size of the thumbnail grid or the size of the thumbnails, the number of pages generated to handle the images changes. The page count, based on your current settings, appears just to the right of the Rows field. The total count of the photos you're about to export appears in the lower-left corner of the window.

Use the Columns and Rows boxes to specify how many thumbnails you want to appear across and down your "index" page. (The little "1 page" indicator tells you how many pages this particular index gallery requires.)

If you'd like a background page color other than white, click the rectangular swatch next to the word Color, and follow the instructions in Figure 11-8. You can also pick a color for the text that appears on each page by clicking the Text Color swatch.

You can even choose a background *picture* instead of a solid background color. To make it so, click the Image button, and then the Set button to select the graphics file on your hard drive. Be considerate of your audience, however. A background graphic makes your pages take longer to load, and a busy background pattern can be very distracting.

5. **Specify how big you want the thumbnail images to be, and also specify a size for the expanded images that appear when you click them.**

The sizes iPhoto proposes are fine *if* all of your photos are horizontal (that is, in landscape orientation). If some are wide and some are tall, however, you're better off specifying *square* dimensions for both the thumbnails and the enlarged photos—240 x 240 for the thumbnails and 640 x 640 for the biggies, for example.

6. **Turn on "Show title" and "Show comment," if desired.**

This option draws upon the titles you've assigned in iPhoto, centering each picture's name underneath its thumbnail. The larger version of each picture will also bear this name when it opens into its own window.

Turning on the "Show comment" option displays any text you've typed into the Comments field for each picture in iPhoto. Depending on which checkboxes you turn on, you can have the comments appear under each thumbnail, under each larger size image, or both.

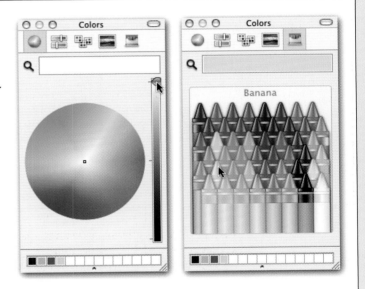

Figure 11-8:
Left: Drag the right-side slider all the way up to see the spectrum of colors available to you. Drag downwards to view darker colors.

Right: Alternatively, click one of the other color-picking buttons at the top of the dialog box. The crayon picker delights with both ease of use and creative color names, like Banana.

7. **Click Export.**

The Save dialog box appears.

8. **Choose a folder to hold the export files (or, by clicking New Folder, create one) and then click OK.**

The export process gets under way.

Examining the results

When iPhoto is done with the export, you end up with a series of HTML documents and JPEG images—the building blocks of your Web-site-to-be. A number of these icons automatically inherit the name of the *folder* into which you've saved them. If you export the files into a folder named Tahiti, for example, you'll see something like Figure 11-9:

- **Tahiti.html.** This is the main HTML page, containing the first thumbnails in the series that you exported. It's the home page, the index page, and the starting point for the exported pages.

- **Page1.html, Page2.html...** You see these only if you exported enough photos to require more than one page of thumbnails—that is, if iPhoto required *multiple* "home" pages.

- **Tahiti-Thumbnails.** This folder holds the actual thumbnail graphics that appear on each of the index pages.

- **Tahiti-Pages.** This folder contains the HTML documents (named Image1.html, Image2.html, Image3.html, and so on) that open when you click the thumbnails on the index pages.

- **Tahiti-Images.** This folder houses the larger JPEG versions of your photos. Yes, these are the *graphics* that appear on the Image HTML pages.

Tip: Some Web servers require that the default home page of your site be called *index.html.* To force your exported Web site to use this name for the main HTML page, save your exported pages into a folder called "index." Now the home page will have the correct name (*index.html*) and all the other image and page files will be properly linked to it. (After exporting, feel free to rename the folder. Naming it "index" was necessary only during the exporting process.)

Figure 11-9:
This is what a Web site looks like before it's on the Internet. All the pieces are here, filed exactly where the home page (called, in this example, Tahiti.html) can find them.

Once you've created these pages, it's up to you to figure out how to post them on the Internet where the world can see them. To do that, you'll have to upload all the exported files to a Web server, using an FTP program like the free RBrowser Lite (available from the "Missing CD" page of *www.missingmanuals.com*).

Only then do they look like real Web pages, as shown in Figure 11-10.

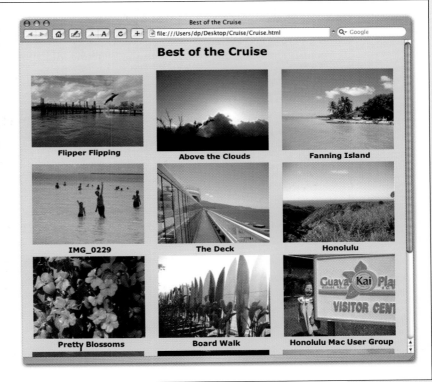

Figure 11-10:
Here's what a Web page exported straight from iPhoto looks like. The no-frills design is functional, but not particularly elegant. You have no control over fonts or sizes. On the other hand, the HTML code behind this page is 100 percent editable.

Enhancing iPhoto's HTML

If you know how to work with HTML code, you don't have to accept the unremarkable Web pages exported by iPhoto. You're free to tear into them with a full-blown Web authoring program like Adobe GoLive, Macromedia Dreamweaver, or the free Netscape Composer (*www.netscape.com*) to add your own formatting, headers, footers, and other graphics. (Heck, even Microsoft Word lets you open and edit HTML Web pages—plenty of power for changing iPhoto's layout, reformatting the text, or adding your own page elements.)

If you're a hard-core HTML coder, you can also open the files in a text editor like BBEdit or even TextEdit to tweak the code directly. With a few quick changes, you can make your iPhoto-generated Web pages look more sophisticated and less generic. Some of the changes you might want to consider making include:

- Change font faces and sizes.

- Change the alignment of titles.

- Add a footer with your contact information and email address.

- Add *metadata* tags (keywords) in the *page header,* so that search engines can locate and categorize your pages.

- Insert links to your other Web sites or relevant sites on the Web.

If you're *not* an HTML coder—or even if you are—you can perform many of these adjustments extremely easily with the BetterHTMLExport plug-in for iPhoto, described next.

Better HTML

iPhoto's Export command produces simple, serviceable Web page versions of your photo albums. Most people assume that if they want anything fancier, they need either HTML programming chops or a dedicated Web design program.

Actually, though, you can add a number of elegant features to your photo site using an excellent piece of add-on software that requires absolutely no hand coding or special editing software.

It's the fittingly named BetterHTMLExport, an inexpensive iPhoto plug-in that extends the features of iPhoto's own HTML Exporter.

You can download a copy of BetterHTMLExport from the "Missing CD" page of *www.missingmanuals.com,* among other places. The version for iPhoto 5 is a $20 shareware program.

Photo Sharing on the Network

One of the coolest features of iTunes is the way you can "publish" certain playlists on your home or office network, so that other people in the same building can listen to your tunes. Why shouldn't iPhoto be able to do the same thing with pictures?

In fact, it can. Here's how it works.

For this example, suppose that you're the master shutterbug who has all the cool shots.

On your Mac, choose iPhoto→Preferences and click Sharing. Turn on "Share my photos" (Figure 11-14).

You might be tempted to turn on "Share entire library," so that no crumb of your artistry will go unappreciated—but don't. Even the fastest Macs on the fastest networks will grind to a halt if you try to share even a medium-sized photo library. You are, after all, attempting to cram gigabytes of data through your network to the other Macs.

It's far more practical to turn on the checkboxes for the individual albums you want to share, as shown in Figure 11-14.

Unless you also turn on "Require password" (and make up a password), everyone on the network with iPhoto 4 or 5 can see your shared pictures.

Finally, close the Sharing window.

Figure 11-14:
If you turn on "Share entire library," you make all of your pictures available to others on the network—and doom your fans to a lifetime of waiting while gray empty boxes fill their iPhoto screens.

Alternatively, click "Share selected albums" and turn on the individual albums that you want to make public.

Either way, turning on Sharing makes only photos available on the network—not movie clips.

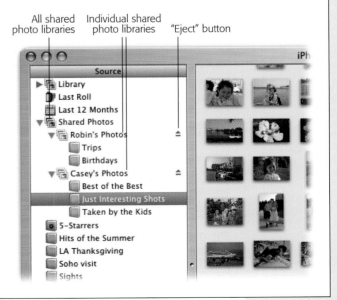

Figure 11-15:
You can't delete or edit the photos you've summoned from some other Mac. But you can drag them into your own albums (or your own Photo Library) to copy them. (The topmost category shown here, Shared Photos, appears only if iPhoto detects more than one shared iPhoto collection on the network.)

When you've had enough, click the Eject button. The flippy triangle, the list of albums, and the Eject button itself disappear. The names of shared collections (like "Casey's Photos" and "Robin's Photos" in this example) remains on the screen, in case you want to bring them back for another look later.

All shared photo libraries   Individual shared photo libraries   "Eject" button

At this point, other people on your network will see *your* albums show up in *their* Source lists, above the list of their own albums; see Figure 11-15. (Or at least they will if they have "Look for shared photos" turned on in their iPhoto Preferences.)

As you may know, when you share iTunes music over a network, other people can only *listen* to your songs—they can't actually *have* them. (The large, well-built lawyers of the American record companies have made sure of that.)

But iPhoto is another story. Nobody's going to issue you a summons for freely distributing your own photos. So once you've jacked into somebody else's iPhoto pictures via the network, feel free to drag them into your own iPhoto albums, thereby copying them onto your own Mac. Now you can edit them, print them, and otherwise treat them like your own photos.

The QuickTime Slideshow

As Chapter 9 makes clear, once you select your images and choose the music to go with them, iPhoto orchestrates the production and presents it live on your Mac's screen as a slideshow.

Which is great, as long as everyone in your social circle lives within six feet of your screen.

The day will come when you want friends and family who live a little farther away to be able to see your slideshows. Sure, you could pack up your Mac and fly across the country, but wouldn't it be easier to simply send the slideshow as a file attachment that people can play on their own computers?

That's the beauty of QuickTime, a portable multimedia container built into every Mac. Even if the recipient uses a Windows PC (every family has its black sheep), your photos will meet their public; QuickTime movies play just as well on HPs and Dells as they do on iMacs and PowerBooks.

The trick is to convert your well-composed iPhoto slideshow into a standalone QuickTime movie. You'll then have a file on your hard drive that you can email to other people, post on your Web page for downloading, burn onto a CD, and so on. When played on the computer or TV screen, your grateful audience will see your photos, large and luscious, accompanied by the music and effects you chose for them.

Exporting an Instant Slideshow

Before you send your "slideshow movie" to hapless relatives who will have to endure downloading it over a dial-up connection, make sure it's worth watching in the first place.

Step 1: Perfect the Slideshow

As you review your presentation, place the pictures into the proper sequence, re-membering that you won't be there to verbally "set up" the slideshow and comment as it plays. Ask yourself, "If I knew nothing about this subject, would this show make sense to me?"

Which photos make the cut

If you're used to the slideshow feature described in Chapter 9, the method for specifying which photos are exported to your QuickTime movie might throw you.

- If *one* thumbnail is selected, that's all you'll get in the finished QuickTime movie—the world's shortest slideshow. (This is the part that might throw you: An iPhoto slideshow would begin with that one selected photo and then move on from there, showing you all the rest of the photos in the album.)

- If *several* thumbnails are selected, only they make it into the QuickTime slideshow movie.

- If *no* thumbnails are selected, the entire album's worth of photos wind up in the show.

When you're ready to convert your presentation to a QuickTime movie, choose Share→Export. The Export Photos dialog box appears, as shown in Figure 11-16. Click the QuickTime tab, where you have some important decisions to make.

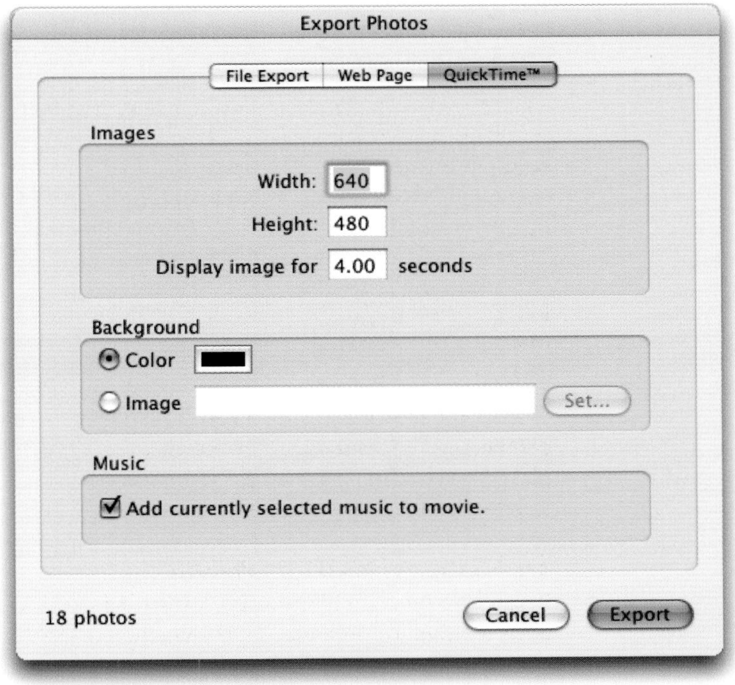

Figure 11-16:
Here's the Export dialog box with the QuickTime tab selected. This is the airlock, the womb, the last time you'll be able to affect your movie before it's born. You're free to change these dimensions, however.

If the movie will be played back from a hard drive, you may want to crank up the dimensions close to the size of the screen itself: 800 x 600 is a safe bet if you're not sure. Remember, though, you have to leave some room for the QuickTime Player controls, so that your audience can start and stop the movie.

Step 2: Choose the Movie Dimensions

Specifying the width and height for your movie affects not only how big it is on the screen during playback, but also its file size, which may become an issue if you plan to email the movie to other people. iPhoto generally proposes 640 x 480 pixels. That's an ideal size: big enough for people to see some detail in the photo, but usually small enough to send, in compressed form, by email.

- **Proportion considerations.** All of these suggestions assume, by the way, that your photos' dimensions are in a 4:3 ratio, the way they come from most cameras. That way, they'll fit nicely into the standard QuickTime playback window.

- **Size considerations.** As you choose dimensions, however, bear in mind that they also determine the *file size* of the resulting QuickTime movie. If you plan to send the movie by email or post it on a Web page, watch out for ballooning file sizes that will slow dial-up sufferers to a crawl.

- **Managing music.** In the Music section of your QuickTime export dialog box, you can turn on "Add currently selected music to movie." (If you want a different soundtrack, click Cancel, click the Play Slideshow triangle beneath the Source list, click the Music tab, choose a different song from, and click Save Settings.)

To save file size, you could turn off this box. That 320 x 240 movie would shrink to a mere 350 K—but you'd also wind up with a silent movie.

Fortunately, there is a middle road; see the box below.

Step 3: Seconds per Photo

How many seconds do you want each picture to remain on the screen before the next one appears? You specify this number using the "Display image for ___ seconds" box in the QuickTime Export dialog box.

When you first open the dialog box, iPhoto proposes whatever frame rate you used in your original slideshow. You're free to change it to other timings. (Although you can *type* a frame rate shorter than one second, iPhoto won't actually create the show with a rate any faster than one image per second. So much for artistic license.)

POWER USERS' CLINIC

Musical Liposuction

By cutting its soundtrack's bit rate (a measure of its sound quality) from 192 to, say, 128 kbps, you can shrink the file size for a hypothetical 320 x 240–pixel movie from 2.1 MB to 1.5 MB, with very little sonic difference.

Start by choosing iTunes→Preferences. In the Preferences dialog box, click the Importing icon. From the Import Using pop-up menu, choose MP3 Encoder. Then, from the Setting pop-up menu, choose "Good Quality (128 kbps)." (A lower quality number will result in even smaller files.) Click OK.

Now highlight the track you want to add to your slideshow, and then choose Advanced→Convert Selection to MP3.

iTunes converts the song into a duplicate with the new, lower sample rate. The song's name appears in the iTunes list just below the original. (You might want to rename it to differentiate it from the original song by highlighting it and then choosing File→Get Info. Click Info in the resulting dialog box.)

Now return to iPhoto. Select your new resampled song as the soundtrack.

When you export the slideshow to QuickTime, you'll find that it's much more svelte, but sounds practically identical to the puffier version.

Step 4: Background Colors

The color or image you choose in the Background section of the dialog box will appear as the first and last frames of the export. It will also fill in the margins of the frame when a vertically oriented or oddly proportioned picture appears. Generally speaking, white, light gray, or black makes the best background.

If you click the Image button and then the Set button next to it, you can navigate your hard drive in search of a *graphics* file to use as the slideshow background.

Step 5: Export the Movie

Having specified the dimensions, frame rate, music, and background for your movie, there's nothing left but to click the Export button in the dialog box. You'll be asked to specify a name and folder location for the movie (leaving the proposed suffix *.mov* at the end of the name), and then click Save. After a moment of computing, iPhoto returns to its main screen.

Press ⌘-H to hide iPhoto; then navigate to the folder you specified and double-click the movie to play it in QuickTime Player, the movie-playing program that comes with every Mac. When the movie opens, click the Play triangle or press the Space bar to enjoy your newly packaged slideshow (Figure 11-17).

Whenever playback is stopped, you can even "walk" through the slides manually by pressing the right-arrow key twice (for the next photo) or the left-arrow key once (for the previous one).

Figure 11-17:
Once you're in QuickTime Player, you can control the playback of the slideshow in a number of ways. If you don't feel like clicking and dragging onscreen controls, the arrow keys adjust the volume (up and down) or step through the photos one at a time (right and left).

Exporting a Saved Slideshow

But what if you've created a more elaborate slideshow, using the new iPhoto 5 Slideshow editing mode? What if there's a Slideshow icon in your Source list at this moment, representing hours you've spent perfecting your pans, fiddling with your fades, and tweaking your timings into a work of art? This creation isn't for posting on the Web. It's designed to be savored in all its glory on a 30-inch Cinema Display. And you want to preserve every nuance when you export your masterpiece to QuickTime.

To do so, click the slideshow icon in the Source list and, once again, choose Share→— Export. This time, though, the Export dialog box (Figure 11-16) asks you to make only three decisions: what you're going to name the file, where you're going to save it on your hard drive, and what its dimensions are. Make your selections, click the Export button, then go walk the dog. iPhoto will take some time to convert your Saved slideshow to a QuickTime movie.

Building a Custom Screen Saver

Mac OS X's screen saver feature is so good, it's pushed more than one Windows user over the edge into making the switch to Mac OS X. When this screen saver kicks in (after several minutes of inactivity on your part), your Mac's screen becomes a personal movie theater. The effect is something like a slideshow, except that the pictures don't simply appear one after another and sit there on the screen. Instead, they're much more animated. They slide gently across the screen, zooming in or zooming out, smoothly dissolving from one to the next.

Mac OS X comes equipped with a few photo collections that look great with this treatment: forests, space shots, and so on. But let the rabble use those canned screen savers. You, a digital master, can use your own photos as screen saver material.

Meet the Screen Saver

When you're ready to turn one of your own photo collections into a screen saver, fire up iPhoto. Collect the photos in an album, if they're not in one already (Chapter 7), and then select the album in the Source list. Or, if you're using Mac OS X [-10.3 or later, simply highlight the photos you want to use as screen saver fodder, whether they're in an album or not.

Tip: Horizontal shots fill your monitor better than vertical ones—the verticals have fat black bars on either side to fill the empty space.

If your camera captures images at a 3:2 width-to-height ratio instead of 4:3, or if you have an Apple widescreen monitor (like the 15-inch PowerBook screen or the 17-inch iMac screen), there's one more step. You might want to crop the photos, or copies of them, accordingly to maximize their impact.

Finally, click the Desktop icon at the bottom iPhoto panel (or, if you don't see it there, choose Share→Desktop).

You go straight to the Desktop & Screen Saver panel of System Preferences (shown in Figure 11-18). Here's the key step (a change from iPhoto 4): Click the Screen Saver tab. You'll see that in the System Preferences "source list," something called iPhoto Selection is selected. Set up your screensaver options as described in the box on the facing page, and then close System Preferences.

Figure 11-18:
In Mac OS X 10.3 and later, all of your iPhoto albums are listed in the Screen Saver panel of the Desktop & Screen Saver preferences window. Just pick the one you want to use as a screen saver, or click iPhoto Selection (in the upper part of the list) to "play" whatever pictures you've selected in iPhoto. Mac OS X turns your photos into a smooth, full-screen slideshow.

Ready to view the splendor of your very own homemade screen saver? If you have the patience of a Zen master, you can now sit there, motionless, staring at your Mac for the next half an hour or so—or as long as it takes for Mac OS X to conclude that you're no longer working and finally begin displaying your images on the screen.

Tip: Your screen saver slideshows look best if your pictures are at least the same resolution as your Mac's monitor. (In most cases, if your digital camera has a resolution of 1 megapixel or better, you're all set.)

If you're not sure what your screen resolution is, go to System Preferences and click the Displays icon (or just consult the Displays mini-menu next to your menu bar clock, if it appears there).

One-Click Desktop Backdrop

iPhoto's desktop-image feature is the best way to drive home the point that photos of your children (or dog, or mother, or self) are the most beautiful in the world. You pick one spectacular shot to replace the standard Mac OS X swirling blue desktop pattern. It's like refrigerator art on steroids.

Creating wallpaper in iPhoto is so easy that you could change the picture every day—and you may well want to. In iPhoto, click a thumbnail and then click the Desktop button on the bottom panel (or choose Share→Desktop). Even though the iPhoto window is probably filling your screen, the change happens instantly behind it. Your desktop is now filled with the picture you chose.

UP TO SPEED

Screen Saver Basics

You don't technically need a screen saver to protect your monitor from burn-in. Today's energy-efficient CRT monitors wouldn't burn an image into the screen unless you left them on continuously for two years, and flat-panel screens never burn in.

No, screen savers are about entertainment, pure and simple.

In Mac OS X, when you click a module's name in the screen saver list, you see a mini version of it playing back in the Preview screen.

You can control when your screen saver takes over your monitor. For example, the "Start screen saver" slider lets you specify when the screen saver kicks in (after what period of keyboard or mouse inactivity).

When you click the Hot Corners button, you're presented with a pane than lets you turn each corner of your monitor into a hot spot. Whenever you roll your cursor into that corner, the screen saver either turns on instantly (great when you happen to be shopping on eBay at the moment your boss walks by) or stays off permanently (for when you're reading onscreen or watching a movie).

If you use Mac OS X 10.3 or later, you can use two corners for controlling the screen saver and the other two to activate Exposé (Mac OS X's window-hiding feature).

In any case, pressing any key or clicking the mouse always removes the screen saver from your screen and takes you back to whatever you were doing.

The Options button reveals the additional settings illustrated here, some of which are very useful. Turn off "Crop slides to fit on screen," for example, if you want the Mac to show each photo, edge to edge (even if it has to use black bars to fill the rest of your monitor); otherwise, it enlarges each photo to fill the screen, often lopping off body parts in the process. (If "Crop slides" is on, you can also turn on "Keep slides centered" to prevent the Mac from panning across each photo.)

And turning off "Zoom back and forth," of course, eliminates the majestic, cinematic zooming in and out of successive photos that makes the screen saver look so darned cool.

Note: If you choose *several* thumbnails or even an album, iPhoto assumes that you intend to make Mac OS X *rotate* among your selected photos, displaying a new one every few minutes on your desktop throughout the day. To confirm its understanding, Mac OS X opens up the relevant panel of System Preferences, so that you can click the Desktop tab and specify *how often* you want the photos to change.

Just three words of advice. First, choose a picture that's at least as big as your screen (1024 x 768 pixels, for example). Otherwise, Mac OS X will stretch it to fit, distorting the photo in the process. (If you're *really* fussy, you can even crop the photo first to the exact measurements of the screen; in fact, the first command in iPhoto's Constrain pop-up menu [page 152] lists the exact dimensions of your screen, so you can crop the designated photo [or a copy of it] to fit precisely.)

Second, horizontal shots work much better than vertical ones; iPhoto blows up vertical shots to fit the width of the screen, potentially chopping off the heads and feet of your loved ones.

Finally, if a photo doesn't precisely match the screen's proportions, note the pop-up menu shown at bottom in Figure 11-19. It lets you specify how you want the discrepancy handled. Your choices include:

- **Fill screen.** This option enlarges or reduces the image so that it fills every inch of the desktop. If the image is small, the low-resolution stretching can look awful. Conversely, if the image is large and its dimensions don't precisely match your

Figure 11-19:
If your photo doesn't fit the screen perfectly, choose a different option from the pop-up menu in the Desktop & Screen Saver preference panel.

While you're in the Desktop & Screen Saver or Screen Effects preferences pane, you might notice that all of your iPhoto albums are listed below the collection of images that came with your Mac. You can navigate through those albums to find a new desktop image. This approach isn't as fast (or fun) as picking pictures in iPhoto, but if for some reason iPhoto isn't open on your Mac (heaven forbid!), you can take care of business right there in System Preferences.

screen's, parts get chopped off. At least this option never distorts the picture, as the "Stretch" option does (below).

- **Stretch to fill screen.** Use this option at your peril, since it makes your picture fit the screen exactly, come hell or high water. Unfortunately, larger pictures may be squished vertically or horizontally as necessary, and small pictures are drastically blown up and squished, usually with grisly-looking results.

- **Center.** This command centers the photo neatly on the screen. If the picture is larger than the screen, you see only the middle; the edges of the picture are chopped off as they extend beyond your screen.

But if the picture is smaller than the screen, it won't fill the entire background; instead it just sits right smack in the center of the monitor at actual size. Of course, this leaves a swath of empty border all the way around your screen. As a remedy, Apple provides a color-swatch button next to the pop-up menu. When you click it, the Color Picker appears, so that you can specify the color in which to frame your little picture.

- **Tile.** This option makes your picture repeat over and over until the multiple images fill the entire monitor. (If your picture is larger than the screen, no such tiling takes place. You see only the top center chunk of the image.)

And one last thing: If public outcry demands that you return your desktop to one of the standard system backdrops, open System Preferences, click the Desktop & Screen Saver icon, click the Desktop button if necessary, choose Apple Backgrounds or Solid Colors in the list box at the left of the window, then take your pick.

iPhoto File Management

When you don't have to buy film or pay for processing, photos have a way of piling up very quickly. Apple says iPhoto can hold an unlimited number of photos and, technically, that's true (as long as you have enough memory and hard drive space). But in fact, once you go much above 25,000 pictures, iPhoto winds up gasping for RAM and acts as if you've slathered it with a thick coat of molasses.

For some photo fans, this comes as a distressing bit of news. You downloaded the software, entrusted your best work to it, even bought a book about it—and now you learn it's going to cop out on you in another couple of years.

Fortunately, a little knowledge—and a handful of blank, recordable CDs or DVDs—can keep you happily in iPhoto at reasonable speeds. The trick is learning how to manage iPhoto's library files. These techniques will also serve you when you want to transfer photos to another Mac or when it comes time to back up your photo collection.

This chapter covers both iPhoto's behind-the-scenes filing system and what's involved in backing it up: swapping photo libraries, burning them to CD, transferring them to other machines, and merging them together.

About iPhoto Discs

iPhoto CDs are discs (either CDs or DVDs) that you can create in iPhoto to archive your entire Photo Library—or any selected portion of it—with just a few mouse clicks.

The beauty of iPhoto's Burn command is that it exports much more than just the photos themselves to a disc. It also copies the thumbnails, titles, keywords, comments, ratings, and all the other important data about your Photo Library. Once you've burned all of this valuable information to disc, you can do all sorts of useful things:

- Make a backup of your whole Photo Library for safekeeping.

- Transfer specific photos, albums, or a whole Photo Library to another Mac without losing all your keywords, descriptions, ratings, and titles.

- Share discs with other iPhoto fans so that your friends or family can view your photo albums in their own copies of iPhoto.

- Offload photos to CD or DVD as your photo collection grows, to keep your current Photo Library at a trim, manageable size.

- Merge separate Photo Libraries (such as the one on your iBook and the one on your iMac) into a single master Photo Library.

Note: One thing an iPhoto CD is *not* good for is sharing your photos with somebody who doesn't have iPhoto! An iPhoto CD from iPhoto 5 is designed *exclusively* for transferring pictures into another copy of iPhoto 5. (iPhoto 5 can read iPhoto 2 and 4 discs, though.) If you just want to share the photos, export them as files (page 265) or a QuickTime slideshow (page 244) and burn the result to a CD .

Burning an iPhoto CD or DVD

All you need to create an iPhoto CD is a Mac with a CD or DVD burner.

1. **Select the photos that you want to include on the disc.**

   You can hand-select some photos (page 115), click a Source list icon (album, book, slideshow), or click the Photo Library icon to burn your whole photo collection.

   In any case, the photo-viewing area should now be showing the photos you want to save onto a disc.

2. **Choose Share→Burn Disc.**

   A dialog box appears, prompting you to insert a blank disc. Pop in the disc; the dialog box vanishes after a few moments.

3. **Check the size of your selection to make sure it will fit.**

   Take a look at the Info panel at the bottom of the iPhoto window, as shown in Figure 12-1; the little graph shows you how much of the disc will be filled up. If the set of photos you want to burn is smaller than 650 or 700 megabytes (for a CD) or about 4.3 gigabytes (for a DVD), you're good to go. You can burn the whole thing to a single disc.

   If your photo collection is larger than that, however, it's not going to fit. You'll have to split your backup operation across multiple discs. Select whatever number of photo albums or individual pictures that *will* fit on a single disc, using the indicator shown in Figure 12-1 as your guide. (Also shown in the figure: the Name box, where you can name the disc you're about to burn.)

For example, you might decide to copy the 2003 folder onto one disk, the 2004 folder onto another, and so on, using the built-in year "collections" in the Source list as your source material.

After burning one disc, select the next set of photos, and burn another CD or DVD. Burn as many discs as needed to contain your entire collection of photos. If and when you ever need to restore your photos from the multiple discs, you'll be able to merge them back together into a single Photo Library using the technique described in "Merging Photo Libraries" later in this chapter.

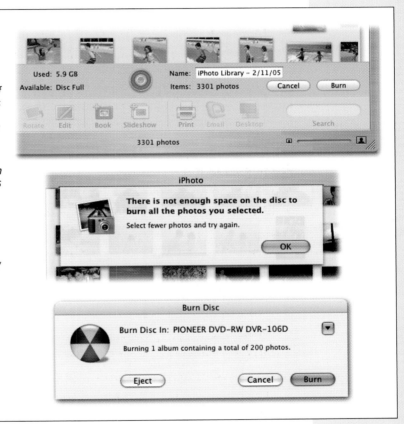

Figure 12-1:
Top: Once you've clicked Burn and inserted a blank disc, this Info panel lets you know how close you are to filling the disc. The indicator icon updates itself as you select or deselect photos and albums to show you how much free space is available on the disc.

Middle: If your photos take up more space than is available on the disc, the little disc icon turns red—and when you click Burn, you see the Disc Full message shown here.

Bottom: If all is well, however, you get this message instead. Click Burn and sit back to enjoy the fruits of your Mac's little internal laser.

4. **Click the Burn button.**

   As you can see in Figure 12-1, you'll either get a "not enough space" message or a "Burn Disc" message. If you get the latter, you're ready to proceed.

5. **Click the Burn button.**

   First, iPhoto makes a disk image—a sort of pretend disk that serves as a temporary holding area for the photos that will be burned. Next, iPhoto copies the photos from your iPhoto Library folder to the disk image.

Finally, the real burning begins. When the process is done, your Mac spits out the finished CD or DVD, ready to use, bearing whatever name you gave it.

Tip: You can safely bail out of the CD-creating process at any time by clicking the Cancel button when the Progress dialog box first appears.

But don't click the Stop button once the Burning dialog box appears. At that point, your CD or DVD drive is already busy etching data onto the disc itself. Clicking Stop will bring the burning to a screeching halt, leaving you with a partially burned, nonfunctioning disc.

What you get

The finished iPhoto disc contains not just your photos, but a clone of your iPhoto Library folder as well. In other words, this disc includes all the thumbnails, keywords, comments, ratings, photo album information—even the unedited original versions of your photos that iPhoto keeps secretly tucked away.

If you want to view the contents of your finished CD in iPhoto, pop the disc back into the drive. If iPhoto isn't running, your Mac opens it automatically.

Moments later, the icon for the CD appears in the Source list of the iPhoto window, as shown in Figure 12-2. If you click the disc's icon, the photos it contains appear in the photo-viewing area, just as if they were stored in your Photo Library.

Figure 12-2:
Pop an iPhoto CD into your Mac and it appears right along with your albums in iPhoto. Click on the disc icon itself or one of the disc's album icons (as shown here) to display the photos it contains. In essence, iPhoto is giving you access to two different libraries at once—the active Photo Library on your Mac's hard drive and a second library on the CD.

You can't make changes to them, of course—that's the thing about CDs and DVDs. But you can copy them into your own albums, and make changes to the copies.

When Not to Burn

The Burn command is convenient for creating quick backups, archiving portions of your Photo Library, or transferring photos to another Mac. But it's definitely *not* the best way to share your photos with Windows users, or even other Mac fans running Mac OS 9.

Think about it: Burning an iPhoto CD automatically organizes your photos into a series of numerically named subfolders inside an iPhoto Library folder, surrounded by scads of special data files like *.attr* files, *Library.cache,* and *Dir.data.* All of this makes perfect sense to iPhoto, but is mostly meaningless to anyone—or, rather, any computer—that doesn't have iPhoto. A Windows user, for example, would have to dig through folder after folder on your iPhoto CD to find and open your photos.

So if the destination of your CD or DVD isn't another iPhoto nut, *don't* use the Burn command. Instead, export the photos using the File Export or Web Page options described in Chapter 11. The pictures won't have any ratings, comments, keywords, and so on, but they'll be organized in a way that's much easier for non-iPhoto folk to navigate.

iPhoto Backups

Bad things can happen to digital photos. They can be accidentally deleted with a slip of your pinkie. They can become mysteriously corrupted and subsequently unopenable. They can get mangled by a crashed hard disk and be lost forever. Losing one-of-a-kind family photos can be extremely painful, and in some documented cases, even marriage-threatening. So if you value your digital photos, you should back them up regularly—perhaps after each major batch of new photos joins your collection.

Backing Up to CD or DVD

The quickest and most convenient way to back up your Photo Library is to archive it onto a blank CD or DVD using iPhoto's Burn command, as described on the previous pages. (If you don't have a disc-burning drive, don't worry; the next section explains how to perform a complete iPhoto backup without burning a disc.)

If anything bad ever happens to your photo collection, you'll be able to restore your Photo Library from the backup discs, with all your thumbnails, keywords, comments, and other tidbits intact.

To restore your photo collection from such a backup, see "Merging Photo Libraries" later in this chapter.

Backing Up (No CD Burner)

Fortunately, even if you don't have a CD burner (and therefore can't use iPhoto's Burn command), backing up thousands of photos is a simple task for the iPhoto maven. After all, one of iPhoto's main jobs is to keep all your photos together in *one* place— one folder that's easy to copy to a backup disk of any kind.

That all-important folder is the *iPhoto Library* folder, which resides inside the Pictures folder of the Home folder that bears your name. If your user name (the short name you use to log into Mac OS X) is *corky,* the full path to your iPhoto Library folder from your main hard drive window drive is: Users→corky→Pictures→iPhoto Library.

As described in Chapter 7, the iPhoto Library folder contains not just your photos, but also a huge assortment of additional files, including:

- All the thumbnail images in the iPhoto window.

- The original, safety copies of photos you've edited in iPhoto.

- Various data files that keep track of your iPhoto keywords, comments, ratings, and photo albums.

To prepare for a disaster, you should back up *all* of these components.

To perform a complete backup, copy the entire iPhoto Library folder to another location. Copying it to a different drive—to an iPod, say, or to the hard drive of another Mac via network—is the best solution. (Copying it to another folder on the *same* disk means you'll lose both the original iPhoto Library folder and its backup if, say, your hard drive crashes or your computer is hit by an asteroid.)

Note: Of course, you can also back up your photos by dragging their thumbnails out of the iPhoto window and into a folder or disk on your desktop, once you've dragged the iPhoto window to one side.

Unfortunately, this method doesn't preserve your keywords, comments, album organization, or any other information you've created in iPhoto. If something bad happens to your Photo Library, you'll have to import the raw photos again and reorganize them from scratch.

Managing Photo Libraries

iPhoto can comfortably manage as many as 25,000 photos in a single collection, give or take a few thousand, depending on your Mac model and how much memory it has.

But for some people, 25,000 pictures isn't a very distant threshold. As your collection of digital photos grows into the tens of thousands (and if you have a digital camera, this will happen sooner than you think), iPhoto eventually starts slowing down as it sifts through more and more data to find and display your pictures. At that point, scrolling the photos in the main Photo Library becomes an exercise in patience that would drive a Zen master crazy.

When your Photo Library becomes too large to manage comfortably, you can always do what people used to do way back in iPhoto 2, when the limit was only *2,000* pictures: Archive some of the photos to CD or DVD using the Burn command described earlier, and then *delete* the archived photos from your library to shrink it down in size. For example, you might choose to archive older photos, or albums you rarely use.

Note: Remember, archiving photos to CD using the Burn command doesn't automatically remove them from iPhoto; you have to do that part yourself. If you don't, your Photo Library won't get any smaller. Just make sure that the CD you've burned works properly before deleting your original photos from iPhoto.

Multiple iPhoto Libraries

Here's a fantastic way to keep your Photo Library from becoming impossibly bloated without transferring part of it to a CD: Start a new one, right there on your hard drive.

Here's what splitting your photo collection into smaller libraries gains you:

- iPhoto itself is *much* faster, especially during scrolling, because there are fewer photos in it.

- You can keep different types of collections or projects separate. You might want to maintain a Home library for personal use, for example, and a Work library for images that pertain to your business. Or you can start a new library every other year.

Creating new libraries

For the first time ever, iPhoto provides a built-in tool for retiring one Photo Library and starting a fresh one. You can use this trick both to create new libraries and, thereafter, to switch back and forth between several of them:

1. **Quit iPhoto.**

   You're going to do the next step in the Finder.

2. **While pressing the Option key, open iPhoto again.**

   When iPhoto starts up, it senses that you're up to something. It offers you the chance to create a new library, or to choose an existing one (Figure 12-3).

Figure 12-3:
If you hide the iPhoto Library from iPhoto, the program invites you either to find it or to create a new one. If your goal is to begin a fresh library for the new year, for example, click Create Library.

Choose Photo Library

iPhoto needs a Photo Library to continue. You may choose an existing Photo Library or create a new one.

Quit   Create Library...   Choose Library...

3. **Click Create Library. In the following dialog box, type a name for the new library** (like *New iPhoto Library*) **and click Save.**

   You're offered not only the chance to create a new library, but even the opportunity to name it anything you like and choose a location for it that's not your regularly scheduled Pictures folder.

   When iPhoto finishes opening, all remnants of your old Photo Library are gone. You're left with a blank window, ready to import photos.

Using this technique, you can spawn as many new Photo Libraries as you need. You can archive the old libraries on CD or DVD, move them to another Mac, or just keep them somewhere on your hard drive so that you can swap any one of them back in whenever you need it, as shown in Figure 12-4.

As for *how* you swap them back in you have two options: Apple's way, and an easier way.

Swapping libraries (Apple's method)

Once you've built yourself at least two iPhoto Library folders, you can use the same Option-key trick (see step 2 above) to switch among them. When the dialog box in Figure 12-3 appears, click Choose Library, and then find and open the library folder that you want to open.

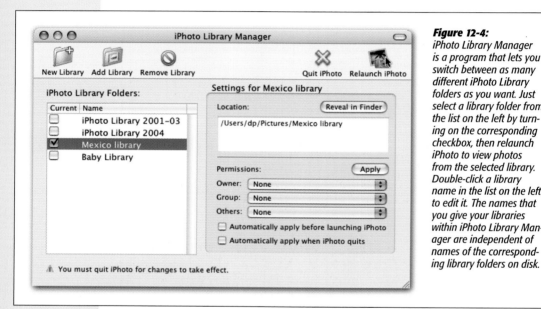

Figure 12-4:
iPhoto Library Manager is a program that lets you switch between as many different iPhoto Library folders as you want. Just select a library folder from the list on the left by turning on the corresponding checkbox, then relaunch iPhoto to view photos from the selected library. Double-click a library name in the list on the left to edit it. The names that you give your libraries within iPhoto Library Manager are independent of names of the corresponding library folders on disk.

When iPhoto finishes reopening, you'll find the new set of photos in place.

Swapping libraries (automatic method)

If that Option-key business sounds a little disorienting, you're not alone. Brian Webster, a self-proclaimed computer nerd, thought the same thing—but *he* decided to do something about it. He wrote iPhoto Library Manager, a free program that streamlines the creation and swapping of iPhoto libraries. Waste no time in downloading it from the "Missing CD" page at *www.missingmanuals.com* or Brian's own site at *http://homepage.mac.com/bwebster*.

The beauty of this program is that it offers a tidy list of all your Library folders; you can switch among them with two quick clicks.

Here are a few pointers for using iPhoto Library Manager:

• The program doesn't just activate *existing* iPhoto Library folders; it can also create new Library folders for you. Just click the New Library button in the toolbar, choose a location and name for the library, and click OK (see Figure 12-4).

- You still have to quit and relaunch iPhoto for a change in libraries to take effect. Conveniently, iPhoto Library Manager includes Quit iPhoto and Relaunch iPhoto buttons in its toolbar.

Tip: You can also switch libraries using the pop-up menu from iPhoto Library Manager's Dock icon.

- iPhoto Library Manager is fully AppleScriptable. If you're handy with writing Apple-Script scripts, you can write one that swaps your various libraries automatically with a double-click.

Merging Photo Libraries

You've just arrived home from your photo safari of deepest Kenya. You're jet-lagged and dusty, but your iBook is bursting at the seams with fresh photo meat. You can't wait to transfer the new pictures into your main Photo Library—you know, the one on your Power Macintosh G5 with 2 gigs of RAM and a 35-inch Apple Imax Display.

Or, less dramatically, suppose you've just upgraded to iPhoto 5. You're thrilled that you can now fit 25,000 pictures into a single library—but you still have six old iPhoto 2 Library folders containing about 2,000 pictures each.

In both cases, you have the same problem: How are you supposed to merge the libraries into a single, unified one?

How Not to Do It

You certainly can combine the *photos* of two Macs' Photo Libraries—just export them from one (Share→Export) and then import them into the other (File→Add to Library). As a result, however, you lose all of your album organization, comments, and keywords.

Your next instinct might be: "Hey, I know! I'll just drag the iPhoto Library folder from computer #1 into the iPhoto window of computer #2!"

Big mistake. You'll end up importing not only the photos, but also the tiny thumbnail versions of each photo (which are stored separately in the iPhoto Library folder) *and* the original versions of any photos that you edited. You'll wind up with duplicates or triplicates of every photo in the viewing area, in one enormous, unmanageable, uncategorized, sloshing library.

No, merging iPhoto libraries is slightly more complicated than that.

Method 1: Use iPhoto CDs as Intermediaries

One way to merge two Photo Libraries is to burn the second one onto an iPhoto CD or DVD, as described earlier in this chapter.

Begin with the smaller library. (In the Kenya safari example, you'd begin with the laptop.)

---

1. **Open iPhoto and burn a CD or DVD containing all the photos you want to merge into the larger Photo Library.**

   Follow exactly the same disc-creation steps outlined in the steps beginning on page 253. If you want to preserve any albums you've created, select the albums, not just the photos themselves, when you burn the discs.

2. **Quit iPhoto. Swap iPhoto Library folders.**

   If you're trying to merge the libraries of two different Macs, skip this instruction. Instead, move to the second Mac at this point—the one that will serve as the final resting place for the photos you exported.

   If you're merging two libraries on the same Mac, swap the iPhoto Library folders using either of the methods described earlier in this chapter. In any case, the master, larger photo collection should now be before you in iPhoto.

3. **Insert the iPhoto CD you just created.**

   iPhoto opens (if it's not already running) and the iPhoto CD icon appears in the Source list of the iPhoto window, as shown in Figure 12-5. Albums on the disc appear underneath the CD icon.

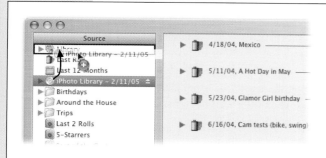

Figure 12-5:
To merge photo libraries, drag and drop albums from an iPhoto CD onto a blank spot in the Source list, or onto the Photo Library icon at the very top.

In this example, the contents of photo albums named Disney World and NYC, which are stored on the iPhoto CD, are being merged into the main Photo Library.

4. **To copy the entire disc's contents to your current iPhoto library, drag its little CD icon onto your iPhoto Library icon (Figure 12-5).**

   You can also drag it into an iPhoto folder icon in your Source list. You just can't drag it onto an album or to a blank spot in the Source list.

   If you don't want the entire disc's worth of pictures, you can also expand its listing (by clicking the flippy triangle) and choosing an album, or several. (You select multiple albums just as you would lists of files in the Finder: Shift-click to select several consecutive albums, ⌘-click to select nonconsecutive albums, and so on.)

   Then drag the selected albums (using any one of them as a handle) to a blank spot at the bottom of the Source list, below all the other albums, onto a folder icon, or onto the Photo Library icon at the very top.

In any case, this is the big moment when the "merge" happens. iPhoto switches into Import mode and copies the selected albums from the iPhoto CD into your main Photo Library. iPhoto also pulls in the photos' keywords, comments, ratings, and titles.

When it's all over, you won't find any new albums. You will, however, find that your Photo Library now contains the merged pictures. (Click the Last Roll icon to see them.)

Using this technique, you can combine the photos stored on any number of CDs into a single library, without losing a single comment, keyword, album, or original photo.

Method 2: Share the Library with Yourself

Burning iPhoto CDs is a great way to merge two or more iPhoto Libraries, because it leaves you with backup discs. And it's a lot simpler than what you're about to read.

Still, you use up a lot of blanks this way, and you spend a lot of time waiting for discs to burn.

If the photo libraries you want to merge are all on the same Mac—in separate accounts, for example, or just in different places—here's another method that doesn't involve burning iPhoto CDs. Instead, it involves using the photo sharing feature described on page 242.

To pull this off, you'll need at least two Mac OS X accounts. You'll also need iPhoto Library Manager, available on the "Missing CD" page of *www.missingmanuals.com*. The steps below look long, but remember that you have to do all this only once.

For clarity, let's say that you want to merge a library called Small Batch into a bigger one called Big Library, both of which are currently in your Pictures folder.

1. **On the Accounts panel of System Preferences, click Login Options. Turn on "Enable fast user switching." Click OK in the confirmation box.**

   This operation also requires at least one account in addition to your own. Take this opportunity to create one, if necessary. Let's call that other account Casey.

2. **Quit System Preferences. Drag the Small Batch library folder into the Macintosh HD→Users→Shared folder.**

3. **Switch into Casey's account. Open iPhoto Library Manager. Click Add Library. Navigate to that Shared folder, click the Small Batch library, and click Open.**

   Now Small Batch is listed in the iPhoto Library Manager list.

4. **Set all three pop-up menus to "Read & Write."**

   You've just made Small Batch accessible to the Casey account.

5. **Turn on the Small Batch checkbox, and then click Launch iPhoto.**

You should now see the photos from Small Batch in Casey's copy of iPhoto.

6. **In Casey's copy of iPhoto, share the albums you'll want to merge.**

   See page 242 for details on photo sharing. Leave iPhoto running.

7. **Switch back to your own account. Open up the Big Library in iPhoto.**

   Now you're looking at the main photo collection—but after a moment, in the Source list, you'll see an icon for Casey's shared photos. (If not, choose iPhoto→Preferences, click Sharing, and turn on "Look for shared photos." Close the Preferences window.)

   Click the flippy triangle to reveal Casey's albums.

8. **Drag Casey's albums into a blank spot in your own Source list.**

   You've just copied the albums from the Small Batch library into your own Big Library. Put another way, you've just merged two iPhoto libraries without having to burn any discs!

   (And they said it couldn't be done...)

9. **Switch back into Casey's account and quit iPhoto.**

   Once you've confirmed that the photos have safely arrived in your main library, you can throw away the Small Batch folder.

Beyond iPhoto

Depending on how massive your collection of digital photos grows and how you use it, you may find yourself wanting more file-management power than iPhoto can offer. Maybe you wish you could organize 50,000 or 100,000 photos in a single catalog, without having to swap photo libraries or load archive CDs. Maybe you'd like to search for photos based on something other than just titles, keywords, and comments—perhaps by file type, creation date, or the camera model used to shoot them. Maybe you have a small network, and you'd like a system that lets a whole workgroup share a library of photos simultaneously.

To enjoy such features, you'll have to move beyond iPhoto into the world of *digital asset management,* which means spending a little money. Programs like Extensis Portfolio ($200, *www.extensis.com*), Canto Cumulus ($100, *www.canto.com*), and iView MediaPro ($160, *www.iview-multimedia.com*) are terrific programs for someone who wants to take the next step up (Figure 12-6). (All three companies offer free trial versions on their Web sites.) Here are a few of the stunts these more advanced programs can do that iPhoto can't:

- Create custom fields to store any other kind of information you want about your files—dates, prices, Web addresses, and so on.

- Track graphics files stored in any location on a network, not just in a specific folder.

- Catalog not just photos, but other file types, too: PDF files, QuarkXPress and InDesign documents, QuickTime movies, sound files, PowerPoint slides, and so on.

- Share a catalog of images with dozens of other people over a network.

- Rename an entire group of images en masse.

- Customize the fonts, colors, and borders of the thumbnail view.

- Create catalogs that can be read on both Mac and Windows.

- Display previews of "offline" photo files that aren't actually on the Mac at the moment (they're on CDs or DVDs on your shelf, for example).

- Handle tens of thousands of photos in a single catalog.

Some of the features in this list were obviously developed with professional users in mind, like graphic designers and studio photographers. But this kind of program is worth considering if your photo collection—and your passion for digital photography—one day outgrows iPhoto.

Figure 12-6:
iView Media, shown here, is one of several programs that do most of what iPhoto does—and a lot more besides.

For example, it can "watch" certain folders on your Mac, so that when new graphics arrive, iView catalogs them automatically. Its photo limit is 128,000 pictures.

Exporting and Converting Pictures

The whole point of iPhoto is to provide a centralized location for every photo in your world. That doesn't mean that they're locked there, however; it's as easy to take pictures out of iPhoto as it is to put them in. Spinning out a photo from iPhoto can be useful in situations like these:

- You're creating a Web page outside of iPhoto and you need a photo in a certain size and format.

- You shot a bunch of 6-megapixel photos, you're running out of disk space, and you wish they were all 4-megapixel shots instead. They'd still have plenty of resolution, but not so much wasted space.

- You're going to submit some photos to a newspaper or magazine, and the publication requires TIFF-format photos, not iPhoto's standard JPEG format.

- Somebody else on your network loves one of your pictures and would like to use it as a desktop background on *that* machine.

- You want to set free a few of the photos so that you can copy them *back* onto the camera's memory card. (Some people use their digicams as much for *showing* pictures to their friends as for *taking* them.)

- You want to send a batch of pictures on a CD to someone.

Exporting by Dragging

It's amazingly easy to export photos from iPhoto: Just drag their thumbnails out of the photo viewing area and onto the desktop (or onto a folder, or into a window on the desktop), as shown in Figure 12-7. After a moment, you'll see their icons appear.

The drag-and-drop method has enormous virtue in its simplicity and speed. It does not, however, grant you much flexibility. It produces JPEG files only, at the original camera resolution, with the camera's own cryptic naming scheme.

Figure 12-7:
This technique produces full-size JPEG graphics, exactly as they appear in iPhoto. Their names, however, are not particularly user-friendly. Instead of "Persimmon Close Up," as you named it in iPhoto, a picture might wind up on the desktop named 200205040035140.JPG or IMG_5197.JPG.

Exporting by Dialog Box

To gain control over the dimensions, names, and file formats of the exported graphics, use the Export command. After selecting one picture, a group of pictures, or an album, you can invoke this command by choosing Share→Export (Shift-⌘-E).

The Export Photos dialog box appears, as shown in Figure 12-8. Click the File Export tab, if necessary, and then make the following decisions:

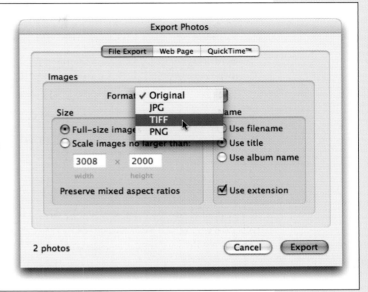

Figure 12-8:
The Export dialog box gives you control over the file format, names, and dimensions of the pictures you're about to send off from iPhoto. The number of photos you're about to export appears in the lower-left corner of the box. You can even tell iPhoto to use whatever names you gave your pictures, instead of the original, incomprehensible file names bestowed by your camera. To do so, click "Use title."

File format

You can use the Format pop-up menu to specify the file format of the graphics that you're about to export. Here are your options:

- **Original.** iPhoto exports the images in whatever format they were in when you imported them. If the picture came from a digital camera, for example, it's usually a JPEG.

  If your camera captured a RAW-format photo (page 98), though, the Original option is even more valuable. It lets you export the original RAW file so that you can, for example, work with your RAWs in a more sophisticated editor like Adobe's Camera Raw (which comes with Photoshop).

- **JPG.** This abbreviation is shorthand for JPEG, which stands for Joint Photographic Experts Group (that's the group of geeks who came up with this format). The JPEG format is, of course, the most popular format for photos on the Internet (and in iPhoto), thanks to its high image quality and small file size.

- **TIFF.** These files (whose abbreviation is short for Tagged Image File Format) are something like JPEG without the "lossy" compression. That is, they maintain every bit of quality available in the original photograph, but usually take up much more disk space (or memory-card space) as a result. TIFF is a good choice if quality is more important than portability.

- **PNG.** This relatively new format (Portable Network Graphics) was designed to replace the GIF format on the Web. (The company that came up with the algorithms behind the GIF format exercised its legal muscle…long story.)

  Whereas GIF graphics generally don't make good photos because they're limited to 256 colors, PNG is a good choice for photos (except the variation called *PNG-8,* which is just as limited as GIF). The resulting files are smaller than TIFF images, yet don't exhibit any compression-related quality loss, à la JPEGs. Not all graphics programs and Web browsers recognize this relatively new format, but the big ones—including iPhoto, GraphicConverter, Photoshop, and most recent browser versions—all do.

Named option

iPhoto maintains two names for each photo: its *original file name,* as it appears in the Finder, and its *iPhoto title,* the one you may have typed in while working in the program. Click either "Use filenames" or "Use titles" to specify what names iPhoto gives the icons of the graphics you're about to export. (When you export just *one* photo, you're offered the chance to name it whatever you like.)

Your third option is "Use album name." It tells iPhoto to name your exported photos according to their album name—and sequence within that album. If an exported photo is the fourth picture in the first row of an album titled Dry Creek, iPhoto will call the exported file "Dry Creek – 04.jpg." Because *you* determine the order within an album (by dragging), this is the only option that lets you control the numbering of the exported result.

Size options

Remember that although digital camera graphics files may not always have enough resolution for prints, they generally have far *too much* resolution for displaying on the screen.

As Chapter 11 makes clear, iPhoto offers to scale them down automatically whenever you email them or transfer them to the Web. If you turn on "Scale images no larger than," and then fill in some pixel dimensions in the boxes, you can oversee the same kind of shrinkage for your exported graphics. Points of reference: 1024 x 768 is exactly the right size to completely fill a standard 15-inch monitor, and 640 x 480 is a good size for emailing (it fills up about a quarter of the screen).

Tip: You can also use this option to de-megapixelize a bunch of photos. Suppose they're all 8-megapixel photos—more than you'll ever need. Export them at, say, 2272 x 1704 pixels (about four megapixels) to a folder on your desktop called "4 Megas" (or something). Delete the originals from your Photo Library, if you like, and then re-import the scaled-down versions by dragging that 4 Megas folder off the desktop and into the album list.

Part Three: iMovie

3

Camcorder Meets Mac

You've captured the raw footage on your camcorder, you've now assembled the ingredients you need, and you're ready to enter the kitchen. Now it's time for the heart of the matter: editing your footage on the Mac using iMovie. This chapter introduces you to both iMovie and FireWire, the high-speed cable system that transfers footage from the camcorder to the Mac, gives you a tour of the iMovie window, and walks you through your first transfer.

Meet Digital Video

Technically speaking, you don't need a camcorder to use iMovie. You can work with QuickTime movies you find on the Web, or use it to turn still photos into slideshows.

But to shoot your own video—and that is the real fun of iMovie—you need a *digital* camcorder. This is a relatively new camcorder format, one that's utterly incompatible with the tapes you may have filled using earlier camcorder types like VHS, S-VHS, VHS-C, 8mm, and Hi-8. At this writing, MiniDV camcorders cost about $400 for a basic model—and prices continue to sink, month by month.

The size of the camcorder is primarily determined by the size of the tapes inside it. A *MiniDV cassette* (tape cartridge) is tiny, so the camcorders are also tiny. Yet the quality is astounding; as you can see in the following table, DV quality blows every previous tape format out of the water. (All camcorders, TVs, and VCRs have the same vertical resolution; this table measures *horizontal* resolution, the number of tiny horizontal stripes of color the playback uses to fill your TV screen.):

Tape Format	Maximum Lines of Resolution
VHS, VHS-C	240
8mm	280
Live TV broadcast	300
S-VHS, Hi-8	400
Digital satellite broadcast	400
MiniDV	500
HDTV	720 or 1080

DV's 16-bit sound quality is dramatically better than previous formats, too. In fact, it's better than CD-quality sound, since DV camcorders record sound at 48 kHz instead of 44.1 kHz. (Higher means better.)

Tip: Most DV camcorders offer you a choice of sound-quality modes: 12-bit or 16-bit. The lower quality setting is designed to leave "room" on the tape for adding music after you've recorded your video. But avoid it like the plague! If you shoot your video in 12-bit video, your picture will gradually drift out of sync with your audio track—if you plan to save your movie to a DVD. Consult your manual to find out how to switch the camcorder into 16-bit audio mode. Do it *before* you shoot anything important.

Digital video has another big advantage, too: You can copy it from DV camcorder to DV camcorder, or from DV camcorder to Mac, dozens of times, making copies of copies of copies. The last generation of digital video will be utterly indistinguishable from the original footage—which is to say, both will look fantastic.

For that reason, although DV tapes may deteriorate over a decade or two, just as traditional tapes do, you won't care. Long before the tape has crumbled, you'll have transferred the most important material to a new hard drive or a new DV tape or to a

---

FREQUENTLY ASKED QUESTION

Two Camcorders Not to Buy

In their never-ending quest to come up with smaller and cooler camcorder designs, electronics manufacturers have already gone well beyond the MiniDV format. Unfortunately, some of these alternative formats are incompatible with iMovie.

Here, then, are two camcorders not to buy:

- **Sony MicroMV.** These camcorders are tiny, all right: they store their footage on a tape the size of a matchbox. Too bad they record in a format that popular editing programs like iMovie don't recognize.

- **DVD camcorders.** Sony, Panasonic, and Hitachi offer camcorders that use miniature DVD discs instead of tapes. Neat, but no FireWire jack.

iMovie HD can now edit video from two camera categories that iMovie 4 couldn't: high-definition footage and palm-sized, USB-connectable "camcorders" that record onto a memory card instead of tape (page 279).

Otherwise, though, stick to MiniDV camcorders. They're inexpensive, their quality is spectacular, and you won't be left behind when the next camcorder-format fad passes.

DVD. Because quality never degrades when you do so, you'll glow with the knowledge that your grandchildren and *their* grandchildren will be able to see your movies with every speck of clarity you see today—even if they have to dig up one of those antique "Macintosh" computers or gigantic, soap-sized "DV camcorders" in order to play it.

Connecting to FireWire

The FireWire jack on the front, side, or back of your computer is marked by a radio-active-looking Y symbol.

If you intend to edit your own camcorder footage, you'll also need a FireWire *cable*, like the one shown in Figure 13-1.

Figure 13-1:
Plug the larger end of the FireWire cable—the six-pin end, as Apple calls it—into the corresponding jack on the Mac. The tiny end may look almost square, but it fits only in one particular way, thanks to a little indentation on one side. Be gentle with it.

On the other end is a much smaller, squarish plug (the four-pin connector). Plug this tiny end into the FireWire connector on your camcorder, which, depending on the brand, may be labeled "FireWire," "i.Link," or "IEEE 1394."

This single FireWire cable communicates both sound and video, in both directions, between the Mac and the camcorder.

Now, if you plan to transfer video to your Mac from a tape in the camcorder, you should turn the camcorder to its *VCR* or *VTR* mode.

Tip: Occasionally, you may even want to capture *live* video into iMovie—to pass whatever your camcorder lens is seeing directly to the Mac, without ever recording it on tape. In that case, put the camcorder into *Camera* mode instead.

For best results, plug in your camcorder's power adapter instead of running it from battery power. At last, you're ready to begin editing video!

Getting into iMovie

After you've connected and turned on your camcorder, open iMovie by double-clicking its icon, or single-clicking it on the Dock. But before you're treated to the main iMovie screen (shown in Figure 13-3), iMovie may ask you to take care of a few housekeeping details.

Monitor Resolution

All modern Mac monitors let you adjust the resolution, which is a measurement of how much it can show as measured in *pixels* (the tiny dots that make up the screen picture). If you choose ⌘→System Preferences→Displays, you'll see the available choices.

Why is it important to understand monitor resolution when you're about to edit video? Because iMovie likes a very big screen—a *high*-resolution monitor. If your monitor is set to one of the lower resolution settings when you launch iMovie, you'll be greeted with an error message prompting you to visit System Preferences to reset the resolution. The bottom line: Choose a setting that's 1024 x 768 or larger. Poor iMovie can't even run at any lower setting.

Caution: If you switch your resolution to a resolution lower than 1024 x 768 *while* iMovie is open, the program has no choice but to quit. (At least it does you the courtesy of offering to save the changes to the project file you've been working on.)

The program is more graceful when you switch between two *higher* resolutions; it instantly adjusts its various windows and controls to fit the resized screen. In other words, whenever you switch resolutions while the program is open, be extra careful not to choose, for example, 800 x 600 by mistake.

The Create Project Dialog Box

If everything has gone well, and iMovie approves of your monitor setting, your next stop is the window shown in Figure 13-2.

You've reached a decision point: You must now tell the program whether you want to begin a new movie (called a *project* in iMovie lingo), open one you've already started, use the new Magic iMovie feature (page 288), or quit the program.

After the first time you run iMovie, you may not see the dialog box shown in Figure 13-2 very often. After that, each time you launch iMovie, it automatically opens up the movie you were working on most recently. If you ever want to see the Project dialog box again, in fact, you'll have to do one of the following:

- Instead of *quitting* iMovie when you're finished working, just close its window, so that the Create Project screen reappears. If you quit iMovie *now,* it won't open any project the next time you fire up the program; it will show the Create Project dialog box instead.

- Discard the last movie you were working on (by trashing it from your hard drive), or move it to a different folder.

- Throw away the iMovie Preferences file (which is where iMovie records which movie you were editing most recently). It bears the uncatchy name com.apple. iMovie.plist, and it's inside your Home→Library→Preferences folder.

Saving a New Project File

If you click Create a New Project (Figure 13-2), you're now asked to select a name and location for the movie you're about to make—or, as iMovie would say, the *project* you're about to make.

Figure 13-2:
Click Create Project to begin working on a new movie, Open Existing Project to open an existing movie, Magic iMovie to let the program assemble a movie unattended, or Quit to back out of the whole thing. The little ? button opens up the iMovie HD Help system.

You'll see a similar box when you first open iDVD and GarageBand.

iMovie HD

Create a New Project

Open an Existing Project

Make a Magic iMovie

Quit

This is a critical moment. Starting a new iMovie project isn't as casual an affair as starting a new word processing file. For one thing, iMovie requires that you save and name your file *before* you've actually done any work. For another, you can't bring in footage from your camcorder without first naming and saving a project file.

Where to save

Above all, the *location* of your saved project file—your choice of hard drive to save it on—is important. Digital video files are enormous. Standard DV footage consumes about 3.6 MB of your hard drive *per second*. Therefore:

This much video	Needs about this much disk space
1 minute	228 MB
15 minutes	3.5 GB
30 minutes	7 GB
60 minutes	13 GB
2 hours	28 GB
4 hours	53 GB

As you could probably guess, high-definition footage is even more massive; each minute of it takes between three and four times as much disk space as standard DV footage.

When you save and name your project, you're also telling iMovie *where* to put these enormous, disk-guzzling files. If, like most people, you have only one hard drive, the one built into your Mac, fine. Make as much empty room as you can, and proceed with your video-editing career.

But many iMovie fans have more than one hard drive. They may have decided to invest in a larger hard drive, as described in the box below, so that they can make longer movies. If you're among them, save your new project *onto* the larger hard drive if you want to take advantage of its extra space.

Tip: People who have used other space-intensive software, such as Photoshop and Premiere, are frequently confused by iMovie. They expect the program to have a Scratch Disk command that lets them specify where (on which hard drive) they want their work files stored while they're working.

As you now know, iMovie has no such command. You choose your scratch disk (the hard drive onto which you save your project) on a movie-by-movie basis.

Note, by the way, that digital video requires a fast hard drive. Therefore, make no attempt to save your project file onto a floppy disk, Zip disk, Jaz disk, SuperDisk, iDisk, CD-R, DVD-R, or another disk on the network. It won't be fast enough, and you'll get nothing but error messages.

Video format

iMovie HD offers a new pop-up menu in the Create Project dialog box called "Video format." The most important lesson to learn about this pop-up menu is that, in general, you should *ignore it.*

Here, you *can* specify what kind of incoming video iMovie should expect, but you don't have to. iMovie detects what kind of camcorder you've attached *automatically*, and it creates the right kind of project no matter what this pop-up menu says.

FREQUENTLY ASKED QUESTION

Saving to External FireWire Drives

I need more hard drive space. What should I do? Can I save a project onto an external FireWire drive?

It's a natural question; most Macs have two FireWire jacks. What better way to capitalize on them than by hooking up the camcorder and an external FireWire hard drive simultaneously?

For example, at the time of this writing, you can get an 80 GB FireWire hard drive for under $160 (from *www.promax.*

com, for example), which is enough to hold over six hours of footage. And the prices are falling rapidly.

Like most FireWire gear, these hard drives have several advantages over hard drives you may have known in the past. They're smaller and faster, can be plugged and unplugged from the computer without turning anything off, and don't require power cords of their own.

---

iMovie Controls

Once you've saved your file, you finally arrive at the main iMovie window. Figure 13-3 is a cheat sheet for what all of iMovie's various screen elements do. Spend no time memorizing their functions now; the rest of this book covers each of these tools in context and in depth.

- **Monitor.** You watch your footage in this window.

- **Clips pane.** These little cubbyholes store the *clips*—pieces of footage, individual shots—that you'll rearrange into a masterpiece of modern storytelling.

  This pane won't always be the Clips pane, incidentally. It becomes the Photos pane, the Audio pane, and so on, when you click one of the buttons beneath it. The one thing all of these incarnations have in common is that they offer you lists of materials you can incorporate into your movie.

- **Pane buttons.** Each of these buttons—Clips, Photos, Audio, Titles, Trans (Transitions), Effects, iDVD—fills the Clips pane area with tools that add professional touches to your movie, like crossfade styles, credit sequences, footage effects (like brightness and color shifting), still photos, sound effects, and music. The following chapters cover these video flourishes in detail.

Figure 13-3:
iMovie HD doesn't look much like any program you've used before—except perhaps earlier versions of iMovie.

iMovie appears in its own window, which you can resize, send to the background, drag to a second monitor, and otherwise manipulate like any other program's window.

- **Clip Viewer/Timeline Viewer.** You'll spend most of your editing time down here. Each of these tools offers a master map that shows which scenes will play in which order, but there's a crucial difference in the way they do it.

When you click the Clip Viewer button (marked by a piece of filmstrip), you see your movie represented as *slides*. Each clip appears to be the same size, even if some are long and some are short. The Clip Viewer offers no clue as to what's going on with the audio, but it's a supremely efficient overview of your clips' sequence.

When you click the Timeline Viewer button (marked by the clock), on the other hand, you can see the relative lengths of your clips, because each shows up as a colored band of the appropriate length. Parallel bands (complete with visual "sound waves," if you like), underneath indicate blocks of sound that play simultaneously.

- **Camera Mode/Edit Mode switch.** In Camera Mode, the playback controls operate your camcorder, rather than the iMovie film you're editing. In Camera Mode, the Monitor window shows you what's on the tape, not what's in iMovie, so that you can choose which shots you want to transfer to iMovie for editing.

In Edit Mode, however, iMovie ignores your camcorder. Now the playback controls govern your captured clips instead of the camcorder. Edit Mode is where you start piecing your movie together.

Tip: You can drag the blue dot between the Camera Mode and Edit Mode positions, if you like, but doing so requires sharp hand-eye coordination and an unnecessary mouse drag. It's much faster to click *on* one of the icons, ignoring the little switch entirely. Click directly on the little camera symbol for Camera Mode, for example, or on the scissors for Edit Mode.

- **Home.** Means "rewind to the beginning." *Keyboard equivalent:* the Home key on your keyboard. (On laptops, you must hold down both the Fn key and the left-arrow key to trigger the Home function.)

Note: In Camera Mode, the Home, Play/Stop, and Full Screen buttons described here are replaced by the Rewind, Stop, Play, Pause, and Fast Forward buttons, as described later in this chapter.

- **Play/Stop.** Plays the tape, movie, or clip. When the playback is going on, the button turns blue; that's your cue that clicking it again stops the playback.

- **Play Full Screen.** Clicking this button makes the movie you're editing fill the entire Mac screen as it plays back, instead of playing just in the small Monitor window. (It still doesn't look nearly as good as it will on your TV, however, as described on page 281. Unless, of course, you have an Apple 30-inch Cinema HD Display, in which case you see every juicy drop of the full, spectacular resolution.)

Tip: The Full Screen button doesn't play your movie back from the beginning. Instead, it plays back from the location of the Playhead. If you *do* want to play in full-screen mode from the beginning, press the Home key (or click the Home button just to the left of the Play button) before clicking the Play Full Screen button.

- **Scrubber bar.** It's like a scroll bar for one piece of footage, or the entire movie.

- **Playhead.** The Playhead shows exactly where you are in the footage.

- **Volume slider.** To adjust your speaker volume as you work, click anywhere in the slider's "track" to make the knob jump there. (You can also boost the Mac's *overall* speaker volume, of course.)

- **Project Trash.** You can drag any clip onto this icon to get rid of it. (Or just highlight a clip and press the Delete key.)

- **Free space.** This indicator lets you know how full your hard drive is.

UP TO SPEED

Special Cases: Recording from iSight, USB, and Hi-Def Camcorders

Recorded footage from a MiniDV tape is by far the most popular source of iMovie video, but it's not the only one. Here are some of the latest new sources.

iSight. The iSight camea (about $150) doesn't take tapes, so you can't prerecord something. But it's an excellent tool for recording live events directly into iMovie. Just connect the iSight's FireWire cable to the Mac. Choose iSight from the little pop-up menu below the Monitor window, and then click Record with iSight.

USB Camcorders. Panasonic, Fisher, Gateway, and other companies sell a new breed of super-tiny microcorders that can capture video directly onto memory cards.

iMovie lets you work with many of these "camcorders," or at least the ones that record in *MPEG-4 Simple Profile* format. When you connect one of these 'corders to your Mac's USB jack, the memory card shows up on your screen as though it's a disk. Double-click it to reveal its contents, which include a folder with all your video recordings in it. Bring them into iMovie by simply dragging their Finder icons into the iMovie Track or Clips pane.

HDV Camcorders. The high-definition video format offers a stunning, high-resolution picture, clear enough to make you feel like you're looking out a window and wide enough to show you, in a single camera shot, the pitcher, the batter,

and the runner on first.

To see high definition, you need a high-def TV set (an HDTV). And to *film* HDTV, you need an HDV camcorder like Sony's HDR-FX1 or HDR-HC1. (HDV isn't a typo. That's the format these camcorders use to store high-def video on ordinary MiniDV tapes.)

Importing and editing high-def video is *almost* exactly like working with regular video. One difference: Your Mac probably isn't fast enough to capture this massive amount of data in real time. That's why you'll see the tiny notation "Capturing HD at 1/4 speed," as shown here. (The fraction fluctuates as the importing goes on.)

In other words, importing high-def footage isn't a real-time operation. Even after the camera is finished playing the tape, iMovie takes a few more minutes to catch up.

Fortunately, it's worth the wait. Once the HDTV footage is inside iMovie, you can work with it with all the speed and fluidity of standard footage. And when the work is finished, you can export the result to iDVD to burn onto a DVD. No, the result won't be a high-definition disc; it will, however, be a widescreen disc (at your option), which will look absolutely spectacular on a widescreen TV.

Importing Camcorder Footage

Suppose you've opened iMovie and clicked the Create a New Project button. At this moment, then, you're looking at an empty version of the screen shown in Figure 13-3. Connect your camcorder to the FireWire cable and turn it on. This is where the fun begins.

Click the little movie-camera symbol on the iMovie screen, if necessary, to switch into Camera Mode, as shown in Figure 13-4.

Tip: If you turn on your camcorder after iMovie is already running, the program conveniently switches into Camera Mode. (iMovie only does so the *first time* you power up the camcorder during a work session, however, to avoid annoying people who turn the camcorder on and off repeatedly during the editing process to save battery power.)

The Monitor window becomes big and blue, filled with the words "Camera Connected." At other times, it may say, "Camera No Tape," "Camera Fast Forward," "Camera Rewinding," and so on.

Now you can click the Play, Rewind, Fast Forward, and other buttons on the screen to control the camcorder (see Figure 13-4). You'll probably find that you have even more precise control by using the mouse to control the camcorder than you would by pressing the actual camcorder buttons. (The Space bar turns the Import button on and off, as described below. Otherwise, though, no keyboard shortcuts control these buttons.)

Camera mode   Playback controls   Import button   Free space

Figure 13-4:
While you're importing footage, the time code in the upper-left corner of the clip on the Clips pane steadily ticks away to show you that the clip is getting longer. Meanwhile, the Free Space indicator updates itself, second by second, as your hard drive space is eaten up by the incoming footage. The square Stop button does exactly the same thing as clicking the Play button a second time. The Pause button also halts playback, but it freezes the frame instead of going to a blank screen.

Tip: The Rewind and Fast Forward buttons work a little strangely. If you *double-click* a button, playback stops and the rewinding or fast-forwarding begins at full speed. If you click and *hold* your mouse button down on a Rewind or Fast Forward button, playback continues with the tape moving at only twice its usual speed.

What you're doing now, of course, is scanning your tape to find the sections that you'll want to include in your edited movie.

The Monitor Window's Video Quality

After reading all the gushing prose about the high quality of digital-video footage, when you first inspect your footage in the Monitor window, you might wonder if you got ripped off. The picture may not look anything like DVD quality.

This video quality is *temporary* and visible only on the Mac screen. The instant you send your finished movie back to the camcorder, or when you export it as a QuickTime movie or DVD, you get the stunning DV quality that was temporarily hidden on the Mac screen.

Still, you'll spend much of your moviemaking time watching clips play back, so it's well worth investigating the different ways iMovie can improve the picture:

- **Good.** If you have a fast Mac, a great way is to choose iMovie→Preferences, click the Playback tab, and then choose "Highest (field blending)." The only reason you'd want to choose one of the lower-quality settings, in fact, is if you experience hiccups during playback, usually in complicated movies on slowish Macs.

- **Better.** Choose iMovie→Preferences, click Playback, and turn on "Play DV project video through to DV camera." You've just told iMovie to play the video *through your camcorder.* If you're willing to watch your camcorder's screen as you work instead of the onscreen Monitor window, what you see is what you shot: all gorgeous, all the time. (You hear the audio only through the camcorder, too.)

- **Best.** The ultimate editing setup, though, is to hook up a TV to your camcorder's analog outputs. That way, you get to edit your footage not just at full quality, but also at full size. This is exactly the way professionals edit digital video—on TV monitors on their desks. The only difference is that you paid about $99,000 less for your setup.

Capturing Footage

When you're in Camera Mode, an Import button appears just below the Monitor window. When you click this button (or press the Space bar), iMovie imports the footage you're watching, storing it as digital-video movie files on the Mac's hard drive. You can ride the Space bar, tapping it to turn the Import button on and off, capturing only the good parts as the playback continues (Figure 13-4).

During this process, you'll notice some changes to your iMovie environment:

- The Import button lights up, as though illuminated by a blue spotlight.

- As soon as you click Import, what looks like a slide appears in the first square of the Clips pane, as shown in Figure 13-3. That's a *clip*—a single piece of footage that makes up one of the building blocks of an iMovie movie. Its icon is a picture of the first frame.

- Superimposed on the clip, in its upper-left corner, is the length of the clip expressed as "minutes:seconds:frames." You can see this little timer ticking upward as the clip grows longer. For example, if it says *1:23:10,* then the clip is 1 minute, 23 seconds, and 10 frames long.

  Getting used to this kind of frame counter takes some practice for two reasons. First, computers start counting from 0, not from 1, so the very first frame of a clip is called 00:00. Second, remember that there are 30 frames per second (in NTSC digital video; 25 in PAL digital video). So the far-right number in the time code (the frame counter) counts up to *29* before flipping over to 00 again—not to 59 or 99, which might feel more familiar. In other words, iMovie counts like this: 00:28...00:29...1:00...1:01.

Tip: Standard DV camcorders record life by capturing 30 frames per second. (All right, 29.97 frames per second; see the box on page 414.)

That, for your trivia pleasure, is the standard frame rate for *television.* Real movies, on the other hand—that is, footage shot on film—roll by at only 24 frames per second. The European PAL format runs at 25 frames per second.

- While the importing is going on, you're free to open other programs, surf the Web, crunch some numbers, organize your pictures in iPhoto, or whatever you like.

  The Mac continues to give processor priority to capturing video, so your other programs may act a little drugged. But this impressive multitasking feat still means that you can get meaningful work or reading done while you're dumping your footage into iMovie in the background.

If you click Import (or press the Space bar) a second time, the tape continues to roll, but iMovie stops gulping down footage to your hard drive. Your camcorder continues to play. You've just captured your first clip(s).

Automatic scene detection

If you let the tape continue to roll, you'll notice a handy iMovie feature at work. Each time a new scene begins, a new clip icon appears in the Clips pane. The Clips pane scrolls as much as necessary to hold the imported clips.

What iMovie is actually doing is studying the *date and time stamp* that DV camcorders record into every frame of video. When iMovie detects a break in time, it assumes that you stopped recording, if only for a moment, and therefore that the next piece of footage should be considered a new shot. It turns each new shot into a new clip.

This behavior lets you just roll the camera, unattended, as iMovie automatically downloads the footage, turning each scene into a clip while you sit there leafing through a magazine. Then later, at your leisure, you can survey the footage you've caught and set about the business of cutting out the deadwood.

In general, this feature doesn't work if you haven't set your camcorder's clock. (JVC's high-definition camcorders are the exception; they don't time-stamp your footage, but iMovie *does* recognize their scene breaks anyway.) Automatic scene detection also doesn't work if you're playing from a non-DV tape using one of the techniques described on page 290.

Tip: If you prefer, you can ask iMovie to dump incoming clips into the Clip Viewer at the bottom of the screen instead of the Clips pane. You might want to do that when, for example, you filmed your shots roughly in sequence. That way, you'll have to do much less dragging to the Clip Viewer when it comes time to edit.

To bring this about, choose iMovie→Preferences and click Import. Where you see "Place clips in," click Movie Timeline. Click OK. Now when you begin importing clips, iMovie stacks them end to end in the Timeline instead of on the Clips pane.

If you would prefer to have manual control over when each clip begins and ends, iMovie is happy to comply. Choose iMovie→Preferences, click import, and proceed as shown in Figure 13-5.

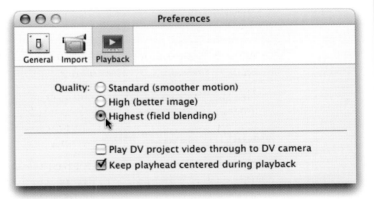

Figure 13-5:
The iMovie→Preferences dialog box gives you control over the automatic clip-logging feature. You can turn off this feature entirely by turning off the "Start new clip at each scene break" option.

Once you've turned off the automatic clip-creation feature, iMovie logs clips only when you click Import (or press Space) once at the beginning of the clip, and again at the end of the clip.

Tip: Tapping the Space bar is the same as clicking the Import button. In fact, if you tap Space when the camcorder is stopped, it begins to play *and* iMovie begins to capture the footage.

The maximum clip length
iMovie veterans are used to a clip-length limit of 9 minutes, 28 seconds, and 17 frames (which is 2 gigabytes of hard drive space). But no more; in iMovie HD, a clip's length

is limited only by the amount of space on your hard drive. You can easily import an entire 60-minute DV tape—if you've got enough hard drive space, of course—as a single icon on your Clips pane, if you like. (That would require, of course, that you've turned off automatic scene detection as described earlier.)

The Free Space readout

As noted earlier, the Free Space display (Figure 13-4) updates itself as you capture your clips. It keeps track of how much space your hard drive has left—the one onto which you saved your project.

This readout includes a color-keyed early warning system that lets you prepare for that awkward moment when your hard drive's full. At that moment, you won't be able to capture any more video. Look at the color of the text just beside the Trash (where it says, for example, "1.83 GB available"):

- If the words are **black,** you're in good shape. Your hard drive has over 400 MB of free space—room for at least 90 seconds of additional footage.

- If the text becomes **yellow,** your hard drive has between 200 and 400 MB of free space left. In about 90 more seconds of capturing, you'll be completely out of space.

- When the words turn **red,** the situation is dire. Your hard drive has less than 200 MB of free space left. About one minute of capturing remains.

- When the Free Space indicator shows that you've got less than 50 MB of free space left, iMovie stops importing and refuses to capture any more video. At this point, you must make more free space on your hard drive, either by emptying your Project Trash or by throwing away some non-iMovie files from your hard drive. (You don't have to quit iMovie while you houseclean; just hide it.)

Managing Project Files

In the iMovie HD era, your movie may appear on the hard drive in one of two formats.

- If it's a new iMovie HD project, it's represented on your hard drive by a single file icon (see Figure 13-6, top). Having a single-icon project document makes it very convenient to open, copy, delete, rename, or move a video project, because you have only one icon to worry about.

- If it's an older iMovie project that you've opened into iMovie HD, it remains just as it was: as a *folder* full of associated files (Figure 13-6, bottom).

You can read more about this distinction later in the chapter. But first, the basics of opening, switching, and converting movie projects.

Starting a New Project

To start a new project after you've been editing another one, choose File→New Project; indicate whether or not you want to save the changes to your outgoing movie (if you haven't already saved them); and off you go.

Switching Projects

To open a different iMovie Project, you can choose either of two routes:

- Close the current project's window. You return to the Create Project dialog box shown in Figure 13-2. Click Open Existing Project. Now you're shown the contents of your hard drive, so that you can find and open the iMovie project you want.

- Choose File→Open Project. Once again, use the resulting dialog box to find the movie you want.

- Choose File→Open Recent, whose submenu lists the last few movies you've worked on.

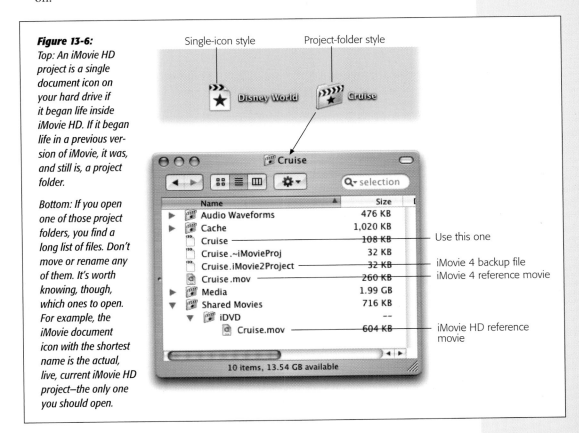

Figure 13-6:
Top: An iMovie HD project is a single document icon on your hard drive if it began life inside iMovie HD. If it began life in a previous version of iMovie, it was, and still is, a project folder.

Bottom: If you open one of those project folders, you find a long list of files. Don't move or rename any of them. It's worth knowing, though, which ones to open. For example, the iMovie document icon with the shortest name is the actual, live, current iMovie HD project—the only one you should open.

Single-icon style   Project-folder style

Disney World   Cruise

Cruise

Name	Size
▶ Audio Waveforms	476 KB
▶ Cache	1,020 KB
Cruise	108 KB	— Use this one
Cruise .~iMovieProj	32 KB
Cruise.iMovie2Project	32 KB	— iMovie 4 backup file
Cruise.mov	260 KB	— iMovie 4 reference movie
▶ Media	1.99 GB
▼ Shared Movies	716 KB
▼ iDVD	--
Cruise.mov	604 KB	— iMovie HD reference movie

10 items, 13.54 GB available

In each case, if you've worked on the current movie but haven't saved the changes yet, iMovie asks you whether you'd like to save them or not. Click Save or Don't Save, as appropriate.

Tip: If you're a keyboard-shortcut fan, you can press ⌘-D instead of clicking Don't Save.

After a moment, the new movie's clips appear on the screen, and you're ready to go.

Converting Older Projects

When you open a project created by an older version of the program, iMovie asks permission to update its file format into the iMovie HD format. If you want to edit the project in iMovie HD, you have no choice; you must click OK. Doing so creates a new project file, and preserves a copy of the original with the filename suffix ".iMovie2Project" (see Figure 13-6, bottom).

Now, even if you click OK, your old iMovie project *folder* doesn't get turned into the new-style, single-icon project *file* as described earlier. Instead, iMovie HD leaves you with the original project folder, with a few new files and folders deposited there for safety. (See Figure 13-6 for an illustration.)

When the conversion is finished, you still have a document inside called Cruise. That's your new iMovie HD project file, the one you should double-click the next time you want to open it (identified in Figure 13-6 at bottom).

Your converted project folder *also* contains a copy of the old, untouched original, now called Vacation.iMovie2Project. That's a backup copy of your original, which iMovie HD thoughtfully deposits there just in case.

Note: Be careful, in the future, not to open the Vacation.iMovie2Project document by mistake. If you try, iMovie will offer to convert it to iMovie HD format again, you'll spin out a second backup copy, and you'll wonder why the editing you did in iMovie HD yesterday isn't showing up. Don't open the version with the ~ symbol, either (Vacation.~iMovieProj); that's your "Revert to Saved" copy, an older draft that iMovie maintains for its own backtracking purposes.

So what if you *do* want iMovie to convert the old project folder into the new-style, single-icon document? After you've opened it up, choose File→Save Project As. Type a name for the newly created package icon and then click Save. After a couple of minutes of file copying and hard drive filling, you wind up with *both* the old project folder *and* the new package icon. (If the conversion goes well, you can now delete the older project folder.)

How iMovie Organizes Its Files

Thousands of people will come to iMovie HD for the first time, observing that each movie is saved as a single document icon. They'll go on through life, believing that an iMovie project is a simple, one-icon file, just like a JPEG photo or a Microsoft Word document.

In fact, though, it's not.

What iMovie HD creates is not really a document icon. It's a *package* icon, which, to Mac OS X aficionados, is code for "a thinly disguised folder." Yes, it opens up like a document when double-clicked. But if you know what you're doing, you can open it instead like a folder and survey the pieces that make up an iMovie movie. If you *don't* know what you're doing, you can hopelessly mangle your movie. Still, now and then, doing just that can get you out of a troubleshooting jam.

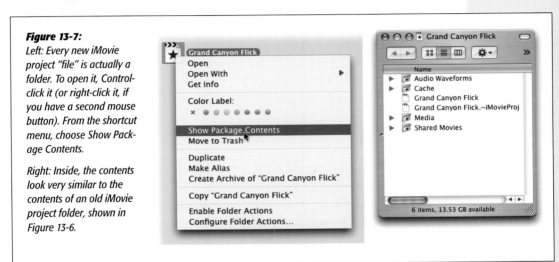

Figure 13-7:
Left: Every new iMovie project "file" is actually a folder. To open it, Control-click it (or right-click it, if you have a second mouse button). From the shortcut menu, choose Show Package Contents.

Right: Inside, the contents look very similar to the contents of an old iMovie project folder, shown in Figure 13-6.

To reveal the contents of this folder-pretending-to-be-a-document, use the Control-key trick revealed in Figure 13-7.

Once you've opened up a package into a folder, it looks and works almost exactly like the project *folder* of older iMovie versions, illustrated in Figure 13-6. Here's a rundown of the files and folders they have in common.

The Project File

The actual iMovie project file—called Grand Canyon Flick at right in Figure 13-7—occupies only a few kilobytes of space on the disk, even if it's a very long movie. Behind the scenes, this document contains nothing more than a list of internal *references* to the QuickTime clips in the Media folder. Even if you copy, chop, split, rearrange, rename, and otherwise spindle the clips *in iMovie,* the names and quantity of clips in the Media folder don't change; all of your iMovie editing, technically speaking, simply shuffles around your project file's internal *pointers* to different moments on the clips you originally captured from the camcorder.

The bottom line: If you burn the project document to a CD and take it home to show the relatives for the holidays, you're in for a rude surprise. It's nothing without its accompanying Media folder. (And that's why iMovie now creates a package folder that keeps the document and its media files together.)

The Media folder

Inside the Media folder are several, or dozens, or hundreds of individual QuickTime movies, graphics, and sound files. These represent each clip, sound, picture, or special effect you used in your movie.

Caution: *Never* rename, move, or delete the files in the Media folder. iMovie will become cranky, display error messages, and forget how you had your movie the last time you opened it.

Do your deleting, renaming, and rearranging in *iMovie,* not in the Media folder. And above all, don't take the Media folder (or the project document) out of the package window. Doing so will render your movie uneditable.

(It's OK to rename the project folder or the project file, however.)

Magic iMovie

Let's face it: millions of people wind up taking camcorder movies, and then never looking at them again. Editing and spicing up those movies is great, but it's *work.*

In an effort to solve that problem, iMovie HD introduces something called the Magic iMovie—a *completely* automated movie-assembly feature. You literally connect the camcorder, choose File→Make Magic iMovie, choose the music and options you want, and then walk away. Without any further attention from you, the program rewinds the tape, creates an opening title, imports all the footage, adds a transition between shots (if you've opted for one), backs it all up with music that you choose (at a volume level you specify), and, if you like, hands off the result to iDVD for quick burning to disc.

Magic iMovie is ideal, in other words, in situations like these:

- You've just captured footage of something—a wedding, a graduation, a school dance—and you want to put something together quickly that you can play at the reception afterward.

- You realize that Magic iMovie can serve as a starting point, with a lot of the grunt work done for you. Once it's done, you can pick through the scenes, deleting the ones you don't need, changing or removing the transitions that don't seem right, and adjusting music volume levels, without having to start from scratch.

- You feel that a DVD is a much better long-term storage depository than a tape, and you'd like Magic iMovie to automate the transfer for you.

Magic iMovie is, however, a fairly limited tool:

- Magic iMovie creates a transition—for example, a crossfade—out of *every single* camcorder shot, even if there are several shots in a row of the same subject. (Of course, it's easy enough to delete these transitions later. Or just turn off the Transition checkbox if you don't want them.)

- You have little control over the specifics of the things the Magic iMovie feature adds, like the length of the duration, the font of the title, and so on. Here again, of course, you can always adjust these manually after the deed is done.

- Left to its own devices, Magic iMovie always imports the entire contents of the cassette; it rewinds the tape before it begins. (There is a workaround, though, as you'll read in a moment.)

Now that you understand what to expect from Magic iMovie, here's how it works:

1. **Choose File→Make a Magic iMovie.**

   From the top of the iMovie window, the box shown in Figure 13-8 appears.

2. **Type a name for the movie.**

   Whatever you type into the "Movie title" box is what will appear on the opening credit, as white text against a black background.

3. **Choose a transition style, if you like.**

   If you like the idea of smooth crossfades between the shots of your video, make sure the first checkbox is turned on. And then choose the transition style you want from the pop-up menu: Circle Opening, Circle Closing, Cross Dissolve, and so on. (See Chapter 15 for details.)

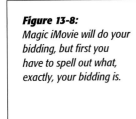

Figure 13-8:
Magic iMovie will do your bidding, but first you have to spell out what, exactly, your bidding is.

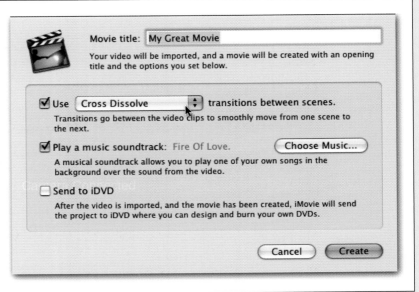

Movie title: My Great Movie

Your video will be imported, and a movie will be created with an opening title and the options you set below.

☑ Use [Cross Dissolve ⬍] transitions between scenes.
Transitions go between the video clips to smoothly move from one scene to the next.

☑ Play a music soundtrack: Fire Of Love. [Choose Music...]
A musical soundtrack allows you to play one of your own songs in the background over the sound from the video.

☐ Send to iDVD
After the video is imported, and the movie has been created, iMovie will send the project to iDVD where you can design and burn your own DVDs.

[Cancel] [Create]

4. Specify what music you want to play as the soundtrack, if you like.

If you'd just like to use the audio captured by the camcorder, turn off the "Play a music soundtrack" checkbox. But if you want to try some background music (you can always remove or adjust it later), click Choose Music. Now a dialog box appears, revealing the contents of your entire iTunes music library. Use the pop-up menu at the top to choose a playlist, if you like.

Just remember that if you don't choose enough music to "cover" all the video, the music will just stop short in the middle. (If you choose too *much* music, the music will end with the video.) Click OK when you're finished setting up the music.

5. Indicate whether or not you want a movie to send the completed Magic iMovie to iDVD in readiness for burning to disc.

At that point, you'll still have to choose a DVD-menu design theme, preview the result, insert a blank DVD, and so on (see Chapter 20). But the work of adding chapter markers and opening a DVD itself—usually a minute-long wait—will at least be handled for you.

And if you *don't* want a movie to hand off the result to iDVD, just turn off the "Send to iDVD" checkbox.

6. Click Create.

iMovie whirls into action.

Tip: If you don't want iMovie to import the entire tape, cue it up before you begin this process. Then, as soon as iMovie starts to rewind the tape, just hit Stop on the camcorder.

Similarly, you can stop the importing process before Magic iMovie reaches the end of the recorded portion of the tape just by turning off the camcorder at that spot.

The important thing to remember is that the resulting iMovie project is fully editable; there's nothing holy about any of the creative decisions that iMovie makes. You can still chop out clips you don't want, remove or edit some transitions, add or remove chapter markers, and so on.

Importing Footage from Non-DV Tapes

We live in a transitional period. Millions of the world's existing camcorders and VCRs require VHS, VHS-C, or 8 mm cassettes—that is, analog tapes instead of digital.

DV camcorders are rapidly catching up; they're the only kind people buy these days. But in the meantime, potential video editors face a very real problem: how to transfer into iMovie the footage they shot before the DV era. Fortunately, this is fairly easy to do if you have the right equipment. You can take any of these four approaches, listed roughly in order of preference:

Approach 1: Use a Recent Sony or Canon Camcorder

If you're in the market for a new digital camcorder, here's a great idea: Buy a Sony or Canon MiniDV camcorder. Most current models offer analog-to-digital *passthrough* conversion. In other words, the camcorder acts as a converter that turns the signal from your old analog tapes into a digital one that you can record and edit in iMovie.

If you've got a drawerful of older tapes, such a camcorder is by far the most elegant and economical route, especially if you're shopping for a new camcorder anyway.

Approach 2: Record onto Your DV Camcorder

Even if your newish digital camcorder doesn't offer *real-time* analog-to-digital conversion, it may have analog inputs that let you record your older material onto a MiniDV tape in your *new* camcorder. If so, your problem is solved.

1. **Unplug the FireWire cable from the DV camcorder.**

   Most camcorders' analog inputs switch off when a FireWire cable is hooked up.

2. **Connect RCA cables from the Audio Output and Video Output jacks on the side of your older camcorder or VCR. Connect the opposite ends to the analog inputs of your DV camcorder.**

   Put a blank DV tape into your DV camcorder.

Tip: If both your old camcorder and your DV camcorder have S-*video* connectors (a round, dime-sized jack), use them instead. S-video connections offer higher quality than RCA connections. (Note that an S-video cable doesn't conduct sound, however. You still have to connect the red and white RCA cables to carry the left and right stereo sound channels.)

---

3. **Switch both camcorders into VTR or VCR mode.**

   You're about to make a copy of the older tape by playing it into the camcorder.

4. **Press the Record button on the DV camcorder, and press Play on the older camcorder or VCR.**

   You can monitor your progress by watching the LCD screen of your camcorder. Remember that the DV cassette generally holds only 60 minutes of video, compared with 2 hours on many previous-format tapes. You may have to change DV cassettes halfway through the process.

When the transfer is finished, you can rewind the newly recorded DV cassette in the DV camcorder and then import it into iMovie exactly as described in this chapter.

Approach 3: Use a Media Converter

If your DV camcorder doesn't have analog inputs, you can buy an *analog-to-digital converter*—a box that sits between your Mac and your VCR or older camcorder. It's an unassuming half-pound gray box, about 3 by 5 inches. Its primary features include analog audio and video (and S-video) inputs, which accommodate your older video gear, and a FireWire jack, whose cable you can plug into your Mac.

Your options include the Canopus ADVC-55 (*www.canopus.com,* $215, shown in Figure 13-9), and the Director's Cut Take 2 box *(www.miglia.com/products/index. html;* about $280).

In either case, you'll be very pleased with the video quality. And when it comes to converting older footage, the media-converter approach has a dramatic advantage over DV camcorders with analog inputs: You have to sit through the footage only once. As your old VCR or camcorder plays the tape through the converter, the Mac records it simultaneously. (Contrast with Approach 2, which requires you to play the footage *twice:* once to the DV camcorder, and then from there to the Mac.)

Unfortunately, you can't control these devices using iMovie's playback controls, as described in this chapter. Instead, you must transfer your footage manually by pressing Play on your VCR or old camcorder and then clicking Import on the iMovie screen. In that way, these converters aren't as convenient as an actual DV or Digital8 camcorder.

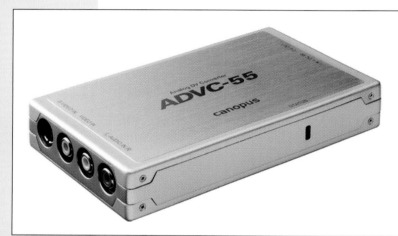

Figure 13-9:
The Canopus box requires no external power because it draws its juice from the Mac, via Fire-Wire cable. It also offers double sets of inputs and outputs, so you can keep your TV and VCR hooked up simultaneously. And it can handle both NTSC (North American) or PAL (European) video signals.

Approach 4: Use a Digital8 Camcorder

Sony's Digital8 family of camcorders accommodate 8 mm, Hi-8, *and* Digital8 tapes, which are 8 mm cassettes recorded digitally. (Low-end models may not offer this feature, however, so ask before you buy.) Just insert your old 8 mm or Hi-8 cassettes into the camcorder and proceed as described in this chapter. iMovie never needs to know that the camcorder doesn't contain a DV cassette.

Actually, a Digital8 camcorder grants you even more flexibility than that. Most Digital8 camcorders also have *analog inputs*, which let you import footage from your VCR or other tape formats, just as described in Approach 2.

Building the Movie

Whether on your Mac or in a multimillion-dollar Hollywood professional studio, film editing boils down to three tiny tasks: selecting, trimming, and rearranging *clips.* Of course, that's like saying that there's nothing more to painting than mixing various amounts of red, yellow, and blue. The art of video editing lies in your decisions about *which* clips you select, *how* you trim them, and *what* order you put them in.

At its simplest, iMovie editing works like this:

1. Trim your clips until they contain exactly the footage you want.

2. Drag your clips from the Clips pane to the storyboard area at the bottom of the screen, where iMovie plays them in one seamless pass, from left to right.

3. Rearrange the scenes by dragging them around.

4. Add crossfades, titles (credits), effects, music, and sound effects.

This chapter is dedicated to showing you the mechanics of the first three tasks. The following chapters cover the fourth step.

Navigating Your Clips

As you're building your movie, you can store your clips in either of two places: the Clips pane or the strip at the bottom of the window. You put clips on the Clips pane before deciding what to do with them, and drag them down to the storyboard area once you've decided where they fit into your movie.

This clip-assembly area at the bottom of the iMovie screen can appear in either of two ways:

- **Clip Viewer.** In this view, each clip appears as an icon, as though it's a slide on a slide viewer. Each is sized identically, even if one is 8 minutes long and the next is only 2 seconds.

- **Timeline Viewer.** This view also shows a linear map of your movie. But in this case, each clip is represented by a horizontal bar that's as wide as the clip is long. Short clips have short bars; long clips stretch across your screen. Parallel bars below the clips indicate the soundtracks playing simultaneously.

Grizzled iMovie veterans are used to switching between these two viewers by clicking the corresponding icon just above them (either the film strip or the clock) or by pressing the viewer-switching keystroke: ⌘-E.

But they might want to consider a different tactic in iMovie HD: not using the Clip Viewer *at all*. In iMovie HD, Apple gave the Timeline Viewer all of the drag-and-droppy talents once reserved for the Clip Viewer. Now, for example, you can drag clips to rearrange them in the Timeline Viewer, drag them back and forth to the Clips pane, drag them to the Finder or programs like iDVD, and so on. In short, there's very little reason left to use the Clip Viewer *at all*.

Note: You can read much more about these two views of your work at the end of this chapter. It's important now, however, to note that Apple hasn't given a name to this bottom-of-your-screen area as a *whole*. To prevent you from having to read about the "Clip Viewer/Timeline Viewer area" 47 times per chapter, this book uses the made-up term *Movie Track* to refer to this editing track, regardless of which view it's showing.

You can do several things to a clip, whether it's in the Clips pane or the Movie Track.

Select a Clip

When you click a clip—the picture, not the name—iMovie highlights it by making its border (the "cardboard" portion of the "slide") or its bar (in the Timeline) blue. The first frame of the selected clip appears in the Monitor window. (If you're in Camera Mode at the time, busily controlling your camcorder by clicking the playback

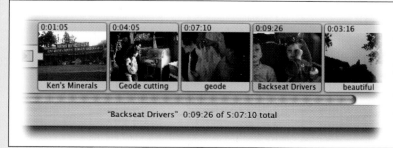

Figure 14-1:
iMovie HD no longer reveals, at the bottom of the window, the date and time a highlighted clip was originally recorded. You can still see those details, though, if you double-click the clip.

controls, iMovie immediately switches back into Edit Mode. The camcorder stops automatically.)

Once you've highlighted a clip, its name and duration appear at the bottom edge of the Movie Track, as shown in Figure 14-1.

To *de*select a clip (all clips, in fact), choose Edit→Select None, or press Shift-⌘-A, or Control-click any clip and choose Select None from the shortcut menu. If you're menu-phobic, just click anywhere *except* on a clip (on the metallic-looking iMovie background, say), or Shift-click the first or last in a series of highlighted clips.

Knowing these five ways to deselect your clips will save you frustration. Just after you create an effect or title, for example, iMovie leaves only that clip highlighted. You'll usually want to deselect it—and to play back what comes *before and after* the effect—to see your handiwork in context.

Select Several Clips

You can use a number of techniques to highlight several clips simultaneously. For example:

- In the Movie Track, click one clip, and then Shift-click the last one. All consecutive clips between them get selected.

- You can also select several clips that aren't next to each other using the same techniques you'd use to select nonadjacent icons in a Finder list view. To do so, click the first clip, then ⌘-click each additional clip. You can also ⌘-click a selected clip to deselect it.

- In the Clips pane, you can either Shift-click or ⌘-click several clips, one at a time. (You may as well learn to ⌘-click, though, so you can use the same shortcut in both the Clips pane and the Movie Track.)

- You can also choose a bunch of clips, either in the Clips pane or in the Movie Track, by *drag-selecting* them. This technique involves positioning the cursor in the gray area outside clips and dragging diagonally over the clips you want to select. As you drag, you create a faint gray selection rectangle. Any clips touched by, or inside, this rectangle become highlighted.

- In either the Clips pane or the Movie Track, you can select all of the clips by choosing Edit→Select All (⌘-A). Or Control-click any clip and choose Select All from the shortcut menu.

Tip: Once you've selected several clips, you can ⌘-click a clip to remove it from the selection, if you like. Also, like the corresponding trick in the Finder, you ⌘-click a stray clip to add it to a Shift-clicked group.

So why would you want to select several clips at once? Let us count the tricks:

- Delete them all by pressing the Delete key, or drag them all to the project Trash.

- Use the Cut, Copy, or Clear commands in the Edit menu to affect all of them at once. You can paste copied clips either to another spot in the same movie, or even into a different iMovie HD project.

- Move them around the Movie Track or the Clips pane—or drag them from one of those locations to the other—by dragging any one of them. The remaining clips slide leftward to close the gaps.

- Drag them all to the Finder, where they appear as individual movie-clip icons, or into another program, like iDVD.

- Apply the same transition, special effect, or Ken Burns photo setting to all of them using the Apply button on the Trans, Effects, and Photo panes. Similarly, you can update them all using the Update button. (Details in Chapters 15 through 17.)

- Consolidate a batch of nonadjacent clips. For example, suppose you ⌘-click clips number 1, 3, 5, and 7. Now you can use Edit→Cut, click a different clip in the movie to pinpoint a landing site, and then choose Edit→Paste. The clips that you cut, which were once scattered, now appear adjacent to each other and in sequence.

Tip: Here's a secret little command that very few iMovie fans even know about: Select Similar Clips.

Here's how it works: Click a clip in the Movie Track, and then choose Edit→Select Similar Clips. (Alternatively, Control-click a clip and then, from the shortcut menu, choose Select Similar Clips.) iMovie thoughtfully selects all clips in the Movie Track that match: all black clips, all photos, all transition effects, all clips that were chopped out of the same original piece of footage, and so on. This command can be a quick, efficient way to delete, move, consolidate, or modify a lot of similar material en masse.

Whenever you've selected more than one clip (either in the Clips pane or the Movie Track), iMovie adds up their running times and displays the total at the bottom edge of the iMovie window. It says, for example, "3 items selected 2:12:01."

Play a Clip

You can play a highlighted clip in the Monitor window by pressing the Space bar (or clicking the Play triangle button underneath the Monitor window).

You can stop the playback very easily: Press the Space bar a second time, or click anywhere else on the screen—on another clip, another control, the Monitor window, the metallic iMovie background, and so on.

Jump Around in a Clip

Whether the clip is playing or not, you can jump instantly to any other part of the clip in one of two ways:

- Drag the Playhead handle to any other part of the Scrubber bar (see Figure 14-2).

- Click directly in the Scrubber bar to jump to a particular spot in the footage. Doing so while the movie is playing saves you the difficulty of trying to grab the tiny Playhead as it moves across the screen.

Tip: To play back a section repeatedly for analysis, just keep clicking at the same spot in the Scrubber bar while the clip plays.

Figure 14-2:
While a clip plays, the Playhead (the down-pointing triangle) slides across the Scrubber bar. If you can catch it, you can drag the Playhead using the mouse, thus jumping around in the movie. Or you can simply click anywhere in the Scrubber bar. Either way, the playback continues at the new spot in the clip.

Step Through a Clip

By pressing the right and left arrow keys, you can view your clip one frame at a time, as though you're watching the world's least interesting slideshow. Hold down these arrow keys steadily to make the frame-by-frame parade go by faster.

Adding the Shift key to your arrow-key presses is often more useful—it lets you jump *10* frames at a time. In time, you can get extremely good at finding an exact frame in a particular piece of footage just by mastering the arrow-key and Shift-arrow-key shortcuts. (These shortcuts work only when the clip isn't playing.)

Scan Through a Clip

The Rewind and Fast Forward keystrokes (left bracket and right bracket—that is, the [and] keys) let you zoom through your footage faster. Press once to start playback, a second time to stop. In iMovie HD, you even hear the audio as you rewind or fast forward (sped up, chipmunk-style).

You don't have to click Play first. The Rewind and Fast Forward keystrokes start your clip playing at double speed even from a dead stop.

Rename a Clip

When iMovie imports your clips, it gives them such creative names as *Clip 01, Clip 02,* and so on. Fortunately, renaming a clip on the Clips pane or Clip Viewer is very easy: Just click directly on its name ("Clip 11") to open the renaming rectangle, and then type the new name. All the usual Macintosh editing techniques work inside this little highlighted renaming rectangle, including the Delete key and the Cut, Copy, Paste, and Select All commands in the Edit menu.

You can also rename a clip in its Clip Info dialog box (see Figure 14-8), which is the *only* way to change a clip's name in the Timeline Viewer. To open this box, just double-click the clip. (Or, if you're billing by the hour, Control-click the clip and, from the shortcut menu, choose Show Info.)

An iMovie clip's name can be 127 letters and spaces long. Be aware, however, that only about the first eleven letters of it actually show up under the clip icon. (The easiest way to see the whole clip name is to double-click the clip icon and then drag your cursor through the Name field in the resulting dialog box.)

The clip renaming you do in iMovie doesn't affect the names of the files in your project's Media folder on the hard drive (see page 288). Files there remain forever with their original names: Clip 01, Clip 02, and so on. That's why, in times of troubleshooting or file administration, the Clip Info box that appears when you double-click a clip can be especially useful. It's the only way to find out how a clip that you've renamed in iMovie corresponds to a matching clip on your hard drive.

Tip: Because you can only see the first few letters of a clip's name when it's on the Clips pane, adopt clever naming conventions to help you remember what's in each clip. Use prefix codes like CU (for "closeup"), ES ("establishing shot"), MS ("medium shot"), WS ("wide shot"), and so on, followed by useful keywords ("wild laughter," "sad melon," and so on). If the clip contains recorded speech, clue yourself in by including a quotation as part of the clip's name.

Reorganize Your Clips

You can drag clips from cubbyhole to cubbyhole on the Clips pane. In fact, you can even drag a clip (or even a mass of highlighted clips) onto an *occupied* cubbyhole. iMovie automatically creates enough new cubbyholes to hold them all, and shuffles existing clips out of the way if necessary.

The freedom to drag clips around in the Clips pane offers you a miniature storyboard feature. That is, you can construct a *sequence* by arranging several clips in the Clips

---

UP TO SPEED

Secrets of the Save Command

As you work in almost any program, you're usually encouraged to choose File→Save (or press ⌘-S) frequently, thus preserving your latest efforts and protecting them against power-failure disaster.

Saving in iMovie is fairly quick; it doesn't require the long, disk-intensive wait that you might expect from a video-editing program. (You're saving only your Project file, not making any changes to the large, underlying DV files in your Media folder.) Better yet, in iMovie HD, saving makes iMovie release unused memory and disk space, making the whole works run slightly faster.

Saving your document does, however, have a few downsides. Each time you save, you wipe out your entire Undo and Redo trail; you can no longer work backward to correct a mistake using the Undo command.

Apple giveth, and Apple taketh away.

pane. When they seem to be in a good order for your finished scene, drag the whole batch to the Movie Track at once.

Navigating Your Clips

Tip: See the little tiny icon next to the name of your project (top of the window)? If you drag that icon to any visible swatch of your Desktop, you create an alias of your project there—a handy, double-clickable launch pad to get you back into this project tomorrow.

Undo, Revert, and Other Safety Nets

As programs go, iMovie is a forgiving one. For starters, the Edit→Undo command is an *unlimited* Undo command, meaning that you can retrace (undo) your steps, one at a time, working backward all the way back to the moment when you created the project. (You can even unimport a clip from your camcorder!)

There's an Edit→Redo command, too, so you can undo your undoing.

Revert to Saved

But iMovie HD also offers, for the first time, a Revert to Saved command. If you *really* botch your work, choosing File→Revert to Saved takes the project all the way back to its condition the last time you used the Save command. It basically undoes every step you took since then.

Still, unlimited Undo, and even Revert to Saved, aren't always ideal. If you made a mistake eight steps ago, you can undo that step, but only by undoing the seven successful editing steps you took thereafter. Even more important, you lose your entire Undo/Redo and Revert to Saved trails *every time you use the Save command!* That little quirk ought to throw cold water on any ⌘-S–happy frequent savers.

Revert Clip to Original

Even then, however, iMovie has one more safety net in store for you: the Advanced→Revert Clip to Original command (called Restore Clip in iMovie 4).

Remember that every time you cut or crop a clip, iMovie doesn't actually disturb the clip itself (the file on your hard drive). Instead, it simply shifts around its own internal *pointers* to the portion of the clip that you want to use. As a result, it's a piece of cake for iMovie to say, "Oh, you want me to throw away those pointers and give you back the original clip as it came from the camcorder? No problem."

In short, the Revert Clip to Original command gives you a convenient safety net, a chance to start with a clean slate on a clip-by-clip basis. (You can also Control-click a clip and choose this command from the shortcut menu.)

When you choose Revert Clip to Original, iMovie returns the clip to its original, precut, precrop condition, even if you've already placed it into the Movie Track. In that case, the clip's bar in the Timeline Viewer grows correspondingly wider, shoving other clips to the right to make room.

The Project Trash

You can get rid of a clip either by selecting it and then pressing the Delete key or by dragging it directly onto the project Trash icon.

The iMovie Trash has a lot in common with the iPhoto Trash, the Finder's Trash, or the Windows Recycle Bin: it's a safety net. It's a holding tank for clips, photos, and sounds that you intend to throw out. They're not really gone, though, until you use the File→Empty Trash command.

In iMovie HD, you can even open the Trash "folder," look over and even play back the clips inside, and rescue or delete *individual* audio and video clips without emptying the whole Trash.

To open the new Trash window, click the Trash icon or choose File→Show Trash.

Tip: If you just want to empty the whole Trash right now, without having to wait for the Trash contents window to open, press the ⌘ and Option keys as you click the Trash icon.

The fact that you can open the Trash window isn't the only startling change in iMovie HD. You should also be aware tha:

UP TO SPEED

Why Emptying the Trash Doesn't Restore Disk Space

OK, this is so weird. I had a ton of stuff in my iMovie Trash. But when I emptied it, the little "free disk space remaining" counter didn't change at all! I had 532 megs available before I emptied the Trash, and the same amount after!

No doubt about it: iMovie HD's revamped editing-and-Trash features are a blessing and a curse.

Here's the blessing: In iMovie HD, you can use the Revert Clip to Original command *any time,* even after emptying the Trash, even months or years later. You can also add back a missing chunk from the middle of a clip that you'd previously lobotomized—again, even after emptying the Trash. You can chop, truncate, split, and shorten clips to your heart's content, and at any time, restore what you'd eliminated. (In previous iMovie versions, emptying the Trash meant that portions you cut from clips were gone forever.)

Here's the curse: These features work because iMovie quietly preserves the *entire* copy of every clip you import. If you split a clip in half, drag the second part to the Trash, and then empty the Trash, you don't get back one single byte of disk

space. iMovie is hanging onto the *entire* original clip, just in case you change your mind someday.

The only time emptying the Trash actually frees up disk space, in fact, is if you've put an *entire clip* into it. If even one frame of it appears in the Timeline, iMovie still preserves the entire original clip on your hard drive.

So what if you've imported a 40-minute tape all in one clip and you intend to work with only the first 5 minutes' worth? Will that iMovie project occupy 40 minutes' worth of space on your hard drive forever?

Yes, unless you the somewhat drastic steps described on page 667. (In short, the process involves exporting the short clip to your hard drive as a full-quality DV movie, deleting all scraps of the original clip from iMovie, and emptying the Trash, which returns all that disk space to you. Finally, you drag the good part of the clip from the desktop *back into* the iMovie window. iMovie will be convinced that this 5-minute segment *is* the entire clip.)

- Whenever you choose File→Empty Trash (or double-click the Trash can), you *lose* your ability to undo your recent steps; the Undo command is dimmed. In fact, emptying the Trash also disables the Revert to Saved command and vaporizes whatever's on your Clipboard. (You can still use the Revert Clip to Original command, however.)

  So when would you ever choose File→Empty Trash? The short answer is, only when you need to reclaim the hard-drive space it's taking up, and perhaps once when your project is finished.

- On the other hand, emptying the project Trash doesn't always restore free disk space, for the technical reasons described in the box on the facing page.

- Emptying the Trash is very fast in iMovie HD, even if there are thousands of clips in there.

Shortening Clips by Dragging

Almost nobody hits the camcorder's Record button at the precise instant when the action begins and stops recording the instant it stops. Life is just too unpredictable. That's why the first thing most people do when they get their clips into a movie is *trim* them—to chop the boring parts off the beginning and ending of each clip before dragging them onto the timeline.

Most of the time, you'll want to adopt one of iMovie's sweetest features instead: *edge dragging.* Instead of chopping off the ends of your clips, you can just *hide* the ends by dragging them inward, as shown in Figure 14-3. (This kind of nondestructive edge-dragging also works with audio clips. It's a common technique in GarageBand, too.)

Tip: Here's a great way to use this technique. First, play back the sequence. Using the arrow keys, position the Playhead so that it pinpoints the precise frame where you want the clip to end. In other words, you're using the Playhead to mark the target for the drag-cropping you're about to perform.

Now grab the *end* of the clip and drag it up against the Playhead. Conveniently enough, the end you're dragging snaps against the ghosted Playhead line, as though it's a bookmark. As a result, you get individual-frame accuracy without having to remember precisely how far to drag. (This trick works only if "Snap to items in timeline" is turned on in iMovie→Preferences.)

The beauty of this approach, of course, is its flexibility. After you crop a clip this way, you can play it back to gauge its impact on the flow of scenes. If you feel that you trimmed a little too much, simply grab the end of the clip and drag it outward a little more. If you don't think you cropped enough, drag it inward.

There's only one limitation to this technique: It works only in the Timeline Viewer. You can't use it to pre-shorten clips while they're still in the Clips pane, or after you've dragged them into the Clips viewer. For those purposes, read on.

And now, three delicious tips pertaining to edge-dragging:

- In general, when you *shorten* a clip, all subsequent clips slide to the left to close up the gap. (That's what the pros call *ripple* editing.) Your overall movie gets shorter.

  In some situations, though, you may want to shorten a clip *without* allowing any other clips to shift. Instead, you want to leave *empty space* behind as you shorten the clip, so that the overall movie stays exactly the same length.

  To make it so, just press the ⌘ key as you drag the clip's edge inward. Now you're creating a gap that, when played back, appears as black space. Later, you can either convert the gap to a clip unto itself (page 311) or fill it with pasted footage.

- On the other hand, when you drag a clip's edge *outward* to expose previously hidden footage, iMovie generally shoves all subsequent clips to the *right* to make room. Your movie, as a result, gets longer.

  Once again, though, the ⌘ key can stop the rippling. If you press ⌘ as you drag outward, you *cover up* some footage in the adjacent clip. Your movie remains exactly the same length.

- Want better precision? Try this technique.

  First, play back the sequence. Using the arrow keys, position the Playhead so that it pinpoints the precise frame where you want the clip to end. In other words, you're using the Playhead to mark the target for the drag-cropping you're about to perform.

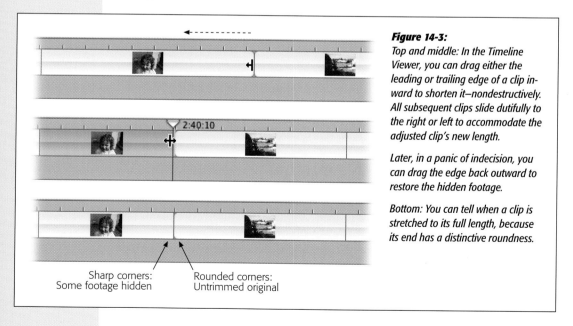

Figure 14-3:
Top and middle: In the Timeline Viewer, you can drag either the leading or trailing edge of a clip inward to shorten it—nondestructively. All subsequent clips slide dutifully to the right or left to accommodate the adjusted clip's new length.

Later, in a panic of indecision, you can drag the edge back outward to restore the hidden footage.

Bottom: You can tell when a clip is stretched to its full length, because its end has a distinctive roundness.

Sharp corners:
Some footage hidden

Rounded corners:
Untrimmed original

Now grab the *end* of the clip and drag it up against the Playhead. Conveniently enough, the end you're dragging snaps against the ghosted Playhead line, as though it's a bookmark. As a result, you get individual-frame accuracy without having to remember precisely how far to drag. (This trick works only if "Snap to items in timeline" is turned on in iMovie→Preferences.)

Three Ways to Trim a Clip

Trimming out the deadwood from your clips, so that you're left with only the very best shots from the very best scenes, is the heart of iMovie—and video editing.

Note: The following three techniques are nondestructive techniques, just like the edge-dragging business described earlier. For example, after you've shortened a clip by hacking a piece off the right end, you can later change your mind, even if you've emptied the Trash and let a year go by. You can restore some or all of the missing footage just by dragging the clip's right edge to the right in the Timeline Viewer.

Highlighting Footage

iMovie works just like other Mac programs: You highlight some footage, then use the Cut, Copy, or Paste commands to move it around. All three of the following footage-trimming techniques, for example, begin with *highlighting*, or selecting, a portion of your footage. Here's how you go about it:

1. **Click a clip to select it.**

    The clip can be either in the Clips pane or the Movie Track.

2. **Position your cursor just beneath the Scrubber bar.**

    See Figure 14-4.

Figure 14-4:
Carefully drag horizontally until the triangles enclose only the scene you want to keep. Finally, when you choose the Edit→Crop command, everything outside of these handles is trimmed away.

3. **Drag until the triangle handles surround the footage you want to keep.**

As soon as you push the mouse button down, the selection triangles jump to the position of your cursor. One remains where you clicked; the other follows your cursor as you drag. (In other words, don't waste time by dragging them painstakingly from the left edge of the Scrubber bar.)

The Monitor window behaves as though you're scrolling the movie, so that you can see where you are as you drag the movable triangle. Also as you drag, the portion of the Scrubber bar between your handles turns yellow to show that it's highlighted. Whatever Edit menu command you use now (such as Cut, Copy, Clear, or Crop) affects only the yellow portion.

Tip: Here's a quick trick for highlighting only the first portion of a selected clip: Shift-click within the Scrubber bar at the point where you'd like the selection to *end*. Instantly, iMovie highlights everything from the left end of the clip to the position of your click.

After you've just dragged or clicked a handle, your arrow key skills come in extremely handy. You can let go of the mouse and, just by pressing the left and right arrow keys, fine-tune the position of the triangle handle on a frame-by-frame basis. (You can tell which triangle handle you'll be moving. It's darker, and it's marked by the Playhead, as shown in Figure 14-4. To move the *other* triangle handle, click it first.) Continue tapping the left and right arrow keys until the Monitor shows the precise frame you want—the first or last frame you'll want to keep in the clip.

Remember, too, that if you press *Shift*-right or -left arrow, you move the triangle handle 10 frames at a time. Between the 10-frame and one-frame keystrokes, you should find it fairly easy to home in on the exact frame where you want to trim the clip.

Tip: After you've highlighted a stretch of the Scrubber bar, you can adjust the selected portion—make it bigger or smaller—by clicking or dragging again beneath any unhighlighted portion of the Scrubber bar (to the right or left of the selected region). Either way, the end of the yellow bar jumps to your cursor as though attracted by a magnet. And either way, you avoid having to redo the entire selection, since one of your two endpoints remains in place.

As you drag the triangle handles, keep your eye on two readouts. First, your precise position within the clip or assembled movie appears just above your cursor, in seconds:frames format.

Second, a notation appears beneath the Movie Track that identifies the amount of footage between the handles. It might say, for example, "Frames selected 0:03:15 of 6:00:02 total." That is, you've selected 3.5 seconds of a 6-minute movie.

Being able to see exactly how much footage you're about to cut (or preserve) can be extremely useful when the timing of your movie is important, as when editing it to accompany a music track or when creating a movie that must be, for example, exactly 30 seconds long.

Tip: If you've really made a mess of your selection, click just *below* the Scrubber bar, on the brushed aluminum iMovie background. The program deselects your footage so that you can try again.

Snipping Off One End of a Clip

Having mastered the art of selecting a portion of a clip, as described in the previous section, you're ready to put it to work. Suppose, for example, that you want to shave off some footage from only one end of your clip. In that case, highlight the footage you want to delete (at the beginning or end of the Scrubber bar), and then choose Edit→Cut (or Edit→Clear), or press the Delete key.

iMovie promptly trims away whatever was highlighted between the triangles. The arrangement should look like Figure 14-5.

Figure 14-5:
To trim footage from one end of the clip, just highlight that much, using the triangle handles. The Monitor window shows you where you are in the footage as you drag the triangles. And once again, you can use the arrow keys to fine-tune the position of the triangle you've most recently clicked.

Cropping Out the Ends of a Clip

If you want to trim some footage off *both* ends of a clip, it's quicker to highlight the part in the middle that you want to *keep*. Just select the footage you want to preserve and then choose Edit→Crop (or press ⌘-K). What used to be the yellow part of the Scrubber bar has now, in effect, expanded to fill the *entire* Scrubber bar. Your clip is shorter now, as a tap on the Space bar will prove.

Chopping Out the Middle of a Clip

In this technique, you *eliminate* the middle part of a clip, leaving only the ends of it in your project. Select the footage you want to delete, and then choose Edit→Cut (or Edit→Clear), or press the Delete key.

If you're not prepared for it, the results of this technique can be startling—and yet it's perfectly logical. If you cut a chunk out of the middle of the clip, iMovie has no choice but to throw back at you the *two end pieces*—as two separate clips, side by side on the Clips pane or the Movie Track. Either way, the name of the newly created clip will help you identify it. If the original clip was called "Cut Me Out," the new, split-off clip is called "Cut Me Out/1."

Splitting a Clip

The techniques described in the previous section work well when you want to remove some footage from a clip. Sometimes, however, it can be useful to split a clip into two separate clips *without* deleting footage in the process. For example, suppose you want the title of your movie to appear 5 seconds into a certain piece of footage. In iMovie, the only way to accomplish that feat is to split the clip into three pieces—the first one being 5 seconds long—and superimpose the title credit on the middle piece. (More on titles in Chapter 16.)

The Split Video Clip at Playhead command is exactly what you need in that case. Just click inside, or drag along, the Scrubber bar until you find the spot where you want to split the clip. (Remember, you can press the right- or left-arrow keys to nudge the Playhead one frame at a time to the right or left. Use Shift-arrow keys for 10-frame jumps.) Then choose Edit→Split Video Clip at Playhead (or press ⌘-T).

As shown in Figure 14-6, you wind up with two different clips, both highlighted. If the original was called "Split Me Up," iMovie calls the resultant clips "Split Me Up"

Figure 14-6:
After you split a clip, iMovie cuts your clip in two and highlights both of the resulting clip icons (Clip Viewer, bottom). If the clip started out in the Movie Track, the Monitor window still lets you scroll all the way through the original clip. Only the telltale slashed number ("/1") on the second part of the clip lets you know that you're actually looking at two different clips side by side.

and "Split Me Up/1." (To remove the highlighting, click anywhere else on the screen, or choose Edit→Select None.)

The Movie Track: Your Storyboard

When you're not trimming or splitting your clips, most of your iMovie time will be spent in the Movie Track—the horizontal strip at the bottom of the screen (see Figure 14-5). The idea is that you'll drag the edited clips out of the Clips pane and into the correct order on the Movie Track, exactly as though you're building a storyboard or timeline.

As noted at the beginning of this chapter, the Movie Track offers two different views: the Clip Viewer and the Timeline Viewer. Both are illustrated in Figure 14-7.

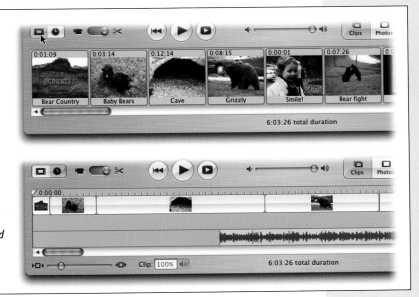

Figure 14-7:
Top: When you click the film strip icon (indicated by the cursor), you see your camcorder footage.

Bottom: Click the clock icon to see the Timeline Viewer, which reveals your audio tracks and shows the relative lengths of your clips. You can even rearrange your clips in the Timeline Viewer, as long as you master the knack of dragging them up (or down) and around the adjacent clips.

In either view, you can freely rearrange clips by dragging them. In the Clip Viewer, just drag them horizontally; in the Timeline Viewer, drag them *up and over* (or down and under) the adjacent clips, rather than directly to the side.

Tip: As you drag over them, the existing clips scoot out of the way, which can drive you crazy. In that case, hold down the ⌘ key until you're ready to let go of the clip you're dragging. They'll stay still.

Moreover, you can freely drag clips back and forth between the Clips pane and the Movie Track. (The ability to drag clips back and forth between the Clips pane and the Timeline Viewer is new in iMovie HD, and really useful.)

Remember, by the way, that you can switch the Movie Track between its two viewers by pressing ⌘-E. It corresponds to the second command in the new View menu, which says either "Switch to Clip Viewer" or "Switch to Timeline Viewer," whichever one you're *not* in.

Readouts in the Movie Track

iMovie identifies the name of your movie at the top of the window (and its format: DV-NTSC, for example, or HD-1080i-30 for "high-definition, 1080 interlaced scan lines, 30 frames per second").

At the very bottom of the window, you can see the name of the selected clip (or how many clips are selected), and how long it is relative to the whole movie.

Tip: The iMovie HD screen no longer tells you when a certain clip was filmed, as did previous versions. But that information is still easy to find: just double-click the clip you're wondering about. The resulting dialog box includes a line for Capture Date, which lets you know when you shot that clip. It's an extremely useful little statistic—like the date stamp on the back of a Kodak print.

Dragging to the Movie Track

There's not much to using the Movie Track: just drag a clip from the Clips pane directly onto it. For your visual pleasure, iMovie shows you a ghosted, translucent image of the clip's first frame as you drag.

Here are a few tips for making the most of this Clips pane–to–Movie Track procedure:

- If you want a clip placed at the *end* of the clips in the Movie Track, drop it in the slice of gray, empty space at the right end.

Tip: It can be difficult to drag a clip to the end of the *Timeline* Viewer, because no gray gap appears there. Depending on the mood of the technology gods, a gap may appear when your cursor actually approaches the right end of the display, making the existing clips scoot leftward to make room. But sometimes that doesn't happen.

If you're having trouble, remember that you can either (a) switch to the Clip Viewer view to tack a clip onto the end or (b) copy the clip from the Clips pane, click the last clip in the Timeline Viewer, and then paste. The clip pops neatly to the right of the last clip.

- If you want to put a clip *between* two clips on the Movie Track, drag your cursor between those clips, and watch as iMovie makes room by shoving existing clips to the right.

- You can also drag clips from the Movie Track *back* onto the Clips pane. You can take advantage of this feature whenever you decide that a sequence of clips isn't quite working, and you're going to postpone placing them into the movie.

- In the Movie Track, you can rearrange clips by dragging their icons horizontally. (Yes, this even works in the Timeline Viewer; see Figure 14-7.) Once again, iMovie makes room between existing clips when your cursor passes between them.

- In the Timeline Viewer, when you drag a clip directly to the right, iMovie leaves an empty gap. This is your opportunity to create a pure black clip (or, in fact, a clip of any solid color), as described on page 311.

- You don't have to drag one clip at a time; it's often more efficient to drag several clips simultaneously. Page 295 describes the various ways you can select several clips (like drag-selecting them or ⌘-clicking to select nonadjacent ones). For example, you might arrange several clips on your Clips pane into a mini-sequence that you then drop into your Movie Track as a unit.

Tip: As you're building your film on the Movie Track, think in terms of *sequences* of shots. By Shift-clicking, you can select, say, six or seven clips that constitute one finished sequence, and drag the selection (or cut and paste it) into a new location in the Movie Track to suit your artistic intentions.

That's an especially terrific tactic, since the *sequence of your Shift-clicking* determines the order of the clips when they get dumped onto the Movie Track. You now have a great way to pluck the best clips out of your video toolbox, no matter where they sit at the moment, and plunk them onto the Movie Track, already in the proper sequence.

Nondestructive Confusion

OK, hold on a sec. You're saying that if I drag the end of a clip, I can stretch it outward to restore some hidden footage. Sounds great, except for one thing: when I drag the beginning of a clip leftward, it shortens the clip before it! I don't want that!

Patience is the path to happiness, grasshoppa.

First of all, it is true that dragging a clip's left edge to the left *looks* like it's eating into the clip before it, which gets shorter and shorter as you drag. But it's just an optical fake-out; the instant you release the mouse, you'll see the squished clip snap back to its original length, as shown here.

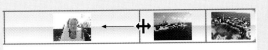

The first clip looks like it's getting shortened.

But when you release, the first clip snaps back to its original length.

OK, but I have another problem. Sometimes iMovie randomly refuses to let me do any edge-dragging at all. The little horizontal-arrow cursor just never appears.

It's true that iMovie sometimes doesn't let you do edge-dragging, but it's not at all random. You can't do edge-dragging when you've got audio levels turned on. Choose View→Show Clip Volume Levels to turn off that feature; you can now drag clip edges as usual.

(Apple no doubt felt that you'd have too much trouble telling the program whether you were dragging an *edge* or an *audio level*, as described in Chapter 17.)

Copying and Pasting Clips

Dragging isn't the only way to move footage around in iMovie; the Copy, Cut, and Paste commands can be more convenient. For one thing, you don't need the mouse.

For another, if you *copy* a clip from the Clips pane instead of dragging it, you leave a copy of the original behind. Later, if you've really made a mess of chopping up the clip in your Movie Track, you can return to the copy—your backup—without sacrificing the other editing work you've done since you made the copy. (Of course, the Revert Clip to Original command can do the same thing, but maintaining a whole, untouched original on the Clips pane is visual and easier to understand.)

For example, you can move a clip from the Clips pane to the Movie Track by clicking it, pressing ⌘-X, clicking in the Movie Track, and then pressing ⌘-V. (You can also *copy* the clip by beginning that sequence with ⌘-C instead.) You can move clips around within the Movie Track in the same way.

In fact, you can cut or copy clips out of one iMovie project and then paste them into a different one. The pasting process may take some time, because iMovie must move huge multimegabyte video files around on your hard drive. But this feature can come in very, very handy.

Note: When you copy and paste clips within a single project, you're never duplicating any files on your hard drive, so copying and pasting clips doesn't eat away at your remaining free space. But when you paste into a *different* project, you may be using far more disk space than you think; see page 667.

You may wonder how you're supposed to know where your cut or copied footage will appear when pasted. After all, there's no blinking insertion point to tell you.

The scheme is fairly simple:

- If there's a *highlighted* clip in the Clips pane or the Movie Track, the pasted clips appear *immediately to the right* of it. iMovie shoves all other clips to the right to make room for the new arrival. In other words, it's always a good idea to click a clip before pasting to show iMovie *where* to paste.

- If *no* clip is highlighted, iMovie pastes the cut or copied clips *at the Playhead position* in the Movie Track, even if that means chopping an existing clip in half to make room. (That's a change from previous iMovie versions.)

- If your intention is to *replace* the existing video in the Movie Track (instead of just shoving it to the right), don't use the Paste command at all. Instead, use the Paste Over at Playhead command, which is described on page 382.

Tricks of the Timeline Viewer

Everything you've read in the preceding pages has to do with the Movie Track in general. Most of the features described so far are available in either of the Movie Track's incarnations: the Clip Viewer or the Timeline Viewer.

But the Timeline Viewer is more than just another pretty interface. It's far more useful (and complex) than the Clip Viewer.

Many of the Timeline's super powers have to do with audio. Soundtracks, narration, music tracks, and sound effects all appear here as horizontal colored bars that play simultaneously with your video. You can read about these features in Chapter 17.

Some of the Timeline's features, however, are useful for everyday video editing—that is, if you consider playing footage in slow or fast motion everyday effects.

Zooming

The Timeline Viewer has a scroll bar, whose handle appears to be made of blue tooth gel, that lets you bring different parts of your movie into view. But depending on the length and complexity of your movie, you may wish you could zoom in for a more detailed view, or zoom out for a bird's-eye view of the whole project.

That's the purpose of the slider shown at lower left in Figure 14-7. It adjusts the relative sizes of the bars that represent your clips.

If you drag the slider handle all the way to the left, iMovie shows the entire movie in a single screen, without your having to scroll. The clip bars may be almost microscopic—you may not even be able to see the thumbnail picture on short clips—but at least you get a sense of the whole. If the handle is all the way at the right side of the slider, only a few frames of video fill the entire width of the Timeline Viewer. You've zoomed in over 50 times!

There's no one best setting for the zoom level. You should adjust it constantly as you work, pulling back when you need to figure out why some sound effects are firing at the wrong moment, zooming in when you want to make fine adjustments to the sound volume in mid-clip, and so on.

Sliding for Blackness

When you drag a clip to the right in the Timeline Viewer, you introduce a gap between the clip and the one to its left; iMovie automatically fills the gap with blackness and silence.

Tip: For greater precision, hold down the Control key and tap the arrow keys to move a clip right or left, making a wider or narrower black clip one frame at a time. Add the Shift key to nudge the clip 10 frames at a time.

You can turn this gap into a bona fide, clickable black clip in either of two ways:

- Flip back to the Clip Viewer. You'll see that iMovie has actually created a new clip, represented by its own icon in the Clip Viewer, called Black.

- Control-click anywhere inside the empty space in the Timeline Viewer. From the shortcut menu, choose Convert Empty Space to Clip.

Either way, you wind up with a new clip that's black and silent.

What you do with this gap is your business. You can leave it black, creating an effective "bookend" between scenes. You can switch to the Clip Viewer and drag the black clip up onto your Clips pane for future reuse. Or you can change its color, as described next.

Note: If there's a transition to the left of a clip (Chapter 15), dragging a clip to the right also drags everything attached to it, including the transition icon and the preceding clip, all in a merry little train.

Colorizing a Black Clip

Turning a black clip into a colored clip is a handy way to create a colored background for some titles or credits, for example. See Figure 14-8 for the secret.

Figure 14-8:
When you double-click a black clip, this dialog box appears. (Other ways to get here: Control-click a clip and choose Show Info from the shortcut menu, or click a clip and choose File→Show Info.)

Click Color to open the Color Picker, where you can choose the color you want (page 5). The Duration box here lets you adjust the length of your color clip with frame-by-frame precision.

Bookmarks

Navigating complex movies—or even simple ones—is a lot easier if you master the Bookmarks feature.

It works like this: Position the Playhead at an important spot in the movie, and then choose Markers→Add Bookmark (or just press ⌘-B, which is a lot quicker). iMovie responds by placing a tiny green diamond at that spot on the ruler (you can see a couple of them in Figure 14-9). Bookmarks are visible only in Timeline Viewer mode.

You'll see the real value of these markers once you've added a few of them to your movie. Now you can:

- Leap from one marker to the next using the Previous Bookmark and Bookmark commands (⌘-[and ⌘-], respectively).

- Align the Playhead with a bookmark by dragging it. You'll feel it—and even hear it—snap against the bookmark, assuming you've turned on Timeline Snapping (in iMovie→Preferences).

- Remove an individual bookmark by clicking it and then choosing Markers→Delete Bookmark. Banish all of them at once by choosing Markers→Delete All Bookmarks.

Note: You can't move a bookmark once you've placed it. If you try to click its diamond, the Playhead jumps to the spot and covers up the bookmark, preventing you from dragging. Deleting the bookmark and installing a new one is your only alternative.

Figure 14-9:
When you drag a clip, a bookmark remains right where it was. As a result, you can bookmark a certain "hit" in the soundtrack and then fiddle with the video, dragging clips into alignment with the bookmark until you find the perfect visual jolt to go with the audio burst.

Bookmarks

Playing the Movie Track

The Monitor isn't limited to playing clips; it can also play the Movie Track. That's handy, because one of iMovie's best features is its ability to show your movie-in-progress whenever you like (without having to *compile* or *render* anything, as you do in some more expensive editing programs).

Playing the Whole Movie

To play back your *entire* Movie Track, press the Home key on your keyboard, which in iMovie means "Rewind to beginning." As a timesaving bonus, the Home key *also* deselects all clips.

Tip: On recent desktop Macs, the Home key is above the number keypad, or stationed together with a separate block of keys like Help, Delete, Page Up, and Page Down. On recent laptop Macs, you simulate the Home key by holding down the Fn key (in the lower-left corner of the keyboard) and tapping the left-arrow key.

Alternatively, you can click the Home *button,* which is beneath the Monitor just to the left of the Play button. Once again, iMovie deselects all clips in the process of rewinding.

When you tap the Space bar, iMovie plays your movie starting from the location of the Playhead in the Scrubber bar; if you've pressed Home, that's the beginning of the movie. iMovie plays one clip after another, seamlessly, from left to right as they appear in the Movie Track.

Playing your movie back is the best way to get a feeling for how your clips are working together. You may discover that, in the context of the whole movie, some are too long, too short, in the wrong order, and so on.

While the Movie is Playing

As the Movie Track plays, the Playhead slides along the subdivided-looking Scrubber bar; if the Timeline Viewer is visible, a duplicate Playhead slides along *it;* and if the Clip Viewer is visible, a bright red, inverted T cursor slides along the faces of the clips themselves (Figure 14-10).

Figure 14-11:
Because every clip icon is the same size but not every clip is the same length, the T indicator speeds up or slows down as it arrives at the left edge of each clip. (You can see it in the center clip here, approaching the right side of the frame.)

While the movie is playing, you can take control in several ways:

- Use the playback controls beneath the Monitor (or their keystroke equivalents) to pause, stop, rewind, and so on.

- Navigate the movie by clicking in the Scrubber bar or dragging the Playhead.

- Deselect the highlighted clips by clicking on any "brushed metal" spot in the iMovie window.

- Adjust the volume by pressing the up-arrow or down-arrow key.

- Add a bookmark by pressing ⌘-B, or a DVD chapter marker by pressing Shift-⌘-M.

- Stop the playback by pressing the Space bar.

- Stop the playback *and* rewind to the beginning by pressing the Home key.

Full-Screen Playback Mode

Whenever you're tempted to play your movie-in-progress, consider clicking the Play Full Screen button (the darkened triangle to the right of the round Play button). It makes the playback—even if it's already under way—fill the entire computer screen.

To interrupt the movie showing, click the mouse or press any key on the keyboard. (The usual Macintosh "cancel" keystroke, ⌘-period, ironically, *doesn't* work in this context.)

Note: The quality of the full-screen playback still isn't the same pristine, crystal-clear playback you'll get when you transfer your finished movie back to your camcorder for TV playback. In fact, it's little more than a blown-up version of what you see in the Monitor window while editing your movie. If it's grainy there, it's enlarged-grainy in full-screen playback.

Transitions and Effects

This chapter is about two iMovie tools—Transitions and Effects—that can make your raw footage look even better than it is. Both of these tools are represented by buttons on the Clips/Effects/Sound panel that occupies the right side of your screen. This chapter covers both of these powerful moviemaking techniques.

About Transitions

What happens when one clip ends and the next one begins? In about 99.99 percent of all movies, music videos, and commercials—and in 100 percent of camcorder movies before the Macintosh era—you get a *cut*. That's the technical term for "nothing special happens at all." One scene ends, and the next one begins immediately.

Professional film and video editors, however, have at their disposal a wide range of *transitions*—special effects that smooth the juncture between one clip and the next. For example, the world's most popular transition is the *crossfade* or *dissolve,* in which the end of one clip gradually fades away as the next one fades in (see Figure 15-1). The crossfade is so popular because it's so effective. It gives a feeling of softness and

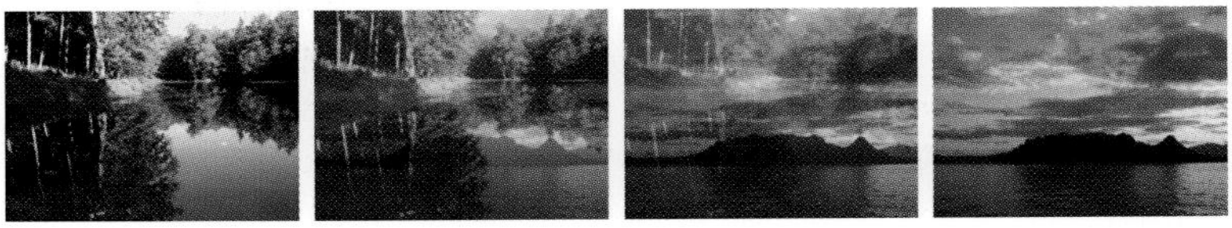

Figure 15-1:
The world's most popular and effective transition effect: a Cross Dissolve.

grace to the transition, and yet it's so subtle that the viewer might not even be conscious of its presence.

Like all DV editing programs, iMovie offers a long list of transitions, of which crossfades are only the beginning. You'll find a catalog of them on page 322. But unlike other DV editing software, iMovie makes adding such effects incredibly easy, and the results look awesomely assured and professional.

When Not to Use Transitions

When you begin to polish your movie by adding transitions, consider these questions:

- **Does it really need a transition?** Sometimes a simple cut is the most effective transition from one shot to the next. Remember, the crossfade lends a feeling of softness and smoothness to the movie, but is that really what you want? If it's a sweet video of your kids growing up over time, absolutely yes. But if it's a hard-hitting issue documentary, then probably not, as those soft edges would dull the impact of your footage.

  Remember, too, that transitions often suggest the *passage of time.* In movies and commercials, consecutive shots in the same scene never include such effects. Plain old cuts tell the viewer that one shot is following the next in real time. But suppose one scene ends with the beleaguered hero saying, "Well, at least I still have my job at the law firm!"...and the next shot shows him operating a lemonade stand. (Now *that's* comedy!) In this case, a transition would be especially effective, because it would tell the audience that we've just jumped a couple of days.

  In other words, learning to have taste in transitions is a lot like learning to have taste in zooming. Transitions should be done *for a reason.*

- **Is it consistent?** Once you've chosen a transition-effect style for your movie, stick to that transition style for the entire film (unless, as always, you have an artistic reason to do otherwise). Using one consistent style of effect lends unity to your work. That's why interior designers choose only one dominant color for each room.

- **Which effect is most appropriate?** As noted earlier, the crossfade is almost always the least intrusive, most effective, and best-looking transition. But each of the other iMovie transitions can be appropriate in certain situations. For example, the Radial wipe, which looks like the hand of a clock wiping around the screen, replacing the old scene with the new one as it goes, can be a useful passage-of-time or meanwhile-back-at-the-ranch effect.

Tip: The Fade In and Fade Out "transitions" in iMovie are exempt from the stern advice above. Use a Fade In at the beginning of *every* movie, if you like, and a Fade Out at the end. Doing so adds a professional feeling to your film, but it's so subtle, your audience will notice it subconsciously, if at all.

Creating a Transition

To see the list of transitions iMovie offers, click the Trans button, as shown in Figure 15-2. The Clips pane disappears, only to be replaced, in the blink of an eye, by a completely different set of controls.

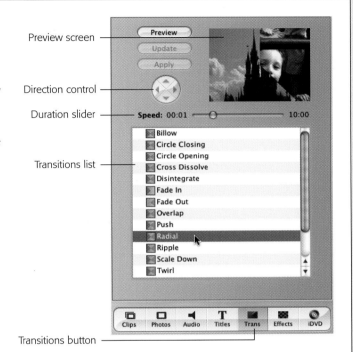

Figure 15-2:
When you click the Transitions button, a list of the transitions available in iMovie appears. When you click a transition's name, the Preview screen above the list shows a simulation of what the effect will look like.

Once you've clicked a transition name, you can press the up or down arrow keys to "walk" through the list.

Preview screen

Direction control

Duration slider

Transitions list

Transitions button

Previewing the Effect

Like most video editing software, iMovie has to do a lot of computation to produce transitions, so it can't show you an instantaneous, full-speed, full-smoothness preview. Therefore, iMovie offers a choice of lower-quality (but instantaneous) previews:

- **The Preview window.** For a very small preview, shown in the tiny screen above the Transitions list, just click the name of a transition.

  This preview plays in real time, endeavoring to make the transition preview last exactly as long as the finished transition will. On slower Macs, you don't see all the frames in this little Preview window, making the transition appear jerky, but rest assured that the finished transition will be extremely smooth.

- **The Monitor window.** To see a preview in a much larger format—big enough to fill the Monitor window—click the Preview button.

Either way, you can drag the Speed slider just above the list to experiment with the length of each transition as you're previewing it. The numbers on this slider—*00:10* (10 frames) at the left side, *10:00* (10 seconds) at the right side—let you know the least and greatest amount of time that a transition can last.

Tip: For more precision, you can bypass the Speed slider. Instead, double-click the timing numbers that appear just above it, in the corner of the black Preview area. Once you've highlighted these digits, you can type new numbers to replace them. These numbers are in seconds:frames format.

When you release the slider, you see another quick preview in the miniature screen above it, and you also see, in the lower-right corner of the Preview screen, the actual length of the transition you've specified.

Tip: The program doesn't yet know which clips you'll want to "transish." Therefore, iMovie uses, for the purposes of this preview, whichever clip is currently highlighted in the Movie Track, into which it crossfades from the previous clip. If the very first clip is highlighted, iMovie demonstrates by transitioning that clip into the second clip.

If no clip is highlighted, iMovie is smart enough to seek out the "clip boundary" that's closest to the Playhead's current position. It uses the clips on both sides of that boundary for the preview—if it's a two-clip transition. If it's a one-clip transition, iMovie uses the clip to the right or left.

Applying the Effect—and Rendering

Once you've set up an effect, place it into the Clip Viewer or Timeline Viewer by dragging its *name or icon* down onto the Movie Track.

Either way, drag until your cursor is between the two clips that you want joined by this transition; iMovie pushes the right-hand clips out of the way to make room. (Most transitions must go *between* two clips, and so they can't go at the beginning or end of your Movie Track. The exceptions are the Fade and Wash effects.) Then a special transition icon appears between the clips, as shown in Figure 15-3.

Tip: The tiny triangles on a transition icon or bar let you know what kind of transition it is. A pair of inward-facing triangles is a standard transition that melds the end of one clip with the beginning of the next. A single, right-facing triangle indicates a transition that applies to the *beginning* of a clip, such as a fade-in from black (or wash-in from white). A single, left-facing triangle indicates a transition that applies to the *end* of a clip (such as a fade or wash *out*).

Almost immediately, a tiny red line begins to crawl, progress-bar-like, along the lower edge of this icon (see Figure 15-3). In the terminology of DV editors everywhere, the Mac has begun to *render* this transition—to perform the thousands of individual calculations necessary to blend the outgoing clip into the incoming, pixel by pixel, frame by frame.

Whether it's an iMovie transition or a scene in a Pixar movie, rendering always takes a lot of time. In iMovie, the longer the transition you've specified, the longer it takes to render. You should feel grateful, however, that iMovie renders its transitions in a matter of minutes, not days (which complex Hollywood computer-generated effects often require).

Furthermore, iMovie lets you *continue working* as this rendering takes place. You can work on the other pieces of your movie, import new footage from your camcorder, or even *play* your movie while transitions are still rendering. (If the transitions haven't finished rendering, iMovie shows you its preview version.)

Figure 15-3:
Top: In the Clip Viewer, a transition shows up as a slide-like icon.

Bottom: In the Timeline Viewer, you get a bar whose width indicates its duration. Each transition has its own red progress bar that creeps along the bottom edge of the icon. After the clip has been fully rendered, this added strip beneath the icon disappears, and the transition is ready to play. (The Movie Track's top edge identifies the transition type and its duration when the transition icon is highlighted.)

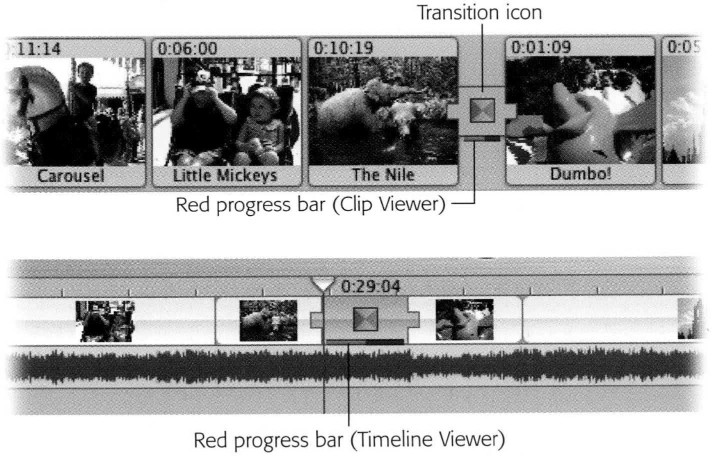

In fact, you can even switch out of iMovie to work in other Mac programs. (This last trick makes the rendering even slower, but at least it's in the background. You can check your email or work on your screenplay in the meantime.)

Applying simultaneous clips

iMovie has always been able to render several transition effects simultaneously, albeit with some speed penalty. iMovie HD, though, offers an even more useful timesaver: you can apply the same transition to several pairs of clips at once. Just click the first clip, then ⌘-click as many other adjacent pairs as you like. Set up a transition the way you like it, and then click the Apply button. iMovie applies the same transition to every selected clip and the one to its right.

When rendering is complete

When the rendering is complete, you can look over the result very easily.

• To watch just the transition itself, click the transition's icon or bar in the Movie Track (it changes color to show that it's highlighted) and then press the Space bar.

- To watch the transition *and* the clips that it joins together, Shift-click the two clips in question. Doing so also highlights the transition between them. Press the Space bar to play the three clips you've highlighted.

- It's a good idea to watch your transition by "rewinding" a few seconds into the preceding footage, so that you get a sense of how the effect fits in the context of the existing footage. To give yourself some of this "preroll," choose Edit→Select None (or just click anywhere but on a clip) to deselect all the clips. Then click a spot on the Scrubber bar somewhere in the clip before the transition, and press the Space bar to play the movie from that point.

- If you don't care for what you've done, choose Edit→Undo.

- If it's too late for the Undo command, you can return to the transition at any time, highlight its icon, and press the Delete key. Your original clips return instantly, exactly as they were before you added the transition.

How Transitions Affect the Length of Your Movie

As you can see by the example in Figure 15-4, most transitions make your movie shorter. To superimpose the ends of two adjacent clips, iMovie is forced to slide the right-hand clip leftward, making the overall movie end sooner.

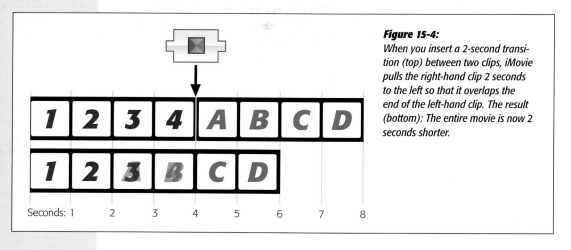

Figure 15-4:
When you insert a 2-second transition (top) between two clips, iMovie pulls the right-hand clip 2 seconds to the left so that it overlaps the end of the left-hand clip. The result (bottom): The entire movie is now 2 seconds shorter.

Under most circumstances, there's nothing wrong with that. After all, that's why you wisely avoided trimming off *all* of the excess "leader" and "trailer" footage (known as *trim handles*) from the ends of your clips. By leaving trim handles on each clip—which will be sacrificed to the transition—you'll have some fade-in or fade-out footage to play with.

Sometimes, however, having your overall project shortened is a serious problem, especially when you've been "cutting to sound," or synchronizing your footage to an existing music track, as described in Chapter 17. Suppose you've spent hours putting your clips into the Movie Track, carefully trimming them so that they perfectly match the soundtrack. And now, as a final touch, you decide to put in transitions. Clearly, having these transitions slide all of your clips to the left would result in chaos, throwing off the synchronization work you had done.

Now you can appreciate the importance of iMovie's Advanced→Lock Audio Clip at Playhead command, which marries a piece of music or sound to a particular spot in the video. If all of your added music and sound elements are attached in this way, adding transitions won't disturb their synchronization. See page 377 for details on locking audio into position.

Tip: Certain transitions—Overlap, Fade In, Fade Out, Wash In, and Wash Out—don't shorten the movie. As described at the end of this chapter, each of these five special transitions affects only *one* clip, not two. They're meant to begin or end your movie, fading in or out from black or white.

How Transitions Chop Up Clips

After your transition has been rendered, you'll notice something peculiar about your Scrubber bar: The transition has now become, in effect, a clip of its own. (In fact, if you open your project "package" icon [page 679] and look in the project's Media folder, you'll even see the newly created clip file represented there, bearing the name of the transition you applied.)

If you click the first clip and play it, you'll find that the playback now stops sooner than it once did—just where the transition takes over. Likewise, the clip that follows the transition has also had frames shaven away at the front end. Both clips, in other words, have sacrificed a second or two to the newly created transition/clip between them. Figure 15-4 illustrates this phenomenon.

Tip: You can rename a transition icon, if it helps you to remember what you were thinking when you created it. To do so, double-click its icon or bar. The Clip Info dialog box appears, in which you can change the name the transition icon displays in your Movie Track.

Editing the Transition

You can edit the transition in several ways: You can change its length, its type, its direction (certain effects only), or all three. To do so, click the transition icon, and then click the Trans button (if the Transitions pane isn't already open). You can now adjust the Speed slider, click another transition in the list, or both. (For the Push and Billow effects, you can also change the direction of the effect.)

When you click Update—a button that's available *only* when a transition icon is highlighted in the Movie Track—iMovie automatically re-renders the transition.

Deleting a Transition

If you decide that you don't need a transition effect between two clips after all, you can delete it just as you would delete any Movie Track clip: by clicking it once and then pressing the Delete key on your keyboard (or by choosing Edit→Clear). Deleting a transition clip does more than eliminate the icon—it also restores the clips on either side to their original conditions. (If you change your mind, Edit→Undo Clear brings back the transition.)

Transition Error Messages

Transitions can be fussy. They like plenty of clip footage to chew on, and once they've begun rendering, they like to be left alone. Here are some of the error messages you may encounter when working with transitions.

When you delete a clip

For example, if, in the process of editing your movie, you delete a clip from the Movie Track that's part of a transition, a message appears that says: "This action will invalidate at least one transition in the project. Invalid transitions will be deleted from the project. Do you want to proceed?"

iMovie is simply telling you that if you delete the clip, you'll also delete the transition attached to it (which is probably just what you'd expect). Click OK. If you first click "Don't ask me again," iMovie will henceforth delete such clips *without* asking your permission.

When the transition is longer than the clip

If you try to add a 5-second crossfade between two 3-second clips, iMovie throws up its hands with various similarly worded error messages. In all cases, the point is clear: The two clips on either side of a transition must *each* be longer than the transition itself.

Put another way, iMovie can't make your transition stretch across more than two clips (or more than one clip, in the case of the Fade and Wash effects).

When you quit while rendering

Creating transitions requires a great deal of iMovie's concentration. If you try to save your project, close it, or empty its Trash, you'll be advised to wait until the rendering is over.

Transitions: The iMovie Catalog

Here, for your reference, is a quick list of each transition, and what editing circumstances might call for it.

Billow

Billow is one of three new transition styles in iMovie HD. It might also be called "Polka-Dot," "Acid Drops," or "Expanding Swiss Cheese." As the clip progresses, a fleet of, well, flying holes descends on the first clip; you can see the second clip through the holes. The holes gradually grow until they occupy the entire frame—and presto, you're now in a new scene. (You can use the directional arrows to specify a general direction for the flurry of UFH's [unidentified flying holes].)

It's kind of hard to imagine when this transition would feel natural, except perhaps in documentaries about cellular reproduction.

Circle Closing

This effect, called *iris close* or *iris in* in professional editing programs, is a holdover from the silent film days, when, in the days before zoom lenses, directors used the effect to highlight a detail in a scene.

It creates an ever-closing circle with the first clip inside and the second clip outside. It's useful at the end of the movie, when the second clip is solid black and the subject of the first clip is centered in the frame. In that setup, the movie ends with an ever-shrinking picture that fades away to a little dot. (If the subject in the center waves goodbye just before being blinked out of view, this trick is especially effective.)

Circle Opening

This effect is much like Circle Closing, except it's been turned inside out. Now the circle grows from the center of the first clip, with the second clip playing inside it, and expands until it fills the frame. (This effect is also called *iris open* or *iris out.*)

Here again, this effect is especially useful at the beginning of a movie, particularly if the subject of the second clip is at the center of the frame. If the first clip in your movie is a solid black frame, your film begins as though the camera's sleepy eye is opening to reveal the scene.

Cross Dissolve

The crossfade, or dissolve, is the world's most popular and effective transition. The first clip gradually disappears, superimposed on the beginning of the second clip, which fades in. If you must use a transition at all, you can't go wrong with this one.

Tip: You can use a very short cross dissolve to create what editors call a "soft cut." When the footage would jump too abruptly if you made a regular cut, put in a ten-frame cross dissolve, which makes the junction of clips *slightly* smoother than just cutting. Soft cuts are very common in interviews where the editors have deleted sections from a continuous shot of a person talking.

Disintegrate

Ever see a film projector get stuck? One frame of film gets stuck in front of the hot projection bulb—and, after a few seconds of heating up, literally melts away to a blank white movie screen?

Imagine your first clip melting away in several spots at once, revealing the second clip beneath, and you've got the idea behind Disintegrate. It looks very, very cool, and is sure to become an everyday effect—among monster-movie makers.

Fade In

Use this effect at the beginning of your movie, or the beginning of a scene that begins in a new place or time. Unlike most transition effects, this one makes no attempt to smooth the transition between two clips. The fade-in overlaps only the clip *to its right*, creating a fade-in from complete blackness.

This transition affects only the clip that follows it, so it doesn't shorten your movie or throw subsequent clips out of alignment, like genuine crossfade-style transitions.

Tip: In general, iMovie doesn't let you place one transition next to another.

The exceptions are the Fade (In and Out) and Wash (In and Out) transitions. Each of these affects only one clip, not two. By placing an In immediately after an Out, you create an elegant fade out, then in to the next shot—a very popular effect in movies and commercials.

Placing an Out just after an In isn't quite as useful, because it reveals only a fleeting glance of the footage in between. But when you're trying to represent somebody's life flashing before his eyes, this trick may be just the ticket.

Fade Out

This effect, conversely, is best used at the *end* of a movie, or the end of a scene that requires a feeling of finality. Like its sister, the Fade In, this one doesn't involve two clips at all; it affects only the end of the clip to its left. As a result, it doesn't affect the length or synchronization of your movie.

It's worth noting, by the way, that a fade-out is almost always followed by a fade-*in*, or by the closing credits. You'll blast your audience's eyeballs if you fade out, sweetly and gracefully—and then cut directly into a bright new clip.

Both Fade In and Fade Out are very useful, and frequently used, effects.

Tip: If you'd rather fade to black and then hold on the black screen for a moment, add a few seconds of blackness after the fade. To do so, switch to the Timeline Viewer and create a pure black clip, as described on page 311. Switch to the Clip Viewer, cut the black clip to the Clipboard, and paste it at the end of the movie. Now iMovie will fade out to black—and hold on to that blackness.

Overlap

Overlap is almost exactly the same as the Cross Dissolve, illustrated earlier. The sole difference: The outgoing clip freezes on its last frame as the new clip fades in. (In a Cross Dissolve, the action continues during the simultaneous fades.) Use it in situations where you might normally use a Cross Dissolve, but want to draw the eye to the second clip right away.

Tip: Unlike the Cross Dissolve, the Overlap transition doesn't change the duration of your movie, which makes it a good choice for movies where you've spent a lot of time synchronizing audio and video. In those cases, a Cross Dissolve might knock things out of sync.

Push

In this transition, the first clip is shoved off the frame by the aggressive first frame of the second clip. This offbeat transition effect draws a lot of attention to itself, so use it extremely sparingly. For example, you could use it to simulate an old-style projector changing slides, or when filming a clever, self-aware documentary in which the host (who first appears in the second clip) "pushes" his way onto the screen.

When you select this transition in the list, the four directional arrows—which are dimmed for most transition types—become available. Click one to indicate how you want the incoming clip to push onscreen: up, down, to the left, or to the right.

Radial

You probably saw this one in a few movies of the seventies. What looks like the sweep-second hand on a watch rotates around the screen, wiping away the first clip and revealing the second clip underneath. This transition suggests the passage of time even more than most transitions, clueing the audience in that the scene about to begin takes place in a new location or on a different day.

Ripple

This effect is gorgeous, poetic, beautiful—and hard to justify.

Ripple invokes the "drop of water on the surface of the pond" metaphor. As the ripple expands across the screen, it pushes the first clip (the pond surface) off the screen to make way for the incoming new clip (the expanding circular ripple). It's a soothing, beautiful effect—but unless you're making mascara commercials, it calls a little too much attention to itself for everyday home movies.

Scale Down

Scale Down, known to pro editors as the *picture zoom* effect, is a peculiar effect, whereby the end of the first clip simply shrinks away. Its rectangle gets smaller and smaller until it disappears, falling endlessly away into the beginning of the second clip, which lies beneath it. The rectangle seems to fly away into the upper-left corner of the second clip, not into dead center.

This kind of effect occasionally shows up on TV news, in documentaries, and so on, after you've been watching a closeup of some important document or photograph. By showing the closeup flying away from the camera, the film editor seems to say, "Enough of that. Meanwhile, back in real life…"

Twirl

Here's your basic *Batman* TV-show transition: The first clip spins away, receding into the black abyss, and then the next clip spins in from the same vanishing point.

Tip: If you transition out of a black clip, you're left with the spinning-in appearance of the second clip without the spinning-away of the first one. In other words, you've just created the spinning-newspaper-headline effect of many an old movie.

Warp In

This effect is very similar to Scale Down, except that as the first clip flies away, it seems to fold in on itself instead of remaining rectangular. That characteristic, combined with the fact that it flies away into dead center of the second clip's frame, makes it look as though the first clip is getting sucked out of the center of the picture by a giant video vacuum cleaner. It's hard to think of *any* circumstance where this effect would feel natural, except when you're deliberately trying to be weird.

Warp Out

You might think that this effect would be the flip side of the Warp In effect, but it's quite different. This time, the second clip intrudes on the first by pushing its way, as an ever-growing sphere, into the frame. What's left of the first clip gets smashed outward, bizarrely distorting, until it's shoved off the outer edges of the picture.

Wash In, Wash Out

These two effects work exactly like Fade In and Fade Out, described earlier, with one big difference: They fade in from, and out to, *white* instead of black.

The Effects Pane

The Effects button summons a panel full of visual effects that you can apply directly to your footage: slow motion, backward, black-and-white, and so on. Some are designed to adjust the brightness, contrast, or color tints in less-than-perfect footage. Most, though, are designed to create actual special effects that simulate fog, rain, earthquakes, lightning, flashbulbs, and bleary-eyed bad LSD.

And if these don't satisfy your hunger for effects, other software companies have had a field day dreaming up new special effects that you can buy and install as plug-ins.

As with transitions, most of these are so out-there and distracting, you should use these only on special occasions.

Selecting the Footage

Before you apply an effect, specify which lucky region of footage you want to be affected:

- **One clip.** Click a clip in the Movie Track or Clips pane; the effect will apply to the entire clip.

- **Multiple clips.** If you highlight several clips in the Movie Track, your selected effect will apply to all of them, treating them as one giant clip. When you click the Apply button, you'll see multiple progress bars marching across the faces of the affected clips in the Movie Track. (Unfortunately, some effects, like the rocketing sparkler of Fairy Dust, aren't smart enough to continue across more than one clip. If you select several clips, the effect starts over at the beginning of each one.)

Tip: Don't forget that you can select several nonadjacent clips. At that point, you can apply an effect to all of them at once.

- **Part of a clip.** If you use the Scrubber bar's selection handles to highlight only a portion of a clip, iMovie will split the clips at the endpoints of the selection, and then apply the effect to the central clip. (iMovie can apply effects only to *entire* clips, which is why this automatic splitting takes place.)

- **Parts of multiple clips.** If you choose Edit→Select None, you can use the Scrubber bar's selection handles to enclose any stretch of clips (or portions of clips) you like. If necessary, iMovie will again split the end clips at the locations of your handles.

Surveying Your Options

Now click the Effects button. Portions of this panel (Figure 15-5) should look familiar. The list of effects, the Preview button, and the Preview pane all work exactly as they do for transitions. (For example, when you click an effect name, the small Preview pane shows a crude, jerky representation of what it will look like; if you click the Preview *button,* you see the same preview in the Monitor window.)

But you'll also find other controls that don't exist anywhere else in iMovie:

- **Effect In, Effect Out.** If you want the chosen effect to start and end exactly at the boundaries of your selection, leave these sliders at their zero points (the far left for Effect In, the far right for Effect Out).

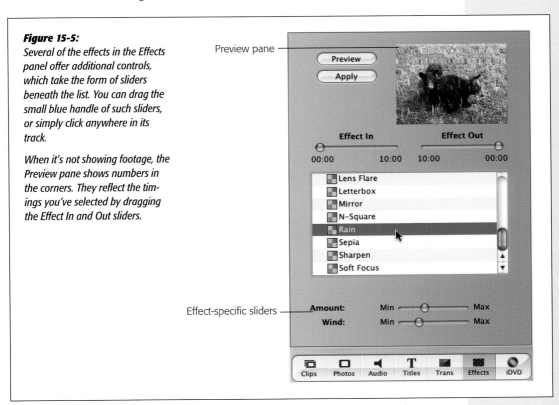

Figure 15-5:
Several of the effects in the Effects panel offer additional controls, which take the form of sliders beneath the list. You can drag the small blue handle of such sliders, or simply click anywhere in its track.

When it's not showing footage, the Preview pane shows numbers in the corners. They reflect the timings you've selected by dragging the Effect In and Out sliders.

Preview pane

Effect-specific sliders

If you like, however, you can make these effects kick in (and kick out) gradually, after the clip has already begun (and before it has ended). That's the purpose of these two sliders: to give you control over when they begin or end.

For example, if you drag the Effect In slider for a Black & White effect to 5:00, the clip will begin playing in full color. After playing for 5 seconds, however, the color will begin to leach out, leaving the rest of the clip to play in black-and-white (a useful effect if you're trying to depict someone slowly going color-blind). You can set the Effect In and Out points no more than 10 seconds from the beginning or ending of a clip.

For example, here's how to make a knockout, professional-looking effect to open your film: Create a still clip from the first frame of a movie, as described on page 400. Split it in half. Convert the first half to black and white, then create a Cross Dissolve between it and the second half. The result: What appears to be a black-and-white photograph "coming to life" as it fades into color and then begins to play normally.

Tip: Instead of using the Effect In and Effect Out sliders, you can gain more precision by double-clicking the timing numbers that appear in at the bottom of the Preview area. (You have to wait until the Preview area is black—that is, until the preview itself has finished playing.) Once you've highlighted these digits, you can type new numbers to replace them. These numbers are in seconds:frames format.

- **Effect-specific controls.** As you click the name of each effect in the list, additional sliders may appear above the Effects panel. They're described in the effect-by-effect descriptions later in this chapter.

- **Apply.** When you click Apply, iMovie begins to render the selected clip—to perform the massive numbers of calculations necessary to bring each pixel into compliance with the effect you've specified. As with transitions, effect rendering telegraphs its progress with a subtle red line, a miniature progress bar that crawls from left to right beneath the selected clip (see Figure 15-6).

Number of effects

Effect indicator

Progress bar

Figure 15-6:
The thin red progress bar lets you know how much longer you have to wait. You can tell at a glance that a clip has had an effect applied, thanks to the checkerboard brand in the upper right. And if there's a digit beside the checkerboard, you've applied more than one effect to the same clip.

Rendering effects works exactly like rendering transitions: You can continue working on other parts of your movie, but things can bog down if you've got several effects rendering at once. Actually, rendering effects takes much longer than rendering transitions, in part because you apply each effect to an entire clip instead of just the last couple of seconds. Press ⌘-period to cancel the rendering.

It's important to note, by the way, that iMovie actually applies the selected effect to a *duplicate* copy of the clip's DV file on your hard drive. iMovie creates the behind-the-scenes duplicate as a safety net for you. It gives you the option of removing or adjusting the effect at any time. (If you're curious, switch to the Finder; open your project package as described on page 379; and open its Media folder. Inside, you'll find a new clip called, for example, Earthquake 01, which represents the modified clip.)

So what happens to the original clip? iMovie puts it into your project Trash. As long as you don't empty your trash, you can recover the original clip (and remove the effect) at any time.

Removing an Effect

If you click a clip and then press the Delete key, you're saying: "Throw away the effect. Bring back my original, unmodified clip." Much though it may feel like you're instructing iMovie to delete the *clip itself,* you're not. (You would have to press Delete a *second time* to achieve that purpose.)

In any case, when you delete an effect in this way, iMovie pulls your original footage out of the project Trash and reinstates it. That is, it does so *if* you haven't *emptied* the Trash. Remember that once you empty your project Trash, you throw away your opportunity to adjust or remove effects forever.

Note: If you do empty the Trash, you'll notice something weird: The little Effect indicator shown in Figure 15-8 *vanishes* from all of your effects clips! That's because as far as iMovie is concerned, those effects are now part of the original clips, married to them forever.

Adjusting an Effect

Despite what the iMovie online help says, there's no Update button on the Effects pane. To adjust the start time, stop time, or other parameters of a special effect, you must first delete the effect altogether, as described above, and then reapply it using new settings.

Superimposing Effects

It's perfectly possible to combine effects by applying first one, and then another. For example, after using the Black & White effect, you may want to use the Brightness & Contrast control to adjust its gray tones. You can even apply a single effect repeatedly, intensifying its effect; for instance, you could apply Fairy Dust several times to make it appear as though multiple fireworks are going off. Or you could apply Rain twice at different intensities to add depth to your simulated deluge.

Once you've applied more than one effect to a certain clip, iMovie thoughtfully adds a "number-of-effects" number next to the effects symbol, as shown in Figure 15-6. When it comes time to *remove* some of your layered effects, you'll appreciate that indicator. It will keep you sane as you peel away one effect after another.

For example, suppose you're making a disaster movie. To one climactic clip, you've applied two Rains, three Earthquakes, an Electricity, and a pair of Fogs.

If you decide that perhaps you've laid it on a bit thick, you can click the clip and then start tapping the Delete key. With each tap, you remove one effect, in reverse chronological order, until only the original clip remains. (Be careful not to press Delete that last time; you'll remove the clip itself!)

Effects: The iMovie Catalog

iMovie HD comes with 23 built-in effects, including five new ones. The following list describes them all.

Adjust Colors

This powerful effect adjusts the actual color palette used in your clip footage. If your footage has an unfortunate greenish tint, you can color-correct it; if you're hoping for a sunset look, you can bring out the oranges and reds; if it's a sci-fi flick taking place on Uranus, you can make it look blue and spooky.

The special sliders for this effect affect the hue, saturation, and brightness of your footage. Hue, saturation, and brightness are cornerstones of color theory; you can read much more about them on the Web, or in books and articles about photo editing. In the meantime, here's a brief summary:

- **Hue Shift (Left—Right)**. Adjusts the overall color tint of the clip. What iMovie is actually doing is rotating the hue around the hue circle, either to the left or the right. In practice, this effect doesn't do anything predictable to an image; you're meant to play with it until you find something you like.

- **Color (B&W—Vivid)**. This slider lets you control the intensity of a color, or its *saturation*. If it's blue, you control *how* blue it is: increasing toward Vivid makes the blue more intense.

- **Lightness (Dark—Bright)**. Use this slider to adjust the overall brightness or darkness of the *colors* in your clip. There's only a subtle difference between these effects and the Brightness/Contrast effect described below; this slider adjusts the brightness of the colors, rather than the overall brightness.

Aged Film

Here you've just spent $500 on a camcorder and a couple thou on a Macintosh, all in the name of attaining perfect purity of video—and then this effect comes along. It's designed to make a clip look like an old, flickering, dusty film, complete with horrible scratches along the celluloid.

Using the Exposure, Jitter, and Scratches sliders, you can control just how faded, shaky-in-the-projector, and scratched up the footage looks (Figure 15-7, top).

Combine this one with Black & White, described next, and you've got yourself something that looks authentically like a horribly preserved reel you dug up from somebody's attic.

Black & White

This effect does one thing very well: It turns your clip into a black-and-white piece of footage, suitable for simulating security-camera footage or TV from the 1950s.

Brightness & Contrast

Footage that's too dark is one of the most common hallmarks of amateur camcorder work. If you're filming indoors without extra lights, you may as well accept the fact that your clip will be too dark.

Figure 15-7:
Top: Modern museum? No—thanks to the Aged Film effect, it's ancient edifice circa 1938.

Middle: Georges Seurat's take on a coffeehouse: a pointillistic mosaic, courtesy of the Crystallize effect.

Bottom: Earthquake! (For a better simulation of what iMovie really does, shake this book rapidly in front of your face.) This effect looks really great when you adjust the Effect In and Effect Out sliders so that the shaking begins gradually and intensifies. (Better yet, apply the effect several times, to make the intensity of the shaking appear to fluctuate.)

Before

After

The Brightness & Contrast controls can help, but they're no substitute for good lighting in the original footage. When you drag the Brightness and Contrast sliders in very small amounts, you may be able to rescue footage that's slightly murky or washed out. Dragging the sliders a lot, however, may make the too-dark footage grainy and weird-looking.

Tip: Using the Effect In and Out sliders, you can control which *parts* of the clip are affected by the Adjust Colors and Brightness & Contrast effects. If you need the colors or brightness to shift several times over the course of a clip, consider chopping up the clip into several smaller clips, each of which is an opportunity to reset the effect settings and timings.

Crystallize

This effect makes your footage look like you shot it through a stained-glass window, or perhaps a translucent honeycomb (Figure 15-7, middle). As you drag the Size slider toward Max, the size of the individual "crystal" facets gets so large, it's more like you're looking at a living stained-glass window. At the Max end, you can't even identify what you're looking at; it's as though you've got an abstract painting that's come to life. This is not, ahem, an effect you'll use often.

Earthquake

Talk about an effect you'll use only rarely!

This one (Figure 15-7, bottom) is designed to simulate *camera shake,* the jittery, shuddering, handheld, no-tripod, stabilizer-off look that you'd get if you felt the earth move under your feet, and felt the sky come tumblin' down. You can use the two sliders to specify *how* the earthquake is tossing your camera around: sideways or vertically, and to what degrees.

Edge Work

Here's another effect that's new in iMovie HD. Its peculiar mission: to reduce the scene to black-and-white moving blobs, as though the entire clip had been constructed of bad Xerox copies.

iMovie creates this effect by setting every *edge* that it detects—borders between light and dark areas—in fat "boldface." The Max slider governs the chunkiness of the rendered black and white blobs. You could easily imagine Edge Work finding a home in music videos, homemade animated movies, or courtroom scenes where you want to mask a witness's identity.

Edges

Again, think "music-video weirdness." This new, amazing-looking iMovie HD effect reduces the entire scene to an *inverted* photocopy. That is, the scene goes black except for the moving edges of things, which are white. You can still tell what you're looking at, especially if you move the Intensity slider to the right, but the whole thing has a weird, ghostly, "erased" look to it.

Electricity

Unlike most of the other effects, which apply equally everywhere in the video frame, this one actually superimposes an image—in this case, a purplish, flickering bolt of lightning—onto any spot of the footage you want. You can use this one to great comic effect; when attached to the end of somebody's wand or walking stick, the electricity looks like it's shooting out. When attached to somebody's head or rear end, the electricity looks like it's zapping that hapless person.

You can probably figure out that the Rotate slider lets you change the lightning bolt's angle (CW = Clockwise, CCW = Counter-Clockwise). But what you may not realize is that you can *click* inside the Preview window to specify the landing (or starting) point of the sparkler. By using the rotation and position controls in combination, you have complete freedom in designing the placement of the zap within the frame. (Alas, you can't make the bolt move *during* a clip. It stays put, crackling away right in place, so it's primarily useful for adding to a tripod shot that you filmed expressly for the purpose of doctoring later in iMovie.)

Fairy Dust

Like Electricity, this effect is designed to superimpose a professional-looking sparkler effect on your footage. In this case, you get a shooting firework that follows a specified arc across the frame; the net effect is something like a burning fuse, except that the path, although visible in the Preview window for your reference, doesn't actually appear once you apply the effect.

Here again, you can click within the Preview frame to position the arc, thereby adjusting the sparkler's trajectory. Use the Direction slider to specify whether the fire flies left to right across the frame, or right to left. (It really has no business being a slider. It has only two positions: left or right. Dragging the handle to an intermediate point does nothing.) The Trail slider, meanwhile, governs the size of the sparkler.

Fast/Slow/Reverse

If you're a veteran of iMovie, you may remember that the Fast, Slow, and Reverse controls used to be at the bottom edge of the Timeline Viewer. It occurred to somebody at Apple that this placement really made very little sense; those are, after all, special effects. Why should they work differently from all the other effects? So Fast/Slow/Reverse is now a card-carrying occupant of the Effects list—and each component has been improved and upgraded in the process.

Flash

This effect simulates flash bulbs going off. You won't have much call for this effect in everyday filmmaking; but when that day arrives that you're trying to depict a movie star arriving at opening night—or somebody getting electrocuted—iMovie stands ready.

- **Count (One—Max).** This slider controls how many flashes will go off in the scene. (The maximum number depends on your Speed slider setting and the length of the clip, but the most you'll get is about one every seven frames, or about four per second.)

- **Brightness (Min—Max).** Controls the intensity of each flash. For true flashbulb effects, you'll want the slider at, or close to, its Max. For storm lightning or nuclear-bomb-watching effects, use lower settings.

- **Speed (Fast—Slow).** Governs how far apart the flashes appear.

Tip: You can use this effect to create a convincing newsreel (or school science film) look. First, turn your clip into black-and-white using the Black & White effect. Now apply the Flash effect with the sliders set to Max, Min, and Fast, respectively.

Fog

You already knew that by letting you edit and add music to your movies, iMovie lets you fiddle with the emotional overtones of your own memories. What you may not have realized is that it also lets you retroactively change the weather.

The Fog effect creates a mist that seems to float in front of the camera lens. It's suitable for atmospheric effects, simulated fire or crash footage, comical hangover clips, and so on.

The Amount slider controls the opacity of the fog, the Wind slider governs how quickly it drifts, and the Color slider lets you specify the color.

Tip: Don't be fooled by the Color slider's Black and White labels. The various positions along the slider actually proceed through all the colors of the rainbow.

Ghost Trails

This effect makes moving portions of the video leave behind "visual echoes." In addition to blurry-vision effects, it can also be handy when you're trying to depict a runner as a superhero with blinding speed. On clips without much motion, this effect does nothing at all.

The sliders let you control the intensity of the effect:

- **Trail (Short—Long).** Governs the length of the ghost images that follow a rapidly moving object in your scene.

- **Steps (Small—Large).** Controls how closely the ghost image follows the object.

- **Opacity (Clear—Opaque).** Lets you specify the transparency of the ghost image.

Glass Distortion

Those nutty Apple programmers must start to go a little stir-crazy after too many long days and sleepless nights. Why else would they introduce, in iMovie HD, a new effect that makes it look like you shot the scene through, ahem, the textured glass of a *bathroom window?*

Anyway, that's exactly what Glass Distortion does. It's incredibly realistic—as long as you are, in fact, going for that public-restroom-window look. (The Scale slider affects the size of the "wrinkles" in the "glass" of the "window.")

Lens Flare

When you aim the camera toward the sun, sunshine can strike the anti-reflective coating on the inside of each lens, resulting in a reflection—a bright spot, or (on complex lens systems) a trail of bright spots—called lens flare.

Ordinarily, photographers try to avoid lens flare. But hey, as long as Apple is on a quest to let you deliberately make your footage look damaged (see Aged Film and Earthquake), why not?

Click within the Preview window to set the rotation point for the lens flare. Then use the Sweep slider to control how broadly the flare line sweeps across the frame, as happens when the camera moved during the shot. (If it did not, in fact, move, do your best to position the Sweep slider handle squarely in the middle of the slider to prevent the flare from moving at all.) The Intensity slider adjusts the size of the primary sunshine blob. (You'll get it as soon as you try it.)

Letterbox

This filter adds black letterbox bars above and below the frame, creating the look of movies (which have 16:9 proportions) as they sometimes appear when presented on a TV (which has 4:3 proportions). You may have seen this look on the Bravo channel, on a Woody Allen video, on some DVDs, or in artsy TV commercials.

The paradox, of course, is that your footage was *already* correctly shaped for a 4:3 TV screen. So to make it look as though the original was movie-shaped, iMovie has no choice but to *chop off* the top and bottom slices of your movie. It works, therefore, only when the subject matter is already vertically centered.

Fortunately, you can use the Shift slider to nudge the original footage upward or downward in the gap between the black bars, or use the Size slider to make the bars themselves more or less intrusive (thinner or fatter).

Mirror

This completely freaky effect makes iMovie split the video picture down the middle—horizontally, vertically, or both (in quadrants). It then fills the left half of the screen with a mirror image of the right half, or the top half with a mirror of the bottom. There's no seam to indicate what's going on; the result is an Alice-in-Wonderland hybrid.

- **Vertical (Top—Bottom).** This slider moves a horizontal "mirror" up and down the frame. At the Top setting, the footage doesn't look any different. At far right, you've flipped the entire frame upside-down.

Tip: If you drag the Vertical slider all the way to Bottom, and the Horizontal slider to Left, you neatly flip your clip upside-down—an iMovie first.

- **Horizontal (Left—Right).** This slider moves a vertical "mirror" left and right across the frame. Pushing this slider all the way to Left removes the horizontal reflections altogether. At far right, you've flipped the entire frame right-for-left. (While the Mirror effect in general doesn't seem to be very practical for most filmmaking, the ability to flip the frame horizontally can be terrifically useful. It can make the actor look left instead of right, make the fire engine drive west instead of east, and otherwise fix continuity problems.)

If you drag both sliders to their center positions, all four quadrants of the picture are, in fact, upside-down and/or horizontally flipped copies of the lower-right quadrant of the original footage.

The Effect In and Effect Out sliders make the mirrors fly in from the top and side of the frame as the clip plays. (Memo to music-video makers: The effect can be truly creepy.)

Tip: Be careful of *signs* (such as road signs) in footage you've mirrored. Their reverse-image type is a dead giveaway that you've rewritten history.

N-Square

If you've been secretly burning to remake *The Fly* from the insect's point of view, this is your effect. It "echoes" the video frame over and over again in miniature, like tiles of a mosaic (Figure 15-8, top).

The **Squares (Min—Max)** controls how many panes the frame contains, each showing the same image. At the Min position, you get four copies; at Max, you get literally hundreds. (Talk about *The Matrix*!)

Tip: If you use the Effect In and Effect Out sliders, you get an interesting variation on the N-Square effect. The clip starts out looking normal; as it plays, the grid of duplicates flies in from the lower right, sliding into its final matrix.

Rain

Here's one of iMovie's most realistic efforts. It makes your clip look as though it was filmed in a driving rainstorm (Figure 15-8, middle).

How driving? You determine that by adjusting the Amount slider (which controls the lengths of the raindrop slashes) or the Wind slider (which specifies how much the drop directions change over time).

Tip: You can create a better depth simulation by stacking this effect onto a clip twice: once with small droplets (farther) and once with long ones (closer). Try throwing in a little Fog, too.

Sepia

You might think of this effect as a more nostalgic version of the Black & White effect. Once again, the color drains out of your clip, but instead of black-and-white, you get brown-and-white, which conveys the feeling of memory (thanks to its resemblance to the look of antique photographs). Don't forget to follow up with the Brightness/ Contrast effect, if necessary, to fine-tune the effect.

Sharpen

You might guess that this effect could help to repair out-of-focus scenes. In practice, however, the Sharpen effect isn't very effective in that role. Instead, it adds a fine grain to your footage, often creating a "solarized" color-banding effect, to the degree you specify using the Amount slider.

Soft Focus

Soft-focus lenses are often used when filming TV commercials that feature aging movie stars, because the fine netting or Vaseline coating on such lenses blurs fine wrinkles. (Soft-focus lenses also give everything a faintly blurry, fuzzy-edged look, but that's the price the stars pay for wrinkle obfuscation.)

Figure 15-8:
Top: The N-Square effect at a low setting looks like this. Higher settings make the video look like Hollywood Squares gone berserk.

Middle: Be grateful. The Rain effect is about the only time you'll ever be able to control the rain, at least in this lifetime.

Bottom: The Soft Focus effect is great for anything misty, nostalgic, or filmed through a nylon stocking.

Before

After

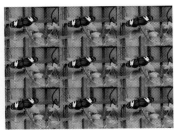

Now you, too, can hide your subjects' wrinkles, by applying this soft-focus effect after the filming is complete (Figure 15-8, bottom). This effect is also good for suggesting dreams, memory, summertime nostalgia, or other hazy situations. At the sliders' extreme positions, the whole frame looks like the nuclear-holocaust scene in *Terminator 2* (especially if you use the Effect In slider to make the glow creep in over time).

Use the Softness slider to adjust the amount of Vaseline on the lens, Amount to specify what percentage of the frame is smeared, and Glow to govern just how radioactive the bright spots look.

Installing More Effects

The effects that come with iMovie certainly aren't the only ones available. For $25 or $30 you can buy dozens of additional effects like Mosaic, Emboss, X-ray, and so on. A quick Google search for *iMovie plug-instrument* will reveal to you a full array of companies that sell these effects online. Some of the best await at *www.geethree.com*, *www.stupendous-software.com*, *www.virtix.com,* and *www.imovieplugins.com*.

These samples, from Stupendous Software (*www.stupendous-software.com*), show you the power of plug-ins (Figure 15-9).

Figure 15-9:

Top: Bluescreen is a common technique in Hollywood, and now on your own Mac. Shoot one image against a blue backdrop, and the plug-in superimposes it on any other clip you like.

Bottom: These plug-ins let you draw or type right on top of the video.

Titles, Captions, and Credits

T ext superimposed over footage is incredibly common in the film and video worlds. You'd be hard-pressed to find a single movie, TV show, or commercial that doesn't have titles, captions, or credits. In fact, it's the *absence* of superimposed text that helps identify most camcorder videos as amateur efforts.

In iMovie, the term *title* refers to any kind of text: credits, titles, subtitles, copyright notices, and so on. You use them almost exactly the way you use the transitions or effects described in Chapter 15: by choosing a text-animation style from a list, adjusting its duration using a slider, dragging it into your Movie Track, and waiting while iMovie renders the effect.

But you don't need to be nearly as economical in your use of titles as you are with transitions. Transitional effects and visual effects interfere with something that stands perfectly well on its own—the footage. Transitions and special effects that aren't purposeful and important to the film may well annoy or distract your audience. When you superimpose text, on the other hand, the audience is much more likely to accept your intrusion. You're introducing this new element for its benefit, to convey information you couldn't transmit otherwise.

Moreover, as you'll soon see, most of iMovie's text effects are far more focused in purpose than its transition and effect selections, so you'll have little trouble choosing the optimum text effect for a particular editing situation. For example, the Scrolling Credits effect rolls a list of names slowly up the screen—an obvious candidate for the close of your movie. Another puts several consecutive lines of text in a little block at the lower-left corner of the screen—exactly the way the text in MTV music videos appears.

Tip: Using the Titles feature described in this chapter isn't the only way to create text effects. Using a graphics program like AppleWorks or Photoshop Elements, you can create text "slides" with far more flexibility than you can in the Titles feature. For example, the built-in Titles feature offers you a choice of only 16 colors and limited choice of type size. But using a "title card" that you import as a graphic, you're free to use any text color and any font size. You can even dress up such titles with clip art, 3-D effects, and whatever other features your graphics software offers.

Credits that you import as still graphics in this way can't do much more than fade in and fade out. When you bypass iMovie's built-in titles feature, you give up the ability to use the fancy animations. Still, the flexibility you gain in the look, color, and size of your type may be worth the sacrifice. For details on this technique, see Chapter 18.

Setting Up a Title

Adding some text to your movie requires several setup steps:

1. **Choose a title effect.**

2. **Type the text.**

3. **Specify the duration and timing.**

4. **Choose a font.**

5. **Specify the size of the lettering.**

6. **Choose an animation direction.**

7. **Turn on the "Over black" checkbox, if desired.**

8. **Choose a color for the lettering.**

9. **Add a backdrop.**

Here are these same steps in more detail:

Choose a Title Effect

Start by clicking the Titles button. The effects list and the other elements of the Titles palette appear, as shown in Figure 16-1.

Tip: If your mouse has a built-in scroll wheel, you can turn it to scroll the list of title effects, even without clicking the clicker, whenever the cursor is in the list area.

When you click an effect's name, you see a short preview in the Preview screen. (Use the catalog at the end of this chapter to guide you in choosing a text effect.) To view the same preview on the full-size Monitor, click the Preview button.

Incidentally, the items in the list with flippy gray triangles next to their names aren't actually titles. They're title *categories.* Click a category name to expand the triangle and see what's inside, as shown in Figure 16-1.

Tip: When showing you the preview, iMovie superimposes the text over whatever Movie Track clip is currently showing in the Monitor window. Drag the Playhead anywhere you like to specify which footage you'd like to see behind this preview. (If you haven't put any clips into the Movie Track, your preview displays only a black background, as though you'd turned on the "Over black" checkbox.)

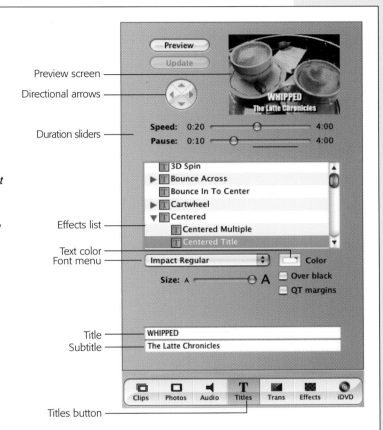

Figure 16-1:
Apple has organized the list by clumping related effects into categories. To expand a title category, you don't have to click the little triangle. Instead, you can click the category name, like Bounce Cross, which gives you a broader target. Click the name a second time to collapse the list of titles.

Each time you start a new iMovie project, the proposed title and subtitle aren't very stimulating. The first title is "My Great Movie," and its subtitle is your name (or whatever you've typed into the Sharing pane of System Preferences). The second title is "Starring," and its subtitle is "Me." You get the idea.

Fortunately, these are quick enough to change: Click in the text box, press ⌘-A to select all of the dummy text, and then type right over it.

Preview screen —
Directional arrows —
Duration sliders —
Effects list —
Text color —
Font menu —
Title —
Subtitle —
Titles button —

Type the Text

Beneath the list of text effects, you'll find a place to type the actual text you want to appear in this credit, caption, or title. Just click the box once to highlight the proposed text and then begin typing. (You don't have to backspace over the factory-installed dummy text first.)

The way this text box looks and acts depends on the kind of title you've selected in the list. They fall into three categories (see Figure 16-2): text blocks, title/subtitle pairs, and pair sequences.

Text blocks

When you choose the Music Video or Scrolling Block text effects, you get a simple text box, into which you can type any text you want. At the end of each line, you can press Return to create a new line or press Return twice to create a blank line, exactly as you would in a word processor. (You can use the Cut, Copy, and Paste commands in the Edit menu to edit this text, too.)

The maximum amount of text you can type or paste here is just under 256 characters—one short paragraph. (See "Music Video" and "Scrolling Block" in the catalog section at the end of this chapter for more details.)

Title/Subtitle pairs

When you click the names of most effects, you're shown only two narrow boxes into which you can type text, as shown in Figure 16-2 at center. Whatever you type into the top box often appears in larger typeface than the one in the bottom box.

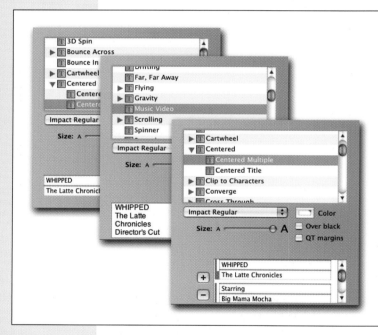

Figure 16-2:
The area into which you can type your text depends on the kind of text effect you've selected. You'll be offered either two lines for a title and subtitle (top left), one big text box (middle), or a virtually unlimited number of two-line pairs (bottom right), suitable for credit sequences at the end of your movie.

Such effects as Bounce In to Center, Centered Title, Flying Letters, Flying Words, Scroll with Pause, Stripe Subtitle, Subtitle, Typewriter, and Zoom fall into this category.

Tip: You don't have to type text into both of these boxes. In fact, *most* of the time you'll probably type into only the top box. The subtitle box underneath is there solely for your convenience, for those occasions when you need a second, usually smaller, line of type underneath the larger credit.

Pair sequences

When you're creating the credits for the end of a movie, you usually want two columns of text: on the left, the list of roles; on the right, the actors who portrayed them. In these situations, you need iMovie to offer *pairs* of slots—enough to accommodate the names of everybody who worked on your movie. It's easy to spot the text effects that offer these two-line pairs because they're the ones with the words "Multiple" or "Rolling" in their names.

After clicking one of these title effects, you see not one but two different text-box pairs. The window offers a scroll bar, plus a + button, so that you can add more pairs and scroll through them (Figure 16-3).

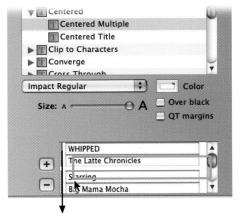

Figure 16-3:
You can rearrange the credits in your sequence by dragging the left edge of a credit pair up or down in the list, and waiting patiently as iMovie scrolls the list (arrow). You can also remove a credit by clicking the – button.

Start by clicking the top box. Drag across the dummy text ("My Great Movie"), or press a quick ⌘-A to highlight it, and then type the first character's name (*Raymond,* for example). Press Tab to highlight the lower box, and then type the actor's name (*Dustin Hoffman,* for example). If there's another empty pair of boxes beneath the one you've just filled, press Tab again, and fill in those boxes, too.

Don't worry, you'll know when you've filled up all the available boxes: You'll either discover that you can't scroll down any more, or that when you press Tab, you'll circle around and wind up in the *first* box you filled in. At that point, click the + button beside the text boxes to add another pair of boxes. Keep going this way—clicking +, typing a pair of names, clicking + again—until you've typed in the names of everybody you want in the list of credits.

Specify the Timing

You have a lot of control over the timing of your titles' animation. Most of the title styles offer two sliders just below the Preview screen:

• The **Speed** slider has different results with different titles. Setting a faster Speed setting makes the Centered Title fade in/out faster, Flying Words fly faster, Typewriter types faster, and so on. For title styles involving motion, it controls the text speed; for title styles that remain still (such as Centered Title), it controls the total amount of time the text spends onscreen. The catalog of title styles at the end of this chapter identifies the Speed slider's effect for each style.

Tip: When precision counts, don't use the Speed slider. Instead, double-click directly on those numbers in the Preview rectangle, the numbers that make up the "05:20 + 01:08 = 6:28" display. Once highlighted, you can type in new numbers with frame-by-frame accuracy (these numbers are in seconds:frames format).

- The **Pause** effect depends on the style, too. For titles that fade in and out, it controls the amount of time the text will be fully manifested onscreen, readable and at full size and brightness, between its fade in and fade out segments. For titles whose text flies or rolls into place (such as Typewriter or Flying Words), Pause controls how long the finished title hangs around after it's complete.

As you adjust these sliders, the readout at the bottom of the preview screen shows you, in the seconds:frames format, the time settings you've specified. (You have to wait until the preview is finished playing before these numbers appear.) For example, if it says "05:20 + 01:08 = 6:28," iMovie is trying to tell you, in its own way:

"You've set the Speed slider to 5:20—that is, you've allotted 170 frames for fading in and out. So I'll make the text fade in over half of that time: 2 seconds, 15 frames. Then you've set the Pause slider to 1:08, so I'll make the text sit there onscreen for 1 second, 8 frames. Finally, I'll take another 2 seconds, 15 frames to fade out."

Take into account your viewers' reading speed. There's only one thing more frustrating than titles that fly by too quickly to read, and that's titles that sit there on screen forever, boring the audience silly. Many video editors use this guideline: Leave the words onscreen long enough for somebody to read them aloud twice.

Preview the Effect

As with the transitions described in the previous chapter, iMovie offers two kinds of preview for titles:

- **Preview box.** If you click a title style's name, you see a real-time preview of your title animation in the small Preview box above the list of titles. It's very tiny, but it lasts as long as the finished title will last, giving you a good idea of your title's readability. (The Speed and Pause sliders affect these previews.)

- **Monitor window.** If you click the Preview *button,* iMovie shows another kind of preview in the Monitor window. This time, you get to see every single frame of the animation, no matter how long it takes your Mac to spew out these images. On slow Macs, you may not see the animation play at real-world speed; you're getting, in essence, a slow-motion version of the full effect.

Choose a Font

Using the pop-up menu just below the list of effects, you can choose a typeface for your text. Consider these guidelines:

- **Use only TrueType or PostScript fonts.** Just don't use *bitmapped* fonts. And if you have no idea what these terms mean, don't worry. *All* the fonts that come preinstalled on your Mac are TrueType fonts, and will look terrific in your iMovie production. You need to worry about the font type only if you've manually installed some additional ones (probably very old ones) onto your Mac.

Note: The beauty of iMovie's titling feature is that the fonts you choose become embedded into the actual digital picture. In other words, when you distribute your movie as a QuickTime file, you don't have to worry that your recipients might not have the same fonts you used to create the file. They'll see on their screens exactly what you see on yours.

- **Be consistent.** Using the same typeface for all of the titles in your movie lends consistency and professionalism to the project.

- **Remember the QuickTime effect.** If you plan to distribute your finished movie as a QuickTime file—an electronic movie file that you can distribute by email, network, CD, disk, or Web page—use the biggest, boldest, cleanest fonts you have. Avoid spindly delicate fonts or script fonts. When your movie is compressed down to a 3-inch square, what looks terrific in your Monitor window will be so small it may become completely illegible. (Look at each illustration in the catalog discussion at the end of this chapter. If the text is hard to read there, you won't be able to read it in a small QuickTime movie either.)

  If your movie is going to be a QuickTime movie, turn on the QT Margins checkbox, too. Doing so increases the maximum font size you're allowed to select using the text-size slider. (See the box on the next page for the explanation.)

  Come to think of it, you might want to choose big, bold, clean fonts even if you're going to play the finished movie on a TV whose resolution is far lower than that of your computer screen. Be especially careful when using one of the text effects that includes a subtitle, as iMovie subtitles often use an even smaller typeface than the primary title font, and may lose legibility if the font has too much filigree.

  Finally, favor *sans serif* fonts—typefaces that don't have the tiny *serifs*, or "hats and feet," at the end of the character strokes. The typeface you're reading now is a serif font, one that's less likely to remain legible in a QuickTime movie. The typeface used in the Tip below is a sans serif font.

Tip: Some of the standard Mac fonts that look especially good as iMovie fonts are Arial Black, Capitals, Charcoal, Chicago, Gadget, Helvetica, Impact, Sand, Techno, and Textile.

Some of the fonts whose delicate nature may be harder to read are Monaco, Courier, Old English, Swing, Trebuchet, Times, Palatino, and Verdana.

Specify the Size of the Lettering

iMovie is extremely conservative with its font-size choices. Even with the Size slider (just to the right of the Font pop-up menu) all the way to the right, and even with "QT Margins" turned on, iMovie doesn't let you make titles that fill the screen. (Keeping your text short may help. If the phrase is very long, iMovie further reduces the point size enough to fit the entire line on the screen, even if the type-size slider is at its maximum. In other words, you can make the font for the credit *PIGGY* much larger than you can *ONE HAM'S ADVENTURES IN MANHATTAN.*)

If you feel hemmed in by the font-size limitations, consider using a still-image "title card" with text as large as you like, as described on page 348.

Choose an Animation Direction

Most of iMovie's text effects are animated. They feature words flying across the screen, sliding from one edge of the frame to the other, and so on. Some feature directional arrows (seen in Figure 16-1, for example) that let you control which direction the text flies or slides in. By clicking the appropriate arrow, you can specify which direction the text should fly. (The directional controls are dimmed and unavailable for other text effects.)

Note: In the case of the Music Video effect, the arrow specifies which *corner* the text block should sit in, motionless.

The catalog of text effects at the end of this chapter identifies those that offer a direction control, and what it does in each case.

The "Over Black" Checkbox

Under normal circumstances, the text you've specified gets superimposed over the video picture. Particularly when you're creating opening or closing credits, however, you may want the lettering to appear on a black screen—a striking and professional-looking effect. In those cases, turn on the "Over black" checkbox.

It's important to note that when you do so, you *add* to the total length of your movie. Adding the "Over black" title is like inserting a new clip, in that you force the clips to the right of your text effect to slide further rightward to accommodate the credit you just inserted. (When the "Over black" checkbox *isn't* turned on, adding a text effect doesn't change the overall length of your movie.)

The "Over black" option is attractive for three reasons. First, it looks extremely professional; it's something people who don't have an editing program like iMovie can't even do. Second, the high contrast of white against black makes the text very legible. Third, the audience will *read* it, instead of being distracted by the video behind it.

Tip: You don't have to limit yourself to adding text over black; you can just as easily superimpose your titles over blue, over red, or over fuschia. The trick is to create a colored clip as described on page 312, and add your titles to *it.* In that case, do *not* turn on "Over black", since you want your lettering to float on top of the existing video, which happens to be a solid, unchanging color.

Choose a Color for the Lettering

By clicking the tiny square beside the word Color, you get a little dialog box known as the Mac OS X Color Picker. (The box on the facing page describes it in detail.) For now, the important thing is to choose a color that *contrasts* with the footage behind the lettering. Use white against black, black against white, yellow against blue, and so on.

Note: iMovie doesn't limit you to TV-safe colors. But be careful. If colors are too bright (saturated), the edges of the letters can smear and tear when played back on a TV.

Add a Backdrop

If you left your education to the Apple online help, you might assume that there are only two kinds of images that can underlie your titles: video footage or a solid black

The TV-Safe Area, Overscanning, and You

Millions of TV viewers every day are blissfully unaware that they're missing the big picture.

In its early days, the little cathode-ray guns inside the TV worked by painting one line of the TV picture, then turning around and heading back the opposite direction. To make sure that the screen was painted edge to edge, these early TVs were programmed to overshoot the edges of the screen—or, to use the technical term, to *overscan* the screen.

TV technology is much better now, but even modern TVs exhibit overscanning. The amount varies, but you may be missing as much as 10 percent of the picture beyond the left and right edges (and often the top and bottom, too).

TV producers are careful to keep the action and titles in the part of the frame that's least likely to be lost in the overscan. But as a film editor, the *TV-safe area* is suddenly your concern, too. The overscanning effect means that when you

show your iMovie productions on a TV, you'll lose anything that's very close to the edges of the frame.

Most of the time, that's no problem; only when you're adding titles does the overscanning effect become a worry.

TV-safe area   Lost when viewed on TV

Fortunately, avoiding text-chopping problems is supremely easy: Just turn *off* the QT Margins checkbox. Doing so makes iMovie shrink the text enough so that it won't get chopped off on a TV—guaranteed.

This business of the TV-safe area *isn't* an issue if you plan to convert your iMovie work into QuickTime movies, which have no such complications. That's why this checkbox is worded as it is: "QT Margins" means "Assume that this movie will be shown as a QuickTime movie, and therefore won't have chopped-off margins." When the QT Margins checkbox is turned *on,* the text-size slider lets you crank your font sizes a few notches higher.

frame. Fortunately, there's a third option that greatly expands your creative possibilities: superimposing your text on a still image, such as a photo or some gradient fill you've created in, say, Photoshop Elements.

Tip: One of the still backgrounds you can download from the "Missing CD" page at *www.missingmanuals.com* is called Color Bars. It lets you begin and end your movie with the standard, broadcast-TV color bar chart like the one shown (in shades of gray) at lower left in Figure 16-4. In professional video work, about 20 seconds of color bars are always recorded at the beginning of a tape. They give the technicians a point of color reference for adjusting their monitors and other reproduction equipment to ensure that the footage looks the same on their gear as it did on yours. Their goal is to adjust the knobs until the white bars look white, not pink, and the black ones don't look gray.

If you intend your movie to be used for TV broadcast, the color bars may actually be required by the station. If not, the color bars make your homemade production look and feel as though you edited it in a $600-per-hour New York editing facility.

To use one of these backdrops, import it into your project as you would any graphics file, as described on page 387. That discussion also explains how to control the length of time a still image appears in your movie. From there, you should have little difficulty superimposing titles as described in this chapter.

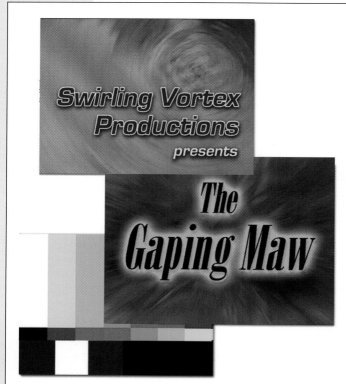

Figure 16-4:
When you hand-build a title using a graphics program like Photoshop Elements or AppleWorks, you lose the ability to animate the words and letters. The results can be much more interesting than plain white text on a black background, yet less distracting than text superimposed over footage.

Another option is to just add color bars (lower left) to make people think you really work in television.

Inserting and Rendering a Title

When you've taken into consideration all the options described so far in this chapter, you probably have a good feel for how this title is going to look once it's inserted into your movie. Now it's time to commit it to digital film.

Dragging the Title into the Movie Track

To place the title you've selected into Movie Track, proceed as follows:

1. **Decide where you want the title to begin.**

   Begin by pressing the Home key on your keyboard, which simultaneously deselects all clips and rewinds the Playhead to the beginning of the Movie Track. Now you can drag the playhead along the Scrubber bar. As you do, a bright red, inverted "T" cursor slides along your Clip Viewer (or a duplicate Playhead slides along your Timeline Viewer) to indicate your position.

   Consider the location of your title carefully. If you're superimposing it on a solid-colored background or a still image, no problem. But if you're planning to superimpose it on moving video, choose a scene that's relatively still, so that the video doesn't distract the audience from the words onscreen. (The exception: If you're using one of iMovie's "see-through" lettering styles, you may want to choose active video to deliberately call attention to the "cutouts.")

   Be particularly careful not to superimpose your titles on an unsteady shot; the contrast between the jiggling picture and the rock-steady lettering on the screen will make your audience uncomfortable.

   Sometimes, such as when you've selected a title style that fades in from nothing, it's OK to put the title squarely at the beginning of a clip. At other times, you'll want to position the title a few seconds into the clip.

2. **If you've selected a starting point for a title that's in the middle of the clip, position the Playhead there and then choose Edit→Split Video Clip at Playhead.**

   It's a fact of iMovie life: A title can begin only at the *beginning* of a clip, never the middle. To make the title seem as though it's starting partway through a clip, therefore, you must *turn* that spot into the beginning of a new clip by chopping the clip in half.

   This is not the only time the title feature will be chopping your clips into smaller clips, as Figure 16-6 illustrates.

3. **Drag the name or icon of your chosen title style from the list of titles directly onto the Movie Track, as shown in Figure 16-5.**

   Drag it just to the left of the clip you'll want to play underneath the title text. All clips to the right scoot rightward to make room for your cursor.

Rendering Begins

Now iMovie begins to *render* the title effect. In other words, it creates a new clip that incorporates both the original footage and the text you're superimposing.

In some ways, this title-rendering process resembles the transition- or effect-rendering process described in the previous chapter. For example, you can stop it by pressing either the Esc key (in the upper left of your keyboard) or ⌘-period.

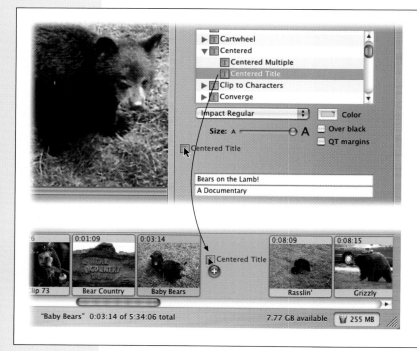

Figure 16-5:
Drag the name of the title you want out of the Titles list directly into the Movie Track.

The clips in the Clip Viewer or Timeline Viewer scoot to the right to make room for the title you're inserting.

The longer the title is to remain onscreen, the longer the rendering process takes. But exactly as when rendering transitions, you can continue to do other work in iMovie (or even in other programs) while the title is rendering. In fact, you can play titles before they're fully baked, to see what they'll look like in your final movie —another handy preview feature that doesn't require you to wait until the rendering is finished. You can even have several titles rendering simultaneously, although iMovie slows down quite a bit if you have more than, say, three titles rendering at once.

The bright red progress bar creeps along the bottom of the clip, as shown in Figure 16-6. In other words, a title in the Movie Track doesn't have its own icon, as a transition does. Instead, you get to see a miniature illustration of what it's going to look like. (Tiny lettering appears directly *on* the superimposed clip icon to help you identify it as a title clip.)

As soon as you've finished dragging a title into the Movie Track, the affected clip's name instantly changes. It takes on the words of your actual title (or as much as will fit; if the name is wider than the clip icon, you see an ellipsis ("like … this"). If the clip was called, for example, "Chris closeup," iMovie renames it "Shoestring Productions presents," or whatever your title says. (You can see this effect, too, in Figure 16-6.) As a bonus, a tiny letter T appears in the upper-right corner of the "slide" in the Clip Viewer, a friendly reminder that you've applied a title to it.

How Titles Chop Up Your Clips

As Figure 16-6 illustrates, it's not enough that you split your clip if you want the title to begin partway into the footage. iMovie may chop up your clips on its own, according to this scheme:

- If the title you've specified is shorter than the clip, iMovie splits the clip in two. The first portion gets the title text embedded into it; the second portion is left alone.

- If the title is *longer* than the clip, iMovie *steals footage* from the next clip to the right (see Figure 16-7). In fact, it continues to eat up as many additional clips as necessary to fulfill the duration you've specified for it. This powerful feature means that you can make a single title sequence extend across a series of short clips, still

Figure 16-6:
If you want a title to begin partway into a clip (top) instead of at the very beginning, you must first chop the clip into two pieces (middle). During rendering, a progress bar keeps track of the rendering progress (bottom).

After the title has finished rendering, you'll find that iMovie has automatically made yet another clip split—at the end of the title (bottom). The result: After you're done inserting a title, that portion of your movie occupied by the title has become a clip unto itself.

Inverted "T" shows where clip will be split

Progress bar —⌐ └— Title text replaces the clip's name

images, transitions, and so on. (By contrast, the transitions and effects described in Chapter 15 limit their appetites to single clips.)

iMovie may still chop up the final clip in the sequence, however, to accommodate the tail end of the title sequence.

Tip: If the title is long enough, it can gobble down a number of individual clips—and turn them into a *single* title clip in your Movie Track. This can be a sneaky way to organize your movie, as described in the box on the facing page.

Figure 16-7:
If your title is longer than its clip, iMovie steals however many seconds of footage it needs from the next clip and incorporates it into the first clip. If you look carefully at the durations of these two clips before (top) and after the title has been applied, you'll see that the second clip has been shortened by one second, and the first clip lengthened, when the stealing process is over (middle).

If you try to apply your title to a too-short clip when there's no subsequent clip from which iMovie can steal frames, on the other hand, you get the error message shown at bottom.

Checking the Result

When the rendering process is complete—or even before it's complete—check out the effect. Click the title clip in the Movie Track and press the Space bar to view the title clip, or Shift-click the clips before and after the title clip (and then press the Space bar) to see how the title looks in the context of the clips around it. Or just drag the Playhead back and forth across the title to see how it looks.

If the title isn't quite what you wanted—if it's the wrong length, style, or font, or if there's a typo, for example—you can change its settings as described in the next section. If the title wasn't *at all* what you wanted—if it's in the wrong place, for example—you can undo the entire insertion-and-rendering process by highlighting the title clip and pressing the Delete key (or choosing Edit→Undo, if you added the title recently). The original footage returns, textless and intact.

Editing a Title

Editing a title is easy. Click the title clip's icon in the Movie Track. Then click the Titles button, if the list of titles isn't already open.

Now you can adjust the title style, the text of the title itself, the title's timing, the direction of motion, or any other parameters described in the first part of the chapter. When you're finished, click the Update button just below the Preview button. iMovie begins the rendering process again, putting in place a brand-new title, and splitting the superimposed footage in a different place, if necessary.

Note: The good news is that your ability to edit the title isn't subject to the availability of the Undo command. In other words, you can revise the settings for a title at any time, even if you've saved the project (and therefore wiped out your Undo trail).

But if you've applied *multiple* superimposed titles, as described in the box below, you can revise only the most recent title you've applied to a particular clip.

Deleting a Title

As noted previously, a title clip is just a clip. You might wonder, therefore, how you can remove a title without also deleting the footage it affects.

Yet sure enough, iMovie remembers what your clips looked like before you overlaid a title. You can click a title clip at any time, press the Delete key, and then watch iMovie restore the original footage. True, pressing Delete on a conventional clip deletes it, but pressing Delete on a title clip simply deletes its "titleness." The clip to its right merges back into its formerly text-overlaid portion, leaving only one clip instead of two.

Now, if you've *moved* the clip that follows the title clip, and you *then* delete the title clip, iMovie will still put back the underlying footage that it consumed, but it may no longer be where you expect it to be. The program can't "splice" the footage back onto the beginning of a clip from which it was split, because iMovie doesn't know where that clip is (you might even have deleted it). If you move the clips back into their original sequence after deleting the title, the footage will still be continuous, but there might now be a cut or break where the title ended, as if you had split the clip at that point.

POWER USERS' CLINIC

Behind-the-Scenes Undo Magic

iMovie can restore an original clip when you delete a title that you've superimposed on it, even weeks later.

Yet as noted in this chapter, iMovie creates titles by *modifying* the original clips—by changing the actual pixels that compose the image. So where is iMovie storing a copy of the original, for use when you decide to delete the title?

In the project's Media folder, that's where (see page 288). There you'll find the original clip from the camcorder (called "Clip 1," for example), untouched. There you'll also find a new clip (called "Typewriter 1," for example), bearing the name of the title style you used. *This* clip contains the modified portion of your original clip.

The iMovie Titles Catalog

This discussion describes and illustrates some of the most useful title effects available in iMovie. Along the way, you'll find out several useful pieces of information about each title:

- How the Speed slider affects the effect.
- Which directions you can make the text move, if any.
- When you might find each effect useful.

Note: Despite the smooth, professional look of iMovie's text effects, many of them may become tiny and illegible when you export your finished movie as a QuickTime movie. They may look terrific in your Monitor window or when played on your TV; however, in a small QuickTime movie frame, especially the kind you might post on a Web page or send by email, the text may shrink away to nothing.

If you have time to experiment with different versions of your movie, exporting each to a QuickTime movie until you find a text effect that's legible, then great. If not, use the notations in this section as a guide. They assume that you've set the text slider to its maximum and turned on the QT Margins checkbox.

Cartwheel

Speed slider: *Controls flying-on speed*
Direction control: *Left, right*

iMovie includes several text effects that involve spinning or tumbling words or letters. You'll probably want to avoid most of them except in special situations. The picture below shows the first of this family.

In this version, all of the letters of your title and subtitle fly onto the screen from one side, each spinning as though pierced on its own axle. You can't actually read the titles until they're finished with their spinning and land in the center.

Read quickly, however, because the letters stand still only for a moment (the moment you specify with the Pause slider), and then spin away again, cartwheeling their way offscreen. If you chose the Cartwheel Multiple version, the next pair of credits now cartwheels on.

Centered Title

Speed slider: *Controls fade in/fade out speed*
Direction control: *None*

The Centered Title is one of the most useful of all the iMovie text effects. iMovie shows a single line of text (or two lines, if you take advantage of the subtitle option), fading in, staying onscreen for a moment, then fading out, making this effect ideal for displaying the title of your movie.

The Centered Multiple variation is ideal for opening credits, because each name (along with an optional subtitle) fades professionally onto the screen, remains there for a moment, and then fades away again. The next name fades in to repeat the cycle. (If you haven't seen this particular opening-credit style used at the beginning of a million TV shows and movies, you haven't watched enough TV.)

Centered Title

This is a tasteful, professional, powerful effect.

Tip: By using several consecutive Centered Titles, you achieve exactly the same effect as the Centered Multiple sequence, except with individual control over the timing of each text pair.

Clip to Characters

Speed slider: *Controls fade in/fade out speed*
Direction control: *None*

Over and over again in Apple's history, its designers have noticed the masses flocking to a certain piece of shareware that fills a feature hole in Apple's own software. In this case, the iMovie team observed how many people were buying add-on title effects from other companies, and decided to spare them that expense by introducing, back in iMovie 4, this powerful title category. All four new text effects described here were once available only as shareware add-ons. (They're called Clip to Characters because the actual letter outlines serve as cookie cutters that clip out video or pictures behind them. You'll get the idea in a moment.)

Animated Gradient

Man, if you're into making mystery movies, you've got your opening credits right here. In this two-toned extravaganza, a moving searchlight seems to be shining out at you from behind the screen, turning the insides of the letters bright yellow as it passes from left to right. It's particularly striking when you turn on the "Over black" checkbox.

Clip Image

Here's a wild new effect with infinite possibilities. In this variation, iMovie fills the hollow outlines of your lettering with a still image—a graphic or photo. You specify which graphic you want to use by clicking the little File button that magically appears below the Size slider, and then using the Open File dialog box to peruse the contents of your hard drive.

If you're just looking for some quick graphic interest, you can choose an interesting photo of texture—a close-up of sandpaper, clouds, or diamonds, for example. If you're aiming for Sundance, you could conceivably spend a few hours in Photoshop creating a more elaborate graphic whose elements are strategically placed to peek out from inside the letters of your title. These could be little silhouetted spy characters, mischievous monkeys, or even tiny words that appear *inside* the larger letters.

Clip Image

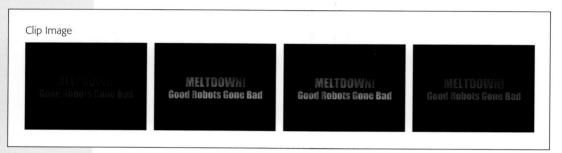

Clip Video

This titling effect wins the award for Most Likely to Save You $30 on Shareware Title Styles. Once again, it makes your letters transparent—but instead of permitting a background still photo to peek through, it actually permits your own video to play inside the lettering. The rest of the screen is black (which is why the "Over black" checkbox is automatically turned on and dimmed when you choose this effect). The Color checkbox has no effect in this case, either.

You can use this title style to create some truly brilliant visuals, video puns, or double meanings. Maybe the title of your short film is "Energy Drink," but we see what appears to be dripping blood inside the lettering. Maybe you've made a movie about a Fourth of July picnic, and you've got some waving-flag video that fills in the hollow letters. Or maybe you're editing a home movie called "Off to Topeka," and a jet plane takes off behind the words, unforgettably appearing and disappearing through and between the letters of the words.

Starburst

Like Clip Image, this effect fills in your lettering with a single image that stretches across the entire title. In this case, though, you don't get to choose which image you get. Like it or not, it's a sunburst, bright yellow in the middle and fading out, with visible radiating lines, toward the outer edges.

The Color box is very important in this case, as it specifies what color the yellow central sunball becomes as its rays reach the outer edges of your words.

Converge

Speed slider: *Controls letter-movement speed*
Direction control: *Left, right (Converge and Converge Multiple only)*

As seen on TV—or in any number of artsy serial-killer movies. The title appears with its letter spacing far too wide—and as you watch, the letters slowly glide inward until they're correctly spaced.

You get four variations. In Converge (for one line) and Converge Multiple (several pairs), the letters on the right or left side remain essentially stationary during the animation, leaving the letters on the opposite side to do all the movement. In the Multiple version, each completed title blinks out of sight to make way for the next title pair.

In Converge to Center and its Multiple variation, the text appears instantly onscreen—but spaced so widely that the right and left parts of it may even be chopped off by the borders of the frame. They immediately float inward to the center until they're readable. Once again, this form of credits has been used now and again during the openings of scary thrillers.

In all four cases, the effect is vaguely menacing and very slick.

Far, Far Away

Speed slider: *Controls flying-on speed*
Direction control: *None*

Star Wars geeks, rejoice! Now you, too, can simulate the legendary prologue text of the Star Wars movies. Your text appears in a block, huge at the bottom of the screen, and then scrolls up and away, in severe perspective, fading out to blackness in the distance as it approaches the top of the screen.

You can't really get away with using this effect for anything but spoofs of the Star Wars movies and tributes to them, because it's so instantly recognizable to just about everyone who's ever been to the movies. But in the right context, and when filled with just the right text, it can be truly hilarious. ("Long, long ago, in a dead-end job far, far away, Larry first saw Charlene, bent over the Xerox machine as she changed the toner cartridge. Thus began the story of their courtship…")

Flying

Speed slider: *Controls flying-on speed*
Direction control: *Up, down*

In the Flying Letters effect, the letters of your title (and subtitle, if you've specified one) fly onto the screen one at a time from the upper-right or lower-right corner of the frame (depending on the directional arrow you click), gradually assembling the phrase you've specified. If nothing else, this effect is certainly offbeat, but it can quickly get boring if you use it more than once.

The Speed slider's maximum time grows according to the length of your title. At its maximum, you and your audience could be sitting there for nearly a full minute while your letters plod onto the screen.

The Flying Words effect is similar, except that entire words fly onto the screen instead of letters. It may be less tedious for your audience to watch, but you should still use it sparingly.

Music Video

Speed slider: *Controls total time onscreen*
Direction control: *Left, right*

If you've ever seen a music video on MTV or VH1, you'll recognize this effect instantly. It places the block of text you've typed—a short paragraph of it, anyway—into the lower-left or lower-right corner of the screen.

The authenticity of this effect is unassailable. It looks *exactly* like the credits that appear at the beginning of actual music videos. Be careful not to make the type too small, though, especially for videos you intend to distribute by email or on the Web.

Tip: The Music Video title is one of the most useful text styles, as it's the only iMovie text style that gives you complete freedom over placement of your text. You can make your title appear off-center, in any corner of the frame, and so on.

The trick is to use "white space" to position the text. By pressing the Space bar before typing each line, you can push your text to the middle or right side of the frame; by pressing Return after the text, you can force the text upward to the middle or top of the frame. Combine these techniques with the left/right directional buttons for various wacky placement effects.

Music Video

Scrolling

Here they are: four variations of the closing-credits effect that wraps up every Hollywood movie you've ever seen. It creates what the pros call a *roll*—text that slides up the screen from the bottom, as though on an endless roll of clear plastic, showing the names of the characters and the actors who played them.

Rolling Credits, Rolling Centered Credits

These effects give you text pairs, like Director/Steven Speilberg and Writer/Robert Towne, or character name/actor name. (The Rolling Credits effect is identical to the Rolling Centered Credits except for the formatting; that is, instead of straddling an invisible "gutter" of empty space, the two columns are separated by a dotted line.)

You can opt to have the text scroll down from the top instead (by clicking the directional arrow), although it looks very weird. (A *crawl*, on the other hand, slides onto the screen from side to side, like the tornado-warning notices that sometimes appear during a TV show. At this writing, iMovie offers no method for creating crawls, much to the disappointment of TV stations in Iowa.)

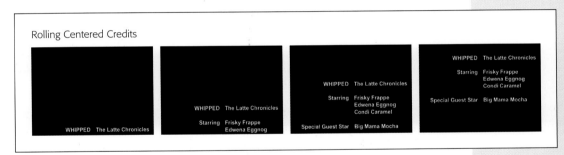

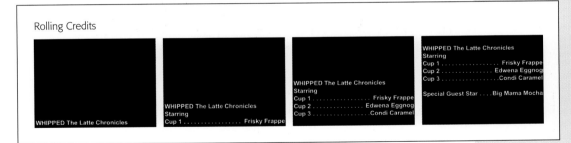

Remember that 45 seconds is the longest scroll you can create, and iMovie automatically adjusts the speed of scrolling to fit all the names you've typed into the duration you've specified. You couldn't fit even 10 percent of the closing credits of *Titanic* into 45 seconds, at least not without scrolling them too fast to read. (On the other hand, you can always use multiple *sets* of Rolling Credits titles, superimposed if necessary [see the next page].)

Scroll with Pause

Speed slider: *Controls scroll-in/scroll-off speed*
Direction control: *Up, down, left, right*

The title and subtitle (if you've specified one) slide, as a pair, from the edge of the screen you've specified (by clicking the directional arrows), pause at the center of the screen for the audience to read, and then continue sliding on their merry way off the screen.

Sure, this isn't an effect you're likely to use often, but it can look quirky and charming if the speed and typeface are right. For example, when your credits slide from left to right, you suggest an old-time slide projector changing slides.

Scrolling Block

Speed slider: *Controls total time onscreen*
Direction control: *Up or down*

This text style is a lot like Far, Far Away, in that a long block of introductory text scrolls slowly upward from the bottom of the screen. In this case, however, it doesn't shrink as it rolls up the screen.

This roll effect is extremely common in commercial theatrical movies. You can use it at the beginning of your movie to explain the plot setup. At the end of the movie, you can use it to provide a postscript or update to the events the audience has just witnessed (like the postscripts at the end of *October Sky* or *A Beautiful Mind*).

POWER USERS' CLINIC

Multiple Simultaneous Superimposed Titles

If you've read this chapter carefully, you may have discovered an intriguing aspect of titles: After iMovie creates one, you don't wind up with a special TV icon in your Movie Track, as you do when you create a transition (see Chapter 15). Instead, the clip that now has your superimposed title is just an ordinary clip—one that you can treat like any other clip. You can move it around in the movie, put it back onto the Clips pane, and so on.

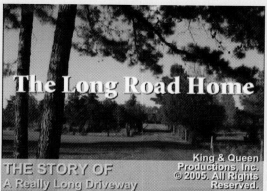

have its own style, animation, duration, color, font, and text. By carefully splitting each title clip in the Movie Track before applying the next title to it, you can stagger the entrance of each title, so that your words fly onto the screen exactly when, and how, you specify.

Furthermore, by combining these titles so that they don't crash into each other—or *do* crash into each other in artistic ways—you can come up with extremely complex

As a result, there's nothing to stop you from applying *another* title to the same clip...and another, and another. Each can title sequences that rival some of the fanciest opening-credit sequences Hollywood has ever dreamed up.

You can also tack one scrolling block onto the end of another, although this tactic is less necessary now that a single Scrolling Block can contain well over 4,000 typed characters. You can also tack a Scrolling Block onto one of the other iMovie scrolling-text effects (it can follow the Rolling Credits effect, for example) to provide a neatly centered copyright, an "in memoriam," or some disclaimer information. As far as the audience is concerned, it will be just one more part of the same smooth scroll.

Furthermore, you don't have to begin this follow-up block after the regular credits (or the preceding Scrolling Blocks) have completely disappeared off the top of the screen. You can make the additional Scrolling Block appear at any moment, even while the previous crawl is still finishing up its movement; see the box on the facing page.

The directional arrows let you control whether this roll proceeds downward from the top or upward from the bottom. You're welcome to make your text block scroll downward, but do so with the knowledge that you're doing something unconventional, even unheard of, in the world of filmmaking.

Stripe Subtitle

Speed slider: *Controls total time onscreen*
Direction control: *None*

This effect creates what the pros call a *lower third*—a stripe across the bottom of the picture where the text identifies, for example, the name and affiliation of the person being interviewed. The tinted background is an unusual touch.

Oddly enough, clicking the Color swatch here *doesn't* let you change the color of the text, as it usually does. (Stripe Subtitle text is always white.) Instead, it specifies the background color of the stripe itself.

Odder still, the stripe always stops just shy of the screen's right edge.

Subtitle

Speed slider: *Controls total time onscreen*
Direction control: *None*

This effect gives you the more traditional look for a "lower third" title, one that identifies the person or place being shown in the footage. The text quietly fades in, centered at the bottom of the screen, and then fades out again. (If you choose the

Subtitle

Multiple variation, the next pair of lines now fades on.) It's a very useful, professional-looking effect.

As the name implies, you can also use this effect to provide captions that translate, say, an opera performance, although that may be a less frequent requirement in your moviemaking career.

Typing

Speed slider: *Controls time for text to fully appear*
Direction control: *None*

Typewriter

You occasionally see the Typewriter effect in the credits of TV police dramas (especially *JAG* and *Homicide*). The letters spill across the screen from left to right, as though being rapidly typed in a word processor.

Tip: When this title style was under development at Apple, it was called *X-Files*—a reference to the animated titles in *The X-Files* that establish the time and date of each new scene. Before iMovie was officially unveiled, the name was changed to Typewriter for obvious reasons (obvious to lawyers, anyway).

Video Terminal

Video Terminal is only slightly different. It adds a blinking insertion-point cursor that gets pushed along as you type—not the vertical one that's familiar to millions of Mac and PC fans, but instead a horizontal underline character like the one on ancient, pre-mouse video terminals. (For some inexplicable reason, Hollywood movies generally depict text appearing on *any* computer screen using this effect, even if it's popping up in a dialog box or error message. The accompanying teletype sound makes Hollywood computers seem even less like the real-world kind.)

The Video Terminal effect is especially useful when you want to recreate the "I'm summing up my day in sentimental, bittersweet prose on my word processor" effect that concluded every episode of *Doogie Howser, M.D.*

Wipe

Speed slider: *Controls speed of reveal*
Direction control: *Left, right, up, down*

The Wipe effect is among the most practical of title styles. Your text is revealed by a soft-edged "spotlight" that, unlike the Animated Gradient effect, reveals the entire width or height of the text at once. (You can direct the wiper to reveal your text from any direction: left, right, up, or down.) The effect is smooth, intriguing, and not overbearing.

During the pause while the audience reads the title, a hint of the shadow is still there, slightly obscuring one edge of the words. Then the wiper moves on, its trailing edge concealing the text that the forward edge revealed a moment earlier.

Narration, Music, and Sound

I f you're lucky, you may someday get a chance to watch a movie whose soundtrack isn't finished yet. You'll be scanning channels and stumble across a special about how movies are made, or you'll see a tribute to a film composer, or you'll rent a DVD of some movie that includes a "making of" documentary. Such TV shows or DVDs sometimes include a couple of minutes from the finished movie as it looked *before* the musical soundtrack and sound effects were added.

At that moment, your understanding of the film medium will take an enormous leap forward. "Jeez," you'll say, "without music and sound effects, this $100 million Hollywood film has no more emotional impact than…my home movies!"

And you'll be right. It's true that in our society, the *visual* component of film is the most, well, visible. The household names are the directors and movie stars, not the sound editors, composers, *foley* (sound effects) artists, and others who devote their careers to the audio experience of film.

But without music, sound effects (called SFX for short), and sound editing, even the best Hollywood movie will leave you cold and unimpressed.

The Two iMovie Soundtracks

Much like traditional film cameras, iMovie separates the audio and video into separate tracks, which you can view and edit independently. In iMovie, you can view the contents of your soundtracks with a single click on the clock icon shown in Figure 17-1.

The top horizontal band of the Timeline Viewer displays the *video* component of your movie. It shows tiny thumbnails that help you identify which clips you've placed in which order. For the most part, you won't do much with this strip when you're editing audio; its primary purpose is to show where you are in the movie.

The two horizontal strips underneath it are your playground for audio clips. Both audio tracks are equivalent; each of them can hold sound from any of these sources, which you're free to drag between the two tracks anytime: iTunes tracks, narration, sound effects, sounds files like MP3, WAV, AIFF, and AAC, music from a CD, plus the original audio from your camcorder.

This chapter covers all of these sound varieties.

Tip: Ordinarily, when playing your movie, iMovie plays the sound in both audio tracks. But you can use the three checkboxes at the right end of these tracks to control which ones play back. When you want to isolate only one track, turn off the other two checkboxes (Figure 17-2). (These checkboxes also govern which soundtracks are exported when you send your finished iMovie production back to tape or to a QuickTime movie.)

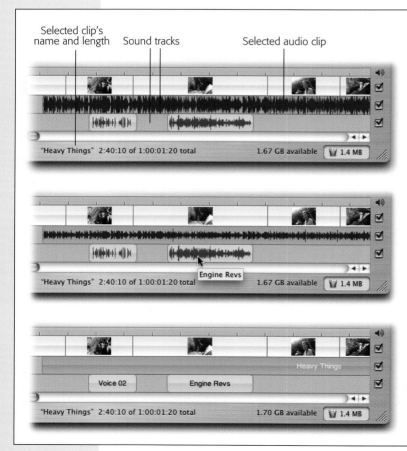

Selected clip's name and length   Sound tracks   Selected audio clip

Figure 17-1:
Top: In the Timeline Viewer, horizontal strips represent narration, CD tracks, music from iTunes, or sound effects.

To identify a sound clip, either click it so that its name appears at the bottom of the window, or just point to it without clicking (middle).

Middle: If the soundwave scribbles are a little distracting, you can adjust their size by tapping the up and down arrow keys. See how the top audio clip has smaller waveforms now? (This doesn't affect the volume level, only the onscreen graphics.)

Bottom: You can also turn off those visual soundwaves altogether by choosing View→Show Audio Waveforms (⌘-Shift-W, or choose the same command from the clip's shortcut menu). Hiding waveforms reduces visual clutter and reveals each clip's name right on the clip—but leaving them visible is a great way to align video with audio "hits."

Audio Clips

In many regards, working with sound files is much like working with video clips. For example, each piece of sound appears as a horizontal colored bar in the Timeline Viewer. You can move a clip around in the movie by dragging horizontally; cut, copy, and paste it; delete it by selecting it and then pressing the Delete key; and so on.

As you work, remember to use the Zoom slider (at the lower-left corner of the Timeline Viewer) to magnify or shrink your audio clips as necessary.

Renaming Sound Clips (or Not)

When you click an audio clip, iMovie intensifies its color to show that it's highlighted. The bottom edge of the Timeline Viewer displays the audio clip's name and duration, as shown in Figure 17-1. (You can also see a clip's name by pointing to it without clicking, as shown at middle in Figure 17-1.)

To rename an audio clip, double-click it. The Clip Info box appears, where you can type a new name into the Name box.

Listening to a Sound Clip

To isolate and listen to a particular audio clip, proceed as shown in Figure 17-2.

Tip: Once your movie is playing, you can *loop* a section of audio (play it repeatedly as you study the effect) by clicking repeatedly in the same spot on the Scrubber bar, keeping the mouse very still. With each click, the Playhead snaps back to replay the segment from the position of your cursor.

Figure 17-2:
A view of the right end of the Timeline Viewer. Drag the Playhead so that the vertical line beneath it strikes the piece of sound you want to listen to. Then turn off the track checkboxes to isolate the track you want. Press the Space bar to begin listening.

Hint: If you've turned on "Snap to items in Timeline" in iMovie→Preferences, the Playhead snaps neatly against the beginnings and ends of audio clips—and bookmarks, chapter markers, and video clips—when you drag it. In fact, it even snaps against bursts of sound within an audio clip, which helps you find the start or end of silent bits. (You can Shift-drag to override the snapping setting.)

1. Position the Playhead.
2. Isolate the track.

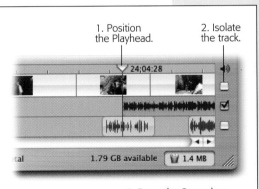

3. Press the Space bar.

Recording Narration

If anyone ever belittles iMovie for being underpowered, point out an iMovie feature that isn't even available in most expensive video-editing programs: the ability to record narration while you watch your movie play.

You can create a reminiscence, narrating as the video plays (thereby creating a *voice-over*). You can identify your home movies—when or where they were shot, for example. Doctors use iMovie to create narrated slideshows, having created a Movie Track filled with still images of scanned slides. Realtors feature camcorder footage of houses under consideration, while narrating the key features that can't be seen ("Built in 1869, this house was extensively renovated in 1880…"). And it doesn't take much imagination to see how lawyers can exploit iMovie.

Preparing to Record

Your Mac's microphone takes one of two forms: built-in or external. The built-in mike, a tiny hole in the facade of the iMac, eMac, or PowerBook, couldn't be more convenient—it's always with you, and always turned on.

If your Mac doesn't have a built-in microphone, you can plug in an external USB microphone (see the Apple Products Guide at *www.guide.apple.com*) or a standard microphone with the help of an adapter (like the iMic, *www.griffintechnology.com*).

Making the Recording

Here's how you record narration:

1. **Click the clock icon so that you're looking at the Timeline Viewer.**

   You'll do all your audio editing in Timeline view.

2. **Drag the Playhead to a spot just before you want the narration to begin.**

   You can use all the usual navigational techniques to line up the Playhead: Press the Space bar to play the movie, press the right and left arrow keys to move the Playhead one frame at a time, press Shift-arrow keys to make the Playhead jump 10 frames at a time, and so on.

3. **Open the Audio panel, if it's not already open.**

   You do so by clicking the Audio button, shown in Figure 17-3.

4. **Click the round, red Record Voice button and begin to speak.**

   You can watch the video play as you narrate.

Note: If the level meter isn't dancing as you speak, the problem may be that your Mac is paying attention to the wrong audio input. Choose →System Preferences, and click the Sound icon. Click the Input tab, then click the microphone input that you want to use. When you're done, quit System Preferences.

If the level meter bars are dancing, but not farther than halfway across the graph (see Figure 17-3), then your narration isn't loud enough. On playback, it'll probably be drowned out by the camcorder audio track.

To increase the volume, open System Preferences, click Sound, and click the Input tab to make sure that your input volume slider is at maximum. If that's not the problem, your only options are to lean closer to the microphone, speak louder, or use an external microphone. (You can learn tricks for boosting the volume of audio tracks later in this chapter, but it's much better to get the level right the first time.)

5. Click Stop to complete the recording.

Now a new stripe appears in the upper soundtrack, already highlighted, bearing the name Voice 01, like the one shown in Figure 17-1. Drag the Playhead to the left—to the beginning of the new recording—and then press the Space bar to listen to your voice-over work.

If the narration wasn't everything you hoped for, it's easy enough to record another "take." Just click the stripe representing your new recording and then press Delete to get rid of it. Then repeat the process.

Figure 17-3:
To summon the narration controls, click the Audio button. If your microphone is correctly hooked up, the round, red Record Voice button is available. (Otherwise, it's dimmed.) Just beside the Record button is a live "VU" level meter. Test your setup by speaking into the microphone; if this meter twitches in response, you're ready to record.

Importing iTunes Music

Nothing adds emotional impact to a piece of video like music. Slow, romantic music makes the difference between a sad story and one that actually makes viewers cry. Fast, driving music makes viewers' hearts beat faster—scientists have proven it. Music is so integral to movies these days that, as you walk out of the theater, you may not even be aware that a movie *had* music, but virtually every movie does, and you were emotionally manipulated by it.

Home movies are no exception. Music adds a new dimension to your movie, so much so that some iMovie fans *edit to music.* They choose a song, lay it down in the audio track, and then cut the video footage to fit the beats, words, or sections of the music.

Tip: Even if you don't synchronize your video to the music in this way, you might still want to experiment with a music-only soundtrack. That is, *turn off* the camcorder sound, so that your movie is silent except for the music. The effect is haunting, powerful, and often used in Hollywood movies during montage sequences.

If you've been using the free iTunes jukebox software to manage your music collection, you're in for a real treat. iMovie is well integrated with the other programs in its iLife software suite—including iTunes. You can view, and even play, your entire music library, complete with its individual playlists, right in iMovie, making it easy to choose just the right piece of music to accompany your video.

(If you've created homemade songs in GarageBand, this feature is your ticket to importing them into iMovie, too. They show up in the iTunes playlist named after you.)

Tip: You can use iTunes to build a music library by converting the songs on your audio CDs into MP3 files on your hard drive, by buying individual pop songs from the iTunes Music Store, or by importing digital audio files you found on the Internet. See *iPod & iTunes: The Missing Manual* for complete instructions.

Here's how you go about choosing an iTunes track for your movie:

1. **Click the Audio button, if necessary (Figure 17-3).**

   The panel changes to reveal your iTunes music collection. (If you don't see your list of songs, choose iTunes Library from the pop-up menu above the panel.)

2. **Find just the right song.**

   The panel is filled with useful controls to help you find the right music. For example, if you've organized your iTunes music into *playlists* (subsets), you can use the pop-up menu above the list to choose the playlists you want to look over. (All other songs are temporarily hidden.) You can also use the Search box at the bottom of the list, as shown in Figure 17-4.

Figure 17-4:
Left: Choose any of your playlists to navigate your massive music collection.

Right: You can also click in the Search box. As you type a song or performer's name, iMovie hides all songs whose names don't match, so that you can quickly home in on a certain song or group of songs from among thousands. (To restore the entire list and delete what you've typed, click the little X button at the right end of the Search box.)

To listen to a song, click its name and then click the round Play button beneath the list. Or, if you think life is too short already, just double-click a song name. (To interrupt playback, either double-click a different song, double-click the same one, or click the round Play triangle button to turn it gray once again.)

3. **Place the music into one of your audio tracks.**

You can go about this in either of two ways. If the Playhead is already parked where you want the music to begin (you can take this opportunity to move it, if you like), just click the song name and then click the Place at Playhead button beneath the song list. iMovie takes a moment to deposit the entire song, beginning at the point you've indicated.

You can also drag the song name directly out of the list and down into the Timeline Viewer. As long as you don't release the mouse button, and as long as the cursor is in one of the two audio tracks, you'll see that you can simultaneously move the Playhead and position the beginning of the song at just the right spot. Release the mouse when the song looks like it's in the right place.

(On the other hand, you can always adjust the starting point of the music after you've placed it, by dragging its audio-clip stripe horizontally.)

Depending on the length of the song you've selected, the importing process can take 30 seconds or more. That's how long it takes for iMovie to copy the iTunes track into a new audio file (in your project's Media folder). When it's complete, a new colored bar appears in the audio track, labeled with the song name.

Try dragging the Playhead back to the beginning of the music bar and pressing the Space bar to play it. If it doesn't have quite the effect you thought it would, click the newly placed music's bar and then press the Delete key, to make room for your next experiment.

CD Music

If you don't use iTunes to organize your music, you can also snag a track or two directly from an audio CD. You just insert your favorite music CD (Carly Simon, Rolling Stones, the Cleveland Orchestra, or whatever), choose the track you want to swipe, and the deed is done.

Here's the procedure:

1. **Open the Audio panel, if it isn't already open.**

Do so by clicking the Audio button shown in Figure 17-3.

2. **Insert the music CD into your Mac.**

After a moment, a list of songs on the CD appears in the list.

At first, they're probably called Track 1, Track 2, and so on. Unfortunately, audio CDs were invented before the advent of computers that could read them, and so the text of their track names isn't stored on the disc. Clearly, it would be a lot easier to find the music you want if you could see the *actual names* of the songs on the CD.

That's why, after a moment, iMovie automatically begins to download the list of songs on your CD, assuming that you're online. (iTunes may also open automatically, depending on how you've set up the CDs & DVDs panel in System Preferences.) Behind the scenes, it's consulting the Gracenote Internet CD database—a worldwide repository of track and album information. After a few moments, switch back into iMovie. You'll see that both the track names and the name of the album have now been typed in for you.

You'll also notice that the pop-up menu above the Audio palette has changed to identify the name of the album.

3. **Find the song you want.**

   To do so, double-click one of the songs in the scrolling list (or click a song and then click the Play triangle button below the list). Click the Play triangle again to stop the music. Unfortunately, there's no way to fast-forward.

4. **Insert the song into one of your audio tracks.**

FREQUENTLY ASKED QUESTION

Fun with Copyright Law

Don't I break some kind of law when I copy music from a commercial CD, or use iTunes Music Store music in one of my movies?

Exactly what constitutes stealing music is a hot-button issue that has tied millions of people (and recording executives) in knots. That's why some iMovie fans hesitate to distribute their iMovie films in places where lawyers might see them—like the Internet.

Frankly, though, record company lawyers have bigger fish to fry than small-time amateur operators like you. You're perfectly safe showing your movies to family and friends, your user group, and other limited circles of viewers. In fact, Apple encourages you to use iTunes Music Store purchases in your movies; after all, Apple is the one who made them available right in iMovie.

You'll risk trouble only if you go commercial, making money from movies that incorporate copyrighted music.

Still, if your conscience nags you, you could always use one of your GarageBand compositions. And even if you're not especially musical, the world is filled with *royalty-free music*—music that has been composed and recorded expressly for the purpose of letting filmmakers add music to their work without having to pay a licensing fee every time they do so.

Some of it's even free. For example, check out *www.freeplaymusic.com,* a Web site filled with prerecorded music in every conceivable style, that you're welcome to use in your movies at no charge.

If that's not enough for you, visit a search page like *www.google.com,* search for *music library* or *royalty-free music,* and start clicking your way to the hundreds of Web sites that offer information about (and listenable samples of) music that you can buy and use without fear. (Many of these sites require a RealAudio plug-in, an add-on for your Web browser that you can download and install from *www.real.com.)*

You can use either of the techniques identified in the previous step 3 (page 369). Either click the Place at Playhead button beneath the song list, or drag the song name out of the list and into position on one of your audio tracks.

A progress bar appears as iMovie copies the song file off the CD and into your project's Media folder. When it's finished, you'll see a new colored bar in your audio track representing the imported song and bearing its name.

When you're finished importing music, you're free to eject the CD (by holding down the Eject button on your keyboard, for example), insert another one, and nab another selection of music. iMovie no longer requires the first CD.

Sound Effects

There's more to a movie soundtrack than music, goodness knows. Fortunately, iMovie also comes with a juicy collection of sound effects, suitable for dropping into your movies. If you choose iMovie Sound Effects from the pop-up menu at the top of the Audio palette, you'll find two flippy triangles, each denoting a collection of professional sound effects. (You don't have to click the triangle to see its contents; you can click directly on the collection's name.)

One, called Skywalker Sound Effects, is named for the Hollywood sound studio from which Apple licensed the effects (Birds, Cold Wind, Creek, and so on)—a list that's been expanded in iMovie HD. The other, Standard Sound Effects, contains the sounds that began life in iMovie 3 (Alarm, Bark, Crickets, and so on).

Across from each sound's name, you see its length, expressed in the minutes:seconds format.

Using a Sound Effect

You add a sound to your audio tracks exactly the way you add an iTunes tune—either by clicking the Place at Playhead button or by dragging the effect's name into either of the audio tracks in the Timeline Viewer. As your cursor moves over a track, the Playhead—accompanied by a cool, fading-out purple stripe—helps you see precisely where the sound will begin. Once placed there, the sound effect appears as a horizontal purple bar, just like any other sound clip. (If the sound effect is very short, you may have to zoom in to see it as a bar, using the Zoom slider at the left edge of the screen.)

A sound-effect clip behaves like any other sound clip. You can edit its volume in any of the ways described in "Editing Audio Clips," later in this chapter. You can slide it from side to side in the track to adjust where it begins, and even shorten, crop, or split it.

Adding or Removing Sound Effects

The list of sound effects in the Sounds palette isn't magical. It's simply a listing of the sound files that came with iMovie. If you know the secret, you can open a special folder and delete, move out, or rename your sound effects—or even install new ones.

1. **Quit iMovie. In the Finder, open your Applications folder. Control-click the iMovie icon; from the contextual menu, choose Show Package Contents.**

The iMovie *package window* appears. You've just discovered, if you didn't already know, that many Mac OS X program icons are, in fact, thinly disguised folders (called *packages*) that contain dozens or hundreds of individual support files. You've just opened up iMovie for inspection.

2. **Open the Contents→Resources folder.**

Welcome to the belly of the beast. Before you, sit hundreds of individual files, most of them the little graphics that make up the various iMovie buttons, controls, and so on. (If you're really feeling ambitious, you can actually open up these graphics and edit them, completely changing the look of iMovie.)

The icon you want is the folder called Sound Effects. It's a folder full of individual sound files—in MP3 format—that make up the list you see in the Audio palette (Figure 17-5).

Tip: *MP3 files* are extremely popular among music fans, since they're compact and sound great. Plus, all kinds of computers can read them.

Looking for even more sound effects? The Internet is filled with downloadable MP3 files that you can use in your iMovie projects. You might start your search at *www.google.com.* Perform a search for *free sound effects.* Many are already in MP3 format; many others are in AIFF format, which you can convert to iMovie-friendly MP3 files using iTunes.

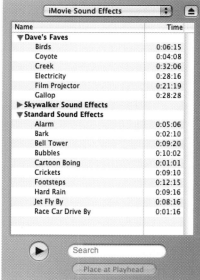

Figure 17-5:
Left: Deep within the iMovie program itself lies a folder called Sound Effects. Any audio file that you download from the Internet, copy from a sound effects CD, create using a shareware sound-editing program, or save out of a QuickTime movie can become an iMovie "sound effect." Just drop it into this folder and relaunch iMovie.

Right: Whatever audio files you put into the Sound Effects folder (and whatever you call them) determine the list of sound effects you see within iMovie.

Feel free to reorganize these files. For example, you can throw away the ones you never use. You can also create new folders in the Sound Effects window to create new categories of sound effects in the Audio palette.

3. **Open iMovie. Click the Audio button. From the pop-up menu above the list, choose iMovie Sound Effects.**

Each folder in the Sound Effects folder forms its own subcategory of effects here.

Editing Audio Clips

Fortunately, you can do more with your audio clips than just insert them into the Timeline Viewer. You can lengthen them or shorten them, make them fade in or out, shift them to play earlier or later in time, and even superimpose them. Best of all—and here's one of the most useful features in iMovie—you can make their volume rise and fall over the length of the clip.

Making Whole-Clip Volume Adjustments

To make a particular clip louder or quieter relative to the other tracks, click its representation in the Timeline Viewer to select it. The clip darkens to show that it's highlighted.

Having selected an audio (or video) clip in this way, you can affect its overall volume level by using the "Clip:" volume pop-up menu shown in Figure 17-6. You can make it so quiet that it's absolutely silent, or you can actually make it 50 percent louder than the original.

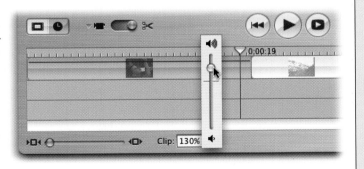

Figure 17-6:
If you set the volume pop-up all the way to 0, you mute the sound completely—for this clip only. If you drag it all the way to the top, you actually boost the volume up to 150%—a terrific way to compensate for weak camcorder microphones.

In any case, adjusting the pop-up menu makes the horizontal volume-level line temporarily appear on the selected clips.

Here are some pointers in this regard:

• You can also type a percentage number into the "Clip:" text box. This isn't a feature only for the obsessively precise; it's a useful way to make sure that each of several audio clips are boosted to the same degree.

• iMovie stores your Volume pop-up menu settings independently for every audio clip. That's why the Volume setting may seem to jump around as you click different audio clips.

- If even 150 percent isn't enough of a volume boost, you can always open the audio clip in GarageBand for a quick boost. Drag the clip from the Finder into a waiting Real Instrument (blue) track, bump up the track's volume, export the result to iTunes, and then reimport the newly amplified file into iMovie.

Volume Adjustments Within a Clip

Being able to make the volume of a clip rise and fall along its length, as you can in iMovie, comes in handy in a multitude of ways:

- It's a rare documentary or news show that doesn't begin a story with a full-volume, attention-getting shot (protesters shouting, band playing, airplane landing, and so on), whose audio fades to half volume after a few seconds, just in time for the reporter to begin speaking.

- Similarly, you can "pull back" the musical soundtrack whenever somebody on camera is speaking, and then bring it back to full volume in between speeches. This technique is incredibly common in movies, TV shows, commercials, and just about every other form of professional video.

- Suppose that the last second of a clip caught the unseemly off-camera belch of a relative at the dinner table. In a flash, you can edit it out, simply by silencing the audio just before the belch.

- You can compensate for the volume drop that occurs whenever your interview subjects momentarily turn their heads away from the camera.

- If you're a parent filming small children, your footage often winds up peppered with parental instructions recorded at a very high volume level, because you're right next to the microphone. ("Honey, stand over there by your brother," or "Watch out for the car!") These parental voice-overs often ruin a clip—but you can rescue them by adjusting the original audio from the camcorder, which you can edit just as easily as imported audio.

- You can make create smooth fade-ins or fade-outs of your music (or the sound from the original video).

Volume "Rubber Bands"

The key to this feature is the new Show Clip Volume Levels command (⌘-Shift-L) in the View menu. (The same command appears in the shortcut menu when you Control-click an audio clip.) When you turn on Show Clip Volume Levels, a horizontal line appears on every audio and video clip, edge to edge. It's an audio-volume graph, which you can manipulate like a rubber band. Here's how it works (consider zooming in for greater control):

- Click directly on the line and drag upward or downward (Figure 17-7, top). The original click produces a small spherical handle, and the drag produces a curve in the line from its original volume level. (Actually, you can simultaneously drag left or right to adjust the timing of this volume change.) Each "knot" in the line (the round handle) represents a new volume level that sticks until the end of the clip or the next volume level, whichever comes first.

- After you create such a curve, the point where the audio deviated from its original volume is denoted by a tiny square handle (Figure 17-7, third from top). To make the volume increase or decrease more or less gradually, drag that tiny square handle

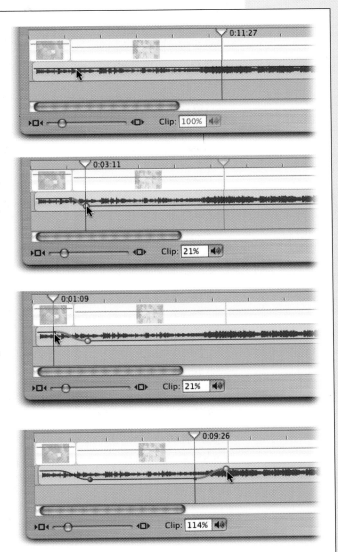

Figure 17-7:

Top: The horizontal line represents the audio clip's standard, 100% volume level. Suppose, in this case, that it's drowning out the spoken dialog in the video track above it. (That's a pretty common occurrence when you add, say, a pop song to your movie as a soundtrack.)

Second from top: As you drag the little "knot" vertically, you have two sources of feedback on how much you've increased or decreased the volume at that spot: the height of the line segment itself (in which the purple clip itself is the piece of graph paper, from 0% to 150%), and the number in the "Clip:" percentage box.

In any case, the orange handle tells you how much volume fluctuation you've introduced, but it doesn't let you specify how gradually you want the change to occur.

Third from top: For that purpose, drag the tiny square (indicated by the cursor) in any direction to control where the volume change begins—both when, and at what level.

Bottom: Repeat the process in reverse when you want to bring the music back up after the dialog portion is over.

left or right, closer to your round adjustment handle or farther from it.

- To make the volume take another dip or swoop, click elsewhere on the volume line and drag again. You've just created a second round orange handle, which you can position independently (Figure 17-7, bottom).

- To remove a volume change, click the orange "knot" to select it, and then press the Delete key. (Or just drag it to the original volume level.) The knot disappears, and the "rubber band" line snaps back to the previous knot, stretched tight.

- To make a volume change extremely sudden, click a knot to highlight it, and then drag the tiny square just to its left. You'll find that you can drag this little square until it's directly above or below the knot—an instantaneous volume change.

- Consider making your volume adjustments *while* the movie plays back. Each time you make an adjustment, the Playhead jumps to that spot. As you keep clicking and adjusting, clicking and adjusting, the Playhead keeps jumping back to that spot, saving you the trouble of having to rewind and play, rewind and play, as you fine-tune the fluctuation.

- To restore the original, straight-line condition of a clip's volume, click each of the orange knots and press Delete until none of them remains.

Tip: When you're finished editing volume fluctuations, you can turn off the View→Show Clip Volume Levels command again. iMovie will remember all of the changes that you've made, and you'll still hear the volume changes on playback. But iMovie hides all of the handles and rubber-band graph lines, making it possible once again to drag clip edges to shorten them (which you can't do while volume graphs are visible).

Adjusting Many Clips at Once

You can adjust the volume levels of more than one clip simultaneously—a technique that comes in handy more often than you might think. For example, you may decide that *all* of the music excerpts you've grabbed from a CD are too loud compared to the camcorder audio. In one fell swoop, you can make them all softer.

You can select as many as you want, even if they're on different audio tracks. Start by selecting the clips you want to affect:

- To select several non-consecutive clips, Shift-click them in any order: clip 1, clip 3, and so on. (Actually, ⌘-clicking works, too.)

- To select several connecting clips, drag-select. That is, begin dragging in any empty part of a track. As you drag, iMovie selects any audio clip that even partly falls within the light gray rectangle you're creating.

- To select *all* of the clips in both audio tracks, highlight *one* clip there. Then choose Edit→Select All.

- To unhighlight a selected clip, Shift-click or ⌘-click it.

Now when you adjust the "Clip:" volume pop-up menu, you're affecting all of the highlighted clips at once. (If you've fiddled around with the clips' rubber-band volume lines, adjusting the volume slider scales the volume of the whole thing up or down proportionally, maintaining the relative sizes of the fluctuations.)

Note: When several audio clips are highlighted, the volume pop-up menu reflects whichever clip has the *highest* volume level.

Locking Audio Clips to Video

Figure 17-8 illustrates a serious problem that results from trying to line up certain video moments (like Bill-Gates-getting-hit-with-a-pie footage) with particular audio moments (like a "Splat!" sound effect). In short, when you insert or delete some video footage *after* lining up audio clips with specific video moments, you shove everything out of alignment, sometimes without even realizing it. This syndrome can rear its ugly head in many video-editing programs.

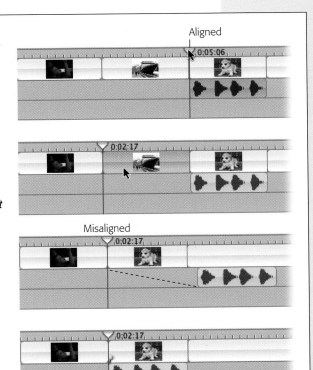

Figure 17-8:
Top: You've carefully lined up a barking sound effect with the beginning of the dog clip.

Second from top: Uh-oh. You've selected the clip right before the dog, in preparation for deleting it.

Third from top: Now you've done it. You've deleted the clip that was just to the left of the dog. The dog clip slides leftward to close the gap—and leaves the barking sound behind, now hopelessly out of alignment with the video above it.

Bottom: If you had remembered to lock the barking clip to the video above it, as indicated by the tiny pushpins, the sound effect would have slid to the left along with the dog clip, remaining perfectly in sync.

You may wind up playing a frustrating game of find-the-frame, over and over again, all the way through the movie, as you try to redo all of your careful audio/video alignments.

In iMovie, the solution is especially elegant. Whenever you place an audio clip that you'd like to keep aligned with a video moment, get it into position and then *lock* it by choosing Advanced→Lock Audio Clip at Playhead (or press ⌘-L). What happens next depends on how you've set things up:

- If you've dragged or nudged the Playhead to the frame you care most about, iMovie locks the audio to the video at that frame, as indicated by the little pushpin (see Figure 17-8). Even if you later trim away some footage from the beginning part of the video clip, the sync moment remains intact.

- If the Playhead isn't anywhere near the highlighted audio clip, iMovie simply locks the beginning of the highlighted audio clip to the video frame it's currently aligned with.

- If you've highlighted several audio clips, once again, iMovie "pushpins" the beginning of each clip at its present video location.

Once you've locked an audio clip to its video, you no longer have to worry that it might lose sync with its video when you edit your video clips. Nothing you do to the video clips to its left in the Timeline Viewer—add, delete, insert, or trim them—will affect its synchronization.

It's important to understand, however, that locking an audio clip freezes its position only relative to the video clip above it. The audio clip isn't locked into a particular *time* in the movie (such as 5:23:12). Put another way, "Lock Audio" actually means "*Don't* Lock Audio (to one spot in the Movie Track); Let It Slide Around as Necessary."

Nor does locking an audio clip prevent *you* from shifting it. Dragging the audio clip will *not* drag the "attached" video clip along with it. You're still welcome to slide the audio clip left or right in its track, independent of any other clips. Doing so simply makes iMovie realign the clip with a new video frame, lining up the pushpin accordingly. (If you *cut* the audio clip and then paste it into a new location, it forgets both its original video-clip spouse and the fact that it was ever "married" to begin with. After pasting, it's pushpin-free.)

To unlock an audio clip, highlight it and then choose Advanced→Unlock Audio Clip (or press ⌘-L again).

Cropping an Audio Clip

As you may remember from Chapter 14, the ability to *crop,* or chop the ends off a video clip, is one of the key tools in video editing. As it turns out, you can adjust the beginning or ending points of any audio clip even more conveniently.

Tip: If you use the Extract Audio command described on page 384, you can even crop the original camcorder audio in this way, without cropping the video clip in the process. Doing so is a convenient way to trim out an audio glitch that appears at the beginning or end of a shot without having to crop the video clip.

You can shorten one of your music or narration clips from either the beginning or the end, just by dragging the corresponding end inward, as shown in Figure 17-9.

For finer adjustments, click one of the clip ends, so that the Playhead snaps to your cursor. Then press the right or left arrow key to move the handle in one-frame increments, or—if you press Shift as you do so—in *10*-frame increments. You might want to zoom in, using the Zoom slider at the left side of the window, if you're finding it hard to see the effects of your cropping maneuvers.

Note: As you drag the audio-clip crop handles inward or outward, any volume fluctuations you've added remain exactly where they were—which means that they might just wind up in nowhere-land. You might drag the end point of a clip so far to the left that you'll never hear the fluctuations you had programmed for the very end of the clip. If your volume fluctuations seem to be missing, turn on View→Show Clip Volume Levels to make your volume graph reappear. You'll see the problem right away.

Figure 17-9:
You can shorten an audio clip without actually deleting any of it, just by dragging the edges inward (shown here before and after). Does this sound familiar? It should...you can do the same thing with video clips.

At any time, you can restore the original length, or part of it, by dragging the edge outward again. (Note, though, that edge dragging doesn't work if Show Clip Volume Levels is turned on in the View menu.)

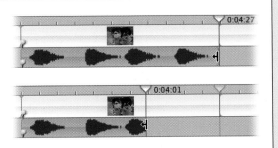

Splitting an Audio Clip

When you drag an audio clip's ends inward, you're not actually trimming the clip. You're simply shortening the *audible portion* of the full-length clip. At any time in your project's lifetime, if you decide that you've overshot, you can slide the clip ends back outward again.

However, you may have good reason to make the cropped-clip arrangement permanent. First, in complex audio tracks, your clips can become cluttered and difficult to "read," thanks to the duplicate clip ends. Second, dragging the ends of clips inward doesn't reduce the amount of disk space that your audio file uses, since iMovie hangs onto the full original in case you decide to uncrop it.

There is an alternative, however. You may remember reading about the power of the Edit→Split Clip at Playhead command, which uses the current Playhead location as a razor blade that chops a video clip in two. In the Timeline Viewer, the equivalent command is called Split Selected Audio Clip at Playhead. As you'd expect, it breaks the *audio* clip beneath the Playhead into two independent clips.

Tip: If your Edit menu doesn't list a command called Split Selected Audio Clip at Playhead, it's because your Playhead isn't in the middle part of a *highlighted* audio clip. If no audio clip is selected, or if the Playhead's vertical insertion point isn't running through it, the command says Split Video Clip instead (and has a very different effect).

Being able to split an audio clip is useful in a number of ways. For example, suppose that you've got a voice recording of a guy recounting his days at the beginning of Apple Computer. One line goes, "We lived in a rundown tenement on the Lower East Side of Cupertino, but nobody cared. We loved what we were doing."

Now suppose you've also got a couple of terrific still photos of the original Apple building, plus a photo of the original Apple team, grinning like fools in their grungy T-shirts and beards. After using the Split Audio Clip command, you can place the first part of the recording ("We lived in a rundown tenement on the Lower East Side of Cupertino") beneath the campus photos, and then *delay* the second utterance ("But nobody cared. We loved what we were doing") until you're ready to introduce the group photo.

Tip: You can't split a clip and then immediately move one of the halves. After the Split command, both clips remain in position, side by side, both highlighted. Whatever you do will affect both pieces, as though you'd never split them at all. Shift-click the piece you *don't* want before trying to drag or cut anything.

Moving an Audio Clip

You can drag audio clips around in their tracks just as you would video clips, or even back and forth between the two audio tracks.

In fact, because precision is often so important in positioning audio relative to the video, iMovie harbors a few useful shortcuts.

For example, whenever you drag an audio clip, the Playhead magnetically attaches itself to the beginning of the clip. As you drag, therefore, you get to watch the video in the Monitor window, corresponding to the precise moment where the sound begins.

GEM IN THE ROUGH

The Invisible Audio "Shelf"

When you're editing video, the Clips pane provides a handy temporary working space where you can set aside clips that you haven't yet placed into the movie. If you've ever worked with a page-layout program like InDesign, you're already familiar with this "pasteboard" effect.

Unfortunately, iMovie doesn't come with any pane or pasteboard where you can temporarily park *audio* clips.

If you think it might be handy to have such a workspace as you manipulate your audio clips, the solution is simple: Drag them, or paste them, far off to the right of the Timeline Viewer, beyond the right edge of your video. Then, just drag them back into place when you're ready for them. (Just don't leave any stray audio clips there by accident. You'll look pretty silly when your movie premieres at Cannes.)

Once the clip is highlighted, don't forget that you can press the left and right arrow keys to move it one frame at a time, or Shift-arrow keys to slide it 10 frames at a time. Even then, you'll see your exact position in the video by watching the Monitor window.

As a matter of fact, you can combine these two tricks. Once the Playhead is aligned with either end of a clip, you can press the arrow keys, or Shift-arrow, to move the Playhead *and* drag the audio clip along with it. You'll feel like the audio is somehow Velcroed to the Playhead.

Superimposing Audio Clips

iMovie may seem to offer only two parallel audio tracks, but that doesn't mean you can't have more layers of simultaneous sound. There may be only two horizontal strips on the screen, but there's nothing to stop you from putting audio clips *on top of each other*. By all means, drag a sound effect onto your already-recorded narration clip, or superimpose two or more different CD music recordings, if that's the cacophonous effect you want. When playing back your project, iMovie plays all of the sound simultaneously, mixing them automatically (Figure 17-10).

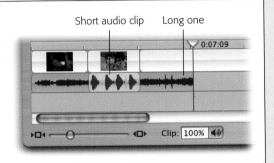

Figure 17-10:
The first time you drag or paste a new audio clip onto an existing one, the situation is fairly clear, thanks to iMovie's tendency to put shorter clips on top of longer ones. It's impossible for a clip to become covered up entirely.

Short audio clip   Long one

If you're having trouble sorting out several overlapping sound clips, consider selecting one and then choosing Edit→Cut. Often, just getting one clip out of the way is enough for you to understand what's going on in its original location. Once you've got your bearings, you can choose Edit→Undo to put it right back where it was.

Another tactic: When you click a clip, iMovie always selects the shortest one in the stack. If you have two overlapping audio clips, therefore, and you intend to select the longer one, click one of its visible ends.

Remember, too, to glance at the top of the Timeline Viewer as you click each audio clip. You'll see its name (if you've turned off the soundwaves, that is), which is another helpful clue when clips collide.

Scrubbing Audio Clips

Scrubbing once meant rotating reel-to-reel tapes back and forth manually, in an effort to find a precise spot in the audio (to make a clean splice, for example). In iMovie

HD, you can scrub by Option-dragging your mouse back and forth across an audio clip. iMovie plays the sound under your cursor.

(This technique is extremely useful, but it works best when you're zoomed in and dragging very slowly. Note that Option is called Alt on some non–U.S. keyboards.)

Overlaying Video over Sound

One of the most popular editing techniques—both with editors and audiences—is the *video overlay*. (On the Internet, you may hear this technique called an *insert edit*, but that actually has nothing to do with pasting video over audio.)

As shown in Figure 17-11, a video overlay is where the video cuts away to a new picture, but you continue to hear the audio from the original clip.

Figure 17-11:
When you overlay video over sound, you can illustrate what the speaker is saying without losing her train of voice.

"What did I love about Edenville? Well, not the odor, that's for sure. And not the plant. No, what I loved most was the old canoe lake. Oh, sure, it was all foamed up with nitrates, and you didn't dare touch the water. But without a doubt, those were some of the happiest days of my life. I'd give almost anything to take one more look at that old lake."

Suppose, for example, that you've got footage of an old man describing his first love. As he gets to the part where he describes meeting her, you want to cut to a closeup of her portrait on his mantelpiece.

The "Extract Audio in Paste Over" Checkbox

It's a piece of cake to paste a piece of video without disturbing the original audio track. First, though, choose iMovie→Preferences, click General, and make sure "Extract audio when using 'Paste Over at Playhead'" is selected.

If this checkbox is turned *on*, you'll paste only the video, preserving whatever audio is already on your audio tracks. If the checkbox is turned *off*, you'll wipe out both the audio and the video in the spot where you paste.

Close the Preferences window. You're now ready to paste over.

Performing the Overlay

To perform the video overlay, follow these steps:

1. **Select the footage you want to paste.**

If it's a complete clip, just highlight its icon on the Clips pane or in the Movie Track. If it's a portion of a clip, use the crop markers to specify the part you want, as described on page 303.

2. Cut or copy the selected footage.

Use the Edit→Cut or Edit→Copy commands.

Now you have to make an important decision. You're about to paste some copied video *over* some existing video. But how much of it do you want to paste? You can either "paste to fit" so that the pasted video begins and ends at precise frames, filling a hole in the existing footage of a particular length; or you can paste it all, without worrying about where the end of the pasted material falls. In this second scenario, you don't want to have to specify a cutoff point (where the existing video cuts in again).

These two cases are illustrated in Figure 17-12.

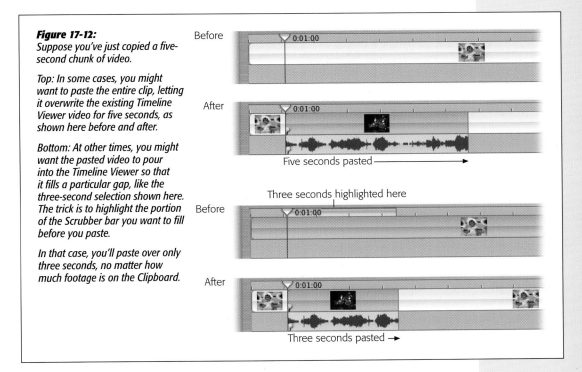

Figure 17-12:
Suppose you've just copied a five-second chunk of video.

Top: In some cases, you might want to paste the entire clip, letting it overwrite the existing Timeline Viewer video for five seconds, as shown here before and after.

Bottom: At other times, you might want the pasted video to pour into the Timeline Viewer so that it fills a particular gap, like the three-second selection shown here. The trick is to highlight the portion of the Scrubber bar you want to fill before you paste.

In that case, you'll paste over only three seconds, no matter how much footage is on the Clipboard.

Before

After

Five seconds pasted ⟶

Three seconds highlighted here

Before

After

Three seconds pasted ➔

3. If you want to paste the entire copied chunk, position the Playhead in the Timeline Viewer exactly where you want the insert to appear. Then choose Advanced→Paste Over at Playhead (or press Shift-⌘-V).

The video you've pasted wipes out whatever was already there, even if it replaces multiple clips (or parts of clips). If the "Extract audio when using 'Paste Over at

Playhead'" checkbox is turned on, as described above, your edit is complete. You've got a cutaway to new video as the original audio track continues.

4. **If you want to paste to fit, highlight the portion of the movie that you want the pasted video to replace. Then choose Advanced→Paste Over at Playhead.**

To select the region that your paste will replace, you can use any of the techniques described in Chapter 14. If you want to knock out only a portion of a single clip, for example, click the clip in the Movie Track and then use the Scrubber bar crop handles to isolate the section that will be replaced (Figure 17-12, bottom). If you want to paste into a segment that spans multiple clips (or parts of clips), choose Edit→Select None, and then use the cropping handles on the entire Scrubber bar map of your movie.

When you paste, one of three things may happen. If the pasted material is *precisely* the same length as the region you've highlighted, great…the pasted chunk drops perfectly into the hole. If the pasted material is longer than the highlighted region, however, iMovie chops off the pasted portion, using as much of the first portion as possible to fit the area you've designated. And if the pasted material is too *short* to fill the reserved space, iMovie creates a "black" clip (see page 311) to fill the remaining highlighted area.

Extracting Audio from Video

iMovie is perfectly capable of stripping the audio portion of your footage apart from the video. All you have to do is click the video clip in question and then choose Advanced→Extract Audio.

As shown in Figure 17-13, the recorded audio suddenly shows up in your first audio track as an independent audio clip; its pushpins indicate that it's been locked to the original video.

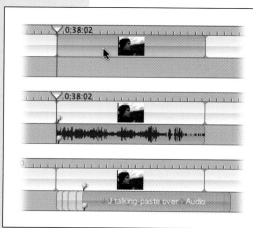

Figure 17-13:

Top: Highlight a camcorder clip and choose Advanced→Extract Audio.

Middle: The camcorder audio appears as an independent clip, which you can manipulate exactly as though it's any ordinary audio clip.

Bottom: You can create a reverb or echo effect by overlaying the same extracted audio several times. (The "soundwave" images have been turned off here for clarity.)

This command unleashes all kinds of useful new tricks that are impossible to achieve any other way:

- **Make an echo.** This is a cool one. Copy the extracted clip and paste it right back into the audio track—and then position it a few frames to the right of the original, as shown at bottom in Figure 17-13. Use the slider at the bottom of the Timeline Viewer to make it slightly quieter than the original. Repeat a couple more times, until you've got a realistic echo or reverb sound.

- **Boost the audio.** The Volume slider at the bottom of the Timeline Viewer is a terrific help in boosting feeble camcorder audio. It does, however, have its limit: it can't crank the volume more than 50 percent above the original level.

  Sometimes, even that's not enough to rescue a line of mumbled dialog, or the distant utterances of eighth-graders on the school stage 100 yards away.

  When all else fails, try this crazy technique: Copy the extracted clip and paste it *right back on top of itself.* iMovie now plays both audio tracks simultaneously, giving an enormous boost to the volume. In fact, you can stack two, three, four, or even more copies of the same clip on top of each other, all in the same spot, for even more volume boosting.

  Now, there's a pretty good reason the Volume slider doesn't go higher than 150%. As you magnify the sound, you also magnify the hiss, the crackle, and whatever other underlying sonic noise there may have been in the audio. When you try this pasting-on-top trick, you may run into that problem, too. Even so, for insiders who know this technique, many an important line of dialog has been saved from oblivion.

- **Reuse the sound.** You can copy and paste the extracted audio elsewhere in the movie. (You've probably seen this technique used in dozens of Hollywood movies: About 15 minutes before the end of the movie, the main character, lying beaten and defeated in an alley, suddenly pieces together the solution to the central plot mystery, as snippets of dialog we've already heard in the movie float through his brain, finally adding up.)

- **Crop the scene's audio.** Trim out an unfortunate cough, belch, or background car honk by cropping the audio. Now the video can begin (or end) in silence, with the audio kicking in (or out) only when required. (Of course, complete silence isn't generally what you want either, as described next.)

- **Grab some ambient sound.** In real movie-editing suites, it happens all the time: A perfect take is ruined by the sound of a passing bus just during the tender kiss moment—and you don't discover it until you're in the editing room, long after the actors and crew have moved on to other projects.

  You can eliminate the final seconds of sound from the scene by cropping or splitting the clip, of course. But that won't result in a satisfying solution; now you'll have three seconds of *silence* during the kiss. The real world isn't truly silent, even when there's no talking. The air is always filled with *ambient sound,* such as breezes, distant traffic, the hum of fluorescent lights, and so on. Even inside in a perfectly still room, there's *room tone*. When you want to replace a portion of the audio track with "silence," what you usually want, in fact, is to replace it with ambient sound.

Professionals always record about 30 seconds of room tone or ambient sound just so that they'll have material to use in case of emergency. You may not need to go to that extreme; you may well be able to grab some sound from a different part of the same shot. The point is that by importing that few seconds of scene into iMovie, extracting the audio, and then *deleting* the leftover video clip, you've got yourself a useful piece of ambient-sound "footage" that you can use to patch over unwanted portions of the originally recorded audio.

- **Add narration.** The technique described on page 365 is ideal for narration that you record at one sitting in a quiet room. But you can add narration via camcorder, too. Just record yourself speaking, import the footage into iMovie, extract the audio, and then throw away the video. You might want to do this if you're editing on a mike-less Mac, or if you want the new narration to better match the camcorder's original sound.

It's important to note that iMovie never actually *removes* the audio from a video clip. You'll never be placed into the frantic situation of wishing that you'd never done the extraction at all, unable to sync the audio and video together again (which sometimes happens in "more powerful" video-editing programs).

Instead, iMovie places a *copy* of the audio into the audio track. The original video clip actually retains its original audio—but iMovie sets its volume slider to zero, thereby muting it. As a result, you can extract audio from the same clip over and over again, if you like. iMovie simply spins out another copy of the audio each time. (When you extract audio, the video clip, too, sprouts a pushpin, but don't let that fool you. It's perfectly legal to extract the audio again.)

If you intend to use the extracted audio elsewhere in the movie *without* silencing the original clip, no problem. Just click the video clip and then drag the volume pop-up menu back up to 100% once again.

Still Pictures and QuickTime Movies

The DV camcorder is the source of iMovie material you'll probably use the most often, but it's not the only source. You can also bring in still images and existing QuickTime movies from your hard drive. In addition, you can *export* still frames from your movie, a much more direct method of producing still images than having to use your camcorder's built-in "digital camera" feature.

Importing Still Images

You might want to import a graphics file into iMovie for any number of reasons. For example:

- You can use a graphic, digital photo, or other still image as a backdrop for iMovie's titling feature (Chapter 16). A still image behind your text is less distracting than moving footage.

- You can use a graphics file *instead* of using the iMovie titling feature. As noted in Chapter 16, iMovie's titling feature offers a number of powerful features, including animation. However, it also has a number of serious limitations. Namely, you can't specify any type size you like, you can't use more than one font per title, and you have only rudimentary control over the title's placement in the frame.

  Preparing your own title "slides" in, say, Photoshop Elements or AppleWorks gives you a lot of flexibility that the iMovie titling feature lacks. You get complete control over the type size, color, and placement, for starters. You can also add graphic touches to your text or to the "slide" on which it appears.

- One of the most compelling new uses of video is the *video photo album*: a smoothly integrated succession of photos (from your scanner or digital camera), joined by crossfades, enhanced by titles, and accompanied by music. Thanks to iMovie's ability to import photos directly—either from your hard drive or from your iPhoto collection—creating this kind of video show is a piece of cake.

Note: Of course, iPhoto can create video photo albums, too. And in iPhoto, you can opt to loop a slideshow (which iMovie can't do); rearranging and regrouping your photos is much easier than in iMovie, too. But building them in a movie has several advantages. First of all, your music options are much greater; you can import music straight from a music CD, for example, or record narration as you watch the slideshow. You have a full arsenal of tools for creating titles, credits, and special effects, too.

As your life with iMovie proceeds, you may encounter other uses for the picture-importing feature. Maybe, when editing a home movie of your kids tussling in the living room, you decide it would be hilarious to insert some *Batman*-style fight-sound title cards ("BAM!") into the footage. Maybe you need an establishing shot of, say, a storefront or apartment building, and realize that you could save production money by inserting a still photo that passes for live video in which there's nothing moving. And maybe you want to end your movie with a fade-out—not to black, but to maroon (an effect described later in this chapter).

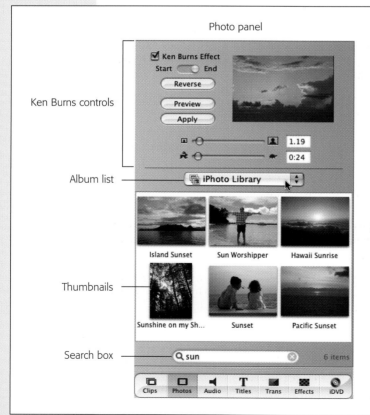

Photo panel

Ken Burns controls

Album list

Thumbnails

Search box

Figure 18-1:
The photo panel shows all the pictures you've imported into iPhoto. Use the Album list pop-up menu to limit the photo display to those in a certain album or folder.

(The dark gray readout at the lower right tells you how many pictures are in that album or folder—or in your entire library, if that's what you're seeing.)

Note the Search box, which debuts in iMovie HD. As you type into it, iMovie smoothly hides all photos except the ones whose names contain matching text. It's an amazingly quick way to pinpoint one photo out of several thousand.

To clear the search box and return to viewing all photos, click the circled X button at the right end of the box.

You have a delicious choice of two methods for bringing still photos into a project. The first and most convenient method is to choose the photo from among those you've organized in iPhoto, using iMovie's window into your picture collection. If you're not using iPhoto to organize your digital photos, you can also use the older method of importing pictures directly from the hard drive.

Snagging Pictures from iPhoto

The more you work with iMovie and iDVD, the more you appreciate the convenience of the way Apple has linked them to the other i-programs, like iTunes and iPhoto. Here's a classic case:

When you click the Photos button (Figure 18-1), you're shown what amounts to iPhoto Lite: a scrolling panel of thumbnail images reflecting the contents of your entire iPhoto Library. Using the pop-up menu just above the thumbnails, you can even limit your view to the contents of one iPhoto *album* or *folder*.

Once you've pinpointed the picture you want, you install it in your movie like this:

Phase 1: Specify the duration

Because you're importing a still image, it doesn't have a *duration,* as a movie clip might. (Asking "How many seconds long is a photograph?" is like asking, "What is the sound of one hand clapping?")

Still, it's a clip, so iMovie has to assign it *some* duration. You can make your graphic appear on the screen for as little as three frames (a favorite of subliminal advertisers) all the way up to 30 seconds (a favorite of all other advertisers).

There's a fast way and a precise way to change this number. The fast way is to drag the rabbit/turtle slider shown in Figure 18-2.

Tip: When you get right down to it, 30 seconds is plenty of time for looking at one particular photo, no matter how good it is. Still, if you need it to last longer—perhaps because you're using it as a background for a series of opening credits—you can always overcome the 30-second limit by placing the same photo into the Movie Track over and over again, side by side, 30 seconds long each.

When more precision is required, you can also type the number of seconds and frames into the Duration box to the right of the slider. You can use a number of shortcuts to edit the numbers in this tiny box:

- Press the arrow keys to walk your cursor from one number to the next. Press the Delete key to backspace over the number to the left of the insertion point, or the forward-delete (Del) key (if your keyboard has one) to delete the number to the right of it.

- Double-click the *portion* of the number you want to change. For example, if a clip's Duration box says 10:00 (10 seconds), double-click the 10 to highlight it, type the new number (such as *07*), and press Enter. (You must type a leading zero in front of a single-digit number, or else you'll get an error message.)

In other words, when efficiency counts, don't waste your time deleting the numbers that are already in the Duration box. Instead, double-click only the portion of it you want to change, and then type right over the highlighted digits.

- Similarly, if you want to change both the seconds and the frames, drag directly across the right pair of numbers in the box. Type the new duration—seconds, a colon, and then frames—and then press Enter.

- If you highlight the entire Duration box (by pressing ⌘-A, for example, or by choosing Edit→Select All), you can rapidly specify the new duration by just typing up the whole thing, including the colon, like this: *05:15.*

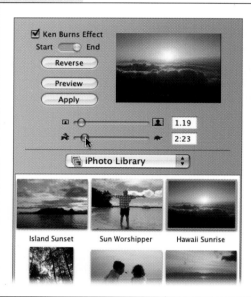

Figure 18-2:
To edit the duration of a still image, click it, either in the Photos panel or in the Movie Track.

Now you can use the rabbit/turtle slider to adjust the photo's duration—that is, the amount of time the picture will appear on the screen, in seconds:frames format.

Or, for greater precision, double-click the actual numbers and then type new numbers over them.

Phase 2: Specify the Ken Burns effect

If you turn on the Ken Burns Effect checkbox at the top of the Photos panel, you unleash a wild and arresting feature: the ability to pan and zoom smoothly across photos, in essence animating them and directing the viewer's attention. Details on page 395.

If you'd rather have your photo just pop onto the screen and remain stationary, make sure that the Ken Burns checkbox is turned off. (If you plan to export the movie to iDVD, however, you might want to read page 677 to find out why you'd want to apply Ken Burns to *every* photo, even motionless ones.)

Phase 3: Insert the photo

At last you're ready to put the picture into the movie (a phrase that would hopelessly confuse Hollywood executives who already refer to movies *as* pictures). You can do so in either of two ways:

- Drag a photo out of the thumbnail palette and into the Movie Track. The other clips scoot out of the way to make room, and the photo becomes, in effect, a new silent video clip with the duration you specified. (If you turned on the Ken Burns effect, iMovie takes a few moments to render the animation. The familiar red progress bar inches across the face of the clip.)

- If you want the photo to drop into the end of the movie—as you might when assembling a slideshow, one photo at a time—click the Apply button.

Tip: Speaking of slideshows: You can also drop a whole bunch of photos into the Movie Track at once. Select them in the Photos palette just as you would clips, then drag them en masse down to the Movie Track. Or click Apply to drop them all at the end of the Movie Track.

You may notice, by the way, that black bars appear above and below (or along both sides of) certain photos, creating the traditional letterbox effect. That happens when a photo doesn't have the proportions that quirkly old iPhoto expects. See the next pages for the fix.

Importing Photos from the Hard Drive

If you want to incorporate graphics that aren't in iPhoto, begin by making sure that no thumbnails are selected in the Photos palette. (If one thumbnail remains highlighted, ⌘-click it.) Then specify the duration for the incoming photo, as described on page 389. If you don't intend to animate or crop your photo, make sure the Zoom slider is set to 1.0, and that the Ken Burns checkbox is turned off.

Finally, choose File→Import File (or just press Shift-⌘-I). When the standard Open File dialog box opens, navigate your way to the desktop (or wherever you put your graphics file), and double-click the file itself. Actually, because you're using Mac OS X, you can select a whole batch of photos to import simultaneously, using the Shift-clicking and ⌘-clicking techniques described on page 115.

The new photo shows up instantly in the Clips pane or the Movie Track, depending on where you've directed incoming clips to go in iMovie's Preferences box. Once again, if black bars appear on the sides or top and bottom of the photo, see page 394.

Tip: iMovie can import graphics in any format that QuickTime can understand, which includes PICT, JPEG, GIF, Photoshop files, and even PDF files, for when an IRS form is exactly what you want to illustrate in your movie. Avoid the GIF format for photos, which limits the number of colors available to the image. But otherwise, just about any format is good still-image material.

After you've imported a graphics file into your project, it's OK to delete, rename, or move the original graphics file you imported. iMovie doesn't need it anymore.

And if you've been lying awake at night, wondering *how* iMovie can display your graphic even after the original file is gone, look no farther than the Media folder inside your movie's project file (or project folder). There you'll find copies of your imported graphics files, with their original names and at full resolution (so that the Ken Burns effect, if turned on, will have enough "margin" to animate your photo). You'll also find clip icons called Still 01, Still 02, Still 03, and so on; these are the rendered video clips, at 640 x 480 resolution, that iMovie made.

Working with Photos

Once you've installed them in the Movie Track, photos behave a lot like standard movie clips. You can rename them, drag them around, click them to view them in the Monitor window, drag them back and forth from the Clip Viewer and Clips pane, delete them, incorporate them into titles or transitions, and so on.

You can also adjust the timing of an imported picture. Just highlight its icon, adjust the Duration slider (or type new numbers into the Duration box), and then click the Update button just above those controls. (The Update button appears only when a single photo is selected. You can't change the timings of multiple photos at once.)

If you haven't applied the Ken Burns effect (described later in this chapter), you can also change a photo's duration by double-clicking it and then typing a new duration into the Clip Info box. Using this method, you save yourself a click on the Photos button.

Tip: If you've used still images in your movie, don't even think about turning your project into a DVD until you've read the troubleshooting steps on page 677. Otherwise, you'll wind up with very jagged photos.

The Dimensions of an iMovie Photo

On the iMovie discussion forums of the Web, the question comes up over and over again: "What resolution should my iMovie-bound photos be?"

That question implies that you're thinking of *changing* them—reducing their resolution from their multi-megapixel original state—and that's generally a bad idea. iMovie can use all the resolution it can get, especially if you intend to give the photos the Ken Burns treatment or edit them for HDTV.

A better question is: "What *proportions* should my photo have?" If your photos don't have precisely the dimensions iMovie expects, you'll get letterbox bars, as shown in Figure 18-3.

Until iMovie HD came along, iMovie expected photos to have 4:3 width-to-height proportions to avoid letterboxing. That was just fine for most people, because 4:3 is exactly how photos come from most digital cameras.

As of iMovie 5.0.1, though, something strange is going on. A perfect 4:3 photo does not perfectly fill the standard-definition 4:3 iMovie screen. Instead, it leaves tiny vertical letterbox bars on the sides. To make the bars go away, you have to use the Ken Burns effect to enlarge the photo slightly—1.06 on the Size slider (for standard DV projects), to be exact.

Note: To make this technique work, click the photo in the Photos pane, then use the Size slider to specify 1.06—don't try typing it into the little box. (The type-into-the-box thing only sometimes works, as thousands have unhappily discovered.)

Even then, you'll see thin letterbox bars in the tiny Preview window—but don't worry. When you proceed by clicking Apply, the photo will neatly fill the standard TV-shaped window.

If you'd rather crop your stills in a program like Photoshop or iPhoto before bringing them into iMovie, you'll have to put up with some pretty peculiar ratios. For example, for NTSC (North American), standard-definition projects, you have to crop photos a width-to-height ratio of *1.364 to 1* if you want them to fit the screen neatly! (For other video formats, see the following table.)

Figure 18-3:
If the dimensions of your graphic aren't in the exact width-to-height ratio that iMovie demands, you'll get letterboxed bars like these.

Top: A portrait-orientation photo.

Bottom: A landscape-orientation photo that's not quite the right aspect ratio.

Graphics from Scratch

What if you intend to design a graphic from scratch? Maybe it's going to be a simple colored square, which you'll fade into between movie segments. Maybe it's going to be a title card that you intend to dress up in a graphics program.

Technically, images 640 pixels wide and 480 pixels tall ought to be perfect for standard TV (assuming you don't intend to zoom or pan with Ken Burns), because that's the resolution of a standard TV screen. Here again, though, iMovie HD has some funny ideas of its own. To prevent letterboxing on a standard-def, NTSC TV, for example, your iMovie-bound graphics files should be at least *720 x 528* pixels!

Confused yet?

Here's the point: If you're going to crop your photos before bringing them into iMovie, look up the "Aspect Ratio for Photos" in the table below. Crop your photos to those width:height proportions to make them fit iMovie's screen perfectly.

And if you're going to create graphics from scratch, consult the "Minimum Graphics Dimensions" in the table below. That, in pixels, is the lowest resolution you should feed iMovie to fit the screen neatly. (If you plan to use the Ken Burns effect, of course, you'll want to use much greater resolution to avoid ugly pixellation—twice the listed resolution, for example, for a 2X zoom effect.)

NTSC Projects (North America, Japan)

Project Format	Screen Dimensions	Aspect Ratio for Photos	Minimum Graphics Dimensions
Standard DV	720 x 528	1.364:1	720 x 528
DV Widescreen	869 x 480	1.818:1	874 x 480
HDV (720p)	1280 x 720	16:9	1280 x 720
HDV (1080i)	1440 x 1080	16:9*	1440 x 1080

PAL-Format Projects (Europe)

Project Format	Screen Dimensions	Aspect Ratio for Photos	Minimum Graphics Dimensions
Standard DV	784 x 587	1.364:1	788 x 576
DV Widescreen	1040 x 576	1.823:1*	1050 x 576
HDV (720p)	1280 x 720	16:9	1280 x 720
HDV (1080i)	1440 x 1080	16:9*	1440 x 1080

* These figures are for Photoshop editing. For some reason, the numbers are different if you're editing in iPhoto. The HDV 1080i aspect ratio should be 16:9.02 (NTSC and PAL). And for PAL widescreen DV, the aspect ratio should be 1.818:1 and the minimum import size should be 1048 x 576.

The Ken Burns Effect

The only problem with using still photos in a movie is that they're *still*. They just sit there without motion or sound, wasting much of the dynamic potential of video.

For years, professionals have addressed the problem using special sliding camera rigs that produce gradual zooming, panning, or both, to bring photographs to life.

But this smooth motion isn't just about adding animation to photos for its own sake. It also lets you draw the viewer's attention where you want it, when you want it. For example: "Little Harry graduated from junior high school in 1963"—slow pan to someone else in the school photo, a little girl with a ribbon in her hair—"little suspecting that the woman who would one day become his tormentor was standing only a few feet away."

Among the most famous practitioners of this art is Ken Burns, the creator of PBS documentaries like *The Civil War* and *Baseball*—which is why Apple, with his permission, named the feature after him.

You can endow any still graphics file with this kind of motion, either at the moment when you place it or import it from your hard drive, or anytime thereafter.

Applying the Ken Burns Effect

In this example, you'll animate a photo that's in the iPhoto palette.

1. **Select the photo.**

   Actually, you can select more than one, to process all of them in the same way.

2. **Turn on the Ken Burns Effect checkbox at the top of the window. Specify how long you want the picture to remain onscreen.**

   Use the Duration controls, just as described on page 389.

3. **Click Start. Use the Zoom controls until the photo is as big as you want it at the** *beginning* **of its time on screen. Drag inside the Preview screen to adjust the photo's position (Figure 18-4).**

   In other words, you're setting up the photo the way it appears at the beginning of the shot. Often, you won't want to do anything to it at all. You want it to start on the screen at its original size—and then zoom in from there.

   But if you hope to create a zooming *out* effect, then drag the Zoom slider to the right (or type a larger number into the box), magnify the photo in the Preview screen, and finally drag the picture itself to center it properly.

Tip: It's actually possible to drag the photo partially or completely *out of the frame,* leaving an empty black void in its place. If you've done this accidentally, just nudge the Zoom slider slightly right, then left. The photo smartly snaps back into centered position. On the other hand, there are certain creative possibilities here. You can make a photo begin offscreen and then slowly slide into place, for example—or even exit the screen by sliding off the opposite side.

---

4. **Click End. Use the Zoom controls to set up the picture's final degree of magnification. Drag inside the Preview screen to specify the photo's final position. (Shift-drag to constrain your dragging to perfect vertical or horizontal adjustments.)**

In short, you've set up the starting and ending conditions for the photo.

Take a moment now to click the Preview button. The animated photo goes through its scheduled motion within the Preview box, so that you can check the overall effect. Repeat steps 3 and 4 as necessary.

Tip: At any time, you can click the Reverse button to swap the settings of the Start and End positions. What was once a slow zoom in, left to right, becomes a slow zoom out, right to left.

---

5. **Drag the thumbnail image out of the Photos palette and into the Movie Track.**

Or click the Apply button; iMovie plunks the image at the end of the movie.

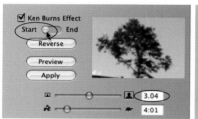 

Figure 18-4:
Top: To set up the Ken Burns effect, establish the position and zoom level of the Start and End points separately. (At top right, you can see the little grabby hand cursor that lets you shift the photo within the frame.)

Bottom: Here are three possibilities. The zoom-out pictured at left results from the Ken Burns settings shown above. The center example makes the camera appear to zoom in on the woman holding the pineapple, even as the photo shifts position to center the pineapple. At right, the Zoom setting was the same (2.0) for both the Start and End points. The only thing that changes over time is the left-to-right position of the photo in the frame.

Zoom out   Pan and zoom in   Diagonal pan

Either way, iMovie now begins rendering your photo effect. You specified the beginning and ending positions of the photo; now iMovie is interpolating, calculating each intermediate frame between the starting and ending points you've specified. The red progress bar crawls across the face of the clip, showing you how much longer you have to wait. (Of course, you're free to work on other aspects of your movie in the meantime, although you may notice a slowdown.)

After the rendering is complete, click the photo clip in the Movie Track and press the Space bar to play your Ken Burns-ized "photo movie" in the Monitor window.

Editing or Removing the Ken Burns Effect

If a photo clip requires adjustment, touching it up is easy enough. Select it in the Movie Track (or wherever it is). Click the Photos button (if the Photos pane isn't already open). Click Start or End, and reprogram the Ken Burns effect just as you did the first time around. (Feel free to edit the duration, too.) When you're finished, click Update. iMovie dutifully re-renders the clip with its new settings.

And what if you want the photo to return to its original, virginal condition? In that case, click the Start button. Drag the Zoom slider all the way to the left, which both re-centers the photo and restores it to its original size. Click the End button and repeat. Finally, click the Update button.

Cropping or Moving a Photo Without Animating It

If you decide that a certain still photo really should be still, click the clip in the Movie Track, turn off the Ken Burns Effect checkbox, and then click Update. The photo is now frozen at its first frame, at the same zoom and position it had when the Ken Burns checkbox was still turned on.

GEM IN THE ROUGH

The Ken Burns Cropping Effect

You already know that the Ken Burns effect can animate a photo over time, slowly (or quickly) zooming, panning, or both, depending on where the picture is when you click the Start and End buttons.

But you can also zoom or shift the photo *without* animating it. In effect, you can use the Ken Burns tools to crop a photo as you place it into your Movie Track. This is a great trick for dealing with a vertical photo that you want to use in the horizontal orientation of a standard television. By zooming in until the black bars disappear, you've chopped off some of the top and bottom of the picture.

To try this out, click a photo, make sure the Ken Burns checkbox is turned off, specify the duration, and then zoom

in. Lastly, drag to shift the photo the way you like it.

Here's a related trick that you may find useful. Suppose you've just Ken Burns-ized a photo. You change your mind. You want it to be still, but you like the way it *ends*.

In that case, Option-click the Start button (in the Photos panel), and then click Update.

Option-clicking copies the End position and zoom level into the Start position. The result is a clip that doesn't move or pan at all, but instead maintains the same zoom level and position for its entire duration. (You can Option-click the End button, too, if the Start position and zoom level are what you want to use for the entire clip.)

What's neat is even when the Ken Burns effect is turned off, the Zoom slider and the little "move my photo around the frame" cursor still work. In other words, you can use the Ken Burns control to enlarge, crop, or shift a still photo *without* animating it.

Still Images as Titles

As noted at the beginning of this chapter, one of the best reasons to get to know the still-image importing feature is so that you can supplement, or replace, iMovie's built-in titling feature. By using still images as your titles, you gain the freedom to use any colors, type sizes, and positions you want.

The only disadvantage to this approach is that you sacrifice the professional-looking animation styles built into the iMovie titling feature.

Even so, imported graphic title cards don't have to be still and static by any means. For one thing, there's nothing to stop you from animating your still-image titles by applying the Ken Burns effect to them—to make the title zoom in from nothing, for example, or slide from left to right. (Just remember to prepare the title as a graphi with high enough resolution for Ken Burns to work with.)

Furthermore, consider the following title tricks.

The Freeze-Frame Effect

If you were a fan of 1970s action shows like *Emergency!,* you may remember how the opening credits looked: You'd be watching one of the starring characters frantically at work in some lifesaving situation. As she looked up from her work just for a moment, the picture would freeze, catching her by lucky happenstance at her most flattering angle. At that instant, you'd see her credit flashed onto the screen: "JULIE LONDON as Dixie McCall, RN." (*Queer Eye for the Straight Guy* does the same kind of thing.)

That's an easy one to simulate—and nobody will guess that it was created using a still image. To pull this off, you must first export the still frame from your footage that you'll want to use as the freeze-frame. (You'll find instructions for exporting a still frame in the next section.) Import the frozen shot into your graphics program, like AppleWorks or Photoshop Elements. Then add the text you want.

Finally, import this touched-up image into iMovie as a still image. Place it at the precise frame in your footage from which you exported the still to begin with, and you've got your freeze-frame title effect.

Tip: If you don't need the added typographical flexibility of your graphics program, you can simplify this procedure by simply creating a freeze-frame, as described on the previous page, and then using iMovie's built-in title feature to add the text over it.

The Layered Effect

In many cases, the most creative use of still-image titles comes from using *several* of them, each building on the last. For example, you can make the main title appear, hold for a moment, and then transition into a second still graphic on which a subtitle appears.

If you have more time on your hands, you can use this trick to create simple animations. Suppose you were to create ten different title cards, all superimposed on the same background, but each with the words in a different size or position. If you were to place each title card on the screen for only half a second (15 frames), joined by very fast crossfades, you'd create a striking visual effect. Similarly, you might consider making the *color* of the lettering shift over time. To do that, create two or three different title cards, each with the text in a different color. Insert them into your movie, join them with slow crossfades, and you've got a striking, color-shifting title sequence.

Creating Still Images from Footage

iMovie doesn't just take still photos; it can also dish them out. It can grab selected frames from your footage, either for use as frozen frames in your movie or for exporting as graphics files. (You might want a still frame to end a Ken Burns zoom, for example, so that the camera seems to hold still for a moment after the zoom.)

Creating a Still Frame

The Edit→Create Still Frame command creates a still image, in the Clips pane, of the frame currently indicated by the Playhead. You can use the resulting still clip just as you would any still clip: Drag it into your Movie Track, apply effects or transitions to it, change its name or duration, and so on.

One of the most obvious uses of this feature is the *freeze-frame* effect, in which the movie holds on the final frame of a shot. It's a terrifically effective way to end a movie, particularly if the final shot depicts the shy, unpopular hero in a moment of triumph, arms in the air, hoisted onto the shoulders of the crowd. (Fade to black; bring up the music; roll credits.)

Here's how you do it. (These steps assume that you're creating a still frame from a clip that you've already placed in the Movie Track. It's possible, however, to create a still frame from a clip that's still in the Clips pane.)

1. **Position the Playhead on the frame you want frozen.**

   If it's the last shot of a clip, use the right and left arrow keys to make sure you're seeing the final frame.

2. **Choose Edit→Create Still Frame (Shift-⌘-S).**

   iMovie places a new clip either in your Clips pane or at the end of the Movie Track, depending on how you've set up the iMovie→Preferences dialog box.

   It's a still image, set to play for five seconds—but it's not the same kind of still photo you're used to. None of the controls in the Photos palette, for example, has any effect on a *Still,* as iMovie calls it. You can't apply the Ken Burns effect to it, for example.

If you created this still clip from the *final frame* of a clip, proceed to the next step. If you created this clip from the *middle* of a clip, however, you should now choose Edit→Split Clip at Playhead. You've just chopped up the clip at the precise source of the still clip, resulting in two side-by-side clips in your Movie Track. Delete the right-hand clip.

3. **Drag the still clip just to the right of the original clip (Figure 18-5).**

   If you play back the result, you'll be impressed at how smoothly and professionally iMovie joins the frozen frame onto the moving footage; there's not even a hint of a seam as the Playhead slides from clip to still.

4. **Adjust the still's playback duration, if necessary.**

   Fortunately, iMovie HD treats still frames the same way it treats video clips. You can change its duration just by dragging its edges in the Timeline Viewer.

Figure 18-5:
A creative way to end a movie: Chop up the final clip and slow down each piece, finally coming to rest on your still image.

Or, for more precision, double-click the still frame. In the Clip Info dialog box, change the number in the Duration box, and then click OK.

Figuring out how to handle the *audio* in such situations is up to you, since a still frame has no sound. That's a good argument for starting your closing-credits music *during* the final clip and making it build to a crescendo for the final freeze-frame.

Exporting a Still Frame

While it's convenient to be able to grab a frame from your footage for use in the same movie (as a freeze-frame, for example), you may sometimes find it useful to export a frame to your hard drive as a graphics file. You can use such exported images in any way you use graphics—for emailing to friends, installing on your desktop as a background picture, posting on a Web page, and so on. An exported frame also makes a neat piece of "album art" that you can print out and slip into the plastic case of a homemade DVD.

This feature is, after all, the reason that most iMovie fans don't really care about the built-in still-photo features of DV camcorders. Basically, iMovie can create still images from *any* frame of regular video footage.

It's worth noting, however, that the maximum *resolution* for a digital video frame—the number of dots that compose the image—is 640 across, 480 down. (By this time in the chapter, these numbers have probably become engraved into your cerebrum.) As digital photos go, that's pretty pathetic, on a par with the photos taken by camera phones these days. That's one-third of a megapixel—a pretty puny number compared with the shots from today's three- to eight-megapixel cameras.

The resolution problem

The standard DV resolution is probably good enough for viewing your captured frames onscreen—that is, for use in Web pages and sending by email. But printing is a different story. You'll notice a certain coarseness to the printouts of frames you export from iMovie.

Exporting a frame

Now that your expectations have been duly lowered, here's how you capture a frame in iMovie:

Open the project from which you want to grab a still photo. Make sure that no individual clips are selected, and then locate the frame you want to capture. Drag the Playhead along the Scrubber bar, for example. Remember that you can press the left and right arrow keys to step through the movie one frame at a time, or Shift-arrow keys to jump ten frames at a time, in your quest for the precise moment you want to preserve as a still image.

When the image you want appears in the Monitor window, choose File→Save Frame (or press ⌘-F). The Save As dialog box (sheet) slides down from the top of the iMovie window (Figure 18-6).

Figure 18-6:
The Save Frame sheet lets you choose a graphics-file format: JPEG or PICT. When the process is over, the saved frame appears with its own icon on your desktop (or wherever you happened to save it).

Use the Format pop-up menu to specify the file format you want for your exported graphic: PICT or JPEG (the better choice if you intend to email it to someone or use it on a Web page). Navigate to the folder where you want this graphic saved (or press ⌘-D to save it onto the desktop). Click Save.

Importing QuickTime Movies

iMovie can import more than still images. It can also import existing digital movies, which you can then incorporate into your footage.

Maybe you've created such QuickTime movies yourself, using other Macs or other software. Maybe you've grabbed a QuickTime movie from a CD-ROM or Web site. Or maybe you've used a digital still camera's Movie mode to grab some short scenes.

In any case, here are three ways to get digital movies into an iMovie project:

- If they're lying on your hard drive, choose File→Import (Shift-⌘-I). In the Open File dialog box, navigate to and open the QuickTime movie you want to import.

- If you used iPhoto 5 to import the movies, you'll find them nestled among the still photos in iMovie's Photos pane.

- With movies stored in iPhoto, you can also drag the thumbnails out of that program's window and into the Clips pane or Movie Track of iMovie. (Of course, you have to first position the windows so that you can see both at once.)

It may take iMovie some time to process the incoming movie. Behind the scenes, it's converting the QuickTime movie into DV format, just like the clips that come from your camcorder. A progress bar keeps you posted.

When it's complete, a new clip appears in your Clips pane, which you can manipulate just as you would any movie clip.

Using the Imported QuickTime Clip

It's worth noting that most of the world's QuickTime movies aren't big enough, in terms of frame size, to fill your entire monitor. In fact, most of the world's QuickTime movies—like all the ones on the Web—play in a window only a couple of inches square.

Therefore, when you play back an imported QuickTime movie, iMovie does what it hopes is the right thing: It blows up the QuickTime movie until the footage fills the entire iMovie playback screen (640 x 480 pixels).

As you probably know by now, however, enlarging *any* graphic on the computer usually winds up degrading its quality, because each pixel that composes the image must be enlarged. The bottom line: QuickTime movies you import into iMovie may look coarse and blotchy unless they were at least 640 x 480 to begin with.

Grabbing Clips from Other Projects

It's worth a reminder: You can also grab clips from one iMovie project and use them in another. Forget all the workarounds you once knew; in iMovie HD, reusing a clip is as simple as highlighting it in Project A, choosing Edit→Copy, opening Project B, choosing Edit→Paste, and then waiting patiently as iMovie, behind the scenes, duplicates the massive video file. (See page 667 for more caveats regarding the Copy command and disk space.)

Finding Your Audience

Unless you edit your movies while keeping your eyes on the camcorder's screen or a TV attached to your camcorder, you've probably been doing your editing work in the Monitor window. But the Monitor window doesn't show you the real thing. It's only an approximation of the smooth, clear video image that your camcorder caught to begin with.

Fortunately, behind the scenes, every shred of crisp, clear, smooth-motioned video is intact on your hard drive. When you export the movie back to your DV camcorder, it appears in all its original, high-resolution glory.

Why Export to Tape

There are any number of reasons you might want to send your finished product back to the camcorder. The following pages outline some of the most popular scenarios.

To Watch It on TV

Once your iMovie creations are back on the camcorder's tape, you can then pass them along to a television. To pull this off, you must connect the camcorder to your TV, using one of the following cables, listed here in order of preference:

- **Component video.** If you're editing high-definition video, sending the result back to your HDTV camcorder is just about the *only* way to play it on a TV. After all, the era of commonplace high-definition DVDs has not yet arrived.

  Your HDTV camcorder came, therefore, with a special cable that ends with three small round jacks colored green, blue, and red. These are *component* video cables, and they must be connected to matching inputs on a high-end (if not high-definition) TV. You'll have to use an additional cable for audio (RCA cables).

- **S-video.** If both your camcorder and your VCR or TV have *S-video* connectors, use an S-video cable to join the two. You'll still have to use RCA cables for the audio.

- **RCA cables.** Most TVs and VCRs don't have S-video connectors, but almost all have *RCA phono* jacks, usually labeled Audio In and Video In. Connect them to the double- or triple-ended cable that came with the camcorder. (If it has *three* connectors at each end, the yellow one is for the video signal, and the red and white ends are for left and right stereo sound.)

Tip: If your TV is very old, it may not have auxiliary input jacks. In this case, plug your camcorder into the *VCR's* auxiliary inputs instead. It will patch the signal through to the TV.

- **Coax inputs.** TVs of a certain era (or price) have only a cable-TV (*coaxial*) input—a round connector about the size of a 24-point capital O, with a single pin in the center. You can buy an adapter at Radio Shack that lets you connect your camcorder's output cables to this kind of jack.

To Transfer It to Your VCR

DV picture quality and sound quality are sensational. Unfortunately, most of the world's citizens don't *have* DV camcorders or DV decks. They have VHS VCRs or DVD players.

Chapters 20 and 22 guide you through turning iMovie masterpieces into DVDs—but that's a stunt you can pull off only if your Mac has a built-in DVD burner. For everyone else, the best way to get your movies to the TV screens of your adoring fans is to transfer them (the movies, not the fans) to VHS cassettes.

You lose a lot of picture and sound quality when you transfer footage to a VHS cassette, whose lines-of-resolution capacity is lower than any other kind of tape reproduction. Still, your viewers will most likely remark how *good* your movies look, not how bad. That's because most people are used to playing back VHS recordings they've made from television, which (unless it's a satellite system) has its own low-resolution problems. The transfers you make from your Mac, even when played back on VHS, look terrific in comparison.

To make a transfer to your VCR, you have a choice: You can either copy the movie back onto a DV cassette in the camcorder, so that you'll have a high-quality DV copy, and then play it from the camcorder onto your VCR; or you can pour the video directly from the Mac, through the camcorder, into the VCR. Both of these techniques are described in the coming pages.

To Offload Footage from Your Mac

Another great reason to transfer your iMovie work back to the camcorder is simply to get it off your hard drive. As you know, video files occupy an enormous amount of disk space. After you've made a couple of movies, your hard drive might be so full that you can't make any more iMovies.

Offloading the movie to your DV camcorder is the perfect solution, thanks to a key advantage of digital video: the ability to transfer footage back and forth between the camcorder and your Mac as many times as you like with *no deterioration in quality*. You can safely unlearn the years of experience you've had with VHS and 8 mm video and feel free to transfer video between your Macintosh and DV camcorder whenever and however you like.

Note: When you transfer an iMovie back to your camcorder—to a fresh tape, if you're wise—the footage remains in perfect, pristine condition. Remember, however, that there's a downside to doing so: Once you've thrown away the digital video files from your Mac, you've lost the ability to adjust titles, effects, transitions, and soundtracks. For best results, therefore, transfer footage back to the camcorder either when you're finished editing the movie, or haven't edited it much at all.

Offloading video to reclaim disk space

After transferring the movie to a DV cassette in your camcorder, you can throw away the corresponding files on your hard drive, which frees up an enormous amount of disk space. The space-consuming digital-video clips sit in the Media folder that lurks within the folder for your project (page 288). In other words, the Media folder is the one taking up all the disk space. Still, you may as well throw away the *entire* project folder (after "backing it up" onto the camcorder), because without the Media files, the actual iMovie document file, and the accompanying *.mov* reference-movie file, are useless.

Transferring Footage to the Camcorder or VCR

The actual steps of transferring the project from iMovie back to the camcorder are fairly simple. The results are almost always satisfying, especially if you've had to look at your footage in its relatively coarse Mac rendition for hours or days. Finally, you get to see your masterpiece at full digital quality. Most people are particularly thrilled by the professional look of iMovie's transitions and titles when they see it on the actual TV (or camcorder LCD panel).

In early iMovie versions, you had to begin the transfer process by sending your finished movie to a DV camcorder as a first step. Now, however, a new possibility awaits: You can play the finished movie directly from the Mac to a VCR, using the camcorder only as a passthrough adapter that doesn't actually record anything. The following discussions cover both methods.

First to DV Tape, Then to VCR

If you'd like your finished movie on DV tape, preserving 100 percent of its original quality, proceed like this:

1. **Insert a blank cassette into your camcorder.**

   Confirm that the tape is unlocked, and—*this is important*—that it's cued up to a part of the tape you're willing to record over.

2. **Put the camcorder into VTR or VCR mode.**

   Confirm that its FireWire cable is plugged into your Mac. Unless you're willing to risk running out of battery power in midtransfer, plug your camcorder into a power outlet, too.

   Open your iMovie project on the Mac, if it isn't already open.

3. **Choose File→Share (Shift-⌘-E, a keystroke designation that's left over from iMovie 3, when this command was called Export).**

   The Share dialog box appears, as shown in Figure 19-1.

Figure 19-1:
The Share dialog box lets you specify whether you're sending your finished movie to a tape, QuickTime movie, DVD, Bluetooth phone, Palm organizer, or whatever.

(Technically, this type of box, which slides down from the iMovie title bar, is known as a sheet.)

4. **At the top of the dialog box, click Videocamera. Change the "seconds of black" numbers in the dialog box, if necessary.**

   The "seconds of black" numbers specify how many seconds of blackness you want to appear on the tape before the movie begins or after it ends; three or four seconds is about right.

   You can also take this opportunity to turn on "Share selected clips only," if you like. This feature lets you split up a long movie into smaller chunks by preselecting only the clips you want before you invoke the Share command.

5. **Click Share.**

   If your project contains certain special effects, iMovie takes this opportunity to say "Your movie contains still, slow motion, and/or reverse clips which need to be rendered for export to iDVD or tape." In that case, click "Render and Proceed."

You're instructing iMovie to generate smoother, more professional looking versions of these scenes—not the quick-and-dirty, temporary ones it's been showing you during editing.

Either way, after a moment, iMovie commands the camcorder to begin recording, and then begins pumping your finished video over the FireWire cable to the tape, from the very beginning of the movie (Figure 19-2). (There's no way to begin playing from the middle of your movie.)

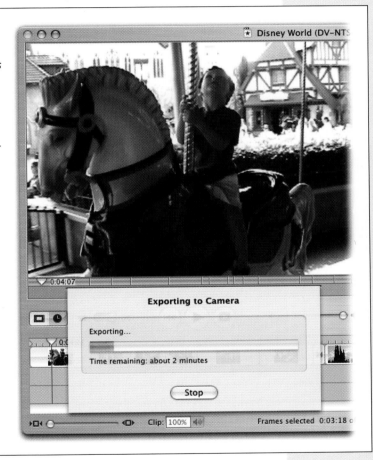

Figure 19-2:
While iMovie sends your finished production back to the camcorder from whence it came, a progress bar shows how much longer you have to wait. Also, you see the playhead ride along your Movie Track to show where you are in the transfer.

You can interrupt the transfer process at any time by clicking Stop. The camcorder stops automatically, having recorded your movie up to the part where you stopped.

While this process is taking place, you might want to open the LCD panel on the camcorder so that you can watch the transfer and listen to the audio. iMovie plays the movie simultaneously in its Monitor window, but the camcorder screen's quality is generally superior.

When the transfer is complete, the camcorder automatically stops recording. Your finished production is now safely on DV tape.

Tip: After the transfer is complete, drag the Camera/Edit switch on your iMovie screen (at the left edge of the screen, just below the Monitor) to its Camera position. Doing so puts iMovie into "I'm controlling your camcorder now" mode. Click Rewind, then Play to watch your newly transferred production.

At this point, you can connect your camcorder to a VCR for transfer to a standard VHS cassette (or any other non-DV format). Connect the camcorder to the Audio and Video input jacks on the VCR. These jacks were once found exclusively on the *backs* of VCRs, but appear on the front panels of many recent VCR models for convenience at times like this.

Make sure that the VHS tape is blank and not protected by its erase tab. If you're smart, you'll label it, too—*now,* before you even record it, so that you won't forget. Put it into the VCR and cue it up to the right spot. Cue up the camcorder, too.

Finally, put your camcorder into VCR or VTR mode, start the VCR recording, and then press Play on the camcorder. If your TV is on, you can watch the footage as it plays into your VCR. Press Stop on both the camcorder and VCR when the transfer is complete.

From Mac Directly to VCR

If your aim is to get your movie onto VHS tape, you don't have to transfer it to your camcorder first. Hook the camcorder to the Mac via the FireWire cable, if it isn't already, and then hook the VCR to the camcorder as described above.

The trick here is to turn on the "Play DV project video through to DV camera" option in the iMovie→Preferences→Playback dialog box.

Press Record on your VCR, then play your movie from the beginning (or from whatever spot you like). iMovie sends the full-quality video through the camcorder and into the connected VCR.

When you reach the end of playback, hit Stop on the VCR.

Tip: If you have an analog-to-DV converter box like those described on page 292, use precisely the same steps. The converter replaces the camcorder in the setup described here.

Of course, this technique bypasses the Export dialog box shown in Figure 19-2, and with it the ability to "lay down" some nice blackness before and after the footage. If you really want those bookends, just add black clips to the movie itself (page 311).

Exporting to a QuickTime Movie

For the best and most cinematic viewing experience, play your finished iMovie productions on TV, via VHS tape or DVD. That way, your public gets to see the full-sized picture that your camcorder captured.

But when you want to distribute your movies electronically, convert them into Quick-Time files instead. Both Mac and Windows machines can play these files right on the screen with little more than a double-click.

Your distribution options for QuickTime files are far greater than for videocassette or DVD, too. You can email a QuickTime file to somebody or post it on the Web for all the world to see. You can put bigger QuickTime files onto a disk, like a recordable CD, a Zip disk, or an Apple iPod, to transport them.

Here's how you do it:

1. **Choose File→Share.**

   The Share dialog box appears.

2. **Click the QuickTime icon at the top.**

   Now the dialog box looks like Figure 19-3.

Figure 19-3:
Using the pop-up menu in this dialog box, you can indirectly specify how much compression you want applied to your movie, and what the dimensions of the finished movie frame will be. The small print below the pop-up menu warns you that many of these settings will reduce the size and quality of the finished product.

3. **Using the Formats pop-up menu, choose one of the preset export formats such as Email, Web, CD-ROM, or Expert Settings.**

   This decision dramatically affects the picture quality, motion smoothness, file size, and window size of the finished QuickTime movie.

   Making a smart choice in this step requires some comprehension of the QuickTime technology itself, so although "Understanding QuickTime" in the next section is many pages long, it's well worth absorbing. It's critical to your grasp of QuickTime movies, what they are, and what they can do.

   That section also describes the choices in this pop-up menu one by one.

4. **Click Share.**

Now the standard Save File dialog box appears, sprouting from the title bar of the iMovie window.

5. Type a name for your movie.

(Unless, of course, you really do want to call your movie "My Great Movie," as iMovie suggests.)

Don't remove the letters *.mov* from the end of the file's name, especially if it might be played on Windows computers. That suffix is a requirement for machines who aren't savvy enough to know a movie file when they see one.

6. Navigate to the folder where you'll want to store the resulting QuickTime file.

You can just press ⌘-D if you want your QuickTime Movie saved onto the desktop, where it'll be easy to find.

7. Click Save.

Now the time-consuming exporting and *compression* process begins. As you can read in the next section, compression can take a long time to complete—from a minute or two to an hour or more, depending on the settings you selected in step 3, the length of your movie, and the speed of your Mac. Feel free to switch into other programs—check your email or surf the Web, for example—while iMovie crunches away in the background.

A progress bar lets you know how much farther iMovie has to go. When the exporting is complete, the progress bar disappears. Switch to the Finder, where you'll find a new QuickTime movie icon (see Figure 19-4). Double-click it to see the results.

Tip: You can click Stop anytime during the export process, but you'll wind up with no exported movie at all.

Figure 19-4:
When you double-click the resulting QuickTime movie on your hard drive (left), it opens into your copy of QuickTime Player, the movie-playing application included with every Mac. Press the Space bar to make the movie play back (right).

Understanding QuickTime

A computer displays video by flashing many still images in rapid succession. But if you've ever worked with graphics, you know that color graphics files are data hogs. A full-screen photograph file might occupy 5 or 10 MB of space on your hard drive and take several seconds to open up.

Unfortunately, most computers are far too slow to open up 30 full-screen, photographic-quality pictures per second. Even if they could, full-screen, full-quality QuickTime movies would still be mostly useless. Each would consume hundreds of gigabytes of disk space, requiring days or weeks to download from the Web or by email—a guaranteed way to annoy citizens of the Internet and doom your movie-making career to obscurity.

That's why most QuickTime movies *aren't* full-screen, photographic-quality films by any stretch of the imagination. In fact, most QuickTime movies are much "smaller"—in three different dimensions:

- **The window is much smaller.** It's rare to see a QuickTime movie that, when played back, fills the computer screen. Instead, most QuickTime movies today play in a much smaller window (see Figure 19-5), therefore requiring far less data and resulting in far smaller files.

Figure 19-5:
Here's the same movie in two standard playback sizes (with the menu bar showing so you can gauge its size). Movies designed for playback from the hard drive are often 640 pixels wide, 480 tall (640 x 480). Movies intended for the Web email are smaller—often 320 x 240. (Movies sent by email are often as tiny as 160 x 120.) The common denominator: Almost all QuickTime movies have the same relative dimensions—a 4:3 width-to-height ratio, which is exactly the same ratio as the picture produced by your TV and your camcorder.

• **The frame rate is lower.** Instead of showing 30 frames per second, many QuickTime movies have far lower frame rates; even fifteen frames per second produces smooth motion. On the Web, especially during live QuickTime "broadcasts," still lower frame rates are common, such as two or five frames per second. This kind of movie is noticeably jerky, but sends so little data that people using telephone-line modems can watch live events in this format.

• **The video is** *compressed.* This is the big one—the technical aspect of QuickTime movies that gives you the most control over the resulting quality of your movie. In short, when iMovie uses QuickTime to compress your video, it discards information that describes each frame. True, the picture deteriorates as a consequence, but the resulting QuickTime movie file is a tiny fraction of its original size. The following section describes this compression business in much greater detail.

The bottom line is that by combining these three techniques, iMovie can turn your 10 GB DV movie into a *3 MB* file that's small enough to email or post on your Web page. The resulting movie won't play as smoothly, fill as much of the screen, or look as good as the original DV footage. But your viewers won't care. They'll be delighted to be able to watch your movie at all, and grateful that the file didn't take hours to download. (And besides, having already been exposed to QuickTime movies, most know what to expect.)

Tip: The later the QuickTime version your Mac contains, the better and faster the movie-exporting process becomes. Mac OS X's Software Update feature is supposed to alert you every time a new version becomes available (if you have it turned on in System Preferences).

About Codecs

As shown in Figure 19-3, at the moment you save your QuickTime movie, iMovie asks you which of several schemes you want to use for compressing your footage. To use the technical terminology, it asks you to choose a *codec* from a long list. That term is short for compressor/decompressor, the software module that translates the pixel-by-pixel description of your DV footage into the more compact QuickTime format—and then *un*translates it during playback.

Each QuickTime codec works differently. Some provide spatial compression, some temporal, some both. Some are ideal for animations, and others for live action. Some work well on slower computers, others on faster ones. Some try to maintain excellent picture quality, but produce very large QuickTime files on the disk, and others make the opposite tradeoff. Later in this chapter, you can read about each of these codecs and when to use them.

In the meantime, all of this background information should help explain a few phenomena pertaining to converting DV movies into QuickTime files:

• **Saving a QuickTime movie takes a long time.** It's nothing like saving, say, a word processing document. Comparing every pixel on every frame with every pixel on the next frame involves massive amounts of number crunching, which takes time. (Some codecs take longer than others, however.)

- **QuickTime movies don't look as good as the original DV.** Now you know why: In the act of shrinking your movie down to the file size that's reasonable for emailing, copying to a CD-ROM, and so on, a codec's job is to *throw away* some of the data that makes a movie look vivid and clear.

- **QuickTime is an exercise in compromise.** By choosing the appropriate codec and changing its settings appropriately, you can create a QuickTime movie with excellent picture and sound. Unfortunately, it will consume a lot of disk space. If you want a small file on the hard drive *and* excellent picture and sound, you can make the QuickTime movie play in a smaller window—160 x 120 pixels, for example, instead of 320 x 240 or something larger—or at a slower frame rate. The guide in this chapter, some experimentation, and the nature of the movie you're making all contribute to helping you make a codec decision.

The Share Presets: What They Mean

iMovie offers several ready-to-use QuickTime compression settings that govern the quality, file size, and playback-window size of the movie you're exporting. Here's a guide to these presets to help you choose the one that's appropriate for your movie-distribution plans.

Each of the descriptions below includes the information about each preset's video codec, size (Figure 19-5), and frame rate. (The frame rate indicates how many individual pictures you'll see per second when the QuickTime Movie plays back. Thirty frames per second is standard NTSC television quality. Ten to fifteen frames per second begins to look less smooth, and anything under ten yields a flickering, old-time movie effect.)

Trivia: Old-time silent movies actually played at *eighteen* frames per second.

- **Audio codec.** This statistic is the sonic equivalent of the frame rate, in that it tells you what kind of sound quality you'll get. At 44.1 kHz, the quality is exactly the same as that of a commercial music CD. At 22 kHz, it's half as good, but you won't hear any difference except when you listen through headphones or stereo speakers. When the sound plays through the *built-in* speaker on the standard Macintosh, most people can't tell the difference between 44.1 and 22 kHz.

- **Time to compress one minute of video.** The "Time to Compress" statistic provided below indicates how long it took a PowerBook G4 to compress a standard sample movie that's exactly one minute long. (Compressing a 10-minute movie, of course, would take about ten times as long.) Of course, the time it will take your movie to get compressed and saved depends on the codec you've chosen, the length of the movie, how much motion is visible on the screen, and your Mac's speed, but the next section offers a rough guide.

- **File size.** The final statistic provided for each option shows you how big the resulting QuickTime file might be (in megabytes). These numbers, too, refer to the sample one-minute DV movie described in the previous paragraph.

Email

Video codec: *H.263*
Size: *160 x 120*
Frame rate: *10 per second*
Audio codec: *QDesign Music 2, mono, 22 kHz*
Time to compress one minute of video: *1 minute*
File size: *1.2 MB*

The movie you export with these settings is fairly blurry, and the size of the QuickTime screen is closer in size to a Wheat Thin than a Cineplex.

Still, the H.263 video codec has two important benefits. First, it makes the exporting much faster than if you used, say, the Sorenson 3 codec (which takes nearly twice as long). Second, the resulting QuickTime file is relatively tiny; at just over 1 MB for a minute-long movie, it's actually within the realm of possibility that you could email this thing to somebody without incurring their wrath. (The Sorenson 3 codec produces a better-looking movie. But its movies are 3.3 MB per minute—far too large for casual emailing.)

Web

Video codec: *H.263*
Size: *240 x 180*
Frame rate: *12 per second*
Audio codec: *QDesign Music 2, stereo, 22 kHz*
Time to compress one minute of video: *1 minute, 35 seconds*
File size: *2.4 MB*

This kind of movie is much more satisfying to watch than the Email type. The image is over twice as big, and the higher frame rate produces smoother motion.

Once again, the Sorenson Video codec could provide far better image quality; but at 2.4 MB per minute, the product of the H.263 codec is small enough to download from a Web page without a high-speed Internet connection.

RARELY ASKED QUESTION

30 fps Drop-Frame

OK, I'll bite. Why on earth did the USA, which is supposed to be so technically advanced, settle on a TV standard that plays at such an oddball frame rate? Why is it 29.97—why couldn't it be rounded off to 30?

The 29.97 frame rate, known in the TV business as *30 fps drop-frame*, dates back to the dawn of color TV. As they prepared to launch color TV broadcasts in January 1954, network engineers wanted to make sure that the expensive black-and-white TV sets of the day could receive the color

shows, too. (Talk about backward-compatible software!)

Trouble was, when they tried to broadcast a color signal at the then-standard 30 frames per second, the extra color information wound up distorting the audio signal. Eventually, they hit upon a discovery: If they slowed down the frame rate just a hair, the distortion disappeared. The video, meanwhile, looked just as good at 29.97 frames per second as it did at 30.

A standard was born.

Web Streaming

In quality and size, this preset is identical to the Web preset described above. The only difference is that this kind of movie comes set up for *streaming* delivery from the Web, meaning it's played on your audience's screens *as* it's being sent from the Web. In other words, your viewers don't have to download the entire movie before playing it.

Streaming means that your movies can be extremely long, even if they're therefore extremely large files. Only a tiny bit at a time is sent to your spectators' computers.

For details on putting your QuickTime movies on the Web, see page 423.

CD-ROM

Video codec: *H.263*
Size: *320 x 240*
Frame rate: *15 per second*
Audio codec: *IMA 4:1, Stereo, 44.1 kHz*
Time to compress one minute of video: *1 minute, 30 seconds*
File size: *6 MB*
As you can see by the specs above, a movie with the CD-ROM setup generally contains too much data to be suitable for live Web delivery. But saving your QuickTime productions into this kind of QuickTime file is ideal if you plan to play it from a hard drive or a CD-ROM that you record yourself. The high frame rate means that motion will seem smooth, and the 320 x 240 dimensions of the window mean that the movie will fill a decent fraction of the computer screen. That's big enough to see a good amount of detail.

Tip: If you're willing to endure more compressing time and a larger resulting file, you can give your CD-ROM movies a dramatic picture-quality upgrade by substituting the Sorenson Video 3 codec for the H.263 codec. (Use the Expert settings described on the next page to do so; duplicate the settings described here, but choose the Sorenson Video 3 codec instead of H.263.)

The only down side is that the resulting QuickTime movie contains too much data for older, slower CD-ROM drives, such as those rated below 12X, to deliver to the computer's brain. The movie will *play* on slower CD-ROM drives, but it will skip a lot.

Full Quality DV

Video codec: *DV*
Size: *720 x 480*
Frame rate: *29.97 per second (for NTSC; 25 for PAL)*
Audio codec: *No compression; stereo, 32 or 48 kHz (depending on source audio)*
Time to compress one minute of video: *1 minute*
File size: *411 MB*
As the numbers (and the example in Figure 19-5) show you, this is the QuickTime format for people whose equipment doesn't mess around. The file size is massive—much too large for playback from a CD-ROM drive.

That's because this setting isn't intended for playback; it's intended to offer you a means of *storing* your iMovie production without sacrificing any video quality. The Full Quality DV setting applies *no compression at all* to your audio or video.

Yet preserving your iMovie work as a giant, single DV clip on the hard drive is still a useful exercise. It can save hard drive space, for one thing, since the resulting Quick-Time file is still far smaller than the collection of DV clips in your project's Media folder from which it was made. After creating a Full Quality DV movie, you could delete the project folder to free up some disk space, confident that you've got your entire movie safely preserved with 100 percent of its original DV quality intact.

The Expert Settings

The canned presets aren't the only ways you can turn your iMovie project into a QuickTime movie. By choosing Expert Settings from the pop-up menu shown in Figure 19-3, and then clicking the Share button, you embark on a tour of crazy nested dialog boxes. Along the way, you'll be offered control of every aspect of the compression process, including which codec it uses, the degree of sound compression, how many frames per second you want, and so on.

The first dialog box to appear is the "Save exported file as" box, where you can type a name and choose a folder location for the file you're about to save (Figure 19-6, top). Resist the temptation, for now.

The real power lies in the buttons and pop-up menus elsewhere in this little box. For starters, the Export pop-up menu (shown at top in Figure 19-6) offers a wealth of conversion options. This is your opportunity to save your film as:

- An AVI file to give to your Windows PC-using friends. (Choose **Movie to AVI**.)

- A huge folder full of still images, one per frame of your movie. (Choose **Movie to Image Sequence.** Click Options to specify the file format—like JPEG or Photo-shop—and how many stills per second you want.)

- A soundtrack. Here's a great opportunity to convert the audio tracks of your movie into standalone sound files. (Choose **Sound to AIFF, Sound to Wave,** or whatever format you want.)

But most of the time, you'll ignore this Export pop-up menu. Most of the time, you'll want to leave it set to "Movie to QuickTime Movie," and then click the Options button to make some settings changes.

As illustrated in Figure 19-6, that Options button opens a very important dialog box: the Movie Settings box. Here's where you can export your finished product with *exactly* the size-smoothness-speed compromise you want.

You'll notice that this box offers three buttons for video: Settings, Filter, and Size. Below that, you get one Settings button for Sound; and at the bottom of the box, you get options for *Internet streaming*. All of these settings are covered in the next few pages.

The Settings Button

The Settings button takes you to the powerful Compression Settings dialog box (Figure 19-7), the heart of the entire Expert software suite. Here's what the controls do:

- **Compressor pop-up menu.** The unlabeled pop-up menu at the top lets you choose one of 27 codecs—or None, which means that iMovie won't compress your project at all. Each codec compresses your footage using a different scheme that entails different compromises. See page 420 to learn about the codecs listed in this pop-up menu. For now, it's enough to note that for live video that will be played on modern computers, the H.264 or Sorenson Video 3 codecs almost always produce the highest quality at reasonably small file sizes.

Figure 19-6:
You're about to burrow down through several nested dialog boxes, only the first two of which are shown here. (See Figure 19-7 for some of the others.)

Top: Use the Export pop-up menu when you want to save just your audio track, or when you want to convert your movie into another movie format (like AVI for Windows machines). Most of the time, though, you'll click Options.

Bottom: The Movie Settings box is just a summary screen for the dialog boxes that hide behind it: Settings, Filter, Size, and so on.

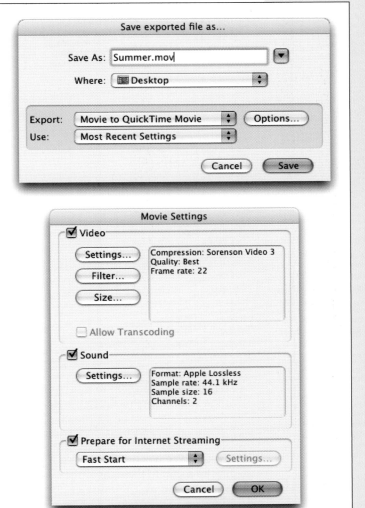

- **Quality slider.** This slider offers another tradeoff between the size of the resulting QuickTime file and the quality of its picture. In general, the proposed value (usually Medium or High) offers the best balance between file size and picture quality. But on important projects, by all means experiment. Export a representative sample of your movie several times, moving the slider each time, so that you can compare the results.

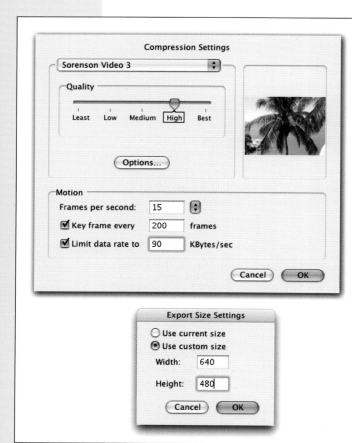

Figure 19-7:
Top: This dialog box gives you point-by-point control over the look, size, and quality of the QuickTime movie you're exporting. Not all of these controls are available for all codecs. That is, depending on what you choose using the top pop-up menu, some of the controls here may be dimmed and unavailable. Furthermore, only some of the codecs offer an Options button in the middle of the dialog box.

In the Sorenson 3 codec controls, shown here, the "Limit data rate to __" option is useful when you're trying to produce a movie that will stream from the Web. Note, however, that this setting overrides the Quality slider setting. (Many people have been baffled by a crummy-looking Sorenson movie that they'd set to Best quality. Now you know why.)

Bottom: Here's where you can specify the dimensions of the movie you're saving, in pixels. (This box appears when you click the Size button shown at bottom in Figure 19-6.)

- **Frames per second.** The number you specify here makes an enormous difference in the smoothness of the QuickTime movie's playback. As always, however, it's a tradeoff—the higher the number, the larger the QuickTime file, and the more difficult it is to email, store, or transfer.

You can type any number between 1 and 29.97 in this box, or you can use the pop-up menu to the right of the "Frames per second" box. Settings like 8 and 10 make very compact, but very jerky movies. 12 and 15 are by far the most common frame rates for today's QuickTime movies online. An actual Hollywood movie plays 24 frames per second, and the European television signal (PAL) plays at 25.

You save a little bit of disk space, while still showing as many frames as people are accustomed to seeing in motion pictures. And 29.97, of course, refers to standard North American TV (see the box on page 414).

- **Key frame every __ frames.** You can read about *key frames* earlier this chapter—they're the full frames that get "memorized" in your QuickTime movie, so that the QuickTime file can store less data for subsequent frames.

  Additional key frames make your QuickTime file bigger, so you have an incentive to make them appear infrequently (that is, to type in a higher number in this box). But if the resulting QuickTime movie is something that your viewers might want to *skip around* in, key frames are very useful. Somebody might scroll back into the movie to a spot with no key frame. When playback begins at that point, the image might be scrambled for a fraction of a second, until the next key frame appears.

- **Limit data rate.** This control is most useful for movies that will be played on the Web. If the movie will be played over a 56K modem, for example, you might want to limit the data rate to 5 K per second to ensure smooth playback; use 20 K for cable modems or DSL. iMovie automatically adjusts the picture quality as necessary, on a moment-by-moment basis, so that the QuickTime movie will never exceed this rate.

The Filter Button

The Filter button opens up a rabbit hole into a world of QuickTime video controls. By opening the various flippy triangles, you'll find a lot of effects you've seen before in iMovie (color balance, brightness and contrast, lens flare, fake old-film grain)—and a few you haven't (blur or sharpen, emboss, edge detection). You can apply any of these to the movie you're about to export.

The Size Button

The Size button summons the dialog box shown at bottom in Figure 19-7, where—after clicking "Use custom size"—you can specify the dimensions for the playback window of your QuickTime movie. See Figure 19-5 for some examples of these different sizes.

Of course, the larger the window you specify, the longer the movie will take to save, the slower it will be transmitted over the Internet, and the larger the resulting file will be.

The huge majority of QuickTime movies play in at one of several standard sizes, such as 160 x 120, 240 x 180, or 320 x 240. All of them maintain this 4:3 aspect ratio. Still, there are dozens of other possible sizes that maintain the correct proportions.

Audio Settings

In the middle of the dialog box shown at the bottom of Figure 19-6, the Settings button lets you specify how your soundtrack is compressed in the exported QuickTime movie (see Figure 19-8), and by how much.

For example, you can specify these parameters:

• **Compressor.** When most people think of codecs—those who've even *heard* of co-decs, that is—they think of *video* compression. But iMovie offers a choice of audio codecs, too. This pop-up menu lets you specify which one you want to use.

Many of them aren't, in fact, appropriate for movie soundtracks. Remember that these codecs are provided by QuickTime, not by iMovie, and that QuickTime is designed to be an all-purpose multimedia format. It's supposed to be just as good at creating pictureless sound files as it is at creating movies. For best results in most movies, use the QDesign or IMA setting.

• **Rate, Size.** A computer captures and plays back sound by capturing thousands of individual slices, or snapshots, of sound per second. As though describing some-body at a wine tasting, computer nerds call this process *sampling* the sound.

The two controls here let you specify how *many samples* you want the Mac to take per second (the sampling Rate) and how *much data* it's allowed to use to describe each sample (the sampling Size). For example, **11 kHz, 8 bits** sounds like you're hearing the audio track over a bad telephone connection. Tinny. Use it only for speech. 662 K per minute. **22 kHz, 16 bits** is fine for playing on a computer equipped with external speakers. 2.6 MB per minute. And **44.1 kHz, 16 bits** is CD-quality audio, suitable for listening to with headphones.

• **Use: Mono/Stereo.** Exporting your QuickTime movie with a stereo format is often a waste of data. Most computers that might play back your movie, including [-some desktop models and iBooks, don't *have* stereo speakers. Therefore, consider using the Mono setting when you're trying to minimize the amount of data required to play back the soundtrack.

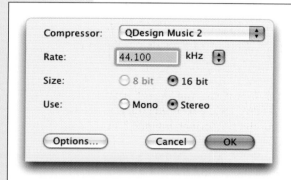

Figure 19-8:
It probably goes without saying that the better the audio quality you specify, the larger your QuickTime movie will be. In any case, this is the dialog box where you make such decisions. Audio isn't nearly as data-greedy as video, so compressing it isn't nearly as urgent an issue (unless you want your movie to play over the Internet).

The Video Codecs

As it turns out, few of these codecs are very useful for everyday use. Many of them are designed for saving still frames (not movies), for storing your movies (not playing them), or for compatibility with very old versions of the QuickTime software. Most of the time, the Sorenson Video 3 compressor (for Internet playback) or H.264 (for

CD, hard drive, or broadband-Web playback) are the ones that will make you and your audience the happiest.

Here, however, are some of the most useful.

Note: The list of codecs that pop up in your dialog boxes may not match what you see here. Your codecs reflect the version of QuickTime that you have installed, which may be older or newer than the 7.0.1 version described here.

- **Animation.** This codec is significant because, at its Best quality setting, it maintains *all* of the original DV picture quality, while still managing to convert files so that they're smaller than files with no compression at all. (As the name implies, this codec was originally designed to process video composed of large blocks of solid colors—that is, cartoons or videos of the Mac screen.) The resulting file is therefore huge when compared with the other codecs described here, but not as huge as it would be if you used the None choice in this pop-up menu.

- **Apple H.263, Apple VC H.263, H.261.** These codecs were designed for video teleconferencing (VC), in which a tiny, jerky image of you is transmitted over a telephone line to somebody who's also equipped with a video telephone. Apple's version, however, does a very good job at maintaining a good picture, while keeping the file size very small. In fact, Apple H.263 should be one of your first choices if you plan to send your video by email or post it on a Web page.

Tip: These codecs work best in footage where very little is going on—like a person sitting in front of a video telephone. The more that the frame remains the same, the better the picture quality, which is yet another argument for using a tripod whenever you can.

- **H.264.** This option appears only if you have QuickTime 7 or later, but it's a doozie. It looks spectacular, and it scales beautifully from cellphone screens all the way up to high-definition TVs. It's not as compact as Sorenson 3, described below—but it delivers a DVD-quality picture in a file less than half the size.

- **DV-PAL, DVCPRO-PAL.** These options are here so that you can export your iMovie masterpiece in the European video format (PAL), while retaining full DV size and frame rate. (DVCPRO is a slight variant of the DV format, intended for use with super-expensive professional broadcast TV video gear.)

Unfortunately, the quality of the video suffers when you make this kind of conversion, especially in action scenes.

- **DV/DVCPRO - NTSC.** Suppose you've just completed a masterful movie, and the thought of compressing it to some much smaller, image-degraded QuickTime movie breaks your heart. You can use this codec to turn your finished, effect-enhanced, fully edited iMovie production into a new, raw DV clip, exactly like the DV clips in the Media folder in your project folder. You might do so if, for example, you wanted to import your entire movie into another DV-editing program, such as Final Cut Express or Final Cut Pro, or if you wanted to turn it into a Video CD or DVD. (*DV*, of course, means digital video; NTSC is the format used in the Western Hemisphere and Japan.)

- **Sorenson Video, Sorenson Video 3.** This codec and H.264 should be your first choices. Sorenson gives you fairly high quality with very good compression, and files so small that you can play them from a CD-ROM or even over the Internet. Sorenson-compressed movies play back on either Macs or Windows computers, too. (Use Sorenson Video 3 if possible. Use the older Sorenson Video—without a number—only if your audience might still be using some ancient version of QuickTime to play back your opus.)

Posting Movies on the Web

After editing your iMovie to perfection, you'll want to show it to the world. Sure, you can preserve your work on videotape, CDs, or DVDs; that's fine if you want to make a handful of copies for a few friends.

But the big time is the Internet. This 200-million-seat megaplex is where the action is, where unknown independent filmmakers get noticed, and where it doesn't cost you a penny to distribute your work to a vast worldwide audience.

Make the Big Screen Tiny

All of the techniques described in this chapter assume that you've exported your iMovie production as a QuickTime movie.

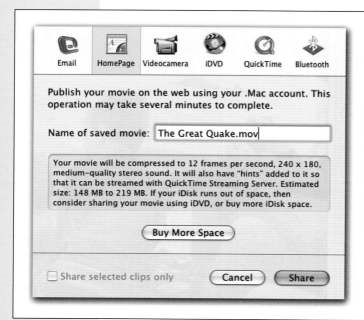

Figure 19-9:
The message here tells you just how small and jerky your movie will be on the Web—12 frames per second, 240 x 180 pixels—and how many megabytes it will occupy. (All of your Web-based movies together can't exceed your 125-megabyte iDisk account limit, unless you pay more money to Apple for more storage.)

Of course, you don't have to post the entire movie online. If you select only specific clips in iMovie before choosing the Share command, you're now offered the "Share selected clips only" checkbox, which posts only the selected stretch of your movie online.

Now, you *could* post your 24-frames-per-second, 640 x 480, stereo-CD-quality sound motion picture on your Web page. But you'd have to include instructions that say, "Please download my movie! It's only 2 GB—about five days of continuous downloading with a 56 K modem. But trust me, it's worth the wait!"

A vast audience still connects to the Internet using an ordinary telephone-line modem, such as a 28.8 K or 56 K model. These modems receive data very slowly, so they're not very well equipped for receiving video from the Internet.

If you expect anyone to actually watch your movies, therefore, you, like thousands of Internet moviemakers before you, will have to make your Web-based movies *tiny*. To make your movie watchable by people with telephone-line modems, use the Expert settings described on page 416.

If the need to downsize your movie like this doesn't crush your artistic pride, the worst is over. Here, then, is how you can make your videos available to the universe.

Posting to Your .Mac Account

By far the easiest way to post your movies on the Internet is to use one of Apple's $100-per-year .Mac accounts (visit *www.mac.com* for details, or open System Preferences, click .Mac, and click Sign Up). A .Mac account gives you a whole raft of Internet-based services and conveniences: electronic greeting cards, synchronizing of calendars and Web bookmarks among the different Macs in your life, a backup program, an antivirus program, the ability to check your email online—and HomePage, which lets you generate your own Web page and occupy it with an iMovie movie.

In iMovie, you can post your finished masterpiece on a .Mac Web page with little more than a couple of clicks:

1. **In iMovie, choose File→Share; in the resulting dialog box, click HomePage.**

   The dialog box tells you how jerky your movie will be online (Figure 19-9).

2. **Type a name for your movie and then click Share.**

   iMovie springs into action, compressing your movie to Web proportions and uploading it to the .Mac Web site. (This is not, ahem, a particularly quick process.)

   When the uploading is complete, your Web browser opens automatically and takes you to the .Mac sign-in page.

3. **Type your name and password. (Capitalization counts.) Click Enter.**

   The HomePage screen appears (Figure 19-10). A miniature version of the movie appears at center, and begins playing automatically for your approval and enjoyment. Farther down the page, you're offered about a dozen standard iMovie Web-page templates, such as Invite, Baby, and so on.

4. **Click the "theater" style you prefer.**

   Next you arrive at the "Edit your page" page (Figure 19-11, top).

5. **Fill in the movie title, description underneath the movie, and so on.**

If you'd like to omit one of the proposed pieces of information (if you don't have any particular directorial notes, for example), edit it anyway, if only to delete the dummy text that appears there (see Figure 19-11).

Figure 19-10:
The "Publish your iMovie" page is a summary of the three page-preparation steps you're about to take. At this point, the most urgent task is step 3, choosing a "frame" for the movie as it will appear on the finished Web page.

Remember that your movie will occupy only a small rectangle in the center of your visitors' screens; the rest is graphic fluff to fill up the window.

6. **Click Preview to see how the Web page will look.**

Click the triangular Play button, shown in Figure 19-11, to try playing your movie over the Internet.

7. **If everything looks good, click Publish.**

When you click the Publish button at the top of the screen, the URL (Web address) for your Web page appears on your screen. You can copy and then email this link to anyone who'd be interested (Figure 19-11, bottom). Finally, your Web page is now available for everyone on the Internet to see.

You can create as many Web pages as you want (within the space constraints of your iDisk). When you return to the HomePage screen, a list of your existing Web pages appears (complete with Edit and Delete buttons). So does the Add button, which you can click to start the process of building another Web page.

Behind the scenes, iMovie builds your movie Web site by placing new Web page (HTML) documents in the Sites folder of your iDisk. If you know how to use a Web-page creation program like Dreamweaver or even Microsoft Word, you can make changes to your Web page by editing these documents.

Posting a Movie on Your Own Web Site

Posting movies on other people's Web pages is one thing. In many cases, however, you might prefer the control and the freedom of putting movies onto your *own* Web page, designed the way you like it.

Figure 19-11:
Top: Here's what your selected movie design looks like. If you don't want the caption to appear beneath it—especially one that says, "Write a sentence or two about your movie here"—delete this dummy text.

Bottom: When it's all over, HomePage tells you the Web address for your new page. Copy this address and publicize it to spread the word about your new masterpiece.

If you click the little arrow button beneath the address, you can send an iCard (electronic greeting card sent by email) to announce it.

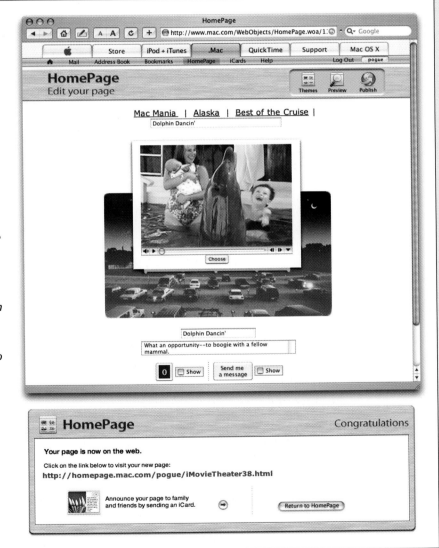

You'll quickly discover that this process is more technical than the ones described so far in this chapter. For example, the following discussion assumes that you do, in fact, already have a Web site.

Setting up streaming playback

QuickTime provides a feature called Fast Start, which means that when a Web page visitor clicks your movie, he can begin to watch it before it's downloaded in its entirety. His copy of QuickTime estimates when enough movie data has been downloaded so that the whole movie can play without having to pause for additional data. The effect is a lot like the *streaming video* feature described earlier, except that there's a considerable pause as the first portion of the movie is downloaded. (On the other hand, you save thousands of dollars on the cost of specialized hardware and software that's required for a true streaming-video system.)

To take advantage of this feature, use the Expert Settings dialog box when you're creating your QuickTime movie from the iMovie project. There, iMovie offers a checkbox called "Prepare for Internet Streaming." If you turn on this checkbox and choose Fast Start from the pop-up menu, iMovie automatically encodes some extra instructions into the resulting QuickTime file that permit your movie to do this "fast starting" when played back from your Web page.

Playing your movie

Once you've uploaded your iMovie, you—and everyone else on the Internet—can watch it just by typing in the correct address. If your Web site's usual address is *www.imovienut.com,* and the name of your movie file is *mymovie.mov,* then the URL (address) for your new movie is *www.imovienut.com/mymovie.mov.* (If you placed it into a folder within your Web site listing—called *flicks,* for example—then the address is *www.imovienut.com/flicks/mymovie.mov.*)

Tip: Mac and Windows computers consider capital and lowercase letters equivalent in Web addresses like these. The Unix machines that dish out Web pages by the millions, however, don't. Therefore, using only lowercase letters is a good precaution to avoid subjecting your visitors to "Web page not found" messages.

If one of your fans types this address into the Web browser or clicks a link that goes to this address, one of three things happens:

- If your visitor's computer has the *QuickTime plug-in* software installed (almost all modern Macs do), a new little movie window opens automatically. (See Figure 19-12.) A few seconds later, it begins to play automatically.

- If your visitor doesn't have this QuickTime plug-in installed, which is possible if she's using a Windows computer, a message appears onscreen. It offers three choices: Track down the necessary plug-in, download the QuickTime movie to the hard drive, or choose another program to play the movie.

Tip: To make it easier for your Windows friends to download the plug-in necessary to watch QuickTime movies, create a link on your Web page that says something like: "To watch this movie, please download the free QuickTime plug-in at *http://www.apple.com/quicktime.*"

- Some browsers have been configured to hand off all downloadable files whose names end with *.mov* to a *helper application,* such as QuickTime Player. In such

Figure 19-12:
The easiest way to put a movie on your Web page is simply to upload it there. Then create a link to it. When clicked, the link makes the movie pop up in its own, separate window. Your viewers can use the Play, Stop, and scroll controls as they see fit.

QuickTime Streaming Server

The Fast Start feature of QuickTime is a great feature. Without it, your movie wouldn't begin to play until its entire multimegabyte mass had been downloaded to your visitor's browser.

That's a good beginning. But in the professional world of Web video, the next step is *QuickTime streaming.* This relatively young technology lets many viewers simultaneously watch your movie in real time, live, as it's played from the host hard drive—without waiting for *anything* to download.

QuickTime streaming makes possible live *Webcasts,* such as the occasional Steve Jobs keynote speech and other historic events.

Serving up QuickTime streaming isn't something that the average Mac can do. It requires a Power Mac equipped with special streaming QuickTime software, a full-time, high-speed Internet connection, and a copy of the Mac OS X Server operating system. Apple's QuickTime Streaming Web site has the details at *www.apple.com/quicktime/servers.*

---

cases, QuickTime Player now opens (independently from the browser), and the movie appears in its window.

Creating alternate versions

If your Web hosting service makes enough hard drive space available, consider creating an alternate version of your movie for viewers who don't have the QuickTime plug-in.

For example, the Windows equivalent of QuickTime is called the *AVI* format. Using QuickTime Player Pro, you can convert your movie into an AVI file, which you can post on your Web page exactly the same way you posted the QuickTime movie. Then you can put two different links on your Web page: "Click here for the QuickTime version (Mac users)," and "Click here for the AVI version (Windows users)."

The HTML code

If you know how to write HTML code (the language of Web pages), you can make the presentation of your movie a little bit more elegant. For example, you can use the <embed> tag to make the movie play right on the Web page, instead of in a separate window. You can also use the <autoplay> tag to make the movie begin playing the instant the browser has received enough data from the server. If you set the tag to false, your visitor must click the Play button.

Movies on Your Phone

When most people hear the word movie, they think "big screen." But high-tech has marched on, small is beautiful, and suddenly we've entered an era when people are content to watch video on *very small* screens. Mind-blowing though it may seem, you can now send movies directly to the screens of certain cellphones, like the Nokia 6600, 3650, 6230, and 6630. No longer must you show people lame wallet photos of your family; you can play them *movies* of your family, right there on the street.

Unfortunately, you can't send your movies to any old cellphone—only those with *Bluetooth* that are *3GPPP-compliant.* Here's what that means:

- **Bluetooth** is a radio technology with a maximum range of 30 feet. The whole idea isn't so much networking as eliminating cables from our lives, which is an idea most people wholeheartedly support.

  Already you can get Bluetooth—either built-in or as a plug-in USB device—for computers, printers, cellphones, cellphone headsets, Palm and PocketPC organizers, Sony camcorders, and so on. Apple's wireless keyboard and mouse both rely on Bluetooth.

  All iMovie cares about, though, is whether or not your Mac has Bluetooth—many models do, including all PowerBooks—and whether your cellphone does. (Technically, iMovie can send movies to more than just phones and Macs; it can send to palmtops, too. At the moment, though, there aren't any 3GPP palmtops.)

- **3GPP** is a video standard for cellphones. (It stands for Third Generation Partnership Program, since you asked.) If your Bluetooth phone is fairly recent, it may be 3GPP-compliant, but check with your cell company.

The phone has to have a movie-playing program on board, too; all 3GPP videophones do.

If you're suitably equipped, here's how the transfer goes:

1. **When your movie is fully edited, save it. Choose File→Share.**

   The Share sheet appears, as shown at top in Figure 19-13.

2. **Click the Bluetooth icon on the toolbar.**

   As usual when you export a movie, you can turn on "Share selected clips only" if you want to send only a piece of your movie (and you highlighted the appropriate clips before choosing File→Share).

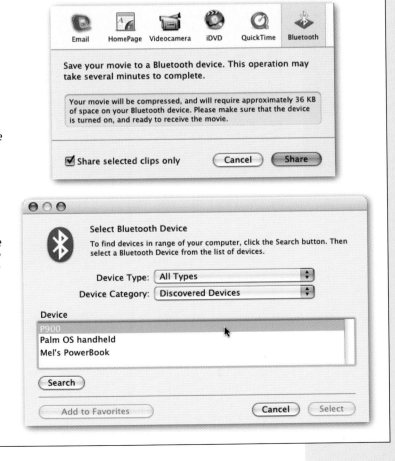

Figure 19-13:
If you're reading this, then congratulations on your very new, very cool phone—specifically, your Bluetooth-equipped, 3GPPP-compliant multimedia cellphone.

Top: On the Bluetooth pane of the Share sheet, the message tells you how much precious memory this movie will consume once transferred to your phone.

Bottom: Once you click Share, iMovie compresses the footage to within an inch of its life, and then uses your Mac's Bluetooth antenna to search for a nearby cellphone that's turned on, "discoverable," and ready to receive your masterwork. Click its name and then click Select to send the film on its merry way.

3. Click Share.

iMovie takes quite awhile to compress your movie. Of course, ordinarily iMovie strives to maintain the best quality possible, with high resolution, full TV-screen size, CD-quality stereo sound, and so on. But for a phone, you want super-compressed, ultra-tiny, monophonic movies, and converting from the high-res format to the low-res one takes some time.

When the compression is complete, the Select Bluetooth Device dialog box appears (Figure 19-13, bottom). Make sure your phone is turned on. Make sure, too, that in its Bluetooth settings, Bluetooth is turned on and *discoverable*, meaning that your Mac can "see" it.

4. Click Search.

After a moment, your phone's name appears in the list.

5. Click the phone's name, and then click Select.

That's all there is to it. On the phone's screen, you'll probably see a message to the effect that it's receiving a file. After a while, the movie's transmission will be complete. Open the phone's media-playing program and play away.

Tip: iMovie stores a copy of the super-compressed movie in your project folder→Shared→Bluetooth folder. Its file name ends with .3gp.

If you're ever inclined to send that movie again—to one of your many other friends who have 3GPP-compliant, Bluetooth phones—you can shoot it right over without having to wait for iMovie to crunch the thing down to pocket size, thus eliminating step 3 above. Use the Bluetooth File Exchange program in your Applications →Utilities folder to do it.

Part Four: iDVD

4

From iMovie to iDVD

i DVD is the software that lets you turn your iMovie movies and iPhoto slideshows into Hollywood-style DVDs that people can watch on their TVs. Visions of Blockbuster may dance in your head, because as you'll see in the following chapters, iDVD 5 is loaded with enhancements that help you make your personal DVD look even more like a commercial Hollywood DVD than ever before.

iDVD lets you add menus, playback controls, and other navigation features to your iMovie movies, resulting in dynamic, interactive DVDs that look amazingly professional. iDVD handles the technology; you control the style.

The software requirement is iDVD. The hardware requirement is a DVD recording drive, preferably an Apple SuperDrive built into your Mac.

Note: The word is *preferably* a built-in SuperDrive, because you don't necessarily need one. For starters, you can do the design work on a Mac that doesn't have a DVD burner, and then burn the actual disc on another machine later. That's a great feature in, for example, school computer labs that have 12 Macs but only two that can burn DVDs. (For step-by-step instructions, see page 497.) Furthermore, now you can even use external, non-Apple DVD burners to create DVDs. See page 500.

Why iDVD?

You already know from Chapter 19 that you can export your finished iMovie project back to a good old VHS cassette, one of the world's most sure-fire distribution methods. Anyone who doesn't have a VCR in this day and age probably wouldn't appreciate your cinematic genius anyway.

But preserving your work on a DVD gives you a boatload of benefits. For example, they're cheaper than VHS tapes. DVDs are also compact. They never need rewinding, either, and they're cheap to ship. They're more rigid and have zero moving parts. They're far more durable, too; whereas VHS tapes begin to deteriorate in 10 to 15 years, DVDs are built to last—up to a century or more, if you believe the manufacturers.

Tip: They'll last, that is, *if* you stick to buying brand-name blanks like Verbatim and Imation. Cheaper brands don't use the same amount of organic dyes and are more likely to suffer premature deaths.

Still, you should be aware that homemade DVDs don't work in as many DVD players as commercially pressed discs do. Check the master player compatibility list at *www.videohelp.com* if you're ever in doubt.

What You're in For

In Chapter 21, you can read about using iDVD *manually,* where you can integrate movies, still pictures, and sound in very flexible ways. But especially at first, most people take one of the two simplest approaches: (a) create the movie in iMovie, and then hand it off to iDVD, or (b) burn your DVD directly using the new OneStep DVD process (page 457).

This chapter guides you through the five broad steps of using iMovie and iDVD together:

1. **Prepare your audio, video, and pictures.**

    In addition to movies, iDVD can incorporate audio and graphics files into your shows. iDVD doesn't, however, offer any way to *create or edit* these files. You must prepare them in other programs first.

2. **Insert chapter markers.**

    In a commercial Hollywood DVD, you can jump around the movie without rewinding or fast-forwarding, thanks to the movie's *scene menu* or *chapter menu.* It's basically a screenful of bookmarks for certain scenes in the movie. (One way to create these useful scene breaks in iMovie HD is to position the Playhead and then choose Markers→Add Chapter Marker.)

3. **Hand off to iDVD.**

    The beauty of iMovie HD and iDVD 5 is that they're tied together behind the scenes. The former can hand off movies to the latter, automatically creating menu buttons in the process.

4. **Design the menu screen.**

    In iDVD terms, *menus* doesn't mean menus that drop down from the top of the screen. Instead, a DVD menu is a menu *screen,* usually containing buttons that you click with the remote control. One button, called Play, starts playing the movie.

Another, called Scene Selection, might take you to a second menu screen full of individual "chapter" buttons, so your audience doesn't have to start watching from the beginning if they don't want to.

DVD menu design is at the heart of iDVD. The program lets you specify where and how each button appears on the screen, and also lets you customize the overall look with backgrounds and titles.

5. **Burn your DVD.**

To create a DVD, iDVD compresses your movie into the universal DVD file format, called *MPEG-2*, and then copies the results to a blank recordable DVD disc. This process, called *burning*, lets you produce a DVD that plays back either in a computer or in most set-top DVD players.

Phase 1: Insert Chapter Markers

If you've ever rented or bought a movie on DVD, you're already familiar with *chapters*, better known as scenes (Figure 20-1).

DVD chapters let viewers skip to predefined starting points within a movie, or pick up where they last left off watching, by either using the scene menu or pressing the Next Chapter or Previous Chapter buttons on the remote control. Thanks to the partnership of iMovie and iDVD, you can add markers to your own movies that perfectly replicate this feature.

Figure 20-1:
Most DVDs offer something called a scene menu like this one (from the movie Ronin*), which lets viewers jump directly to their favorite scenes in the movie. Your DVD scene menus probably won't be quite this elaborate, but you get the idea.*

iMovie HD offers two ways to go about adding chapter markers. The easiest way is to press Shift-⌘-M at each spot where you want a chapter marker, even while the movie is playing. (That's the shortcut for the Markers→Add Chapter Marker command.) Although that's quick and easy, you still have to open up the iDVD chapter-marker palette to *name* the markers (Figure 20-2).

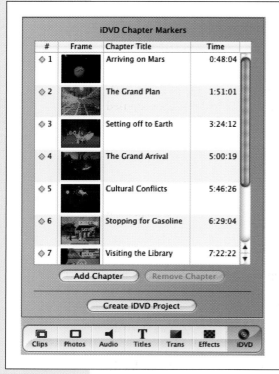

Figure 20-2:
The iDVD palette lets you add, remove, and name chapters—and then publish your iMovies to iDVD. New iMovie chapters are numbered sequentially, as they appear in your movie from left to right. Chapter references appear in your timeline as small yellow diamonds, just above the video track. Amazingly, iMovie can add up to 99 chapters per movie with the iDVD palette.

You can also create and manage chapter markers all in one tidy list, using the older iDVD panel in iMovie. Here's how that goes:

1. **In iMovie, click the iDVD button.**

   You'll find it among the other palette buttons, just to the right of the Effects button, as shown in Figure 20-2. In any case, the iDVD palette now opens. If you've added any chapter markers using the Add Chapter Marker (Shift-⌘-M) method, you'll see them listed here bearing names like Clip 12, Clip 16, and so on.

2. **In the iMovie monitor, drag the Playhead along the scrubber bar to locate the position for your new chapter.**

   You may want to choose Edit→Select None (Shift-⌘-A) first, which ensures that no individual clip is selected. Now you can move the Playhead anywhere in your movie.

Tip: Use the arrow keys for precise Playhead positioning, or press Shift-arrow to jump 10 frames at a time.

3. **Click Add Chapter.**

   You'll find this button near the bottom of the iDVD palette. iMovie adds the chapter to your list, as shown in Figure 20-2.

Tip: You can also use the keystroke Shift-⌘-M at this point, or even choose Markers→Add Chapter Marker.

4. **Type a chapter title into the Chapter Title box.**

   Whatever you type here will wind up as the chapter name in the finished DVD menu. Select a short but meaningful name. (You don't have to delete the proposed name first; just type right over it.)

5. **Repeat steps 2–4.**

   Repeat until you've added all the chapters for your movie.

6. **Save your project.**

   Choose File→Save to save your iMovie project, including the chapter marks you just defined.

Removing Chapters

Suppose you change your mind about where a chapter should begin. Or, you may have added too many chapters to suit your taste, or even put a marker in the wrong place. In any case, you remove a marker by using one of these techniques:

- Click its name in iMovie's iDVD palette and then click the Remove Chapter button.

- Click the diamond-shaped marker in the Movie Track and then choose Markers→Delete Chapter Marker (Option-⌘-M).

Tip: You can also select a bunch of chapters in the iDVD panel at once, using the usual list-keyboard shortcuts—⌘-click individual markers to select them, or select a consecutive batch by clicking the first and Shift-clicking the last. Now clicking Remove Chapter nukes all of them at once.

Changing Chapter Names

To change the name of any chapter that appears in the iDVD Chapter Markers list, just double-click it to open the editing box, and then edit away.

When you press Return or Enter, iMovie accepts the new chapter name and automatically moves to the next chapter. When you're at the last chapter of your project, iMovie cycles back to the first one. As a result, you can edit a bunch of chapter names in sequence with a minimum of mouse clicks. To finish editing chapter names, click the mouse outside the iDVD palette.

Chapter Marker Pointers

Here are a few key points to keep in mind about chapters:

- **Chapter markers appear in the Timeline Viewer.** They appear as small, yellow diamond shapes. (Chapter markers don't appear in the Clip Viewer.)

- **You can't move a chapter marker.** If you've used the wrong start frame when creating your chapter, you have no choice but to delete the chapter marker and create a new one with the correct starting point.

- **You can't drag chapter markers in the iDVD palettes.** Chapter order depends on the associated starting times, which appear chronologically in the palette.

- **When you move (and erase) clips, chapter markers go along for the ride.** iMovie associates chapters with individual clips. Therefore, if you reorder your clips, the chapter markers move with them. If you delete a clip, iMovie removes the included chapters.

- **When you *copy* a clip, you copy chapter markers.** When you duplicate a clip, iMovie copies all of its chapters at their original positions.

- **Frames matter, not timing.** When you slow down or speed up a clip, the included chapter marks slide accordingly, retaining their relative positions within the clip.

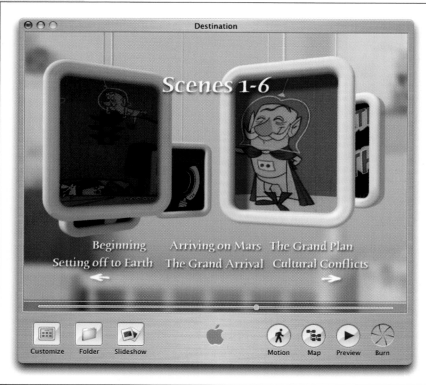

Figure 20-3:
Some iDVD menu themes can accommodate only six or seven buttons per screen. If you've got more than that, left and right arrows appear, so that your audience can navigate to additional screens full of buttons. iDVD automatically adds the scene numbers to your menu title for easier navigation.

- **There's a "secret" unlisted chapter.** iMovie and iDVD always create one more chapter than you see on the iDVD Chapters list. This extra chapter corresponds to the very beginning of your movie (00:00:00), and starts out with the label "Beginning." (You won't see it until you arrive in iDVD.)

- **Your finished iDVD screens can fit up to 12 buttons per screen.** The actual number used depends on the *theme* you pick. (Themes are prebuilt designs with coordinating backgrounds, buttons, fonts, and, if you like, background audio.) When you include more chapters per screen than the theme allows (including "Beginning"), your scene-selection menus will extend to more than one screen, as shown in Figure 20-3.

Phase 2: Hand Off to iDVD

Once you've added your chapter markers in iMovie, you're ready to hand off the whole thing to iDVD, where you can do your menu design and DVD burning.

Start by saving your iMovie project—a necessary step before handing off to iDVD. Then click the Create iDVD Project button at the bottom of the chapter list. If your movie contains slow motion, fast motion, or reverse-motion clips, you'll be asked if you want them to be *rendered* for better quality. Say yes.

Your hard drive whirs, thunder rolls somewhere, and after a few moments, you wind up in iDVD itself. If this is your first time using iDVD, the factory-setting design is called Travel 1, in which empty postcards scroll slowly from right to left, confirming your arrival in iDVD land; if you've run iDVD before, you see whatever design theme you used last. (Those "postcards" are actually *drop zones*—areas of the design that you can fill with your own pictures or movies.)

Tip: To turn off the Apple logo that appears in the lower-right corner of every iDVD Project, choose iDVD→Preferences and turn off "Show Apple logo watermark."

Phase 3: Design the Menu Screen

On the main menu screen now before you, you'll find two buttons:

- **Play.** On the finished DVD, this button means, "Play the movie from the beginning."

- **Scene Selection.** On the finished DVD, this button will take your audience to a second screen, which is filled with individual buttons for the chapters you created. (In fact, this second screen may well have arrows that lead to third and fourth screens, since iDVD menus vary in the number of buttons that fit per screen. Travel Cards holds six buttons per scene-selection menu.)

    If you'd like to have a look at this scene-selection screen, double-click the words Scene Selection. To return to the main menu, click the left-pointing arrow on the scene-selection screen.

Tip: If iDVD seems sluggish when you change screens, it's because the program is busily processing video in the background. To make it work faster, choose iDVD→Preferences, click the General icon, and turn off "Enable background encoding." (Finally, close the General window.)

Creating your DVD at the end of the process will take longer now, because the video hasn't been preprocessed. But at least you'll be able to work in the program without feeling like you're walking through quicksand.

If things are still slow, your Mac may need more memory. iDVD consumes RAM like the ravenous triple-toed dire sloth of the Northern Antipodes consumes white-tailed wombats. (Dire sloths can be very, very ravenous indeed.)

All about Themes

The moving drop zones, any music that's playing, and the font for your buttons are all part of a *theme:* a unified design scheme that governs how the menus look and behave, complete with attractive backgrounds, coordinated typography, and background music. iDVD 5 comes with 15 eye-catching new themes that include a host of visually stunning effects.

It takes a lot of individual design decisions to make a theme. For example:

- **Background image or video.** Whatever art appears in the background, still images, or video clips, is part of the theme. The movement of the desert in the Anime Pop theme is one example of video in action.

Tip: If the repetitive looping of a theme's motion drives you crazy, click the round Motion button below the menu-design screen. The Motion button turns the looping motion on and off while you're working on a DVD. (It also affects the finished DVD, so check its status before you burn the disc.)

- **Button type.** The buttons in iDVD Project can be either little graphics or text phrases that your audience will "click" with the remote control.

- **Button look.** The look of your buttons can vary. Text buttons may have simple backgrounds; graphic buttons may have borders.

- **Button positions.** Each menu can accommodate up to 12 buttons, depending on the theme you've chosen. Themes are preset to place their buttons in certain favored positions.

- **Drop zones.** Drop zones are areas into which you can drag a favorite video clip (sometimes more than one) that plays continuously as a background for the main menu screen. If you've ever seen a commercial Hollywood DVD movie, you've seen this effect. One key scene from the movie plays over and over, looping until you choose one of the buttons on the menu screen—or go quietly insane.

In iDVD 5, advanced *dynamic* drop zones can now move across the screen, even passing in front of each other, providing amazing visual effects.

- **Text boxes.** Text boxes let you freely add text blocks to your menu screens so you can provide, for example, instructions to your viewers, copyright notices, or details about what they're about to see.

- **Font selections.** Themes also specify the color, font size, and typeface for menu titles and buttons.

Figure 20-4 illustrates two very different looks for the same project. The difference lies only in the chosen theme.

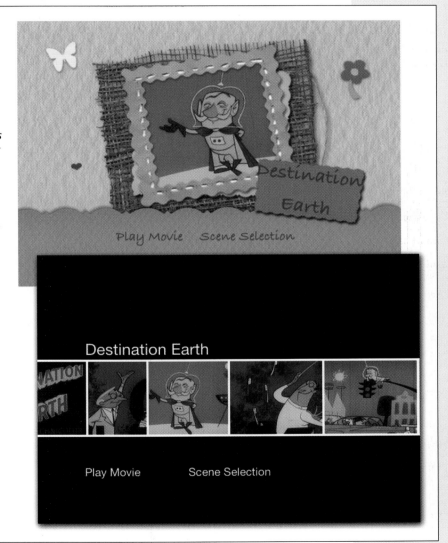

Figure 20-4:
iDVD Themes can create strikingly different menu screens for similar projects.
Top: The Scrapbook theme uses a script font based on handwritten text and a series of drop zones that fly across an animated background video.

Bottom: The Lines theme features a row of drop zones (the series of pictures that, if this weren't a frozen picture on a book page, would be scrolling to the left), a plain black background, and text buttons in an informal font.

Choosing a Theme

Goodness knows, you don't have to be satisfied with the tropically inspired Travel Cards theme. A wide range of canned themes awaits your inspection:

1. **Click Customize to open the Customize drawer, if it isn't already open.**

   The Customize button shows or hides the *drawer* shown in Figure 20-5. (You can also close the drawer by dragging its outside edge inward.)

2. **From the pop-up menu at the top of the drawer, choose a theme set.**

   iDVD offers three built-in theme sets: **5.0 Themes** (15 new themes in this version), **4.0 Themes** (20 designs from iDVD 4), and **Old Themes** (24 themes inherited from iDVD 3, including the excellent Book and Projector offerings). If you've bought additional themes online (Figure 20-6), this pop-up menu may offer other choices. In any case, you can use this pop-up menu to switch between them, or just choose All to see all installed themes in a single scrolling list.

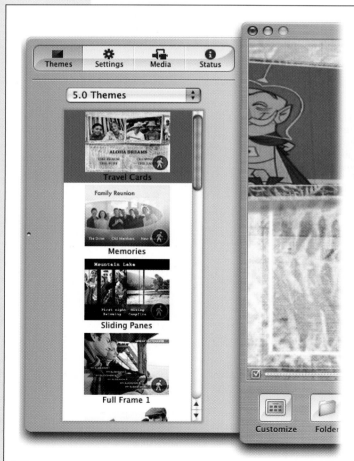

Figure 20-5:
*The Customize button reveals iDVD's Customize drawer. You'll be spending a lot of your time here, so mastering its layout is important. For example, when you click one of the buttons at the top, the pane changes to show its contents. **Themes** lets you choose a design scheme. **Settings** lets you choose motion menu duration, background video and audio, title fonts, and the look and placement of buttons. The **Media** panes reveal the contents of your iTunes and iPhoto collections.*

You'll notice that some of the themes seem to appear twice: "Wedding Theme Bronze One" and "Wedding Theme Bronze Two," for example. That represents another iDVD feature: predesigned screens for *submenu* screens, like the Scene Selection screens you'd find on a commercial DVD. The "Two" designs are intended for these second-level screens full of buttons.

Scroll through the list of themes, clicking each one to see what it looks like in the main work area, or just rely on the little thumbnail icons to get a sense of the theme's overall flavor.

3. **Select a theme by clicking its thumbnail.**

If your DVD menu system consists of only a single screen—the main menu you've been looking at the whole time—it takes on your chosen theme instantly.

A movie you've exported from iMovie, however, probably has chapter markers in it, and therefore your movie probably has at least one additional menu screen: your scene-selection screen.

It turns out that clicking a theme choice in the Customize drawer affects the *current* menu screen only. If you click, say, the Techno B&W theme on the main menu, your scene-selection screen remains unaffected; it still shows the yellow and brown Travel Cards theme. Therefore, follow up like this:

Figure 20-6:
You can buy additional themes, or download free samples, from other companies (such as iDVDThemePAK.com or iDVD-thematastic .com). You install them by creating a folder called Favorites in your Library→iDVD folder (the Library folder in the main hard drive window, not in your Home folder), and then putting them inside.

4. Choose Advanced→Apply Theme to Project.

This command applies the same theme to every screen. Now all of your menu screens look alike.

Tip: If you want all of your menu screens to have the same look except for the main menu, first use the Apply Theme to Project command described here. Then return to the main menu screen and click the theme thumbnail you want for it only.

For example, you might apply Travel 2 to your entire project, and then choose Travel 1 for your main screen.

When you're happy with the way the new theme looks, you're ready to proceed with your iDVD design work. Fortunately, you don't have to commit to a theme at this moment; you can swap in a different theme at any time until you actually burn the DVD.

Editing Menus

If you like the way everything looks when you click a desired theme, terrific. You're good to go. Skip ahead to "Phase 5: Burn Your DVD."

Note, however, that a great deal of flexibility and control await in the meantime. You don't have to accept every element of the theme as it appears when you first select it. You can move your buttons around, change the labels on them, and so on.

Chapter 21 offers the full scoop on these procedures, but here are a few of the most common redesign tasks.

Editing Titles and Buttons

iDVD usually adds a title to your menu screens, often near the top of the page, and usually in a larger font than any other text. You can edit it just as you would a Finder icon name: Click inside it to open up an editing box, type your changes, and then press Enter or Return.

Editing button names works almost the same way, except that you single-click the button first, and then click the text itself to open the editing box.

Keep these points in mind when working with iDVD text:

- **Be succinct.** DVD screens are small, so there's not much room for long and involved text.

- **Be contained.** Don't let one text box overlap another.

- **Spell check.** Nothing speaks worse of your attention to detail than a lovingly crafted masterpiece called "For Mouther's Day."

Tip: If your buttons' text labels are crashing into each other, try making the text wrap into a narrow column, so that it's several lines long. Simply press Return to start a new line; unlike previous versions of iDVD, pressing Return doesn't close the editing box.

Moving Buttons Around

Each theme comes with predetermined locations for your buttons. In fact, internally, each theme stores separate layout maps: one that specifies the button positions if you have *three* buttons, another for *four* buttons, and so on.

iDVD lets you move your buttons around into new positions, but it's not as easy as just dragging them with your mouse. There's no grid to guide you, so the new button positions might not look especially professional. For example, when you play your iDVD disc on a standard DVD player, your menu buttons will sprout glowing rectangles to indicate which button is highlighted. If you've positioned the buttons too closely together, this highlighting might overlap other buttons—with ugly results.

If you're absolutely, positively sure that you want the freedom to drag buttons around into new positions, open the Customize drawer. Click the Settings button at the top, and then in the lower third of the pane, turn on Free Position. Now the buttons are liberated from their grid. (You may want to choose Advanced→Show TV Safe Area so that you don't wind up dragging the buttons off the TV screen.)

Apple disavows all responsibility for the cosmetic quality of the results.

Tip: At any time, you can make your buttons snap back to their original positions by choosing Snap to Grid from the Settings pane.

Reordering Buttons

Apple may not want you to drag buttons randomly around the screen, but reordering them is a different story. See Figure 20-7.

Removing Buttons

To remove a button from a menu screen, click it and then press the Delete key.

Tip: You can also click the first button, and then Shift-click another button, to highlight all of the buttons in between. Or ⌘-click individual buttons to highlight only those.

Of course, if your purpose in removing a button is to move it to a different menu screen, you can use the Cut and Paste commands in the Edit menu. (See page 467 for details on navigating screens.)

Setting Button Images

In some themes—including all of the iDVD 5 designs—the buttons on your menu screen are just bits of text.

In some older themes, though, the buttons can actually be icons, pictures, or tiny movie clips that preview what's in store if viewers click it. In those situations, here's how you specify what that image is.

Moving previews

Suppose you have a button that, when clicked, plays a movie you've created. Here's where you can make iDVD display up to 30 seconds of that movie right there on the button.

Figure 20-7:
Dragging one button on top of another generally swaps the two positions only if they're adjacent. More often, if you drag the first button into the fourth position, the sequence becomes #2, #3, #4, #1 (instead of just swapping #1 and #4). iDVD attempts to maintain as much of the original sequence as possible, so that when your audience uses the remote control's arrow button on the resulting DVDs, the highlighting won't jump around confusingly.

Figure 20-8:
Turn on Movie to create a video button. Use the slider to specify where you want the tiny button movie to begin looping.

Tip: A button can display video only if that button actually links to a video—not to a folder or a slideshow, as described in the next chapter.

1. **Select the button.**

   When you click a button, a slider and a Movie checkbox appear above it, as shown in Figure 20-8.

2. **Turn on Motion, if necessary.**

   If motion isn't already turned on, click the round Motion button at the bottom of the iDVD window. (The button turns green when it's on, gray when it's not.) All the little movie buttons come to life, all playing simultaneously.

Note: If your movie clips don't start playing, don't worry. Some menus, including Kids Theater Two, come with their button loop times set to zero.

To make your video buttons come alive, you have to adjust their timing manually, as described below.

3. **Make sure the Movie checkbox is turned on. Drag the slider to the spot where you want playback to begin.**

   The slider is a map of your entire movie, from start to end. Pinpoint where you want the button's video playback to begin. You've just set what Apple calls the *poster frame* for the linked movie.

   So how do you specify where you want the buttons' looping video to *end?*

4. **Make sure the Customize drawer is open. Click the Settings icon at the top, and then drag the Menu Duration slider to specify how many seconds of video you want your buttons to loop.**

   The maximum loop time varies by theme and project. For some themes, you can specify a loop of up to 30, which should be plenty of time for your audience member to make a selection from the menu screen. In other themes, the loops can last as long as your movies. That's a very long time, menu-wise.

   Note, however, that changing this duration affects the loop times of *all* the menu buttons, *and* the looping time of the background video (see "Drop Zones" on the facing page). Also keep in mind that all your motion menu times added together cannot exceed 15 minutes for your entire project.

5. **Click anywhere on the background to hide the slider and the Movie checkbox.**

   If Motion is turned on, you'll see the video begin playing on the button immediately.

Tip: If your video buttons don't seem to be moving, remember to set their loop lengths to more than 0 seconds, as described in step 4. Also confirm that you've turned on the Motion button at the bottom of the screen, so that it's green.

A still frame from the movie

Instead of a looping video, your button's face can display a still image that comes from a particular frame of the movie. This is a typical style in Hollywood DVD movies, where a still image represents the scene that lies behind each button.

The steps are exactly the same as described in the previous section—except that you turn *off* the Movie checkbox shown in Figure 20-8.

Drop a picture or movie

The picture on a button doesn't have to be a scene from the movie. It can be any graphic you want. Just drag any graphics file right onto the button itself; you'll see the button image change instantly.

This graphic can come from just about anywhere. For example:

- **The Finder.** Drag any graphics file out of a folder window or from the desktop.

- **iPhoto.** In the Customize drawer, click the Media button and choose Photos from the pop-up menu. You now see a list of all of the albums in your Mac's iPhoto collection. You can drag any photo onto a button to install it as the new button face.

Drop Zones

Drop zones let you use video, slideshows, and graphics as the backgrounds of your menu screens. Not every theme offers drop zones, but nearly all of the new 5.0 themes do: Travel Cards, Sliding Panes, Anime Pop, Baby Mobile, and so forth. As if you couldn't guess, the words "Drop Zone" (see Figure 20-9) indicate where the drop zones are.

Tip: If you don't see the telltale phrase "Drop Zone" followed by a number, choose iDVD→Preferences. Click the General icon, and then turn on Show Drop Zones. (This checkbox just hides the words "Drop Zone," not the drop zones themselves.)

Note, by the way, that not all drop zones are onscreen at once. The Scrapbook theme, for example, shows only one of its three drop zones at a time. Similarly, the drop zones in several iDVD 5 themes take their time in parading onto the screen, or rotating through it. To give yourself a quick tour of all the drop zones in your chosen theme, drag the handle of the thin white scroll bar at the bottom of the menu window (shown in Figure 20-9) to cycle through the entire presentation.

Here's how drop zones work:

- **Adding to a drop zone.** Drag any video, photo album, image, or collection of images right into a drop zone outline to install it there. You can drag icons out of the Finder, or directly out of the Media pane in the Customize drawer.

Tip: Albums in drop zones can display 30 images at most. What you'll get is a mini-slideshow, right there within the drop zone. (More on dragging out of the Photos pane in Chapter 21.)

- **Replacing items in a drop zone.** To replace what you've installed in a drop zone, just drag something new into it.

- **Removing items from a drop zone.** To delete an item in the drop zone, drag it away from the spot, just as you'd drag something off the Mac OS X Dock or the Sidebar. You get a cute little puff of smoke to indicate the movie or picture's disappearance. (If you drag it onto a menu button in the process of removing it from the drop zone, it becomes a video menu button.)

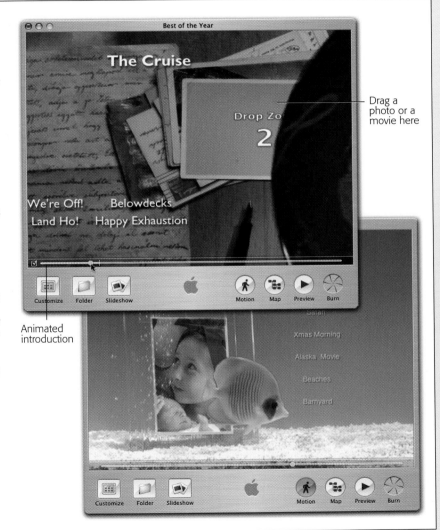

Figure 20-9:
Top: The words "Drop Zone" show you where each drop zone is. In some themes, a preliminary animation appears before your main-menu buttons do; that interval is represented by the notched area on the scroll bar.

Bottom: Drop zones aren't always perfect rectangles or squares, so your video may get clipped around the edges. On the other hand, you can drag the picture or movie around within the drop zone outline so that the most important part shows up. In this theme, the animated fish actually swims around in front of whatever's in the drop zone!

Drag a photo or a movie here

Animated introduction

• **Editing a drop zone slideshow.** If you've decided to create a mini-slideshow within the drop zone, you may wonder how you're supposed to adjust the order of the photos. Figure 20-10 tells all.

Tip: Instead of clicking the drop zone and then clicking Edit Order, you can just double-click the drop zone. You go straight to the Drop Zone Editor window.

Figure 20-10:
Top: When you click the drop zone itself, a transparent control panel appears just above it. Use the slider to specify which photo appears on the button, or click the Edit Order button to open the Drop Zone editor.

Bottom: In the Drop Zone slideshow editor window, a thumbnail display lets you drag the photos around. (The two buttons in the lower-left corner of the editor switch between this column view and an icon-based view.) Reorder the slides until your aesthetic sensibilities are satisfied, and then click Return twice—once to return to the Drop Zone Editor screen (Figure 20-15), and again to go back to the menu editor screen.

• **Add sounds.** Drop zones have no sound, although you can import audio into the menu screen that *contains* the drop zone. See page 489.

• **Turning on Motion.** If you've installed video into a drop zone and it doesn't seem to be playing, click the round Motion button at the bottom of the iDVD window. (When it's turned on, the button is green; when it's turned off, it's gray.) If it still doesn't seem to be playing, the menu duration may be set to 0 (page 447).

Turning off Motion also turns off any background audio track and brings motion menus and motion buttons to a standstill. (Caution: The status of this button affects both your onscreen project and the final DVD.)

• **Locating a drop zone.** As noted above, drop zones in several iDVD 5 themes appear only one at a time. To see them all (so that you can fill them with pictures or movies), drag the thin white scroll bar at the bottom of the menu screen until the zone you want flies into view.

Alternately, you can visit the Drop Zone Editor window, which appears when you either double-click a drop zone or choose Project→Edit Drop Zones. Figure 20-11 shows how to use this new iDVD 5 feature. (Click Return when you're done.)

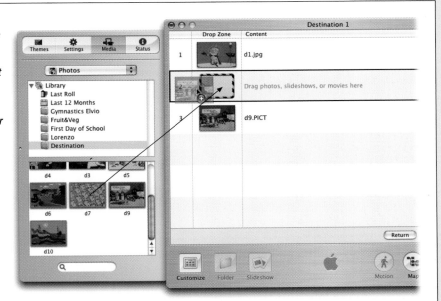

Figure 20-11:
The Drop Zone Editor screen lets you view (and modify) all of a menu's drop zones at once. Drag and drop pictures, movies, or photo albums from the Customize drawer into the broad drop-zone rows, as shown here. To clear a drop zone, drag from the well clear out of the window. You can also double-click a thumbnail to open the corresponding editor (to rearrange a slideshow, for example).

- **Changing the duration.** Use the Settings pane in the Customize drawer to adjust the loop duration for your menus (how long a movie clip plays before starting over). Whatever time you specify here controls the loop length of movies in menu backgrounds, video buttons, *and* drop zones.

Note: If you drag a movie into a drop zone, you can't control where the movie begins as you can with button movies. In a drop zone, a movie always begins at the beginning. Startling, huh?

Redesigning the Theme

You can change every tiny aspect of your theme—the music, the background, the colors, the fonts, and so on—if you have the time and patience. If you're so inclined, turn to Chapter 22 for a full discussion of theme creation.

Phase 4: Burning Your DVD

Once your scene-selection screen is looking pretty good, you're almost ready to burn the DVD. Before you go using up a blank disc, however, you should test it to make sure that it works on the virtual DVD player known as the Macintosh screen.

Previewing Your Project

iDVD's Preview button lets you test your menu system to avoid unpleasant surprises. When you click it, iDVD enters Preview mode, which simulates how your DVD works on a standalone set-top DVD player. You even get a simulated remote control to help you navigate through your DVD's menus, movies, and so on, as shown in Figure 20-12.

To return to iDVD's edit mode, click Exit, Stop (the filled square), or reclick Preview.

fx1 import 1

Widescreen Preview

Customize   Folder   Slideshow   Motion   Map   Preview   Burn

Figure 20-12:
*To "click"
your onscreen
buttons, use
the arrows on
the remote to
highlight the one
you want, and
then click the
Enter button in
the middle of the
remote. Click the
|< or >| buttons
to skip back or
forward by one
chapter, or hold
them down to
rewind or fast-
forward.*

Tip: Instead of using the arrow buttons on the remote to highlight and "click" screen buttons, you can just use your mouse. You'll find it's not only less clumsy, but also a decent indication of how your DVD will play back on computers that can play DVDs.

Previewing Widescreen Footage

iDVD can create widescreen DVDs, just like the ones you rent from Blockbuster—that is, movies that produce a wide, rectangular picture to fit today's wide, rectangular high-definition (and enhanced-definition) TV sets. The key is to make sure that your widescreen movie begins life as a widescreen *iMovie* project, and then hand it off to iDVD from there.

In fact, iDVD-created discs even add letterbox bars automatically when they're played on traditional, squarish sets. That's the effect, in fact, that you see in Preview mode (Figure 20-12). The words "Widescreen Preview" are telling you, in effect, "This is what I'll look like when played on a regular TV. When I'm played on a widescreen set, these gray letterbox bars won't appear."

Note: If you *don't* see the words "Widescreen Preview" during preview, on the other hand, something has gone wrong. iDVD won't treat the footage as widescreen, and will squeeze it horizontally when played on a standard TV. In that event, try reimporting it from iMovie.

Maximum DVD Playback Time

In iDVD 5, you don't have to make the Hobson's choice between 60 minutes of video at best quality and 90 minutes at lower quality, as you did with earlier versions. Apple has thoughtfully raided its own professional DVD creation software (DVD Studio Pro) to bless iDVD with one of its best features: Now any DVD you burn can contain up to 120 minutes of footage at best quality.

To see the on/off switch for this feature, choose iDVD→Preferences. On the General panel (Figure 20-13), you'll see two options under Encoding Settings. Both produce video quality that's superior to what you got from early versions of iDVD:

- **Best Quality.** This option gives you 120 minutes of video at best quality. The tradeoff: It takes a lot longer to burn your DVD, as the program performs quite a bit of analysis before burning.

Figure 20-13:
iDVD 5 offers two ways to compress the video on your masterpiece. Choose Best Performance for up to 60 minutes of excellent-looking footage or Best Quality for up to 120 minutes of video.

When iDVD's work is over, the DVD that pops out of your Mac will come delightfully close to looking and working like a professionally mastered, commercial DVD from Blockbuster. There will, however, be one giveaway: It won't be over two hours long.

- **Best Performance.** Your video will look fantastic, and your Mac will burn the disc relatively quickly. On the downside, the DVD you burn this way can contain a maximum of 60 minutes of video.

In fact, iDVD prefers to burn 60-minute DVDs, because they have the best quality. The instant you try to add the 61st minute of footage to your project, you see the message shown in Figure 20-14. You can change your settings as suggested, or delete some video from the project to make it fit within 60 minutes again.

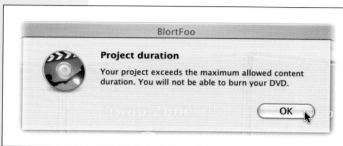

Figure 20-14:
iDVD is telling you that you've put more than 60 minutes of footage onto this DVD. To fit all this video onto your disc, you'll need to use the General Preferences (c-comma) window to switch from Best Performance (60 minutes max) to Best Quality.

A disc that exceeds 60 minutes uses a lower bit rate—that is, it uses less data to describe the video, which allows iDVD to fit more information on the same size disc. (For example, 60-minute iDVD projects depict video using 8 megabits [Mbps] per second; 90-minute projects use 5 Mbps; 120-minute discs use 4 Mbps.)

The tradeoff, of course, is video quality. Higher bit rates generally provide clearer and more accurate picture reproduction than lower bit rates do, especially in action scenes.

If the bit rate of a DVD is *very* low, you get blocky-looking, unclear video. But iDVD's "lowest-quality" mode—4 Mbps—is still above the minimum bit rate needed for clear video for home movies. Don't constrain yourself needlessly to the 60-minute format until you've given the Best Quality format a try.

Burning Your Project

When you've finished editing your disc and testing it thoroughly, it's time to proceed with your burn. This is the moment you've been working toward.

Note: The following steps walk you through the process for burning with an internal Apple SuperDrive (or equivalent). If you want to burn your discs to an external drive, see page 500.

1. **Make sure iDVD is ready to burn.**

   Part of iDVD's job is to *encode* (convert) your movies, music, and pictures into the MPEG-2 format required by standard DVDs.

   Therefore, it's a good idea to open the Customize Drawer, click the Status button at the top, and make sure that the word "Done" appears next to each *asset.* (Apple uses the term "asset" as shorthand for "picture, movie, soundtrack, or what have you.") See Figure 20-15.

Tip: If iDVD doesn't say "Done" for all assets in the list, and yet it doesn't seem to be processing them automatically, make sure you've turned on background compression. Choose iDVD→Preferences, click the General button, and turn on "Enable background encoding."

The only time you'd want to turn off background encoding is when you discover that it's slowing down your Mac as you work.

Figure 20-15:
Look for the word "Done" to the right of each asset. If a status bar appears instead, let iDVD 5 continue encoding until "Done" appears. There's no further action you must take. iDVD encodes in the background without any intervention.

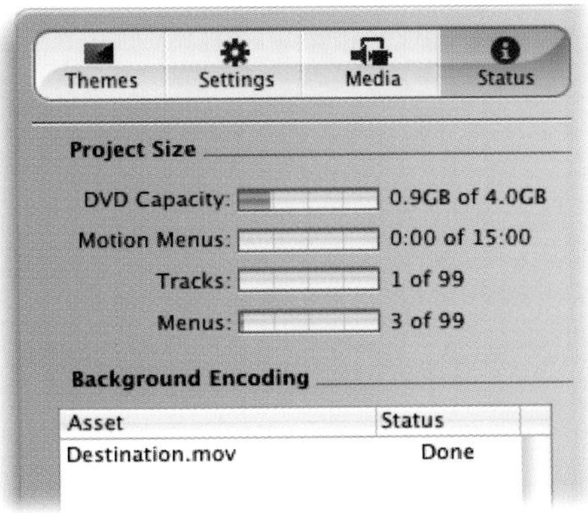

Themes	Settings	Media	Status

Project Size

DVD Capacity: 0.9GB of 4.0GB
Motion Menus: 0:00 of 15:00
Tracks: 1 of 99
Menus: 3 of 99

Background Encoding

Asset	Status
Destination.mov	Done

---

2. **Check your Motion setting.**

   Remember, the Motion button at the bottom of the window determines whether your finished DVD will have animated menus, buttons, and backgrounds, and whether music will play. If the Motion button is green, you'll get all this stuff. If you click it so that it turns gray, motion and audio features won't appear on the final disc.

   (This button has no effect on regular movies and slideshows—only the ones on menu screens.)

3. **Choose File→Save Project.**

   Or press ⌘-S.

4. **Check your disk space.**

   As iDVD rolls along, it needs some extra working space on your hard drive. Be sure there's plenty of free space—at least the amount indicated by the "Project size" statistic on the Status pane of the Customize drawer. If your hard drive doesn't have enough space, do some cleanup.

5. **Click the Burn button twice.**

   See Figure 20-16.

6. **Insert a blank DVD when the Mac asks for it.**

Figure 20-16:
Top: The first click on the gray, closed Burn button "opens" it, revealing a throbbing yellow-and-black button. The second click begins the burning process.

Bottom: During the burning process, iDVD keeps you posted on its progress.

Best Quality/Best Performance: How It Works

When a DVD-burning program goes to work, it faces an important decision. Given that a blank single-layer DVD contains a limited amount of space (4.7 GB or so), how much picture-quality data can it afford to devote to each frame of video?

The Best Performance option in iDVD 5 makes that decision like this: "I'll allot a fixed, predetermined amount of data to each frame of video—enough to make it look great—no matter how many minutes of video my human master has included. A lot of the DVD might wind up being empty if, for example, the project contains less than an hour of video. But at least the burning process will go quickly, and the video will look really great."

The Best Quality option takes a different approach. It says, "I'm going to use every micron of space on this blank DVD. I'm going to analyze the amount of video my human has included, and divide it into the amount of space available on the DVD. The amount of information used to describe an individual frame of video will vary from project to project, and it will take me a lot longer to burn the DVD because I'm going to have to do so much analysis. But at least my human will get two hours of great-looking video per disc."

Incidentally, if you'd like some insight into how iDVD is thinking of the project you're working on at the moment, open the Customize drawer and click the Status button. This panel shows you how close you are to filling up the DVD with your movies, menus, and other elements.

Be sure you're using the correct kind of blank DVD for your DVD burner. For example, don't attempt to burn 1x or 2x blanks at 4x speed. Recent Macs can burn either DVD-R or DVD+R blanks (note the minus and the plus, denoting two incompatible blank DVD formats), as well as their re-recordable, more expensive –RW and +RW counterparts.

7. **Wait.**

It takes iDVD quite awhile to process all of your audio, video, and photos, encoding them into the proper format for a DVD. Your wait time depends on how complex your project is and how fast your Mac is.

Apple says that you should allow two or three minutes of processing per minute of video in your movie, but burning times vary significantly.

After a while, or a bit more than a while, a freshly burned DVD automatically ejects from your SuperDrive.

Note: *After your new DVD pops out, a message says, "Your disc has been created. If you want to create another DVD, insert another disc now." Sure enough, if you want to spin out multiple copies of your project, you can insert another blank DVD right then, so that iDVD can record it while it's on a roll. Otherwise, click Done.*

OneStep DVDs

The new OneStep DVD feature offers a quick method of dumping a tape onto a DVD. You plug in a camera and record directly to a DVD, bypassing iMovie altogether.

This feature turns any camcorder into one that churns out DVDs instead of tapes. It's also a handy way to offload footage from a bunch of tapes, either because blank DVDs are cheaper than tapes, or because tapes have a more limited shelf life.

You should note, though, that the OneStep DVD feature is just as limited as the Magic iMovie described in Chapter 13. For example:

- iDVD can record only from a prerecorded MiniDV tape in a camcorder. It can't record from the TV, a cable box, an analog-digital converter box, or your digital camcorder's video pass-through feature.

- You can't edit the video or choose which parts to include.

- Unless you intervene (details in a moment), iDVD will rewind the tape automatically and transfer the entire thing to the end of the recorded portion.

- You can't customize your project in any way; the resulting DVD won't have a theme, a menu screen, or buttons. Instead, it will be an Autoplay DVD—a disc that begins playing automatically when inserted into a DVD player.

Here's how you use OneStep to copy a tape onto a DVD:

1. **Insert a recorded DV tape into your camcorder, and connect the camcorder to your Mac using a FireWire cable. Turn on the camcorder and set it to VCR mode.**

This mode may also be called Playback, VTR, or Play.

2. **In iDVD, choose File→OneStep DVD.**

Alternatively, just close whatever iDVD project window is open. You arrive at the New Project dialog box; click the OneStep DVD button. If your Mac's DVD drive has a slide-out tray, it now opens automatically.

3. **Insert a blank recordable DVD.**

Close the DVD tray, if necessary.

4. **Wait.**

iDVD takes over your camera, automatically directing it to rewind, play back, and stop. After the capture process is complete, iDVD takes the normal amount of time to compress your video and burn it to disc, so schedule the whole thing for a time (a *long* time) when you won't be needing your Mac. Go get a coffee, found a new spiritual movement, or do something else that will occupy you as the tectonic plates move on inextricably and California continues its long, slow slide into Alaska.

Overriding OneStep

You don't have to live with OneStep's super-simple, super-limited way of doing things. If you're clever, you can work around some of its limitations.

- **You don't have to start from the beginning.** Although OneStep prefers to rewind every tape to the beginning, you can easily override this tendency. That is, *you* can specify where you want the transfer to begin, just by cueing up the tape in the camcorder before you begin the steps above.

  Then, after you insert your blank disc, iDVD displays a "Waiting for Device" message. At that moment, put your finger on the camcorder's Play button. Once iDVD recognizes the blank DVD, OneStep begins the rewinding—but you can interrupt it by pressing Play right away. You've just convinced OneStep that the tape has now been rewound completely. iDVD starts the capture at that point.

- **You don't have to wait till the end.** OneStep ordinarily tries to transfer the entire recorded portion of the tape to the DVD, but you can override this setup, too. Whenever you feel that you've transferred enough of the tape, press the Stop button on your camcorder to end the capture process. OneStep doesn't bat an eye; it moves right ahead to the compression and burning stages.

- **You can bail out at any time.** You can cancel out of the whole OneStep process at any time; just click Stop in the OneStep dialog box. iDVD asks if you want to cancel the recording or continue creating the DVD using the already-captured video.

iDVD Projects by Hand

T he previous chapter showed you how easy it is to convert a finished iMovie project into a bona fide DVD. But iDVD was around long before Apple combined iMovie and iDVD into the glorious package known as iLife. Then, as now, it's capable of much more than turning a single iMovie project into a single DVD.

For example, if all you ever do is click the Create iDVD Project in iMovie, you'll never be able to make a DVD that contains, for example, *six* of your greatest iMovie masterpieces all on one disc. You'll never be able to create a *slideshow* DVD, either, which happens to be one of the world's greatest methods for displaying digital photos. And you'll never know the joy of designing your own navigational menu system, complete with menus within menus.

This chapter has nothing to do with iMovie, and everything to do with iDVD. It shows you how, by doing a few more things manually, you can gain far more power and freedom.

Building iDVDs

Suppose that you've decided to create an iDVD project manually, rather than using the Create iDVD Project button in iMovie. While there's no one best way to put your project together, it helps to have a basic task list to work through. Here are steps for one convenient path through authoring a DVD.

1. **Create a new project.**

   In iDVD, a project file isn't really a single document on your hard drive. It's actually a *package*—a folder that Mac OS X disguises to look like a single icon. The package contains all of your project settings and materials. (As you know from Chapter 13, iMovie projects are package documents, too.)

2. **Choose a theme.**

Use any of iDVD 5's pre-designed, professional-looking design schemes for your project (or add-on themes you've bought on the Web), as described in the previous chapter.

3. **Add movies and slideshows by hand.**

If you've only created iDVD projects from within iMovie, this is the part that's new to you: adding iMovie movies to an iDVD project manually. In fact, you'll *have* to do it this way if you want your DVD to contain a selection of different movies.

You can also create fantastic slideshows this way, as you'll see in this chapter.

4. **Edit your menus.**

Customize the way your menus look. Edit your menu and button titles and add pictures or movies to your drop zones.

5. **Preview and burn the DVD.**

The process ends just as it did in the previous chapter: You look over your work and then feed your Mac a blank DVD to record for posterity.

Creating a New Project

When you're ready to start designing a new DVD, start by creating a project. These steps detail the process you need to follow.

Figure 21-1:
This dialog box pops up the very first time you run iDVD; whenever you close your iDVD project window without quitting the program; whenever you move or delete the iDVD preference file (in your Home→Library→Preferences folder, called com.apple.iDVD. plist); and whenever the most recent iDVD project file has been moved, renamed, or deleted.

1. **Choose File→New (⌘-N). Or, if you're looking at the dialog box shown in Figure 21-1, click Create a New Project.**

   The new iDVD Create Project dialog box (Figure 21-1) is the twin of the one in iMovie. Once again, you'll probably see it fairly rarely.

   All other times, iDVD automatically opens whatever project you just exported from iMovie, or the most recent DVD project you worked on.

   In any case, choosing File→New makes the Save dialog box appear.

2. **Type a name for the project and specify where to save it on your hard drive.**

   If you don't type a more appropriate name, your DVD will be forever known as "My Great DVD."

3. **Click Create.**

   iDVD opens the main menu screen for your new DVD-to-be in the main iDVD window.

Your next step is to choose a visual theme for your DVD's menu screens. Full details appear beginning on page 442.

Adding Movies

When you get right down to it, all iDVD really does is add window dressing—menus, buttons, and so on—to movies, music, and photos created in *other* programs.

Take movies, for example. You already know that you can transfer an iMovie project into iDVD by clicking iMovie's Make iDVD Project button (that's what Chapter 20's all about). But that's just the beginning of the ways you can add movies to your iDVD projects. You can also:

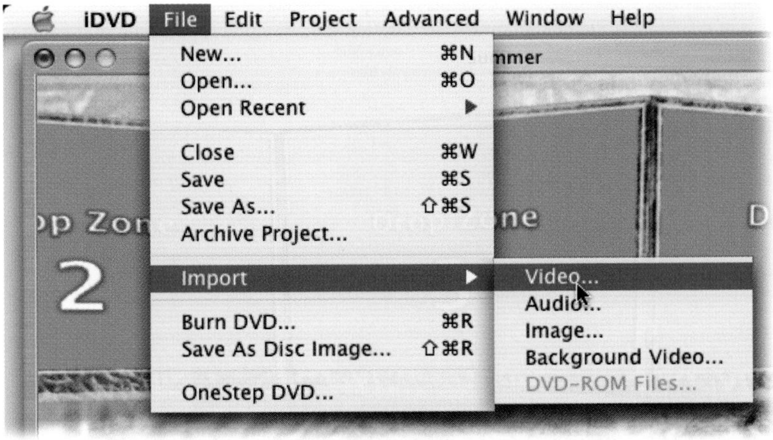

Figure 21-2:
To use the Import command, start on the menu screen you wish to update. When you choose File→Import→Video, the Open File dialog box appears, so that you can navigate to a movie and select it. (You can't select more than one movie to import at a time.) When you click Open, iDVD loads the movie and adds it to the current menu screen.

- Use the File→Import command.

- Drag movies into the iDVD window from the desktop.

- Choose movies from the Media pane of the Customize drawer.

- Drag clips or entire movies directly in from iMovie—a first in iLife history.

The following pages take you through these additional methods..

The Import Command

iDVD's File→Import command lets you install video, audio, pictures, and background movies into your project; see Figure 21-2.

The Finder

Another great way to install a movie into an iDVD menu screen is to drag it there, either right off the desktop or from an open folder window. Figure 21-3 tells all.

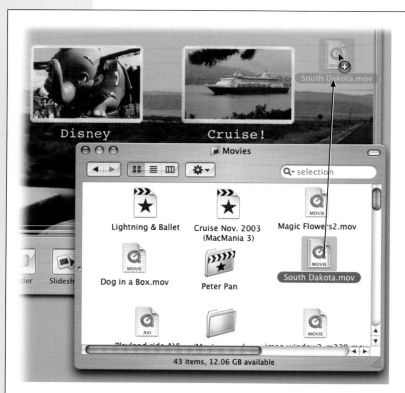

Figure 21-3:
Here's a very quick way to in-stall a movie into one of your menu screens: In the Finder, position the window that contains the movie so that you can see it and the iDVD menu screen at the same time. Then just drag the mov-ies onto the displayed menu and drop them there. (Note, however, that you can't drag iMovie project icons, like the ones with the star icons shown here—only finished QuickTime movies.)

The Movies Media Pane

Dragging files in from the Finder is great, but it assumes that you know where your movies are. Fortunately, if you're a little fuzzy on where you've stored all your movie files, iDVD can help.

Open the Customize drawer (click the Customize button at the bottom of the screen if it isn't already open). Then click the Media button at the top of the drawer and, from the pop-up menu, choose Movies (see Figure 21-4).

The Movies pane opens, showing a list of folders at the top of the pane. At the outset, this list contains only one folder, the Movies folder (which is actually in your Home folder). Click its name to see every digital movie and iMovie project that iDVD can find in that folder (although not in folders *in* that folder.) See the box on the next page for some tips on navigating it. (If you have movies somewhere else on your hard drive, see "Listing more movies," below).

Figure 21-4:
At the top of the pane, you see a list of all the QuickTime movies and iMovie HD project icons in your Home→ Movies folder, or other folders you've told iDVD to search. When you click one of these folders, you see its contents in the pane, exhibited as thumbnail images. Drag your selection into the menu screen to make it part of your DVD-in-waiting.

Listing more movie folders

iDVD starts out displaying only the contents of your Home→Movies folder. This arrangement spares you from looking at a list of the 50,000 individual clips that make up all of your various iMovie projects. The bad news is that it doesn't show you any other folders you have that might contain movies.

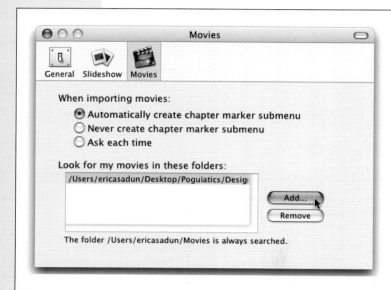

Figure 21-5:
On the Movies preferences panel, click the Add button. Navigate to the folder you need iDVD to search. Click it, and then click Open. iDVD adds the new folder to the list. To remove a file from the list, select it and click Remove. That's the only way you can remove folders from the list (short of trashing your iDVD preference file).

GEM IN THE ROUGH

Useful Pane Tricks

The following tricks and tips may help when using any of the panes (Movies, Audio, or Photos) in the Customize drawer.

Adjust your list panes. Drag the resize bar (the horizontal bar with the small dot that appears between the two panes) to reapportion vertical space between the upper and lower sections of the pane.

Play it. If you double-click a movie or sound, it plays. (You can also click it once and then click the triangular Play button at the bottom of the pane.) Click once anywhere to stop the playback. Use as needed to jog your memory.

Search. If you've got a seething mass of movies to root through, click in the Search box below the list and type a few letters of the name of the movie, picture, or song you want. As you type, iDVD hides all entries except those whose names match. Capitalization doesn't matter, but you can search through only one folder, album, or playlist at a time. (Restore the entire list by clicking the little X at the right end of the Search box.)

Select more than one. You can highlight more than one movie, picture, or song at a time, and therefore save time by dragging them all onto the screen at once. Exactly as in the Finder, you can click the first entry, then Shift-click the last to select an entire group. Or you can ⌘-click random thumbnails to select a nonadjacent set.

Fortunately, you can teach iDVD to list the contents of additional movie folders. To do so, drag new folders from the Finder to the list in the Movies pane, or choose iDVD→Preferences (⌘-comma), click the Movies button, and follow the steps in Figure 21-5. Repeat for as many folders as you want to add.

Clips and Movies from iMovie

If you click the Create iDVD Project button in iMovie, as described in the previous chapter, iMovie creates a brand-new iDVD project. iMovie offers no obvious way to install a *second or third* movie into an existing iDVD project.

That's a shame, because most homemade DVDs are not, in fact, 90-minute opuses, complete with character development and a satisfying narrative arc. (In fact, an hour and a half of *anybody's* home movies is about 80 minutes too long.) Most of the time, people want to fill a DVD with *several* of their finished iMovie projects. They want each button on the DVD's main menu to represent a *complete movie.*

Figure 21-6:
After saving your iMovie project (right), you can drag the entire movie onto an iDVD menu screen (left) by using the project icon in the title bar as a handle. The trick is to hold down the mouse button *on that icon momentarily until it darkens before you begin to drag.*

Alternatively, you can drag individual clips from iMovie (either the Movie Track or the Clips pane) into iDVD, as shown here at bottom.

Fortunately, it's easy enough to create this effect. In iLife '05, you can drag either an iMovie *clip* or an entire iMovie *project* into iDVD—if you know what to drag. Figure 21-6 shows all.

Note: The drag-the-title-bar-icon trick illustrated in Figure 21-6 works only for iMovie projects that have been saved in the new, single-icon iMovie HD project format (page 679). If your project is still represented on your hard drive as a project folder, you can't drag its title-bar icon.

Whichever way you pick, whatever you just dragged turns into a new button on the menu page.

Movies with Chapters

You already know from the previous chapter that if you export a movie directly from iMovie, any chapter markers you've added automatically turn into buttons in iDVD.

But what happens if you drag an iMovie movie, itself containing chapter markers, into iDVD as described above?

Unless you've changed the iMovie settings, iDVD automatically turns those chapter markers into buttons, just as though you'd exported the movie from iMovie. They wind up on a menu screen of their own—a *submenu*.

Unfortunately, you've now created a fairly complex menu structure. To jump to a certain scene in your dragged-in iMovie, your audience has to navigate through three different pages of buttons.

For that reason, you might not always want iMovie to turn your chapter markers into buttons—at least not without asking your permission.

Choose iDVD→Preferences. On the General tab, you have three choices under "When importing movies":

- **"Automatically create chapter marker submenu."** This is the factory setting. When you drag an iMovie project into iDVD, it turns into a folder-icon button. Your audience must "click" that button with the remote control to get to a second screen, where they can either play the movie or access *its* scene-selection menu. (See the following section for more on navigating "folder" menus in iDVD.)

- **"Never create chapter marker submenu."** If you choose this option, dragging an iMovie movie into a menu screen creates a movie button, not a folder button. "Clicking" that button with the remote control makes the movie play immediately.

  Your audience no longer has the option of navigating your movie by viewing a page full of scene markers.

Tip: Even though your viewers won't see individual icons for these scenes, they can still jump to them using the Next Chapter or Previous Chapter buttons on their remote controls.

- **"Ask each time."** When you drag a chapter-filled movie onto a menu screen, iMovie says: "Do you want to add chapter markers for this movie?" Click Yes (if you want to create the nested-menus effect described three paragraphs ago), or No (if you want the invisible chapter-markers effect described two paragraphs ago).

Submenus ("Folders")

Depending on the theme you've chosen, iDVD may impose a limit of six or twelve buttons on a menu screen. Fortunately, that doesn't mean you're limited to twelve scenes in a movie, or twelve movies per DVD. You, or iDVD, can accommodate more movies by creating *submenus*—additional menu screens that branch off from the main menu—and even sub-submenus.

You may have seen this effect already, in fact, if you've tried to create an iMovie DVD containing more than a handful of chapter markers.

You can also create this effect manually. Whenever you click the Folder button at the bottom of the screen, iDVD adds a submenu button to the current menu screen. In some themes, especially those that began life in previous versions of iDVD, this button looks like an actual folder; in most, it's simply a new text button.

Behind the scenes, this button represents a second menu screen, a blank canvas with room for yet another six or twelve buttons.

Navigating Submenus

Navigating iDVD Folders while building your project is pretty easy, once you master these tips:

WORKAROUND WORKSHOP

Temporary Buttons

When you try to add more than twelve buttons to a menu screen, iDVD gracefully announces, "There are too many buttons in the current menu to add a new one."

As with previous versions of iDVD, you can click OK to dismiss the message and return to editing your project—without the new button you tried to add.

But iDVD 5 offers what's often a more convenient alternative: A Temporarily Allow button that lets you add those extra buttons to your menus for now,

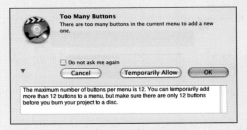

so that you have the convenience of (for example) cutting and pasting them to other menu screens.

But with great power comes great responsibility: iDVD wants you to understand that you can't actually burn a DVD with too many buttons on a menu screen. If you forget to dispose of the extra buttons before clicking the Burn button, another warning message appears (shown here at bottom), and your burning efforts come to a grinding halt.

- **Open by double-clicking.** Double-click any folder or submenu button to "open" it—that is, to bring up the menu screen it represents.

- **Return by clicking the arrow.** Each submenu screen contains a Back arrow. Click this arrow to return to the "parent" menu.

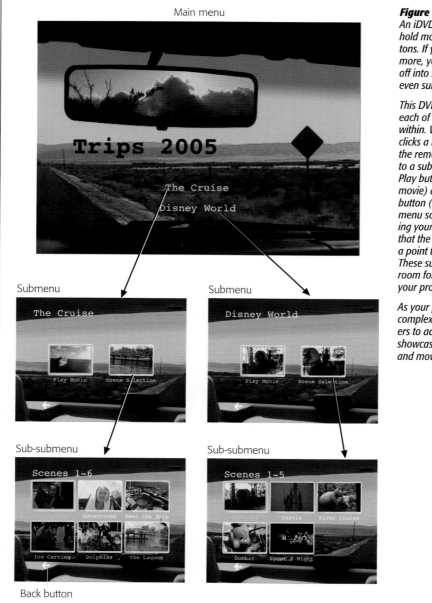

Main menu

Submenu

Submenu

Sub-submenu

Sub-submenu

Back button

Figure 21-7:
An iDVD menu screen can't hold more than twelve buttons. If you try to place any more, you'll have to branch off into submenu screens, or even sub-submenu screens.

This DVD has two movies, each of which has chapters within. When your audience clicks a movie's name (with the remote control), they go to a submenu screen with a Play button (to play the whole movie) and a Scene Selection button (to open yet another menu screen, this one showing your chapter markers so that the audience can choose a point to begin playback). These submenus create extra room for navigation through your project.

As your projects grow more complex, you must use folders to add enough space to showcase all your pictures and movies.

Tip: As you work with your menu and submenu screens, navigating folders may seem painfully slow unless you turn off iDVD's background encoding feature. (Its purpose is to quietly pre-process your video while you're working, so that burning the DVD will take less time.) To do that, choose iDVD→Preferences, click the General button, and then turn off "Enable background encoding."

- **Names may not match.** A folder/submenu button's label may bear no relationship to the title on the submenu screen. You have to edit the text individually in both places if you want to make a change.

- **Themes don't have to match.** Each menu screen can have its own theme. In fact, when you click a theme thumbnail in the Themes pane of the Customize drawer, iDVD changes *only* the menu screen you're looking at right now. If you want that theme to apply to all menu screens, you have to choose Advanced→Apply Theme to Folders.

- **Mind your minutes.** The more folders and more themes you add to your project, the closer you come to iDVD's limit of 15 minutes' worth of menu videos.

Reaching that limit isn't such a remote possibility, either; even one-minute video loops on 15 menu screens will take up all your available space, even if you use the same background video on every menu.

When you try to add a new menu that takes up too much space, you'll see the warning shown in Figure 21-8.

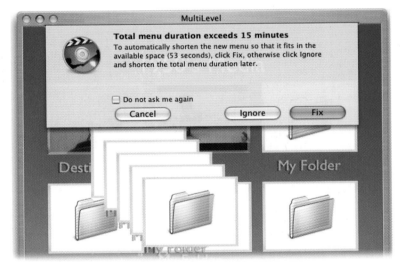

Figure 21-8:
When you try to add a new menu that would exceed iDVD's 15-minute background-video limit, this message appears. Click Cancel to eliminate the new menu. Click Ignore to add the menu despite the warning, with the understanding that you'll have to solve the space issue manually before you burn the DVD. Or click Fix to make iDVD shorten the menu's loop so that it fits within the remaining video menu space on your disc.

If, in that dialog box, you opt to ignore the warning, you're welcome to solve the too-much-background-video problem your own way—just as long as you solve the problem before you burn the DVD. If not, when you go to burn, you'll be prompted once again to lower the total menu minutes.

Tip: You can always peek at the current overall menu duration of your project by opening the Customize drawer and clicking the Status tab. The project size section lists the current total menu duration used by your project.

The DVD Map—and Autoplay

As you can see, menus and submenus can build up with alarming rapidity. At times your projects may grow out of control; pretty soon, you feel like Hansel and Gretel with not enough bread crumbs.

iDVD's Map pretty much eliminates these navigation problems. It's a living, interactive diagram whose icons represent your DVD's menus, videos, and slideshows and reveal

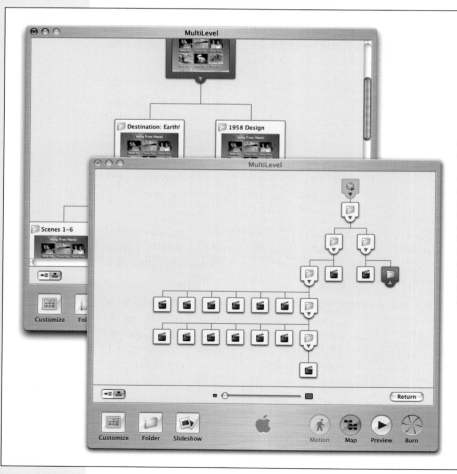

Figure 21-9:
In iDVD 5, the size slider lets you view the map either with large, slide-like icons (back) or with little tiny ones that reveal more of your DVD's structure without scrolling. Here, the right-most folder hides a series of submenus just as detailed as the ones shown in the left branch of the tree—but it's been hidden by collapsing the flippy triangle.

how they're connected. As your menu and button layouts grow more complex, you can use the map screen to help you keep track of your menu structure.

To view the map, click the Map button at the bottom of the main iDVD window. The element you were working on appears with colored highlighting (Figure 21-9).

- **Scroll it** by dragging in any blank space.

- Click one of the **view buttons** to flip the display between horizontal- and vertical-tree layouts.

- The **scale slider** lets you adjust the amount of map detail you can see at once. Working a big, complex project? Move the slider all the way to the left to view more elements at once. Working on a small project? The bigger the tiles, the more project details you'll see.

- Each menu tile now includes a **flippy triangle.** Click it to expand or collapse that limb of the menu tree (Figure 21-9, right).

- **Open a menu or slideshow** by double-clicking its icon in the Map.

- **Click the Map button again** or click Return to return to the menu screen you were working on.

Editing in the Map

Now, in previous versions of iDVD, the Map window provided a visual treat, but you couldn't really *do* anything there. But in iDVD 5, the map is interactive; you can actually do DVD design and editing work all on this single screen.

For example:

- It's easy to delete a bunch of menus or other elements all at once. Just Shift-click the ones you want to target for extermination (Shift-click a second time if you select an icon by mistake), and then press the Delete key.

- Similarly, you can quickly and conveniently apply new themes to the menu screens of your DVD without ever leaving the map. To do so, open the Customize drawer, click the Themes button, select the desired menu icons on the map, and then click the new theme's name.

- You can even add new menu screens and slideshows on the Map screen. Click the icon of the menu screen where you want to put the button that will link to the new menu or slideshow, and then choose Project→New Folder (for a submenu) or Project→New Slideshow. (At that point, you can then specify *which* movies or *which* photos you want on those new entities by dragging them in from the Customize drawer's Media panel.)

- Remember the transitions (cross-dissolve effects) that let you ease from one menu screen to another? You can apply or change these transition styles en masse using the Map, too. Just Shift-click to choose the menu icons you want to transition *out* of, open the Customize panel, click the Settings button, and then use the Transition pop-up menu to choose the style you want for all of them at once.

Autoplay

The DVDs described so far in this book behave like commercial Hollywood DVDs in almost every respect except one: they don't play a certain video clip automatically when the disc is inserted, *before* the menu screen appears. You know—a bright red FBI warning, previews of coming attractions, or maybe just a quick snippet of the movie on the DVD.

iDVD 5 makes creating this kind of "pre-movie" extremely easy. In Map view, the first tile (at the top or the left, depending on the view you've chosen) is technically called the Project tile (see Figure 21-10), but you can think of it as the Autoplay tile. Whatever you drag onto this tile will play automatically when the DVD is inserted, before your viewers even touch their remote controls.

These are the kinds of things you can put there:

- **A video clip.** In the Customize drawer, click the Media button, and then choose Movies from the pop-up menu. iDVD displays all the movies in your Home→—Movies folder (and any other folders you've listed here); drag the one you want directly onto the Project tile to install it there.

- **A still image.** In the Customize drawer, again, click the Media button, but this time choose Photos from the pop-up menu. iDVD shows your complete iPhoto collection, including all of your albums. To use one of these images as a startup screen for your DVD project, just drag it onto the Project tile. (You can add audio to it, too, just as you'd add audio to a slideshow—by dragging in an audio file from the Audio section of the Media pane.)

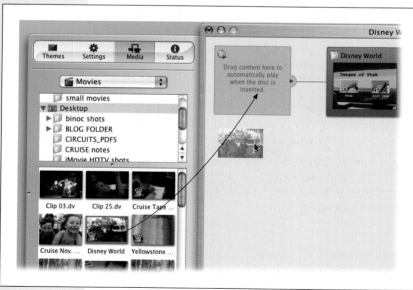

Figure 21-10:
If you decide to add or replace your Autoplay material, just drag new stuff right onto it. Or, to eliminate the Autoplay segment, drag it right off the Project tile. It disappears in a little puff of Mac OS X cartoon smoke.

Tip: If you tinker with the graphics tools in a program like Photoshop or AppleWorks, you could come up with a decent replica of the standard FBI warning that appears as the Autoplay of a commercial DVD. You could precisely duplicate the wording and typographical look—or you could take the opportunity to do a hilarious spoof of the usual warning.

- **A slideshow.** Once you've got the Photos list open in the Customize drawer as described above, you can also drag an entire iPhoto album onto the project icon. Alternatively, you can click and ⌘-click just the photos you want in the Customize panel, and then drag them en masse onto the project icon. In fact, you can even drag photos—as a group or in a folder—right out of the Finder and onto this icon.

To control how long your still image remains on the screen, or how quickly your Autoplay slideshow plays, double-click your Project tile. You arrive at the AutoPlay slideshow editor, a screen like the one shown in Figure 21-10, where you can adjust the timing, transition, and even the audio that plays behind the picture(s).

Tip: It's possible to create a DVD that never even gets to the menu screen—a DVD consisting only of Autoplay material. You could design a project that way for the benefit of, for example, technophobic DVD novices whose pupils dilate just contemplating using a remote control. They can just insert your Autoplay-only DVD and sit back on the couch as the movie plays automatically.

Looping

If you highlight the button for a movie, slideshow, or Autoplay tile—either in Map view or on a menu screen—and then choose Advanced→Loop Movie (or Loop Slide Show), you unleash another raft of possibilities. You can make a DVD that repeats the highlighted material (a slideshow or movie) over and over again and, in fact, *never* gets back to the menu screen.

Tip: In the Map, a small circle appears in the lower-right corner of any element you've set up for looping.

That would be a great way to create a DVD containing a self-running, self-repeating slideshow of digital photos that plays on a TV at a party or wedding reception. You could also use it to create a self-looping kiosk display at a trade show.

In any case, the DVD will loop endlessly—or at least until it occurs to someone in your audience to press the Menu or Title button on the remote, which displays your main menu. At this point, the Menu button redisplays the previous menu screen; the Title button causes a return to the main menu.

DVD Slideshows

The DVD may be the world's best delivery mechanism for digital photos. Your friends and family sit there on the couch—in the comfort of their own living room, as the saying goes. They click the remote control to walk through your photos (or, if you choose, they relax and let the slideshow advance automatically). Instead of passing around a tiny pile of fragile 4 x 6 prints, your audience gets to watch the photos at TV-screen size—accompanied by a musical soundtrack of your choice.

If you've installed movies into an iDVD menu screen, installing photos will seem like a piece of cake. Once again, you can do so using several different methods, each with its own advantages:

- **iPhoto albums.** When you open the Customize drawer, click the Media button, and choose Photos from the pop-up, iDVD presents your entire iPhoto picture collection, complete with the albums you've used to organize them.

  The great thing about this system is that iPhoto albums contain well-defined image progressions—that is, you presumably dragged the photos into an emotionally satisfying sequence. That's exactly how iDVD will present the pictures: as they appear in the album, from the first image to the last.

- **Folder drag and drop.** If the pictures you want to add aren't in iPhoto, you can also drag a folder full of them right off the desktop (or a Finder folder) and onto an iDVD menu screen. iDVD creates a slideshow from the images, all right, but puts them into an unpredictable sequence.

- **Slideshow editor.** iDVD comes with a special window called the Slideshow Editor, in which you can add individual photos to the slideshow and drag them into any order you like. This approach takes a little work, but it gives you the freedom to import images from many different sources without having to organize them beforehand.

Tip: A DVD slideshow (***any*** DVD, not just those produced by iDVD) can contain at most 99 slides, and one DVD can contain at most 99 slideshows. The designers of the DVD format obviously recognized that there's a limit to the patience of home slideshow audiences.

---

iPhoto Albums

You can use either of two approaches to create iDVD slideshows from your iPhoto album collection. One way begins in iPhoto; the other begins in iDVD.

Starting in iPhoto

As part of the much-heralded integration of iPhoto, iTunes, iMovie, and iDVD, iPhoto 5 offers a menu choice that exports albums and slideshows to iDVD. In the iPhoto Source list, click the album or slideshow you want to export, choose Share→Send to iDVD, and then wait as iPhoto transfers the data.

Tip: If you do a lot of this, you can add a Send to iDVD button to your iPhoto toolbar (at the bottom of the window). Just choose Share→Show in Toolbar→Send to iDVD.

Now, although the steps are the same for the iPhoto entities called *albums* and *slideshows,* the results in iDVD are different.

- If you export an iPhoto *slideshow* (a set of photos to which you've applied music, panning and zooming effects, specific crossfade styles, and even individual, per-slide timings), iDVD treats the result as a *movie*. Your audience will see a frozen slideshow when they press the Enter or Play buttons on their remote. They'll see the pictures in the sequence, and with the timings, *you* specified; they'll have no control over the show.

  You can work with this movie as you would any other movie you've imported from iMovie or the Finder.

- If you export an *album* (a "folder" full of photos, assembled and arranged by you), iDVD treats the result as a *slideshow*—a collection of pictures that your DVD audience can peruse, one at a time, using the arrow buttons on their remote controls.

The rest of this discussion applies to these DVD slideshows.

In iDVD, a slideshow looks like a submenu button that bears the name of the album you exported. Double-click it to view the list of pictures inside, change their sequence, and make other adjustments, as described on the following pages.

Tip: If you make changes to your iPhoto album—by adding photos or rearranging them, for example—click iPhoto's iDVD button again. Instead of adding a second copy to your DVD project, iDVD is smart enough to **update** the existing slideshow. Thanks to this smart feature, you can update your albums as often as you like without any adverse affects on your iDVD project.

Note, however, that you don't enjoy this luxury when you use the Photos pane within iDVD. Dragging an album out of the Photos pane onto a menu a second time gives you a second copy.

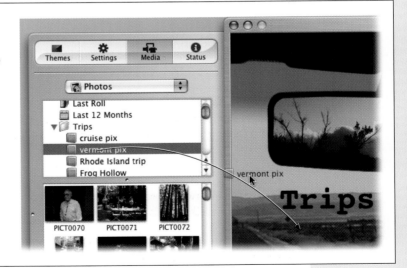

Figure 21-11:
To add a new slideshow, drag any album (from the top pane of the Media Photos pane) onto your iDVD workspace. You can also select more than one album and drag them en masse. (The usual multiple-selection tricks apply: ⌘-click several albums in turn to select all of them, for example.)

Starting in iDVD

If you haven't already been working in iPhoto, there's an even easier way to turn iPhoto albums into living slideshows. Just open the Customize drawer, click the Media tab, choose Photos from the pop-up menu, and voilà: You're presented with the tiny thumbnails of every digital photo in your collection. You even get to see the list of albums, exactly as they appear in iPhoto (Figure 21-11).

Drag Photo Folders from the Finder

Suppose you don't keep all of your pictures in iPhoto. (Hey, it could happen.)

In that case, you may prefer to drag a folder of photos out of the Finder and onto an iDVD menu screen. (Make sure that the folder contains nothing but pictures. If it contains any other kind of document, or even other folders, iDVD may complain that it can't handle the "Unsupported File Type: Unknown Format.")

In any case, the folder shows up on the menu screen as a new slideshow button. You're ready to edit your slideshow, as described below.

Add a Slideshow, Worry about the Pictures Later

If all of your photographic masterpieces aren't already together in iPhoto or even in a Finder folder, you can also bring them into iDVD individually.

To do that, start by creating a new slideshow folder: Click the Slideshow button near the bottom-left of the iDVD window (or choose Project→Add Slideshow). iDVD creates a new, empty slideshow. Double-click it to enter the Slideshow Editor described next.

Editing Slideshows

No matter how you got your slideshow folder button into iDVD, you edit it the same way: by double-clicking it to open iDVD's Slideshow Editor. See Figure 21-12 for a quick tour.

Adding or omitting slides

If you want to add new pictures to the slideshow, use any of the following techniques:

- **Drag from the Finder.** Drag an image, a selection of several images, or a folder of images directly into the slide list.

- **Use the Media Photos Pane.** Open the Customize drawer and click the Media button at the top; choose Photos from the pop-up menu. Drag a picture, a set of several shots, or an iPhoto album into the slide list.

- **Import an image.** Choose File→Import→Image. Navigate to any picture file, select it, and then click Open.

Tip: Before clicking Open, you can highlight several photos to bring them all in at once. If the ones you want appear consecutively in the list, click the first one, and then Shift-click the last one, to highlight all of them. If not, ⌘-click each photo file that you want to import.

Either way, click Open to bring them all into iDVD simultaneously.

To remove a picture from the list, just click it and then press the Delete key. You can also remove a whole bunch of pictures simultaneously by first Shift-clicking them or ⌘-clicking them, exactly as described in the previous Tip, before pressing Delete.

Reordering Slides

Changing the sequence of slides involves little more than dragging them to their new position. Yet again, you can select multiple slides at once (see the preceding Tip) and then drag them en masse.

Slideshow Options

iDVD offers some useful options at the bottom of the Slideshow Editor window:

- **Loop slideshow.** If you turn on the "Loop slideshow" checkbox, the slideshow repeats endlessly, or until your viewer presses the Menu or Title button on the DVD remote control.

Figure 21-12:
The iDVD Slideshow Editor lets you build and customize your slideshows. Each slide appears in order, with its number and a thumbnail; you can move them around by dragging, delete the ones you don't want, or add new ones by dragging graphics from the desktop or the Media pane of the Customize drawer. The buttons in the lower-left corner switch between a list view and an icon view (shown here). Click Return to go back to iDVD's menu-editing mode.

- **Display navigation.** When you turn on this option, you'll see navigation arrows on the screen as your slideshow plays. Your audience can click these buttons with their remote controls to move back and forth within your slideshow.

  Navigation gives your viewers a feeling of flexibility and control. On the other hand, remember that they can always use the < and > buttons on their remote controls to move through the slides, even if no arrows appear on the screen. (Furthermore, you may consider the majesty of your photography marred by the superimposed triangle buttons.)

- **Add files to DVD-ROM.** When iDVD creates a slideshow, it scales all of your photos to 640 x 480 pixels.

  That's ideal for a standard television screen, which, in fact, can't display any resolution higher than that.

  But if you intend to distribute your DVD to somebody who is computer savvy, you may want to give them the original, full-resolution photos. They won't see these photos when they insert the disc into a DVD player. But when they insert your DVD into their *computers,* they'll see a folder filled with the original, high-res photos, for purposes like printing, using as Desktop wallpaper, and so on. (In other words, you've created a dual-format disc that's both a DVD-video disc and a DVD-ROM.)

- **Slide Duration.** This pop-up list allows you to specify how much time each slide spends on the screen before the next one appears: 1, 3, 5, 10 seconds, or Manual. Manual, of course, means that your audience will have to press the Next button on the remote control to change pictures.

  Then there's the Fit to Audio option, which appears in the pop-up menu only after you've added a sound file or a playlist to your slideshow. In this case, iDVD will determine the timing of your slides automatically—by dividing the length of the soundtrack by the number of slides in your show. In other words, if the song is 60 seconds long, and you've got 20 slides in the show, each slide will sit on the screen for three seconds.

Tip: Fit to Audio offers a nifty way to create a simple, no-fuss DVD "mix tape" that you can play on your home theater system. Drop a song into the Audio well (facing page) but add only one photograph, which may be the album art for that song or a graphic showing the song's title. Make a series of "slideshows" this way.

Once you burn the whole thing to a DVD, you can choose a song to start playing in its entirety with the album cover on the screen. (If you add an album-in-a-playlist instead of just one song, you can choose an album to play in the same way.)

- **Transition.** You can specify any of several graceful transition effects—Dissolve, Cube, and so on—to govern how one slide morphs into the next. You can try each of these styles for yourself by selecting one and then watching your slideshow (click Preview to start the show; click it again to return to the editor). Viewing just a few slides will show you how the transitions work on real images.

Note: The transition you specify here affects all slides in the show.

If you don't want any transition animation, choose **None.** iDVD will simply cut from one slide to the next.

Tip: iDVD can put crossfades and transitions between menus, too. That way, when your audience clicks a button on the main menu screen, the screen doesn't just *jump cut* to the selected move or slideshow; it crossfades, wipes, rotates on the face of a cube, or whatever.

To specify which transition you'd like, open the Customize drawer and click the Settings button at the top. Select one or more menu buttons and then use the Transition pop-up menu to specify the effect you want. (In iDVD 5, you can use a different transition for each button.)

Slideshow Audio

Music has a profound impact on the effect of a photo slideshow. You can't appreciate how dramatic the difference is until you watch the same slideshow with and without music playing.

iDVD starts out with whatever music you've selected in iPhoto, but if "Minuet in G" isn't your thing, fear not. You can use any music you like.

The easiest way to add music to your slideshow is to open the Customize drawer, click the Media button at the top, and select Audio from the pop-up. Conveniently enough, iDVD shows your entire iTunes music collection, complete with any playlists you've assembled.

Tip: This list also includes any music you've created yourself using GarageBand (and exported to iTunes). Such songs make great slideshow soundtracks, because you've tailored them to the mood and the length of the show.

When you find suitable musical accompaniment, drag its name out of the iTunes list and onto the rounded rectangle—the well, as Apple calls it—labeled Audio. You can even drag an entire playlist into the well; the DVD will play one song after another according to the playlist, so that the music won't die ignominiously in the middle of the slide show. You can also drag a sound file from any Finder window or the desktop—and directly onto this Audio well.

Tip: When it's empty, the Audio well looks like a small speaker. When it's occupied, its icon identifies the kind of audio file you've installed; the little icon will say, for example, AIFF, AU, or MP3. The icon used when you add a playlist rather than a single song varies, usually showing the first audio file type used in the playlist.

To try out a different piece of background music, drag a new song or audio file into the Audio well. And if you decide that you don't want music at all, drag the file icon directly out of the Audio well and onto any other part of the screen. You see an animated puff of smoke confirm your decision.

Tip: If you can play a sound file in iTunes, you can include it in an iDVD project. If not, use a converter program to bring it into a usable format. For example, iTunes can't import MIDI files, but GarageBand can—and GarageBand can export to AIFF, a format that iTunes understands.

Curiously enough, iTunes can play back soundtracks from iMovie projects. Just drag your iMovie HD project into iTunes and then import them into iDVD from your media pane. You can also drag a QuickTime movie directly onto the Audio well and drop it in. iDVD uses the first audio track.

Leaving the Slideshow Editor

To return to iDVD's menu editor, click the Return button at the bottom right of the Slideshow Editor.

Burning Your Slideshow

Once you've designed a slideshow DVD, previewing it and burning it onto a blank DVD works exactly as described beginning on page 451.

Since most people have never thrilled to the experience of viewing a digital-camera slideshow on their TV sets, a few notes are in order:

- Your viewers can use the remote control's Next and Previous buttons to move forward or backward through the presentation, no matter what timing you originally specified when you designed the show.

- They can also press the Pause button to freeze a certain picture on the screen for greater study (or while they go to the bathroom). Both the slide advancing and music stop until they click Pause or Play button, again.

- If the audio selection or playlist is shorter than the slideshow, the song starts over again.

- Your viewers can return to the main menu screen by clicking the Menu button on the remote.

- When the slideshow is over, the music stops and the main menu screen reappears.

Advanced iDVD

Although iDVD appears simple, straightforward, and direct, there's more power lurking inside than you might expect. You can see, change, and control things you never knew you could—if you're willing to try new and unusual approaches. Some of these approaches require add-on software programs. Others demand nerves of steel and a willingness to dive into hidden iDVD files. And a few even require some familiarity with programming.

In this advanced chapter, you'll discover how some of these sideways (and backwards and upside down) methods can expand your iDVD repertoire.

Designing Your Own Themes

Some of Apple's iDVD themes offer great backgrounds but weak audio. Others provide terrific sounds but terrible text. Some create a nearly perfect package, while others seem broken beyond repair. Fortunately, in the end it doesn't matter, because iDVD lets you adapt themes to your taste and save them as new *Favorites*.

Favorites let you move beyond built-in themes and presets to create truly customized DVD menu systems. You can change font, adjust the length of the looping background video, move buttons around and change their styles, change the fonts and colors for button and menu titles, move text around the screen, substitute new background art or background patterns, replace or remove the audio loop that plays when the main menu is onscreen, and much more. Let the following pages be your guide.

The Themes Pane

All three collections—5.0 Themes, 4.0 Themes and Old Themes—appear in the Themes pane in the Customize drawer. (To view the Themes pane, click Customize to open the Customize drawer, then click the Themes button at the top of the pane.)

As you study the scrolling list of themes, you'll notice that:

- **Favorites appear together.** When you choose Favorites from the Theme Set pop-up menu at the top of the pane, all Favorites (themes that you've created) appear together in the same list. This list is empty when you start out using iDVD.

- **Most non-Apple themes appear separately.** Themes you've bought from other companies (like *www.idvdthemetastic.com* or *www.idvdthemepak.com*) are listed separately in the pane's pop-up menu.

- **View several sets at once.** iDVD 5 lets you view a single set of themes, or all themes at once. To view just one set, select its name from the Theme Set pop-up menu. To view all themes, choose All from that same menu.

- **The walking-man icon means sound or audio.** When you see a small, round, walking-man logo in the lower-right corner of the theme thumbnail, that's your signal that the theme uses a motion background or audio loop.

- **The ribbon means favorite.** A gray prize ribbon appears in the lower-left corner of certain themes. This icon lets you know that the theme is a Favorite—a theme that you created yourself. You'll find out how to create Favorites later in this chapter.

Button Styles

When iDVD was first introduced, its flamboyant button thumbnails generated a lot of excitement. Each button could show a small video or photo, offering visual previews of the linked material.

Times have changed. These days, hyperactive drop zones zoom around the screen, and text buttons have quietly replaced the old button designs. In the 5.0 theme collection, not a single button can display videos or pictures.

If you choose one of the older themes for that reason, you don't have to be content with the proposed button style. To change the look of your buttons, do this:

1. **Open the Customize drawer, if it's not already open.**

   Click the Customize button if necessary.

2. **Click the Themes icon.**

   The Themes pane opens.

3. **From the pop-up menu, choose 4.0 Themes or Old Themes.**

   These are the only themes that contain buttons-with-previews.

4. **Click a theme to see what it looks like.**

   Choose one with non-text buttons, like Fish Two, Brushed Metal Two, or Green Linen Two.

5. **Click the Settings tab at the top of the Customize drawer.**

   The Settings pane appears.

6. **Near the bottom of the panel, click the From Theme pop-up button.**

   You get a pop-up menu of button shapes (Figure 22-1).

7. **Click the button style you want.**

   Choices include gilded frames, file frames, hearts, ovals, and more. Choose T to use a text button (just words, no picture). To revert to whatever button style the theme originally came with, choose From Theme.

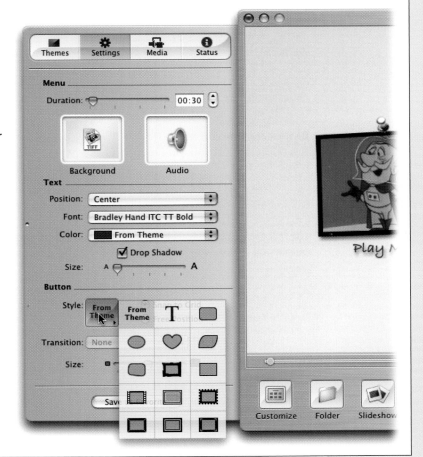

Figure 22-1:
iDVD offers 13 built-in button frames. Note, though, that some iDVD button shapes crop video inappropriately, producing odd-looking and less effective buttons, as shown here. Large subjects, particularly people's faces or still objects, may not appear properly under these conditions. (Unlike drop zones, you can't reposition button videos to produce a better composition.)

Editing and Positioning Text

Although most people focus primarily on iDVD's drop zones, video buttons, and so on, text also plays a critical role. It's a dependable, instantly recognizable part of a DVD menu system.

The text that you can fiddle with falls into three categories:

- **Menu titles** help viewers figure out where they are in the DVD menu system by providing clues to the current context: "Our Vacation," "Pictures (Week 1)," and "Scene Selection Menu," for example. Title text usually appears at the top of the screen, although you can put it anywhere you like.

- **Button text** can appear all by itself, or as labels above, below, beside, or on top of graphic buttons.

- **Text boxes** can appear anywhere on your screen. Thanks to this feature, you can create text boxes on your menu screens and fill them with whatever explanatory text you think is appropriate—instructions, introductions, a description of the project, and so on.

Tip: In iDVD, as in life, don't be too talky. Brevity is the soul of DVD captions.

To add a text block, choose Project→Add Text (⌘-K). Double-click the placeholder text and type away. Use the Settings panel of the Customize drawer to specify the font, color, alignment, and size of the text.

It's a lot easier to edit text in iDVD 5 than in early versions, and a lot more consistent. Just select the text you want to modify and use the Text adjustments in the Settings pane.

Here, for example, is a boatload of techniques to help customize your text. Each method changes the selected text on only the *currently displayed* DVD menu screen.

Tip: Style changes (font, size, color) affect a title, text box, or the buttons on a screen, whichever is currently selected. That is, changes you make to one button apply to all buttons as a group (on the current menu screen).

- **Select the text box.** Click once on it. A brightly colored border appears. Now you can drag the box to move it, press Delete to remove it, Shift-click another text box to highlight both at once, use the Copy command so that you can paste them onto another menu screen, and so on.

- **Change the text.** To highlight a piece of text, double-click anywhere inside it. (If the text is the title of a picture or video button, you must first click the button and then single-click the associated text.)

  You'll note that iDVD automatically highlights the entire phrase, meaning that you can just begin to type, replacing the entire text blob, without first dragging across it. (Of course, if you want to edit only part of the existing text, drag with the mouse first.) Press Return or Enter when you're finished.

- **Choose a font.** To select a new typeface, choose from the Text→Font menu on the Settings pane. You're not allowed to mix and match fonts *within* a text box, but each *kind* of text (button labels, title, and text boxes) can have a different font.

- **Change the text color.** In the Settings pane, choose a new color from the Text→—Color pop-up menu). iDVD offers 18 colors and shades to choose from. Titles, buttons, and text boxes can each use different colors.

- **Add (or remove) a drop shadow.** Use the Drop Shadow checkbox to add a drop shadow—a faint shadow behind and below the text that creates an easier-to-read, almost 3-D effect.

- **Change the font size.** Adjust the Text→Size slider in the Settings pane to choose a new font size for your selected text. As with fonts, you can pick only one font size per text category.

- **Remove the title.** Highlight the text on the menu and then press the Delete key. The empty title text box remains, but it's invisible. Later, if you like, you can click inside the title box to reopen it and type new text.

- **Remove button text.** To remove the labels from your buttons, select any button and then choose No Text from the Text→Position pop-up menu (in the Settings pane). You've just removed labels from *all* the buttons, not just the selected one.

- **Reposition (icon) button text.** iDVD lets you place button text on any side of the button, or even directly in its center. Select a button and then locate the Text→Position pop-up menu in the Settings pane. Choose a button-label position relative to the button graphic: Top, Center, Bottom, Left, and Right.

- **Align text.** To change the alignment of text (titles, text boxes, or text buttons), select the text and then use the Text→Alignment pop-up menu. Choose from Left, Centered, and Right.

- **Position the title or text box.** You can drag titles and text boxes anywhere on the screen you like. (Be careful not to park one where the *overscanning* effect of older TVs [page 347] might chop off some of your letters. To avoid this problem, choose Advanced→Show TV Safe Area before you drag, taking care to keep the text inside the superimposed guideline rectangle that iDVD now puts onscreen.)

Changing Backgrounds

The menu-screen background sets the tone by providing the look and atmosphere that defines the entire screen. As a result, choosing a new background can add a unique twist to an existing theme.

Background Still Images

Using a graphics file as a backdrop is a lot easier than using a video as a backdrop. You don't have to think about timing and loops, and you don't have to worry about how the motion will interact with your buttons and drop zones.

Adding a background image 1: Preserving drop zones

It's incredibly easy to change the backdrop for a particular menu screen: Just drag any graphics file directly onto the existing background. (Your only challenge: To avoid dropping it onto a button or a drop zone.) You can drag a JPEG file, for example, right out of the Finder, out of iPhoto if it's open, or out of the Photos pane of the Customize drawer. iDVD instantly sets the image as your new menu background.

Adding a background image 2: Overwriting drop zones

If you'd rather cover up any existing drop zones, replacing the background with a single image, drag a graphics file into the Background *well*, identified in Figure 22-2.

Tip: Both of the preceding techniques change only the currently displayed menu screen. To apply the change to *all* menu screens, choose Advanced→Apply Theme To Project.

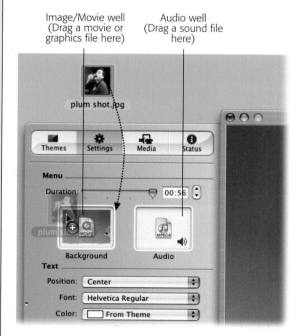

Image/Movie well
(Drag a movie or
graphics file here)

Audio well
(Drag a sound file
here)

Figure 22-2:
In the Customize drawer, click the Settings button. Drag a graphics file into the Background well (from the Finder or from iPhoto, for example). iDVD installs the graphic as the new background. In earlier versions of iDVD, this covered up drop zones but no longer. iDVD 5 fixed this annoying bug and everything now works the way you'd expect it to.

Replacing background images

If you want to try out a different picture in the background, just repeat the steps above. You can drop new graphics as many times as you want; iDVD displays only the most recent one.

Removing background images

If you decide that the original theme's background was superior to your own graphics after all, it's easy enough to restore the original image. On the Settings pane of the Customize drawer, just drag the graphic icon *out* of the Background well. iDVD deletes it, displaying the increasingly familiar puff-of-smoke animation. The original theme's background returns.

Background Video

Instead of a photo background, you can also create moving, animated, *video* backgrounds, just like the ones you find on many commercial Hollywood DVDs. It's far easier to customize your background video than, say, to administer anesthesia to yourself and then extract your own teeth.

Note: In all, iDVD provides three different places to install movies onto your menu screens. The following instructions pertain to only full-screen background videos. Don't confuse video backgrounds with drop zone videos or button videos.

Designing Video Loops in iMovie

Background videos don't have to jump between the end of one play-through and the beginning of the next. If you're willing to take a little time in iMovie, you can eliminate sudden visual changes that create unpleasant jumps. Consider these techniques:

Fade or Wash In and Out: Create a smooth fade out at the end of the movie clip, and a smooth fade in at the beginning, using the Fade In and Fade Out transition styles described in Chapter 15 (or, if you're partial to white, Wash In and Wash Out).

Use Cross Dissolve: If you prefer, you can design your movie so that the end cross-dissolves into the beginning each time it loops.

Move the playhead to 4:02 seconds before the end of your movie. Choose Edit→Split Video at Playhead to break off that 4-second segment into a clip of its own.

Now drag this 4:02-second clip to the front of your movie, add a 4-second cross-dissolve between the transposed clip and the start of your movie, and save your work.

You can choose a different length for the crossfade; just make sure that the transposed clip lasts at least two frames longer than the desired transition time. This method works particularly well on stock footage, such as wind-swept grass, fish in an aquarium, and so forth.

You may discover a couple of drawbacks to this method. First, the start and end audio and video will overlap, and you may not like the results. Second, the background video will, unfortunately, start with the crossfade. There's no way yet to make it start playing from an un-crossfaded spot–iDVD 6, perhaps?

Before you delve into this exciting new career, keep these points in mind:

- **Your video will loop.** Your background video file will play, then restart and play again as long as your audience leaves the menu on the TV screen. There's no way to make a video play just once.

- **iDVD adds both video and sound.** When your imported background video contains a soundtrack, that sound becomes the new soundtrack for the menu screen. It wipes out whatever music came with the theme.

- **iDVD handles timing.** iDVD automatically adjusts the Duration slider (at the top of the Settings pane) to match the length of your movie.

Tip: If you try to drag the Duration slider longer than the length of your movie, weird things happen. Suppose, for example, that you have a 15-second movie, a 20-second bit of audio, and you set the slider to 20 seconds. iDVD plays your movie once, plays 5 seconds more of the start of your movie, and then loops to start your movie again. It's an effect worth avoiding.

Background video selection

Choosing background video can be harder than selecting a still image, for two important reasons:

- **Video moves.** Make sure that the video doesn't hide or overwhelm your titles, buttons, and drop zones. "Audition" your videos and make sure they work with your menus before you burn. In particular, watch for moving objects and scenes that are too bright or too dark.

Tip: You can create a simple washed-out background video by applying iMovie HD's Fog effect. Leave the Wind slider at its factory setting. Drag the Fog slider to "more" and Color to "white," and then click Apply. This effect lightens your video, providing a more suitable backdrop for a DVD menu. Not light enough? Apply it a second time!

- **Motion menus loop.** Unless you take special care when creating your video, menu looping will create sudden, sharp, sometimes distracting transitions between the end and start of your video.

Adding background video 1: Preserving drop zones

iDVD offers two ways to add background video to a menu screen, as shown in Figure 22-2. (Once again, remember that each of them changes only the currently displayed menu screen. To apply the change to *all* menu screens, choose Advanced→Apply Theme To Project after following the steps here.)

This first method ensures that you won't wind up covering any drop zones that are part of your chosen theme.

1. **Bring up the menu screen you want to change.**

   Make sure that the Customize drawer is open.

2. **Switch to the Finder and locate the movie file you want to use as a background.**

   It can be a finished QuickTime movie, the *.mov* reference movie in one of your iMovie project folders, or a new iMovie HD movie project file.

3. **While pressing the Option key, drag the video file onto the menu screen.**

   Avoid all drop zones and buttons. Make sure that the entire menu screen is highlighted (a colored rectangle appears around the edges) before you drop the video.

   Let go of the Option key when the new video appears in the menu background. (The Option key tells iDVD: "I'm installing this movie as a background, *not* as a movie of its own, represented by its own button on the menu.")

Adding background video 2: Covering up drop zones

To replace the background with a single, full-width video that *covers up* any drop zones, press the ⌘ key as you drag a movie file out of the Finder and into the Background well or the background of your iDVD menu. (As usual, avoid drop zones and buttons.) iDVD installs the video (and its audio) as the new background, hiding any drop zones in the process.

Removing background video

If you decide to restore the original background video and audio to your theme, drag the icons out of both the Background well and the Audio well. You'll get an animated puff of smoke with each drag, confirming that you've successfully removed both the audio and video that you had previously installed onto this menu screen.

Choosing Menu Audio

Some of Apple's canned themes come with a preinstalled musical soundtrack, and some don't. If you'd like some music to play during, for example, the Sliding Panes theme, you'll have to install it yourself.

You can also replace the music that comes with any of Apple's themes with a song you like better. In the case of musically challenged themes like Anime Pop, this ability is a true blessing, possibly saving lives and sanity.

- **iTunes method.** If you've got a decent music collection already in iTunes, adding background music is easy. In the Customize drawer, click the Audio button. You'll see a complete list of all your iTunes songs and playlists. Proceed as shown in Figure 22-3.

Tip: Keep in mind that some of the most satisfying and appropriate soundtracks of all are the ones that you create yourself, using GarageBand. Any finished compositions that you've exported from GarageBand show up in this iTunes list, too.

- **Drag-from-the-Finder method.** If you're not a big iTunes user, you can also drag in almost any kind of audio file straight from the desktop. Make sure that you've clicked the Settings button at the top of the Customize drawer, and then drag the audio file directly into the Audio well (identified in Figure 22-2) or onto the menu background.

Incidentally, iDVD doesn't do anything to compensate for background video and background audio that aren't the same length. If the music is too short, it repeats until the video is finished playing, cutting off the music if necessary to start in sync with the video track. If the music is too long, the video repeats until the music ends, cutting off the video mid-repeat. Use the Duration slider in the Settings pane to set the loop time, which applies to both sound and video.

Or, if you're really a perfectionist, you could always use a program like GarageBand to match the soundtrack length to the video. Create a nice fade-out at the end of the audio, and a fade-in at the beginning, so that the looping won't be quite so jarring.

Reminder: This technique affects the background music of only the currently displayed menu screen. To apply the change to *all* menu screens, wrap up by choosing Advanced→Apply Theme To Project. (And make sure you don't exceed your 15-minute total menu-length budget!)

Figure 22-3:
Here's your mini-iTunes, right in the Customize drawer. Use the playlists list at the top, or the Search box at the bottom, to find an appropriate song for your menu screen. Use the Play button (or double-click a song name) to listen to a song before placing it. Finally, drag the song you want directly onto the menu screen to install it there.

Replacing Menu Audio

To replace a custom audio file with another, repeat the steps you used to install the music to begin with. iDVD replaces the current track with the new one.

Removing Menu Audio

To remove audio, drag it out of the Audio well, pictured in Figure 22-2. (When the audio well is empty, it shows a 3-D picture of a speaker.)

If you want to remove *all* audio from your menu screen, you may have to drag twice: Your first drag removes custom sounds, while the second removes the theme sound, if one exists.

Muting Menu Audio

To mute your audio, click the small speaker icon in the corner of the Audio well (Figure 22-3). iDVD disables menu sound and hides the two tiny soundwaves. Click the icon again to restore menu audio. Don't forget to check your audio before burning, as muting the audio in the Settings pane affects the final DVD!

Saving Favorites

After applying all the techniques described so far in this chapter, you may end up creating masterpieces of adapted iDVD themes. Fortunately, iDVD allows you to save and reuse these modified themes after you adjust them to your liking. Here's how to go about it:

1. **Open the Settings pane in the Customize drawer.**

   Click Customize first to open the drawer, if necessary.

2. **Click Save as Favorite (at the bottom of the pane).**

   The Save sheet (dialog box) appears at the top of the window.

POWER USERS' CLINIC

Secrets of the Theme Files

Whenever you save a new Favorite theme, iDVD does a fair amount of administrative work. Behind the scenes, iDVD creates a new theme file on your hard drive. If you decided to share your theme with other account holders, this file appears in the Library→iDVD→Favorites folder. If not, it winds up in your Home→Library→iDVD→Favorites folder. Unlike regular themes, whose names end with the suffix .theme, Favorites use a .favorite file name extension. (See Figure 22-4.)

Why is this important to know? Because it tells you how to remove a saved favorite: Just drag the .favorite file out of the secret folder and into the Trash. The next time you open iDVD, that favorite will no longer appear in the Themes pane pop-up menu.

It's also worth noting that when you create a favorite, iDVD copies all relevant materials, including background audio and video, to the newly created theme. (Don't believe it? To view these materials, navigate to the saved .favorite file. Control-click its icon; from the contextual menu, choose Show Package Contents. Then open the Contents→Resources folder.)

Because iDVD has made copies of your movies, pictures, and soundtrack files, you no longer need to keep the originals, as far as iDVD is concerned. Feel free to discard, rename, or move these components from their original locations on your hard drive.

---

3. **Type the name for your new theme. Turn on "Shared for all users," if you like.**

If you're the only person who uses your Mac, then never mind. But if you share a Mac with other students, workers, or family members, each of whom has a Mac OS X *account,* the "Shared for all users" option makes your new theme available to other people who use the machine. (Otherwise, your masterpiece will appear in the list only when *you* use iDVD.)

4. **Turn off "Replace existing" if you want to create a new entry in the theme list.**

If you turn *on* "Replace existing," iDVD will treat your adapted theme as a replacement for the one you based it on, rather than creating a new entry in the list.

5. **Click OK.**

iDVD saves your theme as a new Favorite. You'll be able to apply it to other DVDs in the future by choosing its name from the Themes pane. (Choose Favorites from the pop-up menu to see its listing.)

Tip: It could happen: You could tire of a saved Favorite. See the box on page 491 for the secret instructions on removing one from your iDVD theme list.

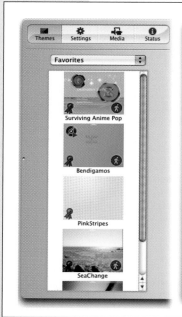

Figure 22-4:
In general, you'll call up your stored Favorite themes by choosing Favorites from the pop-up menu of the Themes pane (left). Behind the scenes, your Favorites are actual icons hidden on your hard drive (right). That's good to know in case someday you want to throw one away.

Buying Sound and Vision

Let's face it. iDVD has a lot of nice themes—but they're not always the *right* themes. Life isn't limited to theaters, road trips, and weddings. There are other holidays, other life events, other styles. If you're celebrating Christmas or Valentine's, graduation day, or a new home, or if you're just looking for a *different* look, then you might want to think about going commercial. With some money to spend, you can expand the way your iDVD projects look and sound.

Third-Party Themes

If you want new themes that work the way built-in iDVD themes do, then buying prebuilt themes can be the way to go. Once installed, third-party themes appear in your iDVD themes list; just click to use. Theme prices start at about $6 for a single theme or about $30 for a pack of six or more. Price, quality, and availability vary. Figure 22-5 showcases several third-party offerings.

Figure 22-5:
You can buy new themes from, for example, www. idvdthemetastic.com or www.idvdthemepak.com. iDVD Themetastic (top) sells themes á la carte, specializing in holiday items. iDVD ThemePak (bottom) sells themes in groups, offering great-looking motion and still graphics. Check their Web sites for some free downloadable samples.

Motion Backgrounds

If you're looking for another way to kick up your DVD productions a notch, then consider buying some commercial video loops for your menu backgrounds. Dozens of companies sell royalty-free video clips for use in movies and television. The price varies from barely affordable to "they've got to be kidding." Page 488 describes how to add a commercial motion background to your iDVD project for a professional flair.

Among the least expensive are Ulead's Pick-a-Video and Pick-a-Video Pro lines (*www.ulead.com/pav_pro*), which, at $60 per disc, cost a fraction of what you'd pay through a normal royalty-free video clearinghouse like FotoSearch (*www.fotosearch.com*). A typical Ulead disc contains about eight motion backgrounds with coordinating still images (ideal for submenus) and video overlays (great for iMovie and Final Cut, not so great for iDVD). The CG Festivities disc (volume 20), for example, has ringing bells, floating balloons, flying stars, streaming ribbons, rotating hearts, and gift boxes, among others.

Stock Art

Don't overlook commercial graphics when customizing your themes. *Stock art* (professional photos and illustrations that you can buy) can add a professional look to your menus without costing a lot of money. The right stock image may look better than the snaps you took with your digital camera.

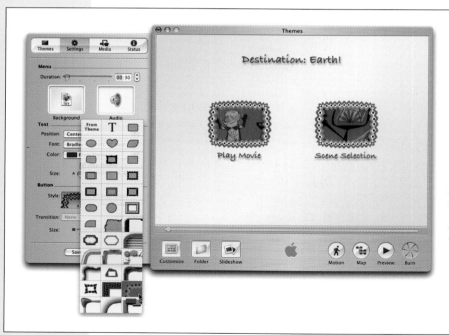

Figure 22-6:
Why buy an entire custom theme when button styles do so much to create an individual feel for your iDVD menus? Mix and match buttons with background art to create a unique look on a budget. These samples are from iDVDThemePak ($40 for 21 custom buttons, or $75 for 42).

Third-Party Buttons

In the crazy, blossoming world of homemade DVDs, there's now such a thing as commercially available *buttons.* They let you add stylish new buttons to your menu screens without having to buy full themes. Stylized buttons can give a personalized twist to even fairly plain backgrounds, as shown in Figure 22-6.

Audio

When you buy songs at the iTunes Music Store, you also buy the right to use them in any iLife creations for your personal use. Why settle for the mayhem of the Kid's Theater audio track when you can throw a buck at Apple and pick the music you really want?

Tip: Stop by *www.freeplaymusic.com* for a vast collection of free, royalty-free music. (It's free for personal, noncommercial use.)

---

iDVD—The DVD-ROM Maker

iDVD's ability to add data files to the DVD-ROM portion of your disc may be its least known feature. When it creates a DVD-ROM, iDVD sets aside a portion of your DVD for normal computer files. This area of the disc won't show up on a DVD player—only on a computer.

With iDVD, you can store any variety of data on your DVD. Here are just a few ways you can use this feature to enhance your disc:

- **Store documents that relate to your DVD contents.** The DVD-ROM area provides a perfect place to store copies of documents that concern the material presented in the DVD. This might include the script used to film a movie, the different versions that eventually led to a final event invitation, extended family narratives, copies of email and other correspondence, and so on. Remember: TV sets aren't much good for displaying text, but a DVD-ROM and a computer can come to the rescue.

  Or store the full-resolution versions of the digital photos featured in your DVD slideshow (one of the most common uses for this feature).

- **Store Web pages.** Web pages are perfect additions to the DVD-ROM disc area. Create a Web site that relates to your DVD and add your source files to the disc. When distributed, your viewers can open these files with an ordinary Web browser. For example, a DVD with a training video can contain supplementary lessons in HTML (Web page) format.

- **Store "email quality" versions of your video.** Use the DVD-ROM area of your disc to store small, compressed versions of your video, or "wallet size" pictures from a slideshow, suitable for email. Now your audience can share your movie experience with other people.

Adding Files to DVD-ROM

iDVD's DVD-ROM file management couldn't be simpler. Just drag icons out of the Finder and into the DVD-ROM Contents list (Advanced→Edit DVD-ROM Contents), as shown in Figure 22-7.

Warning: The DVD-ROM editor in early versions of iDVD 5 (as shown in Figure 22-7) is still fairly buggy. Consequently, your edits may not work as expected. If the program starts acting strangely, stop. Quit from iDVD and relaunch the program before continuing with your DVD-ROM setup.

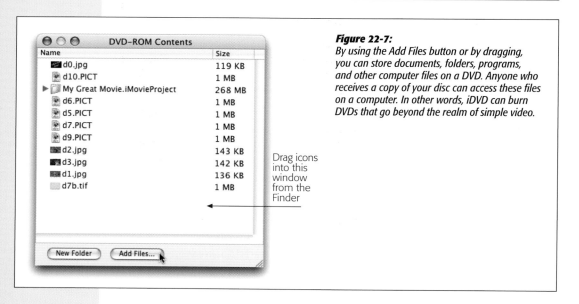

Figure 22-7:
By using the Add Files button or by dragging, you can store documents, folders, programs, and other computer files on a DVD. Anyone who receives a copy of your disc can access these files on a computer. In other words, iDVD can burn DVDs that go beyond the realm of simple video.

Drag icons into this window from the Finder

Organizing DVD-ROM Contents

The DVD-ROM Contents pane lets you organize your files in several ways:

- **Add folders.** Click New Folder to add a folder to your list.

- **Remove things.** Either drag files or folders right out of the list, or select them and then press the Delete key. (Dragging out of the list gives you the cool puff-of-smoke animation.)

- **Move items into or out of folders.** You can drag icons into one of the little folder icons to file them there—or drag them out again to remove them.

- **Reorder the list.** Drag icons up or down the list into new positions.

- **Create subfolders.** Drag one folder into another to create subfolders.

- **Rename a folder.** Double-click the name of a folder to select and edit it. Press Return or Enter when you're finished typing.

- **List/hide folder contents.** You can click a folder's "flippy triangle" to expand it and see what's inside, exactly as in Finder list views.

Archiving Your Project

Ordinarily, iDVD doesn't store any videos, photos, or sounds in your iDVD project file. It remains a tiny, compact file that stores only *pointers* to those files elsewhere on your hard drive.

That's why, if you delete or move one of those media files, iDVD will mildly freak out; you'll see a dialog box listing the pieces it can't find.

In previous versions of iDVD, you couldn't transfer a project from one Mac to another for this very reason. And that meant that you couldn't *design* a DVD on one Mac (one that lacked a DVD burner), and then *burn* it on another. You also couldn't back up your project file, content that you'd included all of its pieces.

Fortunately, Apple packed a solution into iDVD 5. The Archive Project command lets you completely "de-reference" your project, so that the project file *contains* every file that you've incorporated into your project: movies, photos, sounds, theme components, and DVD-ROM files. Your project file is now completely self-contained, ready for backup or transfer to another computer.

It's also now really, really huge.

Follow these steps to produce your archive.

1. **Save your project.**

   If you forget this step, iDVD will remind you.

Figure 22-8:
The Archive Project's Save As panel lets you specify whether you want to include themes and encoded files in your archived project. You can save quite a bit of disk space by leaving these options unchecked. The Size indicator to the right of "Include themes" tells you how much space your project will occupy.

2. **Choose File→Archive Project.**

   The Save As panel shown in Figure 22-8 appears.

3. **Turn the checkboxes on or off, if you like.**

"Include themes" copies your theme files into the project—something that's unnecessary if you're using standard Apple themes. This checkbox is important only if the themes you've used come from other companies, were designed by you, or are modified versions of Apple's originals.

"Include encoded files" is the more important option, because it's very unlikely that all of your sounds, photos, and movies are also on the destination Mac.

Turn the boxes on and off to see how much space you'll recover.

4. **Name the archive file, choose a folder location for it, and then click Save.**

Wait as iDVD builds the new archive. This can take a few minutes, so be patient. You may be working with *very* large files.

Archived projects look like any other projects, in that they use the same .dvdproj extension. But inside, they're very different. For proof, simply open it as a package (page 519). Inside its Contents→Resources folder, new folders called Assets and Themes store the extra archived elements (Figure 22-9).

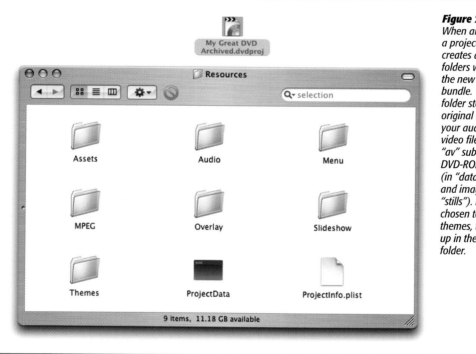

Figure 22-9:
When archiving a project, iDVD creates additional folders within the new project bundle. The Assets folder stores original copies of your audio and video files (in the "av" subfolder), DVD-ROM content (in "data") and images (in "stills"). If you've chosen to save themes, they show up in the Themes folder.

Tip: In order to turn your photos and videos into DVD material, iDVD must encode (convert) them into a format called MPEG. Depending on your Preferences settings, iDVD may constantly be working on this time-consuming task, or it may do the job only when you burn the DVD. Either way, an archived project also stores any MPEG files iDVD has created so far. They'll save you time when you burn the DVD, but they'll make the archive's file size balloon up like a blimp.

If you'd rather keep the file smaller, choose Advanced→Delete Encoded Assets before saving the archive. iDVD removes the remove encoded MPEG files—but you'll pay for this gesture in re-encoding time when you're ready to burn your discs.

Copying the archive to a different Mac

Suppose that you've designed a DVD using a Mac that lacks a DVD burner. Now, as Apple intended, you've used the Archive command to prepare it for transfer to a Mac that *does* have a burner.

Transfer the archive project using any convenient method: copy it across a network, burn it to a CD or a DVD-ROM, copy it onto an iPod, or whatever. (It's too big for email, of course, but you could instead post it on a Web site for downloading.) The

---

Making DVDs Last

Your homemade DVDs (which are "burned" using dyes) probably won't last the 100 years expected of commercial DVDs (which are etched with lasers). But don't get too depressed by the occasional article about homemade DVDs "going bad" in a matter of months. Most cases of "DVD rot" come down to one of two things: problems created during manufacturing or poor handling by their owners.

There's not much you can do about manufacturing errors, apart from buying name-brand blank DVDs.

As for handling, these tips should ensure that your recordable DVDs will last for years:

Store your discs in a cool, dry place. DVD-Rs are sensitive to both temperature and humidity. In an ideal world, DVDs would love to live in a cupboard that's 68 degrees Fahrenheit with 30 to 50 percent humidity. In the real world, room temperature is fine as long as temperature *swings* aren't a fact of life. Recordable DVD's hate large changes in humidity, too.

Keep your discs out of the light. Prolonged exposure to ultraviolet light degrades the organic dyes in the recordable layer, possibly making the data on your discs unreadable. Regular light may also hurt your discs, primarily through heat.

Don't flex your discs. With their laminated polycarbonate layers, recordable DVDs are very sensitive to of bending or flexing. In fact, the quickest way to destroy your disc is to bend it.

So don't. Store your discs in soft envelopes or in cases where you pinch a center hub to release the DVD. Don't store them in CD jewel boxes that have a snap-on hub.

Hold discs by the edges. Fingerprints, scratches, and dust on the disc surface interfere with a laser's ability to read data. DVDs are much more sensitive than CDs in this regard, because the data is crammed together so much more tightly.

Don't stick on labels. Adhesive labels throw off the disc's balance—and might even ruin your drive when the heat makes the glue melt. Instead, use a CD-safe marker to write on your DVD-Rs.

---

project opens normally on the other machine, with all of its pieces intact and ready to touch up and burn.

Disk Images and External DVD Burners

Thanks to a new iDVD 5 feature, you can now save your project as a computer file called a *disk image*. And from there, you can do something that many iDVD fans have always wanted to do: burn DVDs on an *external*, non-Apple DVD burner.

You may have run into the disk-image (.dmg or .img) format before; it's a popular storage format for software you download. It's so popular because you get a single, self-contained file that *contains* many other files, arrayed inside exactly as though they're on a disk. When you open a disk image file, in fact, it turns into a little hard-disk icon on your desktop, with all of its contents tucked inside.

Note: Don't confuse a disk image with a project archive; they're two very different beasts. A disk image is a virtual disk, a bit-for-bit copy of the data that would appear on an actual, physical DVD—it just happens to be stored on a hard drive rather than a DVD.

Project archives, in contrast, contain all the source project material used by iDVD. The only thing that can read or "play back" a project archive is iDVD itself.

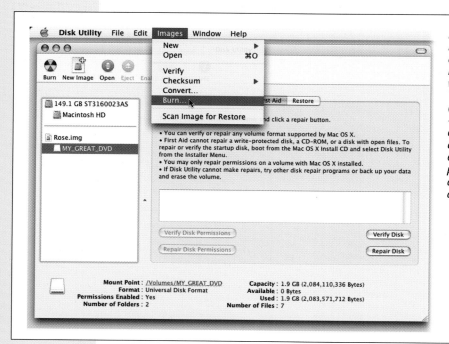

Figure 22-10:
Double-click your disk image in the Finder to make its virtual disk appear. Then open Disk Utility (in your Application-→Utilities folder), click the virtual disk, and choose Imag-es→Burn. Disk Utility prompts you to insert a blank DVD. Do so, and then click Burn.

To turn an iDVD project into a disk image, save it. Then, choose File→Save as Disc Image (Shift-⌘-R). Choose a file name (for example, *Summer Fun.img*) and a location, and then click Save. Now wait as iDVD compresses your movie data and saves it to disk. All of this takes just as long as an actual DVD burning, so now's your chance to catch up on some magazine reading.

When it's all over, you'll find a new .img icon—a disk image—on your desktop.

Disk images are amazingly high-octane, cool stuff for two reasons:

- **You don't have to burn a disc to watch your movies.** Mac OS X's DVD Player program can play back a disk image just as though it's a real DVD. You see all the menus, slideshows, and other iDVD features you've grown to love.

  The trick is to open the Video_TS folder. Never heard of it? Well, it's an important folder on *every DVD ever made*—it's where all the video files reside—and there's one on your disk image, too.

Tip: This is a handy way to test a DVD before you use up a perfectly good blank.

- **You can burn your work to an external drive.** You can use Roxio Toast (a beloved, commercial burning program) or Mac OS X's own Disk Utility program to burn

---

DVD-R, DVD+R, and Drutil

Apple says that iDVD 5 can now record onto more kinds of blank DVDs than ever–not just DVD-R and DVD-RW, but also DVD+R and DVD+RW. (Both kinds of discs play on recent DVD players once they're burned. But most burners can record onto one format or the other–either "-" or "+." Thousands of people, not noticing the difference when they buy blanks at the store, inadvertently buy the wrong kind–and *they* wind up being burned.)

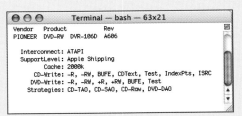

But not all Macs offer this new flexibility. You have to have the right kind of SuperDrive.

So how can you tell? One quick way is to use Terminal, the Unix command program that comes with Mac OS X. It's in your Applications→Utilities folder.

Once the program opens up, you see some Unix codes that end with a $ symbol. At this point, type *drutil info* and press Enter. You've just told Unix to run its *drutil* (disc recorder utility) program.

Instantly, the window fills with useful information about your Mac's disc-recording equipment, including who manufactured it (probably Pioneer).

Near the end of this block of info, you can see, quite clearly, which kinds of DVD it can write (that is, burn). For example, it might say, "DVD-Write: -R, -RW, +R, +RW, BUFE, Test."

If you see only "-R, -RW," then your Mac can't record on DVD+R and DVD+RW blanks. Shop accordingly.

(At this point, you can quit Terminal, unless of course you have other Unix work to do.)

---

the disk image onto a real DVD. Figure 22-10 provides the amazingly simple instructions for this long-sought solution.

- **You can burn copies of your DVD much faster.** The Mac already knows what's on the DVD, and has already encoded it into the proper format. Using Toast or Disk Utility as described above, you can whip out duplicates far faster than you would using iDVD itself.

Professional Duplicating

Maybe you've organized a school play, and you want to sell copies of the performance to parents as a fundraiser. Maybe you want to send out "new baby" videos to your family circle. Or maybe you've used iDVD to create a video brochure of your small business's products and services.

In each of these cases, burning the DVDs one at a time on your own Mac looks more and more like a time-consuming, expensive hassle. Accordingly, when you want to make more than a handful of copies of your DVD, you might want to consider enlisting the aid of a *DVD service bureau*. (DVD service bureaus are middlemen between you and the large replication plants, which don't deal directly with the public.)

Technically, these companies offer two different services:

- **Duplication.** Duplicated discs are copies of your original DVD. Service bureaus use banks of DVD burners, five or ten at a time, that churn out copy after copy on DVD-Rs (the same kinds of blanks as you used).

  You pay for materials and labor, usually by the hour. (Discs with less data burn quicker, producing more discs per hour.) This is the way to go if you need fewer than 100 copies of your disc. (On the other hand, remember that some DVD players don't play DVD-R discs.)

- **Replication.** Replication is designed for huge numbers of copies: 200 and up. In this process, the company actually presses the DVDs just the way Hollywood movie studios do it—and the results play back in virtually every DVD player.

  Replicated discs are produced in factories. When replicated, the data from your master DVD-R is placed on a pressed 4.7 GB "DVD-5" disc—a standard DVDs, not a DVD-R.

  Expect to pay about a dollar per disc for a run of 1,000 discs. Smaller runs will cost more per disc, larger runs less, but $1,000 is about the least you'll pay for a replication job.

Note: DVD service bureaus often call themselves replicators, even though they offer both duplication and replication.

Part Five:
GarageBand

5

Setting Up the Garage

GarageBand is an extremely powerful, easy-to-use program that lets anyone create professional sounding musical recordings. But as you can imagine, not everybody was thrilled when Apple released it.

"They're putting too much power in the hands of amateurs," complained certain professional musicians. "This is like when Apple came out with desktop publishing. Everybody used all 22 fonts in every document, and every flyer and newsletter looked like a ransom note for the next two years."

And sure enough, on the Web sites where people post their GarageBand compositions, you can find a lot of polished, professional sounding, handsomely processed…dreck.

But Apple has a long history of taking elite creative tools, simplifying them, and making them available to the masses. Yes, iMovie lets amateurs make absolutely terrible films—but it has also opened the gates to talented filmmakers who otherwise would have lived in obscurity. One iMovie movie actually won a prize at Sundance in 2003.

In this regard, GarageBand's cultural effects may be even more profound. Until recently, the record companies were the gatekeepers to America's pop-music marketplace, and therefore the dictators of musical taste to the masses. After all, the record companies had sole possession of the two things talented musicians needed to build an audience:

- **Production facilities,** like recording studios, equipment, and engineers, and

- **Distribution channels**—namely, record stores.

As you're already aware, the Internet turned out to be a killer replacement, or at least companion, to the traditional distribution systems. A song, photo, or movie can become popular on the Internet without any help from a record company, publisher, or Hollywood studio—in fact, it can be all over the world in a matter of days. So much for the iron grip the record companies once had on the distribution channels.

With GarageBand, the other shoe has now dropped. Suddenly, no-name singers and undiscovered players can produce recordings that sound like they were made at a $1,000-an-hour recording studio. No longer must great talent remain untapped, or recorded on a tape recorder with an accompaniment by the local church organist. In the *American Idol* era, new artists can grow from the grassroots—and inevitably will.

The Two GarageBand Challenges

Before you fill out your Grammy award application, however, two cautions are in order. First, GarageBand is much more demanding of your Mac than its little i-cousins (iPhoto, iTunes, and so on). It craves memory and processor power like few other programs you'll ever use. Your first challenge in using GarageBand, therefore, is making it comfortable on your Mac.

At first, you may find that job about as exciting as feeding a team of sumo wrestlers who've taken up residence in your guest room. But these pages, especially Chapter 33, will ease the way.

The second challenge you'll face is understanding the two different kinds of musical information that GarageBand can record, edit, and play back (which, not too long ago, required two different pieces of music software).

The point is that if you can overcome these two challenges—the one in your Mac, the other in your brain—GarageBand offers an incredible musical experience. It will let you into a world of music production that was once restricted to people with thousands, or hundreds of thousands, of dollars to invest.

Opening GarageBand

For this guided tour, you need a GarageBand file that's already been completed. You can get yourself one by downloading the GarageBand Examples CD, a "virtual disc" available for free on this book's "Missing CD" page at *www.missingmanuals.com*. (In fact, the rest of this book assumes that you've already done so; see page 508.)

Note: For the moment, don't open GarageBand by double-clicking its icon. (If you do so, the program presents the Project dialog box, which offers you three choices: Start a new project, open an existing one, or quit GarageBand. This box goes away if you switch to the Finder and open a GarageBand song manually.)

Once you've downloaded the GarageBand Examples disk, open the file called "01—Garage Door." After a moment, GarageBand opens and presents you with the simulated studio shown in Figure 23-1.

Playback

You'll probably spend most of your time in GarageBand *playing back* music. That, after all, is the only way to fine-tune and perfect your work.

There's a Play button at your disposal—the big triangle indicated in Figure 23-1—but that's for suckers. Instead, press the Space bar. That's a much bigger target, and a very convenient start/stop control. (You may recognize it as the start/stop control for iTunes and iMovie, too.)

Figure 23-1:
GarageBand isn't just the only iLife program that doesn't start with i; it's also the only program made of "wood." (You can move the window around by dragging any of the wood or "brushed aluminum" surfaces.) At first, the program tends to cower in a smallish window. Click the Zoom button to make it fill your screen—much better!

Zoom button   Playhead   Beat ruler   Timeline (track display)

Track headers   New Track   Play   Tempo   Master volume

Once you've got the 01—Garage Door file open, press the Space bar to listen to this fonky, fonky piece. It's about a minute long.

Tip: If you hear nothing, it's probably because your Mac's speakers are turned down. You can adjust your Mac's overall volume by pressing the volume keys on the top row of your keyboard.

If you have a very old keyboard (or a very non-Apple one), and you therefore lack these keys, you can also adjust the volume by clicking the speaker *menulet* (the ◀)) icon in your menu bar).

(If the speaker control doesn't appear on your menu bar, open System Preferences, click the Sound icon, and then turn on "Show volume in menu bar.")

Whenever music is playing back, you can have all kinds of fun with it. For example:

• **Stop the music.** Press the Space bar again.

• **Slow it down (or speed it up).** Use the Tempo control, as shown in Figure 23-2.

- **Adjust the volume.** You can drag the master volume slider shown in Figure 23-1, or you can press ⌘-up arrow (louder) or ⌘-down arrow (softer). (Hey! Those are the same keystrokes as in iMovie and iTunes!)

- **Jump around in the song.** See the next section for navigation techniques. They work equally well whether the music is playing or not.

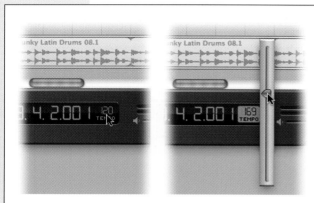

Figure 23-2:
Left: To adjust the tempo (speed) of your piece, position the arrow cursor on the number shown here (which shows how many beats per minute you're getting).

Right: Hold down the mouse button to produce a slider. You're setting the tempo for the entire piece; at least in GarageBand 1.1, you can't program in a change in tempo.

UP TO SPEED

GarageBand Examples CD

A few examples make any learning process easier and more fun—and this book is no exception. Throughout this book, you'll find references to Garage-Band project files, some finished and some intended for you to complete, on something called the GarageBand Examples CD.

You can download these files right now. First, visit *www.miss-ingmanuals.com*. At the top of the page, click the "Missing CD" button.

You arrive at a page listing the downloadable files for the entire Missing Manual series. Under the GarageBand heading, click to download the "GarageBand Examples CD" disk image. It contains all of the sample music you'll work with in this book.

When the download is complete, you'll find on your desktop a file called GarageBand Examples.dmg. That's a disk image file, shown here at lower left.

When you double-click it, you'll find a second icon on your desktop, resembling a hard drive icon, shown here at lower right. (If Safari is your Web browser, just relax and wait as the icon opens automatically.) This is the actual "CD" icon. If you open it up, you'll find all the files for this book. Copy them to a folder on your hard drive, if you like.

If you're in a hurry or using a slow connection, you can also download the various tutorial pieces one at a time. You'll find them listed under the appropriate chapter numbers.

Cycling (Looping)

Looping means playing a certain section of the music over and over again continuously. (That's what musicians call it. Apple calls it *cycling*, because in GarageBand, the word *loop* has a very different meaning. You can read about loops in the next chapter.)

Cycling can be very handy in a number of different situations:

- **Recording.** When you're laying down new music from a MIDI keyboard, Garage-Band merges *everything* you play during all repetitions of the loop. So if your keyboard skills aren't especially dazzling, you can play one hand's part, or even one finger's part, on each "pass" through the loop. GarageBand adds all your passes together.

- **Editing.** In Chapter 26, you'll see that you can edit the notes in Software Instruments sections—adding or deleting notes, rewriting musical lines, and so on. By cycling the section you're editing, you can hear the effects of your edits even while you're making them, in the context of all the other playing instruments.

- **Playing.** Sometimes, it's useful to loop a section just for the sake of listening and analyzing—when a clashing note, for example, is driving you, well, loopy.

To loop a certain section of your piece, start by clicking the Cycle button (identified in Figure 23-3). Or just press the letter C key on your Mac's keyboard.

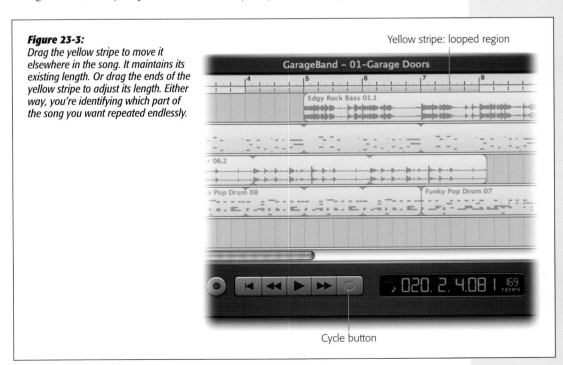

Figure 23-3:
Drag the yellow stripe to move it elsewhere in the song. It maintains its existing length. Or drag the ends of the yellow stripe to adjust its length. Either way, you're identifying which part of the song you want repeated endlessly.

Yellow stripe: looped region

Cycle button

Either way, the Cycle button lights up, and a yellow stripe appears on the beat ruler (the numbered "ruler" strip at the top of the screen). That stripe—the *cycle region*—tells you which part of the song GarageBand intends to repeat.

In a new song, the yellow stripe appears across measures 1 through 4. You can adjust its length and position, though, as shown in Figure 23-3.

If you tap the Space bar now, GarageBand plays *only* the music enclosed by that yellow stripe.

To end the cycling, click the Cycle button again to turn it off, or tap the letter C key again. (You can do that even while the music is playing.)

Navigating the Music

Your current position in the song—that is, the spot from which you'll start recording or playing—is always indicated by the *Playhead* (Figure 23-1) and the moving vertical line beneath it.

You can drag the Playhead around manually, of course; you can also click anywhere in the beat ruler to make the Playhead snap to that spot. You can even jump to a spot in your piece by typing in its time or measures-and-beats position into the digital time display (page 550).

But you'll feel much more efficient if you take the time to learn GarageBand's navigational keyboard shortcuts:

- **Jump back to the beginning.** Pressing either the letter Z key or the Home key rewinds the piece to the beginning without missing a beat.

Tip: On Mac laptops, the Z key is easier to press than the Home key, because triggering the Home function requires first pressing the Fn key in the lower-left corner. Too much trouble.

- **Jump to the end.** Press Option-Z or the End key. That's a great technique for people who like to build up their songs section by section. After you've finished the first part, you can jump to the end of it, ready to begin recording the second.

Note: As far as GarageBand's playback is concerned, the *end* of your piece isn't necessarily where the music stops. It's the point indicated by the small left-pointing triangle on the ruler.

Sometimes you'll trim a piece to make it shorter—and wind up stranding the End marker way off to the right, so that GarageBand "plays" a minute of silence after the actual music ends. In that case, you can fix the problem by dragging the End marker inward until it lines up with the end of the colored musical regions. (You can never drag it inward past the end of the music, though.)

- **Jump back, or ahead, a measure at a time.** As you may recall from your childhood music lessons, a *measure* is the natural building block of musical time. It's usually two, three, or four beats long. (You can think of a *beat* as one foot-tap, if you were tapping along with the music.)

In GarageBand, the measures are indicated on a numbered *beat ruler* (identified in Figure 23-1) that helps you figure out where you are in the music. You can jump forward or back a measure at a time by pressing the left and right arrow keys. (Clicking the Rewind and Fast-forward buttons serves the same purpose.)

Tip: You can also *hold down* the arrow keys, or the onscreen Rewind and Fast-forward buttons, to zoom faster through the piece. Both of these techniques work even when the music is playing.

- **Jump right or left one screenful at a time.** Press the Page Up or Page Down key. (It may feel a little odd to press *up/down* keys to scroll *right/left*, but you'll get used to it.)

- **Zoom in or out.** Once you begin editing your own music, you'll occasionally want a God's-eye view of your whole piece for a visual overview of its structure. Or you'll want to zoom in to see the individual sound waves or notes of a certain musical passage.

  That's what the Control-right arrow and Control-left arrow keystrokes are for. They stretch and collapse the ruler, respectively, making the onscreen representation of your music take up more or less space. (You can also drag the Zoom slider beneath the instrument names, but that's more effort.)

Two Kinds of Music

If you've been reading along with half your brain on the book and half on the TV, turn off the TV for a minute. The following discussion may be one of the most important you'll encounter in your entire GarageBand experience.

Understanding how GarageBand produces music—or, rather, the *two* ways it can create music—is critically important. It will save you hours of frustration and confusion, and make you sound *really* smart at user-group meetings.

GarageBand is a sort of hybrid piece of music software. It can record and play back music in two different ways, which, once upon a time, required two different music-recording programs. They are:

Digital Recordings

GarageBand can record, edit, and play back *digital audio*—sound from a microphone, for example, or sound files you've dragged in from your hard drive (such as AIFF files, MP3 files, unprotected AAC files, or WAV files).

If you've spent much time on computers before, you've already worked with digital recordings. They're the error beeps on every Mac, the soundtrack in iMovie, and whatever sounds you record using programs like SimpleSound, Amadeus, and ProTools. The files on a standard music CD are also digital audio files, and so are the ones you can buy at iTunes.com.

Digital recordings take up a lot of room on your hard drive: 10 MB per minute, to be exact (stereo, CD quality).

Digital recordings are also more or less permanent. GarageBand offers a few rudimentary editing features: You can copy and paste digital audio, chop pieces out, or slide a recording around in time. In GarageBand 2, you can even *transpose* these recordings (make them play back at a different pitch) and change their tempo (make them play back faster or slower), within limits. But you can't delete a muffed note, clean up the rhythms, reassign the performance to a different instrument, and so on.

Now then: To avoid terrifying novices with terminology like "digital recordings," Apple calls this kind of musical material *Real Instruments.*

On the GarageBand screen, Real Instrument recordings show up in blue or purple blocks, filled with what look like sound waves (Figure 23-4).

Software Instruments (MIDI notes)
Green; individual notes visible inside

Figure 23-4:
GarageBand can process two very different kinds of musical material, which Apple calls Real Instruments and Software Instruments. Each offers advantages and drawbacks—but learning the difference is a key part of learning to love GarageBand.

(The color intensifies when a track or region is selected, as shown at bottom.)

Real Instruments (digital audio)
Blue, purple, or orange; sound waveforms inside

MIDI Recordings

You know what a text file is, right? It's a universal exchange format for typed text.

In the early '80s, musicians could only look on longingly as their lyricists happily shot text files back and forth, word processor to word processor, operating system to operating system. Why, they wondered, couldn't there be a universal exchange format for *music,* so that Robin in Roanoke, with a Roland digital piano, could play back a song recorded by Susan on her DX-7 synthesizer in Salt Lake City?

Soon enough, there was a way: the *MIDI file.* MIDI stands for "musical instrument digital interface," otherwise known as "the musical version of the text file." To turn your Mac into a little recording studio, a musician had to rack up three charges on the Visa bill:

- **A MIDI keyboard,** such as a synthesizer.

- **A MIDI interface,** a little $40 box that connects the keyboard to the computer.

- **A MIDI sequencer,** which is software capable of recording, editing, and playing back what you play on the MIDI keyboard.

Although Apple would go bald in horror at using such intimidating language, Garage-Band is, in fact, a *MIDI sequencer.* It can record your keyboard performances; display your performance as bars on a grid, piano-roll style; allow you to edit those notes and correct your mistakes; and then play the whole thing back.

Behind the scenes, GarageBand memorizes each note you play as little more than a bunch of computer data. When it's playing back MIDI music, *you* might hear "Three Blind Mice," but your *Mac* is thinking like this:

```
01|01|000 E3 00|01|000     60
01|02|000 D3 00|01|000     72
01|03|002 C3 00|02|240     102
```

From left to right, these four columns tell the software when the note is played, which note is played, how long it's held down, and how hard the key was struck. That's everything a computer needs to perfectly recreate your original performance.

Musical information that's stored this way has some pretty huge advantages over digital recordings like AIFF files. For example, you can *change the notes*—drag certain notes higher or lower, make them last longer or shorter, or delete the bad ones entirely—whenever you like. You can also transpose a MIDI performance (change its key, so it plays higher or lower) by an unlimited amount, with no deterioration of sound quality. You can even speed up or slow down the playback as freely as you like. When you make such an adjustment, the Mac just thinks to itself, "Add 3 to each pitch," or "Play this list of notes slower."

The downside of MIDI recordings is, of course, that you can't *capture sound* with them. You can't represent singing, or rapping, or sound effects this way. A MIDI file is just a list of notes. It needs a *synthesizer* to give it a voice—like the synthesizer built into GarageBand.

Apple refers to the sounds of GarageBand's built-in synthesizer as *Software Instruments.* They show up in GarageBand as green blocks, filled with horizontal bars representing the MIDI notes that will be triggered. Figure 23-4 makes this distinction clear.

Why It Matters

Why is it important to learn the difference between Real Instruments (sound recordings) and Software Instruments (MIDI data)? Because if you confuse the two, you can paint yourself into some very ugly corners.

For example, suppose you "lay down" (record) the background music for a new song you've written. But when you try to sing the vocals, you discover that the key is way too high for you.

If most of your accompaniment is constructed of MIDI (green) musical material, no big deal. You can transpose the entire band down into a more comfortable range.

But if you'd recorded, say, a string quartet as part of the backup group, you may be out of luck. Those are Real Instruments (digital recordings), and you can't make radical changes to their pitch without some weird-sounding results.

The bottom line: If you began your work by constructing a backup band out of green Software Instruments, you should generally finalize your song's key and tempo *before* you record live audio.

Another common example: GarageBand lets you perform a neat trick with Software Instruments. After recording a part using, for example, a MIDI keyboard, you can reassign the whole thing to a different instrument whenever you like, freely fiddling with the orchestration. You can drag a blob of notes from, say, the Electric Piano track into the Country Guitar track. The Mac doesn't care which sound you use; its job is simply to trigger the notes for "Three Blind Mice" (or whatever).

But although you can drag a blue or purple Real Instrument region into a different Real Instrument track, its instrument sound won't change (see Figure 23-5). In fact, you can *never* change the instrument sound of a Real Instrument.

Figure 23-5:
You can drag a Software Instrument recording into a different Software Instrument track, thereby changing which sound plays those notes. But GarageBand won't let you drag a Real Instrument snippet into a Software Instrument track.

Tracks

When you work in GarageBand, the *timeline* is your primary canvas. It's something like the timeline view in iMovie: a scrolling map of the overall project, marked at the top by a *beat ruler* that helps you figure out where you are in the song.

Tracks are the horizontal, parallel stripes that represent instruments playing simultaneously. Which is lucky, because if this software could play only one instrument at a time, it would have to be renamed GarageSolo.

You'll learn how to *fill* these gray stripes in the following chapters. For the moment, though, it's useful to learn your way around the tracks themselves. After all, like the musicians in a real garage band, they're paid very little, but respond well if you treat them with a little respect.

As you read the following instructions, you might want to follow along by working with the Garage Door song you opened in the previous section (page 506).

Creating a Track

You can add a track in any of three ways.

- **Click the + button below the track names.** You can see this button in Figure 23-1.

- **Choose Track→New Track.** Or press Option-⌘-N.

  Both of these methods open the New Track dialog box shown in Figure 23-6. Click the appropriate tab—Real Instrument or Software Instrument—and then, on the right side of the dialog box, click the *name* of the kind of instrument you plan to add.

  (If you intend to record sound—that is, if what you need is a Real Instrument track—you can bypass the dialog box by simply choosing Track→New Basic Track. Details in Chapter 27.)

Tip: A track's *header* is the dark area at the left edge of the track, where you see its name and icon. To find out which kind of track you're dealing with—Real Instrument or Software Instrument—click the track header. If it turns greenish, you're dealing with a Software Instrument (MIDI) track. If it's purplish, you've clicked a Real Instrument (live recording) track.

You can select one track after another, "walking" through the list of them, by pressing the up or down arrow keys on your keyboard.

Figure 23-6:
A certain track can handle either a Real Instrument (sound file) or a Software Instrument (MIDI notes), so you have to tell GarageBand which sort of instrument you intend to add. If you're going to record a Real Instrument, also specify which effects you want GarageBand to add to the track, like reverb or EQ (equalization). Details in Chapter 28.

If you've installed additional instruments—some of Apple's Jam Packs, for example—you can isolate them by choosing them from the pop-up menu that now says Show All.

• Drag a loop into an empty gray spot in the *timeline* (the track display area). Chapter 24 covers this method in delicious detail.

In any case, a new track appears *below* all the existing tracks.

Tip: If you have a standard, preferred "combo"—drums at the bottom, bass line above that, then piano, then guitar, and so on—you can save a lot of time by building an empty GarageBand template with this track structure. Save this empty file to your desktop. Each time you want to work from this template, open it—and then before filling it with music, choose File→Save As and name the song you're about to create.

The number of simultaneous tracks that GarageBand can play depends on the horsepower of your Mac and which *kind* of tracks they are; Software Instruments make the Mac work a lot harder than Real Instrument recordings. On slower Macs, four or five tracks is about the limit; 10 or 12 tracks is typical on a Power Mac G4. If you have a fully tricked-out, top-of-the-line Power Mac G5 loaded with RAM, then you can build tracks into the dozens.

Fortunately, there's a whole chapter's worth of tips and tricks for helping GarageBand overcome the strain of track-intensive compositions waiting in Chapter 33.

Tip: As you add and work with tracks, keep your eye on the Playhead handle. As described in Figure 23-7, it's an early-warning system that lets you know when you're overwhelming your Mac.

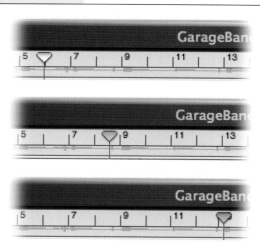

Figure 23-7:
As you play and record music, the Playhead triangle darkens—from white, through ever darker shades of orange and red—to indicate how much trouble your Mac is having. If it spends a lot of time in the red, you're approaching your maximum track limit.

Rearranging Tracks

You can rearrange your tracks' top-to-bottom order just by dragging them vertically. You might, for example, like to keep the track you're working on up at the top where it's easy to find. Or maybe you like to keep your tracks in traditional "score order" (that is, as the instruments would appear in standard full-orchestra sheet music).

Deleting a Track

Before you nuke one of your tracks, scroll through the whole thing to make sure you're not about to vaporize some important musical material. (Consider zooming out—tap Control-left arrow repeatedly—until the entire track fits on your screen.)

Then click the track header to select it. Choose Track→Delete Track, or press ⌘-Delete, to send the track into the great sheet music stack in the sky. (Of course, GarageBand's amazing Undo command can resurrect it if necessary; see the box on page 520.)

Renaming a Track

Click a track's header to select it, and then click carefully, once, on its name. It's now a simple matter to edit the track's name, as shown in Figure 23-8.

Figure 23-8:
If a track header is already selected, click once on the track's name to open its "renaming rectangle." If not, click inside the track header's colored area first, then click the track name. (Just don't double-click the track name; you'll open up a dialog box by accident.) Hold your breath and remain very still. At last, the name-editing box appears.

Edit the name by typing. Then press Return or Enter, or click somewhere else in GarageBand, to make the new name "stick."

Track Characteristics

The importance of the New Track dialog box shown in Figure 23-6 depends on what kind of musical material you intend to record (that is, which of the two tabs you click):

- **Real Instrument.** This tab lists instruments, all right, but they actually refer to *effects presets* that contain canned settings for reverb, echo, and other processing effects that have been optimized for each instrument type. The actual instrument sound is determined by your microphone or whatever electronic instrument you hook up to your Mac. Chapter 27 has details.

- **Software Instrument.** This tab also lists instruments, but here, you're choosing an instrument *sound* that will play when you press the keys of your MIDI keyboard. Details in Chapter 26.

Tip: Either way you can also choose an icon for the track, using the pop-up menu at the lower-left corner. Apple gives you 68 little graphics to choose from—every instrument in GarageBand, plus silhouettes of singers. (These are purely graphic ornaments; they don't affect the sound in any way.)

To open this palette of icons, by the way, you don't have to click the tiny, down-pointing triangle, as you might expect. Instead, click squarely on the icon itself. The broader target means quicker access.

The appearance of the New Track dialog box is not, fortunately, the only chance you get to adjust these parameters.

You can summon the same box at any time, even after recording into the track, by double-clicking the track header, or, if a track is already selected, by choosing Track→Track Info (⌘-I). The resulting dialog box is now called Track Info, but it looks overwhelmingly familiar.

Note: In fact, when you open the Track Info dialog box, you get a Details button at the bottom that you *don't* get in its New Track dialog box. Details on effects in Chapter 28.

You also get a Master Track tab at the top of the dialog box; it's described in Chapter 29.

Muting and Soloing Tracks

Most of the time, GarageBand plays all of your tracks simultaneously—and most of the time, that's what you want.

Sometimes, though, it's useful to ask one track to drop out for a minute. You might want to mute a track when:

- You've recorded two different versions of a part, and you want to see which one sounds better.

- You're trying to isolate a wrong note, and you want to use the process of elimination to figure out which track it's in.

Figure 23-9:
You can tackle the on/off status of your tracks in two ways: either by specifying which ones don't play (by turning on their Mute buttons), or by specifying which tracks are the only ones that play (by turning on their Solo buttons).

- The Playhead is bright red, indicating that the Mac is gasping under its load of tracks. So you'd like to lighten its burden by shutting off a couple of tracks without deleting them forever.

Silencing a track is easy: Just click the little speaker icon below the track's name (see Figure 23-9). Or, if the track header is selected, just tap the letter M key on your keyboard.

The speaker, officially called the Mute button, "lights up" in blue, which means: "I'm shutting up until you change your mind." The regions of notes in that track grow pale to drive home the point. (You can turn the Mute button on or off *while* the music is playing—a great way to compare your mix with and without a certain instrument.)

There's nothing to stop you from muting *more* than one track, either. If you need the entire percussion section to sit out for a minute, so be it.

Of course, if you find yourself muting more than half of your tracks, you should be using the *Solo* button instead. That's the tiny pair of headphones right next to the Mute button.

UP TO SPEED

The Weirdness of the Files

Veteran Mac fans know that some programs, like Word and TextEdit, create documents—that is, individual file icons on the hard drive.

Other programs, like iMovie, create project folders filled with supporting elements like sound and movie clips.

GarageBand falls into a third category unto itself.

When you save a new GarageBand song, it appears to be a standard, self-contained document file. You'll soon discover, though, that it doesn't act like a document file. For example, you can't attach it to an outgoing email message in Entourage unless you first compress it as a .zip or .sit file.

Turns out GarageBand creates a sort of hybrid, a cross between a folder and a file, known as a package. A Mac OS X package looks like an icon, but acts like a folder, in that it contains other files and folders.

In times of troubleshooting—for example, when you're trying to figure out why a certain GarageBand "document" is

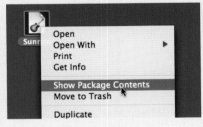

so big—you can actually open up one of these packages to see what's inside.

To do so, Control-click the GarageBand song icon and, from the shortcut menu, choose Show Package Contents, as shown here. Lo and behold, a new window opens, exactly as though you'd opened a folder.

Inside you'll find two important elements. First, there's the project-Data file, which is the actual "edit list" that tells GarageBand what to play when. (If you're familiar with iMovie, the projectData file is the equivalent of the iMovie project document.)

Second, there's the Media folder (again, exactly as in an iMovie project folder). Here, GarageBand stashes several kinds of song component: any digital audio files you've recorded (singing tracks, for example); copies of sound files you added to a composition by dragging them into the program from the Finder; and in some cases, copies of any loops you've used in your masterpiece.

Here again, the point is to control which tracks play, but the logic is now reversed. When you click the headphones (or, if the track header is selected, press the letter S key on your Mac's keyboard), that's the *only* track you hear. The note regions in all *other* tracks grow pale.

Oxymoronic though it may sound, you can actually Solo as many tracks as you like. All *other* tracks are silent.

To turn a track's Mute or Solo button off again, click it again (or press the M or S key a second time).

GEM IN THE ROUGH

There's Undo, and Then There's Undo

GarageBand offers a multiple-level Undo command. That is, you can take back more than one editing step, backing up in time. GarageBand, in fact, can take back the last 30 steps. If you choose the Edit→Undo command (or press ⌘-Z), you can rewind your file closer and closer to its condition when you last saved it. (Or if you haven't saved the file, Undo takes you closer and closer to the moment when you opened it.)

That fine print may startle people who are used to, say, Microsoft Word, which lets you keep undoing even past the point of saving a document. It's a good argument for saving a GarageBand file less frequently—because once you

save the document, you lose the ability to undo changes up to that point.

Of course, if you really do want to rewind your work all the way back to the instant when you last saved the piece, you can bypass all of those Edit→Undos and instead choose File→Revert to Saved. GarageBand tosses out all the work you've done since the last save.

And one last thing: If you rewind too far, and you Undo your way past a good edit you made, you also have a multiple Edit→Redo command at your disposal. In effect, it undoes the Undos.

Loops

Apple claims that GarageBand can be a blast even if your mastery of music never even progressed to the "Chopsticks" stage. And it's true: GarageBand lets you create authentic-sounding, studio-quality music even if you can't carry a tune, let alone a tuba. This chapter, dear nonmusicians, is sure to be one of your favorites.

That's because GarageBand comes with over 1,100 *loops*—short, prerecorded snippets performed in recording studios by professionals who most certainly do know their instruments. According to Apple, some of GarageBand's Motown drum loops, in fact, were played by the original studio musicians who recorded classic Motown hits like "My Girl" and "I Heard It Through the Grapevine."

Loops are only a few seconds long, but they're designed to repeat seamlessly for as long as you specify. That's a serious help when you want to create a drum part, for example.

Using some extremely advanced technological mojo, GarageBand manages to make every loop sound good with almost any other. So all you have to do is choose the drum beat, bass line, and guitar noodling you like (for example), and trust GarageBand to make them all sound like they were recorded in perfect sync. As you'll see, it's all about dragging and dropping.

Starting a New GarageBand Project

If you click Create a New Project in the Project dialog box (when you open GarageBand for the first time), or when you choose File→New, you get the box in Figure 24-1.

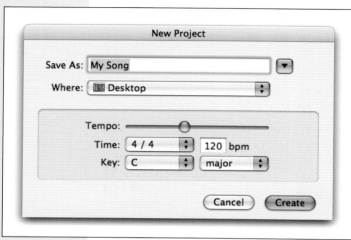

Figure 24-1:
The overwhelming majority of Garage-Band masterpieces that people have post-ed online are built with these settings: 120 beats per minute, 4/4, key of C. Clearly, most people do not, in fact, ever get around to changing these parameters.

Incidentally, if you're interested in learn-ing about time signatures, keys, tempo, and so on, see Appendix A for a crash course.

If you *do* know a little bit about music or the Mac, you can use the New Project dialog box to specify details like this:

- **What to call your new piece.** You'll almost certainly want to type a new title into the Save As box—"My Song" gets old fast.

- **Where to file it.** The program always hopes that you'll keep all your compositions in your Home→Music→GarageBand folder, which the iLife installer created. You can, of course, choose to file it anywhere else (press ⌘-D, for example, to save it onto your desktop). But you'll have to redirect GarageBand in this way each time you create a new piece.

- **The song's tempo.** This means how fast or slow it is, expressed in beats per minute. You can either drag the Tempo slider or type a new number into the "bpm" box just below it.

  You don't really have to know what you're doing at this stage. You can adjust a song's tempo at any time, even after you've recorded it.

- **The song's time signature (meter).** Now you're getting into musician territory; this setting specifies how many *beats* (foot-taps, you might say) there are in a measure. Put another way, the first number in a time signature—like the upper digit in the time signature 4/4—is what you'd count off to your garage band to get it off to a synchronized start. ("And-a one! Two! Three! Four!")

  This is a rather important decision. You *can* change your mind later (page 634), but not without introducing a good bit of chaos into whatever music you've already recorded. (You can't change the time signature midway through a piece, either.)

Note: GarageBand offers a choice of some less common time signatures like 9/8 (think *Jesu, Joy of Man's Desiring*), 2/4 (every march you've ever heard), and 12/8 ("Everybody Wants to Rule the World"). GarageBand's *loops,* however, are designed to work only in 4/4. For most of the other time signatures, no loops at all are available. A couple show up for 2/4 and 6/8, but they're actually mislabeled and don't fit into the beats. The GarageBand Jam Packs expand the selection slightly.

In short, GarageBand is prepared to handle time signatures other than 4/4—but only if you intend to record your *own* musical performances, as described in the following chapters. So, if you want to work with loops, you're stuck with 4/4.

- **What key your piece is in.** The *key* of a piece specifies where it falls on the piano keyboard (for example)—how high or low it is, in other words.

  If you have enough musical knowledge to understand keys, now is the time to choose the one you want. You can *transpose* GarageBand's loops and your own recorded performances at any time (page 577)—that is, move them into a different key. But live digital recordings (made susing a microphone or electronic instrument) and GarageBand's own Real Instrument loops start to distort if you shift them too far from their starting points.

Note: The key you choose also affects which loops are available to you, because GarageBand ordinarily hides the loops that are far from the key you choose. More on this topic on page 534.

Once you've made your choices, click OK. After a moment, you see a screen that looks something like Figure 23-1 on page 507, except that it's empty. GarageBand is now a blank canvas—ready to receive input, captain! It starts you off with a $50,000 Yamaha C7 grand piano sound and (if no external keyboard is attached) a 29¢ onscreen keyboard to "play" it.

For the moment, close the little keyboard by clicking the tiny, round Close button at its upper-left corner. When you get time, you can read all about it on page 554.

The Loop Browser

If you're following along with this chapter, leave the one empty Grand Piano track on the screen. Close the onscreen keyboard for the moment. (If you've been fooling around on your own, start a fresh project by choosing File→New.)

Now, if the plan is to build a piece of music out of 1,100 musical spare parts, you'd better have a *very* organized toolbox. Sure enough, GarageBand offers an extremely clever loop-finding system called the Loop browser. To open it, use one of these three methods:

- Click the eyeball icon below the list of tracks, as shown in Figure 24-3.

- Choose Control→Show Loop Browser.

- Press ⌘-L.

Later, you can hide the Loop browser by repeating the same step (except that the menu command will say Hide Loop Browser).

Tip: When you first open the Loop browser, you're seeing only a sampling of the musical smorgasbord Apple has prepared for you. Only about *half* of the Loop browser buttons—35 of them—are visible.

To view the rest of the buttons, drag the dark gray brushed metal divider bar upward into the Track area, as shown in Figure 24-2.

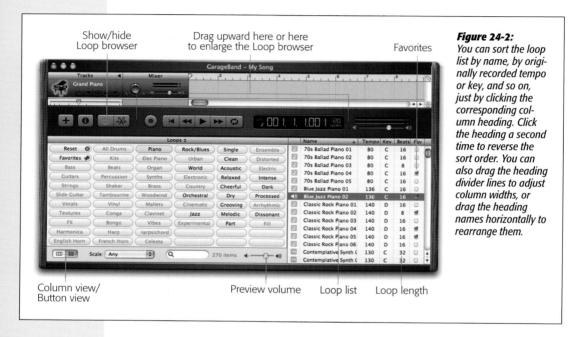

Figure 24-2:
You can sort the loop list by name, by originally recorded tempo or key, and so on, just by clicking the corresponding column heading. Click the heading a second time to reverse the sort order. You can also drag the heading divider lines to adjust column widths, or drag the heading names horizontally to rearrange them.

At this point, GarageBand offers three different ways to search its massive database of juicy sonic tidbits to locate the one you're seeking: Button View, Column View, and the Search box.

Loop Quest 1: Button View

Here's how to use the grid of oval Loop browser buttons:

1. **Click the oval button named for the instrument you want.**

    Eventually, you'll cultivate your own work routine. But in the recording biz, it's common to lay down the *rhythm tracks* first—the bass, guitar, and drums, for example. You can then record the melodic lines, like the vocals or instrumental solos, on top of that background.

    Suppose, then, that you're hunting for just the right drum pattern for a new song you're writing. Click Drums.

At this point, the Drums button remains lit in blue, and the other instrument buttons fade out. The right side of the Loop browser displays a long, scrolling list of drum riffs. These are your loops.

The light gray readout next to the volume slider at the bottom of the window displays how many of GarageBand's 1,100 loops are in the category you're now browsing ("282 items," for example).

2. **To listen to a loop, click its name.**

Immediately, GarageBand plays that prerecorded snippet—cleverly adjusting the loop's speed to match the current tempo of your piece—and then repeats it endlessly. (Now you know why it's called a loop.) A little speaker icon, as well as some colored highlighting, lets you see at a glance which loop is playing.

Drag the slider at the bottom edge of the window to adjust the loop volume.

To stop the playback, either click the name again, or click a different loop name to hear *it*.

GEM IN THE ROUGH

Redesigning the Button Browser

The buttons of the Loop browser are a nifty way to hunt through hundreds of loops. Only trouble is, you now have to hunt through dozens of buttons.

Fortunately, you can rearrange the buttons in the browser in either of two ways.

The point, of course, is to arrange the buttons so they're easy to find. For example, you might want to install the most useful buttons into the cluster of the top 35, making them visible when you initially open the Loop browser. That way, you needn't expand the Loop browser manually every time you open GarageBand.

Method 1: If you grab a button with the mouse and drag it on top of another button, the two buttons swap places when you let go.

Method 2: Control-click any button that you'd like to replace with another. From the shortcut menu that appears, choose the new button name, as shown here. You've just changed the name and function of the button you clicked.

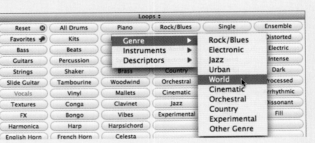

The advantage of this approach is that those shortcut menus offer the complete list of GarageBand buttons, including many that don't generally appear. (The drag-to-swap method, by contrast, only lets you shuffle buttons that are already on the screen.)

Oh, and if you ever want to put all the buttons back where Apple had them, choose GarageBand→Preferences, click General, and click the Reset button.

Tip: Whenever you find a loop that you especially like, or think you'll use again, turn on its Fav checkbox, usually located in the rightmost column. (Make your GarageBand window wider if you don't see this column of checkboxes.) You've just added it to your list of Favorite loops.

At any time, you can recall these favorite loops by clicking the Favorites button at the left edge of the Loop browser. You've just saved yourself the effort of crawling through the 1,100 choices to find that awesome Nordic Fiddle again.

Now, you can have hours of fun just scrolling through this vast list of drum loops, muttering, "Hey! That's the one from 'Brick House'!" But over 275 drum loops come with GarageBand. By the time you find just the right hip-hop beat, hip-hop wouldn't be hip anymore.

That's why GarageBand comes equipped with features that help narrow the loops to just the one that suits the piece you're building.

3. **Click a category or adjective button: Country, Jazz, Relaxed, Acoustic, and so on. In fact, click as many as you like.**

MUSIC CLASS

Scale: Any

The pop-up menu on the bottom edge of the Loop browser, called Scale, offers another way to filter GarageBand's list of loops. It lets you view only the loops that, musically speaking, "go" with certain kinds of scales.

A scale is the series of notes—you know, "Do, re, mi," and so on—that fits a particular key. Most simple melodies are constructed of only the seven notes in a particular scale.

Most GarageBand loops sound good when played simultaneously with other loops—but not all of them. For instance, a guitar loop playing in a major key and a piano loop in a minor key will clash horribly. That's why the Scale pop-up menu exists—so that you can match your loops, major with major or minor with minor.

Your options are:

Any: You're seeing all loops. Nothing is hidden.

Minor: A minor key, and its associated scale, is one that sounds sad or angry. (To hear a melody played using a minor scale, set the Scale pop-up menu to Minor. Then, in the Loop browser, click Reset and then Guitars. Click the

loop called Acoustic Noodling 03.)

Minor keys are fairly rare in pop music, but when you're feeling a little depressed, GarageBand can accommodate you. Choose this option to display only loops played on minor scales.

Major: A major key, and its associated scale, sounds happy. Most pop music uses this kind of scale. To hear the idea, set the Scale pop-up menu to Major. Then click Reset, Guitars, and Acoustic Picking 02.

Neither, Good For Both: Many loops don't have any particular key, pitch, or scale. Drums, for example, have no pitch, so they "go" with music in any key without clashing. Certain bass, guitar, and string loops are more or less scale-less, too—meaning they could go with either major or minor music. (Musicians' Note: Octaves, unisons, and open-fifth "power chords" are some examples. The common thread: You don't hear the third of the chord.)

In any case, after fiddling with this pop-up menu, be sure to set it back to Any, so you won't later wonder what happened to your huge master list of loops.

Each time you click one of these buttons, GarageBand filters its list of loops to show you only the ones that match your description—and dims another set of oval buttons. For example, if you click Drums, and then Electronic, and then Distorted, you wind up with a list of only five loops.

This method isn't utterly foolproof; you might disagree with the categorization of some of the loops. It's not crystal clear how GarageBand is doing its filtering, either. For example, once you've clicked Drums and then Jazz, turning on the Part and Clean buttons doesn't produce any changes in the list.

Still, most of the time, you can find your way to your desired loop in just a few clicks.

Tip: Most people start drilling down by clicking the instrument button (like Piano) first, followed by the category buttons (Clean, Cheerful, and so on). But in fact, you can start with *any* button and work backward: Click Cheerful first, then Piano, and so on.

4. **Once you've added a loop to your piece, or if you give up on your hunt and want to start over, click the Reset button to turn off all buttons and start anew.**

On the other hand, you don't have to return quite that far. It's often less time-consuming just to *back up* in your button-clicking.

To do that, just turn *off* the most recent blue buttons that you've turned *on*. For example, suppose you click Drums, then Electronic, then Cheerful, only to find that there's just one loop in this category. If you decide you've barked up the wrong tree, just click Electronic (for example) to backtrack to the intersection of the Drums/Electronic categories. This way, you can begin drilling down again.

Loop Quest 2: Column View

This business of narrowing your loop quest by clicking successive descriptive buttons is a pleasure, but it isn't right for everyone. Because all 63 of the loop buttons are

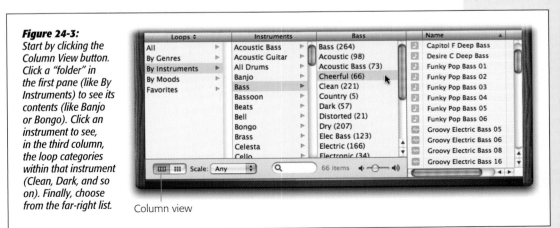

Figure 24-3:
Start by clicking the Column View button. Click a "folder" in the first pane (like By Instruments) to see its contents (like Banjo or Bongo). Click an instrument to see, in the third column, the loop categories within that instrument (Clean, Dark, and so on). Finally, choose from the far-right list.

Column view

displayed in one big nonhierarchical pile, it's not always clear which are instrument categories, which are mood categories, and so on.

Column view solves that problem rather quickly. It turns the Loop browser into a close cousin of the Finder column view, so that you can drill down in successive panes and never lose track of the path you took (Figure 24-3).

Because the third column shows, in parentheses, how many loops fall into each category, Column View provides a good deal of insight into how GarageBand's loops come categorized. There are 11 categories in the Flute group, for example (Cheerful, Orchestral, Acoustic, and so on), but that doesn't mean that you've got dozens and dozens of flute samples. In fact, GarageBand comes with only four flute licks, and the same set of four appears in each of the 11 Flute categories.

Loop Quest 3: The Search Box

Once you've worked with GarageBand awhile, you may not feel quite so browsy as you did when you first began fooling around with it. Eventually, you come to know which loops you have, and then wish for a more direct way to pluck them out of the haystack of music.

That's what the Search box is for (on the bottom edge of the Loop browser). You may not remember, for example, that a certain hyper-funky keyboard loop was played on something called a clavinet; you remember only that its name was something like "Cop Show."

Auditioning: The Loop's Big Break

Once your GarageBand skills grow beyond staying up into the wee hours just clicking loop names and giggling with power-mad glee, you may begin to hunt down the little efficiencies that mark the skilled software master. And when it comes to choosing just the right loop for the piece you're building, that means learning to use loops with cycling.

As described on page 509, cycling is when GarageBand repeats a certain section of the music endlessly. Cycling is a great feature when you're experimenting to find just the right loop to add, or as you practice what you're going to record on top of it.

To loop a certain section of your piece, click the Cycle button (identified on page 509), or press the letter C key. The Cycle button lights up, and a yellow stripe appears on the beat ruler to identify which part of the song GarageBand will repeat. Adjust its length and position, as shown back in Figure 23-3.

If you tap the Space bar now, GarageBand plays only the music indicated by that yellow stripe.

Now here's the cool part: If you click a loop's name in the Loop browser, you'll hear the loop begin playing in perfect sync with the music you've already installed in the piece. It may even wait a moment to start playing the loop, to ensure that the loop will play together with the rest of the "band."

Now, previewing loops by selecting them as the music plays works whether cycling is on or off. But with cycling on, it's easier to audition (listen to) one loop after another, simply by clicking each one's name, rather than having to keep rewinding and starting the playback over. Better yet, just press the up- or down-arrow key to walk through the list of loops, listening to each in turn.

To stop playback, press the Space bar; to turn off cycling, click the Cycle button again to turn it off, or tap the letter C key again.

So you type *cop* into the Search box and press Return or Enter. Instantly, GarageBand reveals all eight of its Cop Show loops, without requiring that you drill down through the categories (see Figure 24-4).

Figure 24-4:
In light gray lettering, the text just to the right of the Search box lets you know how many loop names match your search. (It's sometimes a wake-up call to let you know that you need to scroll the list in the far-right column.)

And now, three notes about the Search box:

- It searches only within the *currently selected* Loop browser category (Bass→Acoustic, for example). If you intend to search the entire GarageBand loop collection, therefore, click the Reset or All button first.

- You can use it to search either for a loop's name or for its category. That is, you can search for terms like *intense* or *strings,* even if those words don't actually appear in any loop names.

- To empty the Search box (and return to seeing all loops), click the circled X at its right end.

Placing a Loop

Suppose that you've used one of the three loop-finding techniques, and you've homed in on just the right loop. Now it's time to install it into your song.

To do that, drag the loop's name upward and into position, as shown in Figure 24-5. The leftmost edge of the loop will align with the spot where you release the mouse.

What happens when you release the mouse depends on *where* you release the mouse.

Drag into a Blank Gray Area

If you drag into an empty track area, you create a brand new track, already set to play the instrument whose name you dragged (Figure 24-5). At the beginning of your song-building session, this is the technique you'll probably use the most. (It makes no difference whether you release the mouse in the light gray area beneath the existing music or the darker gray area beneath the existing track headers.)

Tip: If you *Option*-drag a green Software Instrument loop into an empty track area, GarageBand *converts* that green Software Instrument into a blue Real Instrument loop—and creates a Real Instrument track to hold it.

This is an important trick when your Mac is wheezing under the weight of too many tracks. See the box on the facing page for the explanation.

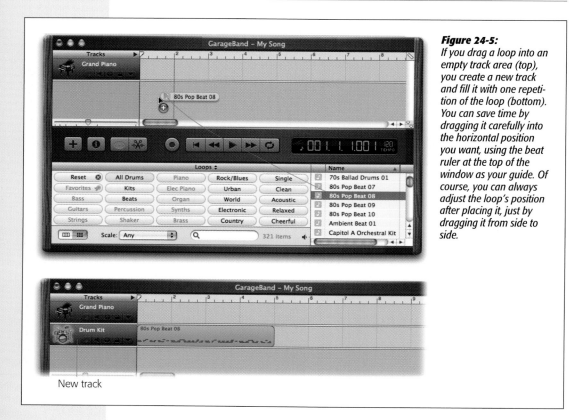

Figure 24-5:
If you drag a loop into an empty track area (top), you create a new track and fill it with one repetition of the loop (bottom). You can save time by dragging it carefully into the horizontal position you want, using the beat ruler at the top of the window as your guide. Of course, you can always adjust the loop's position after placing it, just by dragging it from side to side.

New track

On the other hand, once you've added a track for Cool Upright Bass, for example, there's little point in creating a second or third Cool Upright Bass track for bass licks that occur later in the song. Simply keep all of your Cool Upright Bass in a single track. That's why you can also drag into an existing track. (Read on.)

Drag into an Existing Track

If you drag a loop into a track that's assigned to the *same* instrument sound, you get just what you'd expect. For example, if you drag the Acoustic Noodling 04 loop into an Acoustic Guitar track that you created earlier (by dragging Acoustic Noodling 01 into place, for example), you get more Acoustic Noodling, just as you'd expect.

But suppose you drag a loop into a track whose instrument *doesn't* match the loop you're dragging. For example, suppose you drag Dreamy Guitar Pattern 01 into a Grand Piano track. What now?

GEM IN THE ROUGH

The Secret Lives of Green Loops

If you've managed to grasp the difference between Garage-Band's two kinds of musical building blocks, congratulations. If you've never worked with music on the Mac before, getting over this conceptual hurdle is a huge accomplishment. (To review: Software Instruments = green = MIDI data = editable notes. But Real Instruments = blue or purple = digital audio = frozen as is.)

But wait—there's more.

It turns out that GarageBand's green loops have a little secret. Yes, each contains MIDI note-trigger information, represented by those horizontal bars. But behind the scenes, each one also contains a digital-audio representation of itself—a true-blue AIFF recording. (For proof, switch to the Finder, press ⌘-F, and search for the name of a green GarageBand loop, like Deep Electric Piano. You'll find out that each Software Instrument loop shows up as an .aif file—an AIFF sound file—as it sits in a folder on your hard drive. Each is also far larger than a pure MIDI file would be.)

Go ahead, ask it: What's the point?

Turns out it's actually easier for the Mac to play back digital recordings (blue or purple) than MIDI material (green), because it doesn't have to synthesize the sound itself, in real time. Therefore, if your Mac is having trouble playing back the number of tracks you need, converting green loops into blue ones makes them easier for the Mac to play back. Blue loops require less processing power to play back, so you can use more tracks and effects in a piece.

The downside is that you lose all the great features of MIDI loops, like the freedom to change its notes, transpose it into any key you like, make different notes play louder or softer, adjust its post-processing effects (like reverb), and so on. You're freezing it as it is, complete with whatever effects it came with.

Now, if your Mac isn't having trouble managing all your tracks, you can ignore this entire discussion. But if this MIDI-to-AIFF conversion interests you, here's a summary of the three ways to pull it off.

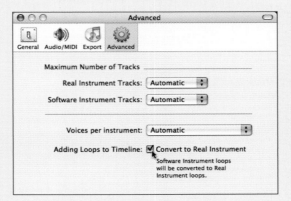

First, you can drag a green loop into a blue (Real Instrument) track.

Second, you can Option-drag a green loop out of the Loop browser into an empty spot in the gray timeline area. GarageBand converts the loop into digital audio and creates a new Real Instrument track to hold it.

Finally, you can request that GarageBand always convert green loops into noneditable blue ones, every time you drag one into your piece. Just choose GarageBand→Preferences, click the Advanced tab, turn on "Convert to Real Instrument" (shown here), and close the dialog box.

At that point, the effect of the Option key changes. Now, Option-dragging a green loop does not make it change into a blue one; GarageBand leaves the green loop green.

To sum up, the Option key always reverses the status of the "Convert to Real Instrument" checkbox in GarageBand's preferences.

Here's where things can get wacky—and confusing. To understand what's going on, you must understand the distinction between Real Instruments (digital recordings—blue or purple in GarageBand) and Software Instruments (MIDI note data—green); see the previous page for a refresher.

In any case, here's what happens when you drag:

- **Green loop→Green track with different sound.** Suppose you drag a Software Instrument loop into a Software Instrument track—but the instrument doesn't match. To use the example above, let's assume you drag Dreamy Guitar Pattern 01 into a Grand Piano track.

  In that case, something rather cool happens: GarageBand plays the *notes* of the loop using the *instrument sound* of the track. Suddenly you're hearing that dreamy guitar pattern played on a piano (Figure 24-6).

  This simple twist vastly multiplies your options as you build a song. When you think about it, you can reassign any green loop to any of dozens of instrument sounds. Apple's categorization is only a starting point for your creativity.

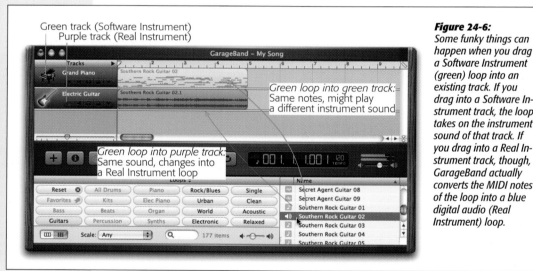

Green track (Software Instrument)
Purple track (Real Instrument)

Green loop into green track:
Same notes, might play
a different instrument sound

Green loop into purple track:
Same sound, changes into
a Real Instrument loop

Figure 24-6:
Some funky things can happen when you drag a Software Instrument (green) loop into an existing track. If you drag into a Software Instrument track, the loop takes on the instrument sound of that track. If you drag into a Real Instrument track, though, GarageBand actually converts the MIDI notes of the loop into a blue digital audio (Real Instrument) loop.

- **Green loop→Blue track.** If you drag a Software Instrument loop into a Real Instrument track, something weird and wonderful happens: GarageBand turns the MIDI loop into a digital recording! Right before your eyes, the green loop turns blue, and its horizontal bars turn into sound waves, indicating that its transformation is complete. Once again, refer to Figure 24-6.

  This behavior isn't exactly consistent with the blue-loop-to-green-track "no go" behavior described below, but it's rather cool nevertheless. It may just give you the speed relief you need when your Mac is straining under the load of your composition; see the box on the previous page for complete details.

- **Blue loop→Blue track with different sound.** This combo produces yet another surprising effect. Dragging a digital-audio (blue) loop into an existing digital-audio track has no effect at all on its instrument sound. Figure 24-7 illustrates this phenomenon.

Note: Although blue loops always play back with their original instrument sounds when added to an existing blue track, they are still affected by the effects and settings of that track—echo, reverb, stereo, and so on. See Chapter 28 for more on track effects.

Figure 24-7:
You can drag any number of different digital-audio loops back-to-back into the same Real Instrument track, as shown here in the second track: Effected Drum Kit, Alternative Rock Bass, and Shaker 4, for example. They'll all play back with the proper instrument sounds, even if the track is called, for example, Acoustic Guitar.

- **Blue loop→Green track.** If you drag a blue loop (Real Instrument) into a green track (Software Instrument), nothing happens at all. GarageBand shakes its little software head "no" and throws the loop back where it came from. You can't park digital audio in a track that expects the horizontal bars of MIDI notes.

All Together Now

In any case, the magic of loops is that most of them sound amazing together, as you'll soon discover.

Now, if your GarageBand window is wide enough, you'll see columns of information for your loops: Key, Tempo, and so on. And you might wonder how a bass loop that's listed as 80 beats per minute, key of D, would sound good with a piano loop that says it's 110 beats per minute, key of C.

Ah, welcome to the magic of software. The listings of tempo and key in the Loop browser indicate the originally recorded tempos and keys. When you actually install a loop into your piece, though, GarageBand automatically tweaks it, nudging into the key and tempo of *your* piece, no matter how it was originally recorded.

Tip: See Chapter 25 for details on working with loops you've placed into your tracks: making them actually loop (repeat), moving them around, shortening them, and so on.

GEM IN THE ROUGH

More Loops Than You Bargained For

When you first peruse the loops that come with GarageBand, you may be pleasantly surprised by how many you have. You may be vaguely aware that you can buy an add-on pack of loops in the form of the Apple GarageBand Jam Pack, but you may not realize that you've got a bunch more loops already on your hard drive. They're just hidden at the moment.

The problem is that GarageBand's different loops were recorded in different keys. (Inspect the Key column in the Loop browser for proof.) If you've ever heard a tone-deaf, slightly drunk karaoke singer at a party, you know how painful it is to listen to clashing keys (two different ones at once). And Apple firmly believes in the old Chinese proverb, "May all your loops sound good together."

Now, one of GarageBand's most amazing features is its ability to transpose its loops (shift them up or down in pitch). If you find a bass loop recorded in the key of D, and drag it into a piece that's in C, it will still sound great, because GarageBand will automatically process it to fit the neighboring key—yes, even if it's a blue (digital-audio) Apple Loop.

So why does GarageBand start out hiding loops that don't match your key?

Apple worries that you might get greedy with that auto-transposing feature. If you choose a blue key-of-F guitar loop, well, that key is rather distant from the key of C. GarageBand's magic software-processing elves will dutifully transpose it into C for you, but the result occasionally sounds

funny—slightly distorted, or, more often, inappropriate for the instrument. (This caveat applies only to blue Real Instrument loops. Green Software Instrument loops sound great in any key.)

Therefore, GarageBand comes set to hide all Real (blue) loops that don't match the key of your piece, to protect you against madcap transpositions.

You can request that it not be such a diva, and show you all of the loops in its bag of tricks. To do that, choose GarageBand→Preferences, click the General icon, and turn off "Filter for more relevant results." Close the dialog box, return to the Loops browser, and click Reset.

Now examine the loops again. As you can see, many more loops appear in the list. For example, if your piece is in C, you now see seven loops in the Bass→Jazz→Cheerful category instead of four.

You may notice that even when "Filter for more relevant results" is turned on, by the way, the listed loops aren't all in your piece's key. For example, scrolling through the list of Bass loops reveals that many of the bass licks were indeed recorded in the key of C. Yet the list also offers you blue loops in keys like C# and D.

The "Filter" option leaves you with blue loops in your song's key and in keys within two half-steps (piano keys) of it. (It also shows you *green* loops in all different keys, because GarageBand can transpose these into any key with no loss of fidelity.)

More Loops

GarageBand comes with 1,100 loops. That should be plenty—for the first half-hour or so!

As your lust for greater musical expression grows, though, you might find yourself wishing you had a more comprehensive sonic palette. You might have noticed, for example, that GarageBand comes with a healthy selection of rhythm parts (bass, drums, guitars, keyboards, mallet instruments), plus some strings and brass—but no solo instruments, like trumpet, clarinet, harp, or solo violin. As noted earlier, GarageBand is also heavily slanted toward music in 4/4 time.

Fortunately, expanding the possibilities is easy enough, since you can add more loops in any of these forms.

Note: As noted at the end of this chapter, you can add almost any sound file to a GarageBand composition just by dragging it into the timeline area. That doesn't make it a loop, however.

A true GarageBand loop comes in *Apple Loop* format. That's basically a dressed-up AIFF file with built-in tags that specify its original length, key, category, and so on. See page 539 for instructions on converting any plain-vanilla loop into a true-blue, smart Apple Loop.

The GarageBand Jam Packs

These $100 expansion packs from Apple each offer 2,000 more loops, additional instrument sounds, more audio effects, and in some cases, more guitar-amp simulators.

The first four Jam Packs were titled Instruments, Loops, and Effects (100 processed or combined versions of the sounds you already have, plus a couple of new solo saxophones, a solo flute, new guitars and bass samples, and sound effects, like a car starting, vinyl record scratching, and phone sounds); Remix Tools (loops and instruments for electronic dance music like techno and hip-hop); Rhythm Section (primarily drum kits and drum patterns); and Symphony Orchestra (sorely needed instrument samples for strings, woodwinds, percussion, a Steinway piano, harpsichord, and organ).

Soundtrack Pro

Think of Apple's $300 soundtrack-creation program, Soundtrack pro, as GarageBand's grandpappy, as it comes with 4,500 Apple Loops of its own. If you've bought Soundtrack—or any of the commercial add-on loop packs for Soundtrack—then you can share its musical riches with GarageBand. Just drag the Soundtrack loops from the desktop into GarageBand's Loop browser, as described below.

Apple Loops from Other Companies

Apple isn't the only company getting into the loop-selling act. There are a few other sources of loops in the Apple Loop format. Some, mercifully, are free. (You'll even find a few free samples on the "Missing CD" page for this book at *www.missingmanuals.com.*)

Tip: The beauty of visiting the Web sites listed below is, of course, that you can actually listen to the loops before you buy them. Most of the sites offer free samples, too, so you can tweak your orchestra without spending a nickel.

- **BandMateLoops.com.** If you're into drums, there's a good chance you'll find what you're looking for among these loop packs: Rock Drums, Electro Beats, Funk Drums, Scratches, and House Beats. Each set costs $18.

GEM IN THE ROUGH

Insta-Samples: Canned Sound Without Loops

Now you know where to find additional loops to buy, download, and install into GarageBand.

In many cases, though, going to all that trouble and expense isn't worth it when all you need is a quick sound effect, or even a sample of a pop song already in your iTunes library. What many GarageBand aficionados don't realize is that you can use any MP3 file, AIFF sound, AAC file (except copy-protected ones), Apple Lossless file, Sony Acid file, or even Windows-format WAV file right in a GarageBand file just by dragging it there, as illustrated here. (Sound files dragged in from the Finder appear as *orange* regions.)

Need a breaking-glass sound to open your new love ballad, "When You Left Me, There Was Only One Way Out"? Zoom over to Google.com, conduct a search for free AIFF sound effects, download a choice candidate, and simply drag its icon off your desktop into the GarageBand Timeline window. That sound effect now plays right along with your music.

Want to sample a killer drum hit from a pop song in your iTunes music library? No problem. Position your iTunes and

GarageBand windows so you can see them both at the same time. Drag the MP3 file's name right out of iTunes and into the GarageBand Timeline window. After the importing dialog box disappears, edit the imported file just as you would any region (see Chapter 25), chopping it up until only the choice moment remains.

Or, similarly, want to create your own version of a pop song? Your first step might be to drag the song into GarageBand from the iTunes window to use as a reference. Adjust the GarageBand tempo control, for example, until the metronome more or less clicks right along with the imported song. Try playing the bass line along with the imported song, or lay down your own singing track on top of it, even if you ultimately intend to delete the imported reference track.

(About that business of copy-protected AAC files, like the ones you buy from the Apple Music Store: If you're desperate to include one, burn a CD of the song, leaving a non-copy-protected copy on the disc. Once when you insert the CD into your Mac, just drag the appropriate song file right out of its desktop window and into GarageBand.)

- **TuneupLoops.com.** Tune-Up for GarageBand includes 500 loops for about $35.

- **Samples4.com.** This British Web site offers a complete line of GarageBand expansion packs at various prices, starting at about $50.

- **BitShiftAudio.com.** 40 free GarageBand loops, all up-to-the-minute in terms of pop-music style.

- **Access-music.de.** This German company offers a 46 MB set of "punchy arpeggiator patterns, fat filter flows, and amazing pad sounds exclusively generated with a Virus C synthesizer"—for free.

And that's just the beginning. Fire up your Web browser, visit Google.com, and search for *free Apple loops*. You'll find plenty of downloads to keep you busy.

How to Install New Loops

Once you've got your hands on a new set of loops, install them into GarageBand just by dragging them there, as shown in Figure 24-8.

What happens now depends on *where* the loops are coming from. In each case, Garage-Band tries to do the smartest thing:

- **From a hard drive.** Some Mac fans have enormous loop collections that they've amassed using other software (like Apple's Soundtrack). These power users are understandably reluctant to let GarageBand *copy* their hundreds of megabytes of loops into its own private loop folder, thus duplicating the loops on the hard drive.

FREQUENTLY ASKED QUESTION

The Case of the Lost Loops

Hey! I installed some new Apple Loops that I downloaded from the Web, and now they're lost somewhere among the 1,100 original GarageBand loops, filed away into the proper instrument or mood categories. How am I supposed to identify which ones are the new ones?

Most loop companies are smart enough to name their supplementary loops with an identifying prefix ("XYZ-Piano Riff 03," for example). If they don't, then sure enough, you may have a hard time

finding your newly installed loops.

That's the beauty of the new Loops pop-up menu shown here. It lists the various loop packages you've installed, so that you can view them one set at a time.

(Behind the scenes, GarageBand stashes newly installed loops in the Library→Application Support→GarageBand→Apple Loops folder on your hard drive. Inside, you should find your newly installed loops in a separate folder of their own.)

That's why, when you drag a folder of loops from a hard drive (whether your own built-in one, an external one, or even a networked one), you get the dialog box shown in Figure 24-8. It's asking how you want to handle this new set of loops. You can opt to have them copied into GarageBand's own Loops folder, or you can have GarageBand *index* them (add them to its list of available loops) but leave the actual files where they are, for the sake of conserving hard drive space.

- **From a CD or DVD.** GarageBand copies the loops into your existing loops folder. It's assuming that this particular disc may not always be in your Mac when you use GarageBand, and that therefore the loops may not always be available—so it copies them to your hard drive for safekeeping.

Once you've installed a loop by dragging into the Loop browser, it becomes available to every GarageBand project you ever work on. It's now a permanent addition to your collection (until you choose to delete it, of course).

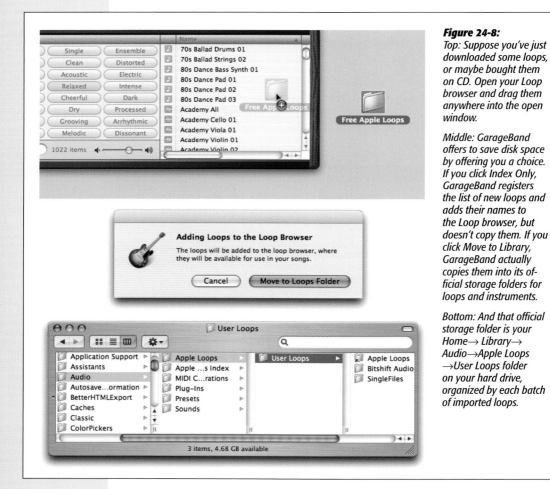

Figure 24-8:
Top: Suppose you've just downloaded some loops, or maybe bought them on CD. Open your Loop browser and drag them anywhere into the open window.

Middle: GarageBand offers to save disk space by offering you a choice. If you click Index Only, GarageBand registers the list of new loops and adds their names to the Loop browser, but doesn't copy them. If you click Move to Library, GarageBand actually copies them into its official storage folders for loops and instruments.

Bottom: And that official storage folder is your Home→ Library→ Audio→Apple Loops →User Loops folder on your hard drive, organized by each batch of imported loops.

Removing Loops and Rebuilding the Index

Not everybody feels straitjacketed by the meager 1,100 loops that come with Garage-Band. Some people actually feel overwhelmed. For them, the trick is not finding new loops to add to their collections—it's deleting the loops they know they'll never need. After all, if your specialty is composing lush, romantic waltzes, it's not immediately apparent how Vinyl Scratch 09 will be useful to you.

Removing loops is a matter of finding them on your hard drive. Open your hard drive→Library→Application Support→GarageBand→Apple Loops folder to find them.

Ordinarily, fooling around with these behind-the-scenes GarageBand folders isn't such a hot idea. Moving, deleting, or renaming the wrong file could profoundly confuse GarageBand.

But if you make your way directly to the Apple Loops folder and don't do anything but remove the loops you really don't want to see, you'll be all right. For sanity's sake, don't simply delete them. Instead, drag them into some other folder on your hard drive, so you can put them back in the unlikely event that you're commissioned to write "The Record Scratching Waltz."

Now, just moving loops out of the Apple Loops folder doesn't actually delete their names from GarageBand's Loop browser. Their names will still appear the next time you fire up GarageBand, because they're still in GarageBand's master *index file* of loops.

But the moment you click the loop's name, you see the dialog box shown in Figure 24-9. Click OK, wait a moment, and then relish your newly pruned collection of loops.

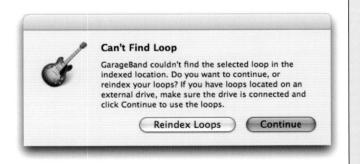

Figure 24-9:
If you delete loops behind GarageBand's back—in the Finder, that is—the program complains with this dialog box. Just click OK, and all will be well.

Can't Find Loop

GarageBand couldn't find the selected loop in the indexed location. Do you want to continue, or reindex your loops? If you have loops located on an external drive, make sure the drive is connected and click Continue to use the loops.

Reindex Loops | Continue

Making Your Own Apple Loops

With very little effort, you can turn your own sonic eruptions into full-fledged Apple Loops, ready for use in your compositions or even for selling online. This technique is also ideal for converting loops originally designed for other music software into official Apple Loops that appear in the GarageBand Loop browser.

In the bad old days of GarageBand 1, you needed a special utility program to do this deed. In GarageBand 2, though, turning a sound into a proper loop is a piece of cake:

1. Select the region in your timeline.

It can be any Real or Software Instrument recording.

2. Choose Edit→Add to Loop Library.

Alternatively, grab your mouse and drag the region directly into the Loop browser. Either way, the Add Loop dialog box appears (Figure 24-10).

You may recognize a lot of the terms on this screen—they're the various category buttons in the GarageBand Loop browser. For example, the Genre pop-up menu controls the primary category this loop will occupy: Electronic, Jazz, World, or whatever. The Mood Descriptors list lets you specify additional categories for this loop: Acoustic, Cheerful, Intense, and so on.

Finally, use the Instrument Descriptors list to identify which instrument produced this sound, or if it's just a sound effect, choose Other Instrument.

3. When you're finished preparing your loop, click Create.

Your recording has now been converted into a living, breathing Apple Loop.

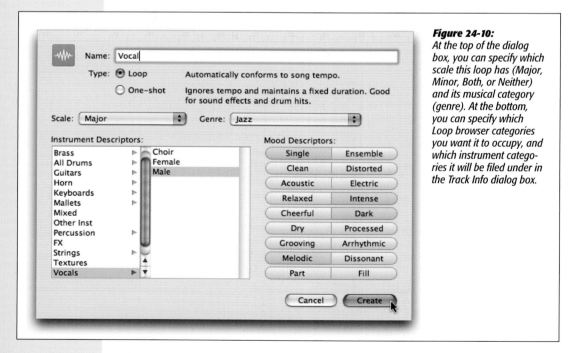

Figure 24-10:
At the top of the dialog box, you can specify which scale this loop has (Major, Minor, Both, or Neither) and its musical category (genre). At the bottom, you can specify which Loop browser categories you want it to occupy, and which instrument categories it will be filed under in the Track Info dialog box.

Regions

A region, in GarageBand lingo, is one of the rounded green, blue, or purple music blocks in the timeline. These are your GarageBand building blocks. A region may contain musical material or silence. Each may last only a fraction of a second, or the entire length of a song. Just by chopping, copying, pasting, and dragging regions around, you can build an infinite number of compositions that have never been heard before.

Loops, described in Chapter 24, are one kind of region (green or blue), but they're not the only kind. In subsequent chapters, you can read about how to record material of your own. Regions containing MIDI note information are always green, Apple Loops containing digital-audio recordings are blue, audio recordings you make yourself are purple, and audio files you drag in from the Finder are orange.

The following discussions tell you how to manipulate regions in general—but these techniques are especially useful for manipulating loops.

Selecting Regions

Before you cut, copy, delete, split, join, or move regions around, you must first select them. This isn't rocket science, of course—you perform the same "Select, then apply" ritual in just about every Macintosh program.

Here's the complete GarageBand region-selecting handbook:

- **Select one region** by clicking it.

- **Select an additional region** by Shift-clicking it. If you Shift-click one by accident, Shift-click it again to deselect it.

- **Select all the regions in one section of the piece** by drag-selecting (Figure 25-1).

- **Select all the regions in one track** by clicking the track header (on the left side, where the track's name and icon appear).

- **Select the entire song** by choosing Edit→Select All (or pressing ⌘-A).

You can tell when a region is selected because its color deepens and its text darkens.

To deselect everything and start over, simply click in any empty gray spot in the timeline.

Zoom slider (drag left to zoom out)

Figure 25-1:
By dragging enormous chunks of your song, you can rearrange sections and experiment with musical arrangements. The trick is selecting so many regions all at once. To do so, start by zooming out. Then, drag a box around the entire area you want to select. Now you can drag any of the selected regions to move them all at once, exactly as with icons in the Finder.

Renaming Regions

Regions usually begin life named after their tracks or instruments. But giving them more descriptive names—like "Vocal Intro," "Bridge," or "Zither Solo"—goes a long way in helping you recognize where you are in your song at any given moment.

To change a region's name, double-click it. As shown in Figure 25-2, an editing window appears. You'll read more about this Track Editor in subsequent chapters, but for now, what you care about is the Track Name box (Figure 25-2).

Dragging Regions

You can change when a region plays by shifting its horizontal position. Just drag it by its center.

Dragging is a very handy tactic. When you drag a region *horizontally*, you make it play earlier or later in time. When you drag it *vertically*, you move it to a different track, according to the rules described on page 530.

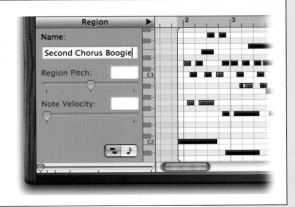

Figure 25-2:
When you double-click any region, the Track Editor appears at the bottom of the window. One key feature is the Track Name box, where you can type a new name for the region. Press Return or Enter to make the name stick.

(Try not to worry about the inconsistency of having to edit the region's name so far away, and not right on the region itself.)

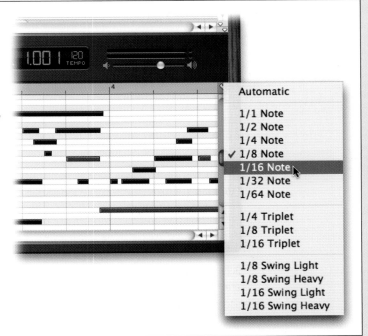

Figure 25-3:
This pop-up menu determines how fine or how coarse the underlying drag-and-drop grid is. It lists basic musical rhythmic units, from largest to smallest (that is, slowest to quickest). In 4/4 time, a region will snap only to the beginnings of measures if you choose "1/1 Note" (that is, a whole note); it will move much more freely if you choose "1/16 Note" (a sixteenth note).

And when you select a huge chunk of your song (Figure 25-1), you can rearrange huge chunks of your piece at once.

The Grid

You may notice that a dragged region tends to snap to positions on an underlying grid, whose vertical lines correspond to the markings on the beat ruler across the top of the window. Here are the keys to understanding this snapping motion:

- In general, the snapping is a good thing. It keeps your loops aligned with one another, so that your GarageBand players have a virtual conductor keeping them together.

- A region you're dragging snaps to the nearest measure, quarter note, and so on. One way to control the fineness of this invisible grid is to use the Grid pop-up menu at the upper-right corner of the GarageBand window, as shown in Figure 25-3 on the previous page.

- If you choose Automatic from the Timeline Grid pop-up menu, the grid expands or contracts according to how much you've zoomed in. As you magnify your music, you get more gridlines per measure, which offers you finer positioning options. (The onscreen gray gridlines show you where GarageBand intends to snap.)

- If you want complete dragging freedom—no snapping grid at all—choose Control→Snap to Grid, or just press ⌘-G. Now you can drag a region wherever you like. (Repeat the command to turn the grid on again.)

Looping Regions

If you install a loop, hit the Home or Z key to rewind, and then press the Space bar to play, you may wonder why you went to all the trouble. The newly installed loop plays once—and then stops.

Fortunately, they're not called loops for nothing. The first and second illustrations in Figure 25-4 show how you can make a loop repeat (or any region, for that matter).

You can make a region repeat as many times as you like. In many songs, for example, you might want the drums to play continuously for the entire song. You can even stop dragging halfway through a repetition, giving you, for example, one-and-a-half repetitions. That might be useful if, say, you want those drums to stop short halfway through a measure to create a dramatic break.

Tip: When you make a loop repeat by dragging its upper-right edge, you're *cloning* the original loop, and the copies remain genetically linked to their progenitor. If you edit the first occurrence, all attached repetitions also change.

If you'd prefer the ability to edit each repetition separately, duplicate the loop region by copying and pasting (or Option-dragging) instead. That way, you create fully independent regions that you can edit separately.

GARAGEBAND

Shortening Regions I

You don't have to use Apple's canned loops in their entirety. By shortening a region from its right end, you can isolate only a favorite first portion of it.

Shortening a region is simple enough: Drag the end inward, as detailed at bottom in Figure 25-4. You'll know you've grabbed the right spot when the cursor changes to a vertical bar with a rightward arrow. (Contrast with the curly cursor that appears when you make a loop repeat.) If you've used iMovie, this movement should feel distinctly familiar. It's exactly the same cropping motion you can use on clips in the Movie Track.

Tip: If the region is blue or purple—a Real Instrument region—you can drag *either* end inward. That is, you can shorten it either from the beginning or end. (You can't shorten a green Software Instrument loop except from its *right* end.)

Figure 25-4:
If you drag a region by its upper-right corner (top), you make it repeat seamlessly (bottom); the curly cursor tells you that you've grabbed the correct corner. The farther to the right you drag, the more repetitions you get.

Middle: The little notches—four of them shown here—illustrate where the region will repeat.

Bottom: If you grab the middle or bottom of a region's right side, you can shorten it by dragging it to the left. (See the difference in the cursor shape?) You can also grab the left side of a blue or purple region and drag inward, cropping out the beginning of the region.

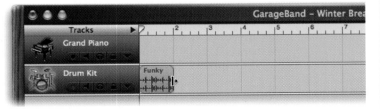

And now some cool mix-and-match editing pointers:

- Once you've shortened a region, you can then drag its upper-right corner to make *just that shortened version* repeat over and over. This trick does amazing things for drum and bass loops, for example, creating fresh, shorter, more repetitive loops that never existed in Apple's imagination.

• The advantage of shortening a region by dragging its end—as opposed to splitting the region and deleting the unwanted portion, as described below—is that you can always restore the region to full length by dragging its end outward again.

• If the *middle* of a blue or purple region is your favorite part, use this technique to crop out both the beginning and ending of it.

Shortening Regions II

If your goal is to shorten a certain drum loop and then place a different region right next to it, try this shorthand: Drag the second region *right on top* of the one you want to shorten, so that they overlap. When you release the mouse, you'll see that you've vaporized the overlapped portion of the stationary region.

In some cases, you'll just leave the dragged region where it is now, so that it plays side-by-side with the shortened one. But once the chopping is done, you don't *have* to leave it where you dropped it. You can drag it right back where it started from, having used it as only a temporary chopper-offer.

Lengthening Regions

You can also make a region longer by dragging its right end to the right. That's not the same thing as dragging the top *right* corner, which makes the loop *loop*. Instead, dragging the loop's right edge extends the loop's width without making it repeat.

You might wonder what the point is, since the extended area of the region is filled with silence. But this trick can be handy when, for example, you recorded only seven measures, but want to loop the region so that it repeats every *eight* measures. By making the region an even eight measures long, you can now drag its upper-*right* corner to make it loop evenly.

Splitting Regions

You don't have to use a region in its entirety. Drum loops, in particular, are fun to split down the middle; the resulting half-loops or quarter-loops often serve as useful *fills* (drum riffs right before a musical moment).

All you have to do is position the Playhead precisely where you want the split to occur, click the region to select it, and then choose Edit→Split (or press ⌘-T). You'll see that the region is now in two separate pieces. You can manipulate, cut, copy, drag, shorten, repeat, or otherwise process each of these two pieces independently.

As noted earlier, what's especially intriguing is that you can split off a snippet of a region, and then make *that* repeat over and over, creating a whole new effect.

And now, some important region-splitting tips:

- It helps to zoom in on your loop before splitting it, so you can see exactly where your knife is about to fall. Drag the zoom slider beneath the track list, or just press Control-right arrow or Control-left arrow key to zoom in or out.

- You can simultaneously split *stacked* regions—that is, parallel regions in several tracks at once. Just make sure that you've first selected the ones you want to split by Shift-clicking each one (Figure 25-5).

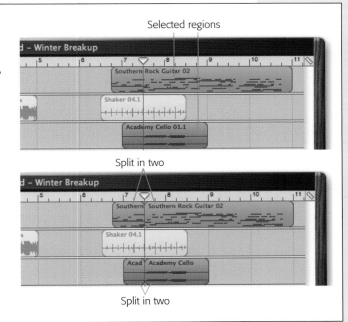

Figure 25-5:
Top: Zoom in, and then position the Play-head where you want to hack up the loop. (Or loops—you can chop several simultaneously, as shown here. Just make sure they're both selected. Here, the middle track is not selected, and so it won't be split.)

Bottom: After the split, the two loop pieces still sound alike when played in succession, but they're now independent entities that you can copy and paste, drag around, and so on.

- After you split a region, both pieces of it remain highlighted. That's great if you now want to copy, delete, or move both pieces as a unit—but if *that* were your aim, why would you have just split them?

No, most of the time, you want to handle them individually. And that's why it's important, just after a split, to click an *empty* track area to deselect them. Only then can you drag or click one of the split pieces all by itself.

You'll use this technique in the tutorial that concludes this chapter.

Joining Regions

What the Split command hath rendered asunder, the Join Selected command shall restore.

Combining two or more regions on a track into a single, unified one has a number of benefits. For example, musical riffs that you've painstakingly assembled and positioned turn into a single, easy-to-manipulate block. Copying, pasting, and dragging regions around is much simpler, too, if you can select the music in question with one quick click, without having to select a bunch of itty-bitty individual regions one at a time. And, of course, you can *loop* a region that you've created by joining them.

There is, however, one condition: The Join Selected command is dimmed if you've selected *blue* regions—that is, Real Instrument Apple loops. It works only on two green regions (MIDI, aka Software Instruments), two purple ones (those you've recorded yourself), or two orange ones (sound files you've dragged in from the Finder).

Tip: According to GarageBand's online help, there are other conditions, too—but don't believe it. For example, the regions you're about to join do *not* have to be adjacent. In fact, you can even Shift-click two regions that are separated by *other* regions! They'll still merge into one long region that appears to float behind the intervening ones—the only time you'll ever see superimposed regions in GarageBand. Weird!

Figure 25-6 shows the routine.

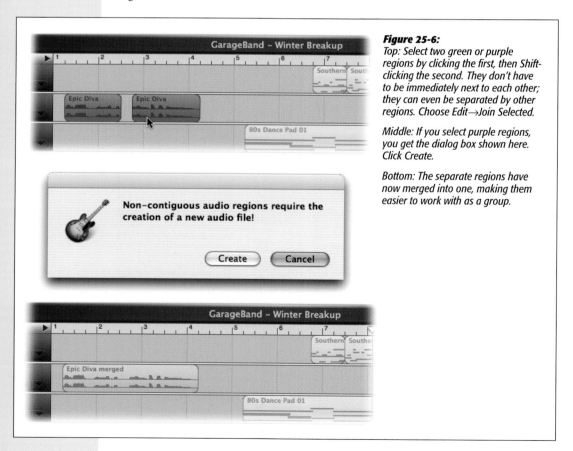

Figure 25-6:
Top: Select two green or purple regions by clicking the first, then Shift-clicking the second. They don't have to be immediately next to each other; they can even be separated by other regions. Choose Edit→Join Selected.

Middle: If you select purple regions, you get the dialog box shown here. Click Create.

Bottom: The separate regions have now merged into one, making them easier to work with as a group.

Copy and Paste

Let's face it: Copy and paste form the cornerstone of the personal-computer religion. If you couldn't copy and paste, where would word processing be? Where would Photoshop be? Where would college students be?

It works with regions just as it does with fields in FileMaker, objects in a drawing program, or icons in the Finder:

1. **Select the region or regions you want to copy.**

   Click to select the first one, Shift-click to select additional regions, either in the same track or in other tracks. Or just "drag out" a huge selection rectangle, as shown in Figure 25-1.

2. **Press ⌘-C (or choose Edit→Copy).**

   You've just placed a copy of the selected music on your invisible Macintosh Clipboard; the original regions remain where they are. If you press ⌘-X (or choose Edit→Cut) instead you place a copy on the Clipboard and *remove* the selected regions from the piece.

3. **Click in the beat ruler to indicate where you want the Clipboard regions to reappear.**

   Or move the Playhead to the proper spot using the arrow keys, the time display, or any other navigation technique.

Note: If your aim is to paste the music at the very end of the piece, you may find that you're not allowed to move the Playhead beyond the end of the existing music. The trick is to first drag the end-of-song marker farther to the right. (It's the tiny, dark purple, left-pointing triangle in the beat ruler.)

---

4. **Press ⌘-V (or choose Edit→Paste).**

   The cut or copied music appears at the position of the Playhead.

The regions always reappear in the tracks from which you cut or copied them; you can't paste into a different track.

Option-Drag

Copy and paste is all very well, but it's a four-step procedure. When you want to copy a region into a nearby spot, there's a much more efficient technique—Option-dragging.

Press the Option key (called Alt on non-U.S. keyboards). While it's down, drag a region to a new position. You peel off a perfect copy of the original. (You may recognize this technique from working with icons in the Finder.)

As with copy-and-paste, this feature is very useful when you drag *horizontally,* because:

- Unlike looping, Option-dragging offers a quick and easy way to make a region repeat *periodically,* as opposed to immediately.

- As noted earlier, Option-dragging creates a separate, fully independent region. That's a handy tactic when you want to *edit* the copy or copies, creating slight variations from the original.

But Option-dragging (or copy-and-paste, for that matter) is also useful when you drag a region vertically into a different track. For example, you can:

- **Set up part doubling.** *Doubling,* in orchestration parlance, means "two instruments playing the exact same notes." Setting up two of the same instrument gives the melody a more intense, louder sound.

  But dragging a green Software Instrument region into a different Software Instrument track gives you the sound of two different *instruments* playing the same line, which creates a new, hybrid sound. Try, for example, dragging the loop called 80s Dance Bass Synth 08 into a track of its own, and then Option-dragging it straight up or down into a green piano or bass track. Because it's now played simultaneously by two different instruments, suddenly the lick has more kick.

- **Chorus yourself.** It's an age-old studio trick made famous by the Beatles. To get this effect, option-drag a region vertically into a second track; then offset the copy by a fraction of a beat by dragging it a hair to the right. (Turn off the grid as described on page 576 before you drag.)

  The result is a cool, reverby, sound-bouncing effect that you can heighten by slightly reducing the volume of the duplicate.

Delete

To delete a selected region or regions, press the Delete key (or, if you're in no particular hurry, choose Edit→Delete).

The Time Display

The Time display is the blue "LED" number counter just below the timeline.

As shown in Figure 25-8 at top, this display can express the position of the Playhead in either of two ways:

- **As measures and beats.** If you're musically inclined, you'll probably prefer the standard musical notation that appears here. It's this format: 025.15.3.100, which refers to measures, beats, *sub-beats* (that is, quarters of a beat), and *ticks* (of which there are 240 per sub-beat).

That's probably *way* more precision than you'll ever need, but hey—overkill is in these days. (Just ask anyone who's bought a Hummer.)

- **As hours, minutes, and seconds.** The Time display can also show you your position in pure time code—that is, how many hours, minutes, seconds, and thousandths of a second you are into the song.

  This mode is especially handy when you're preparing music to accompany, say, an iMovie movie, because you can use it to make sure that the music fits the important moments in the movie exactly.

To switch between these two displays, click to the left of these digits, where you see the tiny clock (absolute time) or musical note (measures:beats).

Note: As you work, remember to save your project (choose File→Save, or press ⌘-S). The dark dot inside the window's red Close button (upper left) lets you know that your project has unsaved changes.

Figure 25-8:
Top: The Time display can show either musical time or stopwatch time.

Middle: The Time display is also a navigation tool. Method 1: Click a number, but keep the mouse button pressed. Now drag up or down to make the number bigger or smaller.

Bottom: Method 2: Double-click a number (which now begins to blink), type new numbers, press the right or left arrow key to jump to the next number, and so on. Press Return or Enter. Either way, the Playhead jumps immediately to the point you specified.

Measure/Beat/Sub-beat/"Tick"   Hour/Minute/Second/¹⁄₁₀₀₀ sec.

Click here to switch between measure display (left) and minutes

Method 1

Click, hold...

...and carefully drag upward.

Method 2

Double-click a number to make it blink.

Type the new number, and then press Enter or Return.

Software Instruments (MIDI)

A s you know from the previous chapters, GarageBand's loops can provide hours of fun and profit even if you don't have a lick of musical training. If you have some semblance of musical chops, though, GarageBand can quickly take you to the next level of creativity. It can record your live keyboard performances, whether you're a painstaking, one-note-at-a-time plunker or a veteran of Carnegie Hall.

To generate the notes that GarageBand records, you can play either an external musical keyboard or an onscreen one. Either way, the cool part is that you can combine your own performances with GarageBand's other tools. For example, some people use GarageBand's loops to create a rhythm section—a backup band—and then they record a new solo on top. Other people ignore the loops altogether and play all of the parts themselves, one instrument at a time, using GarageBand as a multitrack "tape recorder."

Anything you record like this shows up in *green* GarageBand regions. If you made it through Chapter 25, you now know that these regions contain MIDI information (that is, note data that you can edit). If you played a wrong note, no biggie—just drag it onto a different pitch, or delete it altogether. If your rhythm wasn't perfect, so what? No human being's rhythm is perfect (at least compared to a computer's), not even that of rock star millionaires. GarageBand can fix it for you.

How to Feed a Hungry GarageBand

To record a musical performance in this way, you need some way to feed GarageBand a stream of live musical data. You can do so in any of several ways:

• **Use the onscreen, mouse-clicky keyboard.** That is, click the keys of GarageBand's own, built-in, onscreen piano keyboard. Until Apple invents a 10-button mouse, however, this onscreen keyboard limits you to playing only one note at a time. Unfortunately, it's very clunky; it's like playing a piano with a bar of soap.

But it's free, it's built-in, and it's handy for inputting the occasional slow solo line or very brief musical part.

• **Use your Mac's alphabet keyboard.** A great new feature of GarageBand 2 turns your regular typing keyboard into a *musical* keyboard. You don't get much expressive capability, since pressing the letter keys harder or softer doesn't produce any difference in sound. Still, at least you can play chords this way, and you can use your fingers instead of the mouse.

• **Connect a MIDI controller.** MIDI (pronounced "middy"), you may recall from Chapter 23, stands for *musical instrument digital interface.* It's an electronic language that lets musical equipment and computers communicate over a cable.

Because your Mac is perfectly capable of playing any of hundreds of musical-instrument sounds (like the ones built into GarageBand), you don't really need an electronic keyboard that can *produce* sounds. All you really need is one that can *trigger* them.

That's the point of a MIDI *controller;* it looks and feels like a synthesizer keyboard, but produces no sounds of its own. It makes music only when it's plugged into, for example, a Mac running GarageBand.

Apple sells (or, rather, resells) a MIDI controller for $100 called the M-Audio Keystation 49e. If you can live with 49 keys, it's a very nice keyboard. It draws its power directly from your USB jack, so you don't need a power adapter, and it's *velocity-sensitive,* which means that its keys are touch-sensitive. The harder you play, the louder the piano sound, for example.

• **Connect a MIDI synthesizer.** If you already own a MIDI synth—an electronic keyboard that provides an assortment of sounds and has MIDI connectors on the back—there's no point in buying a MIDI controller. You can connect the keyboard directly to your Mac and use it the same way, and simply ignore the keyboard's own sound banks.

Some synthesizers can connect straight to your Mac with a USB cable. Most, however, require a *MIDI interface,* a box with nickel-sized MIDI In and Out connectors on one side, and a USB cable for your Mac on the other.

The following pages explain these musical input methods one by one.

Your FREE! Onscreen Digital Piano

When you fire up a new GarageBand document (on a Mac with no physical MIDI keyboard connected), the GarageBand keyboard appears automatically in a floating window. This onscreen piano is a gift from Apple to people who would like to record notes of their own (instead of just using loops), but don't own a physical MIDI keyboard (Figure 26-1).

Clicking the keys of this little keyboard with your mouse plays the instrument sound of whatever Software Instrument (green) track is currently selected. (The corresponding instrument name appears at the top of the keyboard.)

The onscreen keyboard is a pretty bare-bones beast. For example, it lets you play only one note at a time.

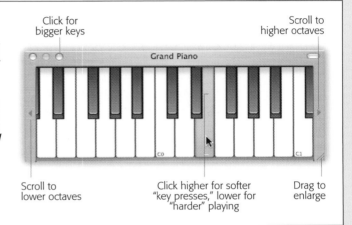

Figure 26-1:
You can make this keyboard appear at any time by pressing ⌘-K (or, if you're charging by the hour, choosing Window→Keyboard). Hide it by clicking its tiny upper-left Close button.

Tip: The keyboard now comes in three sizes. You cycle among them by clicking the green Zoom button identified here, or by dragging the lower-right handle diagonally down and to the right.

Click for bigger keys

Scroll to higher octaves

Grand Piano

Scroll to lower octaves

Click higher for softer "key presses," lower for "harder" playing

Drag to enlarge

MUSIC CLASS

A Different Kind of Velocity

As you get to know GarageBand, and as you get to know the language of electronic music, you'll encounter one term with increasing frequency: *velocity* or *key velocity.*

That's a measurement of how hard you struck the keys of your MIDI controller or synthesizer. GarageBand is required to notice and record that information. If it didn't, how could it play back what you recorded with perfect accuracy?

Now, if you're like most people, your first question is: "Why don't they just say *volume?* I mean, the harder you hit the key, the louder it plays, right?"

And that's where things get tricky. It's true that on a piano, hitting the keys harder makes the music louder. In fact, most of the instrument sounds in GarageBand work like that.

But in the wacky world of computerized music, your key velocity might not affect the loudness of the note. It might change the *quality* of the sound instead, or even what notes are played.

For example, in most of GarageBand's acoustic-guitar sounds (Auditorium Acoustic, for one), pressing a key harder adds a little slide into the note—a grace note, a glissando up the fretboard from the next lower note. In the Fuzz Clav sound, banging harder gives the notes more of an Austin Powers–era "wah wah" sound.

In short, "velocity" means the velocity of your finger coming down on the key. It says nothing about the resulting sound, which is just the way MIDI linguists like it.

But the onscreen keyboard also harbors two secrets that you might not discover on your own. First, it actually has more keys than the 88 of a real piano—well over 10 octaves' worth of keys! To reveal the keyboard's full width, drag its lower-right ribbed resize handle. Or just scroll the keyboard by clicking the tiny gray triangles on either end.

Second, you can actually control how hard you're "playing" the keys. No, not by mashing down harder on the mouse button. Instead, you control the pressure on the keys by controlling the position of your mouse when it clicks. Click higher up on the key to play softer; click lower down to play harder.

Playing harder usually means playing louder, but not always. Depending on the Software Instrument you've picked, hitting a key harder may change the *nature* of the sound, not the volume. More on this topic in the box on the previous page.

For instructions on using the onscreen keyboard to record, skip ahead to page 560.

The Mac Keyboard as Piano

It's nice that Apple provided a little onscreen keyboard so that even the equipment-deprived can listen to GarageBand's amazing sound collection. But you'll never make it to the Grammy Awards using nothing but that single-note, mouse-driven display.

Fortunately, a new feature called Musical Typing lets you trigger notes by playing, rather than clicking. This feature turns your *Mac* keyboard into a *piano* keyboard. It even lets you play *polyphonically*—that is, you can play more than one note at a time. (Six-note chords are the maximum.)

Note: The Mac's keyboard was never intended to be chorded, however. Indeed, it's been carefully engineered to process only one keypress at a time, for word processing purposes. Therefore, playing chords using Musical Typing results in a subtle, mandatory rolling effect, as each note sounds a few milliseconds after the preceding one.

If the effect becomes noticeable, you can always clean up the chords after recording, using GarageBand's *quantizing* feature (page 580).

The row beginning with the letter A represents the "white keys"; W, E, T, Y, U, O, and P in the top row are the "black keys" (sharps and flats). As shown in Figure 26-2, having one row serve as "black keys" means that some computer keys produce no sound at all, because a real piano doesn't have a black key next to every white key. No wonder using Musical Typing takes some getting used to.

Tip: In GarageBand 1.0, the only way to perform using your Mac keyboard was to use the shareware program MidiKeys (part of the "Missing CD" of this book's first edition). In general, the Musical Typing feature is a heck of a lot easier to set up and use, but you still need MidiKeys if you want to play with both hands at once, using two different rows of keys.

Nonetheless, it's a powerful tool for scratching out GarageBand pieces when you're on a plane, on a bus, in bed, and anywhere else where lugging along an external keyboard would get you arrested, expelled, or divorced.

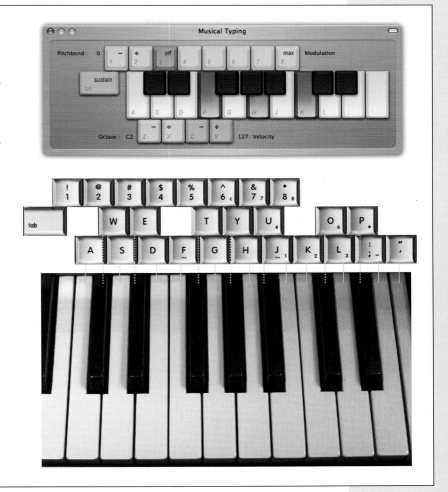

Figure 26-2:
Top: The light gray lettering on the Musical Keyboard "keys" give you some indication as to what notes you'll hear when you press the keys on your Mac keyboard.

Bottom: Here's a more familiar depiction of what notes you'll hear when you press the keys on the top two letter-key rows.

The Tab key simulates a piano's sustain pedal—when it's pressed, notes continue to ring even after you release the keys. The number keys manipulate virtual pitch-bend and mod wheels.

Musical Typing

To use Musical Typing, create a Software Instrument (green) track in GarageBand. (One way is to choose Track→New; in the New Track dialog box, click Software Instrument. Choose an instrument from the right-side column, and then click OK.)

Now open the Musical Typing window by choosing Window→Musical Typing, or by pressing Shift-⌘-K.

Once its keyboard appears (Figure 26-2), try playing a few "keys" on the A row of your Mac's keyboard. You'll see the Musical Typing piano keys change color, you'll hear the corresponding notes play in GarageBand, and you'll see a flickering "light" in the time display (Figure 26-4). It tells you that GarageBand is receiving MIDI musical data.

At this point, you can use Musical Typing like it's a MIDI controller keyboard, including making GarageBand recordings (page 560).

Control of Key Velocity

There's only one problem with using Musical Typing as you've read about it so far: you can't control the key velocity (page 555) as you play. (Apple never designed the typing keyboard to be touch-sensitive, although the idea is intriguing. What would it do—make the letters bolder the harder you hit the keys?)

The solution is to tap the C and V keys—repeatedly, if necessary—to simulate "softer" and "harder" key presses. This is not exactly a simple task when you're using both hands in the middle of a Rachmaninoff concerto, but if you record one hand at a time, riding the C and V keys with the other hand, it's a manageable arrangement.

Of course, you may also want to record your track with *no* velocity adjustments, and then adjust the key velocities later by editing the track (page 558).

Tips and Tricks

Other than handling key velocity, Musical Typing does the best conceivable job of turning your Mac into a bona fide musical instrument. Here are some of its finer points:

- Shift the entire keyboard up or down an octave at a time by tapping the X and Z keys, respectively.

- "Press the piano's sustain pedal" by pressing Tab. Press once to "step on the pedal," press a second time to "release it."

- "Turn the mod wheel" by pressing 4 through 8; see page 569 for details on the mod wheel. (Higher numbers trigger greater turns of the modulation wheel.) Press 3 to turn off modulation altogether.

- "Turn the pitch-bend wheel" by holding down the 1 key, or bend it up by holding down 2. (Alas, you can't control how much you "turn the wheel." You always get a pitch bend of 20 units up or down, on a scale of 0 to 127.)

Tip: Thanks to a bizarro bug in GarageBand 2.0.1, the pitch-bend keys don't work when you're playing certain key combinations, like the notes C, D, and any other "white key" note. Apple says it's working on it.

- While Musical Typing is quite useful for recording new tracks, it's also extremely handy when choosing an instrument sound for a track.

  Think about it: Ordinarily, when the New Track dialog box appears (Figure 26-3), GarageBand offers no way for you to *hear* what each listed sound sounds like (unless you have an external MIDI keyboard). Most people wind up laboriously clicking a sound's name, closing the dialog box, clicking the keys on the Garage-Band onscreen keyboard, double-clicking the track name to reopen the Track Info dialog box, and then repeating the whole ritual over and over.

But with Musical Typing's window open, you can click an instrument's name and then play a few notes on your Mac's keyboard to hear what it sounds like—all without leaving the Track Info dialog box.

If you fool around here long enough, you'll find some surprising selections, including sound effects, exotic percussion instruments, and traditional instruments that have been processed in wild, sometimes musically inspiring ways.

Figure 26-3:
This dialog box appears when you choose Track→New Track. These instrument sounds all look delicious, but how are you supposed to know which one sounds exactly right for your piece? Simple: Press a few keys on your MIDI controller (or, if you're using Musical Typing, the A row of your keyboard). Use your arrow keys to walk through the instrument list, and play a few more keys to hear the next sound.

MIDI Synths and Controllers

The best way to record keyboard performances, though, is to bite the bullet, break the bank, and buy an actual, external MIDI musical instrument. As noted earlier in this chapter, it might take any of these forms:

• **A MIDI controller.** Apple, for instance, sells an M-Audio keyboard for $100. The only cable required is its USB cable, which connects to your Mac's USB port.

That's not the only controller worth considering, of course. If the idea of 49 keys strikes you as a bit confining, the same company also makes a 61-key model that Apple sells for $200. Online music stores like *www.samash.com* sell both of these models and many others, including a full 88-key model (the same number of keys as a real piano) for $300. These more expensive keyboards have semi-weighted keys that feel more like a piano than the spring-loaded plastic keys of the 49-key model.

- **A MIDI keyboard.** This category includes synthesizers, electric pianos, Clavinovas, and so on. Some connect directly to your Mac's USB port, but most require an adapter known as a *MIDI interface,* which costs about $40 at music stores.

- **Another MIDI instrument.** Keyboards aren't the only MIDI instruments. There are also such things as MIDI guitars, MIDI drum sets, and even MIDI gloves. They, too, generate streams of note information that GarageBand can record and play back.

Once you've hooked up a MIDI instrument, create a Software Instrument track and try playing a few notes. You'll hear whatever sound you established for that track, and you'll see the little MIDI activity light blinking in GarageBand's time display (Figure 26-4). Now you're ready to record.

Tip: An external instrument is also great when it's time to *choose* a sound for a new track, because you can walk through the various instrument names without ever having to close the Track Info dialog box. See Figure 26-3 for more information.

Figure 26-4:
The little blue blinky light lets you know that Garage-Band is "hearing" your MIDI instrument as you play it.

Flashing "Incoming
MIDI data!" indicator

Recording a MIDI Track

Whether your keyboard is on the screen or on your desk, virtual or physical, you use it to record in GarageBand the same way. Here's the routine:

1. **Click the track you want to fill with music.**

   Remember, it must be a Software Instrument (green) track.

   If you don't already have a green track ready to record, choose Track→New Track to create one. In the New Track (Track Info) dialog box, click the Software Instrument tab, and then choose the instrument sound you want (Figure 26-3). Click OK.

2. **Turn on the metronome, if you like.**

   A *metronome* is a steady beat clicker that's familiar to generations of musicians. By clicking away "1, 2, 3, 4! 1, 2, 3, 4!" it helps to keep you and GarageBand in sync.

   Use the Control→Metronome command, or the ⌘-U keystroke, to turn the metronome clicker on or off. (See the box on the facing page, too.)

Tip: On the General pane of GarageBand→Preferences, you can indicate whether or not you want the metronome to play during *playback,* or only when you're recording.

---

3. Choose a tempo for recording.

This is a very important step. Because you're using a *sequencer* (recording software) instead of a tape recorder, it makes no difference how slowly you record the part. You can *record* at 60 beats per minute, for example, which is basically one note per second—and then *play back* the recording at a virtuosic "Flight of the Bumblebee" tempo (229 beats per minute, say). Your listeners will never be the wiser.

This isn't cheating; it's exploiting the features of your music software. It's a good bet, for example, that quite a few of the pop songs you hear on the radio were recorded using precisely this trick.

So how do you find a good tempo for recording? First, just noodle around on your keyboard. Find a speed that feels comfortable enough that the music maintains *some* momentum, but is still slow enough that you can make it through the part without a lot of mistakes.

UP TO SPEED

When Not to Use the Metronome

GarageBand is perfectly capable of recording a keyboard performance without clicking away at you with its metronome. In fact, there's a very good reason you may not want the metronome turned on: if the piece you intend to play speeds up and slows down with the mood and the spirit. In those musical situations, a rigid, inflexible tempo would rob your music of all its spontaneity and feeling.

Of course, playing without the metronome means that your sense of where the beats and measures fall won't correspond with GarageBand's. Your measures 1, 2, and 3 won't line up with the beat ruler at the top of the GarageBand window.

That's not necessarily a bad thing. Listen to "03-Expressive Tempo," for example. (It's one of the songs on the Garage-Band Examples CD—see page 506.) It's a perfectly lovely piece. True, its beats and measures are all out of whack with GarageBand's sense of beats and measures. But when people listen to the music, they'll never know or care.

Playing without the metronome does mean, however, sacrificing some very useful GarageBand features. For one thing, you may find it difficult to add another track to the same piece. It's hard to play together with a free-form, flexible-tempo track that you've already recorded.

You lose much of the drag-and-drop region-editing flexibility described in Chapter 25, too. Remember how GarageBand regions' ends snap neatly against the underlying grid of beats and measures? If your more expressive grid doesn't align with GarageBand's, you're out of luck.

Finally, you won't be able to adjust the rhythm of your performance using GarageBand's Align To button (page 581).

In more expensive recording programs (like Digital Performer, for example), you can actually teach the program to follow your own expressive tempo curve as you speed up and slow down; that is, you can make its conception of beats match what you play.

GarageBand, however, is a much more basic program that offers no way to automate a tempo change in the course of a piece. If you're trying to record anything that's more expressive than, say, a typical pop or rap song, you may be forced to go off the grid.

Then adjust the GarageBand tempo slider to match. Hit the Space bar to play the music you've already got in place, if any, and adjust the Tempo control (page 508) during the playback until it matches the foot-tapping in your head.

Tip: If you haven't recorded *any* music, one way to hear the tempo as you fiddle with the Tempo control is to turn the metronome on during playback, as described in the preceding tip. Then play back your empty song, using the clicks as your guide while you adjust the Tempo slider.

Once you've found a good recording speed, stop playback.

4. Position the Playhead to the spot where you want to begin recording.

If that's the beginning, great; just press the letter Z key or the Home key. If it's in the middle of the piece, click in the beat ruler or use the keyboard shortcuts (page 510) to position the Playhead there. (Most often, though, you'll want to put the Playhead a couple of measures before the recording is supposed to begin, as described in the next step.)

5. Set up your countoff.

It's very difficult to begin playing with the right feeling, volume, and tempo from a dead stop. That's why you always hear rock groups (and garage bands) start each other off with, "And a-one! And a-two!" That's also why most orchestras have a conductor, who gives one silent, preparatory beat of his baton before the players begin.

GarageBand can "count you in" using either of two methods. First, it can play one measure full of beats, clicking "one, two, three, go!" at the proper tempo so you'll know when to come in. That's the purpose of the Control→Count In command. When this command has a checkmark, GarageBand will count you in with those clicks.

If you intend to begin playing in the middle of existing music, though, you may prefer to have the music itself guide you to your entrance. This is the second method. For example, you might decide to plant the Playhead a couple of measures *before* the spot where you want to record. As long as doing so won't record over something that's already in your track, this is a convenient way to briefly experience the feel or groove of the music before you begin playing.

6. Get ready to play—hands on the keyboard—and then click the red, round Record button.

Or just press the letter R key on your Mac keyboard.

Either way, you hear the countoff measure, if you've requested one, and then the "tape" begins to roll. Give it your best, and try to stay in sync with the metronome, if you've turned it on.

7. **When you come to the end of the section you hoped to record—it might be the entire piece, or maybe just a part of it—tap the Space bar (or click the Play button) to stop recording.**

On the screen, you'll see the new green region you recorded.

8. **Play back your recording to see how you did.**

Rewind to the spot where you started recording. If you recorded *under tempo* (that is, slower than you intend the playback to be), boost the Tempo slider to a better setting. (Because you recorded a stream of MIDI note information and did not record actual digital audio, you can adjust the playback tempo at any time without changing the pitch of the notes. You couldn't get an "Alvin and the Chipmunks" effect if you tried.)

Tap the Space bar to hear your performance played back just as you recorded it.

Tip: Do what the pros do—record a section at a time. The odds of a good take are much greater when the segment is short. Remember, too, that if your song contains repeating sections, you can reuse one perfect take by copying and pasting it to a different spot in the song.

FREQUENTLY ASKED QUESTION

The Pickup Artist

Hey, how do I make the countoff work if my piece begins with a pickup?

Ah, there's an experienced musician in the audience. Welcome.

A pickup, in musical terms, is a note that begins a melody but doesn't fall on the downbeat (first beat) of the tune; it actually sounds right before the downbeat. In the Broadway song "Tomorrow" (from Annie), the lyrics go, "The sun'll come out, tomorrow." In this case, the word "The" is a pickup (and the downbeat is on the word "sun").

"Tomorrow" a little obscure for you? All right then, what about the national anthem? In "Oh-oh say can you see," that "oh-oh" is a pair of pickup notes. The "say" is the landing note, the beginning of the first full measure.

The reason GarageBand's countoff feature confuses the recording of pickups is that the program always counts off

one full measure of beats before it starts to listen to, and record, your playing. But if you're playing the melody for "Tomorrow," you'd actually count silently "one, two, three," and begin singing on "four." In that situation, GarageBand wouldn't record the first note of the song, because its countoff clicker insists that all four beats be silent.

Even if this discussion leaves you, a musical novice, out in the cold, the bottom line should be clear: If you find that GarageBand just won't record the first note or two that you play when the countoff feature is turned on, let a second nearly full measure of clicks go by before you play. That is, let the countoff go "1, 2, 3, 4, 1, 2, 3"—and then play your pickup.

In that case, GarageBand will "record" empty beats at the beginning of measure 1, so that your pickup will be heard at the end of it.

Retakes

Even before you play back a new recording, you may know if it was a great performance, a good candidate but not necessarily your best effort, or a real stinker that must be deleted immediately. Maybe you messed up a portion of the playing. Maybe you had trouble keeping up with the metronome, or you felt as though it was holding you back.

The beauty of a MIDI sequencer like GarageBand, though, is that you can keep your take, redo it, or trash it, instantly and guilt-free, having used up no tape or studio time.

Here's how to proceed after recording a MIDI performance:

- **Trash the whole thing.** If the whole thing stank, press ⌘-Z to trigger the Edit→Undo command. The new green region disappears. Adjust the tempo, if necessary, and try recording again.

Note: Before you go nuts deleting bad performances, though, remember that it's sometimes more time-efficient just to manually fix what was wrong with it, using the GarageBand track editor. See page 571.

- **Trash part of it.** Use the Edit→Split command to cut the region into pieces, so that you can preserve the good parts but rerecord the bad ones.

- **Keep it.** If the whole thing was great, or mostly great, save your file (⌘-S) and move on to the next track.

- **Mark it "best so far."** Press the letter M key to mute the track you just recorded. Then create a new track and repeat the entire process, hoping to do better this time. After this second attempt—or your third, fourth, or fifth—you can compare your

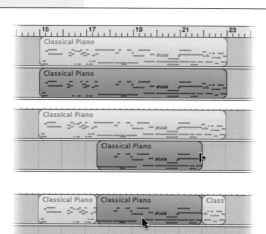

Figure 26-5:
Top: You've recorded this take twice, with mixed results each time.

Middle: Suppose the middle section of the second take was the best performance. Chop off both ends.

Bottom: Drag the remaining middle section upward onto the first take; this obliterates the corresponding moments of the first take. The result: A hybrid final track containing the best portions of each recording.

various takes by muting and un-muting them as they play back. You can also chop up these various regions and use only the best parts of each attempt, yet another extremely common practice in professional recording studios (Figure 26-5).

Tip: One great way to create a new track for the next attempt is to duplicate the first one (choose Track→ Duplicate Track). GarageBand creates a new, empty track just below the first one—with the same instrument sound and effects (reverb and so on) already selected.

Spot Recording (Punch In/Punch Out)

If you're able to record an entire song perfectly the first time, with no mistakes—well, congratulations. Sony Records is standing by.

Most people, though, wind up wishing they could redo at least part of the recording. Usually, you played most of it fine, but botched a few parts here and there.

In the professional recording business, patching over the muffed parts is so commonplace, it's a standard part of the studio ritual. Clever studio software tools can play back the track right up until the problem section, seamlessly slip into Record mode while the player replays it, and then turn off Record mode when it reaches the end of the problem part, all without missing a beat. Recording engineers call this *punching in and out.*

Believe it or not, even humble GarageBand lets you punch in and punch out. Once you master this technique, you'll be very grateful.

Here's how it goes:

1. **Turn on cycling.**

   Page 509 describes *cycling* in the context of playing a section of music over and over again. For recording, the steps are much the same (see Figure 26-6). In this case, though, the beginning and end of the yellow Cycle bar designate your punch-in and punch-out points—the part you're going to rerecord.

2. **Set up your metronome and tempo. Turn on the Count In command (in the Control menu).**

   In this case, Count In is very important; it makes GarageBand play the one measure of music that precedes your punch-in point. (You don't have to position the Playhead for this exercise. Whenever Cycling is turned on, the Playhead always snaps to the beginning of the yellow stripe when playing or recording begins.)

3. **Begin recording (by pressing the letter R key, for example).**

   During the countoff measure, you don't just hear metronome clicks—you also hear the *existing* music in that preceding measure. GarageBand begins recording after the countoff, as the Playhead reaches the yellow cycle area.

As you record, you'll also hear the *old* material—the part you're trying to rerecord. Don't worry, though; it will disappear after you replace it. (If it bothers you, delete it manually before punching in.)

GarageBand doesn't play past the end of the yellow bar. Instead, it loops back to the beginning of the yellow bar and keeps right on recording. (This loop-record feature is the key to *cumulative recording,* described next.) If you nailed it on the first take, just stop playing.

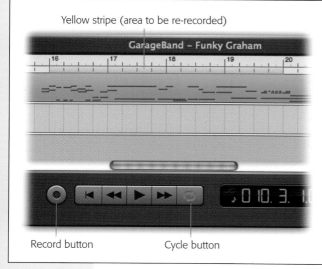

Yellow stripe (area to be re-recorded)

GarageBand – Funky Graham

Record button   Cycle button

Figure 26-6:
Click the Cycle button—or press the letter C key—to make the yellow "repeat this much" bar appear at the top of the screen. Drag the ends of the yellow bar to identify the musical section you'll be loop-recording. (If you don't see the yellow bar, or if you want it to appear in a totally different section of the piece, drag through the lower section of the beat ruler.)

4. Press the Space bar (or click the Play button) to stop recording.

When you play back the piece, GarageBand flows seamlessly from your original take to the newly recorded "patch" section.

Tip: This punch-in/punch-out routine is the only way to go if your goal is to rerecord precisely measured sections.

When the parts you want to rerecord have nicely sized "bookends" of silence before and after, though, there's a more casual method available. Just play the piece from the beginning—and "ride" the letter R key on your keyboard. With each tap, you jump into and out of Record mode as the piece plays. This *manual* punch-in/punch-out method offers another way to record over the bad sections and preserve the good ones.

Cumulative Recording

GarageBand's tricks for people with less-than-stellar musical ability don't stop with the slow-tempo-recording trick and the ability to rerecord certain sections. The Cycle button described earlier is also the key to cumulative recording, in which you record *one note* at a time, or just a few, building up more complexity to the passage as GarageBand loop-records the same section over and over (Figure 26-7).

This trick is especially useful for laying down drum parts. In real life, drummers are surrounded by different kinds of drums; they're constantly reaching out and twisting to hit the different instruments at different times.

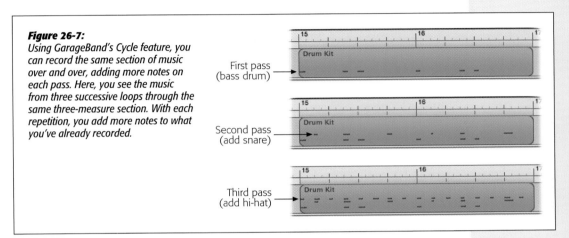

Figure 26-7:
Using GarageBand's Cycle feature, you can record the same section of music over and over, adding more notes on each pass. Here, you see the music from three successive loops through the same three-measure section. With each repetition, you add more notes to what you've already recorded.

First pass (bass drum)

Second pass (add snare)

Third pass (add hi-hat)

When you want to perform your *own* drum parts, you'll probably be using a MIDI keyboard. It turns out that GarageBand's various drum sounds—bass drum, snare drum, tom-toms, and so on—are "mapped" to the various keys of the keyboard (see Figure 26-8). Unless you have an extraordinarily unusual limb structure, you'll probably find it very difficult to play all the drums you want in a single pass, since they're scattered all over the keyboard.

It's much easier to record drum parts in successive passes, as GarageBand continues to record: the bass drum the first time, the snare on the next pass, and so on.

Here's how to set up loop recording:

1. **Turn on cycling.**

   See step 1 of the preceding instructions. Figure 26-6 explains how to adjust the yellow Cycle bar. The point here is to "highlight" the portion of music you want to record.

2. **Set up the recording.**

   Adjust the metronome, the Count In option, and the tempo, just as described in the previous pages. If you plan to record in the middle of a piece, place the Playhead to the left of the cycled region to give yourself a running start. (GarageBand will be in playback-only mode until it reaches the yellow Cycle bar.)

Click a track header to indicate which track you want to record. If you intend to lay down a drum track, fool around with your keyboard to identify which key plays which drum sounds. (The basic setup for GarageBand's drum kit is shown in Figure 26-8.)

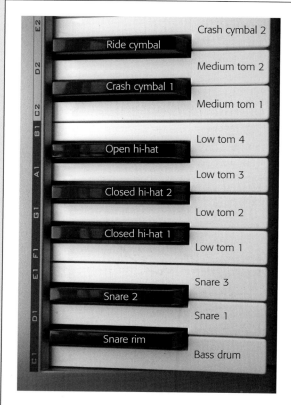

Figure 26-8:
Cumulative recording is especially useful for drum parts, because it lets you focus on only one drum sound at a time. This diagram illustrates how GarageBand's drums are mapped to the keys of your keyboard. (The different drum kits are all mapped identically, although what constitutes a snare or a low tom in the Jazz kit may not sound anything like the one in the Techno kit.)

The bass drum (kick drum), snare, and ride cymbals are the foundation of most drum parts, so these may be the keys you want to "ride" with three fingers as you record.

3. Click the Record button (or press the letter R key).

Each time GarageBand plays through the yellow-striped section, it will record any notes you play. Remember, GarageBand accumulates *all* the notes you play, adding them to the piece even if you play them on different repetitions of the looped passage.

Tip: It's OK to let a pass or two go by without playing anything. You just haven't added anything to the recording in progress, so no harm done. In fact, you might want to consider routinely sitting out a couple of repetitions between recording bursts.

Each time GarageBand loops back to the beginning of the section, you'll notice that it's already playing back what you laid down on previous passes. And when you finally stop (tap the Space bar) and play back the new passage, you'll discover that every note you played during the various repetitions plays back together.

Tip: Believe it or not, you can stop the playback, listen, do other work on your piece, and return much later to add yet another layer of cumulative-recording notes—as long as you haven't disturbed the yellow Cycle bar in the beat ruler. Once you move that yellow stripe or turn off cycling, GarageBand ends your chance to record additional material in that region. The next recording you make there will wipe out whatever's there.

Mod Wheels and Other MIDI Fun

Many of GarageBand's built-in sounds are *samples*—brief recordings of actual instruments. That's why the grand piano sounds so realistic: because it *is* a grand piano (a $50,000 Yamaha, to be exact).

But behind the scenes, GarageBand's sounds have been programmed to respond to various impulses beyond just pressing the keys. They can change their sounds depending on what other MIDI information GarageBand receives from your keyboard.

For example:

- **Sustain pedal.** If you have a sustain or damper pedal, you can ride it with your foot just as you would on a piano. (It's designed to hold a note or a chord even after your hands have released the keys.) Almost any MIDI keyboard—including the $100 M-Audio Keystation—has a jack on the back for a sustain pedal, which costs about $15 from online music stores like *www.samash.com*.

- **Key velocity.** As noted earlier in this chapter, a number of GarageBand sounds respond to key velocity (that is, how hard you strike the keys). Most of the instrument sounds just play louder as you hit the keys harder, but some actually change in character. Acoustic guitars feature a little fingerboard slide; clavichords get

Figure 26-9:
On the M-Audio MIDI controller keyboards that Apple sells, two control wheels liven up the MIDI proceedings. The pitch-bend wheel actually bends the note's pitch. Just turn the wheel either before or after striking the note, depending on the effect you want. The modulation wheel, meanwhile, either produces sound-changing effects or does nothing, depending on the GarageBand sound you've selected.

more of a "wah" sound; Wah Horns also "wah" more; and many of the synthesizer keyboard sounds sound "rounder" as you hit the keys harder.

Using the correct technical language, you would say that these instruments are velocity-sensitive.

- **Pitch and mod wheels.** Some keyboards, including that $100 M-Audio controller that Apple sells, have one or two *control wheels* that also affect GarageBand's sounds (Figure 26-9).

For example, a *pitch-bend* wheel makes a note's pitch slide up or down while you're still pressing the key. It's an essential tool for anyone who wants to make brass or wind instruments sound more realistic, since those instruments are capable of sliding seamlessly from pitch to pitch—something a keyboard, with its series of fixed-pitch keys, can't ordinarily do.

You can use the pitch-bend wheel in either of two ways. First, turn the wheel downward, for example, and hold it (it's spring-loaded). Then, play the key you want—and simultaneously release the key. What you hear is a slide *up* to the desired note.

Second, you can strike the key first and *then* turn the wheel, or even wiggle the wheel up and down. The sound winds up wiggling or bending away from the original note, which is a common technique when you're trying to simulate, for example, the bending notes of a blues harmonica.

Tip: You can hear these effects in the sample file called 04-Control Wheels. It's on the GarageBand Examples CD described on page 506.

The pitch-bend wheel affects *all* GarageBand sounds.

- Your keyboard may also have a *mod wheel,* short for modulation wheel. It's an all-purpose control wheel that produces different effects in different sounds. Here are some of the effects it has on GarageBand's built-in sounds:

Instrument Name	Mod-Wheel Effect
Bass instruments	Brightens the sound
Choir sounds	Vibrato
Drum kits	No effect
Guitars	Vibrato
Most horns	Vibrato
Funk horns	"Fall-off" (slide down) at end of note
Mallets	Vibrato
Most organs	No effect
Vocoder Synth Organ	Searing distortion
Most pianos	No effect
Strings	Vibrato
Most Synth Basics	Vibrato

Star Sweeper	"Sweeps" the sound's phase
Synth Leads	Vibrato
Most Synth Pads	No effect or vibrato
Angelic Organ	"Clicks" through the sound
Aquatic Sunbeam	"Sweeps" the sound's phase
Electric Slumber	"Sweeps" the sound's phase
Liquid Oxygen	"Clicks" through the sound
Tranquil Horizon	"Sweeps" the sound's phase
Woodwinds	Vibrato

Note: *Vibrato* is the gentle wavering of pitch that's characteristic of most professional instrumental soloists and singers. (Real-world pianos and drum sets can't produce vibrato, which is why GarageBand's corresponding sounds don't react to the mod wheel.)

If you've bought the Symphony Orchestra Jam Pack, you'll find an even more amazing range of effects lurking in the mod wheel. The violins and other stringed instruments, for example, play normally (legato) when the wheel is at rest. But as you turn the wheel more and more, the articulation (playing style) changes from staccato (short notes), to tremolo (rapid, back-and-forth bow strokes), to rapid half-step trills, then whole-step trills, and finally—at the top of the mod wheel's rotation—pizzicato (plucked strings).

Woodwinds, brass, and timpani playing styles are similarly affected—for example, turning the mod wheel halfway makes the oboe play with vibrato, the horns swell into a crescendo, and the timpani (kettledrums) play with a thunderous roll.

Learning to use your mod wheel can add a great deal of beauty, realism, and grace to your GarageBand recordings. Remember that you don't have to turn it all the way up; you can turn the wheel only part way for a more subtle effect. Remember, too, that the mod wheel is usually most effective when you turn it *after* the note has begun sounding. It's the contrast of the mod wheel (versus the unaffected note) that produces the best effect.

Editing Software Instrument Parts

Recording MIDI data, as described in the previous chapter, has a huge advantage over recording with a microphone: The results are almost infinitely *editable*. For example, you can delete wrong notes or drag them onto the right ones. If you played a section too loud, you can lighten it up after the fact. You can change the tempo or key of the music, making it faster, slower, higher, or lower, without distortion. If you discover a more appropriate instrument sound for a certain part, you can reassign the whole part.

In fact, GarageBand even lets you edit the invisible data generated by the foot pedal and control wheels.

The key to all of this freedom is the nature of the recordings you make with a MIDI keyboard: GarageBand stores your performance as a series of scheduled note triggers. When you play back your piece, GarageBand plays its own built-in synthesizer in real time. It's not playing back a sound recording.

The Track Editor

The doorway to all of this editing magic is the Track Editor, shown in Figure 26-10.

You can open this window in any of several ways:

- **Double-click a green region in the timeline.** This is the best way to open the Track Editor, because it appears prescrolled to the notes in the region you clicked.

- **Click the scissors icon (✂) beneath the track headers.** The Track Editor opens to the beginning of the first region on the track.

- **Choose Control→Show Editor, or press ⌘-E.** Once again, the Track Editor opens to the beginning of the track.

Tip: When the Editor window first appears, it shows only about an octave's worth of vertical space. Fortunately, you can drag upward on GarageBand's dark gray "brushed metal" divider strip (Figure 26-10) to double the Editor's height. (You might remember having to do this when using the Loop browser, too. Unfortunately, you'll have to do it again each time you open GarageBand.)

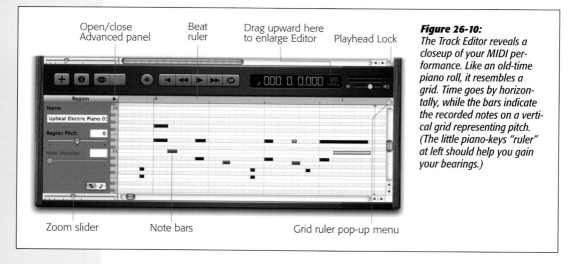

Open/close Advanced panel   Beat ruler   Drag upward here to enlarge Editor   Playhead Lock

Zoom slider   Note bars   Grid ruler pop-up menu

Figure 26-10:
The Track Editor reveals a closeup of your MIDI performance. Like an old-time piano roll, it resembles a grid. Time goes by horizontally, while the bars indicate the recorded notes on a vertical grid representing pitch. (The little piano-keys "ruler" at left should help you gain your bearings.)

Once you know your way around the Editor window, the editing itself is very easy. You can tug on the little note bars with your mouse to move, stretch, or shrink them. More about this in a moment.

For now, gain your bearings by noticing these controls:

- **Note bars.** These are the notes in the green MIDI region. (MIDI regions can be either GarageBand loops or music you've recorded yourself, as described in this chapter.) Longer bars represent longer notes.

  Darker bars represent notes with greater *key velocity*—that is, keys that were hit harder. The lighter the shade of gray, the lighter that note was played.

  This startup view—piano-roll view, for want of a better term—is only one of two editing views in GarageBand 2. You can, if you prefer, view your masterpiece in traditional musical notation, as described in the next section.

- **Beat ruler.** These are the same measures of your piece that are represented by the beat ruler at the top of the GarageBand window.

  But in designing the Track Editor, Apple's programmers faced a quandary. Should this Track Editor window be matched to the timeline area above it, so that when you scroll the top window, the Track Editor scrolls too? Or should you be able to scroll the top and bottom parts of the GarageBand window independently?

  As it turns out, Apple gives you a choice.

- **Playhead Lock button.** When this little icon looks like this 🔒, you can scroll the Track Editor independently of the main GarageBand window. In fact, during playback, the Playhead in the Track Editor screen may chug merrily right off the screen. In this situation, GarageBand scrolls automatically only when the *upper* Playhead hits the edge of your window.

  But when you click the icon so that it looks like this 🔒, both parts of the window scroll together. The Playhead line moves across (and autoscrolls) both parts of the window.

- **Zoom slider.** You can see more of the song at once in the Time Editor by dragging this slider to the left, which causes the beat ruler (and all the notes) to get smaller. To zoom in for finer editing, drag the slider handle to the right, which makes the ruler and the note bars grow.

Tip: You don't have to drag the little slider's handle. It's often faster simply to click *in* the slider. The handle jumps to the spot of your click. (In fact, this tip applies to *all* GarageBand sliders.)

- **Scroll bars.** These scroll bars work like any Macintosh scroll bars, but they're especially important in the Track Editor. If you open the Editor using either the scissors icon or the Show Editor command, the Track Editor window often appears to be completely *blank*. It opens to some portion of the track that has no notes in it. You're left to wonder whether the notes are higher or lower than what's currently on display, or sooner or later. In both of those situations, you'll wind up doing a lot of scrolling.

  This sense of Editor disorientation is a good argument for opening it using the first method described above: by double-clicking a region in the timeline.

Tip: You can also scroll the Track Editor by dragging your cursor through it in the direction you want to go. (Avoid beginning your drag directly on a note bar, though.)

- **Advanced panel.** You can read about the editing controls of this panel in the following pages. For now, just note the tiny triangle that opens and—when you need more space—closes it, as identified in Figure 26-10.

- **Grid ruler pop-up menu.** This little menu works just as it does in the Timeline window. It's a list of basic rhythmic values (1/4 Note, 1/2 Note, and so on) that adjusts the fine vertical grid lines in the Track Editor.

This rhythmic grid comes into play in several situations. First, the beginnings and endings of your note bars automatically snap against these gridlines when you drag, as described below. Second, GarageBand makes *all* selected notes snap to the nearest gridline when you use the Align To command (page 581). Third, this setting determines the value of any new notes you create by ⌘-clicking, as described in the next section.

Notation Editing

Those little piano-roll bars are awfully cute, and they let even nonmusicians see how long and how high the notes are. For musicians, though, skinny horizontal bars are alien life forms that bear little resemblance to standard musical notation.

So what did Apple do? In GarageBand 2, it added standard musical notation.

To see your software-instrument region displayed as traditional notes, click the little musical-note icon in the lower-left corner of the window. Now your fleet of horizontal bars turns into sheet music, with notes, stems, rests, and all of the other goodies described in Appendix A.

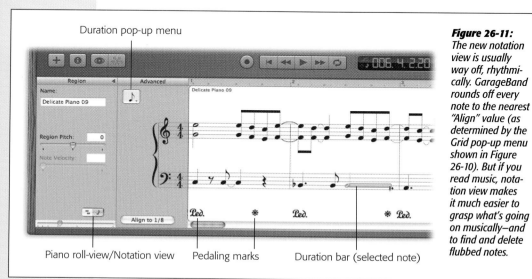

Duration pop-up menu

Piano roll-view/Notation view   Pedaling marks   Duration bar (selected note)

Figure 26-11:
The new notation view is usually way off, rhythmically. GarageBand rounds off every note to the nearest "Align" value (as determined by the Grid pop-up menu shown in Figure 26-10). But if you read music, notation view makes it much easier to grasp what's going on musically—and to find and delete flubbed notes.

Now, the first time they see this new feature, most people who can read music usually have an immediate emotional spike-and-crash cycle. First there's the "Holy cow—this is *sheet music!* I'm a music publisher, baby!" moment.

Which is shortly thereafter followed by the moment best characterized as, "Wait a second—a bunch of the left-hand notes are in the right-hand staff. And the rhythms are all off. That's not what I played! And I can't put in any dynamics, lyrics, articulations, fingerings, slurs, crescendos, or anything else but raw notes!? And I can't even *print* this sucker? What a rip!"

In other words, the first step in mastering notation view is mastering your own expectations. The notation view is very crude. It's intended exclusively for editing in a form that's more recognizable than piano-roll notation. It's *not* for printing, dressing up, playing from, or taking seriously as sheet music.

If you're cool with that, then here's the scoop on editing in notation view:

- You can make the measures wider or narrower by dragging the size slider shown in Figure 26-11.
- You can make the notes larger by enlarging the Track Editor. (Drag the brushed-metal separator bar—the top edge of the Track Editor—upward.)
- Most of the editing techniques described in the following section—adding and deleting notes, adjusting their pitch and duration, and so on—work just as they do in piano-roll view. It helps that when you click a notehead, it sprouts a green horizontal duration bar, which works just like one of the bars in piano-roll view.
- Even so, there are a few notation-only keystrokes that can make this kind of editing go a lot faster. For example, once you've highlighted a note (or a bunch of notes), you can press the right or left arrow keys to slide them left or right on the rhythmic grid. Add *Shift* to make them jump one *measure* left or right.

  Similarly, the up and down arrows make selected notes move up or down by a half-step—and adding Shift makes them jump up or down by an octave (that is, from C to shining C).

The Encyclopedia of MIDI Editing

Now that you know how to navigate the Track Editor, you can get down to the business of using it to rewrite history: changing the recorded music.

Note: Any edits you make to a MIDI region that you've *looped* (by dragging its upper-right corner) appear in *all repetitions* of that loop, which may take you by surprise.

If you'd like to edit only *one* repetition, create it by copying and pasting the original region, so that it's no longer related to the original.

- **Hear a note** by clicking it. (Clicking a note bar also turns it bright green to show that it's selected.)
- **Delete a selected note** by pressing the Delete key.

- **Change a note's pitch** by dragging its note bar up or down, using the center of the note bar as a handle. (If the note won't seem to budge, try zooming in. GarageBand probably considered the note bar too small to make a decent handle.)

Tip: In notation view, you can also shift a note's pitch by pressing the up and down arrow keys.

- **Shorten or lengthen a note** by dragging the right end of its bar. You'll discover that GarageBand forces the note's end to align with the current note grid, described above. (Once again, try zooming in if you're having trouble.)

Note: You can't shorten a note from its left side. If your intention is to lop off the "front" of a note, drag the entire note, as described next, and then shorten the *right* side.

- **Make a note play sooner or later** by dragging its center horizontally. (In notation view, you can also shift a selected note by pressing the right or left arrow keys.)

  You'll notice that as you drag a note, it snaps to the next rhythmic grid line (quarter note, eighth note, or whatever value you've selected from the Grid Ruler pop-up menu shown in Figure 26-10). That's GarageBand's attempt to help keep your music in sync.

  If you'd like to be able to drag freely, choose Control→Snap to Grid (⌘-G), so that the checkmark no longer appears.

- **Duplicate a note** by Option-dragging its bar. This trick works whether you drag vertically or horizontally.

- **Insert a new note** by ⌘-clicking at the appropriate spot. (As soon as you press the ⌘ key, the cursor turns into a little pencil to let you know what's about to happen.)

  In piano-roll view, use the vertical, left-side piano keyboard ruler as a guide to pitch, and the beat ruler to help you figure out where you are in the song.

  You'll soon discover, by the way, that you can't ⌘-*drag* to determine the length of the note you insert. Every new note you create has the same duration. That value (eighth note, for example) is determined by the setting in the Grid Ruler pop-up menu shown in Figure 26-10.

  You can always adjust a note's length once it appears in the Track Editor, of course, by dragging its right end. But when you intend to insert a bunch of notes of similar value, it's worth taking the time to select that duration from the Grid Ruler pop-up menu first.

Tip: Very often, the fastest way to create a new note is not to use the ⌘-click trick at all. Instead, Option-drag an existing note bar to duplicate it; then, before you release the mouse, move it to the proper pitch and time. The first advantage here is that you can duplicate a note that already has the duration and velocity you want; the second is that you can duplicate a *batch* of selected notes at once.

- **Select a few notes** by clicking one, then Shift-clicking each additional note. (Shift-click a second time to remove a note bar from the selected group.)

- **Select a lot of notes** by dragging a selection box around them (Figure 26-12).

  Either way, once you've selected notes, you can perform several editing maneuvers to all of them at once. For example, you can cut or copy them (described next), delete them, Option-drag to duplicate them, stretch or shorten them (drag the right end of any *one* selected note bar), drag them up or down in pitch, drag them left or right in time, and so on. They retain their original timings and relationships.

- **Cut/copy and paste notes to a different spot** by selecting them, choosing Edit→Copy (⌘-C) or Edit→Cut (⌘-X), clicking in the Editor's beat ruler to place the Playhead, and then choosing Edit→Paste (⌘-V). The notes you copied or cut appear at the Playhead position.

  GarageBand *adds* pasted notes to whatever already occupies the paste position, rather than wiping out what's there.

Figure 26-12:
To select a batch of notes, begin dragging diagonally from a blank spot on the Track Editor. Your selection will include any note bar that's even partly enclosed by the resulting box.

When you drag them, they remain in perfect formation.

Transposing Notes or Regions

To *transpose* music means to shift it up or down into a different key, raising or lowering its pitch. In GarageBand 2, you can transpose recordings and loops in both formats: Software Instruments (green) and digital recordings from a microphone. (However, digital recordings—including Apple's own blue loops) start to sound funny if you move them too far from their originally recorded pitches.)

Transposing is a very useful feature. For example, it lets you:

- Adapt a song that was in the perfect singing key for somebody else into the perfect singing key for *you,* without rerecording it.

- Reuse Apple's canned loops in other keys, greatly expanding your palette of chords and harmonies (see Figure 26-13).

- Quickly create an "echo" of a certain musical lick that plays back an octave higher or lower than the first occurrence of that melody.

Now, if you want to transpose only *some* of the notes in a green Software Instrument region, open the Track Editor and use any of the selection techniques described in the previous section. Then drag them up or down, using any one of them as a handle.

The official GarageBand Transpose slider, though, works only on *entire regions*. It goes like this:

1. Select the region you want to transpose.

If you've opened a region for editing in the Track Editor, GarageBand will transpose all of it, regardless of which notes are selected.

You can click a region in the timeline, select a number of regions simultaneously (Shift-click them in the timeline), select all the regions in a track (click the track header), or select the entire piece at once (click in the timeline area and then choose Edit→Select All, or press ⌘-A).

2. Specify how far you want to transpose the region(s).

Use the Region Pitch slider—drag right to transpose the notes higher, left to make them play lower—or type a number into the box just above the slider.

Both of these controls display the number of *half steps* by which you're about to transpose the selected notes. (A half-step is one piano key to the right or left.)

For example, typing *1* here would transpose a middle C up to C sharp, which is the black key just to its right. If you type *2* here, you'd transpose a middle C up to D, the *white* key just to its right.

If you know a little bit about music, you may find the following equivalents handy. To transpose up a major third, enter *4*; up a fourth, enter *5*; up a perfect fifth, type *7*; up an octave, enter *12*.

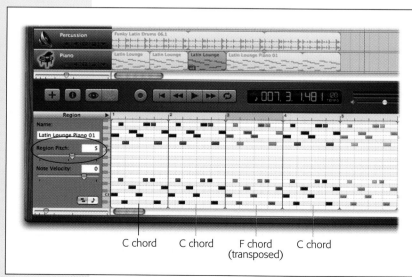

C chord   C chord   F chord   C chord
                                  (transposed)

Figure 26-13:
The loop called Latin Lounge Piano 01 is a great lick. The only problem is that it's a C major chord, now and forever. By transposing copies of this loop, though, you can turn it into any other major chord–F and G, for example–and thereby make it fit the harmonies of many simple pieces.

Note, by the way, the little "+5" indicator, above, on the region itself.

And to transpose the selection *down,* either drag the slider handle to the left, or type a *negative* number into the box (*-12* for an octave down, for example).

You can transpose green Software Instrument regions up to 36 half-steps in either direction (that is, three octaves up or down). You can transpose blue or purple Real Instrument regions 12 half-steps up or down (one octave).

Tip: If you transpose a Real Instrument loop upward and it sounds a little funny—because you've shifted it out of its natural range—try transposing it down a whole octave, so that it lands on the same pitch but in a lower register.

For example, suppose you transpose a bass lick down 4 half-steps, from C to A flat, and it winds up sounding muddy. Think to yourself: *I transposed it by -4; what would be the equivalent pitch 12 half-steps higher? Well, -5 plus 12 = 8.* Drag the slider to 8, and sure enough, you get the same notes, but in a more natural-sounding range.

---

3. **Remain calm.**

   You might expect to see the note bars move higher on the Editor grid when you transpose them upward, or lower when you transpose downward. But instead, the note bars or noteheads remain exactly where they are. (Figure 26-13 proves the point.) Blue loops don't look any different, either.

   Even though they don't *look* different, they do *sound* different. Play back a section that you transposed, and you'll hear the difference immediately.

   Furthermore, you *can* see that a region has been transposed by the little "+5" tag at the lower-left corner of the region in the timeline (a new GarageBand 2 feature). The number there indicates how much the region has been transposed.

If you ever want to restore a region to its original recorded pitch, select it and set the Region Pitch slider to its center position (or type *0* into the box above it).

Quantizing ("Align To" Button)

When Apple representatives demonstrate GarageBand in public, the feature that often gets the most oohs and aahs from the audience is the Align To button. With one quick click, it magically cleans up any recording that has less-than-perfect rhythm. What sounds at first a little ragged, a bit stumbling, suddenly plays back with clean, perfect timing.

Among computer-based musicians, the term for this cleanup is called *quantizing* or *quantization.* In GarageBand, you quantize your music using a button in the Track Editor called Align To.

When you click this button, GarageBand automatically moves all of the notes in a region into perfect alignment with the underlying rhythm grid. In effect, it "rounds off" each note's attack to the nearest eighth note, sixteenth note, or whatever rhythmic value you've specified in the Grid Ruler pop-up menu.

When Not to Quantize

This all sounds wonderful, of course—who wouldn't want a magic button that makes you sound like a better player?—but quantizing is a delicate art. It *can* make your music sound better and cleaner. But it can also create a cacophonous mess.

Many musicians regard quantizing with a certain degree of skepticism. Here's what can go wrong:

- If Align To nudges some notes into alignment with the *wrong* gridlines, your recording may turn into a horrible sounding, clashing crash (Figure 26-14).

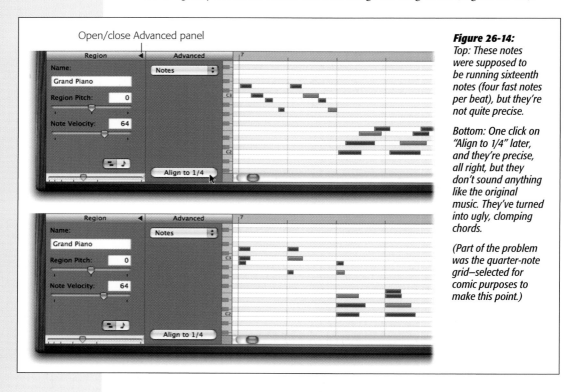

Figure 26-14:
Top: These notes were supposed to be running sixteenth notes (four fast notes per beat), but they're not quite precise.

Bottom: One click on "Align to 1/4" later, and they're precise, all right, but they don't sound anything like the original music. They've turned into ugly, clomping chords.

(Part of the problem was the quarter-note grid—selected for comic purposes to make this point.)

- Quantizing drains a lot of the humanity out of a performance. After all, the tiny quirks and inconsistencies are what give a performance its personality; they make a performance *yours*. When you make every note snap against a fixed-rhythm grid, the music can wind up sounding machine-generated and robotic.

The invention of quantizing software in the '80s helped usher in musical styles that are *supposed* to sound rigidly rhythmic, like disco and rap. But after a while, many musicians grew disenchanted with the way quantizing reduces everything to a machine-gun stutter. Today, professional sequencing programs offer features like *partial* quantization, which lets you specify what *degree* of quantizing you want, and *reverse* quantization (or "humanizing"), which deliberately introduces minor rhythmic inaccuracies into an overly quantized recording to make it sound more human.

GarageBand lacks these less severe quantizing options. It's an all-or-nothing take on quantizing.

- Quantizing flattens out musical effects like grace notes (a lightly played, very quick note right before the main note), glissandos (sliding down the keyboard with a finger), and rolled chords (rolling the hand through a chord rather than striking all notes of it at once). All of the notes in these musical figures get pushed to the nearest eighth-note or sixteenth-note gridline, thereby changing them from delicate special effects into clashing, wrong-note chords.

Tip: On the GarageBand Examples CD (page 506), listen to the file called 05-Quantizing. Double-click the piano region, set the Grid Ruler pop-up menu to "1/8 Note," and then click Align To 1/8.

Now play the file back again to see what's become of the piano part. Let this sample file be a lesson about when *not* to use quantization.

How to Quantize

These downsides notwithstanding, quantizing can still be a very useful cleanup maneuver, especially in the kinds of rock, rap, and hip-hop music for which GarageBand is so well suited. Subtlety and nuance are not necessarily the most prized qualities in those styles.

Here's how to go about fixing the timing of your performance:

1. **Select the music you want to quantize.**

   To quantize an entire region, click its green, rounded rectangle in the timeline (and don't click inside the Track Editor). You can even select more than one region for quantizing just by Shift-clicking them, or an entire track by clicking its header. (You can't quantize more than one track at a time.)

   To quantize only some of the notes in a region, open the Track Editor and select the bars as described on the next page.

2. **Using the Grid Ruler pop-up menu (the tiny ruler icon just above the Editor window's vertical scroll bar), choose the kind of grid you want.**

   If you choose too large a value, like "1/4 Note," all of the faster notes in the region will wind up clumped around the quarter-note gridlines in big, ugly, clashing chords (see Figure 26-14). But if you choose too fine a value, like "1/32 Note," then GarageBand may nudge some of your notes into alignment with the *wrong* gridline—for example, moving certain notes forward instead of backward where you meant them to go. The result is a stuttering, halting disaster.

   The "correct" setting depends on the tempo of your piece, what kind of notes are in it, and the effect you're looking for. Experimentation is the only way to find a setting that works.

3. **Open the Advanced panel, if it's not already open (Figure 26-14). Click the Align To button.**

The exact wording of the button depends on the grid setting you made in step 2. It says "Align to 1/4," for example, or "Align to 1/16." (This is the button that, in GarageBand 1, was called Fix Timing. Apple changed the wording to make it clearer what will happen—that is, what the current rhythmic grid is.)

Give a listen to the results. If the Align To button made a mess of things, you can always choose Edit→Undo (⌘-Z) and try a different setting—or just drag the offending note bars into grid alignment by hand.

Velocity, Pedaling, and Other MIDI Data

As you've probably started to gather by now, there's more to a musical performance than deciding which notes to play when. A keyboard player, for example, adds nuance and interest to a performance using a number of other tools. The *velocity* of the playing (how hard each key is struck), the pedaling (using a sustain pedal connected to the keyboard), and the control wheels (pitch and modulation) can all affect the way the music sounds.

GarageBand records all of this information as you play and lets you edit it later. The key to viewing and editing these kinds of MIDI information is the Advanced panel of the Track Editor (Figure 26-15).

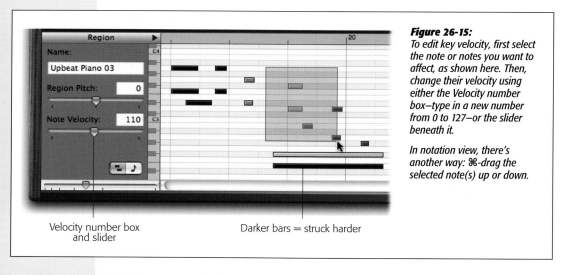

Figure 26-15:
To edit key velocity, first select the note or notes you want to affect, as shown here. Then, change their velocity using either the Velocity number box—type in a new number from 0 to 127—or the slider beneath it.

In notation view, there's another way: ⌘-drag the selected note(s) up or down.

Velocity number box and slider

Darker bars = struck harder

Editing Key Velocity

Key velocity is a digital record of how hard you pressed each key when you recorded a MIDI region. On some instruments, greater key velocity just means "louder," as it does on a piano. But in others, greater velocity means "more vibrato," "crunchier sound," and so on.

Key velocity is measured on a scale of 0 to 127. That may not seem like an especially logical scale to *you*, but (because it's a power of 2) it's very convenient for the Mac to understand. In any case, a velocity of 1 indicates a key pressed with all the force of a falling pigeon feather; a velocity of 127 reflects the force of, say, a second piano falling onto the first. (GarageBand doesn't actually let you change a note's velocity to 0, because that would be a nonsensical value for most musical purposes.)

In the Track Editor, a note bar's *color* indicates its key velocity, as you can see here:

Note color	Key velocity
Light gray	0–31
Medium gray	32–63
Dark gray	64–95
Black	96–127

To edit your notes' key velocities, first open the Track Editor's Advanced panel identified in Figure 26-15. Then proceed as shown in the same figure.

Note: Things can get tricky when you've selected multiple notes with different velocities. In that case, the slider and the number box show the *highest* key velocity among the selected notes. But as you make the adjustment, you're adding or subtracting the *same* amount from all other notes.

If you select three notes, therefore, that have velocity settings of 20, 30, and 40, the Velocity box will say 40. If you drag the slider to shave 10 off the heaviest note, the first two notes will also have decreased by 10. The three notes will now have velocity settings of 10, 20, and 30.

By adjusting key velocities in this way, you can perform a number of different musical-surgery procedures:

- Make an entire *lick* (short musical passage) play with more emphasis. Or less.

- Change the "color" of a chord by lightening up on some notes, and bringing out others.

- Add vibrato to the *money note* (the highest, longest, most important note) of a flute solo.

- Edit an acoustic guitar part so that the sliding grace notes play only where you want them to. (When struck with a key velocity of 124 or higher, most GarageBand acoustic-guitar samples add a little sliding grace note upward from the next lower note.)

Editing Pedaling

If your MIDI keyboard has a sustain pedal—the electronic equivalent of the rightmost pedal on a regular piano—then GarageBand records your foot-presses right along with the key-presses. In the Track Editor, you can even see standard sheet-music pedaling marks, as shown in Figure 26-16.

You can use the Track Editor to edit pedaling you recorded during a performance, of course. But you can also use it to add pedaling to a performance that didn't have any to begin with—a performance you created using Musical Typing (page 556), for example, or a MIDI keyboard that didn't have a pedal.

"Drawing in" pedaling (notation view)

It's light-years easier to edit and insert pedaling in notation view than in piano-roll view, thanks to the prominent *Ped.* markings that indicate when the pedal was pressed. (Note to all beginning piano students: No, it's not a cute little doggie. It's just *Ped.* in a very fancy font.)

If you'd like to experiment, create a new document and insert the loop called Upbeat Electric Piano 03. Its notes are short and sharp, so you'll hear a clear difference when you start adding the sustain pedal.

Then see Figure 26-16 for the details.

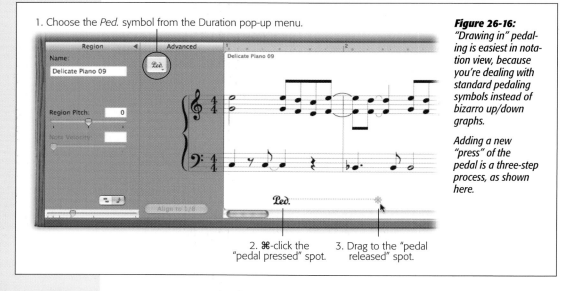

1. Choose the *Ped.* symbol from the Duration pop-up menu.

2. ⌘-click the "pedal pressed" spot.

3. Drag to the "pedal released" spot.

Figure 26-16:
"Drawing in" pedaling is easiest in notation view, because you're dealing with standard pedaling symbols instead of bizarro up/down graphs.

Adding a new "press" of the pedal is a three-step process, as shown here.

"Drawing in" pedaling (piano-roll view)

If notation view isn't your thing, here's how you edit pedaling in piano-roll view:

1. **Open the Advanced panel of the Track Editor.**

   You can see the little triangle to click for the Advanced panel in Figure 26-17.

2. **From the Display pop-up menu, choose Sustain.**

   You've just told GarageBand which kind of invisible MIDI data you want to change.

3. **While pressing the ⌘ key, click a spot along the light gray, top line (labeled 1 in Figure 26-17).**

    GarageBand creates a round handle at the point you clicked. You've just created a "sustain pedal down" event where none existed. (Technically, you can click anywhere in the upper half of the Track Editor window, since GarageBand "rounds off" your click to the top line to indicate a full press of the foot pedal.)

    If you play back your region at this point, you'll hear all the notes get "stuck" at the point where you created the pedal-down event. Unless you enjoy the cumulative, mushy, clashing sound of every note in the piece being held down forever, find a spot to *release* the sustain pedal.

Note: As with key velocity, sustain-pedal motion is recorded on a scale of 0 to 127. Unlike key velocity, however, there's no such thing as a sustain-pedal setting *between* 0 and 127. After all, in the real world, there's no such thing as *half*-pressing the pedal on a piano. So every value is either 0 or 127—which GarageBand tries to simplify by labeling the lines 0 and 1—and your pencil cursor will snap either to the "up" line or the "down" line.

Figure 26-17:
Don't be fooled: When the line is up, the sustain pedal is down, and vice versa. In the world of MIDI software, this particular graph is upside-down from the physical control—the foot pedal—that generates its data. That is, up is "on," and down is "off."

Pedal pressed

Pedal released

4. **Move the cursor to the right, and then ⌘-click a spot on the bottom gray line.**

    Another round handle appears, this time indicating where your virtual player should take his foot off the pedal. A quick playback will prove the point.

Editing existing pedaling (notation view)

You can change the pedaling by dragging the *Ped.* (pedal pressed) and * (pedal released) symbols right or left in the sheet music. You can also delete an entire pedal

---

down-up sequence by clicking either one, so that the dotted line appears, and then pressing the Delete key.

Editing existing pedaling (piano-roll view)

If you've ever edited volume levels of an iMovie video soundtrack, these round handles should seem familiar. They're audio control points, which you can slide around to fine-tune where they appear.

For example, here's what you can do with pedaling points:

- **Drag a handle right or left** to change *when* the pedaling takes place. The control point directly above or below it, if there is one, goes along for the ride, because it takes two to represent one movement of the pedal.

- **Click a handle and then press Delete** to eliminate that handle *and* the one directly above or below it.

   As you'll quickly discover, clicking *one* handle also highlights the one vertically in line with it. For example, if your pedaling map now looks like Figure 26-17, deleting the second pair of vertically aligned points will merge the first pedal-press "mountain" with the second one. You'll be left with a single, but longer, pedal-press.

- **⌘-click the top or bottom line** to introduce a new control point.

Editing Control Wheel Data

Many MIDI keyboards—including the $100 M-Audio keyboard that Apple sells as a companion for GarageBand—have one or two *control wheels* at the left side.

The *pitch wheel* lets you bend a note higher or lower in pitch (like a blues harmonica). Its sibling, the *modulation wheel*, can do a variety of things, like add a sweet vibrato to the sound, change its character, or do nothing at all, depending on which instrument sound you've selected. See page 569 for more on using control wheels.

UP TO SPEED

Beyond Pitch Bend

It's kind of neat that GarageBand records, displays, and edits streams of MIDI information like pitch bend, key velocity, and pedaling. But in the real world of MIDI, those kinds of data are only the beginning. Professional music software can record and play back dozens of other kinds of invisible MIDI data.

Aftertouch, for example, is a measurement of how much pressure you apply to a key after you've pushed it down. Of course, a real piano doesn't respond to aftertouch at all; once you've pressed down a key, pressing harder doesn't give you anything but a thumbache. But on some synthesiz-

ers, bearing down harder on a key after it's already down triggers, say, the vibrato sound on a trumpet.

Program Change data lets you switch to a different synthesizer sound in mid-performance. Breath controller data is generated by a special attachment that, yes, you breathe into, giving you yet another way to change the "shape" of the sound.

GarageBand doesn't record or let you edit these MIDI data types (not that most GarageBand musicians would even care).

Here again, the Track Editor lets you edit any pitch wheel or mod wheel information you generated while recording. It even lets you "turn" one of those wheels after the fact, even if you don't even have a keyboard with control wheels.

To inspect your control wheel data, open the region in the Track Editor, open the Advanced panel (Figure 26-15), confirm that you're in piano-roll view (not notation view), and from the Display pop-up menu, choose either Pitchbend or Modulation.

If pitch wheel or mod wheel information is already a part of the recording, you'll see something like Figure 26-18.

Note: As shown in Figure 26-18, pitch wheel effects usually involve turning the wheel *in between* notes, getting into ready position, and then releasing it, so that it returns to its spring-loaded "at rest" position *during* a note. Or you can do the opposite: Press a key, turn the pitch wheel up or down, and then release both together. Either way, don't be fooled by the up-down and down-up "hills" graphed in Figure 26-18; half of each "hill" actually takes place during the silence between notes.

Most people turn the mod wheel, on the other hand, both up and down during a single note (to make the vibrato gradually begin and end, for example).

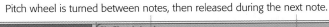

Pitch wheel is turned between notes, then released during the next note.

Figure 26-18:
When you're viewing pitch wheel information, as shown here, the ruler scale goes both upward and downward from 0, because a pitch wheel's "at rest" position is in the middle (see Figure 26-9). You can turn it either up or down. A mod wheel's "at rest" position, though, is turned all the way down, and you turn it only upward, so its scale goes from 0 (at rest) to 127 (all the way up).

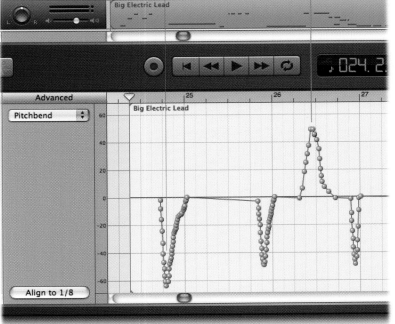

Pitch-wheel data is represented on a scale of 0 (when you're not touching the wheel) to positive or negative 63 (when you've turned the wheel as far as it will go). The mod wheel's scale goes from 0 (at rest) to 127 (turned all the way).

In the case of the pitch wheel, each notch (from 0 to 1, for example) represents one half-step, which is one adjacent key on a piano keyboard. That's useful to remember if you're inclined to add pitch-wheel data to a recording manually (because your keyboard doesn't have wheels, for example).

Once you've got that fact in mind, the techniques for adjusting or creating wheel control points are very similar to the methods for working with sustain pedal data:

- ⌘-click in the Track Editor to create a new round control handle. This is how you'd start "turning" the wheel during a note even if you don't actually have a keyboard with wheels.

- Drag a control handle horizontally to change its timing, or vertically to adjust the intensity of its effect. (Again, 0 means "wheel is at rest.")

- Select a group of control handles to move them all at once; drag any *one* of them as a handle.

This tactic is especially useful when you want to edit pitch-bend or mod-wheel data in a track that you recorded live. As shown in Figure 26-19, using a control wheel during a live performance generates a torrent of control handles. Turning the wheel smoothly and gradually, as you would in a live performance, spits out dozens of control points (0-3-5-11-22-24, and so on). By dragging a whole batch of points

Figure 26-19:
Most instruments' vibratos sound most realistic with the mod wheel turned up only part way—about 50 or so. For added realism, make the vibrato begin and end gradually, and don't begin the wheel turn until a moment after the note has been struck.

at once, you can adjust the timing or intensity of a wheel turn with a single drag. The selected points retain their spatial relationship as you drag them.

- **Delete a turn of the wheel** by selecting all of the representative control points and then pressing the Delete key.

Control wheels: do-it-yourself

If you'd like to experiment with control-wheel data, create a new GarageBand project. Double-click the icon of the Grand Piano starter track, scroll down to Woodwinds, click Pop Flute, and then close the dialog box. (A flute is a great sound for testing control wheels, because its notes are long and sustained so you can hear the effects over time.)

Now open the miniature GarageBand onscreen keyboard (choose Window→Keyboard, or press ⌘-K). Press the letter R key on your keyboard to begin recording, and hold down a long note—C4, for example—on the little onscreen keyboard. Press the Space bar to stop recording after a few seconds of that note.

Now double-click the new green region to open the Track Editor. Make sure the Display pop-up menu says Notes. Zoom in until the note bar you recorded stretches across most of the screen.

Change the Display pop-up menu to say Pitchbend. Now, starting at the 0 midline, go nuts ⌘-clicking control points into a hilly shape, as shown in Figure 26-18. When you play this back, you'll hear the gradual bending of the note over time.

You can repeat the same experiment with the modulation wheel. But this time, start your "hill" from the 0 line at the bottom of the graph, as shown in Figure 26-19. You'll hear your virtual flutist add a gradual vibrato to the note as the "hill" of your mod-wheel graph gets higher.

Importing MIDI Files

Graphics programs can exchange documents in the form of JPEG files. Word processors can exchange text files. Web-design programs can swap HTML documents.

And in the musical world, the common exchange format for finished musical masterpieces is the MIDI file. It's a compact little file that contains no sound data—just note-trigger data that relies on a computer or synthesizer to give it a voice. Hundreds of thousands of MIDI files are all over the Internet, just waiting for you to download. Just go to Google.com, type in *MIDI files "76 Trombones"* or whatever, and in a matter of seconds you've got a list of instrumental versions of that song, arranged and prepared by amateur or professional musicians, ready to download.

Tip: When you click a link to a MIDI file on a Web page, it generally begins to play. That's not the same as downloading the file. In that situation, hit your browser's Back button. This time, Option-click the original link. (Alternatively, Control-click the link and choose from the shortcut menu, "Download Link As" or "Save Link to Disk.") This time, instead of playing the MIDI file, your browser downloads it to your desktop.

The beauty of downloading MIDI files (apart from their being free) is that you can work with them in your music software. You can import a favorite song into Garage-Band, substitute high-quality Software Instrument sounds for the cheesy QuickTime sounds that you hear when you play them online, redo the orchestration by assigning different instrument sounds altogether to each line, add some live recordings to boost the realism, and so on.

This vast Web library of ready-to-play music is ideal for exploits like practicing, karaoke, serving as background tracks for imovie movies and iPhoto slideshows, and so on.

For the first time, GarageBand 2 can directly import MIDI files, so that you can dress them up with effects, add GarageBand's great-sounding drum loops, record some live tracks like vocals, and so on. Figure 26-20 shows the details.

Once GarageBand is showing the imported musical material, you can play it back, change the tracks' instrument assignments, or adjust the tempo or key. (Most MIDI files "know" where their own beats and measures are, so that adjusting GarageBand's tempo correctly speeds up or slows down the MIDI data.)

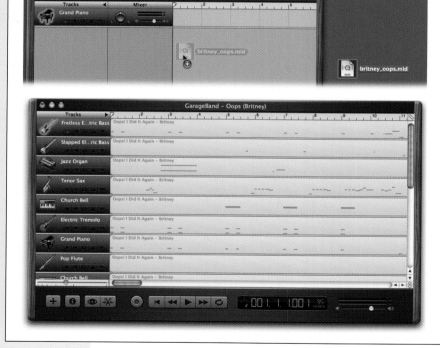

Figure 26-20:
Top: Import a MIDI file by dragging it into an empty spot in the timeline (or into a green Software Instrument track).

Bottom: After a moment, Garage-Band displays the component tracks of the MIDI file. It should sound pretty OK right away, but most MIDI files become dramatically better once you've spent some time reassigning them to GarageBand's more realistic-sounding instruments.

Recording and Editing Live Audio

When you get right down to it, GarageBand is actually three programs in one. It's a loop-building program that lets anyone build great-sounding compositions, even with no musical training. It's a MIDI sequencing program that records whatever you play on a MIDI-compatible keyboard, guitar, or drum set. And now, as you're about to find out, it's also a digital multitrack tape recorder that can record live sound.

That's an important feature, because plenty of musical sources don't have MIDI jacks—including your own voice, not to mention mandolins, harps, violins, castanets, and 8-year-olds burping.

The beauty of GarageBand is that it lets you layer these recordings *on top of* tracks that you've built using its other tools (like loops and MIDI performances), and can play all of it back together at once. The creative possibilities that result are mind-blowing—and make possible a world where Joe Nobody, a guy with a great voice but no money, can produce a studio-caliber demo CD in his living room.

But using GarageBand for *nothing* but its audio-recording features is also perfectly legitimate. Forget the loops, forget MIDI, just use it as a tape recorder with a lot of tracks. You'll still enjoy the freedom to edit your recordings, stack up tracks to create harmony, process them with special sound effects, and mix the whole thing down to a polished, single track.

The Setup

GarageBand can record live audio from two kinds of sound inputs: microphones, and direct line inputs (from electronic instruments like guitars and keyboards, audio interface boxes, and mixers). In version 2, it can even record from several of these sources at once, which is handy if, say, you like to play your guitar and sing.

The Microphone

To record singing, acoustic instruments, or the world around you, you'll need a microphone.

Note: Some acoustic guitars have built-in pickups. If yours does, you don't need a microphone; you can plug the guitar straight into an audio interface, as described next.

This mike can take any of several forms:

- **The built-in microphone on Mac laptops, iMacs, and eMacs.** The drawback of this approach is that you might also pick up the Mac's own fan sounds, and the quality isn't quite studio caliber. But it's cheap, it's built-in, and it works fine for everyday recordings.

- **A cheap USB microphone.** At Amazon.com or Buy.com, you can pick up a microphone that plugs directly into your Mac's USB port for under $20. They come

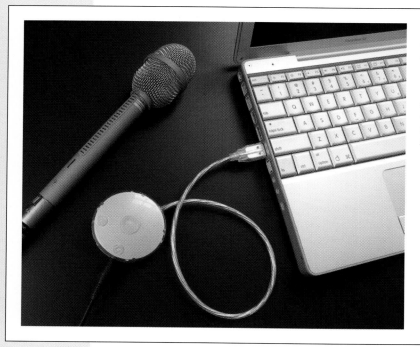

Figure 27-1:
Adapting your microphone to the Mac may require an adapter. Here, a Griffin iMic adapter (preamp) is used for signal boosting for a fancy microphone. The iMic plugs into the Mac's USB jack.

in two forms: headset mikes, designed for use with speech-recognition software, and desktop mikes, which stick up, stalk-like, from a little stand on your desk. Both work fine for recording vocals and—if you position them close to the sound source—acoustic instruments.

- **A regular microphone.** If you have access to a more professional microphone, then by all means, use it. You might run into two problems, though.

First, there's the little matter of fitting the microphone's cable into the Mac's tiny, one-eighth-inch, Walkman-headphones miniplug microphone input. If your microphone's cable ends in a quarter-inch phono plug instead, or even a professional, nickel-sized XLR connector, the cheerful staff at your local Radio Shack will be happy to sell you an adapter. (At Apple's Web site and others, you can buy this adapter in the form of the $20 Monster iStudioLink.)

Second, many microphones (and other sound sources, like record players and tape decks) don't put out enough signal for the Mac's microphone jack. You'll probably need a *preamp* to boost the signal to audible levels.

The most inexpensive option is the $40 Griffin iMic (*www.griffintechnology.com*), which offers not only a built-in preamp but also cleaner sound circuitry than what's built into the Mac. (It's shown in Figure 27-1.)

For even more flexibility, you can use an *audio interface* box like the M-Audio MobilePre USB, which you can also find on the Apple Web site ($150). This more professional box offers three different kinds of input jacks for various microphones and instruments, including both microphone preamp inputs and high-impedance instrument inputs for guitars and basses.

Both the iMic and the MobilePre draw their power from the USB jack, so you don't even have to carry along a power adapter.

Line Inputs

If you have an electric guitar, electric violin, or synthesizer keyboard whose built-in sounds you want to capture, don't bother with the microphone. Instead, connect the instrument's line output cable (which would otherwise go into an amplifier) into an audio interface, like the iMic or M-Audio MobilePre described above. The audio interface then plugs into your Mac's USB port.

In more elaborate setups, you can even connect the outputs from a standalone mixing console. You'd do that if, for example, you wanted to record the playing from several live instruments at once into a single GarageBand track. (Of course, using a very basic program like GarageBand to record from thousands of dollars' worth of recording equipment in this way is a little like using iMovie to edit *The Lord of the Rings*—but hey, whatever floats your boat.)

Because this cable is coming directly from a sound source and not from a microphone, it's called a *line input.*

Introducing the Mac

As you're starting to realize, the Mac is capable of recording sound from a number of different sources: its own built-in mike, an external mike, a line input, and so on. When the moment comes to click the Record button in GarageBand, how will the Mac know what to listen to?

You'll tell it ahead of time, that's how. Figure 27-2 shows the two-step procedure.

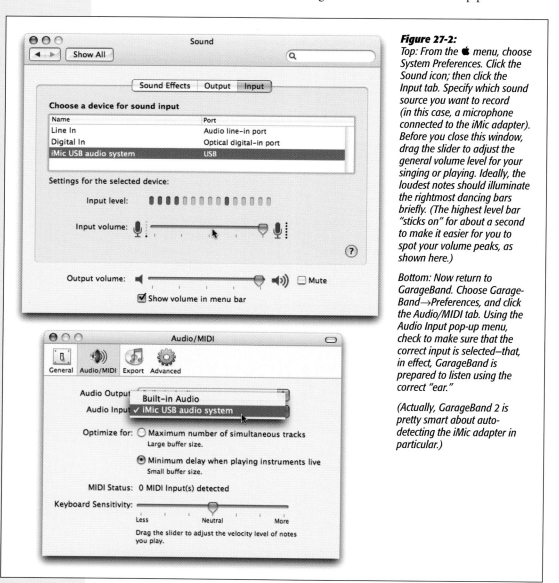

Figure 27-2:
Top: From the ■ menu, choose System Preferences. Click the Sound icon; then click the Input tab. Specify which sound source you want to record (in this case, a microphone connected to the iMic adapter). Before you close this window, drag the slider to adjust the general volume level for your singing or playing. Ideally, the loudest notes should illuminate the rightmost dancing bars briefly. (The highest level bar "sticks on" for about a second to make it easier for you to spot your volume peaks, as shown here.)

Bottom: Now return to GarageBand. Choose Garage-Band→Preferences, and click the Audio/MIDI tab. Using the Audio Input pop-up menu, check to make sure that the correct input is selected—that, in effect, GarageBand is prepared to listen using the correct "ear."

(Actually, GarageBand 2 is pretty smart about auto-detecting the iMic adapter in particular.)

Recording a Live Audio Track

Once you're hooked up, recording a voice or electronic instrument is a lot like recording from a MIDI instrument as described in Chapter 26. In general, though, you'll spend a lot more time in the New Track (or Track Info) dialog box, telling GarageBand about the nature of the sound you're about to record.

Phase 1: Create the Track

What you want is a track that turns bluish when you click it. That's a *Real Instrument* track, as opposed to the green Software Instrument tracks described so far in this book.

Note: When you record digital audio, you create *purple* regions in the timeline. They're the same digital audio as GarageBand's blue, digital-audio *loops,* and you work with them the same way; a single track can contain both blue and purple regions.

Still, the color-coding is a handy means of helping you tell *your* creations apart from Apple's canned ones.

If you don't already have a digital-audio track ready to record, there's a short way and a long way to go about creating one.

The short way is to choose Track→New Basic Track. You get a new, empty Real Instrument track that comes with no effects, monitoring off, and stereo recording on. (You can read about these settings in the following paragraphs.) *Basic* is right!

If you'd like more control over your new track, though, choose Track→New Track instead. This way, the New Track dialog box appears (Figure 27-3).

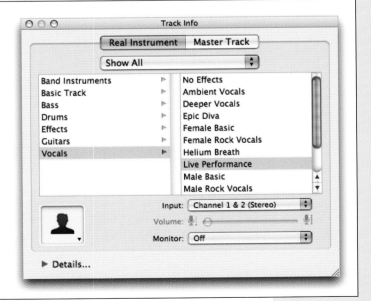

Figure 27-3:
The instruments listed here aren't instrument sounds. They're effect presets that audio engineers consider ideal for the listed instrument types. To use it, click an instrument name in the left column, then an individual effect preset in the right-side list.

Click the Real Instrument tab, and then work through the options as follows:

- **Bass, Drums, Guitars, etc.** It's important to realize that the names listed here don't represent instrument *sounds;* you're going to supply the sound yourself.

  Instead, these are canned sets of *effects,* like reverb and echo, that, in the opinions of GarageBand's creators, are especially well suited to these instrument types. If you plan to sing, for example, you'll find that Live Vocals (in the Vocals category at left) gives your singing sound just a gentle touch of pro-sounding reverb; Male Dance Vocals makes it sound like you're singing in a deserted alley; Ambient Vox sounds like you're at the bottom of the Grand Canyon; and so on.

  Technically, though, there's nothing to stop you from selecting the "wrong" instrument type, such as choosing one of the Horns effects to apply to your guitar playing. Your guitar won't sound like a brass instrument in the least—you're just adding certain processing effects to it—and you might even come up with a strange, spooky sound that's just right for the effect you seek.

Tip: It's a great idea to "walk" through these various effect presets with the up and down arrow keys on your Mac keyboard, listening to each as you play or sing a few notes. Eventually, you'll begin to associate the specific sounds of each preset with its name, and you'll identify your favorites for use in subsequent hit singles.

You can read much more about GarageBand's effects in Chapter 28. For now, though, note that you don't have to make a decision before you record; you can change the effects applied to your live-audio track at any time, before or after the recording session.

To sing without any help from GarageBand's studio-engineer elves, for example, just click the Vocals category, and then click Unprocessed. (On the other hand, a little reverb tends to smooth out the rough edges of the sound, making it sound more professional. As a result, you may feel more comfortable and confident in your singing or playing. That's a psychological byproduct technically called the Singing in the Shower Effect.)

- **Mono or Stereo.** GarageBand can record both the left and right channels of sound from a stereo signal—a stereo microphone, for example, or the left and right outputs from a mixing board. If your sound source does, indeed, produce both left- and right-channel sound, turning on Stereo here tells GarageBand to record them simultaneously. Later, you can use GarageBand's mixing tools to emphasize or de-emphasize one channel or the other, if you like.

  Plenty of instruments, however, produce only a single stream of sound. These are *monophonic,* or mono, sound sources—an electric guitar, for example, or a cheap USB desktop microphone. If that's what you're using, click Mono instead. You'll save a lot of disk space. (Stereo recordings, of course, use up twice as much disk space as mono.)

- **Input.** Even though this pop-up menu appears *above* the Mono/Stereo switch, you'll generally use it *after* making your Mono/Stereo choice. If you've selected

Stereo, this pop-up menu is irrelevant; it always says Channel 1/2 (meaning that it will record from both left and right channels).

This pop-up menu is useful when, for example, you've indicated that you want to record a Mono track, but you've connected a stereo sound source. In that case, this pop-up menu lets you specify *which* channel you want to record: the left (Channel 1) or the right (Channel 2).

The Input pop-up menu is also important when you've connected an audio interface that has enough input jacks for several mikes or instruments at once. Suppose you have an eight-channel box connected, with different microphones or instruments connected to each pair of inputs. In that case, with the Stereo button turned on, you would use the Input pop-up menu to specify which channels you want to record: "Channel 1/2 ," "Channel 3/4," "Channel 5/6," or "Channel 7/8."

- **Monitor: Off/On.** "Monitor," in this case, means "Play what I'm playing through the speaker, so that I can hear it."

Now, your first reaction to this option might well be, "Well, DUH! Of *course* I want to hear myself. It's called an electric guitar, hello! It doesn't make any sound at all unless it's hooked up to an amp or some speakers!"

And sure enough, if you're playing an electronic instrument like a synthesizer or electric guitar, you'll want Monitor to be On. That way, you'll be able to hear your own playing in the context of any other tracks you've already recorded. (You'll also be able to hear yourself when you're *not* recording, so you can rehearse parts before recording them.)

But if you're recording from a microphone, the situation is slightly more complicated. In that case, you can already hear what you're playing or singing. Furthermore, if Monitor is turned on during the recording, your microphone will also pick up *that* sound, coming out of the Mac's speakers.

Unfortunately, that kind of setup produces the ear-splitting, high-pitched whine known as *feedback* (a staple of the standard teen-movie scene in which the doofus principal first steps up to the microphone at the school assembly).

So how do you avoid feedback? Your first instinct might be to turn *off* the Monitor feature. Now you'll hear only the *existing* GarageBand tracks playing as you sing or play—no feedback. Trouble is, GarageBand may then wind up recording both your voice *and* any previously recorded tracks as they play along with you—an ugly situation, because their sound will become a permanent part of your vocal track once you're done.

Fortunately, there's a simple solution to both problems: If you're recording from a microphone, *listen through headphones*. Leave the Monitor feature On, so you can hear yourself as you play or sing.

Tip: Turn Monitor off when you're finished recording. That way, you won't reopen this GarageBand project next week without headphones connected and get a blast of feedback in your ears.

- **Icon pop-up menu.** Use this pop-up menu, if you like, to choose a little picture to represent the recording you're about to make. (It's purely cosmetic, and has no audible link to the instrument sound.) Apple gives you 68 little graphics to choose from—every instrument in GarageBand, plus silhouettes of singers.

Tip: To open this palette of icons, you don't have to click the tiny, down-pointing triangle, as you might expect. Instead, click squarely on the icon itself. That broader target means quicker access.

When you're finished setting up your new Real Instrument track, click OK. You return to the main GarageBand window, where your new, blue track appears, ready for recording.

Phase 2: Prepare the Studio

From here, recording live audio is a lot like the MIDI-recording procedure described in Chapter 26. For most people, the routine goes like this:

1. **Turn on the metronome, if you like.**

   Use the Control→Metronome command, or the ⌘-U keystroke, to turn the metronome clicker on or off.

Tip: GarageBand can even help you tune your instrument (guitar, violin, flute, or whatever).Click the tuning-fork icon at the left of GarageBand's beat counter, or choose Control→Show Instrument Tuner. The display changes to reveal a sort of pitch ruler, with 0 in the center. Play a single note: The tuner displays red lights to the left of the 0 if your instrument is flat, or to the right of the 0 if it's sharp. (It also displays the name of the note it thinks you're trying to play.) If you're perfectly in tune, you get a green light at the 0 point.

---

2. **Choose a tempo.**

   When you record from a MIDI instrument (Chapter 26), the tempo (speed) of the music during your recording makes no difference. During *recording,* you can set the piece so slow, your part is pathetically easy to play. You can stumble along, playing one note per second, like a first-time piano student—and then during *playback,* you can crank up the tempo to make yourself sound like you're some kind of fleet-fingered prodigy. The pop stars do it all the time.

   When you record live playing or singing, however, you lose some of this advantage. When you change the tempo of a piece, audio regions that you've recorded yourself *do* expand or contract to stay aligned with the rest of the music, just as GarageBand loops do. (The fact that live recordings can change speed to fit your new tempo is one of GarageBand 2's coolest features.)

   But the more the tempo changes, the more of a peculiar electronic quality your recorded tracks may gain. Take this moment, therefore, to play back your piece, or at least the hard parts, a few different times at different tempos. (See page 508 for details on using the Tempo control.) Settle on the speed that will suit the finished product.

3. Choose a key.

In GarageBand 1, once you'd recorded a digital-audio track, you were stuck. If you sang in the key of D, the vocal track had to stay in the key of D forevermore; you couldn't transpose digital audio.

The miracle of GarageBand 2, of course, is that it *can* transpose digital audio, even your own singing or live playing. It's no big deal to shift the key higher or lower even after you record.

Here again, though, transposing a live recording changes the sound, even if it's just a tiny bit. And the larger the interval you transpose, the more processed the recording sounds.

Therefore, you should go through the piece a couple of times to make sure it's not too high or too low for your singing voice, or—if you're playing an instrument—to make sure it's in a comfortable key for playing.

FREQUENTLY ASKED QUESTION

Real-Instrument Delay

I've got my synthesizer's outputs connected to the Mac. I'm lovin' this thing! The only trouble is, there's a fraction-of-a-second delay between the time I press a key and the time I hear the sound. The response times are killin' me. What's up with that?

When you press a key, it's taking that much time for the signal to go down the cord to your Mac, undergo processing by GarageBand's effects, and emerge through your Mac's speakers. (In the music biz, this frustrating delay is called latency.)

Most people don't have to contend with latency problems. The issue crops up only on certain Macs and with certain equipment setups.

In any case, GarageBand comes equipped with a latency-reducing feature, right in the GarageBand→Preferences

dialog box. Click the Audio/MIDI button to reveal the controls shown here.

If you click "Minimum delay when playing instruments live," the latency problem should clear up, or at least shrink dramatically.

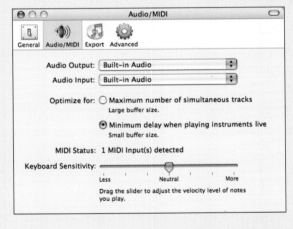

As you can read right in the dialog box, though, there's some fine print: "Small buffer size." In English, that means, "You've just diverted some of GarageBand's horsepower to solving this latency thing. The program therefore has less power available for playing back your piece. If you're using a slow Mac, or if you've got a lot of tracks, GarageBand may have trouble keeping up."

In that case, see Chapter 33 for some GarageBand speed tricks.

---

4. Put the Playhead where you want recording to begin.

To start at the beginning, press the letter Z key or the Home key. To start anywhere else, click in the beat ruler or use the keyboard shortcuts (page 510) to put the Playhead there. Of course, you may find it best to put the Playhead a few measures to the *left* of the part where you want to begin singing or playing, so you'll be able to get into the groove of the music before you begin.

5. Set up a countoff.

As you know, GarageBand can "count you in" with a measure full of clicks at the proper tempo so you'll know when to come in. To turn on the countoff, choose Control→Count In, so that the command bears a checkmark in the menu.

6. Tell GarageBand which track you want to record by turning on the little round, red Record dot in its track header.

In fact, you can turn on *more than one* of these Record-Enabled dots; GarageBand 2 is perfectly happy to record up to seven Real instruments and one Software (MIDI) instrument simultaneously. (You can turn these dots on or off only when the music is stopped or playing back, not during recording.)

To make this work, you need an audio interface (that is, a USB mixer) that sends more than one channel to the Mac via its USB connector. You must also double-click each track's header and, in its Track Info dialog box, assign it to a different channel (or pair of stereo channels) using the Input pop-up menu.

7. Put on your headphones, if you're using them. Get ready to play or sing, and then click the red, round Record button next to the playback controls.

Or just press the letter R key on your Mac keyboard.

Either way, you hear the countoff measure, if you've requested one, and then GarageBand begins to record.

8. When you come to the end of the section you hoped to record, tap the Space bar (or click the Play button) to stop recording.

On the screen, you'll see the new purple region you recorded.

Tip: Instead of stopping altogether, you can also tap the R key on your keyboard to stop recording but *keep playing.* You can then listen for a while, and then tap R again to record a later section.

In fact, you can tap R as often as you like during recording. Each time, GarageBand seamlessly kicks into, or out of, Record mode as it plays.

---

9. Play back your recording to hear how you did.

Rewind to the spot where you started recording. Tap the Space bar to hear your performance played back.

Multiple Takes

As long as you've got yourself a high-quality software studio, you may as well avail yourself of the various cheats that professional recording artists use—and that means mixing and matching the best parts of each "take."

One strategy involves recording your live audio part for the entire song, start to finish. If you mess up, just keep going.

Then prepare for a second attempt like this:

1. **Mute the first track.**

   That is, click it and press the letter M key on your keyboard, or click the little speaker icon in its track header.

2. **Create a second Real Instrument track with the same settings.**

   As it turns out, GarageBand offers a handy shortcut for this step: Choose Track→Duplicate Track (⌘-D). GarageBand gives you a perfect duplicate of the track—empty of notes or regions, but with its settings and effects intact.

Figure 27-4:
Top: In this example, you've recorded two different attempts at the same vocal track. The first take was superior in almost every way—except for the middle part.

Middle: Click the first track and Shift-click the second, so that they're both selected. Position the Playhead just before the messed-up portion and press ⌘-T (the Split command). Then position the Playhead just after that section and press ⌘-T again. You've just chopped up both takes.

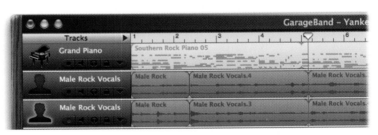

Bottom: Drag the middle segment of the bottom track (the good one) upward so that it replaces the bad portion of the first take. Now you have a single, unified track containing the best of both attempts. Delete the second-take track.

3. Rerecord.

Repeat these three steps until you've got yourself a number of alternate takes to choose from.

Now it's a simple—and, frankly, enjoyable—matter to chop up these various takes, deleting the bad portions and leaving only the good ones, as shown in Figure 27-4. (Of course, you can also copy and paste successful parts—the chorus, for example—without having to redo them.) For a discussion of splitting, recombining, and otherwise editing Real Instrument regions, see Chapter 25.

Punching In and Out

If *most* of the first take was good, but you flubbed a shorter section somewhere in the middle, you may want to record right over the bad spot. That's where *punching in* comes in.

As you can read on page 565, punching in and out is when the software switches from Play mode to Record mode automatically during a segment of the music that you've bracketed in advance (in GarageBand's case, using the yellow Cycle stripe at the top of the window).

Using punch in/punch out for a Real Instrument track is *almost* exactly the same as for a Software Instrument track. Once again, the idea is to turn on cycling (press the letter C key on your keyboard), adjust the yellow Cycle stripe so that it highlights the music you want to rerecord, turn on the Control→Count In command, and then press the letter R key (or click the red, round Record button) and get ready to play. (See Figure 27-5 for the rest of the story.)

Cycle region

Figure 27-5:
When you're set up to punch in (rerecord a specified section), GarageBand plays one measure of music before you come in, and then begins to record whatever you play or sing. When you reach the end of the cycle region (identified by the yellow stripe), GarageBand continues to loop the playback of the cycle region until you click the Play button (or press the Space bar).

There is, however, one big difference between punching into Real Instrument and punching into a Software Instrument. With a Real track, GarageBand records only what you sing or play the *first time through* the cycle region. Then, when the playhead reaches the end of the yellow cycle stripe, GarageBand instantly stops recording and switches to playback-only mode. (In other words, you can't keep playing or singing to build up a cumulative take, one pass at a time, as you can when playing a MIDI instrument.)

The nice part is that if even your punched-in recording wasn't quite right, taking another stab at it is supremely easy. Just tap the letter R key again. GarageBand automatically plays the measure before the yellow stripe, and once again autorecords whatever you play when the playhead reaches the punch-in region. You can repeat this exercise as many times as you need to get the passage perfect.

Editing Real Instrument Regions

When it comes to editing, Real Instrument regions don't offer nearly as much flexibility as Software Instruments. Real Instrument regions are digital recordings of live performances; you can't very well correct a wrong note, boost the emphasis of a sung word, shift the performance in pitch, draw in new notes, or have any of the kind of fun described in Chapter 26.

Still, as Chapter 25 makes clear, you can massage *any* kind of region—Real or not—in a number of useful ways. You can chop them up, rejoin them, drag them around in time, copy and paste them, and so on.

If you double-click a blue or purple region, in fact, you behold the sight in Figure 27-6: actual audio waveforms that make it very easy to isolate certain notes or syllables. You've just opened the Track Editor for a Real Instrument region. (If you've clicked a blue track to select it, you can open the corresponding Track Editor in any of three

Figure 27-6:
By zooming in, you gain incredible precision in selecting portions that you intend to cut or copy.

Note, however, that you can't use this zoomed-in view for the purpose of positioning the Playhead to split a region unless you've turned on Playhead synchronization. To do that, make sure that the button circled here shows two aligned Playheads; if not, click there!

Playhead sync button

Area where dragging moves the region instead of making a selection

other ways: Choose Control→Show Editor, press ⌘-E, or click the ![button] button below the track headers.)

The "mountains" on display in the Track Editor for a Real Instrument region show the bursts of volume in the track—individual notes of an instrument, for example, or words in a vocal track. (A flat straight line means silence.)

There are a few tricks worth noting here:

- The top edge of a region in the Track Editor—maybe about the top eighth of it (Figure 27-6)—is a special zone. Inside it, the cursor changes to this ◀▶ shape. You can now *move* the region by dragging it from side to side.

Tip: When your cursor has that shape, you can also select an entire region with a single click. (Yes, that's easy to do in the *timeline,* but it wouldn't otherwise seem possible in the Track Editor.)

If you click any lower, your cursor becomes a simple cross ✛, and you actually wind up dragging across waveforms and highlighting them. Learning how high to position your cursor for these two different purposes is just part of the game.

- If you drag the upper-right corner of a Real Instrument region *in the Track Editor,* your cursor takes on the curly Loop shape, and you wind up *looping* the region—that is, making it repeat. In other words, it behaves exactly as though you're dragging the upper-right corner of the *un*magnified region up in the timeline, as described in Chapter 25.

- If you drag leftward on the *lower*-right corner of a region in the Track Editor, the cursor changes to this ▶ shape, and you wind up *trimming* the region—essentially hiding the outer notes. It's just like dragging the trailing edge of a region in the timeline (except that you must use only the lower-right corner as a handle—not the entire right edge, as in the timeline).

- If you paste Real region B on top of Real region A, the pasted region wipes out whatever was underneath, just as you'd expect. But suppose you change your mind.

If you then move or cut away the pasted region, you can tug outward on the end of original region A. The wiped-out sound waves *grow right back,* revealing that GarageBand was only hiding them, not forgetting them.

Which gives you a great trivia question for your next bar bet: How is a GarageBand region like the leg of a starfish?

Enhance Timing, Enhance Tuning

As you've surely figured out by now, the two kinds of music that GarageBand processes—MIDI data and digital audio—have very different characteristics. The beauty of MIDI data is that you can edit the recorded notes as though they're typed text in a word processor. Type in new notes, delete others, shift their timing, fix wrong notes.

None of this is possible with digital recordings, which are simply frozen snapshots of a live performance.

Right?

What's mind-blowing about GarageBand 2, though, is that it flagrantly breaks these time-honored rules. Apple has somehow figured out how to fix out-of-tune notes and "off" rhythms even in a digital recording. You just drag a slider to control how much pitch or timing correction you want applied to the recording—a feature that generations of audiences at certain amateur concerts would have given their eye teeth for.

That's not to say that editing digital-audio recordings is every bit as flexible as editing MIDI recordings. Here are some of the limitations:

- You still can't grab a note and drag it, willy-nilly, to a different pitch; all GarageBand can do is round off notes to the closest pitch or beat.

- The Enhance Tuning feature can apply its magic only to recordings of single-note (monophonic) performances like a singer, a flute, or a trumpet. It doesn't work on polyphonic ones (piano, guitar chords, harp).

- You must apply the Enhance Tuning/Enhance Timing features to an entire track at once. You can't wave the magic wand over only a single region (although you can, of course, chop out the problem section and put it on its own track).

- Applying too much Enhance Tuning/Enhance Timing mojo can produce pretty weird results. Use the sliders judiciously.

Even so, it's amazing that you can even fix any timings or tunings at all. Here's how it works (see Figure 27-7).

Figure 27-7:
Apart from the positions of the sliders, you have no visual indication that you've applied GarageBand's tuning or rhythm-fixing features—but you hear it, all right.

Enhance Tuning

Ready to fix a tin ear? Double-click inside the Real Instrument track that contains the out-of-tune notes; the Track Editor opens. Drag the Enhance Tuning slider to the right (Figure 27-7).

For best results, do this while you're playing back (or even cycling) the problem passage, so you can monitor the effect. In general, the more of this effect you apply, the weirder the results may sound. Your goal is to fix the off-pitch notes without making the whole thing sound processed.

Tip: GarageBand tries to nudge each note into alignment with one of the 12 chromatic steps of the scale—that is, to the closest black or white piano key. If you turn on the "Limit to key" checkbox below the slider, though, the effect is even more pronounced. Now you're shoving each note to one of the seven pitches of the song's key (say, G major).

Incidentally, do you remember the weird, electronic, can't-take-your-ears-off-it note-sliding effect that made Cher's 1999 "Believe" such a hit? That's what you get when you sing a song with a fair amount of deliberate sliding between notes, then turn on the "Limit to key" checkbox, and drag the slider all the way to the right.

Enhance Timing

Whereas Enhance Tuning is ideal for performances that had a great feel but a few out-of-tune notes, Enhance Timing cleans up performances that were note-perfect but, here and there, rhythmically sloppy. The steps are similar: Double-click a region in the Real Instrument track that contains the out-of-tune notes. Then, in the Track Editor, drag the Enhance Timing slider a little bit to the right.

Use the pop-up menu below the slider to specify how much GarageBand should round off the music: to the nearest eighth note, sixteenth note, or whatever.

You're adjusting the underlying rhythm grid. Larger note values (like 1/4 note) may distort the melody pretty badly—and even Cher never had a hit with *that* effect.

Transposing a Real Instrument Region

As noted earlier, GarageBand 2 possesses the remarkable ability to transpose a digital-audio recording higher or lower—something that should not, by conventional wisdom, be possible. Just drag the Region Pitch slider shown in Figure 26-13, or type an interval (the number of half-steps) into the text box. Page 577 offers more detail.

Note again, however, that transposing too far from the original pitch can introduce some pretty freaky changes to the sound. Transposing live recordings, therefore, is something best done in moderation.

Effects, Guitar Amps, and Instrument Modules

G arageBand is more than a MIDI sequencer, more than a loop-based music construction set, even more than a multitrack tape recorder. It's also the equivalent of a six-foot-tall, $100,000 rack of studio processing equipment and a room full of guitar amplifiers.

The point is to give you exactly the same professional edge that recording artists have. If your singing sounds a little dry, you can "sweeten" the track with a little reverb. If you're looking for a distinctive keyboard sound for the indie post-grunge trash music you're trying to record, you can bleach out all of the low frequencies and add some stereo tremolo. And if you're a guitarist, GarageBand is pleased to offer you a music store's worth of amplifiers from every decade since 1960.

You can apply these effects to both Real and Software Instruments. You can also apply them on a track-by-track basis (when you're trying to fine-tune one instrument's sound) or to the entire mix at once (when you want to tweak the acoustics of your "garage" space).

Either way, you'll soon discover that the simple, idiotproof face of GarageBand gradually disappears as you begin drilling down into the intricacies of its effects and instrument modules. They offer some of the world's most advanced recreations of real-world, rack-mounted recording machines ever written—and they offer the technical complexity to match.

Instrument-Named Presets

Whenever you double-click a track's header, its Track Info dialog box appears. At the top of it, GarageBand presents a list of what appear to be instrument names (Figure 28-1).

At first glance, these instrument names may seem to have completely different functions for the two kinds of tracks in GarageBand:

- If you've opened a blue Real Instrument track, these instrument names don't refer to instrument sounds; they identify *effects presets*. Each is a carefully adjusted combination of studio processing effects—reverb, EQ (equalization), and so on—that, in the opinion of a professional recording engineer, is well suited to the instrument named in the list.

- If you've opened a green Software Instrument track, you might assume that the instrument names here—Grand Piano, Orchestral Strings, and so on—*are* instru-

These effect presets...

...are composed of these settings.

Figure 28-1:
The Track Info dialog box is a lot like the New Track dialog box. But when you click Details, some important controls appear at the bottom. These are the building-block effects generators that make up the instrument-named presets in the top list. (And the two pop-up menus in the Details panel list the building blocks of those building blocks. It's possible to burrow down very deeply into GarageBand's effects-processing underworld.)

ment sounds. After all, selecting a different instrument in the list changes the sound of whatever's in the track.

But as you'll find out in this chapter, these instrument names also include custom-tailored effects. These are, in other words, instrument-and-effect presets.

For each one, you can modify not only the effect Apple has assigned, but even the sounds themselves, which GarageBand generates from 18 built-in modules—Piano, Strings, Guitar, and so on. For a given instrument named in the list, you can even substitute a different sound module altogether.

When you click an instrument category in the left-side list, the presets are listed in the right-side list. Apple has tried to name them helpfully, to suggest their sonic effect: for example, Edgy Drums, Punk Bass, or (in the Vocals category) Epic Diva. In the Guitar category, most of these presets incorporate the famous GarageBand *guitar-amplifier simulations* (page 616).

Whatever effect preset you choose becomes part of the track. Any sound in that track is affected the same way by those effects.

Save Instrument, Delete Instrument

For want of a better term, Apple calls the effects presets in this dialog box *Instruments.*

In the following pages, you'll learn how to operate the knobs and dials of the individual effect processors (Compressor, Reverb, and so on) that make up each Instrument. The process begins by clicking the Details triangle to expand the dialog box, as shown in Figure 28-1.

It's comforting to know, though, that once you've spent some time tweaking the effects settings for a certain "instrument" (effects preset), you can save your work for use with other tracks and in other GarageBand projects. All you have to do is click the Save Instrument button at the bottom of the dialog box. GarageBand invites you to name your new effect preset. Thereafter, it will appear in the right-side list (see "Giggly Baritone" shown in Figure 28-2).

In fact, GarageBand is so concerned that you might lose hours effects fiddling that, if you try to close the dialog box or select a different "instrument" *without* clicking Save Instrument, it shows you the warning box in Figure 28-2.

So yes, it's very easy to create *new* effect presets. Fortunately, it's also easy to prune the list, throwing away any that you've created that, in the cold light of day, you decide really aren't such masterpieces. Just highlight its name in the right-side list and then click Delete Instrument at the bottom of the dialog box.

Note: You can't use the Delete Instrument button to delete any of *Apple's* effect presets—only your own misbegotten attempts.

Effect Modules

See the flippy triangle next to Details? As noted earlier, clicking it makes the Track Info dialog box expand. You've just revealed a set of building-block effects like Gate, Compressor, Reverb, and so on (Figure 28-3). These are the components of the instrument-named presets in the lists above.

Now, if you've spent the prime years of your life hanging around recording studios, terms like *Gate, Compressor,* and *Equalizer* may already be familiar to you.

If you're anyone else, well, resign yourself to the fact that *reading* about effects is not a very good way to learn about them. The fact is, their names are little more than puny human attempts to describe sounds that are, in many cases, other-worldly and indescribable.

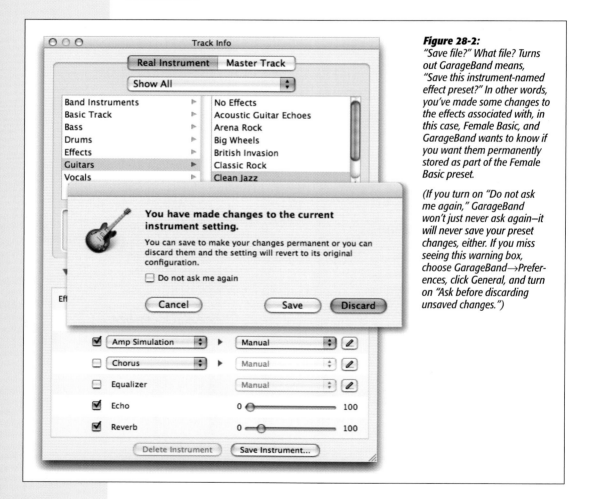

Figure 28-2:
"Save file?" What file? Turns out GarageBand means, "Save this instrument-named effect preset?" In other words, you've made some changes to the effects associated with, in this case, Female Basic, and GarageBand wants to know if you want them permanently stored as part of the Female Basic preset.

(If you turn on "Do not ask me again," GarageBand won't just never ask again—it will never save your preset changes, either. If you miss seeing this warning box, choose GarageBand→Preferences, click General, and turn on "Ask before discarding unsaved changes.")

Still, the prose that follows may be helpful if you read it *while* performing any of these three self-guided exercises:

- Play with the tutorial file called "06—Effects" (on the GarageBand Examples CD described on page 508). It's a project whose tracks are already set up with various guitar-amp simulations.

- As a convenient software quirk, the Track Info dialog box behaves more like a separate program than a true dialog box. That is, even when it's in front of the main GarageBand window, you have full access to GarageBand's controls. You can start and stop playback, add loops, edit notes, and so on.

Tip: You can even click a different track without first closing the Track Info dialog box. You'll see the dialog box update itself instantly to reflect the effects of the currently selected track.

Figure 28-3:
The instruments named in the top part of the dialog box refer to combinations of effects that Apple engineers set up using the Details panel. Yet even these components have components. As you can see here, the true effects aficionado can work this dialog box from the bottom up, first creating a sub-preset for each effect, then naming the collection of presets for the list at top.

To edit one of these sub-presets, click the adjacent pencil button.

If you've already recorded a live performance onto a track, therefore, one great way to experiment with effects is to turn on *cycling playback* for some of it (page 509). Now, in the Track Info dialog box, expand the Details section if necessary, and start the music playing. (You can just tap the Space bar to start and stop the music.)

The music continues to play, looping over and over again, as you tweak its sound with the GarageBand effects controls.

- You can also listen to how each effect changes the sound *while* you play—that is, before you've actually recorded anything. Just connect your microphone or instrument output to the Mac. Play or sing, listening with headphones, as you fiddle with the controls in the dialog box.

In any case, here's a summary of what you'll find in the Details panel. (For a deeper analysis of what these common studio effects do, visit *www.harmony-central.com/ Effects/effects-explained.html.*)

To apply a certain effect to the track you're editing, turn on the checkbox next to its name, and then explore the pop-up menu to its right.

Note: Before you go nuts adding effects to an individual *track*, remember that you can also apply any of these effects to the *entire song,* using the Master Track feature described in the next chapter. Part of the art of mixing is knowing when to process just one instrument, and when to tweak the entire overall mix.

Generator (Software Instruments Only)

This pop-up menu appears only in the Track Info dialog box for Software Instrument tracks. Most people, most of the time, are content to let GarageBand's piano be a piano, its guitar be a guitar, and so on.

You can, however, delve into the sophisticated modeling software that GarageBand uses to produce these sounds, either to subtly tweak the built-in sounds or to radically remake them. In fact, using the Save Instrument button described earlier, you can even create an entirely new Software Instrument, named whatever you please. (You also use this pop-up menu to load new sounds that you've found online.)

The first step is to choose a basic instrument sound from the pop-up menu. Most of them are just what they sound like: Piano, Strings, Horns, Woodwind, Guitar, Bass, Drum Kits. The remaining ten modules are software versions of synthesizers, capable of generating a wild variety of sounds—and not just musical notes (see Figure 28-4).

Familiar instrument names

When you select a traditional instrument name from the Generator pop-up menu, the pop-up menu to its right comes to life. It lists sub-species of the instrument's type: Alto Sax, Tenor Sax, and so on.

If you now click the pencil button, you see a dialog box like the one shown in Figure 28-4. Here's where you can adjust several parameters of the underlying sound. For most instrument sounds, you get three sliders:

- **Volume.** You guessed it: How loud the sound is.

- **Cutoff.** This slider adjusts cutoff frequency for a *lowpass filter*, whose effect is to filter out high frequencies. If you try it on the Grand Piano, for example, dragging the Cutoff slider to the left muffles the sound, as though you're turning down the treble control on a stereo.

- **Release.** This slider governs how long a note "rings" after you've struck the key. In the real world, a piano note, for example, falls silent the instant you take your finger off the key (unless you're pressing the sustain pedal, of course). But by dragging this slider toward Slow, you can make the notes hang in the air longer before fading away.

Note: The Manual dialog box for electric pianos is slightly different. It also offers two options for the underlying Tone: Tines (a bell-like sound, like the classic Fender-Rhodes electric piano of the '80s), and Reeds (a more nasal, oboe-like sound).

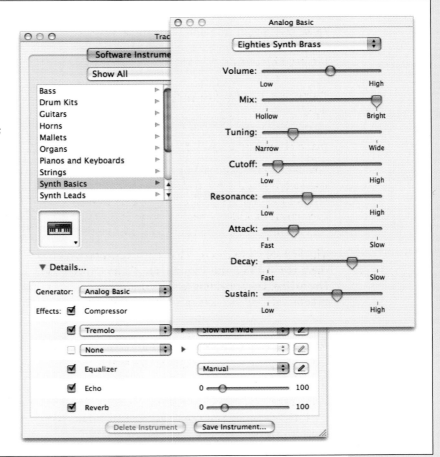

Figure 28-4:
You can adjust the quality of GarageBand's built-in instrument sound generators by clicking the little pencil button. Sometimes you're offered only a few options; sometimes, as with the synthesizers (like the one shown here), you can adjust as many as eight different sliders. In combination, they offer you a nearly infinite number of different sound possibilities.

Synthesizer generators

When you choose one of the synthesizer modules from the first pop-up menu, however, your options multiply considerably. Now when you click the pencil button, the manual-settings dialog box contains a full arsenal of synth controls—and learning what they all do could take you years. In the real world, synth programming is a full-time hobby, if not a full-time job.

In addition to the Volume, Cutoff, and Release parameters described above, the synth generators offer many other sliders. They vary by module, but here's a taste:

- **Tuning.** Some synth sounds are actually composed of multiple "voices" playing simultaneously. Using this slider, you can make the secondary voices play out of tune with the primary one. At the Narrow setting, detuning the voices in this way adds only a subtle piquancy to the sound, an intriguing twang; as you drag the slider toward Wide, the secondary voices begin to sound like completely different notes, farther and farther from the one you're actually playing.

- **Resonance.** Has a lot to do with how rich and full-bodied the synth sounds.

- **Attack, Decay.** A slow *attack* means that when you strike the key, the sound eases in, rather than sounding instantly. A slow *decay* means that after you release the key, the sound eases out instead of cutting off sharply.

- **Glide.** This wacky effect, found in the Analog Mono generator, connects all the notes you play by sliding between the pitches. It sounds like a slide-whistle player gone berserk.

- **Character, Harmonics, Timbre.** These controls, found primarily in the Digital synth modules, change the character of the sound in ways that are impossible to describe in words. Set your Software Instrument track a-playing (or even a-cycling) and drag these sliders to hear for yourself.

- **Drawbars, Percussion Time, Percussion Level, Click, Distortion.** These are all parameters unique to the Tonewheel Organ generator. In combination, they're capable of simulating a huge variety of organ sounds. Choose a preset from the pop-up menu at the top of the dialog box to see some of the possibilities.

Gate (Real Instruments Only)

The *gating* function (often called a *noise gate* by recording geeks) simply eliminates all sound that's quieter than a certain level, which you specify by dragging this slider. The result: total silence in the quieter sections of a track.

In the recording industry, gating can be useful to eliminate hiss from the silent parts of, for example, an old recording. Very few of the GarageBand presets use gating, but you can apply it to your own recordings—for example, when you're trying to get rid of the hum from a microphone or other component.

Compressor

Imagine a graph of your song's volume level over time. A studio *compressor* limits this volume graph so that it doesn't vary so wildly. There's less difference between the loudest and softest parts.

Because compressors can bring out the "highlights" of a track without making the background so low as to be inaudible, they're among the most frequently used effects in today's pop music. A compressor adds punch to a solo or—if you apply it to the Master Track—the overall song. It also helps the music sound better on cheap speakers—like boombox speakers, portable iPod speakers, or your Mac's speakers.

To try out this effect, turn on its checkbox and then drag the slider. 0 means no compression; 100 means maximum compression.

"Additional Effects" Pop-Up Menus

These two unlabeled pop-up menus, near the middle of the Details panel, are complex and deep enough to merit a book of their own. These are fantastically sophisticated software controls that emulate racks full of studio equipment. You can spend hours in here, fiddling with the sliders and checkboxes, in an effort to find the perfect tweak for your vocal or instrumental line.

Note: The two pop-up menus are identical. Apple has given you two of them so that you can apply two effects simultaneously.

Actually, there are a total of *four* pop-up menus. Each time you choose an effect category from a *left-side* pop-up menu, the pop-up menu to its *right* comes to life, pre-stocked with useful presets. (As you're beginning to notice, GarageBand offers presets for the component effects that make up the *instrument-named* presets listed at the top of the dialog box. Presets within presets.)

You may find only three presets in this second pop-up menu (Soft, Medium, Hard) or as many as 20 (Birdish, Club at Next Door, Slow and Deep, and so on). You can dial up your own presets, too (Figure 28-5), and then save them so that they appear in this second pop-up menu (Figure 28-6).

Note: Once you've used the pencil button *once,* GarageBand leaves you stuck in "I Want to Adjust This Effect Manually" mode until you quit and reopen it. That is, *every* time you choose from the first effect pop-up menu, its underlying manual-adjustment dialog box pops up automatically, without your having to click the pencil button.

On the other hand, you don't have to *close* this manual-settings dialog box before choosing a different effect from the first pop-up menu. You can feel free to experiment, choosing different effect names and admiring the way the manual-settings dialog box changes before your eyes each time.

Now that you understand the basic ritual—choose an effect generator from the first pop-up menu, choose a preset from the second, and adjust manually if you like—here's a list of the primary effect generators as they appear in the first pop-up menu.

Note: After each description, you'll find a brief account of what the manual-settings dialog box offers (the one that appears when you click the pencil button).

 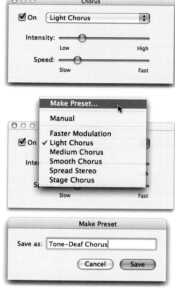

Figure 28-5:
Left: Here, you've selected Chorus; the second menu offers Chorus presets.

Top right: But if you click the pencil button, this box lets you craft your own manual settings.

Middle right: If you come up with some jaw-dropping sound, save your creation by choosing Make Preset.

Lower right: Name this effect. From now on, it will show up in the presets pop-up menu (the one that's shown being opened here at left).

Amp Simulation

If you're an electric guitarist, and you've slogged along this far, here's what you've been waiting for, the gem of GarageBand for guitarists: the amp simulators. These are the effects Steve Jobs and pop artist John Mayer demonstrated onstage when GarageBand was first unveiled at a Macworld Expo; this is the feature that gets true garage-band musicians drooling.

As it turns out, the sound an electric guitar makes is profoundly affected by the amplifier it's plugged into. Various bands of the last 40 years have put both themselves and certain amps on the map by creating trademark guitar sounds.

Unfortunately, amplifiers are expensive, heavy, and impractical to transport in big numbers. To have a single software program on, say, a laptop, that can deliver perfect impersonations of 17 classic amplifiers—with names like Grunge, Scorching Solo, British Invasion, and Seventies Rhythm—is, for guitarists, quite a treat.

(For anyone else, it may be no more than a big yawn. That's an OK reaction, too.)

As you can guess, these amp simulations work best if you have an electric guitar connected to your Mac. (Run its line output into one of the audio interface boxes described on page 597, for example.) Listen on headphones as you experiment and noodle.

Manual options: See Figure 28-6.

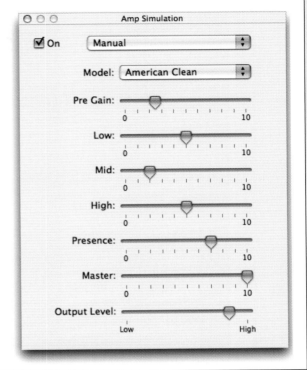

Figure 28-6:
These core effects lie at the heart of the amplifier simulations for guitars. The manual options here are the most elaborate of any GarageBand effect. Beginning with the type of guitar you're playing, these controls let you specify everything about the amp, from its gain (the strength of the incoming signal) to output (the strength of the post-processed signal).

You can tweak the controls to your heart's delight— just as guitarists love to do with their real amps.

Auto Wah

"Wah" here refers to the *wah-wah pedal,* a staple of electric guitar players. The name, as you can probably guess, is an onomatopoeia—the name describes the sound of the effect.

Onstage, guitar players traditionally control the timing and intensity of the "wah" by riding a pedal with one foot. In GarageBand, you can't actually control either the timing or intensity, except in your selection of preset.

Even so, you have an entire music store's worth of wah-wah pedal simulators here, with names like Wow, Duck, and CryBaby. Some of them distort the music beyond recognition; others make you sound like you're playing live from outer space. All of them take the range of sounds you can make with your guitar alone (or whatever your instrument) far beyond what you can play without GarageBand's assistance.

Manual options: Sound (Dark–Bright), Reaction (Light–Strong), Mode (Thick, Thin, Peak, Classic 1/2/3).

Automatic Filter

This pop-up menu unleashes a wide spectrum of truly wild and severe effects. Most introduce some form of pulsing, tremolo, or wobbling. A few highlights among the others:

- **Birdish** adds a high-frequency sweep to the sound, as though your composition were so good, aliens were trying to beam you up.

- **Club at Next Door** is truly hilarious. It removes all frequencies except the very lowest, so that only the throbbing bass remains. It's pretty much exactly what you'd hear of your next door neighbor's stereo through an apartment wall, or, as the name suggests, if a dance club were across the street.

- **Slow Shutter** sounds exactly as though an older brother is covering up your mouth with his hand, then flapping it open and closed while you try to speak or sing. It has an extreme "wah-wah" sound to it.

Manual options: Frequency (Low–High), Resonance (Low–High), Intensity (Down–Up & Down), Speed (Slow–Fast).

Bass Amp

Here's another of GarageBand's now-famous amplifier simulations—but this one's geared for electric basses. The second pop-up menu offers presets like Deep Bass Amp, Funk Bass Amp, Fuzz Bass Amp, Reggae Bass Amp, Sixties Bass Amp, Slap Bass Amp, and many others.

Manual options: Pre Gain (0–10), Low/Mid/High (0–10), Mid Frequency (Low–High), Output Level (Low–High).

Bass Reduction, Treble Reduction

As you might expect, these effects crank down the high or low frequencies of this track's music, respectively. Use Treble Reduction if the source material is too hissy; use Bass Reduction if it's too boomy. (The equalizing options perform much the same function, but with more precision.)

Manual options: Frequency (Low–High).

Bitcrusher

GarageBand generally strives to preserve the maximum sound quality of your instruments. It's capable of CD quality, meaning sound that's described by 44.1 kilobits of data per second.

It wasn't always this way. Primitive computers like the very first Macintosh and the Atari, not to mention AM radios, use far less data. As a result, they sound tinny and flat next to, say, the typical GarageBand instrument.

The Bitcrusher effect is designed to throw away musical data *on purpose,* giving your track a retro, played-over-the-phone-line sound. Its presets include AM Radio, Classic 8-Bit (that is, like the oldest Macs), Meet Atari, and others. Some, like Other World, reduce lyrics to unintelligibility; others, like SR Crush, give vocal lines a buzzing, robotic, Vocoder quality. All of the presets do a real number on the sound quality of your track, blasting it into awfulness for use only in special circumstances. (Ever heard the beginning of the Electric Light Orchestra's "Telephone Line?" The opening verse is meant to sound as though it's sung over the phone—and now you can perform the same processing in the privacy of your own home.)

Manual options: Resolution (Low–High), Sample Rate Reduction (Small–Huge).

Chorus

Chorusing is a famous and frequently used effect in pop music (ever heard Abba?). The fundamental idea is that the computer duplicates your track and offsets the copy by just a millisecond or two, so that you sound like there's two (or more) of you singing or playing together. It also makes the two copies slightly out of tune with each other, which helps with the illusion of multiple voices singing at once.

The presets here are primarily designed to let you control how *much* chorusing you want. Among them, Spread Stereo is among the most interesting, because it attempts to place you and your clones in different spots along the left-to-right stereo "soundstage."

Manual options: Intensity (Low–High), Speed (Slow–Fast).

Distortion

Most musicians go out of their way to make sure that the *input volume* of their microphone or instrument isn't up too high. (That's why you opened System Preferences and adjusted the level slider as described on page 594.) If the input is too "hot," the level meters go off the scale, resulting in the screechy, garbled sound known as *distortion* or *clipping.*

In some musical circles, however—especially heavy-metal ones—distortion is the whole point. It's the trademark sound of guitarists who turn their amplifiers "up to 11," as the cast of *This is Spinal Tap* might say.

Using this option, you can drive *any* musical material into distortion-land, even if the levels were perfectly fine in the original recording.

Manual options: Drive (Low–High), Tone (Dark–Bright), Output Level (Low–High).

Flanger

Here's another classic rock processor, frequently applied to guitars and keyboards by a little foot switch-operated box on the stage floor. And now it's yours, at no extra charge.

You'll recognize it when you hear it: a sweeping, side-to-side, filtery effect. It's something like chorusing described above, but the duplicates of the sound are played back much more out of tune from the original. (Hint: It's most effective in stereo. Go dig out your iPod headphones.)

Manual options: Intensity (Low–High), Speed (Slow–Fast), Feedback (Low–High).

Overdrive

This effect, also common in electric guitar music, is related to distortion. It simulates the sound of an overdriven tube amplifier, adding the intensity of distortion without quite as much "trashiness."

Manual options: Drive (Low–High), Tone (Dark–Bright), Output Level (Low–High).

Phaser

Sometimes called a *phase shifter,* this flanger-like whooshing effect should also strike you as familiar from the pop world. It, too, sounds like somebody is cyclically rotating the dials on some selective-frequency machine, and it, too, sounds especially good on guitars, keyboards, and vocals.

Manual options: Intensity (Low–High), Speed (Slow–Fast), Feedback (Low–High).

Track Echo

The Echo and Reverb effects described on the next pages affect the entire mix. It's as though you're moving your entire band from a garage into an empty stadium.

These presets, though, are independent of the master echo effect; you can set up a different echo setting for each track. Most of the presets are pretty spacey, and you should use them only for special situations; a few, though, are responsible for creating certain recognizable pop sounds.

Manual options: Echo Time (Short–Long), Echo Repeat (Less–More), Repeat Color (Dark–Bright), Intensity (Low–High).

Tremolo

Tremolo is a close relative of *vibrato.* On paper, you might describe it as a subtle up-and-down wobble, either in pitch or in volume—but in the real world of solo voice or solo instruments, you'd describe it as a beautiful, professional sound. It's also a characteristic sound of guitar amps from the '50s and '60s (think The Ventures).

The GarageBand Tremolo effect won't turn a tone-deaf screecher into Pavarotti, though. You can't apply it selectively just to the ends of longer notes, as musicians tend to do in live performance. Many of the presets sound just a hair machine-generated, especially because many of them create the vibrato effect not by subtle waves of *pitch* but by whipping back and forth from left to right in stereo. (Here's another effect that sounds best with headphones on.)

POWER USERS' CLINIC

Audio Unit Effects

Audio Units are plug-ins, in a format created by Apple (but embraced by many other companies) that exploits Mac OS X's sophisticated audio "plumbing." Because GarageBand (and Logic, Final Cut, and Soundtrack) understands Audio Units plug-ins, you've got yourself a quick, easy way to expand its arsenal of pro-quality sounds and effects.

The first mention you're likely to see of Audio Units is at the bottom of each component-effect pop-up menu, where you'll find a long list of effects beginning with the letters AU: AUBandpass, AUDynamicsProcessor, AUDelay, and so on.

These controls give you direct access to some of the Audio Units that come with GarageBand. As you'll soon discover, these controls can be a good bit more technical than what you've encountered so far. Once you start drilling down into the AU labyrinth, you may wish you had the assistance of seasoned studio wonks even to figure out what you're looking at. (And you can get that help, too, by visiting Web sites like *www.osxaudio.com, www.audio-units.com,* and the GarageBand discussion board at *http://discusssearch.info.apple.com.*)

You don't get any presets for most AU effects, as you do with the GarageBand Effects listed above them. For these babies, the right-side pop-up menu usually says Manual, and the only way to adjust them is to click the pencil (if necessary) to bring up the corresponding manual-control dialog box.

As you can see here, these dialog boxes don't even look the same as the others in GarageBand. They're in another realm of tweaky complexity.

Still, some of these options are good to have. Remember, for example, the Equalizer described on page 34? It's nice to have, but it's not a full-blown graphic equalizer like the one in iTunes.

Choosing AUGraphicEQ, however, you get the dialog box shown here, complete with sliders for 31 individual sound frequencies.

Another AU effect that could, in a pinch, be useful is AUDelay. It's something like an echo effect on steroids: the reverberations can continue indefinitely, building and accumulating, until a single spoken sentence turns into the cacophony of 50 drunken people at a frat-house party.

If you do decide to explore the arcane audio settings of the AU set, note that you don't have to do without canned presets altogether. You're perfectly welcome to populate the pop-up menu with your own presets. Just fiddle around in the manual-settings dialog box (like the graphic equalizer pictured here) until you're satisfied, and then choose Make Preset from the pop-up menu at the top of the box. Name your preset, and be AUfully proud of yourself.

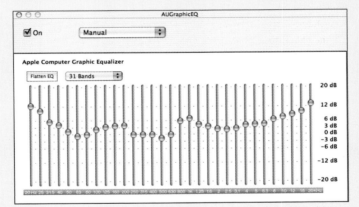

Still, several of these presets can lend interest and magic to a track, especially to a solo line with sustained notes. (If you're a singer and don't have a natural vibrato, try the preset called Soft and Fast, for example. Especially if you've also dialed up a little reverb, as described below.)

Manual options: Intensity (Low–High), Speed (Slow–Fast).

Vocal Transformer

The Effects dialog boxes may look to you like menus within menus and presets within presets. But don't get so lost that you miss the amazing new Vocal Transformer feature.

The pop-up menu to the right lists 13 modules that perform jaw-dropping transformations to any vocal track. Some, like Cartoon Falsetto, Chipmunk, and Monsters, are hilarious-sounding and truly wild. (Got elementary-schoolers in the back seat on a long drive? Hand the iBook to 'em, teach 'em about Vocal Transformer, and try to keep your eyes on the road as they laugh themselves to tears.)

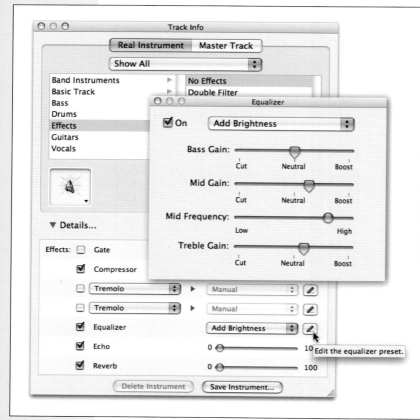

Figure 28-7:
When you click Garage-Band's pencil button (indicated by the cursor), you open the Equalizer dialog box (lower right). Adjust the sliders to boost or reduce the corresponding sound frequencies. If you like, you can then save your settings by choosing Make Preset from the pop-up menu (where it now says Add Brightness). You'll be asked to name the settings, which will thereafter appear in the pop-up menu along with Apple's own presets. (Figure 28-6 shows this process in more detail.)

Other presets keep your voice sounding normal, but transpose it by a certain interval, so that you're singing a strange, monk-like harmony with yourself. (Try this: Over a neutral-key background like drums, duplicate your vocal track twice. Keep one untouched. Use the "Up Major Third" transformation to one, and the "Down Fourth" to the other. Play it back for a wild, crisp, super-hip instant-harmony chorus.)

And some, like "Female to Male" and "Male to Female," are truly useful. They transform your voice into a trans-gendered version of yourself. In effect, you can become your own backup trio (of the opposite gender). Or sing along with yourself an octave or two away by duplicating the main vocal track and then applying these effects to the copy.

Vocal processing: It's not just for record companies any more.

Equalizer

If you've ever fiddled with the *graphic equalizer* on a stereo, or even the software one that's built into iTunes, you already know about these controls. An equalizer lets you boost or repress certain frequencies—like the bass or the treble—to suit different kinds of music. A "graph" for classical music, for example, might slightly boost the low and high frequencies for more sparkle, letting the middle ones "sag"; a pop-rock setting might boost instead the middle frequencies, to bring out the vocal parts.

When you turn on GarageBand's Equalizer checkbox, the pop-up menu to its right offers 21 canned equalizer setups bearing self-explanatory names like Bass Boost, Brighten Strings, and Reduce "S." In the unlikely event that none of these presets is quite what you want, you can click the pencil button to its right to adjust the various frequencies yourself (Figure 28-7).

The truth is, many of the Equalizer presets might make more sense when applied to a finished composition than just one instrument track. But now and again, they can be useful in giving a recording just the right nuance. For example, in the guitar preset called Summer Sounds, the "EQ" of the midrange has been boosted to give your guitar more of a Beach Boys sound.

Tip: If you'd prefer finer control over the various frequencies, don't bother with this user-friendly, quick-and-dirty option. The AUGraphicEq function described in the box on page 621 offers 31 individual sliders for extremely precise adjustment of various sound frequencies.

Echo, Reverb

You might suppose that *echo* and *reverb* are the same thing: the nice echoey sound of, for example, your shower.

Actually, in studio terms, they're different. *Echo,* sometimes called *delay,* is literally an echo, giving you fainter and fainter distinct repetitions of each sound, each separated by a fraction of a second (think Grand Canyon). *Reverb* is a sweet, subtle, professional-sounding reverberation that smoothes the rough edges of a musical performance (think shower stall, empty alley, or concert hall).

You'll probably use Echo only rarely, for special effects. Reverb, on the other hand, is useful for practically any kind of solo. There's not a pop star alive, for example, whose recordings aren't "sweetened" with a little reverb. The audience may not be able to pinpoint why your singing or playing sounds so great, but they'll definitely hear the difference.

Each of these effects has its own on/off checkbox and slider, which goes from 0 to 100 percent.

Note: If the Echo and Reverb checkboxes are dimmed, it's because these effects are turned off in the Master Track (see Chapter 29).

The fix: In the Track Info dialog box, click the Master Track tab, and then turn on the Echo and/or Reverb checkboxes. When you return to the Software Instrument or Real Instrument tab, you'll see these checkboxes come back to life.

The explanation: As it turns out, the individual tracks' Echo and Reverb sliders simply govern how much of these effects are sent to the Echo and Reverb in the Master Track. Studio musician call these *send effects.* (The Track Echo effect in the two unnamed pop-up menus are different; it gives you a truly track-independent echo.) So if Echo and Reverb are turned off for the entire song, they're also turned off for every individual track.

Mixing and Publishing

B y this time, you may have mastered GarageBand. Perhaps you've dialed up your own effects, masterfully combined loops with live audio, honed your mastery of musical arrangements and orchestration, and even added a little mod-wheel tweak here and there. At this point, you may even have the next "Oops, I Did It Again" right there on your screen.

But it's not doing anyone much good sitting in GarageBand. For most people, the whole point of making music is sharing it with others.

This chapter describes how to wrap up your workflow in GarageBand and present it to a wider audience. It's all about fine-tuning your piece, mixing the tracks (adjusting their relative volume levels), and finally handing the whole thing off to iTunes. From there, you can convert the song to any common music file format (like MP3), burn it to a CD, load it onto an iPod, or post it online for your screaming fans to discover.

Mixing Tracks

Next time you listen to the radio, notice how each song ends. A few of them end with a dramatic climactic stopping chord, but most gradually fade out.

GarageBand not only lets you create convincing fade-outs for your songs, but even lets you adjust the volume graph for individual tracks along their lengths. For example, you can make the piano part loud during the introduction of the piece, and then pull back to a softer level when your singing begins.

This business of adjusting the relative volume levels of a song's tracks is called *mixing*. It's both an art and a science; two different people mixing the same song can create totally different psycho-musical effects. You're no longer wearing the composer's hat, or even the rock star's hat. You're now assuming the engineer's and producer's roles.

Here are the tools at your disposal, as described in the following pages:

- You can adjust the relative overall volume levels of the tracks.

- You can create volume fluctuations *within* a track.

- You can adjust the left-to-right positions of your track instruments in the stereo "soundstage."

- You can make overall volume changes—to all tracks at once—to create, for example, a fade-out at the end of the song.

Overall Track Volume

The most basic mixing skill is knowing how to adjust track volumes relative to each other. That is, you might want to make the drum track a little quieter, the vocals a little louder, and so on.

The key to this basic mixing feature is the *track mixer,* a little panel that sprouts when you click the small triangle identified by the arrow cursor in Figure 29-1.

Figure 29-1:
Top: If you point your cursor at various Garage-Band screen controls and wait a moment, a tiny balloon pops up to tell you what it does—in this case, the track mixer.

Bottom: When you click the little triangle, the track mixer panel appears. Here, you can adjust the overall volume level of a track and use the knob to specify where it sits in the left-to-right stereo "soundstage" when you listen with headphones or stereo speakers.

Using the volume slider that you find here is simple enough:

- Drag the tiny, white, round handle to decrease or increase the track volume.

- Click inside the slider to make the volume handle jump to that spot, without having to drag.

- Option-click one of the tiny speaker icons, or anywhere along the slider's length, to restore the track volume to its original factory-set volume level. (Note to studio veterans: Technically, you're setting the track to 0 decibels. Note to everyone else: And why is "normal" zero? It's a long story with its origins in the world of recording-studio equipment, but the bottom line is that on this kind of meter, 0 dB means, "anything higher will distort." Absolute silence, incidentally, is represented on these meters as –96 dB.)

Tip: If you can't seem to adjust the slider at all, it's because you've programmed in volume changes using the Track Volume track described next. The track mixer slider is "live" only if you've never fiddled with the track's volume track.

GEM IN THE ROUGH

Check One, Check Two...

You can use the track volume slider shown in Figure 29-1 even while the song is playing back.

Why is that so useful? Because the two tiny graphs just above the volume slider illustrate the volume level of the left and right stereo channels in real time. They light up with tiny bars, as illustrated here, resembling the digital LED level meters on modern studio equipment.

When you're preparing your song for release to the masses, observe these meters while the song plays back. You want to adjust the volume so that they dance primarily in the green area, slipping into the yellow area only during the loudest passages.

What you don't want is for the graph to extend into the red bars, or, worse, for the two tiny dots at the right end—the *clipping* indicators—to illuminate. That's a sign that the volume is so loud that distortion may result. You'll be pumping out too much signal for the speakers on

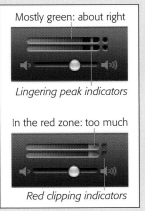

Mostly green: about right

Lingering peak indicators

In the red zone: too much

Red clipping indicators

the other end, resulting in a garbled, overblown sound.

(Once the two clipping-indicator dots have turned red, they stay red to get your attention. They return to black only when you stop and resume playback, telling them, in effect, "OK, OK, I get it—I've got a clipping problem. I'll fix it.")

As the music plays, you'll notice that while these volume meters are bouncing around, every so often, one graph bar will remain illuminated for a second. That's your peak volume meter. It remains illuminated for a moment to help you spot the high points of your track volume.

You can boost or reduce the volume of green Software Instrument tracks whenever you feel like it. But when it comes to Real Instrument recordings, the time to pay attention to these level meters is while you're recording. If the microphone or line input setting was too loud or too soft, adjusting the track volume slider may not rescue the recording.

Volume Adjustments Within a Track

All this time, GarageBand has been concealing a little secret from you. Each track can, at your command, sprout a real-time graph of its volume over time. By dragging this "rubber band" line up or down, you can program in gradual (or sudden) volume changes that GarageBand will incorporate into the playback.

To reveal this graph, use one of these techniques:

- Select a track and then press the letter A key.

- Click the tiny triangle identified in Figure 29-2.

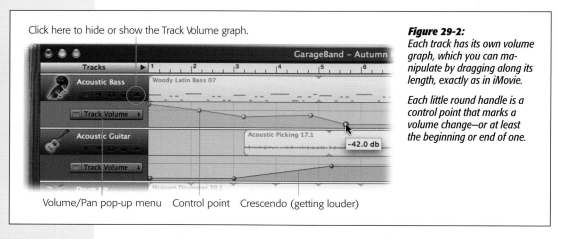

Click here to hide or show the Track Volume graph.

Volume/Pan pop-up menu   Control point   Crescendo (getting louder)

Figure 29-2:
Each track has its own volume graph, which you can manipulate by dragging along its length, exactly as in iMovie.

Each little round handle is a control point that marks a volume change—or at least the beginning or end of one.

To hide the volume track, repeat the same procedure.

This graph of track volume comes in handy in many ways. For example, you can begin the piece with its instrumental introduction at full volume, and then pull back the band so that you can hear the singing. You can also create professional-sounding fade-ins and fade-outs at the beginnings and ends of your songs.

The key to turning on this feature is the Track Volume in the track header. When you turn it on, a horizontal line appears in the volume track, stretching from edge to edge. This line is a graph of the track's volume, which you can manipulate like a rubber band. Here's how it works:

- If you've also opened the track mixer panel (Figure 29-1), adjusting the overall track volume makes this horizontal volume graph float up or down accordingly.

- Click directly on the line and drag upward or downward. The original click produces a small spherical handle, while the drag produces a slant in the line from its original volume level. Simultaneously drag left or right to adjust the timing of this fluctuation.

- To make the volume take another dip or swoop, click elsewhere on the volume line and drag again. You've just created a second round orange handle, which you can now position independently.

- To remove a volume fluctuation, click the orange handle to select it, and then press the Delete key. (Alternatively, drag an orange handle so far to the right or left that it overlaps the adjacent one.) The orange ball disappears, and the "rubber band" of the volume graph snaps back to the previous round orange handle, stretched tight.

- To make a sudden volume change, zoom way in, then drag an orange handle carefully until it's *almost* directly below the previous or next one. (Don't drag it directly underneath—if you do that, the other handle will disappear. In that case, use the Edit→Undo command to restore it.)

- Consider making your volume adjustments *while* the music plays back. GarageBand dutifully changes the mix in real time as you fiddle.

- You can drag a group of handles higher or lower—thus proportionally boosting or decreasing the volume for an entire stretch of music—by selecting them en masse first. You can also drag a group of control points sideways, making the volume fluctuation take place sooner or later. Figure 29-3 has the details.

Tip: In fact, you can use that same trick to drag the *entire* volume graph up or down for the length of the song. To select all of the handles in the entire volume track, click the volume track *header* (marked by the words "Track Volume" at the left edge of the window).

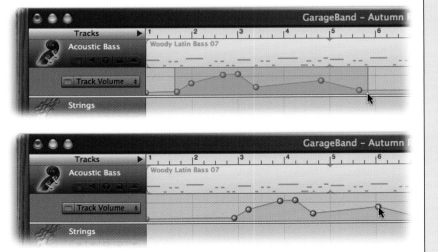

Figure 29-3:
Top: You can select a group of control points either by Shift-clicking the ones you want, or, as shown here, by dragging horizontally through them.

Bottom: Then, you can drag the group either horizontally (to change the timing) or vertically (to change the overall level of the volume change), using one of them as a handle.

- To restore the original, straight-line condition of a clip's volume, select all of the orange handles (see the previous Tip) and press Delete. (Of course, you can also delete only a subset of them by first dragging a selection, as shown in Figure 29-3, at top.)

- When you're finished editing volume fluctuations, you can click to turn off the tiny, square blue "light" next to the words Track Volume (identified in Figure 29-2). GarageBand will remember all of the changes that you've made—you'll still hear the volume changes on playback—but it dims all of the handles and rubber-band graph lines, so you won't drag something out of alignment by accident

At this point, you have another way to adjust the overall volume of the track, maintaining the relative fluctuations you've set up: Use the overall-volume slider shown at bottom in Figure 29-1.

Overall Track Pan Position

The beauty of stereo is that there are *two* speakers or headphones, which happens to correspond very nicely with the number of ears on your head. When you listen to music in stereo, part of the realism stems from the instruments' varied placement in the stereo *sound field* or *soundstage.* In other words, some instruments seem to be coming from the left side of the room, some from the right, and some from directly in front of you, almost as though you were listening to them live.

Over the ages, record producers have become very skilled at exploiting this phenomenon. When they mix the song, they use knobs or software to specify where each track should sound like it's coming from—left, right, center, or anywhere along the scale. In short, they spend a lot of time thinking about the *pan position* of each instrument (that is, its position along the sonic *panorama* before you).

As it turns out, GarageBand provides this flexibility, too. All you have to do is to open the track mixer panel, as described in Figure 29-1.

Unless you intervene, every instrument starts out sounding like it's coming out of both speakers—left and right—with equal volume. Every instrument starts out with

Figure 29-4:
You can't really gauge the effects of the pan control unless you're listening with headphones, or sitting between two stereo speakers. And it probably goes without saying that you should keep the music playing while you make these adjustments.

a *center* pan position; accordingly, every track's pan knob starts out with the little white notch pointing straight up to the center position.

Here's how to work this knob (Figure 29-4):

- Don't even bother grabbing the tiny rim of the knob and then dragging the mouse along it. This will effectively turn the knob, but it requires the precision of a neurosurgeon.

  Instead, click one of the tiny white dots around the *outside* of the knob (or, for extreme panning, click the letter L or R). Instantly, the white notch on the knob turns to face your click.

Tip: Ordinarily, this knob "clicks" into numeric positions that are multiples of 16: 32, 48, and so on. If you press Shift and drag inside the round knob, however, you can dial up any numeric value you want.

- Option-click anywhere on the knob to reset it to center, making its little white notch point straight up again.

Leaving everything set to the center is fine if people are going to be in mono anyway—from a Power Mac speaker, say, or over the Internet in a file that you've distilled down to a single mono track to make it a quicker download.

Most professionally recorded songs, however, feature instruments that are carefully spread out across the stereo field. In general, the most important instruments—the soloist, the drummer, bass player, and maybe the guitars—stick with center positions, but the "flavor" instruments might be spread out to the left and right sides.

You can inject some fun into the process by introducing variations on this formula. If you're singing a duet—maybe even a duet with yourself—you could put the two voices on opposite channels, so it sounds like they're really facing each other. (The more you turn the pan knob, for example, the farther to the left or right you place that instrument.)

Using volume, pan, and reverb together, in fact, you can dial up a pretty convincing sonic impression of a track's position in three-dimensional space.

Pan Adjustments Within a Track

In GarageBand 2, there's more to the panning story than fiddling with that set-it-and-forget-it Pan knob. Now you can make a track's sound *move around* in the stereo field, thanks to the new track panning *curve* feature.

You open and edit this graph exactly as illustrated in Figures 29-2 and 29-3. But once you've opened the volume graph, choose Track Pan from the little pop-up menu identified in Figure 29-2.

At this point, any adjustments you make to the graph affect its right-to-left stereo-field position, not its volume. As the graph line moves upward, the sound shifts to the left ear; downward shifts the sound to the right ear.

The idea here, of course, is to give you the freedom to move "players" around on the "stage." Sometimes you might want a musician to "walk" into center stage during a solo, and then return to the original position; other times, you might want to create a special effect by having a voice or an instrument leap, impossibly quickly, back and forth between the listener's ears.

The Master Track

It's nice that you can control the volume of individual tracks, and of individual sections of music along their lengths. But as a final step before unveiling your masterpiece to the world, you'll want to look over the master volume for the entire mix and set up any master effects, like reverb, that you want to apply to the entire garage band.

Tip: Perform the following adjustments *after* adjusting the mix of your individual tracks.

You apply most of these all-track changes using the *Master Track*. It's an additional horizontal track that appears at the bottom of the track list, as shown below in Figure 29-5.

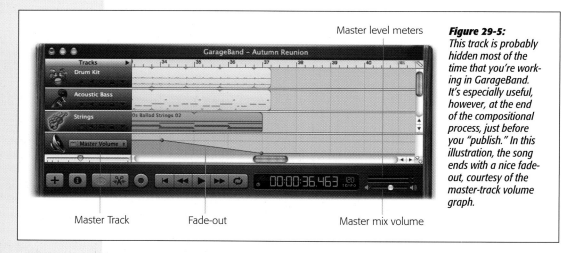

Master level meters

Figure 29-5:
This track is probably hidden most of the time that you're working in GarageBand. It's especially useful, however, at the end of the compositional process, just before you "publish." In this illustration, the song ends with a nice fade-out, courtesy of the master-track volume graph.

Master Track   Fade-out   Master mix volume

To make it appear, choose Track→Show Master Track, or press ⌘-B. (To hide the Master Track again, choose Track→Hide Master Track, or press ⌘-B a second time.)

If you've learned to manipulate the effects, overall volume, and volume graphs for individual tracks, you already know how to operate them for the Master Track. The only difference is that you're now affecting all tracks simultaneously.

Overall Volume

Set the overall volume level for your song using the master volume slider identified in Figure 29-5. Play back the entire song, watching the volume-level meters just above the slider to make sure that they don't cross into the red zone during the loudest portions of the music, and that the two little clipping indicators don't light up. (See the box on page 627 for more detail on using these meters.)

The point is to make sure the music will sound good when other people play it on their computers, iPods, or CD players. Volume that's too low to hear the detail, or so high that you're introducing distortion, will seriously hinder your chances of getting picked for *American Idol*.

Tip: Don't get into the habit of using this master slider to adjust GarageBand's playback volume while you're working on your compositions. For that purpose, use the speaker-volume keys on the top row of your keyboard. Or, if you don't see them on your keyboard, use the ◀)) mini-menu in your menu bar. (And if you don't see *that,* choose →System Preferences, click Sound, and turn on "Show volume in menu bar.")

Use the master output volume slider only to determine the final volume level for your piece, as it will be when you export it to iTunes, post it online, and so on.

Real-time Automated Mixing?

Hey, I was at my buddy's place the other day. He paid $600 for his mixing software, but it does something cool. He can adjust the pan control, or adjust the processing effects for a track, while the music is playing—and the software memorizes it and recreates it automatically the next time the piece plays back. Is there any way to make GarageBand automate the mix like this?

Can GarageBand 2 memorize the movement of its knobs and sliders for fully automated mixes? No.

Can you simulate this effect with a tricky workaround? Yes.

It's possible to export a partial or finished GarageBand mix and then bring it right back into GarageBand as a frozen, but full-quality, unified track. All you have to do is find a piece of software that can record the playback as you fiddle with panning and effects, thus capturing your real-time adjustments for posterity.

Fortunately, exactly such a program exists. It's Audio Hijack Pro, a handy little $32 shareware utility that can capture virtually any sound that's passing through the Mac. Most people use Audio Hijack for things like capturing Internet radio broadcasts, but you can put it to another use entirely. (You can download it from the "Missing CD" page at *www.missing manuals.com*.)

All you have to do is set up Audio Hijack to record the output from GarageBand, as shown here. Play your piece, making any panning or effects adjustments you like during the playback. When it's over, you'll find an AIFF file on your desktop, named after GarageBand.

Drag this icon right back into an empty Real Instrument track in GarageBand. From here, follow the procedure described on page 693.

Fade-ins, Fade-outs

Create fade-ins, fade-outs, and other whole-song volume fluctuations by turning on the Master Volume checkbox and then manipulating the horizontal master-volume graph, exactly the way you would adjust an individual track's graph.

Reverb and Effects

Set up reverb, compression, and any other whole-song processing effects by double-clicking the Master Track's header (where it says Master Volume at the left edge of the window). Doing so produces the Track Info dialog box for the Master Track, as shown in Figure 29-6.

In this dialog box, you can specify a degree of echo, reverb, equalization, or compression. You can also apply any of the GarageBand "additional effects" like Bitcrusher, Chorus, Flanger, and so on, using the pop-up menu in the middle of the Details panel. All of these effects are described at length in Chapter 28.

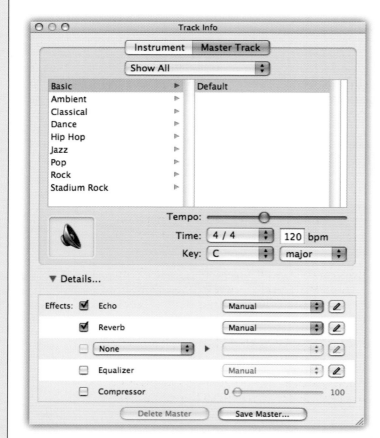

Figure 29-6:
You can get to this dialog box either by double-clicking the Master Track header, or by double-clicking any other track's header and then, in the Track Info dialog box, clicking the Master Track tab. Either way, this is where you set up processing effects for the entire mix.

This is also, incidentally, the only place where you can change the time signature of the piece once you've created the file.

Tip: If you create a combination of effects that sounds particularly appropriate for your style of music, and you think you might use them later for subsequent compositions, click the Save Master button shown in Figure 29-6. You're asked to type a name for this effects preset, and then click Save. From now on, you'll see your new Master Track preset listed in the right-side list of the Track Info dialog box—or at least until you use the Delete Master button to remove it.

Key Changes

If your name is Barry Manilow, you're all over this new feature.

In GarageBand 2, there's a new editable graph, much like the volume and pan curves you've already read about. This one, though, controls the key of the music as it plays. Figure 29-7 shows the details.

Figure 29-7:
If you choose Master Pitch from the pop-up menu in the Master Track (lower left), you get a horizontal line that you can manipulate just like the volume curve shown in Figure 29-3. Control points that move the line upward shift the key higher (each unit of 1 transposes by a musical half-step); downward means lower. Shown here: +5 is a radical ∂ition up a musical fourth (five half steps).

You can spice up your arrangement by taking it up a half-step (+1 on the transposition curve) for the last chorus, for example, or even more—a favorite trick of Mr. Manilow and many a Broadway composer.

What's nice is that GarageBand is intelligent about what it transposes. Loops (green and blue) change key, for example, and so do MIDI regions you've recorded (Software Instruments). But when you use the master pitch curve, GarageBand leaves certain other elements untouched:

- **Drum tracks.** In other words, the actual "keys" being played back won't turn into different drum sounds.

- **Audio files dragged in from the Finder (orange).** Apple's guessing that these are sound effects and other nonmusical items, and that you probably want them left alone.

- **Real-Instrument recordings (purple).** GarageBand can indeed transpose digital recordings like these, but within limits; transposing one by a large increment makes it sound funny. So Apple leaves it to you to transpose your own recordings manually, region by region, as described on page 606.

Publishing the Song

Suppose that the music sounds great, the mix is on target, and everybody who hears the song playing in GarageBand is blown away. This is the moment you've been waiting for. You're about to liberate your tune, freeing it from GarageBand and getting it into a program that's far better at playing and distributing digital music—iTunes. From there, you can burn it to a CD; convert it to an MP3 file; use it as background music for iPhoto, iMovie, or iDVD; and so on.

Here's how the process works.

1. **Choose GarageBand→Preferences.**

   The GarageBand Preferences dialog box appears.

   The music you create in GarageBand will wind up in one iTunes *playlist* (a subset of your music collection that you've built for a certain purpose). Unless you specify otherwise, iTunes will name it "Casey's Playlist" (or whatever your account name is, as identified on the Accounts panel of System Preferences in Mac OS X). Here's your opportunity to assign your collected GarageBand works a more resonant title.

2. **Click the Export tab. Edit the iTunes Playlist, Composer Name, and Album Name boxes (Figure 29-8).**

Figure 29-8:
In iTunes, almost every song displays labeling information: composer name, album name, and so on. All right, maybe you're not much of a composer yet, and you probably don't yet have an album out. But at least you can pretend by filling in the boxes here in Garage-Band's preferences.

(The new options at the bottom of the box are intended for Macs shared by several people, each with a Mac OS X account. These buttons let you specify whether or not you want your masterpiece available to everyone's iTunes collections.)

Once you've filled out the last line of the dialog box, click once in another one of the text boxes to make your changes take.

3. **Close the Preferences box.**

The only information you didn't have to fill in is the name of the song. But of course, iTunes already knows that information—it's whatever name you gave your GarageBand project when you created it.

4. **Specify which tracks you want to export.**

Most of the time, you'll want to export *all* of the tracks. In certain situations, though, you may not want some tracks to be a part of the finished mix. If you really *do* have a garage band, for example, you might want to make yourself a track that includes the backup band but omits your part, so that you can practice by playing along with it.

Note: You may be too young to remember the Music Minus One albums, but they were really cool. Each record was intended to help you learn to play a certain instrument. A full orchestra played on the left stereo channel, and your solo part was recorded on the right. As you got better at playing, you could gradually turn down the right channel until only the accompaniment remained audible—and you, the soloist, provided the missing part.

Maybe, too, your intention is to create a karaoke album of your own greatest hits—that is, minus the vocals.

Or maybe you just want to send a record company's talent scout a couple of different mixes, each with a different instrumentation. (Some people, for example, like to try out a couple of different drum loops for the same song. Each one lends a different flavor to the piece. So for comparison, you can export the song twice, one with each drum track playing.)

Either way, silence the tracks you want omitted by clicking each one and then pressing the letter M key (or clicking the little speaker in the track header). Doing so mutes the track. Now when you export your song to iTunes, they won't be part of the mix.

5. **Specify how much of the song you want to export.**

In most cases, you'll want to export the entire song, which is fine. In that case, skip this step.

But selecting a specific part of the song can be useful now and then. Maybe you've got a shorter version that you want to keep distinct from the extended mix, for example.

Maybe, too, you want to export a region that's *longer* than the song. You might want to incorporate a few seconds of silence at the end, so that your listeners can reflect thoughtfully on the impact of what they just heard. Or, more practically, maybe you've discovered that GarageBand exports only up to the end of the last region, and is therefore chopping off a little bit of reverb that rings past that moment.

In any case, the trick to specifying how much of the song you want to export lies in the cycle region. Figure 29-9 explains.

Yellow bar: Only this much will be exported

Cycle button

Figure 29-9:
Press the letter C key, or click the cycle button, to make the yellow highlighting bar appear at the top of the GarageBand window. Zoom out as much as necessary, and then drag the edges of this yellow bar until it brackets the portion of the song you want to include. GarageBand will export only as much of the song as you've indicated with this cycle region.

6. **Give the piece one last listen.**

   Put on headphones if possible, press the letter Z key to rewind, press the Space bar to play, and watch the output-level meters at the lower-right corner of the GarageBand window to make sure that the two little clipping dots are turning red—or that your piece isn't so quiet that the dancing meter bars never even touch the yellow region. (See the box on page 627.)

7. **Choose File→Export to iTunes.**

   GarageBand takes a moment to create your final mix, merging all those tracks down to just two channels: left and right stereo. In a moment, the iTunes window appears automatically.

   As shown in Figure 29-10, a new playlist has joined the others in the Source list at the left side of the window. This is where you'll find your exported GarageBand masterpieces.

Tip: Of course, you can always change the playlist name in the GarageBand→Preferences dialog box. Doing so will build a second playlist in iTunes, containing all your GarageBand exports henceforth.

To hear your opus now that it's been freed from the protective walls of GarageBand, click the playlist name and then double-click the name of the song displayed to its right.

Having your finished GarageBand pieces stored in iTunes, rather than GarageBand, is a wonderful convenience. iTunes starts up faster than GarageBand, it's easier to search and sort, you can't accidentally mess up your piece by clicking in the wrong place, and the actual music file is much smaller than your original GarageBand project.

Tip: Behind the scenes, your exported GarageBand song is saved as an AIFF file in your Home→ Music→iTunes→iTunes Music→Import folder. Back up this folder if you want to make safety copies of your finished projects.

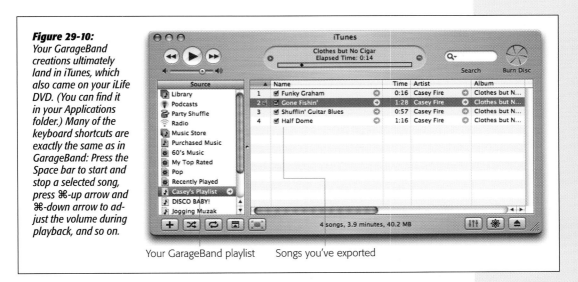

Figure 29-10:
Your GarageBand creations ultimately land in iTunes, which also came on your iLife DVD. (You can find it in your Applications folder.) Many of the keyboard shortcuts are exactly the same as in GarageBand: Press the Space bar to start and stop a selected song, press ⌘-up arrow and ⌘-down arrow to ad-just the volume during playback, and so on.

Your GarageBand playlist   Songs you've exported

Converting to MP3, AAC, WAV, or Apple Lossless

When it arrives in iTunes, your GarageBand masterpiece has been frozen into what's called an AIFF file (Audio Interchange File Format). AIFF files truly sound spectacular. In fact, they're what the record companies put onto commercial music CDs.

These are not, however, what you'd call petite files. A typical pop song occupies 40 or 50 MB on your hard drive, Web site, or iPod. That's a shame, because not many people will tolerate a 50 MB download just to hear your work.

Fortunately, iTunes makes it very easy to convert your songs to other formats, most of which take up far less space. MP3 files, AAC files, WAV files, and Apple Lossless files are all examples of formats you can use. Here's an introduction to each one:

• **MP3 files.** The most popular music files online are MP3 files, which you can find on the Web by the hundreds of thousands. (MP3 is short for MPEG Audio, Layer 3.

And MPEG stands for Moving Pictures Experts Group, the association of engineers that also defined the specifications for DVD video, among other formats.)

And why is it so popular? Well, suppose you copy a song from an Outkast CD directly onto your computer, where it takes up 47.3 MB of hard disk space. Sure, you could now play that song without the CD in your CD drive, but you'd also be out 47.3 megs of precious hard drive real estate.

If you let iTunes convert it into an MP3 file instead, it will still sound really good, but now only takes up about 4.8 MB of space on your hard drive—roughly 10 percent of the original

MP3 files are so small because they omit frequencies that are too high for humans to hear, along with any sounds that are blotted out by louder sounds. All of this compression helps produce a smaller file without overly diminishing the overall sound quality of the music.

- **AAC files.** The Advanced Audio Coding format may be relatively new (it became official in 1997), but it has a fine pedigree. Scientists at Dolby, Sony, Nokia, AT&T, and Fraunhofer collaborated to come up with a method of squeezing multimedia files of the highest possible quality into the smallest possible space—at least small enough to fit through a modem line. During listening tests, many people couldn't distinguish between a compressed high-quality AAC file and an original recording.

What's so great about AAC? For starters, this format can do the Big Sound/Small File Size trick even better than MP3. Due to its tighter compression technique, a song encoded in the AAC format sounds better (to most ears, anyway) and occupies less space on the computer than if it were encoded with the same quality settings as an MP3 file. Encoding your files in the AAC format is how Apple says you can stuff 10,000 songs onto a 40 GB iPod.

The AAC format can also be copy protected (unlike MP3), which is why Apple uses it on the iTunes Music Store. (The record companies would never have permitted Apple to distribute their property without copy protection.)

- **WAV files.** WAV is a standard Windows sound format, although Macs can play these files, too. Windows fans download WAV recordings for everything from TV-show snippets to system-alert noises. A WAV song usually sounds better than the same song in MP3 but takes up more room on your hard drive or iPod.

- **Apple Lossless Encoder files.** As you now know, programs like iTunes create MP3 and AAC files by throwing away some of the audio data (mostly stuff you can't hear anyway). Geeks call these *lossy* formats. But for true audiophiles with impeccable taste and bionic ears, lossy formats make music sound thin, tinny, and screeching.

Of course, WAV and AIFF are lossless—no audio data is lost—but these files take up a huge amount of hard drive space.

In iTunes 4.5 or later, you can use the Apple Lossless Encoder instead. It offers great-sounding files that take up about half the space of an uncompressed CD track. (This format requires not only iTunes 4.5, but also QuickTime 6.5.1 or later.)

How to convert your files

All right, suppose you're now sold on the benefits of converting your GarageBand masterpieces into smaller files. Here's how to proceed:

1. **In iTunes, choose iTunes→Preferences. In the dialog box, click Importing.**

   You see the dialog box shown in Figure 29-11.

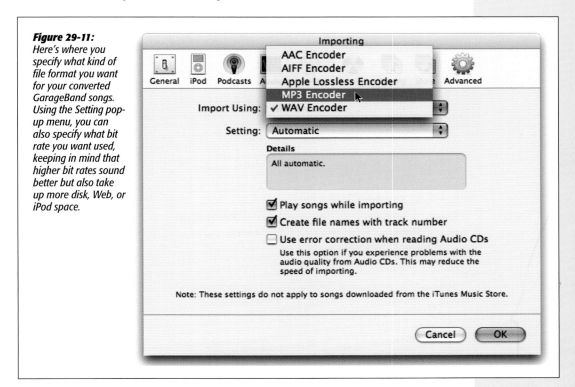

Figure 29-11:
Here's where you specify what kind of file format you want for your converted GarageBand songs. Using the Setting pop-up menu, you can also specify what bit rate you want used, keeping in mind that higher bit rates sound better but also take up more disk, Web, or iPod space.

2. **From the Import Using pop-up menu, choose the file format you want.**

   Choose AAC, Apple Lossless, MP3, or WAV. Also specify a Setting, if you like (see Figure 29-11).

Tip: If you intend to post this masterpiece online or send it by email, consider using MP3. It's the most widely compatible format.

---

3. **Click OK. In your GarageBand playlist, select the song or songs you want to convert.**

To select one song, just click it. To select all of them in the list, choose Edit→Select All (or press ⌘-A). To select a consecutive subset of the songs, click the first one, and then Shift-click the last one. To select a random assortment, click the first, and then ⌘-click each additional song.

4. **Choose Advanced→Convert Selection to MP3.**

   Beware: The menu command changes according to your selection in step 2. For example, it might say Convert Selection to AAC instead.

   iTunes flies into action, simultaneously playing your song and converting it.

5. **To look at the finished product, click the Library icon at the top of the Source list.**

   You'll find your song mixed in with all of your other iTunes files, in alphabetical order (assuming you're sorting your list by song name).

   Of course, the original AIFF version is here, too. One way to tell which is which: Highlight the song's name and press ⌘-I (or choose File→Get Info). The resulting dialog box identifies the file format.

At this point, you can turn the new file into a bona fide, independent file icon by dragging its name out of the list to any visible spot on your desktop. It's now ready to send by email, post on the Web, copy across the network, and so on.

Burning GarageBand CDs

Controlling your own private recording studio isn't the only traditional function that you're whisking away from the big corporate record companies. You're in charge of your own CD-pressing plant, too.

In fact, iTunes can burn your GarageBand hits—or any songs in your iTunes Library—into three kinds of discs:

- **Standard audio CDs.** If your Mac has a CD burner, it can record selected sets of songs, no matter what the original sources, onto a blank CD. (For maximum CD-player compatibility, leave your GarageBand projects in AIFF format for this kind of CD.) When it's all over, you can play the burned CD on any standard CD player, just like the ones from Tower Records. This time, however, you hear only the songs you like, in the order you like, with all of the annoying ones eliminated.

Tip: Use CD-R discs. CD-RW discs are not only more expensive, but may not work in some standard CD players. (Not all players recognize CD-R discs either, but the odds are better.)

- **MP3 CDs.** A standard audio compact disc contains high-quality, enormous song files in the AIFF format. An MP3 compact disc, by contrast, is a data CD that contains music files in the MP3 format.

  Since MP3 songs are much smaller than the AIFF files, many more of them fit in the standard 650 or 700 MB of space on a recordable CD. Instead of 74 or 80 minutes of music, a CD-R full of MP3 files can store *10 to 12 hours* of tunes.

Just about any computer can play an MP3 CD. But if you want to take the disc on the road or even out to the living room, you'll need a CD player designed to read both standard CDs and discs containing MP3 files. Many modern players can play both CDs and MP3 CDs, and the prices are not much higher than that of a standard CD player. Some DVD players and home-audio sound systems can also play MP3 CDs.

- **Backup DVDs.** If your Mac has Mac OS X 10.1 or later and an Apple SuperDrive (that is, it can play and record both CDs and DVDs), you have another option. iTunes 4 can back up 4.7 GB of your music collection at a time by copying it to a blank DVD. (You can't play this disc no matter what kind of player you have; it's merely a glorified backup disk for restoration when something goes wrong with your hard drive.)

Select the type of disc you desire in the Preferences dialog box (Figure 29-12). Then proceed as follows:

1. **Select the playlist you want to burn.**

   To ensure that all of the playlist's songs will fit on a CD, consult the readout at the bottom of the window. It tells you how much playing time is represented by the songs in the playlist.

Note: If it runs out of room on the first CD, iTunes asks you to insert another disc and then picks up where it left off.

Figure 29-12:
Choose iTunes→Preferences, and then click Burning. Here, you select the recorder you wish to use, as well as what kind of CD to make: a standard disc (Audio CD) that will play in just about any CD player, an MP3 CD that will play in the computer's CD drive (and some newer home decks), or a backup just for safekeeping.

2. **When you're ready to roll, click the Burn Disc button at the top-right corner of the iTunes window.**

The icon changes into a yellow-and-black graphic that resembles the symbol used for fallout shelters in the 1950s.

3. **Insert a blank CD into your computer's drive when prompted. Click the Burn Disc button again after the program acknowledges the disc.**

iTunes prepares to record the CD, which may take a few minutes.

Once iTunes has taken care of business, it lets you know that it's now burning the CD. Again, depending on the speed of your computer and CD burner, as well as the size of your playlist, the recording process could take several minutes.

When the disc is done, iTunes pipes up with a musical flourish. Eject the CD (by pressing the Eject key found in the upper-right corner of the Mac keyboard) and label the top of the newly minted music storehouse with a magic marker (or your favorite method).

Tip: You can set up your computer to auto-eject the CD when it's finished ripping—ideal if you plan to copy a bunch of CDs to your hard drive, assembly line–style.

In iTunes, choose iTunes→Preferences (Mac). Click the General icon or tab. Where it says, "On CD Insert," choose "Import Songs and Eject." From now on, each CD spits out automatically when it's done.

"Save as Archive"

As long as you use *only* the built-in Apple loops in your composition, you can freely exchange your GarageBand "document" with any agents, producers, or groupies who also have GarageBand. They'll be able to open the project and hear it exactly the way you did. After all, your composition is made exclusively of built-in Apple Loops, the same ones your audience also has on their Macs, and any Real Instrument recordings that you made, which are embedded inside the GarageBand package icon.

But what about *other* loops? What about Jam Pack loops, or loops you've made yourself, or loops bought from other companies? Your audience does *not* have these on hand. These folks will *not* hear your masterpiece as it exists on your Mac.

The solution is the File→Save as Archive command. It creates what *looks* like a standard GarageBand document icon—but inside, it actually stores copies of all the loops you've used in your piece.

Needless to say, the resulting file takes up a lot more disk space than a regular GarageBand document. In fact, it can be huge. But at least it's self-contained and ready for glitch-free distribution.

Part Six: Troubleshooting

6

Troubleshooting iTunes

When you get right down to it, iTunes is a glorified database. It's a list—a searchable, sortable list—but a very high-profile one with some stiff competition (at least in the Windows world, where iTunes is also popular). For these reasons, Apple has put a lot of effort into making iTunes rock-solid. Not a lot goes wrong in iTunes.

But when the planets don't align your way, may this chapter be your guide to iTunes wholeness.

Rule 1: Get the Latest

Upgrading to iTunes 4.9 or later is the most important step you can take. It cures a long list of glitches that were possible in earlier versions. For example:

- You can't listen to someone else's shared music over the network if they have a big music library. (The "Loading" message appears, but the shared library never does appear.)

- iTunes suddenly crashes when you try to listen to certain radio stations (those whose Web addresses don't begin with *http://*).

- You try to share music with a version of iTunes before 4.5 (and get a "not compatible with this version of iTunes" message).

In these cases and many others, just downloading the free update to iTunes 4.9 or later solves the problem.

Rule 2: Back Up Your Library

Having a backup of your music files is excellent insurance against all sorts of music-library corruption. It's also a safety net for all the music you've bought from the iTunes Music Store; if something goes wrong with your hard drive, and you don't have a backup, you have to buy all of it again.

Backing Up to a Hard Drive or Another Mac

If you've got an external hard drive (the hard drive in another Mac on the network counts), backing up your music collection is extremely easy. Open your Home→Music folder, and copy the iTunes folder inside it. That's it—you're backed up. (In the event of catastrophe, simply restore this backup copy to its original location.)

Backing Up to CD or DVD

You can copy about 650 megabytes of music files to a recordable CD, or (if your Mac has a DVD burner) about 4.7 gigabytes to a blank DVD.

Start by creating a playlist of your entire music library, like this:

1. **In iTunes, click Library in the Source list.**

   Make sure that the Search box is empty—that you're viewing your entire list of songs.

2. **Click a song, and then choose Edit→Select All.**

   iTunes highlights all of your songs.

3. **Choose File→New Playlist From Selection.**

   iTunes asks you to name the new playlist.

4. **Type *Full Backup* (or whatever name you like).**

   Now you're ready to create the backup disc.

5. **Choose iTunes→Preferences; in the Preferences dialog box, click Burning. Click "Data CD or DVD," and click OK.**

   You're going to burn a computer disc, that is, not one intended for playing in stereos.

6. **Select the playlist you created in step 4, and then click the Burn Disc button. Insert a blank CD or DVD (either an -R or -RW blank format), and click Burn Disc again.**

   iTunes backs up all your audio files. If you need more than one disc to hold it all, iTunes will let you know, and invite you to insert a second disc.

Tip: You don't have to back up your entire music library each time. Thanks to the magic of the Smart Playlist, you can back up only the newest arrivals on successive backups.

To do that, note the date and time of the *first* complete backup. Then just create a new Smart Playlist that includes all songs with whose Date Added is after that. When you want to back up that newest batch, just repeat the steps above—but click your Smart Playlist's name in step 6.

Each time you perform one of these so-called *incremental* backups, remember to click the Smart Playlist, choose Edit→Edit Smart Playlist, and change the date to today's date. You've just reset the Smart Playlist so that it will begin collecting *new* new songs.

Store-Bought Songs Won't Play

If you can't play songs you've bought online, the problem almost always boils down to one of these three things:

- **You don't have QuickTime 6.2.5 or later.** You need at least this version of Apple's QuickTime music-and-movie-playing software if you hope to use your store-bought songs in the other iLife programs, like using a song as a background in an iMovie movie.

  To find out what version you have, open System Preferences, click QuickTime, and click the About QuickTime button. If it turns out you don't have the latest version of QuickTime, stay right there in System Preferences. Choose View→Software Update, click Update Software, make sure you can get online, and then click Check Now. After a moment, you'll be offered the opportunity to download the latest, greatest version of QuickTime.

- **Your permissions are scrambled.** An amazing number of mysterious glitches arise because the *permissions* of either that item or something in your System folder have become muddled—that is, Mac OS X's complex mesh of interconnected Unix permissions settings. Music-store songs not playing back is among them.

FREQUENTLY ASKED QUESTION

QuickTime Player vs. QuickTime Player Pro

OK, I tried to update my copy of QuickTime like you said. But the updater asks me for my name, company, and a "QuickTime Pro key!" What the heck is that?

QuickTime Pro is a $30 upgrade (to the free QuickTime you just downloaded). It adds the ability to edit QuickTime movies (instead of just watching them), among other goodies.

If you had paid for this upgrade, this would be your opportunity to plug in the serial number you were sent by email. But if you have no intention of upgrading to Pro, just leave the boxes blank and click Continue. Unlike other programs that sit down and refuse to cooperate if you don't have a serial number, QuickTime lets you *play* for free.

In that case, open your Applications→Utilities folder and open Disk Utility.
Then proceed as shown in Figure 30-1.

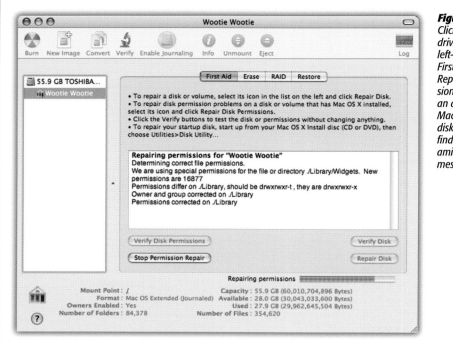

Figure 30-1:
Click your hard drive's name in the left-side list; click the First Aid tab; click Repair Disk Permissions; and then read an article while the Mac checks out your disk. If the program finds anything amiss, you'll see messages like these.

- **You've authorized too many computers.** Remember, once you buy a song online, you're allowed to play it on a maximum of five computers (Macs or PCs).

  Rack your brain: Is it possible you authorized somebody's Mac so they could hear something you bought, forgot to de-authorize it, and now you're over the limit?

  Anyway, you remove a computer from your designated set by choosing Advanced→Deauthorize Computer while you're online. In the resulting dialog box, choose "Deauthorize Computer for Apple Account" and then click OK. If you've already given the computer away, check out the tip on page 71 for a quick fix.

- **You can't listen to store-bought songs across the network.** If you, seated at Computer A, are trying to listen to the music on Computer B using the playlist-sharing feature described on page 42, you may notice that iTunes skips over any songs that came from the iTunes Music Store. That, alas, is normal behavior. Unless you make Computer A one of the five authorized machines for your account, you won't be able to hear Computer B's store-bought tunes.

Playback Problems

Playing back music is a pretty essential and simple task: Just tap the Space bar. Trouble-shooting playback is pretty simple, too:

The Music Is Too Quiet

Remember that you're now contending with two different volume levels: your Mac's own speaker volume (which you can adjust with the volume keys on your keyboard, or using the Sound panel of System Preferences) and the little volume slider at the top of the iTunes window. Adjust both of them.

If you can't hear anything at all, make sure that you don't have external speakers or headphones plugged into your Mac (which cuts off all sound to the built-in speaker).

And if you have an AirPort Express wireless networking base station, make sure that the pop-up menu at the bottom edge of the iTunes window is set correctly. If you're trying to play back the music using your Mac's built-in speakers, make sure this pop-up menu says Computer. And if you're attempting to direct playback to whatever speakers are attached to the AirPort Express, make sure they're turned on and hooked up right.

The Songs Overlap Each Other

It's a feature, not a bug. Choose iTunes→Preferences, click Audio, and turn off Crossfade Playback.

Files Missing in Action

Every once in while iTunes throws you a curveball out of the blue that can range from minorly annoying to downright panic-inducing. Here are a few common issues to look out for:

My Podcast Didn't Get Updated

Keeping current with the latest episode of your favorite podcast is easy with iTunes, since the program does most of the work of checking for—and downloading—fresh installments. If one of your regular shows doesn't get updated, though, the server that actually hosts the program may be down or busy, and iTunes itself can't get through to grab the new installment. In iTunes, click the Update button in the upper right corner of the Podcasts playlist to reach out for the show manually. Or try waiting a while before trying again, in case the server is still having a really, really bad day.

I Get a "Movie File Cannot Be Found" Error

You can play .mov and .mp4 movies right in iTunes 4.8 and later, but the program sometimes gets discombobulated if you have QuickTime "reference movies" in the mix. These reference movies are typically *temporary* pointer files that aimed at the location of the real movie in whatever program it was created in, but they can confuse iTunes when you try to play them.

To fix the error, choose Edit→View Options, check the box next to Kind and click OK. Click Library in the iTunes Source list, then click the new Kind column header you just made to sort your collection by file type. Scroll down to the *QuickTime movie file* section and double-click each file to make sure it plays. If you get the error message, click the Cancel button in the box, select the offending file, and choose Edit→ Clear to boot the bad seed off the list.

I Upgraded iTunes and All My Music Is Gone!

Sure, you think you're doing the right thing by upgrading, but sometimes things can go wacky when you install a new version of iTunes. If you update the program and start it up to find out that *your entire libary has vanished*, take a deep breath, put down the sharp object, and quit out of the iTunes program for a minute.

Just remember that your music is still on the Mac, but this new version of iTunes doesn't know where to look for it.

Now then, go find the folder that iTunes stores your music library's database file. Unless you've fiddled with the default settings, it's in your Home→Music→iTunes folder. Drag the file in there called *iTunes Library* out of the folder and dump it onto your desktop.

Next, go back to that main iTunes folder and open the subfolder called Previous iTunes Libraries that's tucked inside. Find the file called i*Tunes 4 Music Library* in there and drag that out into the main iTunes folder where the old one used to be.

Restart iTunes. You should see all your old music, right where you left it.

Troubleshooting iPhoto

i Photo isn't just a Mac OS X program—it's a *Cocoa* Mac OS X program, meaning that it was written exclusively for Mac OS X. As a result, it should, in theory, be one of the most rock-solid programs under the sun.

Still, iPhoto does have its vulnerabilities. Many of these shortcomings stem from the fact that iPhoto works under the supervision of a lot of cooks, since it must interact with plug-ins, connect to printers, talk to Web servers, and cope with an array of file corruptions.

If trouble strikes, keep hands and feet inside the tram at all times—and consult the following collection of problems, solutions, questions, and answers.

Importing and Opening

Getting photos into iPhoto is supposed to be one of the most effortless parts of the process. Remember, Steve Jobs promised that iPhoto would forever banish the "chain of pain" from digital photography. And yet…

My thumbnails appear as blank, gray rectangles.

Update your copy of iPhoto to 5.0.4 or later. Then rebuild your iPhoto library.

To do that, quit iPhoto. Then, while pressing the ⌘ and Option keys, reopen it. iPhoto will promptly rebuild your library, cleaning out unneeded cobwebs of data and ensuring that all relationships (between thumbnails and full-size images, for example) are healthy and strong.

iPhoto doesn't recognize my camera.

iPhoto generally "sees" any recent camera model, even if it's not listed on Apple's Device Compatibility page (*www.apple.com/iphoto/compatibility*). If you don't see the Import screen even though the camera most assuredly is connected, try these steps in order:

- Make sure the camera is turned on. Check the USB cable at both ends.

- Try plugging the camera into a different USB port.

- Some models don't see the computer until you switch them into a special "PC" mode, using the control knob.

- Try turning on the camera *after* connecting its USB cable to the Mac.

- Turn the camera off, then on again, while it's plugged in.

- If iPhoto absolutely won't notice its digital companion, use a memory-card reader as described on page 96.

iPhoto crashes when I try to import.

This problem is most likely to crop up when you're bringing pictures in from your hard drive or another disk. Here are the possibilities:

- The culprit is usually a single corrupted file. Try a test: Import only half the photos in the batch. If nothing bad happens, split the remaining photos in half again and import *them*. Keep going until you've isolated the offending file.

- Consider the graphics program you're using to save the files. It's conceivable that its version of JPEG or TIFF doesn't jibe perfectly with iPhoto's. (This scenario is most likely to occur right after you've upgraded either your graphics program or iPhoto itself.)

  To test this possibility, open a handful of images in a different editing program, save them, and then try the import again. If they work, then you might have a temporary compatibility problem. Check the editing program's Web site for update and troubleshooting information.

- Some JPEGs that were originally saved in Mac OS 9 won't import into iPhoto. Try opening and resaving these images in a native Mac OS X editor like Photoshop. Speaking of Photoshop, it has an excellent batch-processing tool that can automatically process mountains of images while you go grab some lunch.

Finally, a reminder, just in case you think iPhoto is acting up: iPhoto now imports RAW files—but not from all camera models. For details, see page 98.

iPhoto won't import images from my video camera.

Most modern digital camcorders can store your still images on a memory card instead of DV tape. If you're having a hard time importing these stills into iPhoto with a direct camera connection, try these tips:

- Take out the tape cassette before connecting the camcorder to your Mac.

- Try copying the files directly from the memory card to your hard drive with a memory-card reader. Once the images are on your hard drive, you should be able to import them into iPhoto.

What if I don't want iPhoto to import all the pictures from my camera?

You can't tell iPhoto not to import them all—but you can use Image Capture. A sort of grandfather to iPhoto, this Mac OS X program comes on every Mac. Although it doesn't perform even a hundredth of the feats that iPhoto can, it does offer one feature iPhoto lacks—*selective* importing.

Figure 31-1:
Top: First, make sure that Image Capture, not iPhoto, intercepts and downloads the photos when you connect your digital camera. To do so, open Image Capture, then choose Image Capture→Preferences.

From the Camera Preferences pop-up menu, choose Image Capture. (In fact, you could even choose another program to intervene when your camera is plugged in, by choosing Other from this menu).

Middle: This is the main Image Capture window that now appears when you plug in your camera. To download only some of the photos, click Download Some.

Bottom: This "slide sorter" window is where you can choose the individual pictures you want to download. Or, use the buttons at the top to rotate or delete selected shots from the camera. In slide sorter view, Shift-click or ⌘-click the thumbnails of the pictures you want. In list view, Shift-click or ⌘-click as though they're Finder list-view files.

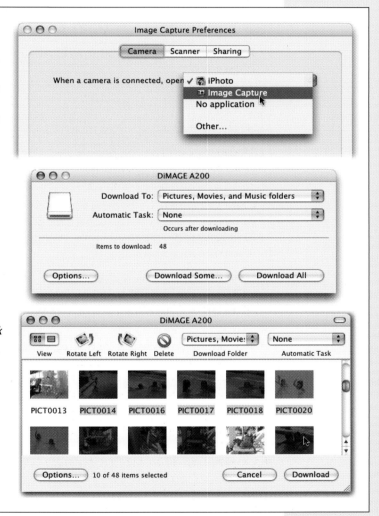

First, however, you must tell iPhoto not to open automatically when you plug in your camera. You want Image Capture to do your importing, instead. To make this change, use the procedure outlined in Figure 31-1. From now on, Image Capture, not iPhoto, will open whenever you plug in your camera.

Once the pictures are on your hard drive, copy them into iPhoto simply by dragging them (or the folder they're in) into the photo-viewing area.

Exporting

Clearly, "Easy come, easy go" doesn't always apply to photos.

After I upgraded iPhoto to the latest version, my Export button became disabled.

This problem is usually caused by outdated plug-ins. If you have any older plug-ins, such as an outdated version of the Toast Titanium export plug-in, disable it and then relaunch iPhoto to see whether that solves the problem.

Here's how to turn your plug-ins on or off:

1. **Quit iPhoto.**

   Return to the Finder.

2. **Highlight the iPhoto application icon. Choose File→Get Info.**

   You may have seen the Get Info box for other files in your day, but you probably haven't seen a *Plugins* panel (Figure 31-2).

3. **Click the triangle to expand the Plugins panel.**

   A complete list of the plug-ins you currently have loaded appears with a checkbox next to each item.

4. **Turn off the non-Apple plug-ins that you suspect might be causing the problem.**

Now open iPhoto and test the export function. If the technology gods are smiling, the function should work now. All that's left is to figure out which *one* of the plug-ins was causing your headaches.

To find out, quit iPhoto. In the Finder, open its Get Info window again. Reinstate your plug-ins one by one, using the on/off switches depicted in Figure 31-2, until you find the offending software.

Once you locate the culprit, highlight its name and then click Remove. (You may also want to check the Web site of the offending plug-in for an updated version.)

Tip: Here's another, somewhat more interesting way to remove a plug-in. Control-click the iPhoto icon; from the shortcut menu, choose Show Package Contents. In the resulting window, open the Contents→PlugIns folder, where each plug-in is represented by an easily removable icon.

Printing

How many things can go wrong when you print? Let us count the ways.

I can't print more than one photo per page. It seems like a waste to use a whole sheet of paper for one 4 x 6 print.

Check the following:

- Have you, in fact, selected more than one photo to print?

- Choose File→Page Setup. Make sure the paper size is US Letter (or whatever paper you've loaded). Click OK.

- Choose File→Print. From the Presets pop-up menu, choose Standard; from the Style pop-up menu, choose N-Up; then choose a number from the "Photos per page" pop-up menu. (Make sure "One photo per page" is turned off.) You'll now see all of your selected images side by side in the preview pane. They're ready to print.

Figure 31-2:
You may be surprised to discover that a number of iPhoto's "built-in" features are actually plug-ins written by Apple's programmers. Most of them are responsible for familiar printing and exporting options. Any others should be turned off in times of troubleshooting. (If you can't remember which plug-ins you've installed yourself, reinstall iPhoto.)

Editing

There's not much that can go wrong here, but when it does, it *really* goes wrong.

iPhoto crashes when I double-click a thumbnail to edit it.

You probably changed a photo file's name in the Finder—in the iPhoto Library folder, behind the program's back. iPhoto hates this! Only grief can follow.

Sometimes, too, a corrupted picture file will also make iPhoto crash when you try to edit it. Use the Show Image File script (one of the free AppleScripts described on page 124) to locate the scrambled file in the Finder. Open the file in another graphics program, use its File→Save As command to replace the corrupted picture file, and then try again in iPhoto.

My Adjust panel is missing most of its sliders!

If your Mac has only a G3 processor inside, them's the breaks. All you get is Brightness and Contrast sliders. (The rest require a G4 processor or later.)

iPhoto won't let me use an external graphics program when I double-click a thumbnail.

Choose iPhoto→Preferences. Make sure that the Other button is selected and that a graphics program's name appears next to it. (If not, click Other, then click Set, and then choose the program you want to use.)

Also make sure that your external editing program still *exists*. You might have upgraded to a newer version of that program, one whose file name is slightly different from the version you originally specified in iPhoto.

My picture doesn't fit right on 4 x 6, 5 x 7, or 8 x 10 inch paper.

Most digital cameras produce photos in a 4:3 width-to-height ratio. Unfortunately, those dimensions don't fit squarely into any of the standard print sizes.

The solution: Crop the photos first, using the appropriate print size in the Constrain pop-up menu (see page 152).

I've messed up a photo while editing it, and now it's ruined!

Highlight the file's thumbnail and then choose File→Revert to Original. iPhoto restores your photo to its original state, drawing on a backup it has secretly kept.

General Questions

Finally, here's a handful of general—although perfectly terrifying—troubles.

iPhoto's wigging out.

If the program "unexpectedly quits," well, that's life. It happens. This is Mac OS X, though, so you can generally open the program right back up again and pick up where you left off.

If the flakiness is becoming really severe, try logging out (choose →Log Out) and logging back in again. And if the problem persists, see the data-purging steps on the next page.

Man, this program's slow!

Installing more memory is by far the best solution to this problem. iPhoto loves RAM like Paris Hilton loves attention.

For an immediate (and less expensive) fix, keep your Photo Library a reasonable size and collapse your film rolls (page 112).

I don't see my other Mac's shared photos over the network.

Chapter 11 covers network photo sharing in detail. If you're having trouble making it work, here's your checklist:

- Make sure you've turned on "Look for shared photos" in the Sharing pane of iPhoto Preferences.

- Is the Mac that's sharing the photos turned on and awake? Is iPhoto running on it, and does it have photo sharing turned on? Is it on the same network subnet (network branch)?

- Do the photo-sharing Macs have iPhoto 4 or later installed?

I can't change the name of an album/book/slideshow icon.

Double-click its name, and then type in the new label.

When I try to choose a soundtrack for a slide show, my iTunes music collection doesn't show up!

First, try opening iTunes before opening iPhoto. That way, iPhoto will be sure to "see" the open iTunes library.

If that doesn't solve the problem, you might have to recreate one of your iTunes preference files, like this:

First, quit all iLife programs. Open your Home→Music→iTunes folder. Drag the file called iTunes Music Library.xml file to your desktop.

Now open iTunes and create a new playlist by choosing File→New Playlist. (Doing so triggers iTunes to build a new .xml file, which is what you want.) Quit iTunes.

When you return to iPhoto, your iTunes library should show up just fine.

I can't delete a photo!

You may be trying to delete a photo right out of a smart album. That's a no-no.

There's only one workaround: Find the same photo in the Photo Library, the Last Roll icon, or the Last Months icon—and delete it from there.

All my pictures are gone! (or)
My thumbnails are all gray rectangles! (or)
I'm having some other crisis!

The missing-pictures syndrome and the gray-rectangle thumbnails are only two of several weirdisms that may strike with all the infrequency—and pain—of lightning. Maybe iPhoto is trying to import phantom photos. Maybe it's stuck at the "Loading photos..." screen forever. Maybe the photos just don't look right. There's a long list, in fact, of rare but mystifying glitches that can arise.

What your copy of iPhoto needs is a big thwack upside the head, also known as a major data purge.

You may not need to perform all of the following steps. But if you follow them all, at least you'll know you did everything possible to make things right.

Fortunately, setting things aright is fairly easy if you know what to do. Follow these steps in order; after each one, check to see if the problem is gone.

- **If you haven't already done so, upgrade to the very latest version of iPhoto.** For example, version 5.0.1 fixed a host of bugs and glitches.

- **Rebuild the photo library.** Quit iPhoto. Then reopen it, pressing the Option and ⌘ keys as you do so.

  iPhoto asks you if you're sure you want to "rebuild your Photo Library," and warns that you might lose some data. What it's referring to here is corrupted data—photo files that are slightly damaged, for example. Since these are probably what's causing iPhoto to misbehave, you probably don't mind losing them. Click Yes.

  In the next dialog box, iPhoto asks you to save the freshly rebuilt iPhoto Library folder somewhere. You can name it, say, "Rescued Library," and save it into your Pictures folder or wherever you like.

  Once you click Save, iPhoto works its way through each album and each photo, inspecting it for damage, repairing it if possible, and finally presenting you with your new, cleaned-up library.

- **Repair your file permissions.** An amazing number of mysterious glitches—not just in iPhoto—arise because file *permissions* have become muddled. Permissions is a complex subject, and refers to a complex mesh of interconnected Unix settings on every file in Mac OS X.

  When something just doesn't seem to be working right, therefore, open your Applications→Utilities folder and open Disk Utility. Click your hard drive's name in the left-side list; click the First Aid tab; click Repair Disk Permissions; and then read a magazine while the Mac checks out your disk. If the program finds anything amiss, you'll see Unix shorthand messages that tell you what it fixed.

Tip: Most Mac mavens, in fact, believe in running this Repair Permissions routine after running *any kind of installer*, just to nip nascent problems in the bud. That includes both installers of new programs and of Apple's own updates.

- **Throw away the iPhoto preferences file.** Here we are in the age of Mac OS X, and we're still throwing away preference files?

  Absolutely. A corrupted preference file can still bewilder the program that depends on it.

  Before you go on a dumpfest, however, take this simple test. Log in using a *different account* (perhaps a dummy account that you create just for testing purposes). Run iPhoto. Is the problem gone? If so, then the glitch exists only when *you* are logged in—which means it's a problem with *your* copy of the program's preferences.

  Return to your own account. Open your Home→Library→Preferences folder, where you'll find neatly labeled preference files for all of the programs you use. In this case, trash the file called com.apple.iPhoto.plist.

  The next time you run iPhoto, it will build itself a brand-new preference file that, if you're lucky, lacks whatever corruption was causing your problems.

- Trash your Thumb.data files. Open your Home→Pictures→iPhoto Library folder. Drag the three Thumb.data files to the desktop, too.

  These three files—ThumbJPG.data, Thumb32.data, and Thumb64.data—store the miniature images of your photos. If they get scrambled, so do your thumbnails. Setting them aside forces iPhoto to start fresh.

If you undertook this mission because your photos seemed to be missing from iPhoto, and all of these steps still didn't restore them, all is not lost. Unless you somehow opened your Home→Pictures folder and, while sleepwalking, manually threw away your iPhoto Library folder, your pictures are still there.

The tool you need is called iPhoto Extractor, and you can download it from *www.missingmanuals.com*. Its sole purpose is to rescue your "missing" photos from a discombobulated iPhoto Library, so it's probably exactly the tool you need right now.

TROUBLESHOOTING

Troubleshooting iMovie and iDVD

Apple wasn't fooling around when it wrote iMovie HD. Big chunks of the program were *completely* rewritten in this version. Put another way, big chunks of this program are in their 1.0 version. And you know what that means, right? Right: bugs.

As of version 5.0.1, a number of peculiar glitches remain. Some offer easy workarounds; some remain baffling and have no simple solutions. Adding to the confusion is the fact that many of these bugs are *intermittent,* striking some people sometimes and other people not at all. Some of the best minds in the business are at a loss to explain the inconsistencies.

Here, though, is the world's most complete compendium of the problems that may occur—and the world's best attempts at solving them.

Two Golden Rules

If there's any common wisdom at all about iMovie, here it is: a pair of golden rules that will stave off a huge number of problems down the road.

- **Use the latest version.** Each ".01" or ".02" upgrade zaps a whole host of bugs and glitches. These updates are free, so when your Software Update program advises you that one is available, jump at the chance to install it.

- **Set your camcorder to 16-bit audio.** The typical digital camcorder can record its audio track using either 12-bit or 16-bit audio. The factory setting is 12-bit, which gives non–computer owners a chance to overlay a second audio track without erasing the original camera sound. Trouble is, 12-bit audio may slowly drift out of sync with the video when you burn the finished project to a DVD.

Use your camera's menu system to switch to 16-bit audio. You, an iMovie aficionado, can easily overlay additional audio using your computer, so you give up nothing—except a lot of frustration. (Make this change *now,* before you record anything important.)

General iMovie Troubleshooting

Let's start general, shall we?

Weird Inconsistent Problems

When a program's preferences file becomes scrambled, all kinds of peculiar behavior can result. Buttons and functions don't work. Visual anomalies appear. Things just don't work right.

If iMovie starts having a bad hair day, suspect its preferences file. Quit the program, open your Home→Library→Preferences folder, and throw away the file called *com. apple.iMovie.plist.*

The next time you run iMovie, it will automatically build a new preferences file. This file will have the original factory settings (for the options in, for example, the Preferences dialog box), but at least it will be healthy and whole.

Keeping Your Hard Disk Happy

Remember the old expression, "If Mama ain't happy, ain't nobody happy"? Well, if your hard disk isn't happy, iMovie won't be happy, either.

Here's a short list of maintenance suggestions. A little attention every week or so may help keep minor hard drive problems from becoming major problems.

- After installing or updating any software, use Disk Utility to Repair Permissions. (Disk Utility is in your Applications→Utilities folder. Click the First Aid tab, click your hard drive, and then click Repair Permissions.)

UP TO SPEED

Really Massive iMovie File Problems

The disk your iMovie HD project sits on must be prepared using the Mac OS Extended formatting scheme, also known as HFS+. All Apple drives come formatted that way, but some people have been known to buy an external FireWire hard drive from another company, plug it in, save an iMovie project onto it, and immediately run into massive problems. The fun may include dialog boxes that complain about file permissions, missing files, and "Icon" documents.

If you've just bought a new drive, check the disk format before using it. Do that by highlighting the disk icon in the Finder and choosing File→Get Info. Under the Format heading in the resulting dialog box, you'll see the formatting scheme identified.

If the format isn't correct, use Disk Utility to reformat the drive (which involves erasing the whole drive).

- Every couple of months, restart your Mac from the Mac OS X CD, choose File→Disk Utility, click the First Aid tab, click your hard drive icon, and click Repair Disk.

- Mac OS X runs three behind-the-scenes Unix maintenance programs at regular intervals between 3 a.m. and 5 a.m. If your Mac is asleep or turned off every night, the maintenance probably isn't being done, because the Mac doesn't wake itself up to do the maintenance.

  If you don't regularly leave your Mac running overnight, take a minute, every month or so, to run MacJanitor—a free program that runs those same maintenance programs, but at your command. (You can get it from the "Missing CD" page at *www.missingmanuals.com,* among other places.)

Starting Up and Importing

Trouble getting going? Here's some advice.

"Some stray files were found" Message

This message is, fortunately, going the way of floppy disks; it occurs very rarely in iMovie HD projects. Even so, it may still pop up occasionally when you're opening older iMovie projects. Here's the explanation.

You're never supposed to move, delete, rename, or fiddle with any of the icons in your project folder's Media folder (page 288). iMovie itself is supposed to manage those clips, behind the scenes.

But if you put a clip into the Media folder *yourself*—a much more difficult proposition in iMovie HD—then the next time you open the project, you get the message shown in Figure 32-1. iMovie doesn't recognize some of the clips it found there, and has moved them to the iMovie HD Trash. It invites you to (a) view the Trash contents, or (b) not.

That's the theory, anyway. In the real world, you'll probably get the "stray files" message from time to time, even when you haven't been anywhere near the Media folder. Sometimes iMovie just gets confused, as may be the case when the program bombs, or when you force quit it.

Figure 32-1:
Movie has discovered clips that it doesn't remember being part of your project. Maybe you put them in the project folder (deliberately or not); maybe the clips were always part of the project, but iMovie somehow forgot.

Some stray files were found in the project, and were moved into iMovie's Trash.

Would you like to view the Trash contents?

Don't View Trash   View Trash

There's no real trouble to shoot here; click the option you prefer and get on with your life.

"Camera not connected"

If you get this message in the Monitor window when you click the Camera button, it probably means one of these things:

- Your camcorder isn't plugged into the Mac with a FireWire cable.

- The camcorder isn't turned on.

- You're using a camcorder whose FireWire circuitry isn't completely compatible with the Macintosh. (Some older JVC camcorders—circa 1999–2000—fall into this category.)

If you get the "Camera not connected" message the very first time you try to connect a new camcorder to your Mac, and you've checked to make sure that the cable is connected properly and the camera is turned on, then you probably need to replace either the camera or the FireWire cable. (The occasional iMovie owner has become frustrated that a new camcorder doesn't work, but upon exchanging it for another of the same model, finds that it works beautifully.)

Import from Camera Stops After 2–3 Seconds

FileVault, a feature of Mac OS X 10.3 and later, encrypts files in your Home folder so that ne'er-do-wells in the neighborhood can't break in when you're not at your desk. If you save an iMovie HD project into your Home folder, the Mac will try to encrypt the video you're importing from the camcorder in real time—and it can't be done.

Either turn off FileVault, or save your iMovie HD project someplace outside your Home folder.

Dropouts in the Video

A *dropout* is a glitch in the picture. DV dropouts are always square or rectangular. They may be a blotch of the wrong color, or may be multicolored. They may appear every time you play a particular scene, or may appear at random. In severe circumstances, you may get lots of them, such as when you try to capture video to an old FireWire hard drive that's too slow. Such a configuration may also cause tearing of the video picture.

Fortunately, dropouts are fairly rare in digital video. If you get one, it's probably in one of these three circumstances:

- You're using a very old cassette. Remember that even DV cassettes don't last forever. You may begin to see dropouts after rerecording the tape 50 times or so.

- You're playing back a cassette that was recorded in LP (long play) mode. If the cassette was recorded on a different camcorder, dropouts are especially likely.

- It's time to clean the heads on your camcorder—the electrical components that actually make contact with the tape and, over time, can become dirty. Your local electronics store sells head-cleaning kits for just this purpose.

UP TO SPEED

Nondestructive Editing: Pros and Cons

Two of the most dramatic changes to iMovie HD involve the Trash and something called nondestructive editing: the ability to restore a clip or adjust the way you've chopped it up, even years after making the movie.

But this overhaul has introduced both blessings and curses—and demands a good deal of new understanding.

The good news:

- You can revert an audio or video clip to its original state at any time, even after you've emptied the project Trash. And even when you shorten or split or crop a clip, iMovie never shortens the original, full-length video file.

- You can even restore or revert clips you've pasted into another project.

- You can pull a clip out of the Trash at any time until the Trash is emptied.

- When you empty the project Trash, you fling the associated video clip into the Mac's Trash (the one in the Finder). That gives you another safety net for recovering something you deleted by accident.

- You no longer have to worry about corrupting your project when you empty the iMovie Trash, as you did in previous versions.

The bad news:

- iMovie deletes a full clip only when you delete the last clip that references it. In other words, if you've used 2 seconds of a 45-minute clip in your movie, iMovie doesn't delete the 45-minute clip or give you back the disk space, even if you empty the project

Trash. As a result, large files always stay large.

- Copying and pasting clips between projects can cause projects to balloon in size. That's because, if you copy that 2-second clip from Project A into Project B, iMovie HD copies the entire, 45-minute underlying source file.

In fact, if you copy two clips ("Laughing" and "Laughing/1") that are both derived from the same original clip, iMovie copies the entire underlying 45-minute source file twice. (Unless you copy both at the same time, that is.)

- When you drag a clip out of iMovie (to the Finder, to iDVD, or anyplace else), iMovie HD copies the entire source file, not just the clip.

To export only the edited clip instead of the full-size original, export the clip instead of dragging it. That is, highlight the clip, choose File→Share, turn on "Share selected clips only," click the QuickTime button, and choose Full Quality from the pop-up menu. (If you're really squeezed for disk space, you can also use this trick to make iMovie "let go" of a full-length original file of which you're using only 2 seconds. Export the 2 seconds, then re-import it; use it to replace the one you exported. Now you can delete the original long one.)

- To recover disk space after emptying the iMovie Trash, you must also empty the Mac Trash.

- Because Trash-emptying rules are complicated, the Trash window sometimes conveys misleading information. For example, when you choose to delete a clip from the Trash window, you're never told whether or not other clips refer to the same original source file, and therefore, you never know whether or not you'll actually regain any disk space.

If you spot the glitch at the same moment on the tape every time you play it, then the problem is on the tape itself. If it's there during one playback but gone during the next, the problem more likely lies with the heads in your camcorder.

Tip: Different DV tape manufacturers use different lubricants on their tapes. As a result, mixing tapes from different manufacturers on the same camcorder can increase the likelihood of head clogs. It's a good idea, therefore, to stick with tapes from one manufacturer (Sony, Panasonic, or Maxell, for example) when possible.

Banding

Banding in the video picture is a relative of dropouts, but is much less common. Once again, it may stem from dirt on either the tape itself or the heads in your camcorder. Most of the time, banding results when the tape was jammed or crinkled on an earlier journey through your camcorder. Now, as the tape plays, your camcorder heads encounter a creased portion of the tape, and then, until they can find clean information to display, fill the screen with whatever the last usable video information was.

If the problem is with the tape itself, the banding disappears as soon as clean, smooth tape comes into contact with the playback heads. If you get banding when playing different cassettes, however, it's time to clean the heads of your camcorder.

iSight Titles and Transitions Look Wrong

Sometimes iMovie HD imports video from an iSight camera with the wrong image size. The video looks fine in the iMovie window, but when titles and transitions are added to the video, they appear in the upper-left corner of the Monitor window.

Actually, the titles and transitions are OK; it's the iSight video that's the wrong size.

The trick is to choose Window→ Show Full Size Resolution before you import the video. Then the iSight video should arrive at the proper size.

Widescreen Video Gets Letterboxed

Some camcorders offer a special shooting mode called 16:9 video (that is, widescreen format). When you import this 16:9 video into a DV Widescreen project, iMovie HD sometimes wants to letterbox it, adding horizontal black bands above and below. (The letterboxing begins as soon as you switch from camera mode to edit mode and click a clip.) Since the video is *already* 16:9, that's probably not what you want iMovie HD to do.

You may be able to avoid this problem by *not* switching modes. That is, instead of switching to Edit mode, stay in Camera mode; save the project; quit iMovie; and turn off the camera. When you reopen the project, the video will stay 16:9.

Title Trouble

For some reason, titles and credits seem to have their own phalanx of problems and issues. For example:

Title Backgrounds Have Jaggies

The quality of the image behind a title in iMovie HD isn't as good as it once was, especially if you burn the movie to DVD. The title looks great, but the background behind acquires *jaggies,* the stair-step lines along hard edges (Figure 32-2).

Figure 32-2:
For some reason, as of version 5.0.1, iMovie HD introduces stairstepped, jagged lines in the video behind a title, as shown here before (top) and after. DV and DV Widescreen projects seem most vulnerable. The quantity of jaggies depends on the type of image and movement in the image. At its worst, the problem is distracting. At its best, it may not occur.

Some things to try to minimize the jaggies:

- Place your title over video that contains natural objects instead of man-made objects. Faces, landscapes, and flowers tend to be better than roof lines, deck railings, and fences. Avoid objects containing straight lines and hard edges.

- Place the title over video that doesn't move. A clip that zooms in on a building—or a Ken Burns clip that zooms in on a picture of the building—may look worse than a clip with no motion.

- When using a Ken Burns photo, import a large-dimension image, not small.

- Before importing the photo, soften the image a bit. Try iPhoto's Edit→Adjust→Sharpness function, or Photoshop's Gaussian blur.

- Before adding the title, export the clip to a DVCPRO - NTSC QuickTime movie, then re-import that to iMovie HD. (If your video is in PAL format, use DVCPRO - PAL instead.)

- Create a title "Over black" instead of a video clip.

The Type Is Too Small

To make sure your title fits onscreen, iMovie limits the text size of the title to what fits within the movie frame. That's a nice feature that keeps all of your text on the screen, without the risk of chopping it off at the sides. Trouble is, even when you drag the type-size slider all the way to the right, the text may still be too small to read, especially when exported as a smallish QuickTime movie.

When making multiline titles, iMovie determines the maximum text size based on the longest line. If you're getting tiny text, then consider shortening the longest line or dividing it in two. You'll see the type size jump up accordingly.

Tip: You also gain another 10 percent size boost by turning on QT Margins. Do that only for movies you intend to save as QuickTime movies, however, not for projects you'll show on TV.

Chopped-off Type on Playback from Tape

The actual dimensions of a TV picture aren't what you'd expect. To avoid the risk that some oddball TV model might display a sliver of black empty space at a corner or edge of the glass, all NTSC television signals are *overscanned*—deliberately transmitted at a size *larger* than the TV screen. Sure, that means that the outer five percent of the picture at each edge doesn't even show up on your TV, because it's beyond the glass borders. But TV directors are aware of this phenomenon, and carefully avoid shooting anything that might get chopped off by the overscanning.

Unfortunately, iMovie has one foot in the world of video, and the other in the QuickTime world, where no overscanning is necessary. QuickTime movies always show *everything* in the picture, perfectly and precisely. Nothing is ever lost beyond the borders of a QuickTime window. That's why some footage that looks spectacular and perfect in iMovie (or in an exported QuickTime movie) gets chopped off around the edges when viewed on a TV.

(This phenomenon explains the "QT Margins" checkbox, described back on page 347.)

Title Flows over Edge of Movie

There's a small bug in iMovie HD that sometimes allows a title to flow off the left and right edges of the movie. The solution is to drag iMovie's text-size slider to make the text smaller, and then try again.

Scrolling Block Title Scrolls Too Fast

Sometimes, scrolling block–style titles scroll by *way* too fast—much too fast to read (which is a definite downside). And iMovie HD doesn't seem to let you set the duration to a longer scroll.

To solve this problem, first note that iMovie HD lets you create scrolling block titles that are much longer than before: They can contain well over 4,000 characters.

The trouble is, as you add text to a long title, iMovie doesn't update the maximum title duration displayed next to the Speed slider. The slider limits you to the maximum duration for a *short* title, say, 20 seconds. So when you apply the settings, it scrolls way too fast.

Here's the trick: After typing your long text in the title, click again on the Scrolling Block style name in the title list. Voilà! Now the Speed slider offers a much longer duration. Set the Speed slider to the duration you want, then redo the title.

Photo Problems

iMovie HD's photo features are, in general, a delight—and they let you get mileage out of iMovie even if you don't own a camcorder. But you may encounter some rough edges.

Can't Change the Duration of a Still Photo

iMovie distinguishes between still *photos* and still *frames,* of the sort that you capture using the Edit→Create Still Frame command. Moreover, it differentiates between photos that exhibit the Ken Burns effect and those that don't.

It's so complicated, you practically need a cheat sheet—and here it is.

- To change the duration of a Ken Burnsized photo (imported from iPhoto or from the hard drive), click the clip and then use the Duration slider (or Duration box) in the Photos palette. Click Update.

- To change the duration of a still frame, double-click it. Change the duration in the Clip Info box.

- To change the duration of a *non*–Ken Burnsized photo, use either method: the Duration slider in the Photos palette, or the Clip Info box.

Ken Burns Accelerates Too Much

When the Ken Burns effect zooms in on an image, the clip sometimes appears to accelerate. There's a pause at the beginning of the clip, then the zooming goes faster and faster, all the way to the end. Most of the time, you probably want, if anything, a *deceleration,* so that the zoom comes to rest gently at the end of the magnification.

You can't eliminate this acceleration, but you can minimize it. These solutions rely on eliminating the pause at the start of the clip, which makes the zooming look smoother:

- Zoom less. A gentle zoom is usually better anyway.

- Add a Cross Dissolve transition before the Ken Burns clip; the transition covers the pause at the beginning. (The length of the pause depends on the duration of the clip and amount of zoom.)

- Set the Ken Burns duration a second or two longer than you actually need. Then, after the clip is finished rendering, crop out the first part of the clip by dragging its left edge to the right.

Ken Burns Zoom Always Shows 1.00

When the Ken Burns checkbox is turned off, it can look like the zoom is stuck on 1.00.

You'll see this situation when two conditions exist: First, the Ken Burns checkbox is turned off when you import a photo; second, the Ken Burns zoom setting is greater than 1.00. For this example, suppose it's 1.48.

When you click the Apply button, the zoom slider immediately jumps to 1.00, making you think that the image was imported with a 1.00 zoom instead of 1.48. That impression is only reinforced when you click the imported clip and see that the zoom slider still says 1.00. (Ordinarily, iMovie HD displays the zoom that was used to import the image when you click the resulting clip.)

In fact, though, the imported clip was imported correctly. These are all just cosmetic bugs. You can prove it by importing the image a second time using a 1.00 zoom, and comparing the two.

iPhoto Slideshow Fails to Import Video

Sometimes, a strange thing may happen when you try to drag a slideshow from iPhoto into iMovie HD: iMovie HD imports the song but skips the video.

In that situation, you've probably selected a copy-protected song, bought from the iTunes Music Store, as background music for the iPhoto slideshow.

If you have QuickTime Player Pro, open the iPhoto-exported movie, remove the audio track, Save, and try importing again. If you *don't* have QuickTime Player Pro, return to iPhoto, remove the song, export to a new movie, and try again.

Remember, you can always import the iTunes song directly into your iMovie HD project.

Problems Editing

All right: Your video is now in iMovie, and you're ready to get to work.

Direct Trimming Doesn't Work

One of iMovie's most delicious features is *edge dragging* or *direct trimming,* which means that you can drag the right or left end of a clip to change its length.

If direct trimming stops working—the cursor never changes to offer direct trimming—you have Show Clip Volume Levels turned on in the View menu. You can't drag edges when the little horizontal volume lines are displayed on your audio clips.

Effects Change a Clip's Color

How's this for weird? You apply an effect to one clip, and the background of the clip suddenly changes color to match the hue of the last *title* you created!

The workaround: delete the effect (select the clip and press the Delete key), save the project, close the project, and reopen it. Now the effects work correctly.

Split Clip Disappears from Clips Pane

Two clips should never occupy the same slot in the Clips pane, of course. But in iMovie HD, it's possible.

The problem can occur when you use the Scrubber bar to select the middle frames of a clip, and then you delete those frames. iMovie splits the clip, leaving behind the clips' ends. (If the original clip is named Clip 01, the new second clip is named Clip 01/1.)

The trouble is, sometimes the new clip gets hidden *underneath* some other clip in the Clips pane—especially when all the top slots in the Clips pane are full.

The workaround, if you call it one: look under the other clips in the Clips pane (by dragging them to other "cubbyholes").

Exporting Troubles

Now suppose that you're able to edit the video successfully, and even edit it into a masterful work of art. The big moment arrives: You're ready to play the movie back onto the tape, or export it as a QuickTime movie, so that you can then play it for friends and venture capitalists. Here are a few things that can go wrong.

You Live in Europe

If you bought your DV camcorder in Europe, it has probably been, as the Internet punsters say, "nEUtered." That is, it's been electronically rigged so that it *can't* record video from a FireWire cable.

Your PAL-format camcorder isn't broken. In fact, it's simply the victim of a European law, enacted under pressure from the motion picture industry, that any camcorder that can accept a video input signal is, technically speaking, a video *recorder,* not a camera. Video recorders are subject to a huge additional tax. Camcorder manufacturers, in an attempt to keep their consumer product line inexpensive, responded by taking out the digital-input feature from the built-in software of *inexpensive* DV and Digital8 camcorders. (More expensive DV camcorders don't have this problem.)

If you're clever with electronics, you can surf the Web in a quest for black market Web sites that explain how to *un*-disable FireWire recording—a simple procedure involving a technician's remote-control unit. Video repair shops in many European cities will perform this task for a small fee, too (but don't expect to see ads for this service). Otherwise, you have no choice but to limit your iMovie productions to QuickTime movies (instead of videotape), or to upgrade to a more expensive camcorder.

Export to Camera Fails to Stop Exporting Selected Clips

You don't have to export your entire movie once it's finished. If, in the File→Share dialog box, you turn on "Share selected clips only," iMovie is supposed to export only the clips that you first highlighted (as long as they're adjacent in the Movie Track).

As of version 5.0.1, however, iMovie HD sometimes fails to stop the export after the last clip. The export continues to the end of the project. The only way to halt the exporting is to click Stop. (Consider adding a 5-second black clip after the last selected clip to give you a clean stopping point.)

Warning: Clicking Stop can sometimes cause weird problems later. You should quit iMovie HD, then reopen the project.

Now, selected clips in the Clips pane (not the Movie Track) *do* stop exporting correctly, although the export order is unpredictable. If you need to export just one or two clips that are now in the Movie Track, Option-drag (to duplicate them) to the Clips pane, then export from there.

Export to HomePage Doesn't Have Fast Start

Fast Start is the QuickTime feature that allows your movie to start playing in your audience's Web browser before the download is complete. Unfortunately, Fast Start doesn't work when you export an iMovie HD movie to your HomePage.

For now, the solution is the shareware program called Lillipot. It lets you add Fast Start to your movie before you upload it to your HomePage. Lillipot is available from the "Missing CD" page of *www.missingmanuals.com.*

Exporting DV Widescreen Doesn't Make a Widescreen Movie

Sometimes, when you export your DV Widescreen project to QuickTime, the exported movie is not, in fact, widescreen.

Once again, the culprit is usually out-of-date iMovie HD plug-ins you've bought from other companies. Old versions can prevent iMovie HD from automatically exporting widescreen projects to widescreen movies.

Tip: Don't be confused by the dimensions shown in the Movie→Share dialog box. For widescreen projects, the text is wrong. It says the exported CD-ROM movie will be 320 x 240, for example, when in fact it will be 320 x 180.

DVD Problems

Exporting to iDVD Fails (Error -43)

As noted here and there throughout this book, you can extend iMovie's effects, transitions, and title styles by installing *plug-ins* from other companies. If you haven't updated your plug-ins to iMovie HD–specific versions, you've found the problem; they can prevent you from exporting to iDVD.

Video and Audio Aren't In Sync

On some longer movie projects (20 minutes or more), everything plays fine in iMovie, but when you turn your project into a QuickTime movie or burn it to a DVD, the audio and video grow slowly, horrifyingly out of sync. The longer the movie plays, the farther apart they drift.

The most important thing to check is the audio recording settings of your camcorder. As described at the beginning of this chapter, most camcorders come set to record *12-bit audio,* which lies at the heart of the video/audio drift problem. Change it to 16-bit audio, using the camcorder's own menus. (If you use a video converter like the Formac Studio or Dazzle Hollywood Bridge, make sure it, too, is set to import 16-bit audio, not 12-bit.)

If it's too late for that step, here are two possible fixes.

The back-to-camcorder solution

Set your camcorder to 16-bit audio. Once editing is complete, export the entire movie to your camcorder (see Chapter 19).

Then start a new iMovie project file and import the camcorder's footage right back into your Mac (Chapter 13). This time, you should be able to export the project without the drift.

The export-as-QuickTime solution

For this trick, you'll export the project as a high-quality QuickTime movie.

Chapter 19 offers details on exporting iMovie projects as QuickTime movies. For this particular task, though, these steps guide you through the proper settings:

1. **Choose File→Share.**

   The Share options sheet appears.

2. **Click the QuickTime icon at the top of the window. From the "Compress movie for" pop-up menu, choose Expert. Then click Share.**

   The Save Exported Movie dialog box appears.

3. **From the Export pop-up menu, choose "Movie to QuickTime Movie." Click Options.**

   The Movie Settings window opens.

4. **Turn on Video and click the Settings button.**

   Now the Compression Settings dialog box shows up.

5. **From the pop-up menu, choose DV/DVCPRO - NTSC. (For PAL videos, choose DVCPRO - PAL.) Specify Best quality, 29.97 frames per second (for PAL, 25). Click OK.**

   You return to the Movie Settings window.

6. **Click Size.**

   You meet the tiny Export Size Settings dialog box.

7. **Click "Use custom size." For a standard DV project, set the Width to 720 and Height to 480; for a DV Widescreen project, set Width to 869 and Height to 480.**

   The numbers are slightly different if you're working in the PAL format. For standard DV, set the width and height to 768 and 576; for widescreen, use 1040 and 576.

8. **Click OK. Back in the Movie Settings window, turn on the Sound checkbox, and then click on the Settings button.**

   The Movie Settings sound box opens.

9. **From the pop-up menu, choose None. Set the Rate to 48.00 kHz, Size to 16 Bit, and "Use" to Stereo.**

The resulting summary box should look like Figure 32-3.

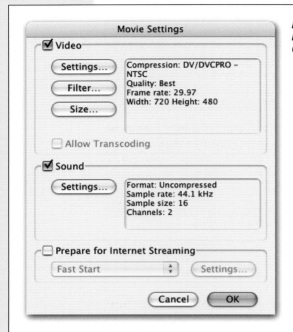

Figure 32-3:
Here's how to properly set up for an export of a perfect QuickTime copy of your movie.

10. **Click OK, and OK again.**

You return to the Save dialog box.

11. **Name the movie, choose a folder location for saving it, and click Save.**

If all went well, you now have a very large, perfect-quality QuickTime movie on your hard drive.

If your project contains no DVD chapter markers, drag this exported movie into the iDVD window to place it there—with no audio-video sync problems, if the programming gods are smiling. If the project *does* require chapters, import the exported movie to a new iMovie HD project, add chapters, and *then* send it to iDVD as usual.

White Frames at Chapter Markers in Slideshows

You've created a gorgeous slideshow in iMovie. You've added chapter markers to help your audience navigate. And you've burned it to a DVD—and you've cringed at the blinks of white that appear at each chapter marker.

The workaround: *don't* put chapter markers in your main project file. Instead, once your movie is otherwise ready, export it as a Full Quality QuickTime movie. (Choose

File→Share, click the QuickTime button, choose Full Quality from the pop-up menu, click Share. Use any name and folder location.)

Import the exported movie into a new iMovie HD Project, and add chapter markers at *this* stage. Finally, export to iDVD and burn your disc as usual.

Photos Look Jaggy and Awful on DVD

All over the world, every single day, more Mac fans try to turn their digital photos into DVD slideshows using iMovie—and find out that the photos look *terrible*. What makes this syndrome so baffling is that the photos probably began life with super high resolution and look fantastic in Photoshop or iPhoto. But once they arrive on a DVD, the pictures look lousy.

It turns out that when you click the Create iDVD Project button in iMovie (the usual way to hand off the project to iDVD), iMovie offers to process any still photos—to *render* them, turning them into what amounts to motionless video. "Your movie contains still, slow motion, and/or reverse clips," it says. If you click "Render and Proceed," iMovie does a pretty poor job at converting them into video, resulting in jaggy blockiness. (This conversion is permanent in iMovie. Once it's done, your photos will always look bad in iMovie until you reinsert the originals.)

The solution is to bypass iMovie's low-quality photo-rendering cycle altogether. You can do that in either of two ways.

The Ken Burns Method

If you turn your photos into digital video clips, then iMovie doesn't consider them stills any more, and won't attempt to render them. Here's how to do that:

Turn on the Ken Burns Effect checkbox (page 395), configure the pan or zoom settings, then import the image.

After the bright red progress bar finishes its trip across your photo clip, you're left with a very high quality "still" video clip that iMovie won't attempt to process when you hand off to iDVD.

Repeat this process for any other still photos in your movie.

At this point, your still photos are no longer still photos. Clicking the "Create iDVD Project" button is now safe. iMovie will make no attempt to render your stills, because they've already been rendered by the far superior Ken Burns feature.

The Drag-into-iDVD Method

The second way to bypass iMovie's still-photo rendering feature is to avoid the "Create iDVD Project" button altogether. As you may remember from Chapter 21, there's another way to bring an iMovie movie into iDVD: drag its title-bar icon right into the iDVD window. See page 465 for the proper technique.

If you do that, iMovie's weak photo-rendering software doesn't touch your stills—and iDVD's own, much better rendering software processes them instead. You may find that the Ken Burns technique looks slightly better on some photos, but of course, it's much more work than the drag-into-iDVD method. Either way, though, you'll be delighted with the results.

At disc-burning time, iDVD will perform the photo processing itself, with much better results.

Project Corruption

Most of the time, iMovie stops people's hearts only with the beauty and magnificence of its creations. Unfortunately, every now and then, it can stop your heart in a much more terrifying way. At some random moment when you least expect it, some iMovie project that you've worked on for days or weeks refuses to open.

FREQUENTLY ASKED QUESTIONS

How to Save Your Project for Future Generations

OK, I'm done editing my iMovie. How do I back up my project to reclaim the hard drive space?

That's an excellent question. Considering the hours you've probably spent building your masterpiece, preserving a full-quality copy, preferably in editable form, is probably extremely important.

(As you know, exporting the movie to QuickTime, cellphones, the Web, or VHS entails a huge deterioration in video and audio quality. Surprisingly, even burning to DVD involves losing some of the original quality, because the video is stored on the disc in a compressed form.)

In the end, there are only three ways to preserve a movie at its full original quality.

First, you can store it on a hard drive. This method is getting less expensive every day, and offers fast and convenient storage of your entire project. Because you can store your entire project package or folder, you'll be able to re-edit the project next year when iMovie 6 comes out with enhancements you can't resist.

Second, you can use a backup program like Retrospect to copy your project folder onto multiple DVDs (not video DVDs, but DVD-ROMs—like glorified blank CDs). It takes a

handful of these blanks to store one hour of video. But this solution is certainly cheap. And in a pinch, you'll be able to reconstruct your entire project folder, with full editing capability.

If the project is small enough to fit on a DVD, you can use the File→Burn Project to Disc command.

Finally, you can send the movie back out to your DV camcorder, as described in Chapter 19. MiniDV tapes have about a 15-year life span, but they store the original video quality, even if you rescue the footage by copying it onto a fresh tape once every 10 years.

You lose the ability to edit your titles and substitute new background music, of course, but you don't lose all editing possibilities. If you ever re-import that movie back to iMovie, most of the clips will still appear as distinct, rearrangeable clips in your Movie Track (because clip boundaries are nothing more than breaks in the originally recorded time code).

(The exception: Clips that you create within iMovie, as opposed to those captured from a camcorder, don't have a time stamp, so they'll re-import as one conjoined clump of scenes.)

The odds of project corruption in iMovie HD are lower than in any previous version, but if it happens, that's little consolation.

Using the Timeline Movie to Recover the Project

If the worst should happen, you may be able to rescue the project by importing its *timeline movie* to a new, fresh, iMovie project file. (More on the timeline movie in a moment.)

If you read page 679, you know that the modern iMovie "document" is, in fact, a tricky kind of folder. To open it, Control-click the project's Finder icon; from the shortcut menu, choose Show Package Contents. In the window that opens, double-click the Cache icon. Inside, you'll see an icon called Timeline Movie.mov.

The Timeline Movie is a *reference* movie. That is, it contains no video or audio of its own—just pointers to the video and audio files stored in the package's Media folder. If those files are intact, then the reference movie will play the project just as iMovie HD did.

Create a new iMovie project, and then drag the Timeline Movie.mov icon from the Finder window right into the Timeline Viewer of the new project.

Now, the resulting movie will contain all of the original movie project, but you should be aware that it will show up in the new project as a single, giant clip. You won't be able to edit the titles and transitions, but at least everything will play in the proper order.

Problems with Sound

Sound problems are especially frustrating when you're working with digital video, because they bear no resemblance to sound problems with more familiar equipment. In any other situation, if sound is too low or too loud, for example, you can adjust it with a knob. But what you do about random electronic beeps and buzzes that weren't there on the original tape?

Sound Is Too Soft

If one particular clip is too soft, see page 373.

If, however, the entire movie soundtrack plays back too quietly, it's probable that iMovie has nothing to do with the problem. Instead, your overall Mac volume is probably too low. Visit the Sound panel of System Preferences and adjust the output volume of your machine, or tap the Volume Up key on the top row of your keyboard. Make sure that iMovie's own volume slider (just above the Movie Track) is up all the way, too.

Random Electronic Beeps

It's hard to imagine anything more frustrating than finding a permanent—or, worse, intermittent—buzzing, crackling, or popping in the audio tracks of your project.

This problem has been on many minds, and its victims have come up with various solutions. Fortunately, most people manage to solve it by following one of these steps:

- Just as there are video dropouts, as described in the beginning of this appendix, cheap tapes may sometimes give you *audio* dropouts. The problem is exactly the same: a tiny bit of dirt or a nonmagnetized particle on the tape. But this time, it affects the audio, not the video. Try cleaning the heads of your camcorder, and then reimport the video.

- If cleaning the heads doesn't solve the problem, consider turning off the Audio Filtering feature. To do so, choose iMovie→Preferences. Turn off "Filter audio from camera." Click OK.

  Again, try reimporting the video to see whether the sound-buzzing problems have disappeared.

Of course, these workarounds assume that the audio glitch began life on the camera, rather than within iMovie itself.

If the pop is intermittent, there's not much you can do. But if you hear the pop in the same place every time you play your movie, you may be able to repair it using a sound-editing program, like this:

1. **Export the audio of the video clip as a sound-only AIFF file.**

   That is, turn on only the relevant audio-track checkboxes (at the right end of the Timeline Viewer). Then Choose File→Share. In the Share dialog box, choose the Expert Settings option, and then click Export. In the following dialog box, use the pop-up menu to choose Sound as AIFF.

   The result: You've just exported the soundtrack of your movie as a standalone audio file.

2. **Using GarageBand, cut out the beeps.**

   GarageBand lets you highlight the specific sound waves that represent the beeps and change their volume, or replace them with pieces of sound you've copied from neighboring moments in the soundtrack.

3. **Reimport the AIFF sound file into your iMovie project.**

   For example, choose File→Export to iTunes, and then, in iMovie, use the Audio panel to import that "track" from iTunes.

   Once it has appeared on an audio track, you can turn off the existing camcorder audio track.

Pops at Transition or Scene Breaks

Audio pops or snaps sometimes materialize where clips intersect—that is, at transitions and scene breaks. Fortunately, these audio defects don't survive to any DVDs you may burn.

If a DVD isn't the final destination for your project, the workaround is slightly more involved. First, remove the transition or title as described in Chapters 15 and 16.

Next, select the video clip that will be affected. Finally, choose Advanced→Extract Audio.

iMovie HD places the audio from that video clip into one of its two audio tracks. If you apply the title or transition now, iMovie HD will leave the audio—now an independent entity—alone.

Relinking Missing Files

When you're working with regular projects (not archived ones), iDVD is pretty helpless if you move or rename any of the photo, movie, or sound files that it expects to use in your DVD (see Figure 32-4).

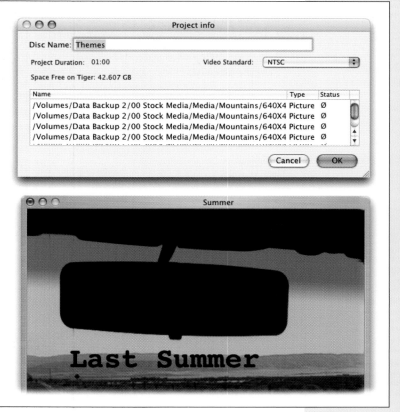

Figure 32-4:
Top: If you open a project whose original movies, photos, or sounds have been moved or renamed, you see this message. Click Cancel to proceed without those files, or click Find File to show iDVD where the file is now.

Bottom: The broken link image indicates a file that iDVD can't find. Avoid this problem by keeping all your source files on the hard drive until after you've burned your project.

If you encounter the dialog box shown in Figure 32-4 at top, click Find File, navigate to a folder that contains at least one of the files, and click Open. iDVD dutifully inspects that folder for *any* missing files. Repeat until you've located all the missing files.

If you *can't* find a file—say, you deleted one by accident—then keep showing iDVD the files you *can* find. At the end of the process, click Cancel.

Your project will open just fine, but you'll see a big black space (Figure 32-4, bottom) where the missing file ought to be. At this point, you can replace it with a file that you do have.

Where to Get Help Online

You can get personal iMovie help—help on any iLife program, actually—by calling Apple's help line at (800) 500-7078 for 90 days after you bought the iLife DVD or a new Mac. (Technically, you can call within the first 90 days of ownership, but the clock really doesn't start until your first call.) After that, you can either buy an AppleCare contract for another year of tech-support calls ($170 to $350, depending on your Mac model), or pay $50 per individual call!

Beyond 90 days, however, consider consulting the Internet, which is filled with superb sources of fast, free technical help. Here are some of the best places to get your questions answered:

- **Apple's own iMovie HD discussion forum.** Here, you can read user comments, ask questions of knowledgeable users, or hang out and learn good stuff (*http://discussions.info.apple.com*).

  The iMovie FAQ link (Frequently Asked Questions) is at the top of the first forum page. Check it first—you'd be surprised at how likely it is that other people have had the same question or problem that you're having. Try using the Search box on the first page of the iMovie forum, too.

  Tip: The Search box on the first forum page searches the entire forum. A Search box on an individual discussion page searches only that discussion thread.

- **MacDV List.** This outstanding resource is a *mailing list,* which is like a public bulletin board, except that each message is emailed to everybody who has signed up for the list. To post a message yourself, you just email it to a central address. It's attended by both iMovie fans and Final Cut Pro users, but the group tolerates both beginner and advanced questions.

  You sign up for this free feature at *www.themacintoshguy.com/lists*. Note that you can sign up either for the one-message-at-a-time membership, which sends about 20 messages a day to your email box, or for the Digest version, in which you get just one email each day containing all of the day's messages.

- **iMovie List.** Here's a mailing list—several, actually—dedicated to iMovie and only iMovie. In some of these lists, the level of technical discussion is much lower than the MacDV List—in other words, it's a perfect place to ask questions without embarrassing yourself. Sign up by visiting *www.egroups.com* and searching for *imovie*.

Where to Get Help Online

- **The Unofficial iMovie FAQ.** iMovie fan Dan Slagle stocks this site with useful accumulations of iMovie tips, workarounds, and information (*www.danslagle. com/mac/iMovie/iMovieFAQ.html*).

- **Official iMovie help pages.** Apple doesn't freely admit to bugs and problems, but there's a surprising amount of good information in its official iMovie answer pages (*www.info.apple.com/usen/imovie*).

- **Official iMovie HD tutorials.** Apple offers step-by-step instructions and movies at *www.apple.com/support/imovie/index.html*.

TROUBLESHOOTING

Troubleshooting GarageBand

The truth is, most of the troubleshooting you'll do in GarageBand has to do with accommodating its horsepower demands. You'll know there's a problem when you see the Playhead turn orange or red, get skips in the music, or see a note that "Some parts were not played." That's why most of this chapter is devoted to solving speed and horsepower problems.

Still, a few other things can go wrong, or at least can baffle you. Here, for your headache-relieving pleasure, are recipes for solving the most common problems.

The Speed Problem

GarageBand, as you may recall from Chapter 23 (or as you may have discovered on your own), is a power hog. It thrives on memory and processor speed, eternally craving more, more, and more. Even a handful of tracks is enough to redline your system, turning the Playhead orange, then red, and finally summoning the dreaded dialog box shown in Figure 33-1 as playback grinds to a halt.

There's no cause for panic, though. In the end, it's you who's made GarageBand gasp for air, by overextending your Mac—and therefore it's you who can undo the damage, too. This chapter presents the accumulated wisdom of thousands of online GarageBand fans sharing their workarounds, plus Apple's own suggestions. They're presented here in decreasing order of importance and urgency. (Better yet, try the first steps first!)

Set the Stage

You can avoid many overburdened-Mac situations just by taking the time to set up your GarageBand environment smartly. For example:

- Quit as many other programs as possible. GarageBand needs all the memory it can get.

- Every PowerBook, iBook, and Power Mac G5 lets you switch your computer's brain into a slower, reduced-power mode to save heat and battery charge. But for GarageBand, that's just asking for trouble; it needs every hair of horsepower it can get.

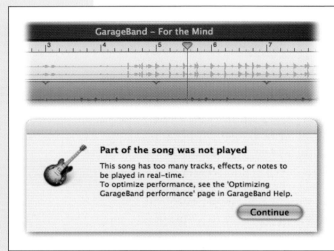

Figure 33-1:
Top: When GarageBand starts having trouble keeping up with everything going on in your tracks, the Playhead begins to change color. It turns from white, through orange, and finally to deepening red, as you approach the system-overload point. It's your early-warning system that your piece is approaching GarageBand BogDown.

Bottom: When GarageBand absolutely reaches the end of its ability to process all of the music, this message appears. Time to read this chapter.

So choose →System Preferences, click Energy Saver, then click the Options tab. Now from the pop-up menu, choose Highest. Close the window.

Your laptop battery won't last quite as long, and your G5's fan might spin up a little more, but at least you'll be able to get some meaningful work done in GarageBand.

- Don't try to play a song, loop, or audio file that's on a CD or DVD. Copy it to your hard drive first.

- Turn off FileVault, if you're using it, by choosing →System Preferences, clicking Security, and clicking Turn FileVault Off. (FileVault is a Mac OS X security feature that encrypts your entire Home folder; you'd remember turning it on.) It slows down data transfer from your Home folder dramatically.

Alternatively, copy your GarageBand projects to a location outside your Home folder—into the Shared folder, for example. That way, you can leave FileVault turned on without any speed penalty.

Mute Some Tracks

If GarageBand announces that "Some parts were not played," at least *you* should be the one determining *which* parts. As you work, you can mute the tracks whose playback you consider expendable for the moment. (Click each track and press the letter M key, or click the little speaker icon in the track header.)

Any track that you silence like this is one more task crossed off the Mac's real-time To Do list. By selectively muting and unmuting tracks, you should be able to get your piece mostly ready. Afterwards, you can either export the thing, convert some Software Instrument tracks to Real Instruments, or even bounce the whole thing into iTunes and back. Both of these radical tactics are described later in this chapter.

Lock Some Tracks

This new GarageBand 2 feature is designed precisely for the gasping-Mac scenario described on these pages. It can help out by taking a lot of the processing load off the Mac's shoulders.

Ordinarily, GarageBand spends a lot of its playback attention on two kinds of music:

- **Software Instruments.** These regions (green) contain MIDI data, nothing more. The *sounds* triggered by this note information are something GarageBand has to synthesize in real time during playback, and that takes a lot of processing power

- **Real Instrument effects.** Real instruments (digital-audio recordings) are generally much easier for GarageBand to play back, because it doesn't have to do any calculating or real-time sound production. There's an exception, though: the *effects* described in Chapter 28 (reverb, EQ, and so on). They represent the state of the art in software simulators, but it's still quite a feat for the Mac to pass the sound of your various tracks into these software modules, calculate the new, post-processed sound, and then send it back out your speakers—all in real time.

When you *lock* a track as shown in Figure 33-2, you take a snapshot of it. You freeze it. GarageBand memorizes its playback sound and stashes it on the hard drive, in essence turning all of it into digital-audio files with no effects or sounds that must be calculated in real time. You should find that GarageBand is now capable of playing back complex arrangements that used to reduce it to a limp puddle.

You do pay a small price for this luxury, however:

- Locking a track can take a long time.

- Once the track is locked, you can't edit it. Sometimes, of course, that's a good thing; it means that you can freeze a track that's already perfect, protecting it from accidental modification. (In other words, some people's reason for locking tracks has nothing to do with reducing the processing load.)

  If you do attempt to make changes, though, you'll get only the error message shown in Figure 33-2. Fortunately, it's a simple matter to unlock the track to make your changes, and then lock it again afterward, if you like.

• The amount of power you restore to GarageBand by locking tracks has to do with the speed of your hard drive, because that's where the tracks' playback now originates. On laptop drives, full drives, or older, slower hard drives, you may not get much of a boost out of track locking.

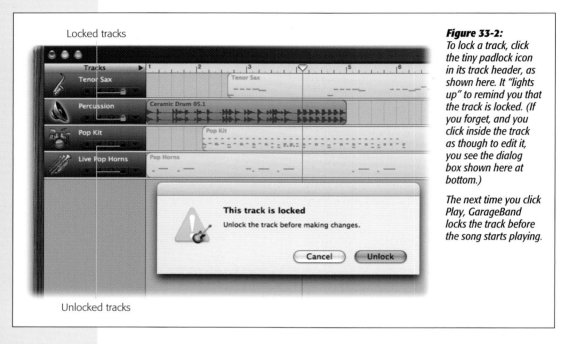

Locked tracks

Unlocked tracks

Figure 33-2:
To lock a track, click the tiny padlock icon in its track header, as shown here. It "lights up" to remind you that the track is locked. (If you forget, and you click inside the track as though to edit it, you see the dialog box shown here at bottom.)

The next time you click Play, GarageBand locks the track before the song starts playing.

Temporarily Squelch the Effects

Here's another approach to relieving the Mac's speed burden: Turn off some effects. (Double-click a track to open the Track Info dialog box, expand the Details panel, and start turning off checkboxes.) You can always turn them on again before you export the finished piece to iTunes. This trick changes the sound, of course, but may be much quicker than locking tracks.

Tip: Amp Simulation is among the most processor-intensive effects of all. If you're a guitarist and you ache for the flexibility of having different guitar effects, but your Mac doesn't have the muscle for GarageBand's simulators, consider buying an inexpensive multi-effects box from a company like Digitech or Korg (under $100). These boxes apply the effects *before* the sound reaches GarageBand, so you can leave the Amp Simulations turned off.

It's worth considering, too, whether you'll actually *hear* individual track effects. Once you've added master effects like reverb, not all individual track effects are even audible.

Combine Tracks

Playing more tracks makes GarageBand work harder. In many cases, though, you can combine the *material* from several tracks into a single one.

It's especially easy to combine blue Real Instrument tracks. Figure 33-3 shows the procedure.

Combining green Software Instrument tracks is more difficult, because dragging a region into a different track usually means that its instrument sound changes. Not to worry: You can always turn Software Instrument regions into Real Instrument regions, as described on page 532, and then merge them.

Enlarge Your Buffer

In GarageBand→Preferences, click the Audio/MIDI button to see the controls shown at top in Figure 33-4. Setting it to "Maximum number of simultaneous tracks" devotes more of the Mac's energies to playing back your piece.

The disadvantage of this setting is that when you record from a MIDI keyboard, you may experience *latency*—a frustrating, fraction-of-a-second delay between each keypress and the playing of its sound.

The trick, then, is knowing when to switch this setting. Leave it on "Minimum delay when playing instruments live" when you're recording, and compensate by turning off some tracks if the Mac begins gasping. After the recording, change the setting to "Maximum."

Figure 33-3:
Top: These three Real Instrument tracks are making this old Power Mac's heart race. There's no good reason for them to occupy different tracks, since their regions aren't playing simultaneously.

Bottom: By dragging all of their regions into a single track, you ease your Mac's burden considerably. The only downside is that you've lost the ability to specify different effect settings for each track.

A reminder: Use this trick only on regions that don't overlap.

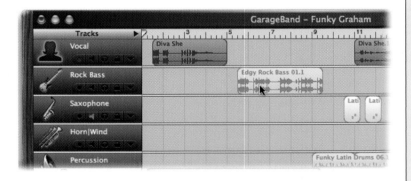

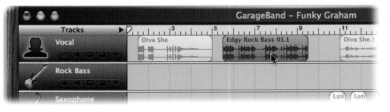

Lose Some Software Instrument Voices

Some instruments, like flutes and kazoos, can play only one note at a time—in software parlance, one *voice* at a time. A piano, meanwhile, can theoretically play 88 notes at once, although you'd need a few friends to help you press the keys if you wanted to hear more than 10 notes simultaneously.

But the more Software Instrument voices GarageBand must play, the more your Mac sweats. As shown in Figure 33-4 at bottom, a certain pop-up menu in the Garage-Band Preferences dialog box lets you limit the number of voices that get played. In a

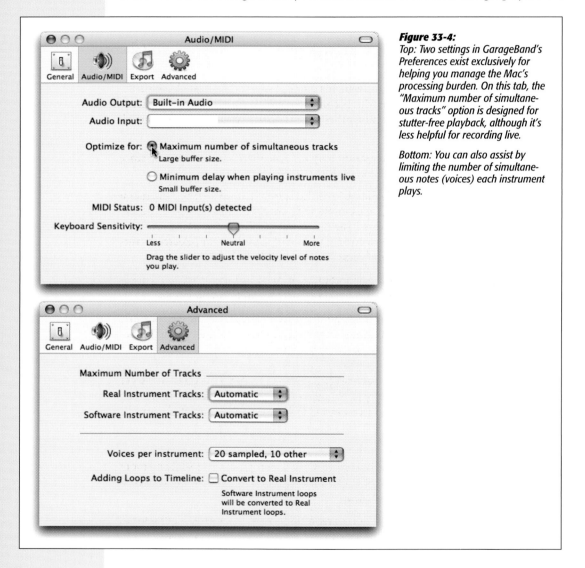

Figure 33-4:
Top: Two settings in GarageBand's Preferences exist exclusively for helping you manage the Mac's processing burden. On this tab, the "Maximum number of simultaneous tracks" option is designed for stutter-free playback, although it's less helpful for recording live.

Bottom: You can also assist by limiting the number of simultaneous notes (voices) each instrument plays.

pinch, you can set a limit on these voices, thus saving GarageBand further effort and sometimes making an unplayable song playable again on your Mac.

The wording of this dialog box is a tad cryptic, in that it refers to "sampled" and "other" voices. To comprehend this lingo, it helps to understand the two different ways that GarageBand can create Software Instrument sounds:

- **With samples.** A *sampled* instrument sound began life as a recording of a real-world instrument playing one note in a real-world studio. Pressing a key on a MIDI keyboard triggers a playback of that short recording. In the case of woodwind instruments, the sampled sound seamlessly repeats for as long as you press the key.

  In GarageBand, all the woodwind, brass, piano, guitar, bass, strings, and drum sounds are sampled sounds.

- **With synthesis.** The rest of the Software Instrument sounds are created using software algorithms; in essence your Mac becomes a musical synthesizer. GarageBand's clavinet, organ, electric piano, and synthesizer Software Instrument sounds are all created this way.

  Synthesized sounds put a greater strain on your Mac than sampled sounds, since GarageBand must compute these sounds on the fly.

When you inspect the dialog box in Figure 33-4, the options in the lower pop-up menu should make more sense. Suppose, for example, that you choose "10 sampled, 5 other." You've just specified that no Software Instrument will be allowed to play more than five notes simultaneously if it's an electronic keyboard sound (organ, electric piano, and so on), or more than 10 notes at once for any other Software Instrument.

Now, you might be aghast at this suggestion. Surely eliminating notes from your chords would eviscerate your harmonies, leaving them sounding hollow and empty.

In truth, though, you might never miss the notes that GarageBand leaves out of a busy orchestration. Meanwhile, thinning out the voices could make all the difference in a GarageBand composition that's too complex for your Mac.

Tip: Speaking of voices: When keyboard players attempt to create guitar parts by playing a MIDI keyboard, they often forget that a guitar has only six strings. If you play freely with both hands on the keyboard, using all 10 fingers, you may inadvertently create a guitar part that would be unplayable on an actual guitar.

Reduce the Track Overhead

Every time you create a new GarageBand project file, the program allots some memory to hold a certain number of tracks. (The exact number depends on the speed of your Mac and how much memory is installed.)

But if you intend to create nothing but a single-line kazoo recording, that's a lot of memory being set aside that could be used for other purposes…like keeping up with playback.

That's why, as soon as you know how many total tracks your piece will have, you should choose GarageBand→Preferences, click the Advanced tab, and change the Maximum Number of Tracks pop-up menus (Figure 33-4, bottom).

You're telling the program: "I intend to use no more than eight Software Instrument tracks and eight Real Instrument tracks" (or whatever), "so please put whatever additional memory you were holding back into the pot. I could use it right about now."

Convert Software Instrument Loops

As you may have read in Chapter 23, Software Instruments are much more trouble for the Mac to play back than Real Instruments.

Now, at first glance, that statement might seem to be illogical—in fact, reversed. After all, green Software Instrument regions contain very little data—only a list of note triggers ("Play middle C for one beat, then C sharp for two"). MIDI *files* take up only a few kilobytes on the hard drive. They're absolutely minuscule compared with digital recordings like Real Instrument regions, which take up 10 MB per minute. So why isn't it easier for the Mac to play the little files than the big ones?

Because it must also *generate the instrument sounds,* not to mention processing them with effects, as it plays each MIDI note. It's not the triggering that's so much work; it's the synthesizing.

To play a blue or purple Real Instrument region, on the other hand, the Mac just plays back a bunch of sound data that's already fully formed on the hard drive.

In any case, exploiting this little quirk of Software and Real Instruments is an excellent way to reduce the load on your Mac's processor, because GarageBand makes it easy to *convert* the former into the latter.

For example, GarageBand offers at least three ways to convert green loops into blue ones that are easier for the Mac to play:

- If you press the Option key before dragging a green loop out of the Loop browser and into an empty spot on the timeline (and keep the key down), GarageBand creates a blue Real Instrument track. It then converts your loop into the familiar blue sound waves found in a Real Instrument region.

- If you enjoy that auto-conversion so much that you'd *always* like GarageBand to convert green loops, choose GarageBand→Preferences, click the Advanced tab, and turn on "Convert to Real Instruments." From now on, every loop you drag out of the Loop browser (into a blank spot in the timeline area) creates a blue Real Instrument track and region.

Tip: Pressing the Option key simply reverses this Preferences setting. If "Convert to Real Instruments" is turned on, for example, then Option-dragging a green loop does *not* convert it to a blue one.

- You can drag a green loop that's already *in* a track into a blue Real Instrument track. GarageBand converts it to a Real Instrument region as described on page 532.

Remember, though, that once converted to digital-audio form, a loop loses much of the editing flexibility it once had. You can no longer change individual notes inside it, for example.

"Bounce Down" Many Tracks into One

And now, one of the most useful and powerful tools in the GarageBand musician's arsenal. It involves exporting several tracks, or even *all* of your tracks, and boiling them all down into one.

Suppose, for example, that your Mac can play only five tracks at once before bogging down. However, you've got 20 tracks' worth of music in your head! Using the "bounce down" trick, that's no problem. You could simply proceed as shown in Figure 33-5.

Here's the step-by-step version:

- Export all five tracks to iTunes (Figure 33-5, top). Reimport the result into GarageBand as *one* track (Figure 33-5, middle and bottom). Delete the original five component tracks, or just mute them. Now you're free to add another four! (Effective total now: nine tracks.)

- Export *these* five tracks (which sound like nine) to iTunes. Reimport into Garage-Band as *one* track, delete the original five—and add yet another four. (Effective total: 13.)

The one big caution here is that each time you export your tracks, you're freezing them. You're giving up any ability to adjust their effects, rebalance their volume levels, change the song's tempo, and so on. Take care to finalize each semi-mix as much as possible before exporting.

Tip: You might also want to use the File→Save As command along the way, preserving each set of exported tracks before you delete them, so you can return to the original GarageBand files if necessary. (Like when you finally get that dual-processor Power Mac G5 with 1 gig of RAM.)

Install More Memory

After a certain point, bending over backward to accommodate all of these work-arounds, settings, and cheats just isn't worth it. If you're still getting "Parts were not played" messages after following all, or even some, of the steps in this chapter, you should just break down and give your Mac the gift of more memory.

With more RAM, GarageBand can hold more of the sampled audio (blue Real loops, your purple Real recordings, and green, sampled Software Instruments) in memory, and therefore doesn't have to read as much information from your hard drive, which is what slows GarageBand down.

In particular, if your Mac has only 256 or even 512 megabytes of memory, you're living at the edge, as far as GarageBand is concerned. (To find out how much you have, choose ▲→About This Mac.) Hie thee to *www.ramseeker.com,* choose your Mac's model name from the pop-up menu, and see just how inexpensive a memory upgrade can be these days.

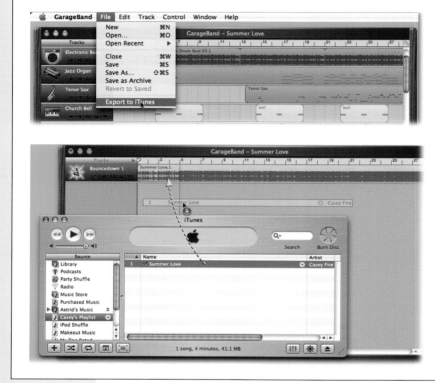

Figure 33-5:
Top: A bunch of tracks, just crackling with music. Finalized and polished to within an inch of their life. And pushing the Mac to its max. How will you gain the headroom neces-sary to add the four vocal tracks you have in mind?

Easy—just export the half-finished mix to iTunes, and then delete the tracks from GarageBand.

Bottom: Then bring it all right back in as a single track, as shown here. Now you've got a nearly empty track canvas in which to add four more tracks.

You've just created what studio musicians call a submix.

Trouble with Loops

Loops, as described in Chapter 24, are among the greatest joys of GarageBand. So when they don't work, they're among the biggest disappointments.

Your Loop Browser is Empty

Adding more loops to GarageBand isn't just a matter of stuffing them into a certain folder on your hard drive. You also have to make GarageBand aware of them. To do that, you force GarageBand to *index* any new loops, building an internal card catalog of which loops you have and where they're stored.

If anything goes wrong with GarageBand's loop index, you may discover that all of the buttons in the Loop browser are dimmed and no loops appear in its list. Other wackiness can result, too, like loops that exist in name only or simply misbehave.

In all of these situations, the solution is to *rebuild* the GarageBand loop index. You do it like this:

1. **Quit GarageBand. In the Finder, open your hard drive window. Then open the Library→Audio→Apple Loops Index folder (see Figure 11-1, top).**

   Inside, you'll see the actual text files that constitute your current index.

2. **Drag the index files to the Trash.**

   GarageBand will rebuild fresh, healthy ones in just a moment.

3. **Open GarageBand and click the Loop Browser (eyeball) button.**

   GarageBand suddenly realizes that it has no loops, and shows the dialog box at bottom in Figure 11-1.

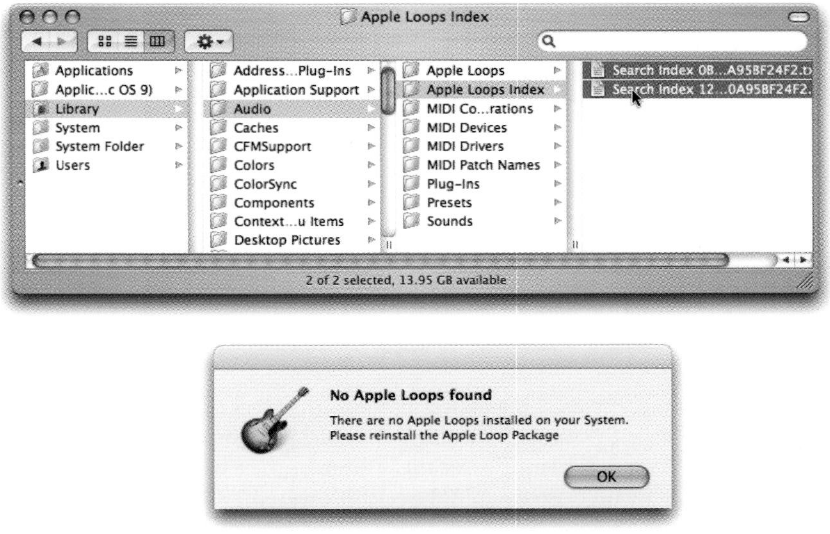

Figure 33-6:
Top: You've found your secret stash of index files, buried deep within the GarageBand folder. If you're having loop problems, throw them away; Garage-Band will recreate better ones.

Bottom: Garage-Band, too, knows that you've fooled with its indexes.

4. **In the No Apple Loops Found dialog box, click OK.**

   Now return to the Finder.

5. **Open your hard drive→Library→Audio folder again. Drag the Apple Loops folder directly into any visible portion of GarageBand's Loop browser.**

   GarageBand dutifully recreates its loop index, based on the current location and contents of that Loops folder.

Note: If you've installed any Jam Packs, drag *their* folders (also in the Library→Application Support→ GarageBand folder) into the Loop browser, too.

New Add-On Loops Don't Show Up

It's a nice perk that GarageBand can accommodate additional loops that were designed for other music-software programs. Note, however, that:

- You should install them by dragging them into GarageBand's Loop browser, *not* by dragging them into a folder in the Finder. Dragging them into the Loop browser ensures that GarageBand indexes the new loops (that is, adds them to its internal database).

- Occasionally, non-Apple loops don't show up in the Loop browser even when you've installed them correctly. In that case, you may have no choice but to drag them from the Finder directly into the GarageBand timeline area, bypassing the Loop browser entirely.

Some Loop Buttons are Dimmed or Missing

Remember that most of the time, GarageBand shows you only a *subset* of the 1,100 loops that it comes with. For example:

- It shows you only the loops that you've requested by choosing from the Loops pop-up menu (Figure 33-7).

- It shows you only the loops that fit your song's time signature, and hides the rest. (They wouldn't sound right anyway.) If your song is in 7/4 time, for example, you won't see any loops *at all.* The vast majority of Apple loops are in 4/4 time.

- It shows you only the loops that fit your song's *key,* or are close to it. See page 534 for details, and for the workaround.

- Remember that each time you open GarageBand, you see only 30 loop buttons. But you can drag the prominent, dark gray, brushed-metal divider bar upward, using the spot on either side of the time display as a handle, to reveal 24 more.

- By Control-clicking individual buttons in the Loop browser, it's possible to choose new identities for the buttons you see here. That's a great feature, because it means that you can put the buttons *you* consider important in more easily reached positions.

  Of course, it also means that you (or some meddlesome interloper) can duplicate buttons, hide buttons, and so on.

  If you suspect that something's amiss, choose GarageBand→Preferences. Click the General button, and then click the Reset button at the bottom of the dialog box. All buttons return to their original Apple factory-set positions.

Recording and Editing Problems

What can go wrong during the main working phase? Let us count the ways.

There's a Delay When Playing Live

On slower Macs, you may experience an annoying lag between the time you press a key on your instrument and the time the sound comes out of the Mac's speakers. That's *latency,* baby, and there's one—and only one—step you can take to solve it.

See page 689 for the details.

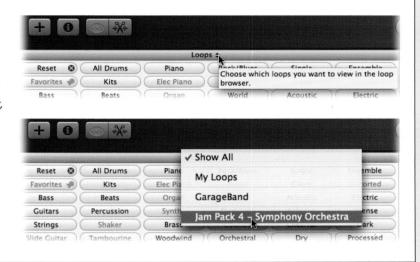

Figure 33-7:
If you don't seem to be seeing all of your loops, it's possible that you're viewing only one of your loop sets. Loops that came with GarageBand, loops that came with a Jam Pack, and loops that you've created yourself are all listed separately in this subtle pop-up menu.

Trouble Staying with the Beat

If you're having trouble playing new music in step with the current tempo, consider these techniques:

- **Slow the tempo.** Later, you can always crank it back up again for final playback.

  This is, alas, a trick you can use only if you're recording Software Instrument tracks (from a MIDI keyboard controller, for example). If you're playing a live instrument or singing, you must record at the final tempo.

- **Eliminate the delay problem.** It may be that what you're experiencing is the *latency* problem described, and solved, on page 689.

- **Mute some tracks.** If you mute the other tracks, you'll hear nothing but yourself and the metronome.

- **Add a drum part.** Sometimes, making the drum part more prominent (by silencing the other tracks for the moment) makes it easier to hear the beat. You may even want to consider *adding* a drum part for a song that doesn't need one, just for recording purposes. You can always delete the drums later.

Weird, Phase-Shifty Sound During Recording

Mac OS X comes with a program, in the Applications→Utilities folder, called Audio MIDI Setup. You may have other audio setup programs, too.

Most people never even see these programs, and that's fine. But if you, a power user with a lot of gear and a fancy MIDI setup, have used these programs to configure your equipment setup, note that the Playthru feature of Audio MIDI Setup *duplicates* the effect of the Monitor setting in GarageBand. (Double-click a track's header to turn Monitor on or off.)

If both Playthru (in Audio MIDI Setup) and Monitor (in GarageBand) are turned on at once, the Mac tries to play what you're recording *twice,* nearly simultaneously, resulting in the odd phase-shift sound you're hearing. Turn one of those two features off.

No Sound from a Microphone or Real Instrument

If GarageBand doesn't seem to be "hearing" anything from your microphone or line input, the problem is usually that the Mac hasn't been taught to "listen" to the right audio source. Review the steps on page 594, including visiting System Preferences and choosing the correct input in the GarageBand→Preferences panel. Otherwise, double-check these points:

- Make sure that you've clicked a blue Real Instrument track. If a green Software Instrument track is selected, GarageBand ignores your microphone or instrument.

- Also make sure you haven't muted this track, or soloed another one. (The speaker icon in your track's header should be lit up in blue, and no other instrument's headphones icon should be blue.) While you're at it, make sure that the track's volume slider isn't set to zero (page 626).

- It's possible that GarageBand is set up to listen to the wrong channel (mono instruments). Double-click the track header and check the Input pop-up menu and Format (mono/stereo) buttons, as described on page 600.

- Are you getting *any* sound from GarageBand? Is your Mac's speaker turned up? Did you turn on Monitor in the Track Info dialog box? Check by double-clicking the track header.

- If you're using a mixer or audio interface, is its volume turned all the way down?

- Are you getting any sound from the instrument? If it's electric, do you have it turned on, with the volume turned up? Make sure all the connections are good—especially if you've incorporated plug adapters into the mix.

Tip: Are you using a Griffin iMic adapter to connect your microphone or instrument to the Mac? Make sure you've connected the mike or instrument to the iMic's input jack (the one with a microphone symbol). Also make sure to switch the iMic's selector toward the microphone symbol.

Finally, in GarageBand, choose GarageBand→Preferences, click the Audio/MIDI button, and, from the Audio Input pop-up menu, choose "iMic USB audio system." You should be ready to roll.

No Sound from a MIDI Instrument

Are you having trouble getting GarageBand to "hear" an external MIDI instrument, like a keyboard controller or MIDI guitar? In that case, use the MIDI status light identified in Figure 33-8 as an assistant detective.

The status light doesn't flicker when you play

If that little light isn't flashing when you play your MIDI instrument, the MIDI information isn't reaching GarageBand, for some reason. Here are two things to try:

- Make sure the instrument is turned on and connected to the Mac. If a MIDI interface box is involved, pay close attention: It's easy to get the MIDI In and MIDI Out cables confused. (You want one cable to run from the instrument's MIDI Out jack to the interface's MIDI In jack, and another cable going from In to Out.)

- Choose GarageBand→Preferences. Click the Audio/MIDI button. See the MIDI Status line? It should say "1 MIDI Input(s) detected" (or 2, or whatever number you have).

  If not, it's remotely possible that you're using a MIDI interface that requires driver software of its own. Visit the manufacturer's Web site to seek out a Mac OS X–compatible driver. Without this software installed, the MIDI interface may not work at all.

The status light flickers when you play

If that little indicator *does* flicker on and off, then everything is correctly hooked up and working.

In that case, here's your checklist:

- Make sure you've selected a green Software Instrument track. Otherwise, Garage-Band won't produce sound for your MIDI instrument.

- Make sure that you haven't muted this track or soloed another one, or set your track's volume to zero.

- Choose Window→Keyboard and click a few keys on the onscreen keyboard to make sure that the selected track has a working instrument selected. (Incidentally,

---

Figure 33-8:
This handy little light flickers blue whenever GarageBand is receiving note data, either from its own onscreen keyboard, an external MIDI instrument, or an onscreen virtual keyboard like MidiKeys or LoudK.

Flashing MIDI indicator

---

playing a few notes will also help you find out whether your Mac's speaker is turned down all the way.)

You might also try double-clicking the track header to open the Track Info dialog box. Make sure you've selected an instrument and effects preset in the top two lists. In the Details panel, consider turning off some effects until you find the problem. (Believe it or not, it's technically possible to fiddle with the effects so much that no sound emerges.)

- Do you, in fact, have any Software Instruments available? (Double-click a track header to see if anything's in the list.) If you or somebody else has been doing some naughty playing in the Library→Application Support→GarageBand folder, the files may be so dismantled that you need to reinstall GarageBand to get it going again.

No Sound from External Speakers (or Audio Interface)

Ordinarily, GarageBand sends the sound of its own playback through your Mac's audio circuitry, whether that's through your Mac's built-in speakers or speakers connected to its headphone jack.

But what if you've bought fancy external USB speakers? Or what if you've connected an audio interface box that's hooked up to its own sound system?

In those cases, choose GarageBand→Preferences. Click the Audio/MIDI button. Use the Audio Input Driver pop-up menu to choose the name of your external speakers or interface box. (This assumes, of course, that it's *listed* in the pop-up menu, which often means that you've installed some driver software that came with the speakers or audio box.)

Mixing and Publishing Glitches

There's nothing more annoying than something going wrong when your masterpiece is finished. Here's what to do.

Finished Song Is Too Quiet

If your GarageBand masterpiece arrives in iTunes playing far too softly relative to your other tunes, revisit Chapter 29 for tips on setting the master volume level before exporting.

But if the master volume slider is turned all the way up and the music is *still* too soft, you can also:

- **Add the Compression effect before exporting.** (Double-click the track header, turn on Compressor, and then drag the slider to the right.) Doing so boosts the softest passages and flattens the loudest ones, so that the whole thing remains at a more consistent volume level.

- **Use the iTunes preamp after exporting.** Once the song is in iTunes, you can also boost the volume there. Figure 33-9 has the details.

Tracks Panned to One Side Still Play in Both Speakers

Here's a tricky one. Suppose you've used the Pan knob (page 630) to "place" a certain track's instrument all the way to the left side of the stereo field, or all the way to the right. Yet when you listen with headphones, you still hear the darned thing coming out of both speakers!

There are two possibilities:

- Most of the time, the culprit is the Echo or Reverb effect that you've applied to that track. When you turn on these checkboxes for one track, you're actually telling GarageBand how *much* of the *master* track's Echo and Reverb to apply. You're not really applying a *different* echo or reverb to this individual track.

  What you're hearing, then, is the sound of your fully panned track reverberating through both speakers, courtesy of the master echo or reverb. And the solution is to turn *off* the track's individual echo or reverb effect. (Double-click its track header and turn off the corresponding checkboxes.)

- Turning on the Compressor effect for the master track also makes all tracks play in both left and right channels. (In this case, though, turning off Compressor for an individual track makes no difference. What matters is the Compressor effect on the *master* track.)

See Chapter 28 for much more detail on these effects, including how to turn them on or off.

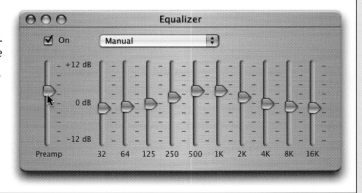

Figure 33-9:
To open this graphic equalizer in iTunes, choose Window→Equalizer, or press ⌘-2, or click the tiny equalizer button in the lower-right corner of the iTunes window. Drag the Preamp slider upward to boost this song's playback level, being careful not to overdo it.

Tail End of the Song is Chopped Off in iTunes

If you've applied reverb or echo to your song (or individual tracks), you might be frustrated to discover that GarageBand ends its export with the last measure containing notes. It doesn't especially care that the reverb on those notes might want to ring over into the following, empty measures. The result is an alarmingly abrupt cutoff of the sound in the exported tune.

The solution is shown in Figure 33-10.

Exported Song Won't Appear in iTunes

If a dialog box or alert message is open in iTunes at the moment you export from GarageBand, the handoff won't be successful. Click OK to dismiss whatever's going on in iTunes, and then try exporting again.

Drag Cycle strip past the end of the notes

Cycle button

Figure 33-10:
When you export the whole song to iTunes, heavy reverb, echo, or other time-based effect may get chopped off when the music ends—in this case, at the end of measure 29.

The solution: Turn on the Cycle button, identified here. Then drag the yellow cycle stripe all the way from measure 1 of the piece, well past the end of the notes (top). Include enough in your selection to give the effect time to die away.

You've just told GarageBand exactly how much you want exported, even if some of it is "silence."

TROUBLESHOOTING MOMENT

Sound, but in the Wrong Account

Help! My brother and I both use GarageBand. I've switched into my account using Fast User Switching—and now when I play my MIDI keyboard, the sounds are coming out in his copy of GarageBand, which is still running in his account!

Pretty cool, though, isn't it? You both are logged in at once, and you're both running GarageBand—but anything you play is being intercepted by his copy!

Gotta love being alive to see this kind of thing.

Anyway, GarageBand works fine with Fast User Switching (a feature of Mac OS X 10.3 and later)—but only one person at a time can use a MIDI interface. You have no alternative but to switch into your brother's account and quit GarageBand.

Now your account has the MIDI instrument's full attention.

Index

Index

Colophon

This book was written and edited in Microsoft Word 2004 on various Macs.

The screenshots were captured with Ambrosia Software's Snapz Pro X *(www. ambrosiasw.com)*. Adobe Photoshop CS and Macromedia Freehand MX *(www.adobe. com)* were called in as required for touching them up.

The book was designed and laid out in Adobe InDesign 3.0 on a PowerBook G4, and Power Mac G5. The fonts used include Formata (as the sans-serif family) and Minion (as the serif body face). To provide the and ⌘ symbols, custom fonts were created using Macromedia Fontographer.

The book was then generated as an Adobe Acrobat PDF file for proofreading, indexing, and final transmission to the printing plant.

Related Titles from O'Reilly

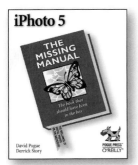

Missing Manuals

Access: The Missing Manual, *Startup Edition*

AppleScript: The Missing Manual

AppleWorks 6: The Missing Manual

Creating Web Sites: The Missing Manual

Dreamweaver 8: The Missing Manual

eBay: The Missing Manual

Excel: The Missing Manual

Excel: The Missing Manual, *Startup Edition*

FileMaker Pro: The Missing Manual

FrontPage 2003: The Missing Manual

GarageBand 2: The Missing Manual

Google: The Missing Manual, *2nd Edition*

Home Networking: The Missing Manual

iLife '05: The Missing Manual

iMovie HD & iDVD 5: The Missing Manual

iPhoto 5: The Missing Manual

iPod & iTunes: The Missing Manual, *3rd Edition*

iWork '05: The Missing Manual

Mac OS X Power Hound, *Panther Edition*

Mac OS X: The Missing Manual, *Tiger Edition*

Office 2004 for Macintosh: The Missing Manual

Photoshop Elements 3: The Missing Manual

QuickBooks: The Missing Manual

Switching to the Mac: The Missing Manual, *Tiger Edition*

Windows 2000 Pro: The Missing Manual

Windows XP Power Hound

Windows XP: The Missing Manual, *Startup Edition*

Windows XP Home Edition: The Missing Manual, *2nd Edition*

Windows XP Pro: The Missing Manual, *2nd Edition*

Our books are available at most retail and online bookstores.

To order direct: 1-800-998-9938 • *order@oreilly.com* • *www.oreilly.com*

Online editions of most O'Reilly titles are available by subscription at *safari.oreilly.com*

Keep in touch with O'Reilly

Download examples from our books

To find example files from a book, go to: *www.oreilly.com/catalog* select the book, and follow the "Examples" link.

Register your O'Reilly books

Register your book at *register.oreilly.com* Why register your books? Once you've registered your O'Reilly books you can:

- Win O'Reilly books, T-shirts or discount coupons in our monthly drawing.
- Get special offers available only to registered O'Reilly customers.
- Get catalogs announcing new books (US and UK only).
- Get email notification of new editions of the O'Reilly books you own.

Join our email lists

Sign up to get topic-specific email announcements of new books and conferences, special offers, and O'Reilly Network technology newsletters at:

elists.oreilly.com

It's easy to customize your free elists subscription so you'll get exactly the O'Reilly news you want.

Get the latest news, tips, and tools

www.oreilly.com

- "Top 100 Sites on the Web"—PC Magazine
- CIO Magazine's Web Business 50 Awards

Our web site contains a library of comprehensive product information (including book excerpts and tables of contents), downloadable software, background articles, interviews with technology leaders, links to relevant sites, book cover art, and more.

Work for O'Reilly

Check out our web site for current employment opportunities:

jobs.oreilly.com

Contact us

O'Reilly Media, Inc.
1005 Gravenstein Hwy North
Sebastopol, CA 95472 USA
Tel: 707-827-7000 or 800-998-9938
    (6am to 5pm PST)
Fax: 707-829-0104

Contact us by email

For answers to problems regarding your order or our products:
order@oreilly.com

To request a copy of our latest catalog:
catalog@oreilly.com

For book content technical questions or corrections: **booktech@oreilly.com**

For educational, library, government, and corporate sales: **corporate@oreilly.com**

To submit new book proposals to our editors and product managers:
proposals@oreilly.com

For information about our international distributors or translation queries:
international@oreilly.com

For information about academic use of O'Reilly books:
adoption@oreilly.com
or visit:
academic.oreilly.com

For a list of our distributors outside of North America check out:
international.oreilly.com/distributors.html

Order a book online

www.oreilly.com/order_new

Our books are available at most retail and online bookstores.
To order direct: 1-800-998-9938 • *order@oreilly.com* • *www.oreilly.com*
Online editions of most O'Reilly titles are available by subscription at *safari.oreilly.com*